THE

CENTENARY EDITION

OF THE WORKS OF

NATHANIEL HAWTHORNE

Volume XV

THE LETTERS, 1813-1843

EDITORS

General Editors

William Charvat, 1905–1966

Roy Harvey Pearce

Claude M. Simpson, 1910–1976

Thomas Woodson

Fredson Bowers, *General Textual Editor*

L. Neal Smith, *Associate Textual Editor*

Bill Ellis, *Assistant Textual Editor*

A PUBLICATION OF

THE OHIO STATE UNIVERSITY CENTER

FOR TEXTUAL STUDIES

NATHANIEL HAWTHORNE

THE LETTERS, 1813-1843

Edited by

Thomas Woodson

L. Neal Smith

Norman Holmes Pearson

Ohio State University Press

Copyright © 1984 by the Ohio State University Press
All Rights Reserved.

Library of Congress Cataloging in Publication Data
Hawthorne, Nathaniel, 1804–1864.
The letters, 1813–1843
(The Centenary Edition of the works of
Nathaniel Hawthorne ; v. 15)
"A publication of the Ohio State University
Center for Textual Studies"—p.
Includes bibliographical references and index.
1. Hawthorne, Nathaniel, 1804–1864—Correspondence.
2. Novelists, American—19th century—Correspondence.
I. Woodson, Thomas. II. Smith, L. Neal.
III. Pearson, Norman Holmes, 1909–1975.
IV. Ohio State University. Center for Textual Studies.
V. Title. VI. Series:
Hawthorne, Nathaniel, 1804–1864. Works. 1962 ; v. 15.
PS1850.F63 vol. 15 [PS1881.A4]   813'.3s   83-27336
[813'.3]
ISBN 0-8142-0363-9

PREFATORY NOTE

The Centenary Edition will publish Hawthorne's letters in five volumes, four of personal letters from 1813 to 1864, followed by *Consular Letters from Liverpool, 1853–1857*. Each of the first four volumes will have an index of proper names; a conflated comprehensive index will conclude the fifth.

We present every known surviving letter by Hawthorne for which the text is available, and letters by others in which he had a hand. It was the custom in the Manning family during Hawthorne's youth that two or three correspondents share the same cover. After his marriage, he often made brief contributions to letters by his wife and children. In these cases, we give the other writer's work in full, with historical annotation, but with less attention in the Textual Notes.

Hawthorne would have appreciated the irony that it has taken a period equal to the length of his lifetime to bring the first volumes of his letters to the public. The present edition traces its history to the efforts of Professor Stanley T. Williams, of Yale University, a pioneer of American literary studies, who began to collect the letters as early as 1924. By the late 1920s, he was joined by his student Randall Stewart, whose work culminated in an influential biography in 1948. In the early 30s, another Yale student, Norman Holmes Pearson, joined the endeavor, and soon thereafter, Manning Hawthorne, the author's great-grandson, who obtained the permission of the Hawthorne family to publish and ultimately passed that permission to the Centenary editors. Pearson wrote an undergraduate essay on Hawthorne's college career; Manning Hawthorne devoted his master's thesis to "The Youth of Hawthorne" and published letters of that period in several biographical articles.

By the late 1940s, Professor Pearson took charge of the

letters project, his collaborators having turned to other tasks; until his death in 1975, he continued to search for, to transcribe, and to annotate Hawthorne's letters, and shared his files with many scholars who came to see him in New Haven. Pearson's literary executors, Professor Louis L. Martz and Dr. Donald C. Gallup, kindly agreed to lend his papers to the Centenary editors as the basis for the present edition. Pearson had recognized that his notes were expansive, providing "information in great detail," even "over-full," as his friend Arlin Turner remarked in an obituary tribute in the Hawthorne Society's *Newsletter*. In accordance with "his goal of thoroughness," Professor Turner concluded, Pearson intended "to compress later, when full information would be in hand." The Centenary editors have winnowed extensive quotations, have added much new information, reorienting emphasis when a broader view seemed to warrant it, and have made frequent use of manuscripts and published scholarship that have become available only since 1975. Much of Pearson's research remains, though in a form different from that remembered by those who sought it out in his office in the Sterling Memorial Library, and we retain the name of Norman Holmes Pearson as an editor of this edition, with gratitude for his pioneering example.

For permission to publish, and in many cases for providing photocopies, we thank the following owners: Mrs. Richard K. Agnew, Winnetka, Illinois; Universiteits Bibliotheek, Amsterdam; Antioch College Library; Roger W. Barrett, Chicago; Berkshire Museum, Pittsfield, Massachusetts; Boston Public Library; Bowdoin College Library; Bancroft Library, University of California, Berkeley; William Andrews Clark Memorial Library, University of California, Los Angeles; Chicago Historical Society; Columbia University Library; Concord Free Public Library, Concord, Massachusetts; Cornell University Library; Dartmouth College Library; Essex Institute, Salem, Massachusetts; Fruitlands

Museum, Harvard, Massachusetts; Isabella Stewart Gardner Museum, Boston; Adam Gimbel; Mrs. Gordon S. Haight, Woodbridge, Connecticut; Gordon Hall, Wilmette, Illinois; Harvard College Library; Manning Hawthorne, The Colony, Texas; Donald Henry; Thomas L. Hinckley, Boston; Dinand Library, College of the Holy Cross; Huntington Library; University of Illinois Library; Lilly Library, Indiana University; Iowa State Education Association; Iowa State Historical Department; Maine Historical Society; Marietta College Library; Henry Bradley Martin, New York; Massachusetts Historical Society; Abernethy Library, Middlebury College; Milburn Collection of Hawthorniana, Owen D. Young Library, St. Lawrence University; Pierpont Morgan Library; Stephen V. C. Morris, Lenox, Massachusetts; New Hampshire Historical Society; New Haven Free Public Library; New York Historical Society; the following Divisions of the New York Public Library: Anthony Collection, Henry W. and Albert A. Berg Collection, Duyckinck Collection, Ford Collection, Gansevoort-Lansing Collection, Goddard-Roslyn Collection; Library of the State University of New York, Buffalo; Historical Society of Pennsylvania; Carl and Lily Pforzheimer Foundation, Inc.; Carl H. Pforzheimer Library; Walter L. Pforzheimer, Washington, D.C.; The Library Company of Philadelphia; Mrs. Erastus Plummer, Raymond, Maine; Princeton University Library; Rhode Island Historical Society; University of Rochester Library; Stephen T. Rudin, Manhasset, New York; St. John's Seminary, Camarillo, California; Robert R. Spaulding, Providence, Rhode Island; Stanford University Libraries; Sutro Library, San Francisco, California; Robert Taylor; Humanities Research Center, University of Texas; The Master and Fellows of Trinity College, Cambridge; University of Virginia Library; Wellesley College Library; Wesleyan University Library; Beinecke Rare Book and Manuscript Library, Yale University.

Librarians to whom we owe especial gratitude include Herbert Cahoon and Pamela White, Pierpont Morgan Library; Arthur Monke and Dianne Gutscher, Bowdoin College Library; Irene Norton, Essex Institute, Salem; Marcia Moss, Concord Free Public Library; Nina Myatt, Antiochiana Collection, Antioch College Library, where the Robert L. Straker Collection of typed transcriptions of many letters by members of the Peabody family proved invaluable. C. E. Frazer Clark, Jr., was generous in allowing our use of his unparalleled Hawthorne collection, deposited in 1983 at the Essex Institute.

For their advice on the historical annotation and introductory essay we thank Professors B. Bernard Cohen, Michael J. Colacurcio, Edward H. Davidson, and Raymona E. Hull. For his searching critique, on behalf of the Committee on Scholarly Editions of the Modern Language Association, of our preparation of Hawthorne's text, we thank Professor S. W. Reid. Others who have helped with specialized historical information include Professors Peter Balakian, Thomas Cooley, Rita Gollin, Margaret Neussendorfer, and the late Arlin Turner. We owe particular thanks to Professor David Burchmore for his help in clarifying the biographies of his ancestors.

Indispensable assistance with matters historical and textual as well as with the preparation of indexes has come from a series of Graduate Research Associates in the Department of English, Ohio State University: Jamie Kayes, Gary Keith, Mary C. Kelly, Ruth Rauch, James Rubino, and Jessica Rubinstein.

We gratefully acknowledge the support of the National Endowment for the Humanities of the National Foundation on the Arts and Humanities, and of the following Divisions of the Ohio State University: the Department of English, the Graduate School, the University Libraries, and the Research Foundation.

The Editors.

CONTENTS

ABBREVIATIONS AND SHORT TITLES

References to Hawthorne works are to the Centenary Edition (Columbus: Ohio State University Press, 1962–) with the exception of *PAN: Passages from the American Notebooks*, and *EN: The English Notebooks*, which are individually identified. In the editorial matter, library locations of manuscripts indicate that their texts have been quoted or cited.

AL	*American Literature*
AM	*Atlantic Monthly*
AN	*The American Notebooks*
Bancroft	Bancroft Library, University of California, Berkeley
Barrett	Clifton Waller Barrett, "Gleanings in a Field of Stubble," *Autograph Collector's Journal*, IV (Summer, 1952), 5–11.
Berg	The Henry W. and Albert A. Berg Collection of the New York Public Library
Birdsall	Richard D. Birdsall, *Berkshire County: A Cultural History* (New Haven: Yale University Press, 1959)
BPLQ	*Boston Public Library Quarterly*
BR	*The Blithedale Romance*
Clark	C. E. Frazer Clark, Jr., *Nathaniel Hawthorne: A Descriptive Bibliography* (Pittsburgh: University of Pittsburgh Press, 1978)

Critical Heritage	J. Donald Crowley, *Hawthorne: The Critical Heritage* (New York: Barnes and Noble, 1970)
DAB	*Dictionary of American Biography,* ed. Allen Johnson and Dumas Malone (New York: Scribner, 1943)
Die Entwicklung	Alfred Weber, *Die Entwicklung der Rahmenerzählungen Nathaniel Hawthornes: "The Story Teller" und Andere Frühe Werke (1825–1835)* (Berlin: Erich Schmidt, 1973)
EIHC	*Essex Institute Historical Collections*
EN	*The English Notebooks,* ed. Randall Stewart (New York: Modern Language Association, 1941)
Essex	Essex Institute, Salem, Mass.
Faust	Bertha Faust, *Hawthorne's Contemporaneous Reputation: A Study of Literary Opinion in America and England 1828–1864* (Philadelphia: University of Pennsylvania Press, 1939)
FIN	*The French and Italian Notebooks*
Gollin	Rita K. Gollin, *Portraits of Nathaniel Hawthorne: An Iconography* (DeKalb: Northern Illinois University Press, 1983)
Gordan	John D. Gordan, "Nathaniel Hawthorne, The Years of Fulfilment 1804–1853," *Bulletin of the New York Public Library,* LIX (1955)
Harris	Sheldon Howard Harris, "The Public Career of John Louis O'Sullivan," Ph.D. dissertation, Columbia University, 1958
Hawthorne	James T. Fields, *Hawthorne* (Boston: James R. Osgood, 1876)
Hawthorne and His Publisher	Caroline Ticknor, *Hawthorne and His Publisher* (Boston: Houghton Mifflin, 1913)
HSG	*The House of the Seven Gables*

Huntington	Henry E. Huntington Library, San Marino, California
JMN	Ralph Waldo Emerson, *Journals and Miscellaneous Notebooks* (Cambridge: Harvard University Press, 1960–82)
Kesselring	Marion Louise Kesselring, *Hawthorne's Reading* (New York: New York Public Library, 1949)
Lathrop	George Parsons Lathrop, *A Study of Hawthorne* (Boston: James R. Osgood, 1876)
Leach	Joseph Leach, *Bright Particular Star: The Life and Times of Charlotte Cushman* (New Haven: Yale University Press, 1970)
LL	*Love Letters of Nathaniel Hawthorne* (Chicago: Society of the Dofobs, 1907), Vol. 1, 1839–41; Vol. 2, 1841–63
Longfellow, *Letters*	*The Letters of Henry Wadsworth Longfellow,* ed. Andrew Hilen (Cambridge: Harvard University Press, 1966–82)
Longfellow, *Life*	*Life of Henry Wadsworth Longfellow,* ed. Samuel Longfellow (Boston: Ticknor & Co., 1886)
LT	*Letters of Hawthorne to William D. Ticknor, 1851–1864* (Newark: Carteret Book Club, 1910), Vol. 1: Nov. 14, 1851–Jan. 17, 1856; Vol. 2: Feb. 16, 1856–March 18, 1864
Melville Log	Jay Leyda, *The Melville Log: A Documentary Life of Herman Melville* (New York: Harcourt Brace, 1951)
Memories	Rose Hawthorne Lathrop, *Memories of Hawthorne,* 2nd ed. (Boston: Houghton Mifflin, 1923)
MHS	Massachusetts Historical Society, Boston
MF	*The Marble Faun*

MOM	*Mosses from an Old Manse*
Morgan	Pierpont Morgan Library, New York
Mott	Frank Luther Mott, A *History of American Magazines 1741–1850* (New York: Appleton and Co., 1930)
NEQ	*New England Quarterly*
Nevins	Winfield S. Nevins, "Nathaniel Hawthorne's Removal from the Salem Custom House," *EIHC*, LIII (1917)
NH	Nathaniel Hawthorne
NHHW	Julian Hawthorne, *Nathaniel Hawthorne and His Wife* (Boston: James R. Osgood, 1884)
NHJ	*Nathaniel Hawthorne Journal* (by year)
Nichols	Roy Franklin Nichols, *Franklin Pierce: Young Hickory of the Granite Hills,* 2nd ed. (Philadelphia: University of Pennsylvania Press, 1958)
PAN	*Passages from the American Notebooks,* ed. Sophia Hawthorne (Boston: Ticknor & Fields, 1868)
PBSA	*Publications of the Bibliographical Society of America*
Pickard	Samuel T. Pickard, *Hawthorne's First Diary* (Boston: Houghton, Mifflin, 1897)
Recollections	Horatio Bridge, *Personal Recollections of Nathaniel Hawthorne* (New York: Harper and Brothers, 1893)
SEG	Boston *Saturday Evening Gazette* (cited from Sunday morning editions)
SH	Sophia Hawthorne (Sophia Peabody before marriage)
SI	*The Snow-Image*
SL	*The Scarlet Letter*
Swift	Lindsay Swift, *Brook Farm* (New York: Corinth Books, 1961)
TS	*True Stories from History and Biography*
TT	*Tanglewood Tales*
TTT	*Twice-told Tales*

Turner   Arlin Turner, *Hawthorne as Editor*
                          (University: Louisiana State Univer-
                          sity Press, 1941)
Virginia   Alderman Library, University of
                          Virginia
WB/TT   A *Wonder Book* and *Tanglewood Tales*
Works   Riverside Edition, *The Complete
                          Works of Nathaniel Hawthorne* (Bos-
                          ton: Houghton, Mifflin, 1883); 12
                          vols.
Writings   Autograph Edition, *The Writings of
                          Nathaniel Hawthorne* (Boston: Hough-
                          ton, Mifflin, 1900); 22 vols.
WA   *Wide Awake*, XXXIII (November,
                          1891)
Wilson   Carroll Atwood Wilson, *Thirteen Au-
                          thor Collections of the Nineteenth Cen-
                          tury* (New York: Scribner, 1950)

THE LETTERS, 1813-1843

INTRODUCTION: HAWTHORNE'S LETTERS, 1813–1853

WHEN *Love Letters of Nathaniel Hawthorne,* containing 160 letters, was privately printed in two volumes in 1907, a reviewer—one of few—concluded: "The letters are very tender and characteristic, but they add little to our knowledge of Hawthorne, and it is not to be regretted that they are to remain practically unpublished."[1] Three years later, another two-volume set, again privately printed, with 146 letters, *Letters of Hawthorne to William D. Ticknor, 1851–1864,* was as little noticed until Houghton, Mifflin brought out much of its contents in 1913 as *Hawthorne and His Publisher.* A reviewer found that here "the personality of the writer is revealed with the frankness of intimacy," but a later, more-informed judgment was that these letters "show the man of affairs, the outer Hawthorne."[2] None of the subsequent publications of smaller groups of letters has elicited much excitement, but it may nevertheless be expected that the present volumes and those to come, containing all the surviving letters, will provide the materials for new approaches to the biography of one of America's most enigmatic writers, a man who firmly opposed self-exposure during his life and who professed the wish that no biography ever be written.

[1] *Nation,* LXXXV (August 22, 1907), 160. The letters were edited by Roswell Field for the Society of Dofobs, a Chicago book club.

[2] *Dial,* LVI (January 1, 1914), 13; Austin Warren, ed., *Nathaniel Hawthorne: Representative Selections* (New York: American Book Company, 1934), pp. lxxxviii–lxxxix. The letters were printed for the Carteret Book Club, Newark, N. J.

Of course, there are by now many biographies of Hawthorne. Though the "complete" letters have not previously appeared, biographers beginning with Julian Hawthorne in 1884 have made extensive use of those available, always trying to reveal "the frankness of intimacy." Like some other American writers of his time, Hawthorne became through his writings an increasingly important, and increasingly remote, personality for following generations. A function of familiar letters has been, at least since the early eighteenth century, to show an author's simple and natural self, his informal, relaxed, colloquial writing. "Talking upon paper," Alexander Pope put it: "Having windows in our breasts."[3] When he published Emerson's *Letters* in six volumes in 1939, Ralph L. Rusk wrote in his introduction that though his "confessions of coldness and restraint are common and are sometimes justified . . . the whole body of Emerson's correspondence goes to prove that he was capable of much more warmth and enthusiasm in his friendships, as well as in his domestic relations, than has been supposed. . . . Letters about his children, or to them, add more than enough evidence to put an end to the legend of the stoic."[4] Just as typically, Andrew Hilen claims that Longfellow's early letters reveal a "different" self than that of Samuel Longfellow's authorized biography. Though still "a well-mannered young man with the instincts of the genteel age," the personality of the letters "appears now with all his shortcomings and peccadilloes, all his worries and yearnings and regrets, and . . . the self-portrait is more interesting than the brother's idealized one."[5] Similarly, Randall Stewart published twenty letters of Hawthorne to the Salem Custom House officer and Democratic politician William B. Pike to

[3] Pope to Lady Mary Wortley Montagu, August 18, 1716 (Pope, *Correspondence*, ed. George Sherburn [Oxford: Clarendon Press, 1956]), I, 353.

[4] (New York: Columbia University Press), I, xvi–xvii.

[5] Longfellow, *Letters*, I, 4.

show the falsehood of the received image of Hawthorne as a remote, eccentric, alienated man: "Several passages in the following letter suggest an active and sagacious participation in local political movements." The Hawthorne of these letters is "worldly and pragmatic," shrewd, skillful in diplomacy, possessing "a remarkable sense of humor."[6] The reader will be able to judge how all his surviving letters humanize Hawthorne and what legends they may end or begin.

Readers will notice that from the time of his graduation from Bowdoin to his work as editor of a Boston magazine in 1836 only twelve letters appear. Since many of his most admired tales were first published during this period, the lack will certainly be regretted by anyone hoping for authorial comment on these works. The lack seems to exist because he felt in a particularly protective way about this period of his life, feelings he was quite eager to confess to Longfellow in a now famous letter of June 1837. He set out to destroy systematically the epistolary record of those years. His closest friend, Horatio Bridge, recalled: "Many years ago Hawthorne requested me to burn the letters he had written me in his youth and early manhood. On reading them over, I found them full of passages of beauty and details of his own plans and purposes, hopes and disappointments. They were, however, too free in their expressions about persons and things to be safely trusted to the chances of life; and all his early letters were destroyed. Many of these were signed 'Oberon,' and others the familiar 'Hawthorne' or 'Hath'." Hawthorne confirms this account in a letter to Bridge from his second year in England, in response to something about lending the letters: "As regards those letters of mine, I wish you would burn them the moment you regain possession of them. I certainly do not wish to read them; nor do I see why you

[6] "Hawthorne and Politics: Unpublished Letters to William B. Pike," *NEQ*, V (1932), 240, 243–44.

should." Two years later, at the moment he resigned the consulship at Liverpool, Hawthorne repeated the request with even stronger emotion: "Those old letters of mine—are they destroyed? I beg you not to leave this matter at loose ends." At an earlier transitional moment, just before sailing for Europe in June 1853, he confided to his notebook that he had just "burned great heaps of letters and other papers. . . . Among them were hundreds of Sophia's maiden letters—the world has no more such; and now they are all ashes. What a trustful guardian of secret matters fire is!"[7] In "The Devil in Manuscript" (1835), told about the writer Oberon, and "Fire Worship" (1843), told by the writer resident in the Old Manse, fire is the ambivalent symbol of the imagination, suggesting Promethean creativity, conventional domesticity, and retributive destruction. All of these seem contained in the personification "trustful guardian of secret matters." And the destructive tendencies emphasized in the 1835 story did not recede after Hawthorne attained fame and prosperity. James T. Fields told the English writer Mary Russell Mitford that Hawthorne's was "a difficult mind to deal with. . . . If I had found the slightest fault" with *The House of the Seven Gables*, "he would instantly have flung the whole MS. into the fire."[8]

We may explain this apparently desperate neuroticism by speculating that Sophia is not recorded to have objected to the destruction of her love letters precisely because they were

[7] *Recollections*, p. 49; Hawthorne to Bridge, December 14, 1854; Hawthorne to Bridge, February 13, 1857; MSS, Bowdoin; AN, p. 552. Sophia Hawthorne wrote to James T. Fields, October 14, 1865, as she began to prepare the American Notebooks for publication: "If he journalized before 1835, he destroyed the books. Alas for it" (MS, Boston Public Library). See Randall Stewart, "Editing Hawthorne's Notebooks: Selections from Mrs. Hawthorne's Letters to Mr. and Mrs. Fields, 1864–1868," *More Books*, XX (September, 1945), 303.

[8] *The Friendships of Mary Russell Mitford as Recorded in Letters from Her Literary Correspondents*, ed. A. G. L'Estrange (London: Hurst & Blackett, 1882), p. 362; March 11, 1852. Compare Letters 542 and 543, and the statement about "condemned manuscript" in the Preface to *Twice-told Tales*, 1851, and see Letters 173, 222, 327, and especially 401.

"too free in their expressions about persons and things," whereas his letters to her could be retained if they were made to emphasize the lover's fanciful lyricism, literally cutting out the facts and opinions that reveal too much. Hawthorne wrote in "The Old Manse," his first major excursion into autobiography, that "the stream of thought that has been flowing from my pen" is "shallow and scanty . . . compared with the broad tide of dim emotions, ideas and associations, which swell around me from that portion of my existence! How little have I told!" And, writing a public letter to Bridge as preface to *The Snow-Image,* he again seems proud that, while speaking "as friend speaks to friend," he and his correspondent remain "cautious, however, that the public and critics shall overhear nothing we care about concealing." Like the epistolary novels of the eighteenth century that enchanted his youth, Hawthorne's correspondence is often a self-conscious game of purposeful disclosures and reticences.

He sometimes seems obsessively concerned about suppressing what was not carefully and fully thought out. He destroyed all early drafts of his fiction (except for the unfinished romances of his last years), and his notebooks and letters both show frequent signs of copying from earlier versions. In the Preface to her edition of his English Notebooks, Sophia Hawthorne justified her creative editing by claiming a great difference between writing "given to the world by his own hand," which presents his condensed "*conclusions,*" and journalizing, where "Mr. Hawthorne is *entertaining,* not *asserting,* opinions and ideas. He questions, doubts, and reflects with his pen, and, as it were instructs himself."[9] By all accounts not a ready conversationalist, Hawthorne often mistrusted spontaneity in writing as well.

But this is not to say that he wrote weak, careless, or uninformative letters. What he and his widow allowed to

[9] *Passages from the English Note-Books,* ed. Sophia Hawthorne (London: Strahan, 1870), pp. 9–10.

survive provides his readers with much to consider. He was born into a world in which gentlemen were expected to be able to write letters as an exercise not only of sociability but of character. Like Longfellow's father, Hawthorne's Aunt Mary and Uncle Robert required him as a boy to write frequently and at sufficient length to demonstrate his intellectual mastery of the subjects discussed and his concern for method and style. His famous letter of March, 1821, to his mother about the problem of vocation shows the firm command of that epistolary persona his teachers in school and college set as a model. During his decade after college, he practiced the genre of the narrative or traveling letter, both in his descriptions of Salem happenings to John Stephen Dike and in his accounts to his family of his own summer excursions. "This is not intended for a public letter," he wrote to Louisa in 1831, "though it is truly a pity that the public should lose it. When John Stevens's [sic] epistles are published, this shall be inserted in the Appendix." By the time he met Sophia, herself a devoted letter-writer, he had become used to expressing his distaste for letters; she reported to her sister, Elizabeth, that this mysterious Salem author "said it was a great thing for him to write a letter." He maintained this attitude with varying degrees of intensity for the rest of his life, and Sophia came to accept "his excessive aversion to writing a letter," as she put it to Louisa in 1843, and his "utter detestation of pen, ink and paper," as she informed Bridge in 1846.[10] He would write to close friends like Burchmore of his "inveterate habit of shirking all correspondence," and to strangers that he was always "sluggish" in answering letters. After 1850, as he began to see himself as a literary

[10] Sophia Hawthorne to Elizabeth Peabody, April 26, 1838 (MS, Berg); Sophia to Louisa Hawthorne, January 29, 1843 (MS, Berg); Letter 449. He gave Sophia the task of corresponding with his sister, sometimes adding a postscript or marginal comment to her letter. On a few occasions, he contributed to her letters to the Peabodys and Horatio Bridge.

lion, he would apologize for awaiting a "genial mood" or an "eminently epistolary mood."

Sophia Hawthorne made use of "extracts from his private letters" of 1839–41 to supplement the journals in her edition of the American notebooks in 1868, concluding with his remarkable performance of October 4, 1840: "Here I sit in my old accustomed chamber, where I used to sit in days gone by. . . . Here I have written many tales,—many that have been burned to ashes, many that doubtless deserved the same fate. This claims to be called a haunted chamber, for thousands upon thousands of visions have appeared to me in it; and some few of them have become visible to the world. If ever I should have a biographer, he ought to make great mention of this chamber in my memoirs. . . . " As *his* biographer she omitted the parts of the letter about her, about her role to "reveal me to myself," but these appeared in their son's *Nathaniel Hawthorne and His Wife* in 1884.[11] What statement by an author could be a more pregnant germ for his official biography?

When she began reading over his letters in May 1867, she, feeling her widowhood, first thought that they would be "a glory" to publish, for "the world never contained such letters before"; but still it was "impossible" that "prosaic men" be allowed to see them: "I even feel like veiling myself when I read them."[12] By use of scissors and heavy overscoring, she settled her problem with respect to some passages that the world will never see. But she remembered that on their first wedding anniversary Hawthorne had written a letter to her in the Old Manse journal that they shared.[13] Other passages of journal, such as "Twenty Days with Julian & Little

[11] *NHHW*, I, 222–23; compare Letter 225, where he turns this theme to burlesque.

[12] Sophia to Fields, May 31, 1867 (MS, Boston Public Library); see Stewart, "Editing Hawthorne's Notebooks," 311.

[13] *AN*, pp. 390–91.

Bunny," were an even more "intimate domestic history," so she replaced that in her volume with carefully selected extracts from twenty-three letters. Even these she objected to Fields's printing in the *Atlantic Monthly*, for "there is a certain intimateness of revelation in even these extracts from the letters which I cannot bear to go into a public journal."[14] Nevertheless he did persuade her to let them appear in the January, 1868, *Atlantic*. This incident seems typical of the history of the love letters, and of Hawthorne's letters as a whole: Reluctance has seemed to conspire with Revelation alternatively to show a vision and to draw a veil, until now we can hope that the spell is broken, and that everything that can be found is on public display.

II

Hawthorne was born July 4, 1804, in Salem, in a house at 21 Union Street. His paternal grandfather, Daniel (1731–96), a legendary Revolutionary War naval hero known as "Bold Hathorne,"[15] had bought it in the 1750s (though Hawthorne once claimed that this "maritime personage" had built it).[16] His father, born in 1775 and also named Nathaniel, the favorite name in the family since the seventeenth century, was another ship captain; he died of yellow fever in South America in early 1808. Since his estate totaled less than $300, his widow moved with her children to her father's house at 12 Herbert Street, directly behind the Union Street

[14] Sophia to Fields, January 30, 1868, and November 3, 1867 (MSS, Boston Public Library); see Stewart, "Editing Hawthorne's Notebooks," 312.

[15] The author changed the spelling and pronunciation of his surname in the mid-1820s, so that, he wrote an autograph-seeker in 1837, "no other person spells the family name in the same manner"; see also "Time's Portraiture" (1838), where he jokingly rebukes himself for having "seen fit to transmogrify a good old name" (*SI*, p. 331).

[16] In the autobiographical sketch he sent to R. H. Stoddard in 1853 for publication in the *National Magazine;* see *NHHW*, I, 95.

house, and it was there that Hawthorne passed most of his childhood. In both houses lived numerous relatives. On Union Street his grandmother Rachel Phelps Hathorne (1734–1813) presided over two unmarried daughters, Eunice (1767–1827) and Ruth (1778–1847), a childless widowed daughter, Sarah (1763–1827), and an unmarried son, Captain Daniel (1768–1805), as well as Captain Nathaniel and his wife and children. Two other daughters could afford houses of their own nearby in which to raise their children: Rachel (1757–1823) and Judith (1770–1829). Of the five sons and sons-in-law, all of whom followed the sea, only one, Rachel's husband Simon Forrester (1748–1817), an Irish protégé of "Bold Hathorne" whom Hawthorne was to mention in "The Custom–House" as one of the "princely merchants" of Salem, died at home at a venerable age. The young Daniel Hathorne died at sea in 1805; Captain John Crowninshield, husband of Sarah, died in 1786 at the age of twenty-five of a fever contracted abroad; Captain George Archer, husband of Judith, died at sea in 1799, leaving four small children.

Hawthorne's mother was Elizabeth Clarke Manning (1780–1849), second daughter of Richard (1755–1813) and Miriam Lord Manning (1748–1826). He was a blacksmith who came to Salem from nearby Ipswich in 1774; in the 1790s he began, with his sons, a stagecoach line, the Boston & Salem; as he prospered, he soon bought considerable land in Raymond, Maine, inland from Portland on Sebago Lake. In 1808 Betsey Hathorne and her children returned to a house inhabited not only by her parents but by her three unmarried sisters and four unmarried brothers, who ranged in age from thirty-one to seventeen years. Another brother had gone to sea in 1802 or 1803 at the age of fourteen or fifteen, and was never heard of again.[17] One of the sisters

---

[17] Hawthorne recalled his Uncle John in his notebook on June 30, 1854: Miriam Manning "never gave up the hope of his return, and was constantly hearing

and two of the brothers were to marry, the first not until 1816; the first of Hawthorne's full cousins on the Manning side was not born until 1826. After an aunt married a widower in 1817, there were two half-cousins, but one of these died in 1820. Under these circumstances, it is not surprising that the Manning aunts and uncles indulged and pampered the children. Several Hathorne-side cousins are mentioned in the letters, suggesting that there was considerable more social intercourse with them than the author's published autobiographical writings were to suggest, but of course the Mannings were the most important childhood influences.

During Hawthorne's childhood his Grandfather Manning died, and his Aunt Maria (1786–1814) soon afterward. Neither Mary (1777–1841) nor William (1778–1864), the oldest sister and brother, ever married. It was Mary who transferred her share in the Salem Atheneum to Nathaniel in 1828, allowing him to borrow books, a privilege he made much use of until he moved to Boston in 1839. She was a devout Calvinist, strict with children, and parsimonious like her mother. Accepting their mild rebelliousness and frequent teasing, she staunchly maintained her faith in their earthly fortunes, particularly Nathaniel's, encouraging him to be the first member of either family to attend college. William, whose personality appears less striking, took over management of the stage operation, but lacked an aggressive business sense. By the time the railroad replaced the stagecoach in the late 1830s, he was unable to adjust: he ended his long life a bachelor in a rented room. His benevolence to Hawthorne during his college years was returned to him in his old age, when he received a place as custodian in the Custom House,

---

stories of persons whose description answered to his. . . . And even to this day, I never see his name (which is no very uncommon one) without thinking that this may be the lost uncle" (*EN*, p. 64). This case is fictionalized briefly in *The House of the Seven Gables* as Hepzibah's uncle, who, she hoped, might return from India after fifty years of silence "and make her the ultimate heiress of his unreckonable riches" (*HSG*, p. 64).

and money from his by then moderately prosperous nephew, who apparently chose to overlook William's niggardly attitude at a moment of crisis, the return from the Old Manse to Salem in 1845.

Richard (1782–1831), the second son, chose to move to Raymond immediately after his father's death. He managed the family property there, ran a general store, married a local woman, and won honor as a leading citizen. In 1817 Priscilla (1790–1873), the youngest daughter, married John Dike (1783–1871), a Salem widower with two children, Mary (1805–20) and John Stephen (1807–91). The younger John Dike seems to have been as close a family male companion as Hawthorne had in his adolescent years. In 1830 he went to Ohio, but his father remained in Salem, following various mercantile enterprises connected with the port and its shipping, sometimes prospering and sometimes not. Though Hawthorne seems never to have been close to either Priscilla or John, they became after the deaths of his mother and sister Louisa his chief family link with Salem.

Samuel (1791–1833), the youngest son, became a companion to Hawthorne after his return from Bowdoin. His speciality was the purchase of horses for the family's stagecoaches. Fond of travel, of taverns, and of sharp and irreverent perceptions about people on the road, Sam was much more like an older brother than a parental authority and resembled some of the men whose company Hawthorne later preferred in Salem. He died of tuberculosis in his early forties.

A document surviving at Bowdoin states that Hawthorne's Uncle Robert (1784–1842), together with John Dike and Samuel Manning, paid the college $100 for their nephew's expenses in 1823. William and Mary also helped, but Robert seems the principal benefactor and father substitute. The third son and fifth child, he was the most able and successful. He was associated with William in the stage operation from 1813 to 1821, when he went to live in Raymond to develop an orchard. By 1823 he was back in Salem as president of the stagecoach company, with William as its "agent" or manager. Robert acquired land on the northern outskirts of the town for a "pomological garden . . . a laboratory for testing, proving, and selecting fruits."[18] First at Raymond and then at Salem, he imported many varieties, particularly of pears and apples, from England, Belgium, and France, to find which were hardy enough to withstand the New England winters. He was a founder of the Massachusetts Horticultural Society, and soon became known for his extraordinary talent in identifying different varieties and in establishing a coherent and systematic nomenclature. By his death he had collected more than two thousand varieties, with a special interest in pears, but including apples, peaches, plums, and apricots. He built a house on Dearborn Street near his experimental garden, at about the time of his marriage in 1824. By 1828 he was able to add a cottage for his sister Elizabeth and her children, who lived there until they returned to Herbert Street in 1832.

Hawthorne seems to have indicated his lack of interest in these projects at the outset in 1823, in his last letter to Robert that has survived. But we can speculate that he was encouraged then and later to join the quest for sturdier and more succulent pears and apples. In his only published book, a descriptive catalogue called *The Book of Fruits,* Robert defended the nobility of his vocation: "To a young man with the advantage of fortune and a familiarity with the modern languages, researches of this nature would open an inexhaustible source of enjoyment. He could scarcely be more honorably and usefully occupied than in collecting and identifying fruits, and introducing them to the notice of his countrymen; nor better rewarded than in witnessing his anticipation, from

---

[18] Albert Emerson Benson, *History of the Massachusetts Horticultural Society* (Boston: For the Society, 1929), p. 73.

year to year, continually realized and continually renewed."[19]
We cannot know if these "pretty sentences" are the work of
the author's literary nephew, but we can see that Hawthorne
kept an interest that expressed itself at unexpected moments,
as in Rappaccini's garden or Hester Prynne's visit to the
Reverend John Wilson's house; or in his own initial encounter with the English countryside at Poulton Hall in Cheshire,
where the peaches and pears looked "miserable enough," the
trees flattened against a brick wall "like the skin of a dead
animal nailed up to dry." A year later he felt the same aversion to an Englishman's comparing a peach to a melon: "Just
think of this idea of the richest, lusciousest of all fruits."[20]
At such moments, Hawthorne was proud to remember his
uncle's expertise. Among his characters, the hypocritical,
villainous Judge Pyncheon, "the christian, the good citizen,
the horticulturist, and the gentlemen," who benefits horti-
culture "by producing two much-esteemed varieties of the
pear," is balanced by his antagonist Holgrave, who when
finally civilized by Phoebe pledges "to set out trees, to make
fences . . . even . . . to build a house for another
generation."[21]

More problematical, perhaps, than his feelings toward
Robert Manning was his relationship with his mother. His
last letter to her that we have is of 1832, seventeen years
before her death. There is, moreover, no hint of a correspondence that was destroyed. This fact would seem to support
his son Julian's characterization in *Nathaniel Hawthorne and
His Wife*: "His mother, a woman of fine gifts but of extreme
sensibility, lost her husband in her twenty-eighth year; and,
from an exaggerated, almost Hindoo-like construction of the
law of seclusion which the public taste of that day imposed

[19] Robert Manning, *Book of Fruits* (Salem: Ives & Jewett, 1838), p. 10. For
Hawthorne "correcting" his uncle's prose into "pretty sentences," see Letter 52.
[20] *EN*, pp. 7, 64.
[21] *HSG*, pp. 24, 230–31, 307.

upon widows, she withdrew entirely from society, and permitted the habit of solitude to grow upon her to such a degree
that she actually remained a strict hermit to the end of her
long life, or for more than forty years after Captain Hawthorne's death."[22] Many biographers have accepted this view,
but letters by her published in the last few decades suggest
quite a different situation, at least for the first fifteen years
of her widowhood. While she lived in Raymond, from 1818
to 1822, she took an active interest in her children's activities, in her property, and in the Sunday school she founded
and conducted there. In Raymond she found freedom from
the authority of her mother and her older sister. If she had
become a hermit, her son hardly would have included in his
private family newspaper, *The Spectator*, on January 31,
1822, humorous announcements that "she has opened a
PUBLIC HOUSE at her residence in Raymond," and that
"the RAYMOND HOTEL, kept by Mrs. E. C. Hathorne,
[is] the usual resort of all Strangers of Distinction."[23] Earlier, about 1816, she appears in a similar verbal picture at
home in Salem. Lucy Ann Sutton, a cousin from Portland,
made her first visit to the Hathornes: "Aunt Mary took me
by the hand and led me to the sitting room, where Nathaniel
was standing by the side of his mother and reading aloud.
Mrs. Hawthorne kindly noticed me, and then Aunt Mary
said to Nathaniel: 'This is your cousin, and I want you to be
very polite to her'."[24] Lucy Ann recalled the incident almost
seventy years later, but it has the tone of truth: the widow
quietly but fiercely proud of her son as he declaims his Goldsmith or Thomson or Pope. Mother and son were, his sister
Elizabeth wrote to Sophia Peabody on the eve of the marriage, of the same disposition. But already by 1820 the son is

---

[22] I, 4–5.

[23] MS, Essex.

[24] Manning Hawthorne, "A Glimpse of Hawthorne's Boyhood," *EIHC*,
LXXXIII (1947), 179.

concerned that his mother will "wear a cap" to symbolize her retirement, and his pleas to her to not return to Salem from Raymond indicate the intimacy of their relationship and their mutual need for retirement. Nevertheless, when Nathaniel left Salem in the summer of 1821 for college at Bowdoin, he stopped at Raymond with her for only a few hours, though he had not seen her for two years.

His older sister, Elizabeth (1802–83), was by all accounts, including his own, a remarkable woman, and she often seems the person closest to his creative resources. She was his confidante about his reading and his literary ambitions during his school days; she borrowed books for him from the Salem Atheneum during his decade of apprenticeship after college; it was to her that he expressed his hopes and plans as well as his pride in the first English review of his tales in 1836. She collaborated in producing the *American Magazine of Useful and Entertaining Knowledge,* and in its sequel, the "history of the universe," under the general and seemingly ubiquitous name "Peter Parley," Samuel Goodrich's highly profitable device for popular education, and it was she that he first asked to work with him in 1841 on the project that became *Biographical Stories for Children.* Later she worked on a translation of Cervantes's *Tales,* for which he gave assistance. He supported her while he was in Europe, and near the end of his life tried to find her a position as a librarian, noting that "she is the most sensible woman I ever knew in my life, much superior to me in general talent, and of fine cultivation . . . she has both a physical and intellectual love of books, being a born book-worm."[25]

As a young girl, she had some social life, visiting friends and relations in Salem and nearby Newburyport, though even then she disapproved of gossiping visits. Her activities Nathaniel described jokingly as "a vortex of dissipation," and

[25] Hawthorne to William D. Ticknor, May 17, 1862 (MS, Berg).

when in 1821 she apparently was sought in marriage by a forty-year-old widower, Captain Jeremiah Briggs, her brother's prose turned cartwheels in affectionately sarcastic appreciation.[26] Within a few years, this bustle ended; and as her mother gradually withdrew from society, Elizabeth joined her. By 1837, when the Hawthornes met the Peabody family, she was, Mary Peabody noted, the author's "very remarkable sister who lives even more to herself than he has done."[27] She was an "impossible correspondent," and she entertained what Hawthorne called "naughty notions" about politics, always opposing his; but she shared his love of the wilder nature of Raymond, and of long "rambles" on the seashore and in the woods near Salem. Her nearsightedness caused sometimes humorous confusion when she walked with him or his friends. The Peabodys soon discovered that "there was not the least bit of sentiment about her, but she was strongly intellectual," and that "extreme sensibility makes her a hermitress."[28] Finally, just before his marriage, Hawthorne tried to explain to his bride the "strange reserve" in his family, and Elizabeth herself wrote to Sophia of her dislike of "any responsibility not forced upon me by circumstances beyond my control." She had difficulty thinking of marriage as a way of life for herself, or for anyone. It was the same independence, expressed in a more powerfully positive, almost Melvillian way, that led her to answer her brother's request for her opinion of *The House of the Seven Gables*. She found the great charm of both it and *The Scarlet Letter* in

[26] Briggs (1780–1844) was not to remarry until ten years later; his first wife had died in 1810. Hawthorne's description of Captain Briggs in *The Spectator* as "a young man of rank and accomplishments" should be compared with that by the Reverend William Bentley: "A man of excellent natural genius, as cultivated as his opportunities could admit, but capable of great development and of powerful and persevering action." See *EIHC*, LXXIII (1937), 187–88.

[27] November 16, 1837 (MS, Berg).

[28] Elizabeth Peabody, quoted by Julian Hawthorne (MS, Morgan); see Norman Holmes Pearson, "Elizabeth Peabody on Hawthorne," *EIHC*, XCIV (1958), 254; Sophia to Elizabeth Peabody, May 13, 1838 (MS, Berg).

"the perfect ease and freedom with which they seem to be written; it is evident that you stand in no awe of the public, but rather bid it defiance, which it is well for all authors, and all other men to do."[29]

His younger sister, Louisa (1808–52), was the most sociable of the Hawthornes. Her letters to Sophia show a keen mind, though she lacked the dedication to literature of Nathaniel and Elizabeth. As a child, Louisa was Nathaniel's audience, and his helper for his family newspaper, *The Spectator,* to which she contributed a quatrain, "Address to the Sun." She also served the Pin Society, another of his inventions, as "second Pin Counter." From Bowdoin and afterward, she was the recipient of his letters about his travels and adventures. By the late 1830s, she had joined him and his friends Conolly, Roberts, and Susan Ingersoll in a club for playing cards, where she was known as "the Empress"; he was "the Emperor." She thus took an interest in the Salem politics and gossip that Hawthorne found refreshing—until the furor over his dismissal from the Custom House soured him forever on his native town. Louisa provided a steady flow of Salem papers when he lived in Concord and Lenox, and she kept up her end (after considerable prodding) of the correspondence with Sophia about such matters as darning socks, making baby clothes, furnishing rooms, and preserving fruit. Of literature she tended to mention only her brother's productions, which she read faithfully as they appeared. "It does me good to see something of his," she wrote. She disapproved mildly of the indifference to church attendence shared by Elizabeth, Nathaniel, and Sophia. In Salem she wrote to Sophia, "People have been going to meeting all winter, and we hear of little else, but that is not in *your* line, you being *beyond* the Church, as Mr. [Theodore] Parker says."[30] She also shows a wry attitude toward other family

[29] May 3, 1851 (MS, Berg); NHHW, I, 439.
[30] February 15, 1844; March 4, 1843 (MSS, Berg).

foibles, as when Uncle William balked at renting a room when the Old Manse suddenly had to be vacated: "If any one wants anything of him, it is sure to acquire a new value in his eyes, and he finds out that he wants it himself."[31] She was willing to leave Salem to visit in Concord, Lenox, and West Newton. She adored her nieces and nephew in a more active way than her sister and mother. Ironically, when she took the longest journey of her life, in the summer of 1852, accompanying her uncle John Dike to Saratoga and returning by way of New York City, the steamboat *Henry Clay* caught fire, and she jumped into the Hudson and drowned.

III

It was soon after the publication of *Twice-told Tales* on March 6, 1837—Hawthorne's attempt, as he later described it, "to open an intercourse with the world"[32]—that the world began to come to him. It came first in the form of a fellow resident of Salem, the Transcendentalist teacher and author Elizabeth Palmer Peabody (1804–94), who had become used to finding men of genius. After teaching with her mother in Salem before 1820, she had opened a school in Brookline in 1822, had studied Greek then with Ralph Waldo Emerson, had served as secretary and amanuensis to the Reverend William Ellery Channing intermittently from 1826 to his death in 1842, and had joined A. Bronson Alcott in his controversial experimental school in Boston in 1834–35. Disappointed that Alcott's imparting of transcendental wisdom to children by Socratic questioning was not appreciated by the Boston intelligentsia, she had returned to Salem in 1836, and was to live there with her family for four years, without employ-

[31] September 3, 1845 (MS, Berg).
[32] Preface to *Twice-told Tales*, 1851, *TTT*, p. 6.

ment, restless and ever searching for new challenges. She
was naturally excited to learn that the author of *Twice-told
Tales* lived in Salem, and first thought it was Elizabeth Hawthorne, whom she had known slightly as a child. With the
first visit of Nathaniel and his sisters to the Peabody house
on Charter Street on November 11, 1837, she seems to have
made a strong impact on this family of "extraordinary seclusion." She cultivated Elizabeth and Louisa, both for themselves and to learn more about the previous life that had made
Nathaniel, as she immediately recognized, "a man of first
rate genius, surpassing *Irving* even." Treasuring some un-
named "document" of his, she wrote to Louisa: "Nathaniel
has appointed me his future biographer."[33] But we may suspect that however much Hawthorne wished now to come out
of the dungeon of his solitude, he was not, and never would
become, prepared to live in the glare of Elizabeth's busyness.
She conducted an extensive correspondence with him in
1838–39, which she found as full of "moral sentiment" as his
fiction, but none of these letters has been found: he probably
later ordered their destruction, much to the chagrin of his
would-be biographer.

When he looked ahead in 1837, he contemplated more
such "drudgery" as writing children's books and editing magazines of "useful and entertaining" knowledge. Elizabeth
Peabody soon began to help him. She told Horace Mann that
Hawthorne's "one great moral enterprise" was "to make an
attempt at creating a new literature for the young," but that
he had "no genius for negotiation with booksellers," and she
would propose, for him, that Mann persuade Massachusetts

---

[33] Elizabeth Peabody to Horace Mann, March 3, 1838 (MS, MHS); Elizabeth
Peabody to Louisa Hawthorne, November 9, 1838 (MS, Berg). She was to resume
her function as his biographer in a small way after his death. In a letter to
Horatio Bridge, June 4, 1887, she still planned to give the "most true psychological biography of him as I got it from his own account to me in 1838–39 of the
growth of his mind" (MS, Bowdoin). She was to provide information and opinion
to Moncure D. Conway for his *Life of Nathaniel Hawthorne* (London: Walter
Scott, 1895).

to adopt this literature for its schools. She was not successful in this or in her effort in 1842 to make him editor of the *Boston Miscellany,* a struggling literary monthly. But she was a principal force in obtaining employment for him at the Boston Custom House in 1839 and at the Salem Custom House in 1846. She must also have encouraged him to join the Brook Farm experiment in 1841, for by then she had opened her bookstore on West Street in Boston, which soon became one of the most important meeting places in American literary history. It was here already in 1840 that the leaders of New England thought congregated. George Ripley, Margaret Fuller, Theodore Parker, and Frederick Hedge came there, as well as Emerson; the *Dial* was for a time published there, and on her own press she printed three of Hawthorne's books for children, among the antislavery pamphlets and translations of German metaphysics.

Elizabeth's qualifications as the archetypal female Transcendentalist are impeccable, from her personal untidiness and unladylike bustle to her seemingly constant endorsement of utopian educational schemes. Henry James was to make her the Miss Birdseye of his *Bostonians,* and she was long remembered for her legendary reaction to having walked into a tree in Lenox: "Yes, I saw it, but I did not realize it."[34] In her initial enthusiasm (mixed perhaps with a more erotic desire) for Hawthorne, she reviewed *Twice-told Tales* for Park Benjamin's *New-Yorker.*[35] Her review begins: "The Story without an End, of which all true stories are but episodes, is told by Nature herself." For her, Hawthorne as storyteller was an exponent of Wordsworth and Emerson and an example of the superiority of genius to talent. At least usually, for she did discriminate between "the wild imagina-

[34] See Harriet Hosmer, *Letters and Memories* (London: John Lane, 1913), p. 32.

[35] V. (March 24, 1838), 1-2; reprinted in Arlin Turner, "Elizabeth Peabody Reviews *Twice-told Tales,*" NHJ 1974, pp. 75–84.

tion of Germany" in "The Great Carbuncle" and the mere "faculty of fancy" in "Fancy's Show Box." She deplored his penchant for "the odd and peculiar, and especially the fantastic and horrible" in such tales as "The Prophetic Pictures," and must have been more dismayed when she read the pieces he had already published but did not collect in 1837. Ten years later, she was to reject politely "Ethan Brand" for *Aesthetic Papers,* and to welcome the "more cheerful" historical sketch "Main-street" in its place.[36]

Her insistent high-mindedness was shared by others in her family, especially her mother, also named Elizabeth Palmer Peabody (1778–1853), who was the daughter and granddaughter of Revolutionary War generals, sister-in-law of the jurist and dramatist Royall Tyler, and aunt of the publisher George Palmer Putnam. She had become a schoolteacher in her teens, and was preceptress of the girls' academy in Andover, Massachusetts, in 1801, when she met her husband, the boys' preceptor. Nathaniel Peabody (1774–1855) came from a much less brilliant milieu, from a family that arrived in Salem in the seventeenth century but had produced for the most part only farmers in nearby Topsfield. He graduated from Dartmouth in 1800 and, after his fling at teaching, married Betsey Palmer in 1802. Then he suddenly turned his interests to medicine, apparently because his bride preferred the dignity of that profession. By the time their second daughter, Mary, was born in 1806, he had centered his in-

---

[36] Elizabeth's taste was not simply informed by the sentimental optimism common to her contemporaries. She had written in the mid-1820s a series of six essays, "Spirit of the Hebrew Scriptures." After the first three, "Creation," "Temptation, Sin and Punishment," and "Public Worship: Social Crime, and its Retribution," were published in the *Christian Examiner* in May, July, and September, 1834, the editor, Andrews Norton, suppressed the remainder as subversive of Unitarian orthodoxy. See Margaret Neussendorfer, "Elizabeth Palmer Peabody: The Current State of Research," December, 1977 (unpublished). Hawthorne was impressed enough to copy a passage, from the unpublished essays or a journal, into his notebook in 1838; see *Hawthorne's "Lost Notebook," 1835–1841,* ed. Barbara S. Mouffe (University Park: Pennsylvania State University Press, 1978), p. 83.

terests in the unglamorous field of dentistry; and by Sophia's birth in 1809, the family had settled in Salem. The three sons who followed resembled their father as the girls had their mother: both Nathaniel Cranch (1811–81) and George Francis (1813–39) attended Harvard but were expelled for small offenses; Wellington (1816–38), suspended from Harvard, ran up debts, and was in New Orleans studying medicine when he succumbed to yellow fever. George went into business, also in New Orleans, but returned to Salem in 1838 to die of a lingering paralysis caused by consumption of the spinal marrow. A seventh child, Catherine, had died in infancy in 1819.

The younger Nathaniel had followed his father's path by administering schools in Maine and outside Boston until in 1845 he became a homeopathic apothecary, working with his father on the same premises on West Street, Boston, where Elizabeth had sold books and encouraged philosophic conversations. Later Nathaniel lived in West Newton, where he ran boardinghouses for students at the normal school. He was the only Peabody to marry young. His wife, (Sarah) Elizabeth Hibbard (1814–99), of Boston, had no intellectual or artistic pretensions, and their daughters, Ellen Elizabeth (1836–1906) and Mary Cranch (1837–1917), grew up painfully aware of being undistinguished members of a remarkable family.

Mrs. Peabody anticipated Elizabeth's prominence as an educator by conducting schools that assumed the latent genius of all pupils. In 1810 she published in Salem a catechism, *Sabbath Lessons; or, an Abstract of Sacred History,* that may have come to the attention of Elizabeth Hathorne and Mary Manning in the course of their evangelical efforts at Raymond. Twenty-five years later, she published a prose children's version of the first book of *The Faerie Queene,* imitating the Lambs' *Tales from Shakespeare.* In her Preface

to *Holiness; or, The Legend of St. George, . . . by a Mother,*
she announced that similar treatments of the rest of the poem
were in manuscript, "a source of delight to such young persons as have access to them" and were ready to "come forth
at the call of the public."[37] Though that call did not occur,
her passion for Spenser opened a mutual interest with her
future son-in-law, and he and Sophia were to name their
firstborn for Spenser's (and Mrs. Peabody's) heroine.

The second and third Peabody daughters became famous
through the men they married. Mary Tyler (1806–87) helped
her older sister in several schools; in 1832 she and Elizabeth
met Horace Mann (1796–1859), a lawyer and state legislator,
who boarded with them at Mrs. Rebecca Clarke's house in
Boston. Both were attracted to Mann, whose wife had recently died after only a year of marriage. It became clear by
the mid-1830s that he would not propose to Elizabeth, but it
was not until 1843 that he married Mary, who often helped
as a secretary with his educational and legislative projects.
Mary seemed, a recent biographer has argued, to lead "a life
of self-denial and service to others," but this impression
"concealed . . . intense moral convictions which at times
bordered on fanaticism." She favored the Whig attitude
toward republican government, Emersonian idealism applied
to educational theory, and the abolition of slavery without
compromise or delay. "Carefully she placed the seed of an
idea" in Horace Mann's mind, "then helped it grow until he
thought he had originated it and went to her for
reassurance."[38]

Soon after she met Hawthorne in 1837, Mary proposed
that he write a novel about slavery in Cuba, based on the
experience that she and Sophia had there in 1833–35, and

[37] (Boston: E. R. Broaders, 1836), p. iv.

[38] Jonathan Messerli, *Horace Mann: A Biography* (New York: Alfred A. Knopf,
1972), pp. 190–91.

that Sophia recorded at length in letters to her mother.[39] He did not take up the idea, and fifty years later, she was to write the book herself. She was more successful with her request that he keep a journal of his stay in western Massachusetts in the summer of 1838: "He at first said he should not write anything, but finally concluded it would suit him very well for hints for future stories."[40] Of course, he had been keeping a journal for such purposes at least since 1835, and the concession was only apparent. Mary's attitude toward fiction seems to have combined Elizabeth's platonism with the sterner Puritanism of Mann, who replied to Elizabeth's proposal of March, 1838, for Hawthorne with the flat observation that *Twice-told Tales* had insufficient moral significance, and that "something nearer home to duty & business" was needed.[41] Mann had become the first secretary of the Massachusetts Board of Education in 1837, and during the twelve years of his incumbency produced a remarkable series of annual reports as well as editing a semimonthly magazine, the *Common School Journal,* in which he regularly expounded "the great idea of social improvement . . . the sublime law of progression . . . ever-upward ascension in the scale of being."[42] Thus he took a prominent place among the Unitarian ministers and Whig political thinkers of the time.[43] In 1848 he ran for Congress, for the seat recently

[39] Mary Peabody to Sophia (MS, MHS), dated "ca. 1839" by Claire Badaracco, "The Night Blooming Cereus: A Letter from the 'Cuba Journal' 1833–35 of Sophia Peabody Hawthorne, with a Check List of Her Autograph Materials in American Institutions," *Bulletin of Researach in the Humanities,* LXXXI (1978), 58.

[40] Sophia to Elizabeth Peabody, May, 1838, in *NHHW,* I, 192.

[41] Horace Mann to Elizabeth Peabody, March 10, 1838 (MS, MHS). See Messerli, p. 345.

[42] *Common School Journal,* IV (January, 1842), 7.

[43] On the closeness of Mann's reforms to the educational ideas of Daniel Webster and Edward Everett, see Daniel Walker Howe, *The Political Culture of the American Whigs* (Chicago: University of Chicago Press, 1979), pp. 36–37, 218–19.

held by John Quincy Adams, and won. In 1852 he ran unsuccessfully for governor, having progressed from a "conscience" Whig to a Free-Soiler. He then accepted the
presidency of Antioch College in Ohio, just opened to practice educational principles such as those he had formulated
for Massachusetts. He served there until his death. Temperamental and intellectual differences kept Hawthorne and
Mann from close familiarity, though the two families lived
briefly together or as neighbors in Concord, Boston, and
West Newton. As a Whig congressman, Mann became Hawthorne's court of last appeal when he was expelled from the
Custom House in 1849. The families were alike in that the
children were of the same age: Horace Mann, Jr. (1844–68)
is best known as the companion of Henry Thoreau's last
excursion to Minnesota; his brothers were George Combe
(1845–1921) and Benjamin Pickman (1848–1926).

Hawthorne met his wife, Sophia Amelia Peabody (1809–
71) through her sister Elizabeth, as Mary had met Horace
Mann. Sophia was the sickly sister, having suffered from
migraine headaches and nervous disorders since the age of
fifteen, when she also (perhaps not coincidentally) began to
study drawing. She was frequently and for extended periods
confined to her chamber, where she drew, painted, and
sculpted, and read the books and periodicals that Elizabeth
brought home or mentioned in her letters. Before she was
twenty, she had begun her lifelong habit of writing "journal
letters" to family members and close friends. These were
often daily accounts of a week or more of her visits or visitors,
her reading, the news, and gossip, and were done in a frequently lively, breathless style. When she and Mary spent
almost a year and half on a plantation in Cuba in 1833–35,
her "Cuba Journal" sent back to Boston became widely
known there and in Salem as evidence of Sophia's epistolary
genius. Elizabeth called the letters "gentle masterpieces,"
and prepared them for publication in the *American Monthly*

Magazine in the autumn of 1834, more than a year before Hawthorne's work began to appear in its pages.[44] Though they did not reach (and never have reached) print, the letters had such readers as Bronson Alcott and Sophia Ripley. When Hawthorne met the Peabodys, he was, of course, shown them, and copied several passages into his notebook. It is worth mentioning that these are not romantic effusions but rather detailed descriptions of Cuban social activities. He intended, or at least promised, to use her letters as sources for his fiction. She wrote to Elizabeth on May 14, 1838, a few months before she and Hawthorne discovered their mutual love: "I enquired whether the story of the picture was written yet, & he replied no but this week he was going about it—I said that I should be very proud if I should be ever so indirect a means of causing a creation—& he replied 'that he could make a great many stories *from my works.*' . . . "[45] The "story of the picture" became "Edward Randolph's Portrait," in which the character of Alice Vane, Lieutenant-Governor Hutchinson's niece, resembles Sophia. "She was clad entirely in white, a pale, ethereal creature, who, though a native of New England, had been educated abroad, and seemed not merely a stranger from another clime, but almost a being from another world." She had lived several years "in sunny Italy, and there had acquired a taste and enthusiasm for sculpture and painting," which included knowledge of restoring works of art.[46] She could thus reveal, for only a moment, the true meaning of the portrait. In fact, Sophia in Cuba had actually restored a painting, as Hawthorne noted.[47]

Just before leaving Salem in July for his North Adams excursion, Hawthorne returned her journal, with a joke

[44] Badaracco, p. 59.

[45] MS, Berg.

[46] *TTT*, p. 259.

[47] *Hawthorne's "Lost Notebook,"* p. 64: "Cleaning an obscure old picture." See Louise Hall Tharp, *The Peabody Sisters of Salem* (Boston: Little, Brown, 1950), pp. 97–98, 348.

about its weight: "He said he took up my journal to bring, but my 'works were so voluminous he concluded to send them'— . . . He told me Saturday that I was the Queen of Journalizers. This matter of my Journal seems like a baseless vision. It is all moonshine to me for I cannot realize that it is anything so mirabile [*sic*]. But I shall ever thank my stars that I have given him so much pleasure."[48] During the four years until their marriage, Hawthorne wrote rather little. In the flood of stories he did write at the Old Manse, Sophia's character is not readily apparent, though subtly present. One change from courtship to marriage is clear: they imagined that he would write stories based on the descriptions in her continuing journal ("when thy husband is again busy at the loom of fiction, he would weave in these little pictures," he wrote to her on May 29, 1840), allowing them to share not only the isolated Eden of their home but the same thoughts and words in a constant collaboration; but by the end of 1843, she ruefully noted that he retired habitually to his study after breakfast. Sometimes he allowed her to read, or read aloud to her, the story or sketch just before he sent it to be published, as with "The Christmas Banquet" on December 12; sometimes, as with "Fire Worship" on December 6, her first view was of the published work.[49] By this time, she recognized, and even exulted in, Hawthorne's uniqueness as a thinker and stylist, his difference from the Transcendental idealism to which she was so accustomed. In a letter to her mother a little more than a year after the marriage, she wrote: "The longer I live with Mr Hawthorne, the more I revere & wonder at his almost unerring eye, & with it his heavenly charity. . . . He rebukes my hasty opinions, my Rembrandt lights & shadows with the marble precision & justness & still

[48] Sophia to Elizabeth Peabody, July 23, 1838 (MS, Berg).
[49] "A Sophia Hawthorne Journal, 1843–44," ed. John J. McDonald, *NHJ* 1974, pp. 13, 6.

light of his. . . .I have not known a person before who *never* used expletives nor superlatives—(except in regard to *one* subject—) whose talk was always marmoreal—just like his style in writing, in which you can never find language trying to exhaust itself & diluting the thoughts it is meant to strengthen & adorn." She therefore began to try to "put off my 'verys,' 'mosts' and '-ests.'" She concluded: "Words with him are worlds—suns & systems—& cannot move easily & rapidly."[50] The influence of style worked, of course, both ways; and one explanation for the idealistic passion of Hawthorne's love letters is that he was intrigued by—perhaps in fact came to even half believe in—the "'tyrannising Unity' in every thing" that Sophia described in an early letter as symbolized by a bouquet of violets, quoting from the beginning of "Prospects" in Emerson's *Nature*. (She reported of the same flowers' odor that "Mr Hawthorne thinks them too overpowering, but I do not.")[51] At this time he was reading and quoting from her Cuba journal. He copied a passage from a letter by Mary from Cuba that described Sophia awakening from a nap, looking "as if she were just made," and in his next entry speculated on "the perception of the true unreality of earthly things."[52] Here may be the beginning of the Adamic pose in the love letters and the writings of the Old Manse period. Also in the love letters, Hawthorne responds to the epistolary extravagances of Sophia and her family. She came to address him as "Apollo" or "Hyperion" or "Ithuriel," just as her sister Elizabeth was "Dido, Queen of many hearts," and Mary (after her sons were born) "Cornelia of the Gracchi." The Hawthornes' daughter Una was as a baby showered with appropriate literary epithets, and Julian, though his father preferred "Bundlebreech," was to her an "Olympian baby, my infant Hercules." The following will

[50] Sophia to Mrs. Peabody, September 3, 1843 (MS, Berg).

[51] Sophia to Elizabeth Peabody, April 30, 1838 (MS, Berg).

[52] *Hawthorne's "Lost Notebook,"* p. 62; the second entry is also in *AN*, p. 168.

have to serve as a brief sample of the flavor of her love letters, almost all of which were later destroyed, under circumstances described above:

> My life—how beautiful is Brook Farm! I was enchanted with it & it far surpassed my expectations. Most joyfully could I dwell there for its own beauty's sake; independently (were such an honor possible) of thy presence, which would make any place a virtual paradise. I do not desire to concieve [sic] of a greater felicity than living in a cottage, built on one of those lovely sites, with thee. Tell me, ye angels, is your Elysium sweeter or more satisfactory than this will be: Cannot we, ye flaming ministers, walk with GOD on those green hills, as well as on the amaranths of Heaven? Is He there more than here? Oh how plainly, in some sharp moments of intellectual vision, do I see that our Heaven is wherever we will make it.[53]

Hawthorne joined Sophia's family and friends in praise of her writing, but after their marriage, he never permitted her to seek public outlets, purportedly because of his prejudice against women of letters. As late as 1859, when James T. Fields suggested that her journal appreciating the art and culture of England and Italy be serialized in the *Atlantic Monthly,* Hawthorne wrote to discourage the eager editor; it was not until after his death that Sophia, facing poverty, prepared and published *Notes in England and Italy* with her cousin George Palmer Putnam.[54]

She enjoyed even greater admiration among her friends as an artist. At times in the mid-1830s, she shared a studio in

[53] Sophia to Hawthorne, May 30, 1841 (MS, Berg).

[54] (New York: G. P. Putnam, 1869). While they were touring England in 1857, he wrote to Ticknor that "Mrs Hawthorne altogether excels me as a writer of travels. Her descriptions are the most perfect pictures that ever were put on paper; it is a pity they cannot be published, but neither she nor I would like to see her name on your list of female authors" (June 5, 1857; MS, Berg). On August 13, 1857, he wrote to Elizabeth Peabody that he would "entirely yield the palm to Sophia on the score of fullness and accuracy of description" (MS, Berg). Finally, on November 28, 1859, he replied to Field's suggestion: "I have never read anything so good as some of her narrative and descriptive epistles to her friends, but I doubt whether she could find sufficient inspiration in writing directly for the public" (MS, Hawthorne-Fields Letterbook, Harvard).

Boston with her friend Mary Newhall, where she worked industriously on copies of such classic works as landscapes by Salvator Rosa and on some of her own ideas. There she met the Boston artists George Flagg, Chester Harding, Francis Graeter, and Thomas Doughty, and—most important— received the attention and praise of Washington Allston. Her first published illustration was of Bronson Alcott talking to children at his school; it appeared as the frontispiece to the second volume of Alcott's *Conversations on the Gospels* in 1837. She followed it with "The Puritan and the Gentle Boy," which Hawthorne encouraged for the special edition of his tale in January, 1839. This engraved drawing illustrated an early moment in the story: "The boy had hushed his wailing at once and turned his face upward to the stranger." Hawthorne in his Preface noted that through the story he had "wrought an influence on another mind, and—thus given to imaginative life a creation of deep and pure beauty," adding that Sophia's greatest recompense for the sketch was "the warm recommendation of the first painter in America"—Allston.[55] His letters to her of September, 1841, suggest that she do similar sketches of important moments in the colonial history he retold in the 1842 enlarged edition of *Grandfather's Chair.*

Sophia also did busts and bas-reliefs, beginning with one to commemorate her brother George. A similar work to honor Emerson's brother Charles led eventually to the choice of Concord as the first home she was to share with Hawthorne. But as with her writing, marriage did not bring about the collaboration they had looked forward to. After Una's birth, Sophia did little to continue the practice of her art; her later efforts took the form of changes in the manuscript of *The*

[55] *TTT*, p. 568. For Allston's impact on Sophia and her group, see William H. Gerdts and Theodore E. Stebbins, Jr., "*A Man of Genius": The Art of Washington Allston* (Charlottesville, University Press of Virginia, 1979), pp. 132–41.

Marble Faun that reflected her understanding of Italian culture and art, and her now notorious editions of his notebooks after his death, as well as her treatment of these letters. She rivaled her sister Mary as wife and mother, and in other ways; once she wrote to Mary, with wistful envy: "If I could help my husband with his labor, I feel that that would be the chief employ of my life."[56]

The first of the Hawthorne children, Una (1844–77) was born at the Old Manse; Julian (1846–1934) in Boston; and Rose (1851–1926) in the Red House at Lenox. Hawthorne's sense of Una of course contributed to the characterization of Pearl in *The Scarlet Letter*. She was a quiet, bookish girl, who became known in her mother's family by the age of ten as a letter-writer who promised to rival her mother's achievements.[57] But she was never to reach her potential in that, or in art or music, partly because she never fully recovered from the malaria that threatened her life in Rome in 1858–59. Julian, whose earlier career resembles more the fumblings of his Peabody uncles than his father's steadily controlled promise, eventually became an editor, a literary journalist, and the author of more than a score of novels. But none of his writing attained distinction; he could not escape awareness of his father's example. Rose married hastily at the age of twenty when her mother's death left her alone. Her marriage was unhappy, though George Lathrop was a literary man who wrote the first critical biography of her father. The tales and poems she produced were published only because of her name. The Lathrops became Catholics in 1891; after their separation in 1895 and his death three years later, Rose became a nun, eventually Mother Mary Alphonsa. She spent the remainder of her life nursing victims of incurable cancer.

[56] April 6, 1845 (MS, Berg).
[57] Miss Love Rawlins Pickman to Mary Mann, June, 1854 (Transcript, Straker Collection, Antioch).

IV

Soon after his arrival at Bowdoin College in the late summer of 1821, Hawthorne met three boys whose friendships with him were to last their lifetimes. For one of these, Jonathan Cilley (1802–38), no letters by Hawthorne have survived, if we except their written wager of November 1824: Cilley promised to pay a barrel of the "best old Madeira wine" if Hawthorne were not to marry during the subsequent twelve years.[58] He lost the bet, and was to lose his life in a duel before he could make good the wine. Trained in the law, Cilley soon made political connections and was elected to the Maine legislature in 1832, as Hawthorne noted, certainly with a glance at himself," at a period when most young men still stand aloof from the world."[59] He rose to the United States Congress in 1836, and was killed by a southern representative over a trivial matter of gentlemanly honor in what the historians of Bowdoin were to call many years later "one of the saddest traditions of our political history."[60] In his biographical sketch commemorating Cilley in the *Democratic Review,* Hawthorne recalled him in college as "a popular leader" whose "influence among his fellow-students" came from "a free and natural eloquence—a flow of pertinent ideas, in language of unstudied appropriateness, which seemed always to accomplish precisely the result on which he had calculated."[61] Hawthorne was to be always fascinated by men of political action, starting with Andrew Jackson, the hero of his youth, whom he was to characterize thirty years later as "surely . . . the greatest man we ever had" because

[58] *Recollections*, pp. 47–48. See also Cilley's letter to Hawthorne, November 17, 1836, recalling the wager and encouraging his friend to publish; *NHHW*, I, 144–45.

[59] "Biographical Sketch of Jonathan Cilley," *Democratic Review*, II (1838), 71.

[60] Nehemiah Cleaveland and Alphonsus Packard, *History of Bowdoin College, with Biographical Sketches of Graduates* (Boston: James Ripley Osgood, 1882), p. 298.

[61] "Biographical Sketch of Jonathan Cilley," 70.

of his "power of presenting his own view of a subject, with irresistible force, to the mind of his auditor."[62] Another such man was Franklin Pierce (1804–69), who became his close friend in college, and for whom he was to write the campaign biography that contributed to Pierce's election in 1852 as fourteenth president of the United States. Pierce and Cilley (Hawthorne was more searchingly critical of the latter in his notebook)[63] shared, to Hawthorne's perception, his own desire to convert expertise with language into persuasion of an audience both elite and democratic; but unlike them, he was always to shrink both from the posturing oratory of the platform and the spontaneous debate of the caucus room.

Franklin Pierce's rise to prominence after college and the study of law was as swift as Cilley's. He was followed by good fortune almost always till he reached the summit, only then to stumble and fall into the oblivion and mild taint of those presidents remembered for their ineffectiveness. As Hawthorne's surviving letter of 1832 almost predicted, Pierce was successively justice of the peace, town moderator of his native Hillsborough, New Hampshire, state representative, Speaker of the House, congressman—all these before he was thirty—senator, 1837–42, general during the Mexican War, and president, 1853–57. Pierce was more fascinating to Hawthorne than Cilley because his father, General Benjamin Pierce, "a noisy, foul-mouthed, hard-drinking tavern keeper,"[64] had fought in the Revolution and had become governor of New Hampshire at just the moment of the long-awaited triumph by Jackson in 1828. Young Pierce attained through school and college a slight polish of manner and some respect for culture, but in his keen gregariousness, he embodied raw, Western, Jacksonian qualities for Hawthorne,

[62] *FIN*, pp. 366–67. Compare Hawthorne's appreciation of Pierce's "miraculous intuition" and "magic touch" in *FIN*, pp. 513–14.

[63] *AN*, pp. 61–63.

[64] Donald B. Cole, *Jacksonian Democracy in New Hampshire, 1800–1851* (Cambridge: Harvard University Press, 1970), p. 59.

whose enthusiasm for "Old Hickory" was instantaneous in spite of (or because of) Salem's preference for Federalist orthodoxy. And after all, "Bold Daniel" Hathorne had been a Republican (a Jeffersonian Democrat), and had loudly objected to his daughter Rachel's marriage to Simon Forrester, a Federalist.[65]

Pierce gave up his senate seat in 1842 to return to New Hampshire politics, for which he recognized his talents were better suited. His genius was for management and consensus, the creation and enforcement of party loyalty. But when the unexpected opportunity came to him in the Democratic convention of 1852 as a compromise candidate, he was unable to resist the prize he had dreamed of from boyhood. Distracted by the tragedy of his sons' deaths and his wife's inconsolability, Pierce was psychologically incapable of handling the challenge that faced him on inauguration. Having won by a landslide, a truly fated leader might have dealt with the problems of slavery and sectional strife by decisive action, but Pierce would do little to keep the country from its drift toward armed conflict.

Many years after Hawthorne's prophecy of 1832, and even long after his *Life of Franklin Pierce,* he insisted on a public sharing of his friend's disgrace by dedicating *Our Old Home* to Pierce. This was in the summer of 1863, at the height of the war. The reason was simple: Pierce had provided Hawthorne the opportunity to live in England and write about it. Much to the disgust of Elizabeth Peabody and Mary Mann, Hawthorne wrote a letter to defend not only the "steadfastness and integrity" of Pierce as morally superior to "adapting one's self to new ideas, however true they turn out to be," but even Benjamin Pierce's heroic "simplicity."[66] Though

[65] Bernard Farber, *Guardians of Virtue: Salem Families in 1800* (New York: Basic Books, 1972), p. 120.

[66] Hawthorne to Elizabeth Peabody, July 30, 1863 (MS, Harvard).

Pierce had sometimes not come up to Hawthorne's expectations on particular issues and events, he never faltered in his defense. It was only during his idyllic removal from politics and public affairs during the first year at the Old Manse that Hawthorne could feel that Pierce had "faded out of my affections." When the author's need for a federal position at Salem became acute in 1845, Pierce was glad, in spite of his involvement in the intricacies of New Hampshire politics, to throw his influence behind his friend's candidacy.

The third of Hawthorne's Bowdoin friends is the most important for the reader of Hawthorne's letters, perhaps because he never attained fame in public life or as a literary man. Horatio Bridge (1806–93) was, like Hawthorne and Cilley, a member of the class of 1825. He was the person closest to Hawthorne's aspirations as a writer through the whole range of his career. Bridge claimed in his *Personal Recollections* that "for the forty-three years of his subsequent life" after their meeting as freshmen their friendship "was never for a moment chilled by indifference or clouded by doubt."[67] Hawthorne confirmed this by writing in his Preface to *The Snow-Image,* in the form of a letter to Bridge (though like none of his private letters), of the "very long and unbroken connection" between them; and in the first preserved letter to Bridge calls him "the best friend I ever had or shall have."[68] Both are suggesting what we would not otherwise know: that throughout the decade of Hawthorne's silence, almost void of biographical documents, Bridge was a sounding board for his literary plans. This correspondence Bridge burned at Hawthorne's request; he is also the only correspondent besides Sophia to censor the later letters Hawthorne permitted him to perserve.[69] But we should not inflate the

[67] *Recollections*, p.4.
[68] *SI*, p. 5; Letter 81.
[69] *Recollections*, p.49.

importance of what we can never hope to know: Bridge was not a "literary man," and Hawthorne's confessions to him would not likely have the detail we would most appreciate.

Bridge was born in Augusta, Maine, third son of the Honorable James Bridge, an esteemed judge and wealthy banker and financier. He had the knack of befriending men of importance. After college he studied law; his first partner, James Ware Bradbury, was a classmate who was later a United States senator. With his older brothers, both also lawyers, Horatio financed the construction in 1836 of a dam for the Kennebec River, to be used as a mill site. Two years later, a disastrous flood wiped it out, as well as the twenty-room ancestral home and the three brothers' entire fortunes. Bridge then sought and received an appointment as a purser, or supply officer, in the United States Navy, stationed at the nearby Portsmouth, New Hampshire, Naval Base. He was assigned to the sloop-of-war *Cyane,* which was soon dispatched to the Mediterranean, and in 1842 transferred to the *Saratoga,* which cruised off the west coast of Africa to prevent the slave trade and protect American interests. In 1846–48 he again cruised the Mediterranean and African coasts in the frigate *United States.* He returned to a command assignment at Portsmouth in 1849–51. Next he was with the sloop-of-war *Portsmouth* in the Pacific, from whence Pierce eventually called him to Washington as chief of the Bureau of Provisions and Clothing in October 1854. Bridge held this important post for fifteen years; he was recognized for outstanding service during the Civil War. Upon mandatory retirement in 1869, he was styled chief inspector of clothing, and later pay director. These were civilian positions he held until 1873, when he was finally detached from all naval duty, retiring to his country home in Athens, Pennsylvania.[70]

Hawthorne dramatized Bridge's importance to him by his

[70] Most of this information is summarized from an article by Doyle W. Selden in the Brunswick, Maine, *Record,* March 3, 1955; 14: 1–4.

dedicatory Preface to *The Snow-Image:* "If anybody is responsible for my being at this day an author, it is yourself." He
refers to their days in college as "two idle lads" and Bridge's
"prognostic . . . that he was to be a writer of fiction." More
practically, it was Bridge who in 1836 pledged $250 to guar-
antee the publishers of *Twice-told Tales* against loss, this
"interposition" occurring without Hawthorne's knowledge.
Early in his visit to Augusta in July, 1837, the grateful Hawthorne put into his notebook his appreciation of his friend's
"high and admirable qualities, of that sort which make up a
gentleman . . . polished, yet natural, frank, open and
straightforward, yet with a delicate feeling for the sensitiveness of his companions: of excellent temper and warm heart,
well-acquainted with the world, with a keen faculty of observation, which he has had many opportunities of exercising. . . . " At this point, Sophia Hawthorne later erased
more than a line, probably removing something about Hawthorne's and Bridge's mutual curiosity about prostitution or
the conversation of tavern habitués. Bridge was a man of
impressive physical proportions. He satisfied Hawthorne's
elitist and egalitarian sympathies by his status with the Irish
and French-Canadian squatters on his family lands, for
whom he was "the umpire of their disputes, their adviser . . . a protector and patron-friend."[71] For Hawthorne
he was apparently as close a friend as he would want or need:
one who opened new experiences and would share his passion
for the "queerer" phenomena of life without actually participating in the process that transformed observation into fictional creation.

Bridge's friendship was manifested by his generosity with
money: in May, 1845, he sent $100 to alleviate the Haw-
thornes' severe straits at the Old Manse, and in September

---

[71] AN, pp. 32, 41. Longfellow wrote in his journal, after their first meeting
since college: "Bridge is gigantic; and stands and looks plumb-down onto the top
of my head" (March 17, 1838; MS, Harvard).

$150, when they abruptly left Concord to board with Nathaniel's family in Salem. More important, Bridge was always ready with cheering advice concerning worldly matters about which Hawthorne felt uncertain: he was on hand to try to place Hawthorne as historian of Charles Wilkes's exploring expedition to the South Seas in 1837; he contributed to the effort that succeeded in gaining the surveyorship of Salem in 1846; while Hawthorne was consul in Liverpool, Bridge was his Washington connection and his means of indirect contact with President Pierce; as late as 1863, Bridge used his influence to improve the salary of Hawthorne's old friend Burchmore at the Salem Custom House. Beyond his persuasion of senators and federal officials, Bridge took it upon himself to approach editors and publishers for Hawthorne's sake, first for the financing of the original *Twice-told Tales,* and later in 1849, at his friend's low ebb after expulsion from the Custom House, to provide steady literary employment with *Blackwood's Edinburgh Magazine,* just as Elizabeth Peabody was working towards a similar end with Horace Greeley's New York *Tribune.*

It turned out that Hawthorne needed neither of these: he was to write *The Scarlet Letter* for Ticknor & Fields and attain a measure of financial stability. It was characteristic that he wrote to Bridge after the latter had finished reading *The Scarlet Letter* as the author's "oldest and friendliest critic," recalling that in 1837 Bridge had published a review of *Twice-told Tales* in an Augusta newspaper.

Bridge's only literary effort before his *Recollections* was also inspired by Hawthorne, as a means of recording his adventures on the *Saratoga,* and in an effort to make some money in the period when such tales as "Rappaccini's Daughter" and "The Artist of the Beautiful" were bringing in almost nothing. Hawthorne proposed to arrange the sketches and correct the style of the *Journal of an African Cruiser,* which he and Evert Duyckinck aimed at a large audience as the first of Wiley & Putnam's "Library of American Books." As work progressed, he admitted to "working up" Bridge's original journal observations, "developing" ideas and putting in "occasional patches of sentimental embroidery," or "trimmings and varnishing out of the question." He always protested that he would not tamper with the facts, for Bridge was "a man of some cultivation, good feeling, and excellent practical sense," as he wrote to Duyckinck. The result was for Hawthorne an amalgamation of his own literary sensibility with the "solid and material . . . substance" that came from Bridge's journal, part of which is now preserved in the Berg Collection. Patrick Brancaccio, the only close student of the authorship, has found that the *Journal*'s "thematic organization and ironic and morally ambiguous point of view clearly betray Hawthorne's hand;[72] but present scholarly opinion seems to continue to accept the report of the title page, which describes the book as "By an Officer of the U.S. Navy. Edited by Nathaniel Hawthorne."

A fourth Bowdoin undergraduate who was to become Hawthorne's devoted friend was Henry Wadsworth Longfellow (1807–82), the best-known poet ever to write in America. He was also a member of the class of 1825, though he did not take up residence until his sophomore year. Longfellow was born in Portland, Maine, the second of eight children in a distinguished provincial family. His father was a lawyer, philanthropist, and briefly a Federalist congressman; perhaps for this reason Longfellow joined the more conservative Peucinian literary society, rival to the Athenaean, which enrolled Hawthorne, Bridge, Pierce, and Cilley. Whereas Hawthorne and Bridge were not diligent in their studies, as they enjoyed recalling in later years and as Hawthorne stressed in his epistle dedicatory to *The Snow-Image,* Longfellow was so outstanding a student that the college administration awarded

---

[72] "'The Black Man's Paradise': Hawthorne's Editing of the *Journal of an African Cruiser,*" *NEQ,* LIII (1980), 33.

him immediately upon graduation the just-established professorship in modern languages, stipulating that he travel and study in Europe for preparation.

Already during college, he had published several poems in newspapers, literary periodicals, and gift books. Some of these were on local themes or celebrated legendary associations, such as "Lover's Rock," on a spot near the outlet of Sebago Pond, in the vicinity of Hawthorne's Raymond, where, as for many other places, an Indian maiden was fabled to have thrown herself into the lake to protest her jilted love. In favoring such material, the young poet may have been encouraged by a new teacher at Bowdoin, Thomas Coggswell Upham, a champion of an independent American literature who had published *American Sketches* in emulation of Sir Walter Scott's richly imagined native land. Hawthorne may also have felt the force of Upham's example; in the spring of 1825, he must have noticed Longfellow's "Ode Written for the Commemoration at Fryeburg, Maine, of Lovewell's Fight," occasioned by the centenary of an encounter with Indians on the border of Maine and New Hampshire. Longfellow enjoyed the satisfaction of attending the celebration, mingling with the guests of honor at the local judge's mansion, and hearing the assembled company sing his own verses in solemn ceremony. What an auspicious moment for an eighteen-year-old poet! The six stanzas of the ode barely touch on the moral and psychological problems that Hawthorne was to place at the center of "Roger Malvin's Burial," written sometime between 1825 and 1830. This masterpiece should be seen as, in a sense, Hawthorne's answer to his classmate. It is characteristic of their relationship as authors: Longfellow was the epitome for their contemporaries of the socially responsible man of letters, whereas Hawthorne, in choosing a theme remote from public rituals but more central to basic human experience, was to command the same attention from the more doubting and sober generations to come in another hundred years.

But neither saw themselves then or later as in competition. Longfellow may well have contributed to Hawthorne's professional preparation by his precocious example as an unabashed aesthete in a society he characterized in 1825 as "practical, operative and thorough-going," a utilitarian society. First in his commencement oration of 1825, and in an important article in the *North American Review* in 1832, Longfellow championed a national literature purely for its own values, demanding public respect for "our native authors," for their "deep and thorough conviction of the glory of their calling, an utter abandonment of everything else, and a noble self-devotion to the cause of literature." Whether or not Hawthorne was inspired by these words when he heard them at the commencement, he acted upon them when he returned to Salem. Seven years later in his review of a new edition of Sidney's *Defence of Poesie* for the *North American*, Longfellow took up the relation of literature to history, a matter much in Hawthorne's thought in 1832. Longfellow echoed Sidney's claim for the superiority of literature because it "exhibits [intellectual] phenomena more perfectly and distinctly than history does"; whereas history would give America "the external symbol of its character," poetry "is the spirit of the age itself." To say this five years before Emerson's "American Scholar" took courage as well as insight. It pointed clearly to what Longfellow called the "bare, brawny, muscular utility"[73] that controlled American attitudes, and called for the power of imagination against the dessicated rationalism of what Emerson was to label "Unitarian and commercial times."

[73] *Every Other Saturday*, I (April 12, 1884), 116–17; *North American Review*, XXXIV (January, 1832), 56–78; both reprinted in Richard Ruland, ed., *The Native Muse: Theories of American Literature, Volume I* (New York: E. P. Dutton, 1972), pp. 238, 250, 242.

While Hawthorne was working in Salem on *Fanshawe* and his projected collections "Seven Tales of My Native Land" and "Provincial Tales," Longfellow wrote from Europe to publishers about a "Sketch Book of New England," in imitation of Washington Irving, to contain both an account of the American author abroad and "recollections of My Native Land." His American theme Longfellow realized partially in tales and sketches he published anonymously in the 1832 and 1833 editions of *The Token*, the *New England Magazine*, 1831–33, and the *Knickerbocker*, 1834–35.[74] Hawthorne's equally anonymous writings were appearing in the same places. But while he was keeping his secret both as an author and a man, Longfellow was becoming a prominent man of letters in those years: after six years' teaching at Bowdoin, he accepted in 1835 the Smith Professorship of Modern Languages and Belles-Lettres at Harvard, again preparing for his duties by an extended stay in Europe, this time especially in Scandinavia and Germany. In 1835 he also anticipated Hawthorne by publishing his first literary book, *Outre-Mer*, a loose collection of tales and sketches derived from his first European sojourn, and a comfortable imitation of Irving's *Sketch-Book*.[75] Hawthorne resumed his acquaintance and began his friendship with Longfellow by his letter to accompany a complimentary copy of *Twice-told Tales;* he would not have approached his classmate without providing a tangible token of his membership in the invisible fraternity of writers, the fraternity that Longfellow had joined with such apparent ease at such an early age. (It was in the same way, with a copy of his *Wonder Book*, that Hawthorne finally introduced himself to Irving fifteen years later.) In the exchange of letters that followed, leading to Longfellow's gracious review in

---

[74] Robert Stafford Ward, "Longfellow's Roots in Yankee Soil," *NEQ*, XLI (1968), 185–86; Longfellow, *Letters*, I, 408.

[75] See Thomas N. Pauly, "*Outre-Mer* and Longfellow's Quest for a Career," *NEQ*, L (1977), 30–52.

the *North American,* we can clearly see the shock of recognition passing between them: the poet praises the tales in which Hawthorne most clearly suggests a writer's unique powers, and Longfellow then places his countryman in the self-conscious company of Jean Paul and Carlyle; Hawthorne responds with a remarkable confession that combines sincerity and posturing in a unique way, and may even be his pale aesthete's version of Carlyle's "Everlasting No" and "Center of Indifference."[76] From this point until Longfellow's funeral elegy of 1864, the two maintained a mutual respect and admiration that is clearly mirrored in their correspondence and in the reports we have in Longfellow's journal of their meetings. Hawthorne saw the poet as, in outward circumstances and contemporary reputation, at least, his ideal of the American writer. He went to dine at Craigie House in Cambridge without any of Emerson's misgivings about how the aristocratic trappings, the servants with their fine coats, and "the bottles of different coloured wines" made it impossible to talk with Longfellow as one would like to talk to Socrates.[77] Hawthorne accepted gratefully a charm and a "harmonizing temper" that made it easy for a shy conversationalist to participate without embarrassment. Longfellow was also a sympathetic listener to his complaints about the "anti-literary" atmosphere of custom houses, being himself tied to te-

[76] In the *North American Review,* XLV (July, 1837), 59–73 Longfellow, like Elizabeth Peabody, singled out for praise "The Great Carbuncle"; also like her, he emphasized Hawthorne's spiritual insights, "dwelling in the universal mind of man, and in the universal forms of things," as evidence, not so much of his Transcendentalism as of his standing as a "true poet," in whom the imagination is "set free . . . to lift . . . the roofs of the city, street by street" to reveal the many "wild and wondrous things" in an outwardly "dull, commonplace and prosaic" New England.

[77] *JMN,* XIII, 38, ca. August, 1853. In 1861 Hawthorne wrote to Henry Bright about Longfellow at the Saturday Club that "though he was not brilliant, and never said anything that seemed particularly worth hearing, he was so genial that every guest felt his heart the lighter and warmer for him" (November 14, 1861; MS, Trinity, Cambridge). On two occasions, Hawthorne was reminded of Longfellow by Richard Monkton Milnes, the consummate English host and litterateur; see *EN,* pp. 87, 457.

dious rote teaching of languages until 1854, when he followed Hawthorne's advice and tore himself from these duties by pleading "the helpless state of my eyes."[78] Biographers make much of the friendship of Hawthorne and Melville in the Berkshires in 1850–51, and rightly so; but we should not forget that at this time Hawthorne was disappointed by Longfellow's decision not to vacation at the farm in Stockbridge his father-in-law had left him. Significantly, it was Longfellow who gave the farewell dinner before Hawthorne's embarkation for England in 1853, an occasion that honored Hawthorne by bringing together many of the literary leaders of Boston. In fact, Hawthorne admired and respected Longfellow through all the vicissitudes of their lives. It is tempting, perhaps, to quote his letter to Sophia in the summer of 1843 about his recently married friend's radiant happiness— "Longfellow appears perfectly satisfied, and to be no more conscious of any earthly or spiritual trouble than a sunflower is,—of which lovely blossom he, I know not why, reminded me"—and to conclude, as Robert Penn Warren has, that "Hawthorne seems to have had little taste for literary and intellectual company," especially of those writers who had no "sense of the tragic tensions of life."[79] Hawthorne was sensitive to his friend's happiness because he knew how Longfellow had suffered after the sudden death abroad of his first wife and how desperate was his apparently fruitless courtship of Fanny Appleton before she accepted him. Hawthorne often avoided writers, but for other and personally complicated reasons, and there is no evidence that he ever avoided Longfellow.

So much having been said, we should not forget Longfellow's consciousness, on his side, that his friend's fancies

[78] Carl L. Johnson, *Professor Longfellow of Harvard* (Eugene: University of Oregon Press, 1944), p. 82.

[79] *American Literature: The Makers and the Making* (New York: St. Martin's Press, 1974), p. 434. Warren is restating a point made by F. O. Matthiessen in *American Renaissance* (New York: Oxford University Press, 1941), p. 227.

were not only "strange" and "original" but that *The House of the Seven Gables* was a "weird, wild book," and *The Marble Faun*, though "wonderful . . . in its way," showed "the old, dull pain that runs through all Hawthorne's writings"[80]—a pain that his own poetry and prose rarely expressed. Furthermore, as has been recently argued, beneath Longfellow's stance as "representative poet of his age" there lie "antithetical concerns . . . deep within the fabric of his poems." Like Hawthorne, he was sometimes able to see civic authority, Puritan and contemporary, as "cruel and hard," and to oppose in his fictional world the artist as society's leader to "the alienated, antisocial artist," whose "darker powers" parallel those of the political leader.[81] We can only wonder how far their conversation may have entered into such attitudes.

The circumstances of Hawthorne's efforts to publish his early work, including *Fanshawe*, may never be known because he succeeded so well in destroying the record of those times. The first correspondent of this kind we can identify is Samuel Griswold Goodrich (1793–1860), known to contemporaries as "Peter Parley" because of his numerous and widely sold educational publications for children under that name. He was born in Connecticut into a family known in the clergy and the law, and educated himself and entered bookselling and publishing in Hartford in his early twenties, arriving in Boston in 1826. The first of more than a hundred Parley books appeared the following year. "In these books a kindly and omniscient old gentlemen is represented as talking to a group of priggishly inquiring children, and instruction is given a thin sugar-coating of fiction."[82] Hawthorne was to make use of a similar narrative frame in his own books for

---

[80] MS journal, Harvard: October 27, 1846; April 16, 1851; March 1, 1860.

[81] Robert A. Ferguson, "Longfellow's Political Fears: Civic Authority and the Role of the Artist in *Hiawatha* and *Miles Standish*," *AL*, L (1978), 187–215.

[82] William B. Cairns, "Samuel Griswold Goodrich," *DAB*.

children, beginning with *Grandfather's Chair;* earlier he was
to edit in 1836, with his sister Elizabeth, the two volumes of *Peter Parley's Universal History on the Basis of Geography,* a hackwork job that sold well over a million copies.
But Goodrich's first interest in Hawthorne came much earlier; he wrote in his *Recollections* that after the publication in
1828 of *Fanshawe* he claimed to have recognized in it "extraordinary powers. I inquired of the publishers as to the
writer, and through them a correspondence ensued between
me and 'N. Hawthorne.' This name I considered a disguise,
and it was not until after many letters had been passed, that
I met the author, and found it to be a true title, representing
a very substantial personage."[83] Of these "many letters," only
two by Hawthorne have survived, from 1829–30, near the
beginning of the relationship; a handful of notes by Goodrich,
most from 1836–37, appear in Julian Hawthorne's and G. P.
Lathrop's biographies.[84] In spite of Goodrich's recollection, it
is equally likely that Hawthorne initiated the correspondence, because in 1827 Goodrich performed one of his greatest services to American literature by publishing the first
collected edition, in six volumes, of the novels of Charles
Brockden Brown. Hawthorne must have read the long appreciation of Brown's "fatal power" by Richard Henry Dana in
the *United States Review,* for he recognized Brown's "classic
reputation" (as he mentioned in sketches almost twenty years
later)[85] and perhaps his anticipation of his own literary
qualities.

When Goodrich printed his unflattering portrait of Hawthorne in 1856, the latter was quick to react to the account

[83] Goodrich, *Recollections of a Lifetime* (New York: Miller, Orton & Mulligan,
1856), II, 270.

[84] *NHHW,* I, 131–57, *passim;* Lathrop, p. 166; see also Wayne Allen Jones,
"Hawthorne's First Published Review," *AL,* XLVIII (1977), 495.

[85] "P's Correspondence" and "The Hall of Fantasy"; see *MOM,* pp. 380, 174.
See also *Critical Essays on Charles Brockden Brown,* ed. Bernard Rosenthal (Boston: G. K. Hall, 1981), p. 50.

of "my personal appearance" and to "the airs of a patron" the
editor assumed, though he assured Elizabeth Peabody (who
had, as mentioned above, long since concluded that he had
"no genius for negotiation with booksellers") that he had "not
the slightest inclination to defend myself or to be defended,"
publicly. He proceeded to write a memorable description of
Goodrich, which he must have assumed Elizabeth would
eventually bring to light: the editor "was born to do what he
did . . . as maggots to feed on rich cheese."[86] In letters of
1836, Hawthorne had found him an "unscrupulous" but "ridiculous" man, but apparently one he much needed to work
with until another, more reliable person came along.

It is difficult, lacking so many documents, to sort out Hawthorne's attitudes toward his editors. Some facts are, however, clear: in a two-month period in 1830–31, five pieces
appeared in the Salem *Gazette,* a newspaper edited by Caleb
Foote (1803–94), a lifelong local friend. Twenty-eight pieces
first appeared in *The Token,* the Boston giftbook annual edited by Goodrich, between 1831 and 1838. Another editor,
Park Benjamin (1809–64), published twenty-four pieces between 1834 and 1838, all but one in magazines, the *New-
England* of Boston and *American Monthly* of New York.[87] In
late 1837 Hawthorne replaced both Goodrich and Benjamin
by John Louis O'Sullivan (1813–95), of the *Democratic Review* of Washington and New York, who published twenty-
three pieces until 1845.

In Hawthorne's tale "The Devil in Manuscript," published by Benjamin in November, 1835, the apparently autobiographical hero Oberon laments the indifference of
American publishers to American writers, noting that only
one of seventeen booksellers has "vouchsafed even to read my
tales; and he—a literary dabbler himself, I should judge—

---

[86] August 13, 1857 (MS, Berg).

[87] Benjamin published "Little Annie's Ramble" in *The Youth's Keepsake* for
1835, a gift book.

has the impertinence to criticize them, proposing what he calls vast improvements."[88] If this is an allusion to Goodrich, Hawthorne was quick to adopt a more conciliatory tone in the review he wrote, at the author's request, of Goodrich's *The Outcast and Other Poems,* for a Boston newspaper in February, 1836.[89] Park Benjamin, a poet several ranks higher than Goodrich, was then pursuing a feud with the latter, having characterized him as the literary equivalent of a "quack vendor of universal nostrums in medicine." Benjamin had also shortly before first publishing Hawthorne's work described it as "some of the most delicate and beautiful prose ever published this side of the Atlantic."[90] In reviewing Goodrich as poet, Hawthorne carefully controlled his urge toward satire: "We think he might safely trust to homely nature and sober truth, and not etherealize so much." Benjamin said the same with scathing irony in his review a few months later, seeming to realize the satiric potential in Hawthorne's thought: "As a poet, we should say that he seems pitifully bewildered in the realms of fancy, and enveloped in glorious obfuscation, when treading the heights of imagination; but . . . when he condescends to enter into the door of common sense, and to walk in the halls of fact, his step becomes more steady and his vision almost clear."[91] Hawthorne was to show restraint again, in 1849–50, when he reviewed privately and for a considerable fee the similarly vapid poems of a successful upstate New York storekeeper, Lewis Mansfield.

Goodrich seems seldom to rise above the status of a useful

[88] *SI,* pp. 172–73.

[89] Boston *Atlas,* February 23, 1836, 2:3; reprinted in Jones, "Hawthorne's First Published Review," 497–98.

[90] *New-England Magazine,* VIII (October, 1835), 295; VII (October, 1834), 331.

[91] *American Monthly Magazine,* n.s. I (May, 1836), 524. Hawthorne approached this kind of satire in his comment on Goodrich's *Universal Geography* in the *American Magazine of Useful and Entertaining Knowledge,* II (August, 1836), 503–4; reprinted in Turner, pp. 223–24; see Wayne Allen Jones, "The Hawthorne-Goodrich Relationship and a New Estimate of Hawthorne's Income from the *Token,*" *NHJ* 1974, p. 121.

operative in relation to Hawthorne's work, but Benjamin is a more intriguing character. We have only one vital fact about him from Hawthorne himself; in his 1857 letter to Elizabeth Peabody, he mentioned casually that "for instance, it was Park Benjamin, not Goodrich, who cut up the 'Story teller,' " the collection Hawthorne was preparing in the mid-1830's. There are also suggestions that Benjamin was unwilling or unable to pay promptly or in the amount expected. We must rely on Bridge's quotation from a Hawthorne letter that has not survived, a "bitter malediction" on Benjamin as not the generous patron he wished to appear but one who took "from a penniless writer material incomparably better than any his own brain can supply."[92] Recent students have even suggested that it was Goodrich whom Bridge meant here to describe.[93] In any case, Benjamin remains the critic who first praised Hawthorne's work, when it was still entirely anonymous, in his reviews of The Token for 1833, 1835, and 1836. And in October 1836 he finally put "NATHANIEL HAWTHORNE" in capital letters, suggesting that next year Goodrich "employ Hawthorne to write the whole" Token. It is apparent from Bridge's and Cilley's exasperated encouragement in letters of that time that Hawthorne needed a rude shove to accept the publicity of fame: "You must be aware of the necessity of coming out as you are," Bridge wrote; and Cilley echoed, "Don't turn up your aristocratic nose" to remain a "writer for immortality who hides himself from his own generation in a study or garret."[94]

[92] Recollections, p. 69.

[93] Jones, "The Hawthorne-Goodrich Relationship," p. 109; Lillian Gilkes, "Hawthorne, Park Benjamin and S. G. Goodrich: A Three Cornered Imbroglio," NHJ 1971, pp. 102–3. For Hawthorne's later friendly relations with Benjamin, see Arlin Turner, "Park Benjamin on the Author and Illustrator of 'The Gentle Boy'," NHJ 1974, which also suggests a possible source of this tension between author and editor: in a note on the expanded Twice-told Tales of 1842, Benjamin remarked that the "more ambitious" tales Hawthorne had now chosen to include were "failures" compared with those of the original 1837 volume.

[94] American Monthly Magazine, n.s. II (October, 1836), 406; NHHW, I, 139, 145. It is worth noting that in naming Hawthorne Benjamin went out of his way to claim that the works of Nathaniel Parker Willis, a friend of Goodrich, were

Hawthorne's next major editor, O'Sullivan, had the personality to keep up the pressure, and, like the Bowdoin classmates, he was more a political than a literary person; more important, he was a man whom Hawthorne could make into a lasting and helpful friend. His exotic, romantic background was new in Hawthorne's experience: he had been "born on shipboard, on the coast of Spain, and claims three nationalities. . . . He has hereditary claim to a Spanish countship. His infancy was spent in Barbary, and his lips first lisped in Arabic. There has been an unsettled and wandering character in his life."[95] Hawthorne did not write down these details until 1854, but he and his family had fondly known O'Sullivan for years as "the Count," after his claim for resemblance to an ancestor, a legendary Irish warrior of the Elizabethan age. Other adventurous forebears had been intimate with Charles Stuart, the Young Pretender, and connected with John Paul Jones during the American Revolution. Circumstances of the American and French revolutions drove the family to America, and his father had been American consul at Teneriffe and Mogador near the time when O'Sullivan was born. After his infancy on the Barbary Coast he went to school in France, and briefly in England, coming to New York with his mother in 1827 after his father's heroic death in a South American shipwreck. He graduated from Colum-

---

"far inferior to those of this voluntarily undistinguished man of genius," and Goodrich in his memoirs twenty years later persisted in making an extended contrast between the "cheerful and confident" Willis and the "cold, moody, distrustful" Hawthorne. A sign of Hawthorne's temporizing is in "Little Annie's Ramble": for Benjamin in 1835 he wrote that Annie "is deeply read in Robin Carver's tomes"; when reprinting the story in Twice-told Tales, 1837, under Griswold's auspices, he changed "Robin Carver," pseudonym of a Boston juvenile writer, to "Peter Parley"; see TTT, pp. 124, 586. Internal and external evidence suggest that Benjamin was also the author of the American Monthly Magazine's review of Twice-told Tales in March, 1838, which Faust and Crowley (Critical Heritage) assign to his coeditor Charles Fenno Hoffman. Actually, Hoffman left the Monthly in 1837, according to Mott, I, 620.

[95] EN, p. 60. This account, written when O'Sullivan visited the Hawthornes in Liverpool on his way to his chargéship in Lisbon, is an important source for his principal biographer, Harris.

bia College in 1831 an outstanding student, particularly of languages. (Hawthorne was to characterize him in letters as "a scholar.") He taught briefly while studying law, and after admission to the New York bar moved with his family to Washington in 1835. By March 13, 1837 (one week after *Twice-told Tales* was published in Boston), he was able with his brother-in-law Samuel Langtree to propose the *United States Magazine and Democratic Review*.[96] The project received support from leading Democratic politicians and from a large financial reward won from the government concerning the controversial activities of O'Sullivan's late father. O'Sullivan learned of Hawthorne from Congressman Jonathan Cilley, who was eager to bring the retiring author into public view.[97] (It was at this moment that Pierce was negotiating, apparently at Hawthorne's request, for an editorial position for Hawthorne on Francis P. Blair's Washington *Globe,* the powerful, semiofficial organ of the Democratic party.)[98] O'Sullivan wrote to Hawthorne on April 19 to ask that he become a regular contributor, guaranteeing as much as $5 a page, "handsome remuneration."[99] Hawthorne, perhaps still clinging to a hope of accompanying Wilkes's exploring expedition, delayed answering, and O'Sullivan apparently came to Salem, where he succeeded in "engaging him." "The Toll-Gatherer's Day" appeared in the first number of the *Review,* October, 1837.[100]

The purpose of the *Democratic Review,* Hawthorne wrote in his preface to "Rappaccini's Daughter," was to lead "the defence of liberal principles and popular rights," and this

---

[96] Harris, p. 60.

[97] "John O'Sullivan to Henry A. Wise," *NHJ 1971,* p. 121. The letter is dated November 24, 1843.

[98] *NHHW,* I, 135.

[99] *NHHW,* I, 159; Harris, p. 77, characterizes the letter as "extravagant."

[100] *NHHW,* I, 163; Conway, p. 33, reporting the recollection of Elizabeth Peabody. For the first number, O'Sullivan succeeded in recruiting also Bryant and Whittier.

O'Sullivan did, he said, "with a faithfulness and ability worthy of all praise."[101] In spite of his scholarship, O'Sullivan was less of a literary man than even Goodrich; his interests were in the political program of the radical wing of the Democratic party, the faction known as "Young America." O'Sullivan is known today, if at all, as the author of the phrase "manifest destiny"—it is "our manifest destiny to overspread the continent alotted by Providence for the free development of our yearly multiplying millions"—which he first wrote in a leading article for the annexation of Texas.[102] His rhetoric was expansive, extravagant, often revolutionary in content. His idea of "the literary spirit" was firmly connected with "the spirit of liberty": "The moralist, the historian, and the poet, the three intellectual characters who include all others, are essentially democratic." Like Hawthorne, the great poets Milton and Dante, Wordsworth and Bryant, were "the warmest partizans" of liberty. The "latest of the great historians," George Bancroft, Hawthorne, and the great moralist Channing "expressed themselves plainly in terms of the democratic creed." On the other hand was the aristocratic writer who, like Edmund Gibbon, possessed the "most brilliant intellectual power" but in "the absence of high moral and religious affections . . . Society has interests more vital, infinitely more important, than the gratification of *taste*, or the pleasures of imagination."[103] He would not think of aiming such a charge at Hawthorne, who served him as an example of the "genuine originality and excellence" deserved by democratic nations, and recognized by the citizens as the

[101] *MOM*, p. 93.

[102] *Democratic Review*, XVI (July–August, 1845), 426. See Julius W. Pratt, "The Origin of 'Manifest Destiny'," *American Historical Review*, XXXII (1927), 795–98.

[103] "Democracy and Literature," *Democratic Review*, XI (August 1842), 196–200; "Gibbon," *Democratic Review*, XX (June 1847), 524. See John Stafford, *The Literary Criticism of "Young America": A Study of the Relationship of Politics and Literature, 1837–1850* (Berkeley: University of California Press, 1952), pp. 85, 89–90.

results of "our free institutions." Thus O'Sullivan reviewed *Twice-told Tales*, 1842, as work "not imported" but inspired by Hawthorne's "own mind, with the accumulated experiences of New England life." Thus far he anticipated the review by his friend and collaborator Evert Duyckinck, as Duyckinck anticipated the review by *his* friend Herman Melville. But otherwise Hawthorne's work had for O'Sullivan qualities like those found by Elizabeth Peabody and Longfellow: "His short, unambitious tales steal upon us with the silent charm of a melody heard, now among the singing of birds, and cheerful voices, and now in the pensive twilight, amid the mournful shadows of some dark mouldering ruin. Nothing forced, affected, or vicious, disturbs the harmony of the effect." He concluded by reporting his "great pride" that some of such "exquisite" tales had first appeared in the *Democratic Review*, and looked forward to more.[104]

Most of Hawthorne's fiction had little to do with the "spirit of liberty" as O'Sullivan conceived it, but there was no problem because the latter's radicalism did not keep him from being a clever editor who could persuade many of the most talented writers of the day to contribute, and also to offer them artistic freedom. Only unsigned articles needed to maintain ideological purity, as Hawthorne's friend Thoreau found upon submitting his review of a utopian tract by J. A. Etzler. O'Sullivan, more sympathetic to "communities" than Thoreau, proposed "additions and modification . . . to suit my peculiar notion on the subject" and to satisfy the editorial need for "a certain pervading homogeneity." Thoreau did not concur; O'Sullivan backed down, and the article appeared without revision.[105]

As an editor and politician, O'Sullivan was a fast-talker,

---

[104] *Democratic Review*, X (February, 1842), 197–98.

[105] O'Sullivan to Thoreau, July 28, 1843; Thoreau, *Correspondence*, ed. Walter Harding and Carl Bode (New York: New York University Press, 1958), p. 130. Emerson did not fare so well with his review of Ellery Channing's poems for the September, 1843, number; see his *Letters*, III, 196–97.

most observers felt, but not oppressively aggressive. The diplomat Benjamin Moran first saw him in his mid-forties and decided that in spite of his "slight" build and "thin face" he was "altogether decidedly a man of mark such as one would notice in a crowd." Literary men were less impressed: for Longfellow he was "a young man, with weak eyes, and green spectacles . . . a *Humbug.*" Thoreau thought him "rather puny-looking," but "at any rate, one of the not bad"; but when Emerson met him at dinner, he decided that "*Washington* is supposed in every line of the 'Demo. Review'," and later concluded gloomily, with O'Sullivan in mind, that "Democracy becomes a government of bullies tempered by editors. The editors standing in the privilege of being last devoured."[106]

Hawthorne recognized faults in his friend, but never deviated from public commitment to O'Sullivan and his various causes, although he soon recognized that as an editor he was "certain to disappoint me as any pitiful little scoundrel."[107] Waiting for payment could be exasperating, but from 1838 onward Hawthorne could count on O'Sullivan, no less than on Bridge and Pierce, to press without stint and sometimes with persuasiveness to obtain him government employment commensurate with the needs and the dignity of his literary vocation. It was O'Sullivan who earned the honor of becoming godfather to Una Hawthorne and who showed his pleasure by bringing to the Old Manse a large dog named Leo for the newborn lady's protection. Ten years later, during the

---

[106] Benjamin Moran, *Journal, 1857–1865,* ed. Sarah Agnes Wallace and Frances Elma Gillespie (Chicago: University of Chicago Press, 1948), p. 7, February 4, 1857; Longfellow to George W. Greene, July 23, 1839, *Letters,* II, 162–63; Thoreau to Emerson, January 24, 1843, *Correspondence,* p. 77; Emerson to Margaret Fuller, February 12, 1843, *Letters,* III, 147; Emerson, *JMN,* IX, 413, 1846 or 1847.

[107] Letter 265. When he mentioned O'Sullivan in "The Hall of Fantasy," Hawthorne chose to single out his current "pet" reform, the abolition of capital punishment. See *MOM,* p. 637; Harris, p. 136.

winter of 1855–56, he solved the family's problem of enduring the English climate by offering his hospitality in Lisbon and Madeira to Mrs. Hawthorne and her daughters. But when Sophia wrote about the magnificence of his hospitality and his angelic character, Hawthorne replied with unusual candor: he did not wish for "an undue and undesirable familiarity" in calling O'Sullivan "John." Though he wished Sophia might take him for a friend "more than any other man I ever knew," he was not "the man in whom I see my ideal of a friend." O'Sullivan had " a quick, womanly sensibility, a light and tender grace," but "he never stirs me to any depth beneath my surface; . . . neither of my best nor of my worst has he ever, or could he ever, have a glimpse."[108] Hawthorne was willing to be part of various dubious schemes, such as some New York real estate for which he lost his $3,000; but by 1861, when he invested allegedly $10,000 in a Spanish copper mine, he knew O'Sullivan as a connoisseur of lost causes: "I shall hardly share his hopes at present, after knowing him so many years, and seeing him always on the verge of making a fortune, and always disappointed."[109]

Like stump politicians, desperate gamblers seem to have always fascinated and intrigued Hawthorne. When in Washington for the first time in April, 1853, he saw Franklin Pierce among his political friends, among them George Sanders of Kentucky, O'Sullivan's successor as editor of the *Democratic Review,* and soon to be United States consul to London for the new administration. Hawthorne told a young office-seeker who was at Sanders's raucous supper party at the Willard Hotel that, though not political himself, "some men possessed a kind of magnetic influence over him which he

[108] February 7, 1856, (MS, Huntington).

[109] Hawthorne to Franklin Pierce, December 3, 1861, (MS, Library of Congress). On the mine scheme, see Julian Hawthorne, *Hawthorne and His Circle* (New York: Harper & Brothers, 1903), p. 135; Harris, pp. 375–76.

could not resist, however it might lead him."[110] Historians of the Pierce administration link O'Sullivan with Sanders and others as "dashing and bizarre diplomats, . . . undiplomatic, or worse," and "hotheads . . . wild-eyed expansionists."[111] Of these, O'Sullivan seemed the most moderate, and of course was a safe friend of many years; but Hawthorne cultivated the others, especially regretting Sanders's recall to Washington for conduct embarrassing to the American government.

O'Sullivan's adventures had really begun when he gave up editing the *Democratic Review* in 1846, working from New York to promote a wild revolutionary scheme first to buy Cuba from Spain, and, when that failed, to conquer the island through a "filibustering expedition," a forerunner of the Bay of Pigs fiasco. The upshot was that he was twice indicted for violation of the neutrality laws, and so dishonored for a time, but not convicted. It was also in character that he should make public his proslavery bias at the most inauspicious moment, as the southern states were seceding in 1860. His succession of business speculations, from the "dry-dock humbug" Hawthorne heard of in 1846 to a fiber factory of the 1880s, were as unvaryingly unsuccessful as his political schemes. Through all this he came almost regularly to visit the Hawthornes and to tell of his adventures: twice at the Manse, once at Lenox, more often at Liverpool and Lon-

---

[110] Waldo H. Dunn, *The Life of Donald G. Mitchell* (New York: Charles Scribner's Sons, 1922), p. 257. Compare the characterization of O'Sullivan in Hawthorne's *English Notebooks*, October 19, 1854: "A wanderer, a man of vicissitudes, as if his native waves were all the time tossing beneath him" (*EN*, p. 95).

[111] Nichols, pp. 539, 330; Ivor Debenham Spencer, *The Victor and the Spoils: A Life of William L. Marcy* (Providence: Brown University Press, 1959), p. 231. In 1870 O'Sullivan somehow had dinner with Bismarck at Versailles after the German victory; O'Sullivan gave him gratuitous advice on "how to settle with France," and was sent away the next day in humiliation, but he persisted in publishing his account of the incident; see John Bigelow, *Retrospections of an Active Life* (Garden City, New York: Doubleday, Page, 1913), IV, 446–47.

don, where he seemed most in his element. Julian Hawthorne, who shared some of his characteristics and much of
his humbug, wrote two eloquent sketches of him: "Under
disappointments which would have crushed (one might suppose) hope itself, he remained still hopeful and inventive;
and it was difficult to resist the contagion of his eloquent
infatuation." "He was like a beautiful, innocent, brilliant
child, grown up, endowed with an enchanter's wand, which
was forever promising all the kingdoms of the earth to him,
but never (as our modern phrase is) delivered the goods."[112]
In 1886, when the Statue of Liberty was unveiled, O'Sullivan is alleged to have been chosen, because of his mastery of
French, to deliver a speech to the donors, but newspaper
accounts of the ceremonies do not mention his name.[113]

V

Hawthorne's social life in Salem was a controversial matter
for his early biographers. Lathrop, accepting Oberon's "mor-
bid" self-portrait in "Fragments from the Journal of a Solitary
Man" as a confession rather than an exaggeration of Hawthorne's experience, felt obligated to respond that "Hawthorne believed himself to possess a strongly social nature,
which was cramped, chilled and to some extent permanently
restrained" by his early seclusion. Salem society, he explained, was open to Hawthorne as scion of an old local
family, but was "peculiarly constituted," dominated by "a
strong circle of wealthy families" who "maintained rigorously
the distinctions of class" and "prescribed certain fashions,

[112] NHHW, I, 160; Hawthorne and His Circle, p. 135.
[113] Julius W. Pratt, "John L. O'Sullivan and Manifest Destiny," New York
History, XIV (1933), 233.

customs, punctilios, to disregard which was social exile for the offending party. . . . "[114]

Henry James found this excuse "easy to believe. . . . But in fact Hawthorne appears to have ignored the good society of his native place almost completely; no echo of its conversation is to be found in his tales or his journals." James was satisfied by the compensation Lathrop claimed Hawthorne had found, for as James said, "like almost all people who possess in a strong degree the story-telling faculty, Hawthorne had a democratic strain in his composition and a relish for the commoner stuff of human nature. . . . He liked to fraternize with plain people."[115] Salem gossip had already claimed that these "were for the most part stipendiaries of the Customhouse and dubious hangers-on, who were not only Democrats but quaffers of strong waters, tellers of stories unfit for ears refined, and men whose walk and conversation were not improving." Reporting this, George P. Holden, one of the first students of Hawthorne's life, concluded: "Undoubtedly all this may be to some extent true."[116] Understandably, Julian Hawthorne entered a vigorous denial that his father was either possessed by "a superhuman and monstrous shyness" or that he was "a tippler . . . the victim of an unsatiable appetite for gin, brandy and rum."[117] But other biographers persisted with qualifications: in 1895

---

[114] Lathrop, pp. 158-59, 137. Compare Hawthorne's statement in "The Sister Years" (1839) predicting that the new railroad between Salem and Boston would lead to "a probable diminution of the moral influence of wealth, and the sway of an aristocratic class, which, from an era far beyond my memory, has held firmer dominion here than in any other New England town" (*TTT*, pp. 338–39). Compare also the problem of Hawthorne's contemporary, the Democratic leader Robert Rantoul, Jr., "confronting first in Salem and finally in Boston the snobbish exclusiveness of the Whig upper class"; see Marvin Meyers, *The Jacksonian Persuasion: Politics and Belief* (1957; New York: Vintage, 1960), p. 207.

[115] Henry James, *Hawthorne* (1879; Ithaca, N.Y.: Cornell University Press, 1956), pp. 36–37.

[116] "Hawthorne and His Friends," *Harper's New Monthly Magazine*, LXIII (1881), 264.

[117] *NHHW*, I, 84–85.

Moncure Conway quoted George B. Loring, who had known both Hawthorne and Salem politics well:

Salem was full of cultivated and brilliant people at that time, but Hawthorne could not be induced to visit them. He was really too shy for such social intercourse; his brain was too busy with its creations; and he had no gift whatever for ordinary conversation. His life had been too long secluded. His daily official associates [when he had returned there after marriage] were a group of men, all of whom had remarkable characteristics, not of the best many times, but original, strong, highly-flavoured, defiant democrats, with whom he was officially connected, who made no appeal to him, but responded to the uncultivated side of his nature, and to whose defects he was blind on account of their originality. If they were given to excesses, as perhaps one or two of them were, he took no part with them in that side of their lives.[118]

In his volume for the "American Men of Letters" series, George Woodberry added: "Hawthorne was not personally popular with the merchants as a class. He kept them at a distance just as he did men of letters, and could not mix with them on even and frank terms. . . . He was inoffensive, but he was not liked, and took no pains to make himself one of the community; he was ignored by the citizens of the place because he ignored them, and when his Washington friends lost power, there was no one else interested in keeping him in office, and he had no influence of his own on the spot."[119]

In evaluating such judgments, we should recall the oppressively moralistic tone of nineteenth-century American polite society and the antics the opponents of conventionality put on. The best evidence may be still the letters themselves.

David Roberts (1804–79) grew up in Salem and graduated from Harvard in 1824. By 1827 he had opened law offices on Essex Street, where he practiced for many years. He never married. He served a term in the Massachusetts legislature

[118] Conway, pp. 116–17.
[119] George E. Woodberry, *Nathaniel Hawthorne* (Boston: Houghton Mifflin, 1902), pp. 175–76.

in the 1830s, and was elected mayor for 1866–67. He published papers on maritime law, and contributed a lecture on Benjamin Franklin to the Salem Lyceum in the 1836–37 season.[120] Hawthorne seems to have known him since boyhood; his first surviving letter to Roberts, from North Adams in 1838, suggests a long friendship. Hawthorne and Louisa played cards for several years with Roberts, Horace Conolly, and Susan Ingersoll; Roberts was known in the group as "the Chancellor." Hawthorne spent time in his office, discussing politics and local gossip. Roberts was a Democrat, but he seems to have maintained cordial relations with local Whigs, including the Reverend Charles W. Upham.[121] He entertained Longfellow and Hillard when they visited Hawthorne in 1846, but did not provoke a comment in the poet's journal beyond a general lack of enthusiasm for the ambience of Salem. Sophia Hawthorne had made clear, however, her distaste for his shabby manners when Roberts visited the Old Manse without invitation in 1843. Hawthorne, on the defensive, wrote only in their joint notebook: "My wife shall describe him." She gave her description not there but in a letter to Louisa, where she called Roberts an "intolerable heavy lump of stupidity & clownishness. . . . Ah Louisa, it was such an infliction!!! Nathaniel acknowledged he had no idea of him before."[122] After Hawthorne's fame their friendship continued by letter and, when Roberts moved his practice to Boston, by meetings there. He was not invited to Lenox, but by 1861 both a world-weary Hawthorne and a reconciled Sophia were eager for his visits to the Wayside. Roberts had supplied information during 1856–57 about the early American years of the Hathorne family.

Another bachelor, Horace Lorenzo Conolly (1810–94) was

[120] *EIHC*, LXXII (1936), 141–42.
[121] *Hawthorne's "Lost Notebook,"* pp. 59–60; Letter 416.
[122] *AN*, p. 362; Sophia to Louisa Hawthorne, September 13, 1843 (MS, Berg).

the illegitimate child of the housekeeper for Miss Susan Ingersoll (ca. 1785–1858), a second cousin of Hawthorne whose old house on Turner Street, Salem, is thought to be the original House of the Seven Gables. He was a bright and charming boy; Miss Ingersoll adopted him to educate him for the Episcopal ministry, first at Yale, which he entered in 1828, and later at Trinity College, Hartford. After holding the rectorship of Saint Matthew's Church, South Boston, he organized a church in Philadelphia, but tired of his ministerial career and returned to Salem about 1840 to study law at Harvard. By this time he was a good friend of David Roberts, and in the card games with the Hawthornes was nicknamed "the Cardinal"; his guardian, Miss Ingersoll, was "the Duchess." Soon Conolly had law offices on Essex Street, and was involved with Democratic politics, scheming to support the winning side of any controversy. By 1842 Hawthorne was annoyed by his "intolerable rudeness," perhaps a sign of his own lack of promise among the local politicians, but with affectionate contempt invited him to the Old Manse during Sophia's absence to cook for him, as he did other male friends. Conolly seems to have enjoyed Hawthorne's verbal abuse, but by the time of the latter's expulsion from the custom house, Conolly had characteristically switched parties, voting against Hawthorne and leaving his name on Upham's infamous Memorial. He then became "Mr. Ex Cardinal," and Hawthorne's complimentary copies were accompanied by curses when sent to his "pet serpent." By the time of Pierce's nomination, both Conolly and Roberts were sure, they told Louisa, of Hawthorne's "glorious" future as a political appointee.[123] In the 1850s Conolly left the law and politics for the study and practice of medicine, a third career. In 1858 Miss Ingersoll died, leaving him her house and her

---

[123] Louisa Hawthorne to Hawthorne, July 1, 1852 (MS, Berg).

name, which he assumed. He gradually squandered his inheritance; by 1879 the house was sold to pay his debts, and he lived thereafter on the charity of friends.

As Hawthorne wrote to Longfellow in 1846, Conolly was "a devoted admirer" of the poet and of "Poesy"; he took a particular pride in supplying these two writers with the materials of their trade. In a series of letters to a Salem friend in the 1880s, he claimed to have met Hawthorne in New Haven in 1828, and to have directed him to the graves of the Regicides and the Judge's Cave there. These visits led to "The Gray Champion," but not to the romance Hawthorne expected to write. In May, 1840, Conolly went on, Hawthorne sent him a letter about first noting the seven gables of the Duchess's house, and about her suggesting he use a chair there as "Grandfather's Chair" in a children's book.[124] We have included this as Letter 157, though its style has more in common with Conolly's other letters than with Hawthorne's. Less questionably, Hawthorne recorded in his notebook the story of Evangeline as told him by Conolly, who had heard it from a parishioner. Longfellow was to use it as the basis of his poem.[125]

William Baker Pike (1811–76), also a bachelor, was born in Salem and trained as a carpenter before going into party politics. He gradually demonstrated talents for public speaking, both at Democratic meetings and as a Methodist lay preacher, and shortly before Hawthorne met him spent six weeks as editor of the Salem *Advertiser,* the Democratic paper.[126] He was appointed a measurer at the Boston Custom House at the beginning of February, 1839; Hawthorne soon recorded in his notebook some of his conversation about skeletons and ghosts in Salem, and was enough struck by his

[124] Manning Hawthorne, "Hawthorne and 'The Man of God'," *Colophon,* n.s. II (1937), 262–82.

[125] *Hawthorne's "Lost Notebook,"* p. 82; AN, pp. 182, 600.

[126] *EIHC,* LXXII (1931), 76.

personality to picture him—"a shortish man, very stoutly built . . . a heavy, yet very intelligent countenance."[127] Though he did not wish to be associated with all of Pike's political preferences, he strongly supported him for a position at the Salem Custom House in 1847, and tried to persuade him to come to England in 1854 as consul to Manchester: "There is no man whom I should like so much to have for a companion, and I never see anything interesting without thinking of you."[128] Pike was appointed collector of the port of Salem by Pierce in 1857, and held that position until 1861. Hawthorne's special feeling for him came out casually to Longfellow in 1851: "A man of no letters, but of remarkable intellect." In 1857 Hawthorne had mixed feelings about Pike's political success: "Ever since I knew you, I have wanted you to do some higher and better thing than other men are able to do."[129] His commitment to Pike impressed Hawthorne's children. Rose recalled that when he visited the Wayside in the 1860s, "he was so short, sturdy, phlegmatic of exterior, and plebeian, that I was astounded at my father's pleasure in his company, until I noticed a certain gentleness in his manner of stepping, and heard the modulations of his voice, and caught the fragrance of his humility." Julian with his usual positiveness claimed of Pike that "he probably knew Hawthorne more intimately than any other man did; for he had the faculty of calling forth whatever was best and profoundest in him."[130] We would be able to judge their friendship better if Pike had published his "Memories of Hawthorne," which he did not complete but burned shortly before his death, perhaps because he had said more than Hawthorne would want. One anecdote of the early 1860s tends to confirm the accounts by Loring and Holden about

---

[127] AN, pp. 189–92.
[128] Hawthorne to Pike, December 21, 1855 (MS, Bowdoin).
[129] Hawthorne to Pike, March 27, 1857 (MS, Bowdoin).
[130] Memories, p. 154; NHHW, I, 444.

Hawthorne's companions: Hawthorne, along with former President Pierce, Dr. Loring, and other former Salem Custom House officials, met at Pike's farm outside Salem. "At the banquet in the evening, Pike was preeminent, and his sentiment expressed was that 'water was useful for floating ships, turning water-wheels and washing dishes, when they needed it, a necessary beverage for cows and horses, but mankind should use it cautiously, and then only when properly reinforced.'"[131]

Zachariah Burchmore, Jr. (1809–84), one of Hawthorne's favorite correspondents, has a prominent if anonymous place also in his published writings. He is in "The Custom-House" the "one man, especially, the observation of whose character gave me a new idea of talent." Like Cilley and Pierce in politics, this "man of business" was "prompt, acute, clear-minded; with an eye that saw through all perplexities, and a faculty of arrangement that made them vanish, as by the waving of an enchanter's wand." As Hawthorne wrote to Horace Mann after his dismissal, Burchmore was the "actual head" of the custom house, or, as he put it in softer terms in the sketch, "the main-spring that kept its variously revolving wheels in motion." Zack's grandfather, Captain Zachariah Burchmore (1743–1807), was a well-known Salem mariner; and his father, Captain Stephen Burchmore (1781–1850), had been a shipmaster before he became an inspector in the custom house. He also appears in Hawthorne's sketch: "Scarcely a day passed that he did not stir me to laughter and admiration by his marvellous gifts as a story-teller. Could I have preserved the picturesque force of his style, and the humorous coloring which nature taught him how to throw over his descriptions, the result, I honestly believe, would have been something new in literature."[132] Zack himself had entered there in his teens, and retained the connection for

[131] Augustus A. Smith, quoted by David Mason Little, "History of the Salem Custom House," *EIHC*, LXVII (1931), 266–67.

[132] *SL*, pp. 24, 37.

nearly thirty years, as clerk, deputy naval officer, and deputy collector. He was dismissed soon after Hawthorne because his business activities were closely tied to work for the Democratic party, as one Whig accuser put it, "an active political intriguer."

Burchmore, who was married and had fathered six children, then kept a small shop in Salem, where he sold liquor among other things. He was for a while the British consul for the port. By November 1853 he returned to the Custom House as a "special appraiser," at the same time that Hawthorne's Uncle William Manning became "superintendant of repairs." He had since his dismissal become an alcoholic. Hawthorne chastised him for it, but not severely. By 1857 he had to beg Pike to "let poor Zack have a little foothold within your precincts."[133] During the Civil War, Burchmore was a clerk and a watchman at the Charlestown Navy Yard. Hawthorne gave him money and asked Bridge to get him a pay increase. After the war, he was dismissed; he died in poverty in Boston. Hawthorne, though disgusted by his drinking, continued to admire him as "a true man," a more candid friend than Pike even. As late as May 1863, he relied on Burchmore for help in applying for money from the government under a relief act: "I was always stupid as a blind horse about the accounts of the Salem Custom House. . . . I don't doubt you are right. . . ."[134] But his most intriguing characterization of Burchmore came during their happy days together in 1848. On January 27 of that year, Burchmore wrote a note: "For value received I promise to pay Nath¹ Hawthorne on order Four pence in Sixty years." Over this was written: "Pay the within to the Wandering Jew Nath¹ Hawthorne."[135]

[133] Hawthorne to Pike, February 27, 1857 (MS, Bowdoin).

[134] Hawthorne to Burchmore, May 2, 1863 (MS, Anderson).

[135] A photograph of this document, entitled "An Autograph of Hawthorne," is opposite page 328 of Hawthorne's *Miscellanies*, volume XVII, *Writings*. See also Conway, pp. 109–10.

VI

A final group of principal correspondents comprises the professional literary men who furthered Hawthorne's career by publishing and publicizing his work. The only one of these not primarily associated with Boston is Evert A. Duyckinck (1816–78), the New York editor and critic who is now best known as Melville's friend, and for introducing Melville and Hawthorne at a summer picnic in 1850. Duyckinck more than any other contemporary first suggested what would become the modern critical response to Hawthorne's writings. He was the son of a publisher whose family had lived in New York for seven generations, a staunch Episcopalian, and an apologist for urban life who began with a prejudice against New England's cultural and literary traditions. In 1838, at the outset of his editorial career, however, he chose to visit Longfellow in Cambridge, and armed with a letter of introduction that recorded his "wonderment and delight" in *Twice-told Tales,* came to Salem with his brother and a friend, as Hawthorne remembered fifteen years later, "the first individuals who ever thought it worth while to pay me a visit as a literary Man."[136] Duyckinck must have followed Hawthorne's progress in Park Benjamin's *American Monthly Magazine* before *Twice-told Tales* was published; he had himself become known for the humorous sketches he wrote for Benjamin in 1838 under the name "Felix Merry," in imitation of Irving's "Geoffrey Crayon."[137]

It is remarkable that during his first European tour in 1838–39 Duyckinck made a point of recording his reading of Hawthorne's latest tale; when he began in late 1840 his own

[136] Longfellow, *Letters,* II, 84; Hawthorne, Letter 625. See also Leland Schubert, "A Boy's Journal of a Trip into New England in 1838," *EIHC,* LXXXVI (1950), 97–105.

[137] *American Monthly Magazine,* n.s. V (February, May, and June, 1838), 134–39, 413–16, 566–69.

monthly, *Arcturus: A Journal of Books and Opinions*, he first inquired of Longfellow about Hawthorne's activities, and included a glowing review of *Grandfather's Chair* in an early number.[138] Although he seems to have had no part in the generation of *Twice-told Tales* into two volumes in 1842, Duyckinck had already begun public planning to collect a third and a fourth volume of tales, as he was actually to do in publishing *Mosses* in 1846; in *Arcturus* he made clear his choices for preeminence in the developing Hawthorne canon.[139] His article of May, 1841, though it acknowledges Longfellow's "admirable eulogy of the 'Twice Told Tales'" and Benjamin's "worthy" review, breaks new ground in interpretation not only in his suggestion that Hawthorne's imagination has "much of Hamlet" but in quoting "confessions" from "Fragments from the Journal of a Solitary Man" that "betray the secret of the sombre half-disappointed spirit that breathes through his pages."[140] This excerpt from the concluding part of "The Story Teller" had been in Benjamin's *American Monthly Magazine* in July, 1837; Hawthorne never collected it, for James T. Fields missed it when he searched for such papers in 1854.[141] It presents to one modern critic "the fundamental antithesis of Hawthorne's thinking about the artist,"[142] and as interest in Hawthorne's

[138] Duyckinck, diary, April 28, 1839 (MS, NYPL); *TS*, pp. 293–94; *Arcturus*, I (January, 1841), 125–26.

[139] In addition to the editorial accounts in *MOM*, pp. 511–12, and *TTT*, p. 527, see Duyckinck, "Nathaniel Hawthorne," *Democratic Review*, XVI (April, 1845), 384: "A third and fourth volume are yet behind, unpublished in book form, unknown to the shelves of the trade." Benjamin had urged collecting Hawthorne's works when revealing the author's name in October, 1836, and then in reviewing *Twice-told Tales* in March, 1838, both in the *American Monthly Magazine*; see note 94 above.

[140] "Nathaniel Hawthorne," *Arcturus*, I (May, 1841), 332–34.

[141] See *MOM*, "Historical Commentary," pp. 523–26. For an account of how the "prescient Duyckinck" may have influenced Hawthorne's writing of "The Christmas Banquet" through his *Arcturus* review, see David Cody, "Invited Guests at Hawthorne's 'Christmas Banquet': Sir Thomas Browne and Jeremy Taylor," *Modern Language Studies*, XI (1980–81), 20–22.

[142] Millicent Bell, *Hawthorne's View of the Artist* (New York: State University of New York Press, 1962), pp. 142–43.

biography deepens, it may provoke valuable speculations about his self-appraisal in the years for which no letters survive. Its own speculations are like what Longfellow might mention in a letter, but Duyckinck made them matters of central concern.

His second major statement about Hawthorne was in the *Democratic Review,* for which O'Sullivan had just made him literary editor, at the moment in the spring of 1845 when *Twice-told Tales* was reissued, when Hawthorne's need for a government appointment was becoming acute, and when he himself had contracted with Wiley and Putnam to edit a "Library of Choice Reading" (European books reprinted) and a "Library of American Books." These series were to include more than ninety and twenty-five titles, respectively, by the end of his stint in 1847. "Nathaniel Hawthorne," in the April issue of the *Democratic Review,* had two functions. As a literary nationalist, writing for the vehicle of "liberal principles and popular rights," as Hawthorne had put it, Duyckinck called attention (as he had in *Arcturus*) to Hawthorne's originality and profundity, and observed that such an introspective habit of mind would not likely lead to popularity, or coincide with "money-making pursuits." Such authors should benefit from a governmental "Literary Pension Fund," for they are "the immediate ornaments of the State, as the good they confer is general, and their honor and prosperity contribute so largely to the [national] life and enjoyment." Perhaps at O'Sullivan's suggestion, he called attention to six writers and intellectuals serving the new Polk administration, implying that Hawthorne should be added to their number. The second purpose was to provide "a systematic examination" of the writings, distinguishing their balance of "masculine" and "feminine" qualities and extending his analysis in *Arcturus* of the dark revelation essential to Hawthorne's "novel and original" qualities: "'I fear thee, Ancient Mariner!' No conventionalist art thou, or respecter of show and outside, but as keensighted a moralist as tempest-stricken Lear, whose sagacity flashes forth from his exceedingly vexed soul like the lightning from the storm-driven clouds." To illustrate these qualities, Duyckinck again quoted from an uncollected tale, "the incidents of which fully disclose the secret of many of his writings. It is called 'Young Goodman Brown'." His excerpt is almost the whole second half of the tale; for the first time a critic called attention to the aspect of Hawthorne's genius that would continue his reputation through the twentieth century. But true to his instincts as an editor and reviewer, Duyckinck "makes amends for this gloomy night-picture by the sunshine of . . . 'Little Annie's Ramble'," which appears entire. Five years later, Melville in "Hawthorne and His Mosses" was to feature Lear's "sane madness of vital truth" and "Young Goodman Brown" as evidence of the "blackness in Hawthorne," and he was to contrast that blackness to the "Indian-summer sunlight on the hither side of Hawthorne's soul." It is hard to believe that Melville had not read and remembered the main outlines of Duyckinck's analysis.

The first volume of the "Library of American Books" was Horatio Bridge's *Journal of an African Cruiser,* edited by Hawthorne; *Mosses from an Old Manse* became volumes 17 and 18. *Tales by Edgar A. Poe* was volume 2, *Poe's Raven and Other Poems* volume 8, and *Herman Melville's Typee* volumes 13 and 14. Duyckinck thus provided opportunities for three contemporaries who were to gain fame, and who needed someone like him at just this moment; Emerson could fend for himself (though Duyckinck made overtures), and Thoreau could not expect Duyckinck's interest after Hawthorne's letter characterizing him.[143] Poe came to New York from Philadelphia in 1844 counting on Duyckinck's help to find a proper editorial position; he received the help and the

[143] Letter 318. "The Library of American Books" was the first publishing venture to include only original American works and to pay royalties to the authors. See George T. Goodspeed, "The Home Library," *PBSA,* XLII (1948), 110.

position, for in spite of temperamental and cultural differences, the New Yorker found him a "man of genius," and
encouraged O'Sullivan to solicit "Marginalia" for the *Democratic Review*. He lent Poe books from his large personal library, and encouraged him, while feeling distaste for the
squabbling Poe was prone to engage in.[144] On Melville his
effect was more dramatic and decisive. He published the
young former sailor's first effort; he defended the broad humor and easy morality of *Omoo;* he provided convivial evenings and the freedom of his library during the extraordinary
gestation of *Mardi* in late 1847 and early 1848. By this time,
Duyckinck had left Wiley and Putnam, and had gained and
lost the editorship of a new weekly, the *Literary World*. From
the time he could purchase this paper, in October, 1848,
until it ceased publication at the end of 1853, he was able,
with his brother George (1823–63) as collaborator, to provide
the best and most complete literary journalism yet in America. Melville's rapid intellectual development took place
within his view; as he passed from mentor to puzzled critic
to satirized enemy through the succession of *Mardi, Redburn,
White-Jacket, Moby-Dick,* and *Pierre,* his opinion of Hawthorne's work underwent a similar, though much less dramatic, transformation. As a canny reviewer who was also a
fervent advocate of the writers whose genius he recognized,
Duyckinck went through the greatest torture of his career in
writing about *Mardi*. Knowing that its extravagant literary
experiments would prove fatally tedious to most of the public
that had bought *Typee,* he wrote: "Many a reader will turn
back again and again after he has concluded this
book. . . . Indeed, we despair in any way of giving an account of the multifold contents of this well-filled book, laden
deep as a Spanish argosy. . . . " Still the book did not sell,

[144] See Arthur John Roche, "A Literary Gentleman in New York: Evert A.
Duyckinck's Relationships with Nathaniel Hawthorne, Herman Melville, Edgar
Allan Poe, and William Gilmore Simms," Ph.D. diss., Duke University, 1973,
pp. 77–104.

and he must have agreed with Hawthorne's comment to him (after he had sent him a copy) that "one scarcely pardons the writer for not having brooded long over it, so as to make it a great deal better."[145] But in reviewing *Moby-Dick,* Duyckinck was in the process of leaving the author's sympathy for that of the typical reader: "We do not like to see what, under any view, must be to the world the most sacred associations of life violated and defaced." Hawthorne did not agree, seeing "much greater power" in the writing and complaining that the review "hardly seemed" to do "justice to its best points."[146] In March, 1850, Duyckinck had praised *The Scarlet Letter* as a "perfect creation," but saw its author as "less companionable" than in his sunlit sketches: now he was "a reviewer of witchcrafts and of those dark agencies of evil which lurk in the human soul." Finally, Hawthorne was the truest literary "product of the American soil, though of a peculiar culture."[147] Four months later, when they met at the picnic in Berkshire where Duyckinck introduced him to Melville, Hawthorne was dubbed "Mr. Noble Melancholy" by his New York friends; and he remembered that, even as he thanked Duyckinck for appreciating "the sunny side of justice" in *The House of the Seven Gables.* When the Duyckinck brothers returned to Lenox in the summer of 1851, Hawthorne mentioned them in a letter to his wife only as "two other gentlemen" who called with Herman Melville.

Duyckinck's limitations as critic might have been foreseen even in his 1845 article on Hawthorne. Reacting with awe and shock to the moral power he had put before his reader in reprinting the climax of "Young Goodman Brown," he suddenly drew back from his author by alluding to Isabel's re-

---

[145] *Literary World,* IV (April 21, 1849), 351, 352; Letter 448.

[146] *Literary World,* IX (November 22, 1851), 404; Letter 525. Leon Howard has observed that Duyckinck "commented upon *Moby-Dick* like a missionary on *Typee*"; see *Herman Melville: A Biography* (Berkeley: University of California Press, 1951), p. 191.

[147] *Literary World,* VI (March 30, 1850), 323–25.

proof of Angelo in *Measure for Measure:* "How dramatically is
the truth conveyed, how naturally are these strange scenes
managed! They show the possession of a power which it is
'excellent to have' but 'tyrannous to use'." If his conventional
prejudices kept him from appreciating what he understood in
The Scarlet Letter and *Moby-Dick,* Duyckinck was less prepared to cope with *Pierre* and *The Blithedale Romance.* In
reviewing these, he looked back from Melville's present "immoral *moral*" and "unintelligible . . . transcendentalism"
to his literary origins "in the hale company of sturdy sailors,
men of flesh and blood"; Hawthorne's latest romance
"means . . . no literal decipherable interpretation of the
real world" such as might come from Dickens's "large,
healthy, observing eye," and Duyckinck is clearly heartily
tired of promoting Hawthorne's chosen role as a "delicate
spiritual anatomist."[148] Melville had long since cut his company by cancelling his subscription, but Hawthorne wrote to
Duyckinck days before sailing to ask that the *Literary World*
be sent to him in Liverpool, and even offering to provide
gossip for its columns, an offer never fulfilled because of the
paper's demise a few months later.

There was little correspondence during Hawthorne's years
abroad, and apparently none after his return to the Wayside.
In a lengthy article for their *Cyclopedia of American Literature*
in 1855, the Duyckinck brothers adapted the reviews of the
romances in the *Literary World,* treating *The House of the
Seven Gables* at the greatest length. The article alluded only
indirectly to Evert's pioneering essays of 1841 and 1845, noting that the neglect of Hawthorne's early writings "is the
more remarkable, as there is scarcely a trait of his later writings which did not exist in perfection in the first told
tales. . . . This neglect was the more extraordinary looking
at the maturity and finished execution of the early writings,

---

[148] *Literary World,* XI (August 21, 1852), 118–20, and (July 24, 1852), 52.

which contained something more than the germ of the author's later and more successful volumes." Here again is Duyckinck's anticipation of the twentieth-century understanding of Hawthorne, though in his choice of texts for extracts, "The Gray Champion" and "Sights from a Steeple," he affirms his participation in his contemporaries' taste. His comments on *The Marble Faun,* in later editions of the *Cyclopedia,* are consistent with his reservations about the romances he had reviewed: "The prevalent tone of the book is sombre and melancholy, and in some measure revolting, but it is redeemed by art. . . . "[149] For his part, Hawthorne looked back on his relationship with the New York editor with characteristic polite distance. For a minor English poet visiting America in 1855, he wrote a note of introduction, characterizing Duyckinck in a covering letter as "a person of leisure, who interests himself in all matters of art and literature."[150]

Hawthorne's oldest friend among the Boston *literati* was George Stillman Hillard (1808–79), a Whig lawyer and orator, and Brahmin critic and editor, who became in 1840 his personal attorney, and was to give important advice and help at times of crisis in Hawthorne's government appointments. After the author's death, he was executor of the estate and Mrs. Hawthorne's embarassed ally in her struggle with James T. Fields over the money she believed her husband's writings had earned. Hawthorne seems to have met Hillard, probably through Elizabeth Peabody, when he came to Boston to work in the custom house, for he was soon to be "delightfully situated, with a little parlor and bed-room" in the home of his friend on Pinckney Street, Beacon Hill. Sophia and her sisters had known him at least since 1832,

---

[149] *Cyclopedia of American Literature* (Philadelphia: William Rutter, 1875), II, 358, 363. On Hawthorne's precocious maturity in his early writings, compare the comment to Duyckinck in Letter 334.

[150] To an unknown recipient, July 24, 1855 (MS, Virginia).

when he first came to Salem to lecture at the Lyceum on "The Comparison of Ancient and Modern Literature."[151] Born in Machias, a seaport of northern Maine, Hillard had been to Boston Latin School and was graduated from Harvard in 1828. While studying law at Northampton, he taught at the experimental Round Hill School, where George Bancroft and Joseph Green Cogswell had established an American version of the German *Gymnasium*. He became law partner of Charles Sumner in Boston in 1834. Their association was to continue for more than twenty years, though disagreement over the issue of slavery was to cool their friendship by the late 1840s. Hillard married Susan Howe, daughter of a Northampton judge, in 1834; their only child, a son born the next year, died before his third birthday. The marriage became unhappy: Hillard restlessly tried to express his literary ambitions while a sense of personal unworthiness came to dominate him.

In 1843 Hawthorne described him as "a melancholy shadow of a man," for whom "outward triumphs are necessary."[152] He was an unconvincing debater, cursed by an effeminate voice. In the formal oratorical exercises, his cultivation and taste and his mastery of rhetorical strategies gave pleasure, but rarely moved his auditors. On one occasion, however, he seems to have found the fame that otherwise eluded him: at the Dinner for Charles Dickens in Boston on February 1, 1842, Hillard was a vice-president of

[151] Sophia, writing to Mary Peabody on November 10, 1832, indicated that Hillard was to stay at the Peabody house while in Salem. Sophia wrote to Elizabeth Peabody "care of G Hillard Esq Boston" May 26, 1838 (MSS, Berg). This was a different residence than where Hawthorne was to board in November, 1839.

[152] Hawthorne mentioned him in the *Pioneer* version of "The Hall of Fantasy" as editor of Spenser's *Faerie Queene*, "though he might well have preferred a claim on his own account" as a poet (*MOM*, p. 636). His name appears in a casual anecdote in "The Old Manse" (*MOM*, pp. 17–18), and with more point in "The Custom-House": "After growing fastidious by sympathy with the classic refinement of Hillard's culture . . . it was time, at length, that I should exercise other faculties of my nature . . . " (*SL*, p. 25).

the event and responsible for the toast. His was "the admired speech of the occasion," and the toast itself—"The *gifted minds of England*—Hers by birth; ours by adoption"—became a keynote of his contributions to culture in the years ahead.[153]

Hillard's literary acquaintance was enormous, and his role as friend and confidant of writers, in Boston and London, made its contribution. But his personal ineffectuality has left him obscure, without even a single twentieth-century scholarly article to summarize his accomplishments. At the time of his debut as a Lyceum lecturer in the early 1830s, he began to publish sketches and essays, among them series of "Selections from the Papers of an Idler" and "Literary Portraits" of Bryant and other poets, for the *New England Magazine* of Joseph T. Buckingham, 1831–34; this was two to four years before Hawthorne's first appearance in its pages. Park Benjamin, who succeeded Buckingham, had been his roommate at Harvard; and Oliver Wendell Holmes, the magazine's leading contributor, was also a classmate. From 1831 to 1864, Hillard wrote a total of twenty-three major reviews for the *North American Review*, the most widely read and internationally respected American periodical. Its former editor, Edward Everett, had been his teacher and was to remain a lifetime friend; and he was also close to Jared Sparks, John Gorham Palfrey, and Alexander H. Everett during their terms as editor.

For the *North American*, Hillard reviewed works of fiction and poetry, memoirs, orations, biography and history, and studies of law and education. His first appearance, in January, 1831, was the most important literary criticism he was

[153] For Hillard's speech, see William Glyde Wilkins, *Charles Dickens in America* (New York: Charles Scribner's Sons, 1911), pp. 42–48. For Dickens's reaction, see his *Letters*, ed. Madeline House, Graham Storey, and Katheleen Tillotson (Oxford: Clarendon, 1974), III, 67. Hawthorne's attendance is doubtful. Hillard had planned a party for Dickens at his house three days earlier, where Hawthorne may have been staying, but Dickens had been unable to attend, "on grounds of exhaustion" (*Letters*, III, 32). See also Letter 226 below.

to write, a lengthy review of Catharine Maria Sedgwick's
latest novel, *Clarence*. He took a stand on the theory of American fiction that relates in an interesting way to Hawthorne's
practice, by raising the question how a writer like Miss Sedgwick might "give a highly romantic interest to events occurring in our own prosaic age and country," asking in effect
whether the realistic observation of the novel could be expressed through American materials. Hillard concluded that
"the Protean forms which society assumes in our wide continent" would provide "abundant food for speculation" to the
novelist, and that the newness of American society was in its
favor, for "vigorous and fantastic shoots of character are not
nipped by the frost of hoary convention" and "the materials
of romance in the old world are waxing threadbare, but the
charm of unworn freshness is here like morning-dew."[154]
The contrary opinion had been expounded in the *North
American*, and by other American critics who saw Walter
Scott's historical romances as a model for Americans, to cul-
tivate the now legendary early history of colonization rather
than current society. Recently James Fenimore Cooper had
described "the poverty of materials" for American fiction in
Notions of the Americans (1828). Hillard, however, taking his
cue from the subject of his review, argued that contemporary
American society was adequate material, especially in "the
gay throngs that chase amusement from one watering-place
to another, and in the lowly virtues that cluster round our
farm-house hearths." The resorts that Hillard had in mind
(now abandoned places like Lebanon Springs and Trenton
Falls, both in upstate New York) were American equivalents
to Bath, as it appeared in the British "fashionable novel."[155]

[154] *North American Review*, XXXII (January, 1831), 84, 95.

[155] See Neal Frank Doubleday, "*Redwood* and Bryant's Review," in *Variety of
Attempt: British and American Fiction of the Early Nineteenth Century* (Lincoln:
University of Nebraska Press, 1976), p. 150. On the preference for romance as
expressed in the *North American*, see the articles by E. T. Channing (1819) and
W. H. Gardner (1822), reprinted in Ruland, *The Native Muse*, pp. 118–30, 186–

Unlike the "fantastic shoots of character" that were to appear in Hawthorne's tales and romances, Hillard's ideas about character (and about the other elements of fiction) were firmly based on the precedent of English models.

In advocating that fiction celebrate rural "lowly virtues," he seems also not in tune with much of Hawthorne's fiction. In his praise for *Clarence's* "high and pure tone of moral and religious feeling," he noted that the author "never makes vice interesting or virtue repulsive. . . . She draws no beings, half-gods and half-fiends, with a veil of splendid and romantic qualities, covering but not hiding the darkest and foulest traits of character, and constraining us to admire the actor, though we detest the guilt." He thus shows no prospect of sympathy with Hawthorne's adaptation of Gothic and Byronic hero-villains. Twenty years later, soon after he finished reading *The Scarlet Letter*, Hillard wrote to its author to praise this "remarkable book," and to announce a confession:

> You are, intellectually speaking, quite a puzzle to me. How comes it that with so thoroughly healthy an organization as you have, you have such a taste for the morbid anatomy of the human heart, and such knowledge of it, too? I should fancy from your books that you were burdened with secret sorrow; that you had some blue chamber in your soul, into which you hardly dared to enter yourself; but when I see you, you give me the impression of a man as healthy as Adam was in Paradise. For my own taste, I could wish that you would dwell more in the sun, and converse more with cheerful thoughts and lightsome images, and expand into a story the spirit of the Town Pump. But while waiting for this, let me

---

94; also in Ruland are Cooper's statement (pp. 222–29), Hillard's conclusion (pp. 210–11), and W. C. Bryant's review of *Redwood* discussed below (pp. 212–21). Hillard, as a Whig "son of the Puritans," did not dispute the value of early American history: for his address to the New England Society of New York in 1851, "The Past and the Future," see Cephas and Eveline Brainerd, eds., *New England Society Orations* (New York: Century, 1901), II, 137–62; and J. V. Matthews, "'Whig History': The New England Whigs and a Usable Past," *NEQ*, LI (1978), 193–208.

be thankful for the weird and sad strain which breathes from "The Scarlet Letter," which I read with most absorbing interest.[156]

At one moment in *The Blithedale Romance,* Coverdale leaves the "Bedlam" of "the Community" to "go and hold a little talk with . . . the writers of the North American Review."[157] His affection and sympathy for "all those respectable old blockheads," who so disliked such reformers as Hollingsworth represented, may constitute a response to Hillard's sentiments.

But Hillard's idea about the future of American fiction in his first review was not original, for William Cullen Bryant had drawn a similar conclusion about Miss Sedgwick's "ennobling" of "the pecularities in the manners and character of our countrymen" in his review of her novel *Redwood* in the *North American* in 1825.[158] Hillard copied other details of Bryant's argument; the editors must have noticed this lack of originality because for the remainder of his career he was often not given the most important books by members of the Brahmin establishment, but had to be content to review them

---

[156] *Memories,* pp. 121–22. In his Phi Beta Kappa address of 1843, "The Relation of the Poet to his Age," Hillard "perfectly expressed the genteel temper: in times when sensitive people were 'constantly repelled by some iron reality,' the poet's task was 'to idealize life; to connect the objects of thought with those associations which embellish, dignify and exalt, and to keep out of sight, those which debase and deform'," according to David B. Tyack, *George Ticknor and the Boston Brahmins* (Cambridge: Harvard University Press, 1967), p. 150. Tyack explains that such statements came in part from anxiety, for the Brahmins "attributed such power to literature that they believed that an author could undermine the moral foundations of the family and even shake the state." In his Fourth of July address in Boston in 1835, Hillard emphasized the social need of "spontaneous reverence"; see Jean V. Matthews, *Rufus Choate: The Law and Civic Virtue* (Philadelphia: Temple University Press, 1980), pp. 86–87.

[157] *BR,* p. 141.

[158] *North American Review,* XX (April, 1825), 271–72, reprinted in Bryant's *Prose Writings* as "American Society as a Field for Fiction." See note 155 above, and Robert Eugene Streeter, "Critical Thought in the *North American Review,*" Ph.D. diss., Northwestern University, 1943, pp. 115, 117, 169, 175.

in the *Christian Examiner,* a lesser vehicle of Boston Unitarian opinion.[159]

His bland gentility and urbanity have similarly reduced his recognition as a representative of Boston culture in England. He spent much of 1847–48 in Europe, gathering notes for his most popular publication, *Six Months in Italy* (1853), and reestablishing his friendships with Dickens and the actor William Charles Macready. He was also able to meet Thomas Babington Macaulay. He discussed literature, culture, and America with these gentlemen, with apparently mixed results. But it seems no coincidence that in recent scholarly editions of the letters of Dickens and Macaulay he does not appear, either because he is confused with his brother John, a London merchant of no discernible literary importance, or because his visit was so minor as to leave him an "unidentified recipient" for Macaulay's cool refusal to consider an American tour.[160]

Only a month before Hillard became deeply involved as Hawthorne's legal adviser and as a friend of prominent Boston Whig politicians in the effort to reinstate the author in the Salem Custom House, he tried to help William Macready out of somewhat similar difficulties. Macready's appearance on the stage in New York had led to the Astor Place riot, a demonstration by supporters of his rival, the American actor Edwin Forrest, in which several people were killed and Ma-

---

[159] For example, in 1850 W. H. Prescott reviewed George Ticknor's *History of Spanish Literature* in the *North American,* and Hillard in the *Examiner;* C. C. Felton reviewed Edward Everett's *Orations and Speeches* in the *North American;* Hillard in the *Examiner.*

[160] See *The Diaries of William Charles Macready,* ed. William Toynbee (London: Chapman & Hall, 1912), II, 395, and Dickens, *Letters,* V, 330, to connect Hillard with their dinner of June 13, 1848. Macready had seen Hillard in Boston in 1843 (*Diaries,* II, 235). Hillard's dinner with Macaulay in May, 1848, led to an invitation to visit the United States, which Macaulay declined in a letter to "an unidentified recipient" of May, 1849, but Longfellow's journal for May 2 mentions Hillard receiving this letter; see Macaulay, *Letters,* ed. Thomas Pinney (Cambridge: Cambridge University Press, 1974–83), IV, 365–66; V, 39–40; Longfellow, *Life,* II, 139.

cready's own life brought into danger. When Macready reached Boston on May 11, 1849, Hillard, his indignant friend and adviser on things American, offered legal services as well as moral support.[161]

Hillard's closest literary friend over the years was Longfellow. It was at Longfellow's dinner parties that Hawthorne saw him most frequently. In 1837 Hillard and Longfellow had formed, with Sumner, Henry Russell Cleveland, of Salem, and the Harvard professor C. C. Felton, the "Five of Clubs," meeting for dinner and literary conversation on Saturdays. Hillard and Sumner were Longfellow's legal advisers. It is Hillard's closeness to Longfellow that has led scholars to attribute the *North American*'s brief notice of *Twice-told Tales* (1842) to the poet, whereas recent documentary evidence proves Hillard's authorship.[162] The similarity to Longfellow's review of 1837 comes, of course, from Hillard's having studied that, as he must have studied Bryant's review of Miss Sedgwick ten years earlier. It is not surprising, then, that his notice should emphasize Hawthorne's originality: "He does not see by the help of other men's minds, and has evidently been more of an observer and thinker, than of a student. . . . His style strikes us as one of marked and uncommon excellence. It is fresh and vigorous, not formed by studying any particular model, and has none of the stiffness which comes from imitation; but it is eminently correct and careful."[163] His longest and last public statement about Hawthorne as author came almost thirty years later, as a major

[161] Macready, *Reminiscences and Diaries*, ed. Sir Frederick Pollock (New York: Macmillan, 1875), pp. 616, 621, 623–24.

[162] Rodney G. Dennis, "Attribution of Critical Notices in the 'North American Review'," *PBSA*, LVIII (1964), 292–93. Faust and Crowley (*Critical Heritage*) attributed this notice to Longfellow. Dennis's list reveals that Hillard also wrote the notice of *Grandfather's Chair* in the *North American Review*, LII (January, 1841), 260–61.

[163] *North American Review*, LIV (April, 1842), 496–99. Hillard's article, "Henry Wadsworth Longfellow," in *Graham's Magazine*, XXII (May, 1843), 288–93, gives an interesting contrast: he emphasizes Longfellow's "careful intellectual training and familiarity with the best models in every language," and his

review of *Passages from The English Notebooks* in the *Atlantic Monthly*. Freed by his subject's death and increasing fame to give a personal assessment, Hillard moved from a now familiar mention of the author's shyness, his terror before "the claims and courtesies of social life," to his independence of mind; each phrase points the contrast with Hillard's own intellectual personality:

> Unlike most men who are at once intellectual and shy, he was not a lover, or a student, of books. He read books as they came in his way, or for a particular purpose, but he made no claim to the honors of learning and scholarship. A great library had no charms for him. He rarely bought a book, and the larger part of his small collection had come to him by gift. His mind did not feed upon the printed page. It will be noticed that in his writings he very seldom introduces a quotation, or makes any allusion to the writings of others. The raptures of the bibliomaniac, fondling his tall copies, his wide margins, his unique specimens, his vellum pages, were as strange to him as are the movements of a violin-player's arm to the deaf man's eye. In the summer of 1859 the writer of this notice—who confesses to an insatiable passion for the possession of books, and an omnivorous appetite for their contents—saw him at Leamington, and was invited by him into his study, the invitation being accompanied with one of his peculiar and indescribable smiles, in which there lurked a consciousness of his friend's weakness. The study was a small, square room, with a table and chair, but absolutely not a single book.[164]

In view of these opinions it is amusing that Hillard, who edited the first American edition of *The Faerie Queene* in 1839, questioned Hawthorne's taste in naming his daughter Una (and we do not know what he thought of naming a cat Pigwiggen). The sizable squad of Hawthorne scholars that has adduced numerous allusions to Spenser will find his

---

accumulated "stores of various and elegant learning . . . in the companionship of a large and well-chosen library."

[164] *Atlantic Monthly*, XXVI (September, 1870), 258–59.

bookish friend particularly obtuse on this point. Moreover, the anecdote about the empty room is probably true, but Hillard had forgotten that when he arrived in Leamington for one hour's stay on October 29, 1859, the family had been there only two weeks: Hawthorne had just finished most of *The Marble Faun,* and had sent the manuscript to London two days earlier; he was now enjoying a brief break before going back to the last portion, which he sent off November 9.[165]

What disturbed Hillard most about reading the notebooks was Hawthorne's comment on his public speaking in England. Reflecting on the occasion of opening William Brown's free public library in Liverpool in April, 1857, he had written: "I question much whether public speaking tends to elevate the orator, intellectually or morally; the effort, of course, being to say what is immediately received by the audience, and produce its effect on the instant. I don't quite see how an honest man can be a good and successful orator; but I shall hardly undertake to decide the question on my merely post-prandial experience." Hillard was about to publish a schoolbook on oratory and elocution, containing an anthology of patriotic and sentimental passages for boys to read and memorize. He took many of these from Dickens and from his friends among the Boston Whig intellectuals and statesmen.[166] He responded with understandable defensiveness to "Hawthorne's opinion . . . this startling doctrine," but concluded weakly with the admission "Most popular speakers, at least, are superficial thinkers."

This review barely mentioned *The Marble Faun,* perhaps because Hillard had reviewed it at length ten years before, and made almost no allusion to Hawthorne's year and half in

[165] See Hawthorne's Pocket Diary for 1859, in *FIN*, pp. 695–700.

[166] Actually Hawthorne's comment was inspired by another public occasion in Liverpool a few months earlier; see *EN*, pp. 440–41. Typical of Hillard's anthologies was *The Franklin Fifth Reader for the Use of Public and Private Schools* (Boston: Brewer & Tileston, 1874).

Italy, the scene of Hillard's best remembered writing. In his Italian notebook, which Mrs. Hawthorne was preparing to edit at the time she sought Hillard's legal advice in her quarrel with Fields, Hawthorne had made a few references to *Six Months in Italy*. When Hillard visited Hawthorne so briefly in 1859, he was in the midst of a literary pilgrimage to Great Britain, sending back frequent descriptive letters to the Boston *Courier*, a paper in which he held a part interest. These did not mention Hawthorne, and were never published in book form. Hillard's most discernible curiosity about his friend's years abroad is in the *Atlantic* review, where he listed many of the cultural monuments of England that Hawthorne did *not* visit or describe: "the stately houses . . . the National Gallery," music, opera, theater, cricket, yachting, fox hunting, horse racing. On this negative note, which suggests the "items of high civilisation" that Henry James was to list as "absent from the texture of American life" in his biography of Hawthorne, their relationship seems to end, at least from Hillard's side. In a letter to Fields from England, Hawthorne mentioned Hillard's "excellent notice" of *The Marble Faun* in the *Courier;*[167] but aside from casual meetings at the Saturday Club, on those occasions when Hillard was invited as a guest and when Hawthorne chose to come, there is no record of their continued relationship.

Hillard's most significant effort for Hawthorne was to raise the money that enabled the recently dismissed surveyor of the custom house to survive until *The Scarlet Letter* was published, and he found a financial arrangement with his new publishers, Ticknor, Reed & Fields, that kept him for the rest of his life from the discomfort and embarrassment of pinched finances. Hawthorne's letters to Hillard, accepting the money, and then triumphantly returning it four years later, are among his most eloquent, evoking memories of the

[167] April 26, 1860 (MS, Huntington). Boston *Courier*, April 5, 1860, 1:5–6.

grace of generosity in Augustan England. Hawthorne's eloquence also shows some debt to the personal distance that
was necessary to their friendship.

Writing *The Scarlet Letter* opened a new phase of Hawthorne's career in several ways. For one, with this work he
found a new publisher, a firm for which he was to write until
his death; the partners, James T. Fields (1817–81) and William D. Ticknor (1810–64), became his good friends. Another of their associates, Edwin Percy Whipple (1819–86), a
critic for several periodicals of national importance, came to
help Hawthorne to "see" his work as no one apparently yet
had done. Since most of his correspondence with these men
came in the time after Hawthorne went to Europe in 1853,
we will defer fuller biographical treatment to the Introduction to a subsequent volume.

Some later biographers have questioned Fields's account of
his part in making *The Scarlet Letter*. In *Yesterdays with Authors* (1871), he wrote that he came to Salem "in the winter
of 1849," a few months after Hawthorne had been ejected
from the custom house; he claimed, in effect, to have forced
the author to allow him to discover the manuscript, through
begging and cajolery; it was his advice that led Hawthorne to
elaborate an original short story to book length. Fields may
have been influenced by the "Custom-House"'s own fiction
about discovering "a small package" containing "documents . . . of a private nature" and "a certain affair of fine
red cloth." Later, after Sophia Hawthorne had occasion to
wish him ill, she wrote that Whipple had accompanied Fields
to Salem, and that it was he who first recognized the value,
potential or actual, of what Hawthorne had written.[168] In

[168] Fields, *Yesterdays with Authors*, pp. 48–51. Sophia wrote to Hawthorne's
cousin Richard Manning February 12, 1871, of Fields's "absurd boast" that he
was "the sole cause of the Scarlet Letter being published. . . . It was Mr
Whipple, the clever critic, and really literary man of careful culture,
who . . . told him that a splendid work it was" (MS, Essex). Recent study of
The Scarlet Letter by Watson Branch suggests how Hawthorne may have enlarged
an original short narrative to the present book, in a much more specific way than

any case, the earliest letter by Hawthorne that Fields could quote dates from January, 1850, when all but three chapters had been completed.

Fields was Hawthorne's correspondent in the company until the autumn of 1851, when he sailed to Europe, and Ticknor came to take his place. One of their main functions soon became financial: they served as Hawthorne's bankers, providing money on demand from a fund created by the royalties his books earned, based on fifteen percent from the romances and ten percent from collections of tales and from children's books.[169] For the rest of his life, he had only to ask for money. At first he preferred to deal with Fields, who was the more outgoing, even flamboyant personality, and who as a promoter was revolutionizing the selling of literature in America and, to some extent, in Great Britain. Fields cultivated the friendships of authors—Dickens, Thackeray, De Quincey, Tennyson, Browning, and Longfellow, Holmes, Emerson, and Lowell. Equally or more important, he built up "vital relationships in the world of critics, editors, and reviewers"— with men like Whipple and Evert Duyckinck, who by advertising, reviewing, preliminary gossip-writing, prepublishing of extracts, and other such activities, became "molders of public taste."[170]

Hawthorne came to appreciate Fields's genius, as he said in a letter of 1861: "I care more for your good opinion than for that of a host of critics, and have excellent reason for so doing; inasmuch as my literary success, whatever it has been or may be, is the result of my connection with you. Somehow or other, you smote the rock of public sympathy on my behalf; and a stream gushed forth in sufficient quantity to quench

---

Fields suggested; see "From Allegory to Romance: Hawthorne's Transformation of *The Scarlet Letter*," *Modern Philology*, LXXX (1982), 145–60.

[169] See Ellen B. Ballou, *The Building of the House: Houghton Mifflin's Formative Years* (Boston: Houghton Mifflin, 1970), pp. 62, 146–48, 597.

[170] William Charvat, "James T. Fields and the Beginnings of Book Promotion, 1840–1855," *Huntington Library Quarterly*, VIII (1944), 88.

my thirst, though not to drown me."[171] He included Ticknor in this praise; in fact, the senior partner became a closer friend than Fields, receiving many more letters. At first, however, Ticknor was only "at bottom a bookseller," who could not replace Fields when the latter was abroad. Hawthorne early recognized that the sober, accounting side of business was only "accidental" to Fields, "while your native and essential characteristics assimilate you with my own wretched brotherhood."[172] Hawthorne later saw that Ticknor, the home-loving Baptist father of seven, skilled in investment and banking as well as the love of literature, was as essential to the partnership as the self-centered Fields, whose enthusiastic accomplishments in charm and flattery made him less reliable, even less companionable.[173] As Ticknor's daughter was to put it, her father "supplied just that which Hawthorne felt he lacked and understood precisely what was needed before the other asked for it," and so resembled Franklin Pierce, to whom Hawthorne also became close in his last years.[174] Ticknor's loyalty was remarkable: he accompanied Hawthorne to Washington in the spring of 1853, and even to England in the summer of that year. In 1862 they made a second trip south together; in 1864 it was for Hawthorne's health that they were in Philadelphia when Ticknor unexpectedly died, only a month before Hawthorne

[171] February 28, 1861 (MS, Huntington).

[172] Letter 551.

[173] Sophia wrote in her letter of February 12, 1871, to Richard Manning: "Mr Fields was never admitted to the *intimacy* of Mr Hawthorne, and is not a man with whom he could deeply sympathize at all. He has caught up some culture, but is not a truly literary person, and has no original opinions. His comical vein and a sort of good-fellow-way, amused my husband, and he believed him faithful and upright" (MS, Essex).

[174] *Hawthorne and His Publisher*, pp. 6–7. There is evidence that in the 1830s Hawthorne sought similar shelter from, and access to, the social world from Samuel Goodrich and Park Benjamin; see Merle M. Hoover, *Park Benjamin: Poet and Editor* (New York: Columbia University Press, 1948), p. 62; Daniel Roselle, *Samuel Griswold Goodrich, Creator of Peter Parley* (Albany: State University of New York Press, 1968), p. 88.

was to succumb in New Hampshire, in the company of Pierce.

Whipple's importance for Hawthorne was more purely intellectual. He resembled a combination of Hillard's taste and learning and Duyckinck's incisive critical judgment. All three of these new acquaintances, these men who would be so important to Hawthorne in the 1850s, had come from provincial beginnings into Boston in their teens, and had found their way to a junior partnership or the equivalent by their early twenties. Hawthorne had received earlier opportunities, in attending Bowdoin, and the luxury of a prolonged apprenticeship to the art of writing, with no need immediately to satisfy a commercial master. In spite of the success that his associations with Ticknor, Fields, and Whipple would bring, he kept his own sense of his achievements and limitations: no one penetrated to "the inner passages of my being," as he had warned the reader of "The Old Manse" that no one would.

T. W.

A CHRONOLOGY OF
NATHANIEL HAWTHORNE'S LIFE TO 1853

1801	August 2	Nathaniel Hathorne and Elizabeth Clarke Manning married.
1802	March 7	Elizabeth Manning Hathorne born.
1804	July 4	NH born at Union Street, Salem.
1808	Winter	Father dies at sea.
	January 9	Maria Louisa Hathorne born.
	April	Word of father's death arrives; family moves in with grandfather Richard Manning at Herbert Street, Salem; NH begins instruction with Elizabeth Carlton.
1809	September 21	SH born Sophia Amelia Peabody in Salem.
1813		Attends school run by Joseph Worcester.
	April 19	Grandfather Manning dies; Uncle Robert Manning assumes guardianship.
	November 10	Injures foot; lame for next fourteen months.
1816	Summer	Hathornes board at Manning property in Maine.
1818	Late October	Hathornes move to Raymond, Maine.

	Mid-December	Attends school of the Rev. Caleb Bradley in Stroudwater, Maine.
1819	Late January	Leaves school, returns to Raymond.
	July 5	Enters Samuel H. Archer's school, Salem.
1820	By March 7	Prepares for college under Benjamin L. Oliver in Salem.
1821	Early October	Enters Bowdoin College, Brunswick, Maine; meets Jonathan Cilley, Franklin Pierce, Horatio Bridge.
1822	May 29	Fined for card-playing.
	Fall	Longfellow enters Bowdoin; he and NH meet.
1823	May	Vacations in Augusta with college friends (perhaps Bridge?).
1824	November 14	Cilley wagers that NH will not still be a bachelor in 1836.
1825	Summer	Shows first literary works to sister Elizabeth.
	September 7	Graduates from Bowdoin; returns to live with family at Herbert St., Salem.
1828	October	*Fanshawe* published anonymously at NH's expense, soon after suppressed by him. Robert Manning builds two houses on Dearborn Street, Salem; Hathornes move into one. By now NH has added 'w' to spelling of his last name.
1829	August	Travels to New Haven and Deerfield.

	December 20	Sends "The Gentle Boy," "My Uncle Molineux," "Alice Doane," and "Roger Malvin's Burial" to S. G. Goodrich for publication in the *Token*.
1830	April 7	Captain Joseph White murdered in Salem; NH follows the ensuing investigation and trial.
	May 6	Sends "Sights from a Steeple" to Goodrich, proposes to publish a collection of stories titled *Provincial Tales*.
	Summer?	Visits Martha's Vineyard?
	October	"Sights from a Steeple" (first acknowledged sketch) published in 1831 *Token*.
	November–December	First known articles in Salem *Gazette*.
1831	August	Visits New Hampshire with uncle Samuel Manning.
1832		Hathornes return to Herbert St. house.
	September–October	Travels extensively in Vermont and New York, visiting the White Mountains, Fort Ticonderoga, Lake Champlain, Rochester, and Niagara Falls, perhaps going as far on the Great Lakes as Detroit.
1834		Proposes another collection of sketches, called *The Story Teller*.
	November	Begins contributing to *New-England Magazine*.
1835		Contributes "The Wedding-Knell," "The Minister's Black Veil," and "The May-Pole of Merry Mount" to 1836 *Token*.

1836	January	Becomes editor of *American Magazine of Useful and Entertaining Knowledge;* moves to Hancock Street, Beacon Hill, Boston.
	March	First of NH's issues of *American Magazine.*
	May	Agrees to write (with sister Elizabeth) *Peter Parley's Universal History, on the Basis of Geography.*
	August	Resigns editorship; returns to Salem.
	September	*Peter Parley's Universal History* completed.
	November 15	Wins bet with Cilley.
1837	March 6	*Twice-Told Tales* published; mother and sisters accept "Hawthorne" spelling.
	March 7	Begins corresponding with Longfellow.
	Spring	Becomes acquainted with Mary Silsbee.
	July	Travels to Maine to visit Bridge; returns after August 12.
	November 11	NH and his sisters first visit the Peabodys; NH meets SH on a second visit shortly after.
1838	February 24	Cilley killed in a duel; NH writes his biography.
	July 23	Leaves Salem for "three months seclusion from old associations"; in North Adams July 26–September 11, with trips in the Berkshires, New York, Vermont, and Connecticut. Returns to Salem September 24.

	November	Breaks off relationship with Mary Silsbee. Offered post of Boston Custom House inspector by George Bancroft; declines.
1839	January 11	Accepts position of measurer in Boston Custom House; begins work January 17.
	March 6	First surviving love letter to SH.
	July 24	Proposes marriage to SH in letter; subsequently refers to himself to her as "thy husband."
1840	April 1	SH completes medallion of Charles Emerson for Elizabeth Hoar of Concord.
	May	*Grandfather's Chair* finished (published in December).
	June	SH moves to Salem from Boston, visits Emerson at Concord; she and NH begin to plan to build "our cottage" there.
	August	Peabodys, including SH, move to Boston.
	November	Resigns from custom house, effective January 1; considers settling at Brook Farm.
	December	*Famous Old People* finished.
1841	Mid-January	Leaves custom house, returns to Salem.
	April 12	Arrives at Brook Farm.
	Late August	Takes vacation in Salem; decides to return to Brook Farm as a paying boarder, free from labor obligations.
	September 29	Appointed a trustee of Brook Farm and director of finance; purchases two shares in the project, intended toward a house in which to live.

	Late October	Leaves Brook Farm for Boston.
	November	Arranges second edition of *TTT* in two volumes with added material.
1842	January 13	*TTT*, 2nd ed., published.
	May 7	NH and SH look at the Old Manse, Concord, and, on May 10, agree to rent it from Samuel Ripley. (SH had visited with Emerson and Elizabeth Hoar earlier.)
	May 25	Declines to join the Northampton community.
	July 9	NH and SH married at the Peabody home in Boston; they settle at the Old Manse.
	October 10	Robert Manning dies.
	October 17	Resigns from Brook Farm project; asks to withdraw his stock.
1843	February 1	Sends "The Birthmark" to the *Pioneer*.
	Early February	SH miscarries.
	March	Begins publishing monthly articles in *Democratic Review*.
1844	March 3	Una born.
	Mid-November	"Rappaccini's Daughter" finished.
1845	January	Begins editing Bridge's *Journal of an African Cruiser*.
	March	Ripleys request possession of the Old Manse in the following spring.
	Early April	*African Cruiser* finished; NH proposes new collection, *Mosses from an Old Manse,* to Duyckinck.
	July 24	Visits Bridge to try to meet Senator Atherton and arrange a political appointment.

	Late August	NH and SH plan to leave the Old Manse in November and rent a room from William Manning at Herbert St., Salem.
	September 6	Sues George Ripley and Charles Dana for remainder of his investment in Brook Farm.
	September	Samuel Ripley asks the Hawthornes to vacate the Old Manse; NH agrees to be out by October 1; they move to Herbert St., Salem.
	Early November	Salem Democrats propose NH for custom house surveyor.
1846	January	Edits Benjamin Frederick Browne's "Papers of an Old Dartmoor Prisoner."
	February 4	Bancroft recommends NH's appointment to President Polk.
	February 22	Sends Duyckinck copy for Volume II of *MOM*.
	March 7	Awarded $585.70 in suit against George Ripley and Charles Dana; none apparently collected.
	March 23	Learns that Polk has nominated him for surveyor.
	April 9	Sworn in at Salem Custom House.
	April 15	Sends copy for *MOM*, Volume I, "The Old Manse."
	April	SH moves to 77 Carver Street, Boston; NH follows her in May, commutes to Salem Custom House.
	June 5	*MOM* published.
	June 22	Julian born.
	August	Hawthornes rent house on Chestnut St., Salem.

1847	September 27	Hawthornes rent larger house on Mall St., Salem; NH's mother and sisters live upstairs.
1848	June-July	SH and children in Boston with her family.
	November	Becomes corresponding secretary for Salem Lyceum; invites lectures from, among others, Thoreau, Emerson, Fields, Mann.
	December 15	Sends "The Unpardonable Sin" (later called "Ethan Brand") to C. W. Webber.
1849	Early March	First intimations that NH will be turned out of office.
	June 7	Dismissed from custom house; controversy results.
	June 18	Defends himself in public letter to Hillard.
	July 6	Salem Whigs oppose NH's reinstatement in memorial drafted by Upham.
	July 31	Mother dies.
	August 8	Responds to memorial in letter to Horace Mann; proposes to "bid farewell forever" to Salem; considers moving to Portsmouth, N.H.
	Late August	NH and SH consider moving to Lenox.
	Early September	Writes "immensely" on "The Custom-House" and *The Scarlet Letter*.
	September 3-8	SH visits Caroline Sturgis Tappan in Lenox.
	Late October	Visits Lenox.
1850	January 15	Sends copy for *SL*, less the three final chapters.

	Early January	Hillard takes a collection for NH's support.
	February 3	*SL* finished.
	March	Hawthornes engage Tappan's house in Lenox.
	March 16	*SL* published by Ticknor and Fields.
	May 23	Hawthornes arrive in Lenox, live with Tappans for about a week, then move into "Red Cottage."
	August 5	Attends literary picnic with David Dudley Field, Oliver Wendell Holmes, Cornelius Mathews, James T. Fields, Evert Duyckinck; meets Melville.
	August	Writing *The House of the Seven Gables*.
	August 17, 24	Melville, "Hawthorne and His Mosses," in *Literary World*.
	October 1	NH agrees to new edition of *TTT*.
	November 22	*True Stories* published (reissue of *Grandfather's Chair* and *Biographical Stories*). ·
1851	January 12	Sends preface for *TTT*, 3rd ed.; reports *HSG* nearly finished.
	January 27	Sends *HSG* to Ticknor & Fields.
	March 8	*TTT*, 3rd ed., published.
	April 9	*HSG* published by Ticknor & Fields.
	Early April	Proposes *A Wonder-Book* to Duyckinck.
	May 20	Rose born.
	June-July	Writing *WB*.
	July 15	Sends last of *WB* to Fields.

	July 28–August 16	SH in West Newton; NH keeps chronicle of his and Julian's activities.
	September 5	Quarrels with Mrs. Tappan over use of fruit grown on rented land.
	September 19	Discusses renting the Manns' house in West Newton for winter; SH agrees September 23.
	November 3	Sends preface to new collection, *The Snow-Image,* to Ticknor.
	Ca. November 14	*Moby-Dick,* dedicated to NH by Melville, published.
	Mid-November	Hawthornes leave Lenox for West Newton.
	December 18	*SI* published.
1852	April 2	Buys Alcott house in Concord from Emerson and Sewell (to be renamed the "Wayside").
	April 30	*The Blithedale Romance* finished.
	Late May	Hawthornes move to the Wayside.
	June 5	Pierce nominated for president; NH offers June 9 to write his campaign biography.
	July 14	*BR* published by Ticknor & Fields.
	July 27	Louisa Hawthorne killed in steamer fire near New York City.
	Ca. August 12–27	Sends parts of *Life of Pierce* to Ticknor.
	Before September 8	Zachariah Burchmore proposes to ask Pierce to offer NH the Liverpool consulate; NH initially cool.
	September 11	*Life of Pierce* published.
	October 13	Writes Bridge that he would accept the consular appointment.
	November 2	Pierce elected.

	By December 11	Pierce assures NH of diplomatic appointment.
1853	January	Writing *Tanglewood Tales*.
	March 15	Sends *TT* to Ticknor.
	March 26	NH's appointment as U.S. consul at Liverpool and Manchester confirmed by Senate, effective August 1.
	April 21–May 2	Visits Washington to confer with Pierce.
	June 14	Longfellow gives NH a farewell dinner, attended by Emerson, Lowell, Clough, Charles Eliot Norton, and Samuel Longfellow.
	July 6	Hawthornes sail from Boston to Liverpool.

THE LETTERS, 1813-1843

Salem Thursday December 9 1813

Dear Uncle

I hope you are well
and I hope Richard[1] is too   My foot is no better[2]   Louisa
has got so well that she has begun to go school but she did
not go this forenoon because it snowd   Maam[3] is going to
send for Doctor Kitridge[4] to day when William Cross[5] comes
home at 12 o clock and maybe he will do some good for Doctor
Barstow[6] has not and I don't know as Doctor Kitridge will it
is now 4 weeks Yesterday, since I have been to school and I
dont know but it will be 4 weeks longer before I go again   I
have been out in the office[7] two or three times and have
set down on the step of the door and once I hopped out
into the street. Yesterday I went out in the office and had
4 cakes Hannah[8] carried me out once but not then Elizabeth
and Louisa send their love to you   I hope you will write to
me soon but I have nothing more to write so good bye dear
Uncle your affectionate Nephew.[9]

Nathaniel Hathorne.

1. NH's uncle Richard Manning had moved to Raymond after his father's death
in April; there he managed family holdings in land and property, and a general
store.

2. His foot had been injured playing ball on November 10, and his lameness
continued for fourteen months, requiring crutches. Mrs. Hathorne wrote to
Richard on January 20, 1815, that she "had many Doctors to him and used

various remedies, but all to no progress. Doctor Smith of Hanover, ordered cold water to be poured on his foot every morning. I think this was of more service to him than any thing I did for him" (MS, Bowdoin). Family tradition has it that one doctor consulted was Nathaniel Peabody, father of SH.

3. His mother.

4. Probably Oliver Kittredge (1786–1823), the Manning family physician; possibly Jacob Kittredge, who had opened a practice earlier in 1813.

5. A teen-aged clerk in the office of the stage line, of which his father Henry Cross was a partner with NH's youngest uncle, Samuel Manning, and Holton Dale.

6. Gideon Barstow (1783–1852), who had married Nancy Forrester, a cousin of NH, in 1812. He was later a merchant, and a member of Congress, 1821–23.

7. Of the stage line, nearby on Union Street.

8. Hannah Lord (1788–1869), a niece of NH's grandmother Miriam Manning, had been for some time a helper in the household.

9. Robert answered at once, to encourage NH and his sister Elizabeth to write frequently to him (Arlin Turner, *Nathaniel Hawthorne* [New York: Oxford University Press, 1980], p. 18).

2. TO ROBERT MANNING, RAYMOND

,

Salem. Monday. July 27th. 1818

Dear Uncle.

All the family are well, and I hope you are the same. Elizabeth has not returned from Newbury-Port[1] yet and we have not heard from her. Ma'am, Louisa, & I, Mr & Mrs Dike, John, & Mary[2] have been to Nehant,[3] we had a very pleasent time, fish are very thick there. Is not the house almost finished?[4] I think I had rather go to dancing school[5] a little longer before I come to Raymond. Does the Pond[6] look the same as it did when I was there? it is almost as pleasent at Nehant as at Raymond. I thought there was no place here that I should say so much of. I suppose you have a great many berries, we have very few. the garden I think looks as well as when you was here though there is not much done to it. I have written all I can think of.

Good bye,
Nath[l] Hathorne

1. Sixteen-year-old Elizabeth had begun to make social visits of several days' and weeks' duration to friends in Newburyport, twenty miles north of Salem.

2. John Dike, a coal and wood merchant and a widower, had married NH's aunt Priscilla Manning in 1817. John Stephen and Mary W. were children of his first marriage.

3. Nahant, a popular oceanside resort between Salem and Boston.

4. Robert in the summer of 1817 had begun the building of a large house intended to accommodate the entire Manning family. It was not completed until

November, 1818, a month after the Hathornes returned to Raymond expecting to live in it.

5. "Master Turner" was a resident of Boston who taught dancing in Salem each Monday and Wednesday during the summer. See "Notes on Old Times in Salem," *EIHC*, LXXIV (1938), 366.

6. Raymond is located on the north shore of a body of freshwater called Sebago Lake, Sebago Pond, or Great Pond.

Raymond March 24th 1819

Dear Uncle

I hope you arrived safely at the end of your Journey. I suppose you have not heard of the death of Mr Tarbox and his wife who were froze to death on Wednesday last.[1] they were brought out from the cape on Saturday and buried from Capt Dingleys[2] on Sunday. How soon do you intend coming down[3] Louisa says she wants to see you very much. The snow is going off very fast and I dont thinke we shall have much more Sleighing I hope we shall not for I am tired of winter. You ordered me to write as well I could but this is bad paper I am writing with a bad pen. and am in a hurry as I am going to Portland at noon with Mr Leach.[4]

your affectionate Nephew
Nathl Hathorne.

PS this paper was two cents a sheet

Dear Mary   I am sorry to trouble you to get another gown made but Elizabeth thinks she cannot have a gown made only in Salem   she wishes you to have it fixt fashionable the bosom lined   if trimmins are worn she would like to have it trimed   I should have sent the money to pay for the making and triming but I hope William or Robert can supply you and charge it to me   she wishes to have this silk gown longer than the one she left in Salem

I am anxious to hear from Robert hope he will not hurry
down   I shall endeavour to take all possible care in his
absence

it is needless for me to say how much
I want to see you all
Yours
E C Hathorne

1. The Samuel Tarbox family lived at Raymond Cape on Lake Sebago, five
miles south of the village. During a nine-day March blizzard, Tarbox walked to
Raymond to replenish their exhausted food supply. He was unable to reach the
house on his return because of drifting snow, and when his wife heard his calls
and came out to help, both perished, leaving five orphaned children. A friend in
Raymond, William Symmes, recounted that NH wrote a ballad on the "Tarbox
Tragedy"; see Pickard, pp. 9, 64–65. The incident is a "Saco Valley Fireside
Tale" in G. T. Ridlon, *Saco Valley Settlements and Families* (Portland, 1895; rpt.
Rutland, Vt.: Charles E. Tuttle, 1969), pp. 374–76. Also see 11.3.

2. Samuel Dingley (1757–1825), one of the first settlers at Raymond, had a
sawmill and gristmill there. His daughter Susan had married NH's uncle Richard
Manning in 1816, and NH attended school at Stroudwater with his son Jacob.

3. The prevailing southwest breeze made the voyage from Salem to Maine
downwind, "down," and the contrary voyage to Massachusetts was against the
wind, "up."

4. Mark Leach (1771–1841) worked in Richard Manning's store. His son Mark
was a friend of NH.

4. TO ROBERT MANNING, SALEM

Raymond May 16th 1819

Dear Uncle

We have received your letter and are all very well. The grass and some of the trees look very green. the roads are very good. there is no snow on Lymington Mountains.[1] the Fences are all finished and the garden is laid out and planted. Two of the goats are on the island and we keep the other one for her milk. the ram threatened to kill Louisa without any provocation and has behaved so bad that Mother did not think it safe to keep him and Mr Ham[2] has got him. I have shot a partridge and a henhawke,[3] and caught 18 large trout out of our brooke I am sorry you intend to send me to school again.[4] Mother says she can hardly spare me We hear nothing of Dr Brown[5] and expect he is lost in the woods. I hope you will soon recover your health as I wish to see you very much.

Nath¹ Hathorne

1. Twenty miles southwest of Raymond. Mrs. Hathorne and her children had returned from a visit to Salem in early May. See Louisa to Robert Manning, May 19, 1819 (MS, Bowdoin).

2. Ben Ham, a neighboring farmer.

3. Richard had given NH a fowling-piece that had once belonged to the boy's father; see 7, 8, 9, 10.

4. NH had attended the school of the Reverend Caleb Bradley in Stroudwater, near Portland, from mid-December 1818 till late January 1819, when he returned to Raymond homesick and rebellious. His Uncle Robert and Aunt Priscilla arranged that he enter Samuel H. Archer's school in Salem on July 5, 1819.

5. Winthrop Brown (b. 1784), a physician from Salem, had been asked by the Mannings to come to Raymond to practice. He did eventually arrive there, and remained until 1835.

5. TO ROBERT MANNING, RAYMOND

Salem Monday July 26th 1819

Dear Uncle

I hope you and all our friends in Raymond are well. E. M's[1]
letter is received. I have begun to go to school and can find
no fault with it except it's not being dear enough only 5
dollars a quarter, and not near enough for it is up by the
Baptist Meeting House.[2] I am as well contented here as I
expected to be, but sometimes I do have very bad fits of home
sickness. but I know that it is best for me to be up here as I
have no time to lose in getting my schooling.[3] I wish when
you come you would bring Ebe with you not for her sake,
for I do not think she would be half so well contented here
as in Raymond but for mine for I have nobody to talk to but
Grandmother, Aunt Mary & Hannah[4] and it seems very lonesome here. there is a pot of excellent guaver jelly[5] now in the
house and one of preserved limes and I am afraid they will
mould if you do not come soon for it's esteemed sacrilege by
Grandmother to eat any of them now because she is keeping
them against somebody is sick and I suppose she would be
very much disappointed if everybody was to continue well
and they were to spoil. we have some oranges too which Isaac
Burnham[6] gave G mother which are rotting as fast as possible
and we stand a very fair chance of not having any good of
them because we have to eat the bad ones first as the good
are to be kept till they are spoilt also. I hope you will excuse
this writing as school keeps late and I have not much time.

I have exhausted my whole stock of news and

remain your affectionate nephew
Nath[l] Hathorne

1. Elizabeth Manning Hathorne, NH's sister, whose most frequently used nickname was "Ebe," as in a following sentence. She had written from Raymond on June 23 to her Grandmother Manning: "We have received no letter from Salem since Uncle Sam and Nathaniel left us, and we wish much to hear from them. . . . Nathaniel must write next week if he has not written already. . . . I shall write to Miss Manning and Nathaniel soon, and hope to receive letters from all our friends" (MS, Bowdoin).

2. Samuel Archer's school was on Marlborough Street, now Federal Street, approximately eight blocks from Herbert Street.

3. Mary Manning had written July 6 to Mrs. Hathorne that NH "sighs for the woods of Raymond, and yet he seems to be convinced of the necesity of prepairing to do something. I think after he gets engaged in buisness his views of things will be much altered, we all endeavour to make him as comfortable & happy as we can" (MS, Bowdoin).

4. Miriam Lord Manning, Mary Manning, and their helper Hannah Lord.

5. By association with the limes and oranges, not "quaver" but NH's try at "guava."

6. (1795–1825), grandmother Manning's distant cousin, a son of Major Thomas Burnham of Ipswich. See 9.2.

6. TO LOUISA HATHORNE, RAYMOND

Salem Tuesday Sept 28 1819[1]

Dear Sister

We are all well and hope you are the same.
I do not know what to do with myself here. I shall never be
contented here I am sure. I now go to a 5 dollar school, I,
that have been to a 10 dollar one.[2] "Oh Lucifer, son of the
morning, how art thou fallen!"[3] I wish I was but in Raymond
and I should be happy. But "twas light that ne'er shall shine
again on lifes dull stream."[4] I have read Waverly, The Mysteries of Udolpho, The Adventures of Ferdinand Count
Fathom, Roderick Random, and the first vol. of Arabian
Nights.[5]

Oh earthly pomp is but a dream
And like a meteor's short lived gleam
And all the sons of glory soon
Will rest beneath the mould'ring stone

And Genius is a star whose light
Is soon to sink in endless night
And heavenly Beauty's angel form
Will bend like flower in winter's storm

Though those are my rhymes, yet they are not exactly my
thoughts. I am full of scraps of poetry can't keep it out of my
brain

I saw where in his lowly grave
Departed Genius lay.
And mournful yew trees oer it wave
To hide it from the day.

I could vomit up a dozen pages more if I was a mind to so turn over.[6]

Oh do not bid me part from thee
For I will Leave thee never
Although thou throwst thy scorn on me
Yet I will love forever.

There is no heart within my breast
for it has flown away
And till I knew it was thy guest
I sought it night and day

Tell Ebe she's not the only one of the family whose works have appeared in the papers.[7] The knowledge I have of your honour and good sense Louisa gives me full confidence that you will not show this letter to anybody. you may to mother though

My respects to Mr and Mrs Ham.

I remain your humble servant and affectionate brother

N H

Your's to Uncle received[8]

1. It is notable that of letters 6 through 31 twenty-two were written on Tuesday.

2. The "5 dollar school" was Archer's at Salem, and the "10 dollar one" probably was Bradley's at Stroudwater. Mary Manning on August 3 wrote to Mrs Hathorne of NH that "since he went to school his health and spirits appear to be much better . . . this morning he got up before six o'clock to study his lesson. we shall be happy to see Brother R[obert] whenever it is convenient for him to come but I beg he will not hurry home on N's account, we think ourselves capable of taking care of one Boy" (MS, Bowdoin).

3. Isaiah 14:12.

4. Thomas Moore, "Love's Young Dream," in *Irish Melodies* (1808).

5. Sir Walter Scott, *Waverley; or, 'Tis Sixty Years Since* (1814); Ann Radcliffe, *The Mysteries of Udolpho* (1794); Tobias Smollett, *The Adventures of Ferdinand Count Fathom* (1753) and *Roderick Random* (1748); *The Arabian Nights' Entertainments* was available in a number of American editions, most translated from the French of Antoine Galland (1704).

6. A direction for Louisa to turn the manuscript page.

7. Elizabeth, Julian Hawthorne reported, told him that NH had at the age of sixteen sent poems "to a Boston Newspaper" (*NHHW*, I. 102). These have not yet been identified.

8. Robert was at this time in Salem, agent for the Mannings' stage line to Boston and, beginning in November, another stage north to Andover. He also rented horses and carriages at his stable on Union Street.

Salem Tuesday March 7th 1820

Dear Mother,

As we received no letter last week, we are in anxiety about your health. All of us are well. Mrs Forrester & Mrs Crowninshield[1] are better. I have left school, and have begun to fit for College under Benj^m L. Oliver,[2] Lawyer. So you are in great danger of having one learned man in your family.[3] Mr. Oliver thought I could enter College next commencement,[4] but Uncle Robert is afraid I should have to study too hard. I get my lessons at home, and recite them to him at 7 °clock in the morning. I am extremely homesick. Aunt Mary is continually scolding at me. Grandmaam hardly ever speaks a pleasant word to me. If I ever attempt to speak a word in my defence, they cry out against my impudence. However I guess I can live through a year and a half more, and then I shall leave them. One good effect results from their eternal finding-fault. It gives me some employment in retaliating, and that keeps up my spirits. Mother I wish you would let Louisa board with Mrs Dike[5] if she comes up here to go to school. Then Aunt M. can't have her to domineer over. I hope, however, that I shall see none of you up here very soon. Shall you want me to be a Minister, Doctor or Lawyer? A Minister I will not be. I beleive M. Louisa has not written one letter to me. Well, I will not write to her till she does. Oh how I wish I was again with you, with nothing to do but to go a gunning. But the happiest days of my life are gone. Why was I not a girl that I might have been pinned all my life to my Mother's apron. After I have got through college I will come down and learn Ebe. Latin and Greek. I rove from one subject to another at a great rate.

I remain[6] your affectionate and dutiful son, and most obedient and most humble servant, and most respectful, and most hearty well-wisher.

Nathaniel Hathorne.

1. Rachel Hathorne Forrester and Sarah Hathorne Crowninshield, NH's aunts.

2. Benjamin Lynde Oliver (1757–1843), born in Marblehead, was the author of books on law and music; his *Practical Conveyancing: a Selection of Forms of General Utility* (Boston: Cummings & Hilliard, 1816) is among NH's books preserved at the University of Virginia. In 1823 he became editor of a newly established weekly paper, the Salem *Observer*. See Herringshaw's *Encyclopædia of American Biography*.

3. There had been much discussion in the Manning family for the past two months about NH's future. His mother had written on January 25 to Robert that she hoped Nathaniel had "given up the thoughts of going to sea for some years at least"; Robert wrote to Louisa on February 8, intending to amuse her, that he had no employment for NH and that "as a last resort we can bind him for 7 years to turn a Cutler's wheel" (MSS, Bowdoin). Then Mary wrote to his mother: "we must not have our expectations too much raised about him, but his Master speaks very encourageingly respecting his talents &c. and is solicitous to have him go to Colleg. Buisness is very dull, and Brother R. does not know what to do with him he would send him if he thought he could easyly defray the expences, I am willing to put down for 100 Dollars perhaps it will be said thats but a drop. well but it's a great drop and if everyone of his Relations who are as near to him as I am would put down as much I think his buckett would be full, but to be more sedate it appears to me the prospect for his makeing a worthy & usefull man is better in that way than in any other" (February 29, 1820, MS, Bowdoin).

4. In early autumn.

5. Their Aunt Priscilla.

6. Following "I remain," NH inscribed the close in a zigzag pattern of one or two words on a line, down three-quarters of the page to his signature.

8. TO LOUISA HATHORNE, RAYMOND

Salem. March 21st. 1820

Dear Louisa,

I have received two letters from you, for which I lay under great obligations. I did not know Mother had been so unwell as to require a nurse. I am glad that she is recovering. All your friends in Salem are in tolerable health. I think you have improved in your hand writing very much. I am almost ashamed of my own. I hope mother is not going to wear a cap.[1] I think it will look horribly. I wish very much to see you all; and though you and I could never keep the peace when we were together, yet I believe it was almost always my fault. I am outrageously mad with Ebe for not writing, and this is the last time I will mention her 'till she does write. "Oh that I had the wings of a dove, that I might flee hence and be at rest."[2] How often do I long for my gun, and wish that I could again savagize with you. But I shall never again run wild in Raymond, and I shall never be so happy as when I did. I hope Mother will upon no account think of returning to Salem, and I don't much want you to come either. Uncle Richard's letter was received. I went to a Concert a few days ago.[3]

I remain your affectionate Brother
Nath¹ Hathorne

1. An indoor cap, as of muslin, in place of hair dressing; a symbol of retirement.
2. Psalm 55:6.
3. On March 14 the Handel Society of Salem had performed "an Oratorio selected from works of Handel, Haydn, and other composers," at Dr. John Prince's Meeting House (*Essex Register*, March 11, 1820).

9. TO ELIZABETH C. HATHORNE, RAYMOND

Salem March 28th 1820

Dear Mother,

I hope you have quite recovered your health, though from our not receiving a letter last week I am afraid you have not. Grandmaam, Mrs Mary Manning,[1] Mr Dike, Rebecca Burnham,[2] Susan Giddins[3] have all had bad colds. The roads are nearly dry, and the lilack bushes had begun to bud two or three days ago. Aunt Mary threatens to come down with Uncle Robert. [*obliteration*] I wish I were coming down now. I hope Uncle Richard and Aunt Susan are well. Samuel Manning is staying in Boston. I went to Boston on Saturday. I shall go to the theatre soon I beleive

How does Louisa employ herself. I am in fear lest you should send her up here this Summer. How does the kitten do? I hope you have not condemned her to the same fate, that you did her unhappy Mother

I hope my gun still remains in the closet.

I suppose that little sausage Clark[4] still remains with you. [*obliteration*] Uncle Robert wants to know whether Louisa's sick hen has recovered its health. Miss Manning has got a gown fixed for you. Do Louisa or Jane[5] or any of the rest of the family want one   If they do they must speak now for this is the last opportunity they will have. Uncle Robert is coming down when you write him word he can get down with a chaise

Your affectionate son
Nath[l] Hathorne

1. NH's maiden aunt, "Mrs." by a title of civility.

2. Rebecca Dodge Burnham (1797–1869), sister of Isaac, was to marry Robert Manning in 1824.

3. Susannah Giddings (1767–1847), Newburyport, whose mother was a sister of NH's Grandmother Manning.

4. Peter Clark, a boy who worked on Mrs. Hathorne's farm.

5. A girl from Salem who worked for Mrs. Hathorne.

Salem, May 2d. 1820.

Mr Robert Manning
Dear Uncle,

I was happy to hear you had arrived at home safe. Received Miss Manning's letter Saturday.[1] I am going to the Theatre tommorrow.[2] Am sorry I did not begin in the middle of the paper as I have not much to write. We are all well. It is training day.[3] I hope Mother is well by this time. My Gun has got a very large charge in it, and I guess it will kick.[4] Do you intend to stay much longer? I sleep very comfortably alone.[5] I am afraid you will scold at me if I stop here, but as one excuse I must beg leave to represent that I have from ten to fourteen pages of Latin to parse and translate.

I remain your affectionate Nephew,
Nath[l] Hathorne.

I hope Uncle Richard and Aunt Susan are well. The reason I did not send last Tuesday's Palladium[6] was that I staid at our Reading room[7] till it was too late. How many of her Books has Aunt Mary given away.[8]

---

1. Mary had accompanied Robert to Raymond a few days earlier, for a month's visit.

2. A performance at Washington Hall by a Boston company, of August von

Kotzebue's *Lovers' Vows* (*Das Kind der Liebe*), a sentimental and didactic melodrama of seduction and repentance, followed by a farce, *The Weathercock; or, What Next?*, by J. T. Allingham. See Pat M. Ryan, Jr., "Young Hawthorne at the Salem Theatre," *EIHC*, XCIV (1958), 244–48.

3. An inspection and parade of local militia: the Independent Cadets, the Salem Light Infantry, the Salem Artillery, and the Mechanic Light Infantry.

4. The tense suggests that NH's gun had been sent to him, and that he had charged it in readiness for the training exercises.

5. An allusion to having to share a bed with Robert when the latter was in Salem; see 19.

6. The *New England Palladium and Commercial Advertiser*, published in Boston.

7. Either at the Athenaeum, where his Uncle William held a membership, or a circulating library.

8. Mary distributed Bibles and Testaments in Raymond to support the Sunday School that Mrs. Hathorne had founded there.

11. TO ELIZABETH C. HATHORNE, RAYMOND

Salem July 11 1820

Dear Mother,

Uncle Richard's letter is rec'd. We are all well and hope you are the same. Uncle Robert is gone to Boston to day. He intends coming down very soon. Louisa seems very well contented.[1] Is much pleased with going to Dancing School.[2] It is a long time since we have had any rain. I have learned to swim, which I suppose you will be glad of. You must excuse my bad writing as I am in a hurry. Louisa sends her love to Uncle Richard and Aunt Susan, and Elizabeth T. Manning.[3] I wish Elizabeth[4] would write to me. She has not written me but one letter since I came from the Eastward. I am 16 years old. In five years I shall belong to myself.[5]

I am
your son
Nathaniel Hathorne

1. Robert and Mary had brought Louisa with them to Salem on June 1 to further her education and to provide companionship for NH. In a letter June 6 to Mrs. Hathorne, Mary commented: "Nathaniel is well and is even more pleased than I expected he would be, with having his sister with him; they are both much pleased with being together" (MS, Bowdoin).

2. Mr. Turner's Dancing School. See 2.5.

3. Elizabeth Tarbox Manning, the youngest child of the dead Tarbox couple, had been adopted by Richard and Susan Manning. See 3.2.

4. His sister.

5. On July 4, NH's birthday, Louisa wrote to Mrs. Hathorne: "Nathaniel delivered a most excellent Oration this morning to no other hearers but me. . . . Nathaniel has not laughed at me quarreled with me or pestered me more than once or twice since I came up." A year later, July 4, 1821, Mrs. Hathorne wrote to Elizabeth: "I suppose Nathaniel does not view the return of this day with quite as much rapture as he did six or seven years past" (MSS, Bowdoin).

Salem July 25th 1820

Dear Mother,

Your's of last week was not received, I suppose because it was not written. All the family are in tolerable health except Uncle Robert who has the headache. Mrs. Sutton[1] has been here. I should like to come down with Mr. Manning to see you but I suppose it is in vain to wish it. I went to Baker's Island[2] yesterday in a sloop, after some horses. Caught some fish. It is a very warm day. Louisa seems to be quite full of her dancing acquirements. She is continually putting on very stately airs, and making curtisies. Uncle Richard's Phaeton is finished. Mr. Dike's schooner has arrived.[3] If Elizabeth never intends writing to me again, I wish her to write me word of her intention. Do not know when U. R.[4] is coming down. Aunt Eunice and Ruth[5] are as well as usual. Ditto Aunt Forester and Crowninshield. Louisa was at Mrs. F's[6] last Saturday. [*obliteration*]
I have been for some time endeavouring to read what I have written above, but owing to the legibility of my writing find it scarcely possible.

Sum tui amans filius
Nathaniel Hathorne.

Cara Mater,

Non possum dicere, ne potes legere Latinam linguam. Sed scribam te nonnihil in eam, et Ebe leget.

tui Filius

N. Hathorne.[7]

Do not show the above to the Doctor[8] or any other learned man, for it is nonsense.

Hope Uncle Richard and Aunt Susan are well.

---

1. Lucy Lord Sutton, a grandniece of NH's Grandmother Manning, married to Captain Richard Sutton of Portland.

2. Five miles east of Salem harbor.

3. A 124-ton coastal schooner, *The Favourite*, built at Newbury, used for trading to Portland.

4. Uncle Robert, the "Mr. Manning" of the fourth sentence.

5. Eunice Hathorne and Ruth Hathorne.

6. I.e., Aunt Forrester's.

7. "I am your loving son Nathaniel Hathorne. Dear Mother, I cannot speak, nor can you read, the Latin language. But I will write you a little something in this, and Ebe may read it. your Son, N. Hathorne."

8. Dr. Winthrop Brown (4.5).

13. TO ROBERT MANNING, RAYMOND

Salem Aug 15th 1820.

Dear Uncle,

I hope you have arrived safe. Mother's letter was received. The sloop in which the Dog is to sail has not gone yet. She is expected to sail tomorrow. Watch[1] is afflicted with a difficulty of breathing, owing I am afraid to his excessive eating. I give him nothing at all to eat, but he gets a great deal at Hannah's house. The first volume of the Analectic is returned.[2] Do you wish me to send you the Gazettes.[3] The Register has bestowed "Much praise, but *no* reward beside"[4] upon you. As it is nearly dark I hope you will allow me to conclude,

Your affectionate Nephew,
N. Hathorne.

P. S. we are all well. Louisa is going to see the Temple of Industry this evening.[5]

---

1. Robert had bought a dog, Watch, which was to be sent to Raymond.

2. Robert had advertised in the *Essex Register* for the return of the first two volumes of the *Analectic Magazine*, "lent to some persons not recollected."

3. The Salem *Gazette*.

4. The Salem *Register*. Adapted from Alexander Pope, "Second Epistle of the Second Book of Horace," line 43: "Much praise, and some reward beside."

5. An exhibition of a "Mechanical Panorama, or Temple of Industry," with automatons that appeared to perform a variety of musical numbers, at Foster's Tavern, Court Street.

Salem September 12. 1820

Dear Uncle,

Your letter to Mr. D.[1] was received. You did not particularly mention whether the dog arrived safe. All the family are well. Your letter was shown by Mr. Haskell[2] to John Andrew Esq.[3] and I am very sorry there was so bad an account of Raymond in it.[4] I am afraid you will not sell much of the land. There has been some rain here to day. Having nothing more to say, I must of course conclude

Your affectionate
Nephew,
Nath[l] Hathorne.

Am not I very economical to use so little paper.

1. John Dike.

2. John W. Haskell (1781–1849), of Portland. His wife, Elizabeth, was a niece of NH's Grandmother Manning.

3. John Andrew (1774–1849), a merchant who owned land at Raymond. His wife, Rachel Forrester, was NH's first cousin on the Hathorne side.

4. The summer drought at Raymond had killed fruit trees and the potato crop, and had much reduced the growth of wheat, rye, oats, and grass. NH reported in his hand-lettered newspaper *The Spectator,* August 21: "By a letter from a gentleman in the State of Maine, we learn that a Famine is seriously apprehended, owing to the want of rain. Potatoes could not be procured in some places" (MS, Essex). See Elizabeth Chandler, ed., "Hawthorne's *Spectator*," *NEQ,* IV (1931), 301.

15. TO ELIZABETH C. HATHORNE, RAYMOND

Salem Septem 26. 1820

Dear Mother,

We are all well. We received no letter last week. I was very glad of the Inkstand. I should like to have you send my Stamp.[1] I am at present a man of many occupations. I study Greek in the Forenoon and write for Uncle William in the Afternoon for which I receive one dollar a week.[2] Uncle William intends to give me a new suit of Clothes. I was happy to hear that Uncle Richard had arrived to the high station of Justice of Peace.[3] Though he is lame yet he outstrips all of his Brothers. It is nearly 9 now and Cannot write any more. Moreover I have nothing more to write

I am
Your affectionate Son
N Hathorne.

1. For marking books and other articles: "N. Hathorne."

2. Bookkeeping in the stagecoach office. In *The Spectator*, No. 5, Monday, September 18, 1820, NH described his own activities: "In the first place, we study Latin and Greek. Secondly, we write in the employ of Wm. Manning Esq." (MS, Essex). See "Hawthorne's *Spectator*," *NEQ*, IV (1931), 318.

3. *The Spectator*, No. 6, Monday, September 25, 1820, announced: "Mr. Richard Manning has been appointed Justice of the Peace, by his Excellency Gov. King, with the advice and consent of the Council. From the talents of the Gentleman, we are confident, that the arduous duties of his exalted station, will be well discharged" (MS, Essex). See *NEQ*, IV (1931), 324.

16. TO ELIZABETH C. HATHORNE AND TO ELIZABETH M. HATHORNE, RAYMOND

Salem October 31st 1820

Dear Mother,

Your Letter & Uncle Richard's were received. We are all well. If Uncle Robert's Letter was not rec'd last week, he wishes you to send to Mr. Coburn's for 3 Bundles Trees & bushes (Freight Paid,) and to Dr Dupee's for 14 trees.[1] They must be planted immediately with 2 shovels of Manure to each tree. The Bushes are to be planted in the Borders with Manure. I am happy to hear that the Storm did no damage to our territories. Uncle Robert says he shall bring me down the next time he comes. I do not know how soon that will be. It is nearly a Year now since I saw you. I still continue to write for Uncle William, and find my Salary quite convenient for many purposes.[2] Please to present my respects to Richard Manning Esquire and Lady, and to Elizabeth T. Manning.

I remain Your Affectionate Son
Nathaniel Hathorne

I shall expect a letter from you this week or next.

Dear Sister,

I am very angry with you for not sending me some of your Poetry, which I consider as a great piece of Ingratitude. You will not see one line more of mine, untill You return the confidence which I have placed in you. I have bought the Lord of the Isles,[3] and intend either to send or to bring it to you. I like it as well as any of Scott's other Poems. I have read Hoggs Tales, Caleb Williams, St Leon & Mandeville. I admire Godwin's Novels, and intend to read them all.[4] I shall read the Abbot by the Author of Waverly as soon as I can hire it. I have read all Scott's Novels except that.[5] I wish I had not, that I might have the pleasure of reading them again. Next to these I like Caleb Williams. I have almost given up writing Poetry. No Man can be a Poet & a Book-Keeper at the same time. I do find this place most horribly "dismal." And have taken to chewing tobacco with all my might, which I think raises my spirits. Say nothing of it in your letters, nor of the Lord of the Isles. Louisa seems very well contented. I do not think I shall ever go to College. I can scarcely bear the thought of living upon Uncle Robert for 4 years longer. How happy I should feel, to be able to say, "I am Lord of myself."[6]

You may cut off this part of my letter, and show the other to Uncle Richard. Do write me some Letters in Skimmed Milk.[7] I must conclude as I am in a "monstrous" Hurry.

Your Affectionate Brother
Nath. Hathorne.

P.S. the most beautiful Poetry I think I ever saw, begins

> "She's gone to dwall in Heaven, my Lassie,
> She's gone to dwall in Heaven;
> Yer'e owre pure quo' a voice aboon,
> For dwalling out of Heaven."[8]

It is not the words but the thoughts. I hope you have read it, as I know you would admire it.

OCTOBER, 1820

1. Robert imported fruit trees from Boston and New York to replace those lost at Raymond in the drought. Coburn's coffee house and Dr. Dupee's office were convenient places for the transporting vessels to deliver them in Portland.

2. According to Robert's letter to Mrs. Hathorne of October 20, NH and Louisa were spending much time and money preparing for a ball of their dancing school, at the New Assembly Room on October 26 (MS, Essex). NH had advertised in *The Spectator*, September 18: "Money Wanted. Good security will be given for a small sum of money, to be repaid in one month" (MS, Essex). See *NEQ*, IV (1931), 321.

3. Sir Walter Scott, *The Lord of the Isles* (1815).

4. James Hogg, *Winter Evening Tales, Collected among the Cottagers in the South of Scotland* (1820); William Godwin, *Caleb Williams* (1794), *St. Leon* (1799), *Mandeville* (1817); Godwin's other fiction was *Damon and Delia, Italian Letters, Imogen: A Pastoral Romance* (all 1784), and *Fleetwood* (1805).

5. Sir Walter Scott, *The Abbot* (1820). Scott's novels between *Waverley* and *The Abbot* were *Guy Mannering, The Antiquary, The Black Dwarf, Old Mortality, Rob Roy, The Heart of Midlothian, The Bride of Lammermoor, A Legend of Montrose, Ivanhoe,* and *The Monastery*.

6. John Oldham, "A Satire addressed to a Friend That is about to leave the University, and Come abroad in the World," (1683), lines 121–22: "Lord of myself, accountable to none, / But to my conscience, and my God alone."

7. An elementary form of invisible writing, which could be revealed by heating the paper.

8. The first stanza of a pseudo-traditional ballad by Allan Cunningham (1784–1842) published in R. H. Cromek's *Remains of Nithdale and Galloway Song* (1810). NH probably read these lines in an article on Cromek's book by John Wilson, who in *Blackwood's Magazine*, VI (December 1819), 317, identified Cunningham as the author and characterized the lines as "perfectly beautiful" and Cunningham as "a man of genius" who wrote "in the very spirit of antiquity." NH's quotation, apparently from memory, is not entirely accurate.

17. FRAGMENT, TO ELIZABETH M. HATHORNE, RAY-
MOND[?]

[Ca. 1820–21]

I have read all most all the Books which have been published for the last hundred Years. Among them are. Melmoth
by Maturin. Tom Jones and Amelia by Fielding. Rosseau's
Eloisa which is admirable. Memoirs of R. L. Edgeworth. The
Abbot. Romantick Tales by M. G. Lewis.[1] I hear [MS torn][2]

N. Hathorne

1. Charles Robert Maturin, *Melmoth the Wanderer* (1820); Henry Fielding,
Tom Jones (1749) and *Amelia* (1751); Jean-Jacques Rousseau, *Julie, ou la Nouvelle
Héloïse* (English trans., *Eloisa*, 1761); Richard Lovell Edgeworth, *Memoirs . . . Begun by Himself and Concluded by His Daughter* [Maria, the novelist]
(1820); Sir Walter Scott, *The Abbot* (1820); Matthew Gregory ("Monk") Lewis,
Romantic Tales (1808), a four-volume anthology, chiefly of long stories translated
and adapted from the German. In a letter to James T. Fields, December 26,
1870, Elizabeth Hawthorne recalled receiving a letter from NH about his reading
in Scott and Rousseau "when my brother was about fourteen." Her memory
seemed to have conflated letters 16 and 17. See Randall Stewart, "Recollections
of Hawthorne by His Sister Elizabeth," *AL*, XVI (1944), 324. Una noted on the
verso of this manuscript, "Written when Papa was about fifteen."

2. The phrasing suggests that he heard a bell, as would be likely at college.

Salem March 6th 1821

Dear Sister   I hope a letter is allready on the way containing an account of those Bibles, if it is not and nothing special takes place to prevent do write me the next maile. the Bible Society[1] hold thier quarterly meeting a week from to morrow and I should like to have presented the account before that time as it is a long while since I recieved them. do write me a very particular statement of the manner in wich you disposed of them, and wheather you found it difficult to sell them. and I want to know how many Bibles & Testaments you have on hand for the Sabbath School, and how many other Sabbath School books you have and what you think of the improvement made by the scholars.
we have not heard from Brother Richard & Sister Susan for some time   are they well do ask them to write to me
N and M.[2] are in good health & spirits
Mother and all the Family are in tolerable good health
I wish E. M.[3] would write to me
how does old Mrs Dingley do   I think this winter must have been a time of grate affliction to her & all her Family
how does Old Cap[t] Dingley do this winter.
it is a very cold spell now and I suppose it is not much different with you. your Friends on the Hathorne side are I believe all tolerable well

yours affectionately
M. Manning

Dear Mother

I dont know as I shall have much time to write but I must
write faster. We shall have an examination in about three
weeks, I dread it. Aunt Mary says that she does not think
she shall take me away from Mrs Curtis's,[4] which I am very
glad of. I should like to have Ebe send up Fergusons
Astronomy[5] if she can   Mrs Curtis wants me to study it,
I study Aikins Geography,[6] Parsing, Globes, and Arithmetic.
I beleive that is all I shall say at the examination, I am sure
I hope it is. we study Dr. Lowells Bible Questions[7] Sundays.
Nathaniel went to Boston to the theatre yesterday and came
back to-day, he saw Mr Kean perform, he liked him very
much. I mean to write to Ebe soon, and I want her to write
to me. how does Betsy[8] do. give my love to Uncle Richard
and Aunt Susan; I want to see you all very much. the wind
blows quite hard tonight. there is a beautiful slide out in the
garden.

I remain your affectionate daughter
Maria L Hathorne

Dear Mother

I must contribute my share to fill up this Letter, though I
have nothing of importance to say. I have been to Boston and
seen Mr Kean in King Lear.[9] It was enough to have drawn
tears from millstones. I could have cried myself, if I had been
in a convenient place for such an exploit. I almost forgot that
I did not live "in Regis Learis seculum," "in the age of King
Lear." I shall probably see you in September, and stay 4
weeks with You.[10] I hope you will remain in Raymond during
the time I am at college, and then I can be with you 3 months

out of the year. I am very much afflicted at the loss of Watch.[11] It is now going on two Years since I saw you. Do not you regret the time when I was a little boy. I do almost. I am now as tall as Uncle Robert. I beleive that either the 5th—6th or 7th of this Month is Ebe's birth day.[12] Do not show this to Uncle Richard.

Your Affectionate Son
Nathaniel Hathorne.

1. The Board of Trustees of the Bible Society of Salem and Vicinity met on March 14 (Salem *Gazette*, March 13, 3:3). In a letter of March 7, Mrs. Hathorne sent an account of her selling and giving away Bibles in Raymond (MS, Bowdoin).

2. Nathaniel and Maria Louisa.

3. Elizabeth Manning Hathorne, her niece.

4. Amelia Palmer Curtis (1784–1854), SH's aunt, kept a school in Salem, which Louisa had attended since June 1820. See 168.

5. James Ferguson, *An Easy Introduction to Astronomy, for Young Gentlemen and Ladies*, first published in London in 1768.

6. John Aikin, *Geographical Delineation; or, A Compendious View of the Natural and Political State of All Parts of the Globe*, first published in London in 1806.

7. Probably Charles Lowell (1782–1861), pastor of the West Church, Boston, and father of James Russell Lowell.

8. Betsey Tarbox Manning.

9. The play's engagement at the Boston Theatre began on March 5. Edmund Kean (1787–1833) played Nahum Tate's version of Shakespeare's tragedy.

10. Before matriculating at Bowdoin College.

11. The dog sent to her the previous August (see 13.1) had strayed.

12. Elizabeth was born on March 7, 1802.

Salem. March 13th. 1821

Dear Mother,

Yours of the   was received.[1] I am much flattered by
your being so solicitous for me to write, and shall be much
more so if you can read what I write, as I have a wretched
pen.[2] Mr Manning is in great affliction concerning that
naughty little Watch, and Louisa and I are in the like dolorous condition. I think it would be advisable to advertise him
in the Portland Papers. How many honours are heaped upon
Uncle Richard! He will soon have as many titles as a Spanish
Don.[3] I am proud of being related to so distinguished a personage. What has become of Elizabeth? Does she never intend to notice me again? I shall begin to think she has eloped
with some of those "Gay Deceivers" who abound in Raymond, if she does not give me some proof to the contrary.
I dreamed the other night, that I was walking by the Sebago,
and when I awoke was so angry at finding it all a delusion,
that I gave Uncle Robert (who sleeps with me) a most horrible kick. I don't read so much now as I did, because I am
more taken up in studying. I am quite reconciled to going to
College, since I am to spend the Vacations with you. Yet four
years of the best part of my Life is a great deal to throw away.
I have not yet concluded what profession I shall have. The
being a Minister is of course out of the Question. I should
not think that even you could desire me to choose so dull a
way of life. Oh no Mother, I was not born to vegetate forever
in one place, and to live and die as calm and tranquil as—A

Puddle of Water. As to Lawyers there are so many of them already that one half of them (upon a moderate calculation) are in a state of actual starvation. A Physician then seems to be "Hobson's Choice," but yet I should not like to live by the diseases and Infirmities of my fellow Creatures. And it would weigh very heavily on my Conscience if in the course of my practice, I should chance to send any unlucky Patient "Ad inferum," which being interpreted, is "to the realms below." Oh that I was rich enough to live without a profession. What do you think of my becoming an Author, and relying for support upon my pen. Indeed I think the illegibility of my handwriting is very authorlike. How proud you would feel to see my works praised by the reviewers, as equal to proudest productions of the scribbling sons of John Bull.[4] But Authors are always poor Devils, and therefore Satan may take them. I am in the same predicament as the honest gentleman in Espriella's Letters.

> "I am an Englishman and naked I
>   stand here
> A musing in my mind what
>   garment I shall wear"[5]

But as the Mail closes soon I must stop the career of my pen. I will only inform you that I now write no Poetry, or anything else. I hope that either Elizabeth or you will write to me next week.

I remain,
Your Affectionate Son,
Nath[l] Hathorne.

Do not show this Letter

1. NH could not recall the date, and left a space for it.

2. In her letter to Mary Manning of March 7, Mrs. Hathorne wrote: "It is a long time since Nathl wrote if he has not time to write long letters he must write short ones" (MS, Bowdoin).

3. Richard had been chosen a selectman of Raymond.

4. NH may be recalling here the notorious question of Sydney Smith in the *Edinburgh Review*, XXXIII (January, 1820), 79: "In the four corners of the globe, who reads an American book?", and Francis Jeffrey's answering prediction in the *Edinburgh Review*, XXXIV (August, 1820), 160, that Washington Irving's *Sketch Book* "will form an era in the literature of the nation to which it belongs [as] the work of an American, entirely bred and trained in that country. . . . Now the most remarkable thing in a work so circumstanced certainly is, that it should be written throughout with the greatest care and accuracy, and worked up to great purity and beauty of diction, on the model of the most elegant and polished of our native writers." See 562.

5. Robert Southey, *Letters from England: By Don Manuel Alvarez Espriella* (1807), Letter 49. NH's quotation is not entirely accurate.

Salem. May 8th 1821

Dear·Uncle,

We are all well as usual. Mother's Letter, I forget the date, was received. There is no news of importance here. I hope your trees are all alive, and suppose that you will make the "Wilderness blossom like the rose."[1] The "Boston & Salem Stage Company" have had no Clerk since your resignation, but Mr. Manning[2] talks of getting one Soon. I have not been to see the boat since you went away, and do not know whether she is finished. Our dinners are not so plentiful or so luxurious as when you were here; one day we have Bacon & potatoes, and the next Potatoes & bacon. It is said that there is to be a Mob the day that Clark[3] is hung. I beleive, at least I have heard, that Mr. Oliver wrote that peice concerning him, in Saturday's Register.[4] The weather is now warm and pleasant.
If I can find any subject for a postscript I will write one after Supper which is now ready.

Your affectionate Nephew
Nath Hathorne.

P.S. I can think of nothing of which I can possibly manufacture a postscript.
My best respects to the Esquire & his Lady.[5]

1. Isaiah 35:1. Robert had recently moved to Raymond.

2. William.

3. Stephen Merrill Clark, seventeen years old, was hanged at Winter Island, Salem, on May 10, for setting fire to a stable in Newburyport. The blaze spread to destroy a house. There was much indignation against Clark.

4. Benjamin Lynde Oliver, NH's teacher. The anonymous letter in the *Essex Register* opposed the execution of Clark, arguing in favor of his youth.

5. Richard and Susan Manning.

Salem May 15th 1821

Dear Sister we recieved Elizabeth's letter to Mother and were very thankfull to heare that Brother Robert had arived, and that you were all well, and had recieved the Trees & goods safe, and were pleased with the Frock with pink and white ribbon for E. M. because it is fashionable here, but the most valuable artical was sent by Sister Priscilla and was in the box with your bonnet. I hope you will excuse what I put into your bonnet it was in the Evening when I packed it & I was in a hurry.

M. L. appears to have recoverd her health she looks well has a good appitite & a great relish for Amusements

I hope the Sabbath-School is begun do write to me very particular about it, how many of the Bibles & Testaments and other Book's have you on hand. what other Books are most wanted, perhaps I may be able to send some more. if poor Steven Clark had attended a Sabbath-School he might have escaped the dreadfull End to which he has come, his situation & fate, excited a greatdeal of Pitty. Mr Cornelius & Mr Carlile[1] were very kind and attentive to him. Doc^t. Prince[2] preached last Sabbath on the occasion from Proverbs chap^r 4 verse 14, and Mr Cornelius Preached a Sermon which I hear is to be printed we are all well and send our love to Brothers & Sisters and Neese & all inquiring Friends

Yours Affecttionately
M. Manning

Dear Mother,

Please to tell Uncle Robert that his Ducks died in the shell on account of the late cold weather. I have been down to see the boat this afternoon. She is caulked, and I beleive finished all but the painting. Uncle William has hired Mr. Foster that wrote for Colcord.[3] Mr Oliver is in good health. [*obliteration*] I did not send the last Palladiums because I could not find them. [*obliteration*] I did not go to see Stephen Clark executed. It is said that he could have been restored to life some time after his execution. I do not know why it was not done.

My health never was better than it is now.

In little more than 3 months I shall be in the land of promise.[4] I hope it will prove something more than promise to me. I go to meeting constantly, which has the effect of an "Auctor Somni," which is being interpreted "Causer of Sleep." Aunt Eunice & Ruth are in good health, although I have not ocular evidence for it. I do not care whether Ebe writes to me or not. If she does not it will save me the postage of the Letter, which in the present state of my affairs is a matter of the first importance. I congratulate you upon having overcome all the dangers and difficulties of Mrs. Manning's bad spelling and my bad writing.[5]

I remain,
Your affectionate Son
Nath Hathorne.

1. Elias Cornelius (1794–1832), pastor of the Tabernacle Church, and Thomas Carlile (1792–1824), rector of St. Peter's Episcopal Church, had become young Clark's "spiritual confessors"; "he ascended the scaffold between the two Rev. Gentlemen, when an address to the assembled spectators written with his own hand, was read by Mr. Cornelius" (Salem *Gazette*, May 11, 3:3). The Rev. Mr. Cornelius's sermon was not published.

2. The Rev. John Prince (1751–1836), pastor of the First Church, Salem. The text reads: "Enter not into the path of the wicked, and go not in the way of evil men."

3. The new clerk and bookkeeper had done the same work at the Colcord stable in Salem.

4. The Mannings and other settlers used "land of promise" to describe Raymond and Maine in general. For NH, thinking of Bowdoin, it seems to mean a personal test of accomplishment in a strange place; compare Longfellow, *Letters,* I, 102.

5. Mary was apparently used to such criticism. She wrote to Robert Manning on December 1, 1818: "Do not look for any bad spelling or any ungrammatical sentences in my letter, but reade it as if spelt & wrote well." She ended her letter to Robert of November 19, 1827: "Do not criticize the writeing spelling &c of your affectionate Sister Mary Manning" (MSS, Essex).

Salem May 29th 1821

Dear Mother,

Elizabeth's Letter was received. There must be some particular reason for Uncle Robert's silence. Mr. Manning[1] was
much disappointed at not receiving a letter from him. Louisa
went to Newburyport yesterday with Mr. Dike & John and
returned to day. All the family are in good health. Richard
Manning of Ipswich[2] died last week. Mr Dike has moved,
and Louisa, as usual, favours them with a great deal of her
Company.[3] Please to ask Uncle Robert where I am to procure
my Greek and Latin Books, now that the Constitution of the
Stage Company is altered.[4] I went to the Theatre last Night.[5]
Please to present my respects to Mr Manning & Lady.[6]

I remain
Your Affectionate Son
Nath Hathorne.

P.S. I can send but one of the Palladiums, as we have not
had the other. Excuse the shortness of this Letter, there
being not an Iota of News.

1. Presumably William.
2. (1777–1821), a first cousin of Mrs. Hathorne.

3. The Dikes now lived on William Street. Mary W. Dike, Louisa's cousin, had died in early December. Louisa continued a close attachment to the Dikes, and after her mother's death in 1849 went to live with them.

4. Robert was not now a partner in the company. For William's contributions to NH, see 24 and 26.

5. The popular Gothic tragedy *Douglas* (1756), by John Home, acted by the Philo Dramatic Society of Boston at the Essex Coffee House. See Pat M. Ryan, Jr., "Young Hawthorne at the Salem Theatre," *EIHC*, XCIV (1958), 249–54.

6. The Richard Mannings.

Salem June 12th. 1821.

Dear Mother.

We arrived here in health and safety on Saturday at five o'clock, found our friends well and met with a most welcome reception. I hope you have by this time recovered your spirits, and that you will not feel any concern on my account, as I am much pleased with my situation, though I hope I shall return soon, as Uncle Robert says he shall go to Raymond in a month. I hope you will be very careful of your health, and ride out often.[1]

Dear Mother   Ebe has got to go down to Aunt Forresters this evening and has commissioned me to finish her letter we were very glad to see Ebe but did not expect her we all want to see you very much I should think you would be very lonesome without any body with you there is no news here. Nathaniel did not know Ebe at first till he saw Uncle Robert and then he stood transfixed with astonishment he was not at home when they came he says he shall want to write some in this letter so I suppose I must leave some paper for him I believe I have written all the news how do you all do give my love to Uncle Richard and Aunt Susan it is very warm here and I suppose it is so at Raymond we are all well I remain your affectionate daughter

Maria Louisa Hathorne

Dear Mother,

That you might receive a Letter from all your Children at once, I have concluded to trouble you with a few lines. I was very happy to see Elizabeth, but hope she will return to Raymond soon, because I know you must be very lonesome without her. She seems very well contented, but prefers Raymond to Salem. I beleive you were never before deserted by all your Children at the same time.

I remain
Your Affectionate Son
Nathaniel Hathorne.

1. Elizabeth was interrupted; there was no signature.

Salem June 19th. 1821.

Dear Mother,

I received your letter, and am glad you are well. I beleive you were never before deserted by all your children at once. Uncle Robert intends to bring Louisa down with him, and leave Elizabeth till I come down in September.[1] He talks of starting next week, but I do not think he will get away so soon. Uncle William has given Elizabeth a Leghorn Bonnet, of the moderate price of 15 Dollars. It is so large that the most piercing eye cannot discover her beneath it. She seems very well contented here, but prefers Raymond to Salem. I hope, Dear Mother, that you will not be tempted by any entreaties to return to Salem to live. You can never have so much comfort here as you now enjoy. You are now undisputed Mistress of your own House. Here you would have to submit to the authority of Miss Manning.[2] If you remove to Salem, I shall have no Mother to return to during the College Vacations, and the expense will be too great for me to come to Salem. If you remain where you are, think how delightfully the time will pass, with all your children round you, shut out from the world, and nothing to disturb us. It will be a second Garden of Eden.

> "Lo what an entertaining sight,
> Are Kindred who agree."[3]

Elizabeth is as anxious for you to stay as myself. She says she is contented to remain here for a short time, but greatly prefers Raymond as a permanent place of Residence.[4] The reason of my saying so much on this subject is, that Mrs. Dike and Miss Manning are very earnest for you to return to Salem, and I am afraid that they will comission U. R.[5] to persuade you to it. But, Mother, if you wish to live in peace I conjure you not to consent it. Grandmother I think is rather in favour of your staying.

If you can read this letter (of which I have great doubts) I shall be much rejoiced.

I remain Your Affectionate Son
Nath Hathorne

Do not show this Letter.

1. To attend Bowdoin College.

2. Mary.

3. Isaac Watts, *Hymns and Spiritual Songs* (1707), I, 44, "Brotherly Love," (Psalm 133): "Lo! what an entertaining sight / Are brethren that agree, / Brethren whose cheerful hearts unite / in bands of piety!"

4. On December 15, 1818, Elizabeth had written from Raymond to Priscilla Dike: "I do not feel at all surprised that people think it strange we should remove from Salem, but I assure you we are extremely well contented here, and that nothing could induce us to return" (MS, Bowdoin).

5. Uncle Robert.

25. FRAGMENT, TO UNKNOWN RECIPIENT[1]

[Salem, ca. June 1821?]

That Ass brought the book, and gave it directly to your aunt Mary. I hope you were wise enough to pretend to know nothing of the matter, if she has said anything to you about it.

Nath. Hathorne.

1. Julian Hawthorne printed this note in *NHHW*, I, 104, and placed it "on the evidence of the handwriting" as "about Hawthorne's eighteenth year." It seems likely to have been a note within the house, passed to Louisa (July, 1820–July, 1821) or, more probably, to Elizabeth (June–August, 1821), to evade the censure of Mary while visiting her.

Salem August 28th 1821.

My Dear Mother,

I received Louisa's letter, for which I thank her. All the Family are well. Mrs. Dike has rode over here once. Elizabeth has gone to stay a week at Mrs G. Archer's.[1] I beleive she is much pleased with her Situation. The time of her visit there will be out tomorrow. Mr Oliver says I will get into College, therefore Uncle Robert need be under no apprehensions. I should be very sorry if "ineluctabile Fatum"[2] should prevent my seeing you before January; for as Solomon saith, "Hope deferred maketh the Heart sick."[3] If Mr. Oliver should accompany me to Brunswick, it would be impossible for me to come. I think there will be no need of Uncle Robert's coming up here for me. If I should not be otherwise provided he can meet me in Portland, which will be a great saving. I suspect that Uncle William intends to give me the cloaths I shall want at my departure, and perhaps the Books; which will be another great saving. You must say nothing about these things in your letters. I fear Elizabeth is too deeply immersed in the vortex of Dissipation to wish to visit Raymond very soon. There are few People of so much constancy as myself. I have preferred, and still prefer Raymond to Salem, through every change of Fortune. This will probably be the last Letter I shall have time to write while I remain here. I hope you write to me Soon.

I remain Your Affectionate Son,
Nathaniel Hathorne.

My Respects to Mr & Mrs. Manning.[4]

1. Judith Hathorne Archer, NH's aunt, widow of George Archer (1755–99), a Salem sea-captain who was lost at sea.

2. "Inevitable Fate."

3. Proverbs 13:12.

4. The Richard Mannings.

Brunswick, Octr. 9th. 1821.

Dear Uncle,

I suppose you have heard that I have entered College.[1] I passed through my examination as well as most of the Candidates. I am very well contented with my situation, and do not wish to come back to Salem this some time.[2] My Chum[3] is the Son of the Hon. Mr. Mason of Portsmouth. He has money enough, which is perhaps unfortunate for me, as it is absolutely necessary that I should make as good an appearance as he does. The Students supply the Furniture for their own Rooms, buy their own wood, and pay 2 dollars a term for washing, 1 dollar for sweeping and bed making besides various other expences.

I board at Professor Newman's[4] with three other Students. The Laws of the College are not at all too strict, and I do not have to study near so hard as I did in Salem.

The 5 dollars you gave me, has been of great use to me, and I did not tell Uncle Robert that I had it, so that I was richer when he left me than he supposed.[5] I hope I shall have no occasion to call upon you for any more this term. If I should be in want of any, I shall confidently apply to you.

If Elizabeth has returned from Andover, I should like to have her write to me. I hope that Grandmother, Aunt Mary, Mr. & Mrs. Dike, Uncle Sam, Aunt Eunice & Ruth, and all my other friends are well.

I remain
Your affectionate Nephew,
Nathaniel Hathorne.

1. NH had come with his Uncle Robert from Salem to Raymond the previous week, and stayed less than a day with his mother, though he had not seen her for two years. Robert wrote to his mother, Miriam Manning, on October 5 of their arrival at Brunswick, and NH's concern about the entrance examination: "During the whole journey he was doubtfull. & after he returned from the Presidents he was positive he should not pass & requested me to be ready to return Immediately. I encouraged him as much as possible. at 2 OClock he attended & in 1 hour returned. having been examined passed & a Chum appointed him. . . . " See Manning Hawthorne, "Nathaniel Hawthorne at Bowdoin," *NEQ*, XIII (1940), 247–48.

2. In his letter of October 5, Robert Manning wrote: "I left Nathaniel yesterday morning. The Introductions to Students Tutors & citizens the civilities disipline & punctuality which the Laws of the Institution demand were Irksome at first to him but habit already began to have a very perceptable Influence" (MS, Bowdoin).

3. Alfred Mason (1804–28), whose father Jeremiah (1768–1848) was attorney general of New Hampshire, 1802–5, and U.S. senator, 1813–17. Alfred prepared at Phillips Academy, Exeter; after graduation from Bowdoin, he became a physician, but died of fever during the first weeks of his internship at Bellevue Hospital, New York.

4. Samuel Phillips Newman (1797–1842), professor of Latin and Greek, 1819–24, and of rhetoric and oratory, 1824–39.

5. Robert wrote in his October 5 letter: "The Tuition Board &c was as low as I had anticipated but Furniture Books &c took so much of my money that I regretted I could leave Nathaniel so small a sum as after Buying wood & candles will be sufficient to procure him those small articles which are absolutely necessary." He also remarked that NH had observed that in buying the furniture he "had traded more than he ever did before."

Brunswick, Octr. 17th. 1821

Dear Mother,

I suppose Mr. Watkins was mistaken about the money which he said was in the Desk,[1] as it is no where to be found. I am in no immediate want of any at present, but shall want some at the end of the Term, to pay my bills for Washing, Sweeping, Bedmaking &c which will amount in all to between 3 and 4 Dollars.

I am very well contented with my situation. I have a very good Chum, and find College a much pleasanter place than I had expected, but still I shall look forward with impatience to the Vacation, when I shall rejoin my Friends, "by absence made more dear"

I have not heard from Salem since I have been here. I wrote last week. I hope Uncle Robert will call here before he returns, as I should like to have some instructions about the manner in which I am to get home.[2]

I have subscribed for some Catalogues of the Students, which I will send to you by the first opportunity. They are not printed yet.

I have nothing more to write, and am

Your Affectionate Son
Nathaniel Hathorne

I wish you or Louisa would write to me once a week.

1. Jacob S. Watkins (1783–1855), a Raymond farmer, probably carted to Portland a mattress and bedstead sent to NH from Raymond by stage the week before (Robert Manning to John Dike, October 23; MS, Essex). Robert did not mention a portable desk, which by NH's reference had interior compartments.

2. Robert, in his letter to Dike, said that he had received a letter from NH making this request, but that he did not intend to "spare time to go to Brunswick."

Brunswick, Octr. 28th. 1821

Dear Sister,

As Mr McKeen[1] offers to carry a Letter for me, I will endeavour to find some subject for one. I am very well contented with my situation, and like a College Life much better than I expected. I have not yet been under the necessity of studying more than 3 hours a Day, though by the Laws of the College I should study 7. The Lessons are so short that I want employment the greatest part of the time. Yet I generally make the time pass very tolerably, by dint of playing Cards, at which all the Students are great adepts, and other unlawful occupations, which are made more pleasant by the fines attached to them if discovered. The Laws of the College are not very strict, and they are not half of them obeyed. Some of them are peculiarly repugnant to my feelings, such as, to get up at sunrise every morning to attend prayers, which law the Students make it a custom to break twice a week. But the worst of all is to be compelled to go to meeting every Sunday, and to hear a red hot Calvinist Sermon from the President, or some other dealer in fire and brimstone. Our President[2] is a short, thick little lump of a man, with no talents, and, as I have been told, no extraordinary learning. He is quite an inoffensive little animal, and causes me no trouble except to put my hand to my hat when I meet him. The College is a much more civilized place than one would expect to find in this wilderness. There are two Societies composed of the Students,[3] one containing 1200 and the other 600 volumes. The Books are generally well chosen, and they have many of the best English Authors. There is also a theological Society and Library, into which, owing to a fib of my Chum's who said that I was religious, I should have been elected, had I not rescued myself by taking the name of the Devil in vain, which had a very great and marvellous effect. The peculiarly pious expression of my countenance, which was so much noticed in Andover,[4] has caused me many inconveniences in this place, insomuch that it is with great difficulty I can keep clear of Conferences,[5] and other meetings of the Righteous. By far the greater proportion of the Members of College are yet in the "bond of bitterness and the gall of iniquity,"[6] but there is a considerable congregation of Saints.—The first bell rings and I must dress myself to attend meeting.

Afternoon— Meeting for this day is over. We have had a Minister from the Andover Mill, and he "dealt damnation round"[7] with an unsparing hand, and finished by consigning us all to the Devil.

I suppose Caroline Archer[8] is married before this time. If you should have any thoughts of entering into the Holy State yourself, I hope you will ask my advice.[9] I noticed that Mr. L.[10] looked very remarkably well, considering that he has been "crossed in hopeless Love."[11]

The winter Vacation will commence on the 19th. of December, and continue 7 weeks. I am sorry that you will not be in Raymond this winter, as that would add much to the happiness I expect to enjoy. I suppose you will go to the Assemblies,[12] and in the round of pleasure and dissipation lose all remembrance of the Friends you have left. I do not wish however to have you think that I have grown sentimental for I was never in better spirits in my life, than since I have been here.

I must close my letter as I have a Bible Lesson to get to recite after prayers. I believe it is not the custom in any other

College to recite Lessons from the bible, and I think it a very foolish one.

I hope you will remember that no letter has been sent me since I have been here, which is now nearly a month. I do not think you can have any excuse for not writing, as you must have sufficient time.

Praying that you may in time arrive in safety at the end of this letter I take my leave,

Your Affectionate Brother,
Nathaniel Hathorne.

I need not caution you not to shew this.

1. John McKeen (1789–1861), a son of the Reverend Joseph McKeen (1757–1807), first president of Bowdoin, after graduation had kept a small store in Brunswick, where he had offered NH a position as clerk. He was acquainted with the Manning and Dike families through business dealings in Raymond and in Beverly, Mass., his original home. On this trip he reported to John Dike that NH was "getting along finely"—news that Dike relayed on October 31 to Robert Manning in Raymond (MS, Bowdoin).

2. William Allen (1784–1868), a native of Pittsfield, Mass., had graduated from Harvard in 1802 and, after preparing for the ministry, compiled *The American Biographical and Historical Dictionary* (1809); as pastor of the First Congregational Church of Pittsfield, 1810–17, "he insisted upon strict compliance with the letter of the law and his unyielding disposition and rigorous enforcement of church discipline made him many enemies" (*DAB*). After two years as president of Dartmouth, he was chosen president of Bowdoin in 1819. By the 1830s, his unpopularity with students and trustees led to legal efforts, eventually successful, to remove him.

3. The Peucinian and Athenaean were social and literary societies whose rivalry was chiefly expended on their libraries. NH joined the Athenaean, and Longfellow became prominent in the Peucinian. See 38.2.

4. This town northwest of Salem, served by the Mannings' stagecoach line, was the site of a Calvinist theological seminary opened in 1808 to oppose the Unitarianism of Harvard Divinity School.

5. Annual assemblies of governing bodies of religious organizations. See *OED*.

6. Acts 8:22–23: "Repent therefore of this thy wickedness, and pray God, if perhaps the thought of thine heart may be forgiven thee. For I perceive that thou art in the gall of bitterness, and in the bond of iniquity."

7. Pope, "Universal Prayer" (1738), 25–28: "Let not this weak, unknowing hand / Presume thy Bolts to throw / And deal Damnation round the land / On each I judge thy Foe."

8. NH's cousin (b. 1798) had gone with her mother, Judith Hathorne Archer, in 1816 to live in Baltimore with her sister Sarah (b. 1794), wife of Robert Hawkins Osgood.

9. In a leaf of *The Spectator* issued in Raymond, January 31, 1822, NH wrote: "We have received letters from Salem, dated January 29. They contain little information of importance to the Public. A report was in circulation that the beautiful Miss E. M. Hathorne, formerly of this place, had consented to enter the holy state of Matrimony, in company with Capt. Jeremiah Briggs, a young gentleman of rank and accomplishments. 'Oh, there's nothing half so sweet in life, as Love's young Dream'" (MS, Essex). The quotation is from Thomas Moore, "Love's Young Dream," in *Irish Melodies* (1808).

10. Unidentified.

11. A conflation of two famous lines from Richard Brinsley Sheridan's farce *The Critic* (1779), III, 1: "Tho' hopeless love finds comfort in despair," and "An oyster may be cross'd in love."

12. Dances at Hamilton Hall in Salem. See "Reminiscences of the Old Assemblies . . . " in "Notes on Old Times in Salem," *EIHC*, LXXIV (1938), 365.

Brunswick, Octr. 30th. 1821.

Dear Mother,

I received Louisa's letter, and will write to her soon. I have not had a Letter from Salem since I have been here, and think Elizabeth neglects me very much. I had an opportunity of writing yesterday by Mr John McKeen, who has gone to Boston.

I continue to be well contented here, though I had much rather be at home. My Chum and I live together in the greatest harmony.

I should make no objection to some money, as I have had to buy Webber's Mathematicks[1] which cost 3.00, and am now almost out of Cash.

I hope that Uncle Robert will call here before he returns to Salem, as I long to see somebody from home.[2] I do not think that you write to me often enough.

I have nothing in particular to write, except that I shall not want a feather-bed.

I remain
Your affectionate Son
Nath Hathorne.

P.S. The Vacation commences, the 19th of December.

---

1. Samuel Webber, *Mathematics . . . Intended to be the Text-Book of the Course of Private Lectures on these Sciences in the University of Cambridge*, first published in Boston in 1801.

2. Mrs. Hathorne had written to Mary Manning from Raymond in mid-September: "I think Robert will return to Salem by the 1 of January" (MS, Bowdoin).

Brunswick. November. 13th. 1821

My Dear Mother,

I Received a Bundle which was left at Dow's[1] by the Stage, and I suppose was sent by you, but I hear nothing of any Letter, and have had but one from Raymond since I have been here.

I have for several days past been quite unwell with the Measles, but am now recovered. Mr. & Mrs. Newman treated me with much care, and I staid at their house while I was sick. It is very necessary that I should have some money to pay the Doctor's Bill, which at present I cannot do. He visited me five times, and supplied me with all my medicines. I have some thoughts of writing to Uncle William for some money, in compliance with his request, but I feel rather unwilling to do so.[2]

The Vacation will commence in 5 weeks from Wednesday, and I shall be heartily glad when it comes.

I have nothing more of importance to write,

and remain
Your affectionate Son,
Nathaniel Hathorne

1. The principal public house and the stage stop.

2. Mary Manning wrote to Mrs. Hathorne on November 21: "Brother William received a letter from Nathaniel yesterday dated November 17 informs him he had just recovered from the Measles. W. writes to him this evening" (MS, Essex).

Brunswick Dec 4, 1821

Dear Uncle,

I rec'd your Letter inclosing 10 Doll. Also one from Uncle W. on the same day inclosing 5. Having paid the Doctor's Bill, and settled accounts with my Chum for Wood and other expences, I have about 7 dollars left.
The term closes in a fortnight from Tommorrow.
The bill for tuition and Board need not be paid till next term.
Those for washing & Bedmaking will amount to about 3 or 4 dollars.
I hope you will call for me, for I long to get home.[1]
It is Recitation time and I must conclude.

Your affectionate Nephew
N. Hathorne

1. On December 11 Louisa wrote from Raymond to Elizabeth in Salem: "We expect Nathaniel next week" (MS, Essex).

Raymond, January 15th. 1821 [1822]

Dear Uncle,

Your Letter was received. We were glad to hear of your safe arrival. I send the measure of my foot. The Boots will be very acceptable as mine are not fit to be seen.

I have not three weeks longer to stay,[1] and think that the pantaloons had better be made with all convenient speed. If Mr Derby[2] has not kept my measure I can get them made in Portland.

I hope Uncle Sam will come to Brunswick, if I should not be in Raymond when he comes down. I have nothing of importance to write,

and Remain
Nath Hathorne.

Measure of my Foot[3]

1. Before returning to college.
2. John Derby, Jr., & Son, Salem tailors.
3. "Measure of my Foot" is inscribed along left margin, accompanied by a bracket marking 10 1/2 inches.

Brunswick, February 20th. 1821 [1822]

Dear Uncle,

I hope you and all the family are well. I have nothing in particular to write. I have left Mr. Newman's, and now board at Mrs. Adam's.[1] I am very comfortably situated, except that I am without money, and in debt to my Chum for wood.[2]
I wish you would write me word if you have sent my pantaloons, as they have not arrived.
You complained very much of the shortness of my Letters, but I hope that you will beleive that the occasion of it is not the want of will, but the want of subject, I would willingly write more if I could find anything to write about.
I have not heard from Salem since I have been here, and I hope to receive Letters soon. It is late and I have not got my Lesson.[3]

I remain,
your Affectionate Nephew.
Nathaniel Hathorne.

1. Mrs. Adams, widow of a Brunswick physician, lived opposite the president's house.
2. Robert wrote to Mrs. Hathorne on March 6: "Rec'd a letter from Nath'l he was well & I have forwarded him some money" (MS, Essex).
3. Louisa wrote from Raymond on February 20 to Robert: "We have not heard from Nathaniel since he went to Brunswick" (MS, Essex).

Brunswick. April 14th. 1822.

My Dear Sister,

I received your Letter of April 10th, and also one which was dated the 20th of March. How it could have been so long on the road, I cannot conceive. I hope you will excuse my neglect in writing to Mother and you so seldom, but still I beleive there is but one Letter due from me to you, as I wrote about the middle of March.[1] My health during this term has been as good as usual, except that I am sometimes afflicted with the Sunday Sickness,[2] and, as that happens to be the case to day, I employ my time in writing to you.

My occupations this term have been much the same as they were last, except that I have, in a great measure, dis-continued the practice of playing cards. One of the Students has been suspended lately for this Offence, and 2 of our Class have been fined. I narrowly escaped detection myself, and mean for the future to be more careful.

I beleive our loss by the fire is or will be nearly made up.[3] I sustained no damage by it, except having my Coat torn, but it luckily happened to be my old one. The repairs on the Building are begun, and will probably be finished by next commencement.

I suppose Uncle Robert has arrived at Raymond. I think I shall not want my pantaloons this term, the end of which is only three weeks from Wednesday. I look forward with great pleasure to the Vacation, though it is so short, that I shall scarcely have time to get home. A great part of the Students intend to remain here.

I hope [*MS torn*] will endeavour to answer. I received a Letter from Elizabeth last week, and wrote one to her. I was very much surprised to hear of Mr. Carlile's failure.[4]

I have some cash at present, but was much in want of it the first part of the term. I suppose you have heard that a Letter containing money which Uncle Robert sent me some time ago, was lost. I have since received some by Joseph McKean.[5] I beleive Mother has written me but one Letter this term. I shall expect both of you to write to me before the end of the term. Excuse my bad writing.

I remain,
Your affectionate Brother
Nath Hathorne.

You need not show this

---

1. Louisa had written to her sister on April 10: "We have had no letter from Nathaniel for nearly six weeks, since the College was burnt, we write to him but do not know whether he recieves our letters, when you write do let us know when you hear from him" (MS, Bowdoin).

2. Laziness.

3. On March 4, Maine Hall was destroyed by fire. NH and Alfred Mason escaped easily. While the hall was rebuilt, they roomed as well as boarded with Mrs. Adams.

4. The Reverend Thomas Carlile declared bankruptcy in early April. His wife, Eleanor, daughter of Simon and Rachel Hathorne Forrester, was NH's first cousin.

5. Joseph McKeen (1787–1865), a Brunswick merchant, brother of John (28A.1).

Brunswick, May 1st. 1822.

My Dear Mother,

I am happy to inform you that the Vacation will commence on the 8th of May, which is a week from tomorrow. I have not money enough to get home by the stage, and therefore hope you will send for me. If Uncle Robert has not yet arrived I should like to have Mr Leach[1] come after me, if convenient. There will not be time enough to send me any money.

I hope Elizabeth will be in Raymond during the Vacation. I received a Letter from her some time since,[2] together with a Watch, with which I am much pleased, and cut a great dash.

The Breakfast-bell rings. I am very hungry

and remain,
Your affectionate Son
Nathaniel Hathorne.

1. See 3.4.

2. Elizabeth's letter of May 14 to her mother, describing her unhappy life with the Manning relatives in Salem, is in Gloria Erlich, "Hawthorne and the Mannings," *Studies in the American Renaissance 1980*, pp. 106–7. Elizabeth concludes, "I have not heard from Nathaniel for a long time."

Brunswick May 30th 1822

My Dear Mother,

I hope you have safely arrived in Salem.[1] I have nothing particular to inform you of, except that all the Card Players in College have been found out, and my unfortunate self among the number. One has been dismissed from College, two suspended, and the rest, with myself, have been fined 50 cts. each. I beleive the President intends to write to the friends of all the delinquents.[2] Should that be the case you must show the letter to nobody. If I am again detected I shall have the honour of being suspended. When the President asked what we played for, I thought proper to inform it was 50 cts. although it happened to be a Quart of Wine, but if I had told him of that he would probably have fined me for having a blow.[3] There was no untruth in the case, as the wine cost 50 cts. I have not played at all this term.
I have not drank any kind of spirit or wine this term, and shall not till the last week.

I remain
N H.

I must have some money, for I have none left, except about 75 cts.

Do not show this.

1. Mrs. Hathorne had on May 22 moved permanently to Salem, though retaining her house in Raymond.

2. The letter of William Allen to Mrs. Hathorne, May 29, 1822, is published in Manning Hawthorne, "Nathaniel Hawthorne at Bowdoin," *NEQ*, XIII (1940), 260.

3. "A merry frolic with drinking; a spree" (Benjamin H. Hall, *A Collection of College Words and Customs*, 1851).

37. TO MARK LEACH, JR.,[1] RAYMOND

Brunswick, May 31, 1822.

My Dear Friend,

As I intend that you shall have no cause of complaint for my neglect this term, I take this early opportunity of writing to you. There is no news here, except that all the Card-Players in College have been found out. We have all been called before the Government, two have been suspended, and several more, myself among the number, have been fined. The President has written to all the parents of those who were found out, and to my Mother among the rest. If Uncle R.[2] hears of it he will probably take me away from College. I noticed in the paper that No. 15885 had drawn a prize of 1000. Is not that one of your tickets? If it is, I congratulate you upon your good fortune, and only wish it had been 100000.[3]

I have been much more steady this term than I was last, as I have not drank any kind of spirit, nor played cards, for the offence for which I was fined was committed last term. The reason of my good conduct is that I am very much afraid of being suspended if I continue any longer in my old courses.

I hope you will write to me very soon, and tell me all about your prize. I must conclude my letter as it is nearly recitation time, and it is probable that you will not be able to read half that I have written.

I remain,
Your Friend,
N. H.

1. (1792–1831); see 3.4.
2. Robert.
3. Mark is mentioned several times in Manning family correspondence as an enthusiast of lotteries.

Brunswick, August 5th. 1822

My Dear Sister,

I admire your policy in carrying the war into the enemy's country, when you cannot defend your own frontiers. Most assuredly you are the last person from whom I should have expected a rebuke on account of the shortness and infrequency of my letters. If you will please to recollect you will find that my letters exceed yours considerably in number this term, and as for length (though neither of us have anything to boast of) mine are at least equal to yours.

To quiet your suspicions, I can assure you that I am neither "dead, absconded, nor anything worse." I have involved myself in no "foolish scrape," as you say all my friends suppose; but ever since my misfortune have been as steady as a Sign post, and as sober as a Deacon, have been in no "blows" this term, nor drank any kind of "wine or strong drink." So that your comparison of me to the "prodigious Son" will hold good in nothing, except that I shall probably return pennyless, for I have had no money this six weeks. My only reason for not writing has been that I have had nothing to write.

The President's Message is not so severe as I expected. I perceive that he thinks I have been lead away by the wicked ones, in which however he is greatly mistaken. I was full as willing to play as the person he suspects of having enticed me, and would have been influenced by no one. I have a great mind to commence playing again, merely to show him that I scorn to be seduced by another into anything wrong. I have not read either of the Novels you mention. I began some time ago to read Hume's History of England,[1] but found it so abominably dull that I have given up the undertaking until some future time. I can procure Books of all sorts, from the library of the Athenean Society,[2] of which I am a Member. The Library consists of about 800 Volumes, among which is Ree's Cyclopedia,[3] and many other valuable works.

The Commencement will be on the 21st of this Month, which is a fortnight from Wednesday. All the students will have liberty to go home one Friday before Commencement, which is a week from next Friday, and if I receive money for my expenses in time, I shall take my departure then. I hope it will be sent on as quick as possible. I received Mother's Letter, and wrote one the day before I received it, which I hope has reached you.

Our class will be examined on Tuesday for admittance to our Sophomore year. If any of us are found deficient we shall be degraded to the Freshman Class again; from which misfortune may Heaven defend me.

If you have any conscience you will certainly be satisfied with the length of this Letter.

I am
Your affectionate Brother,
Nath. Hathorne.

Do not forget to tell Uncle Robert that I shall want some money to get home with.

---

1. David Hume, *History of England*, 1754–62.

2. The Athenaean Society, one of two literary clubs at Bowdoin, was described by NH in *The Life of Franklin Pierce*, chapter 1, as "typifying . . . the progres-

sive or democratic" party. No record of withdrawals from its library has been preserved.

3. Abraham Rees, *The New Cyclopaedia; or, Universal Dictionary of Arts and Sciences . . . Biography, Geography, and History,* 1802–20, 45 volumes. NH was to borrow eleven volumes of Rees from the Salem Athenaeum between 1827 and 1830 (Kesselring, p. 48).

Brunswick. May 4th. 1823.

My Dear Sister,

I recieved your Letter, and was glad of it, for they are "like angel visits, few and far between."[1] However, to say the truth, I believe I have not much right to complain of the dilatory nature of our correspondence.

I am happy to hear that Uncle Robert has arrived safe, and was pleased with his Journey. I should have thought a longer stay would have been necessary to make observations sufficient for a reasonable book of travels, which I presume it is his intention to publish.[2]

The bundle of books which you mention I saw, with my own eyes, put into the desk where all orders for Sawin[3] are deposited. As it was a stormy day Sawin did not come himself, but sent a boy.

There is in the medical Class a certain Dr. Ward[4] of Salem, where he intends to settle, after taking his degree of M.D. which will be given him this term. I shall give him a letter of introduction to you, when he returns to Salem, which he intends in about a fortnight. He is the best scholar among the Medicals, and I hope you will use your influence to get him into practice.

I am invited by several of the students to pass the vacation with them. I believe I shall go to Augusta if Mother and Uncle R. have no objections. The stage fare will be about $5, and I should like about $10 dollars as spending money, as I am going to the house of an Honourable.[5] As Mr. McKean is sick, I think the money had better be directed to me than to him. The term ends in a fortnight from Wednesday next.

I wish to recieve instructions about my thin cloathes, whether I am to get them made here, or have them sent down to me. I have but one good pair of pantaloons, the others being in rather a dilapidated condition.

I do not believe you can tell whose profile the inclosed is.[6]

If I had time I would tell you a mighty story, how some of the students hung Parson Mead[7] in effigy, and how one of them was suspended. Mother need not be frightened, as I was not engaged in it.

Give my love to all and sundry.

Your affectionate brother

N. Hathorne

Excuse my bad pen.

1. Thomas Campbell, *The Pleasures of Hope* (1799), 2.378.

2. Apparently a pleasantry.

3. Jabez Sawin (1808–70) was a driver for the Maine Stage Coach Company, between Portland and Brunswick. Robert had sent the books from Salem to Richard in Raymond.

4. Malthus Augustus Ward (1792–1863) graduated an M.D. from Bowdoin in 1823, and then practiced in Salem. He was superintendent of the Marine Museum in Salem, 1825–31.

5. Probably the Hon. James Bridge (1765–1834), father of NH's classmate Horatio; a judge and wealthy financier, now retired. In *Recollections*, Horatio Bridge does not mention the proposed visit, and it may not have occurred.

6. Apparently the silhouette that appears among his class's profiles in the Bowdoin library. See Hubert H. Hoeltje, "A Forgotten Hawthorne Silhouette," *AL*, XXVIII (1957), 510–11; Gollin, pp. 16–17.

7. The Reverend Asa Mead (1792–1830) was pastor, 1822–29, of the Brunswick Congregational Church, which was supported by the college and townspeople. He was finally repudiated by the college trustees, after earning the dislike of many students for the rigor of his orthodoxy and because he enforced compulsory attendance at his sermons.

Brunswick, August 12th. 1823

My Dear Uncle,

I recieved your Letter in due season, and should have answered it in due season, if I had not been prevented, as Louisa conjectures, by laziness. The money was very acceptable to me and will last me till the end of the term, which is only three weeks from next Wednesday. I shall then have finished one half of my College Life. Louisa mentioned in her last letter that Aunt Archer was in town, but did not say how long she had been there, or whether Caroline or Mrs. Osgood[1] were with her. I should be very happy to see her, and hope I shall return home before she goes away.

I suppose your farm prospers, and I hope you will have abundance of fruit, and that I shall come home time enough to eat some of it, which I should prefer to all the pleasure of cultivating it.[2]

I have heard that there is a Steam boat which runs twice a week between Portland and Boston. If this is the case, I should like to come home by that way if Mother has no apprehensions of the boiler's bursting.

I really have had a great deal to do this term, as in addition to the usual exercises we have to write a theme, or essay of three or four pages every fortnight, which employs nearly all my time, so that I hope you will not impute my neglect of writing wholly to laziness.

The breakfast bell has rung. I am very hungry and must hasten to a conclusion. Please to remember me to all my friends.

Your affectionate Nephew
Nath. Hathorne

If you please I should like to have the money for my travelling expenses sent to me rather before commencement (the 1st Wednesday in September,) as I wish to buy some furniture.

---

1. See 28A.8.

2. It was during this year that Robert established his fruit tree nursery on Dearborn Street in a sparsely populated area of North Salem. His work there for almost twenty years led to his fame as the leading pomologist in America.

Brunswick. August 11th. 1824.

My dear Louisa,

I have just received your Letter, and you will no doubt wonder at my punctuality in answering it. The occasion of this miracle is, that I am in a terrible hurry to get home, and your assistance is necessary for that purpose. In the first place I will offer a few reasons why it is expedient for me to return to Salem immediately, and then proceed to show how your little self can be instrumental in effecting this purpose.

Firstly—I have no clothes in which I can make a decent appearance, as the weather in this part of the world is much too cold for me to wear my thin clothes often, and I shall therefore be compelled to stay at home from meeting all the rest of the term, and perhaps to lie in bed the whole of the time. In this case my fines would amount to an enormous sum.

Secondly—If I remain in Brunswick much longer I shall spend all my money, for, though I am extremely prudent, I always feel uneasy when I have any cash in my pocket. I do not feel at all inclined to spend another vacation in Brunswick, but if I stay much longer I shall inevitably be compelled to, for want of means to get home.

Thirdly—Our senior examination[1] is now over, and many of our class have gone home. The studies are now of little importance, and I could obtain leave of absence much easier than at any other time.

Fourthly—It is so long since I saw the land of my birth that I am almost dead of homesickness, and am apprehensive of serious injury to my health, if I am not soon removed from this place.

Fifthly—The Students have now but little to do, and mischief, you know, is the constant companion of idleness. The latter part of the term preceding commencement is invariably spent in dissipation, and I am afraid that my stay here will have an ill effect upon my moral character, which would be a cause of great grief to Mother & you.

I think that by the preceding arguments I have clearly shown that it is very improper for me to remain longer in Brunswick, and we will now consider the means of my deliverance. In order to effect this you must write me a letter, stating that Mother is desirous for me to return home, and assigning some reason for it. The letter must be such a one as is proper to be read by the president, to whom it will be necessary to show it. You must write immediately upon the receipt of this, and I shall receive your letter on Monday. I shall start the next morning, and be in Salem on Wednesday. You can easily think of a good excuse. Almost any one will do. I beseech you not to neglect it, and if Mother has any objections your eloquence will easily persuade her to consent. I can get no good by remaining here, and earnestly desire to be at home.

If you are at a loss for an excuse, say that Mother is out of health, or that Uncle R. is going a journey on account of his health, and wishes me to attend him, or that Elizabeth is on a visit at some distant place and wishes me to come and bring her home. Or that George Archer[2] has just arrived from sea, and is to sail again immediately, and wishes to see me before he goes. Or that some of my relations are to die or be married, and my presence is necessary on the occasion. And lastly, if none of these excuses will suit you, and you can think of no other, write, and order me to come home without any. If you do not, I shall certainly forge a letter, for I *will* be at home within a week. Write the very day that you receive this. If

Elizabeth were at home she would be at no loss for a good excuse.

If you will do as I tell you I shall be

Your affectionate Brother, Nath. Hathorne.

My want of decent clothes will prevent my calling at Mrs. Sutton's.[3] Write immediately. Write immediately. Write immediately.

Haste, Haste, Post haste, ride and run, until these shall be delivered. You must and shall and will do as I desire. If you can think of a true excuse, send it, if not, any other will answer the same purpose. If I do not get a letter by Monday, or Tuesday at farthest, I will leave Brunswick without liberty.

1. Qualification for entrance to the senior year.
2. Son of Judith Hathorne Archer (b. 1793).
3. See 12.1.

Brunswick. October 1st. 1824.

My Dear Sister,

As we have no recitations this week I have thought proper to favour you with a letter. I met with no uncommon occurrence on my journey, except that I was squeezed to death by the multiplicity of passengers, and drowned by the rain. Since my arrival I have put on my gold watch-chain, and purchased a cane; so that, with the aid of my new white gloves, I flatter myself that I make a most splendid appearance in the eyes of the pestilent little freshmen.

I had the pleasure of seeing my dear cousin, T. H. Forester, Esq.[1] in Portland, in as delectable a state as could well be imagined. He employed himself a part of the time in reading aloud, to the great edification of the company. He did not recognize me, and I was of course not very anxious to assert my relationship. He is now in Brunswick, but intends, I beleive, to leave town tomorrow.

The lady[2] was very much delighted with the purse, but, as I feared that the price would not be so much to her satisfaction, I with the greatest generosity refused to receive any remuneration.

I am very low-spirited, and I verily beleive that all the blue devils in Hell, or wherever else they reside, have been let loose upon me. I am tired of college, and all its amusements and occupations. I am tired of my friends and acquaintances, and finally I am heartily tired of myself. I would not live over my college life again, "though 'twere to buy a world of happy days"[3]

I must now come to the serious part of my letter, and truly I do it with a sad heart. There has been a new code of laws promulgated since the last term, from which I extract the following section, for the edification of all concerned: "If any bill is not paid within one month after the commencement of the next term, interest shall be charged; and if not paid within *six months* from the date of the bill, there shall be an assessment of twenty cents for *every days neglect,* and the student, against whom the bill is made, *may be dismissed from College*." My term bills remain unpaid for more than a year past. I do not ask for money, but I thought it best that you should know how delightful are my prospects.

I can write nothing-else that will be interesting to you. I hope that I shall hear from you soon, and do let your letters be long. Notwithstanding I was so weary of home, I shall rejoice when I return to it, whether by dismission from College, or from any other cause.

I am your affectionate brother, N. H.

Gardiner Kellog[4] has entered college, but I have heard nothing of my protegee, T. M.[5]
Remember me in a suitable manner to yourselves and the family.

---

1. Thomas Haley Forrester (1791–1830), a Salem merchant, the son of Simon and Rachel Hathorne Forrester, drank habitually and heavily. See NH to R. H. Stoddard and to E. B. Stoddard, January 8 and 26, 1863 (MSS, St. Lawrence, Berg).

2. Unidentified.

3. Shakespeare, *Richard III*, I.iv.6.

4. Gardiner Kellogg (1802–41), Bowdoin B.A. 1827. His father, Gardiner Kellogg (1765–1826), a Calvinist preacher at Windham, Maine, frequently vis-

ited the Mannings and Mrs. Hathorne at Raymond. In his January, 1822, *Spectator*, NH facetiously announced that the Reverend Dr. Kellog [*sic*] had come to Raymond to "attend to the duties of his profession in this place. From our knowledge of the eloquence and piety of this venerable Servant of the Lord, we doubt not that many through his means will be brought out [of] darkness into light &c &c &c" (MS, Essex).

5. Thomas Manning (1805–39), who with his father, Joseph, a blacksmith of New Gloucester, Maine, often visited their cousins in Raymond. Thomas entered the Bowdoin class of 1829, and was later a teacher in Pennsylvania, Alabama, and Tennessee.

[Brunswick, ca. October 31, 1824]

I have been introduced to Gardiner Kellog. A few weeks ago, as I was entering the door of the College, somebody took hold of my cloak, and said that "Kellog wished the honour of Mr. Hathorne's acquaintance." I looked round, and beheld a great, tall, awkward booby, frightened to death at his own boldness, and grinning horribly a ghastly smile. I saw his confusion, and with that condescending affability which is one among my many excellencies, I took him by the hand, expressed my pleasure at the meeting, and inquired after his sister and friends. After he had replied to these queries, as well as his proper sense of my superiority would admit, I desired to see him at my room as soon as convenient, and left him. This interesting interview took place before numerous spectators, who were assembled round the door of the College. He has since been at my room several times, and is very much pleased (how should it be otherwise?) with my company. I am however very much displeased with him for one thing. I had comfortably composed myself to sleep one Saturday afternoon, when I was awakened by a tremendous knocking at the door, which continued about 10 minutes. I made no answer, but swore internally the most horrible oaths. At last, the gentleman's knuckles being probably worn out, he retired; and upon looking out of the window, I discovered that my pestilent visitor was Mr. Kellog. I could not get asleep again that afternoon.

I made a very splendid appearance in the Chapel last Friday evening, before a crowded audience.[1] I would send you a printed list of the performances, if it were not for the postage.

1. On October 29, NH delivered a dissertation, "De Patribus Conscriptis Romanorum" ("Of Roman Senators"). The text and a translation appear as Appendix II of Lathrop's *Study*. See Hubert Hoeltje, "Hawthorne . . . at Bowdoin," *EIHC*, XCIV (1958), 208–10.

Brunswick. November 26th. 1824

My Dear Aunt,

Elizabeth has informed me that you wish me to write to you, and as I am always ready to oblige, I shall endeavour to find materials for a letter. There is so little variety at College that you will not expect much news, or if you do, you will be disappointed. If my letter should happen to be very short, you will excuse it, as I attend to my studies so diligently that I have not much time to write.

A missionary society has lately been formed in College, under the auspices of a gentleman from Andover;[1] but it does not meet with much encouragement. Only twenty two of the students have joined it, and most of them are supported by the Education Society;[2] so that they have not much to give. I suppose you would be glad to hear that I was a member, but my regard to truth compels me to confess that I am not.

There is a considerable revival of religion in this town, and those adjoining, but unfortunately it has not yet extended to the College. The students have generally been very steady and regular this term, but religion is less regarded than could be desired. This is owing in part to the unpopularity of Mr. Mead, whom the Students dislike so much, that they will attend to none of his exhortations.

I sincerely sympathize with Uncle Robert and the family, in the pleasure they must feel at the approaching event.[3] I wish that it were possible for me to be present, in order that I might learn how to conduct myself, when marriage shall be my fate. I console myself with the hope that you, at least, will not neglect to give me an invitation to your wedding, which I should not be surprised to hear announced. Elizabeth says that you are very deeply in love with Mr. Upham.[4] Is the passion reciprocal?

The weather has lately been very cold, and there is now snow enough to make some sleighing. I keep excellent fires, and do not stir from them, unless when it is absolutely necessary. I wish that I could be at home to Thanksgiving, as I really think that your puddings and pies and turkies are superior to anybody's else. But the term does not close till about the first of January.

I can think of nothing else that will be interesting to you, and as it is now nearly recitation time, I must conclude. Please to give my love to Grandmother, Mother &c. I shall expect a letter from you very soon, otherwise I shall not write again.

Your affectionate nephew,
N. Hathorne.

1. A professor or student from the Andover (Mass.) Theological Seminary.

2. Founded at Andover in 1815 to support students preparing for the ministry.

3. Robert married Rebecca Dodge Burnham on December 20, 1824.

4. NH is teasing Mary about her staunch orthodoxy. The Reverend Charles Wentworth Upham (1802–75), was to be installed as associate pastor of the First Church (Unitarian) of Salem on December 6. He was in 1849 influential in the dismissal of NH from the custom house, and is thought to be a model for Judge Pyncheon in *HSG*. See *DAB*.

Brunswick, April 21st 1825

My Dear Sister,

I have been very negligent in answering your letter, but you know my habits too well to be at all concerned about it. Nothing of any importance has taken place lately; my health has been very good, and I have neither been suspended nor expelled.

The term, I beleive, will close in about three weeks from the present time. I feel extremely anxious to see you all, and unless the Government[1] should compell me to stay in Brunswick during the vacation (of which there is little danger) I shall certainly return home. Mr. Leach was extremely anxious that I should accompany him on a visit to Raymond this spring, but I think I shall decline the honour.[2]

I hope Mother's health continues to improve, and that I shall find her as well as ever, when I return. You ought to give me a more particular account of yourselves and all that concerns you, as, though it might appear trifling to others it would be interesting to me. I suppose Louisa has by this time returned from Newburyport, and gives herself all the airs of a travelled lady.

I betook myself to scribbling poetry as soon as I heard of Lucy Ann's[3] Album, and, after much labour, produced four lines, which I immediately burnt. I fear I shall be unable to write anything worthy of the immortality of such a record.

I have been thinking all the term of writing to Uncle William, according to his request, and shall expect a good scolding when I return for neglecting it. I beleive I promised to write to him, but promises are not always performed. He is so engaged in business, however, that he will never think of it.

I have scarcely any money, and wish to have 15 dollars sent me in about a fortnight. I am not sure whether the term ends in three or in four weeks. If it is more than three, I will write after receiving the money.

I have nothing more to write except my respects to all the family and friends.

I am,
Nath. Hathorne

1. The college administration.

2. A letter of Richard to Robert of June 18 places NH at that time in Raymond (MS, Bowdoin).

3. Lucy Ann Sutton, of Portland, a great-grandniece of NH's Grandmother Manning. See 12.1. She described her first acquaintance with NH, when he may have been twelve to fourteen years old, including their shared literary interests; her article, "Nathaniel Hawthorne's Boyhood," in the New York *Observer*, August 4, 1887, was reprinted in Manning Hawthorne, "A Glimpse of Hawthorne's Boyhood," *EIHC*, LXXXIII (1947), 178–84.

Brunswick. June 1825

My dear Sister,

Mr. Dike[1] wishes me to write, and though I have nothing to say, I will endeavour to oblige the young gentleman. I arrived without accident, and am now comfortably settled. Lucy Ann Sutton went to Portland in the Accomodation Stage, the day that I left home. Gilman,[2] of Exeter, who was in the stage with her, was highly enraptured with her, and mentioned her to me (before he knew of my relation to her) as one of the prettiest little girls he had ever seen. I tell you this, that you may repeat it to L.A.S. Mr. Dike and J. McKean called on me yesterday afternoon, and found me endeavouring to take a comfortable nap, which I should have preferred to their company. He will give a most glorious account of my diligence. I hope Grandmother, Mother &c are all well   I am in great haste and must conclude

Nath. Hathorne

Write soon

1. John Stephen Dike, not his father, as Julian Hawthorne wrongly surmised (*NHHW*, I, 122).

2. John Taylor Gilman (b. 1806), of Exeter, New Hampshire, was a member of the Bowdoin class of 1826. He later practiced medicine in Portland and became a trustee of Bowdoin College.

Brunswick, July 14th. 1825

My Dear Sister,

I received your letter in due season, and shall not attempt an excuse for not answering it before. I am not very well pleased with Mr. Dike's report of me. The family had before conceived much too high an opinion of my talents, and had probably formed expectations, which I shall never realise. I have thought much upon the subject, and have finally come to the conclusion, that I shall never make a distinguished figure in the world, and all I hope or wish is to plod along with the multitude. I do not say this for the purpose of drawing any flattery from you, but merely to set Mother and the rest of you right, upon a point where your partiality has led you astray. I did hope that Uncle Robert's opinion of me was nearer to the truth, as his deportment toward me never expressed a very high estimation of my abilities.

Mr. Dike has probably discovered before this, that the lead mine which we discovered is nothing more than a vein of *Mica Slate,* a mineral which is very common, and of no value. I received but little pleasure from my visit to Raymond, and do not desire to return there again. Uncle Richard seemed to care nothing about us, and Mrs Manning was as cold and freezing as a December morning.

Did the President write to you about my part? He called me to his Study, and informed me that though my rank in the class entitled me to a part, yet it was contrary to the laws to give me one, on account of my neglect of Declamation. As he enquired Mother's name and residence, I supposed that he intended to write to her upon the subject. If so, you will send me a copy of the letter. I am perfectly satisfied with this arrangement, as it is a sufficient testimonial of my scholarship, while it saves me the mortification of making my appearance in public at commencement. Perhaps the family may not be so well pleased with it. Tell me what are their sentiments upon the subject.

I shall return home in three weeks from next Wednesday, & if I should not write, I wish to have 15 dollars sent me, about a week before that time. You must answer this letter immediately, as I feel very anxious to hear from you all.

I am &c
Nathaniel Hathorne.

Salem August, 11th. 1829

My dear Uncle,

Your letter has been received, and as Uncle Robert is very busy, he wishes me to answer it. He says that there is no news, except that Doctor Robbins, of Boston,[1] has failed for nine hundred thousand dollars. I do not know the man, but I suppose you will. All the family are as well as usual. I have seen Aunt Mary only once or twice, since you left town. She drinks nothing but sweetened water, and never offers me any porter; so that there is not so much inducement to visit the house as when you were here.[2]

I shall have much pleasure in coming to New-Haven, if possible; and I do not at present see any thing to prevent me. Uncle Robert desires me to say, that if I should be unable to leave town, he will come himself. I rather think, however, that I shall not put him to the trouble.

We shall expect to hear from you soon. The family send their love to you &c.

I am, your affectionate Nephew,
Nath: Hawthorne.

Aunt Mary says that you must take care of yourself and not sit with your back to an open window.[3]

1. The Boston *Directory* for 1830 lists a Chandler Robbins, Jr., physician.

2. Robert had built a house next to his own on Dearborn Street, and Mrs. Hathorne and her childen had moved into it at Christmas, 1828. They remained

there until 1832, when they returned to Herbert Street. See Winfield S. Nevins, "The Homes and Haunts of Hawthorne," *New England Magazine*, IX (1893), 291–92.

3. Samuel had gone to New Haven to buy horses for the family's stage company, and to recover from what seems to have been a pulmonary disorder. He had been dangerously ill the previous October, and the condition had persisted into the summer.

[Deerfield, Mass., ca. August 24, 1829][1]

We did not leave New Haven till last Saturday . . . and we were forced to halt for the night at Cheshire, a village about fifteen miles from New Haven. The next day being Sunday, we made a Sabbath day's journey of seventeen miles, and put up at Farmington. As we were wearied with rapid travelling, we found it impossible to attend divine service, which was (of course) very grievous to us both. In the evening, however, I went to a Bible class with a very polite and agreeable gentleman, whom I afterward discovered to be a strolling tailor of very questionable habits. . . . We are now at Deerfield (though I believe my letter is dated Greenfield) . . . with our faces northward; nor shall I marvel much if your Uncle Sam pushes on to Canada, unless we should meet with two or three bad taverns in succession. . . .

I meet with many marvellous adventures. At New Haven I observed a gentleman staring at me with great earnestness, after which he went into the bar-room, I suppose to inquire who I might be. Finally, he came up to me and said that as I bore a striking resemblance to a family of Stanburys, he was induced to inquire if I was connected with them. I was sorry to be obliged to answer in the negative. At another place they took me for a lawyer in search of a place to settle, and strongly recommended their own village. Moreover, I heard some of the students at Yale College conjecturing that I was an Englishman, and to-day, as I was standing without my coat at the door of a tavern, a man came up to me, and asked me for some oats for his horse.

1. The conjectured dating is by association with 47.

Salem, Decr 20th, 1829

Dear Sir,

I am obliged to you for your willingness to aid me in my
affairs, though I perceive that you do not anticipate much
success. Very probably you may be in the right, but I have
nevertheless concluded to trouble you with some of the tales.
These which I send[1] have been completed (except prefixing
the titles) a considerable time. There are two or three others,
not at present in a condition to be sent. If I ever finish them,
I suppose they will be about upon a par with the rest.[2]
You will see that one of the stories is founded upon the
superstitions of this part of the country. I do not know that
such an attempt has hitherto been made; but, as I have
thrown away much time in listening to such traditions, I
could not help trying to put them into some shape. The tale
is certainly rather wild and grotesque, but the outlines of
many not less so might be picked up hereabouts.[3]
Before returning the tales, (for such, I suppose, is the most
probable result) will you have the goodness to write to me,
and await my answer? I have some idea that I shall be out of
town, and it would be inconvenient to have them arrive during my absence.

I am &c,
Nath. Hawthorne.

P.S. None of the pieces are shorter than the one first sent
you.[4] If I write any of the length you mention, I will send

them to you; but I think I shall close my literary labours with
what I have already begun.

1. Goodrich's reply of January 19, 1830, names "The Gentle Boy," "My Uncle
Molineux," "Alice Doane," and "Roger Malvin's Burial" (see *NHHW*, I, 131–
32).

2. Elizabeth Lathrop Chandler proposed that "four other tales, 'Dr. Bullivant,'
'The Gray Champion,' 'Young Goodman Brown,' and 'The May-Pole of Merry
Mount,' published within a few years, were written at this time or before June,
1830, when NH speaks of the 'Provincial Tales' as completed" (*A Study of the
Sources of the Tales and Romances Written by Nathaniel Hawthorne before 1853*
[Northampton: Smith College Studies in Modern Languages, 1926], p. 12).

3. Probably "Alice Doane," published as "Alice Doane's Appeal" in the *Token*
for 1835; it is set in Salem and refers to the witchcraft incidents of 1692.
Goodrich in his January 19 reply wrote: "About 'Alice Doane' I should be more
doubtful as to the public approbation."

4. "Roger Malvin's Burial," according to Goodrich's reply.

Salem, Feb[y] 18th. 1830

Dear John,

I was very glad to receive your letter, but there is so little news of any kind stirring, that I am quite at a loss how to answer it. Everything goes on in the same way as when you were here, except that the times are considerably duller. However, I will do my best to find something to tell you. Your father, as you already know, has removed to Aunt Mary's house, and now occupies the sitting room as a parlour.[2] I often go in to see him and your mother, and find them quite contented and comfortable. I saw Mrs. Dike this evening. She is in very good health, and so is your father, who has been in Boston for the last two or three days, attending the General Court. He appears to be in excellent spirits, and looks younger than when you were here.—Uncle Richard has been very sick, of a complication of disorders. He wrote to Uncle Robert that if he wished to see him alive, he must come down to Raymond immediately.[3] He went, and found him recovering slowly; though still very feeble.—You have a new cousin, a fine little boy, who is named Richard. I have not seen him, but they say he is handsomer than either Maria or Robert.[4] I suppose there will be half a dozen more, before you travel this way again. Maria (Uncle Robert's Maria, I mean) has been staying at Ipswich about two months.—John Treadwell, son of John W. Treadwell of this town,[5] shot himself a short time since, at Cambridge. He was a student there, and was so dissipated that he had been sent away once or twice. He borrowed a pair of pistols of another student,

and requested him to load them well, saying that he had been
attacked by a man in the night. He was found dead, in the
dusk of the evening, about three miles from the colleges on
the road to Boston. He had been very unsteady for about a
fortnight previous. The newspaper tells us that he was subject to fits of mental derangement.—There is to be a great
ball in town, the evening of Washington's Birth-Day. You
know my habits too well to suppose that I shall be there. The
theatre was opened in the first of the season, but has been
closed several weeks for want of encouragement. A Lyceum
is shortly to be established here, and they could not apply the
theatre to a better purpose than to deliver lectures there.[6]—
It is said that a son of Dr. Warren, of Boston, killed a man
last night. He was in company with several persons, and
behaved so improperly that they turned him out of the room.
He came back, and was again turned out. He then went to
his lodgings and returned with a dirk, with which he stabbed
one of the gentlemen. I do not know whether he is in cus-
tody, but if the story is correct, he certainly deserves death,
and will very probably be brought to the gallows.[7] He is said
to be a person of dissipated habits. You must not mention
this story on my authority, as it is only a report, and has not
yet appeared in the newspapers.—Perhaps you will like to
hear of some new engagements. Miss Mary Hodges to Vin-
cent Brown, a commission merchant in Boston. Nathan Rob-
inson to Miss Hannah Ropes, an old maid. Miss Betsey Varney to Mr. Jonathan Perkins.[8] Aunt Mary does not think of
getting married at present. Louisa has told me of these engagements, and it is all the intelligence I am able to get out
of her. She has been staying at Newburyport several weeks,
and returned a few days since.—Mr. Paddison, the Baptist
Minister in this town, has requested a dismission from his
people, and desired them not to ask his reasons till the day of
judgement. His reasons may be easily guessed without asking; for he has received a louder call in Providence. His salary

here is but eight hundred dollars, and they offer him fifteen hundred there.[9]—I saw some of your letters describing your journey, and was much interested with them. I should like to travel the same route, but I believe that I shall be detained here some time longer.—Theodore Morgan Jr.[10] got married very suddenly (perhaps you knew it before) and has sailed for Rio Grande with his wife. Nath[l] Carlile has arrived at Bahia with his wife, who was sick the whole passage, and arrived almost dead.[11]—I have now told you all the news I can collect, and I hope you will be able to read it. My pen is bad, and I write in a great hurry.—I intend to send you some newspapers with this. I understood that Nathan Pierce[12] was to send you a good many of them from the News-Room.—I hope you will write often, as I shall always be glad to hear from you.

Your affectionate cousin,
Nath: Hawthorne

1. Following the failure of his father's dry goods business in 1829, John Stephen Dike moved to Steubenville, Ohio, where an uncle had settled in 1816, and he soon became partner in a general store. See Edward B. Hungerford, "Hawthorne Gossips about Salem," *NEQ*, VI (1933), 445-69, to which many annotations of letters 50, 52, and 54 are indebted.

2. The elder John Dike's house and land on Pickman Street had been offered for sale by the Commercial Bank, his creditor, and were sold at auction on March 31.

3. See 52.3.

4. Richard (1830–1904), Maria (1826–1917), and Robert (1827–1902) were children of NH's Uncle Robert. A second daughter, Rebecca, was to be born in 1834, and to live until 1933.

5. The elder Treadwell was a banker, a director of two local insurance companies and of the Salem Laboratory Company. His eighteen-year-old son was a student at Harvard.

6. The first meeting of the Salem Lyceum took place February 24 at the Methodist Chapel, Sewall Street.

7. The victim was not seriously wounded, and according to the newspapers was well recovered a week later.

8. Miss Hodges and Brown were married July 26, 1831; Hannah Ropes (1791–1862) died unmarried; Miss Varney's engagement with Perkins was apparently broken, for both later married other persons.

9. Robert Everett Pattison was to become pastor of the First Baptist Church of Providence, Rhode Island.

10. Morgan (b. 1807), was Dike's relative; his mother, Abigail Manning Morgan, was Mrs. Dike's first cousin.

11. Mehitabel B. Carlile survived to give birth to three children in Brazil.

12. Secretary of the Oriental Insurance Company in Salem.

51. TO S. G. GOODRICH, BOSTON

Salem May 6, 1830

Dear Sir,

I send you the two pieces for The Token.[1] They were
ready some days ago, but I kept them in Expectation of hearing from you. I have complied with your wishes in regard to
brevity. You can insert them (if you think them worthy a
place in your publication) as by The Author of Provincial
Tales,[2] such being the title I propose for my volume.
I can conceive no objection to your designating them in this
manner, even if my Tales should not be published so soon as
The Token—or indeed if they never see the light at all.
An unpublished book is not more obscure than many that
creep into the world, and your readers will suppose that the
Provincial Tales are among the latter.

I am &c,
Nath Hawthorne

S. G. Goodrich Esq.

1. The *Token*'s literary contents were assembled by Goodrich in the spring of
each year, illustrations were ordered, and printing was done in the autumn. The
volume referred to here (published by Gray & Bowen), is that edited in 1830 to
be ready for sale at Christmas and New Year's as the *Token* for 1831. "Sights
from a Steeple" was printed, pp. 41–51, without attribution; it was included by
NH in *TTT*, 1837. His second piece is generally agreed (in spite of its lack of
brevity) to be "The Haunted Quack. A Tale of a Canal Boat. By Joseph Nichol-
son," pp. 117–37, never collected by NH.

2. For speculation on this volume's proposed contents, see *TTT*, "Historical
Commentary," pp. 489–91, and Richard P. Adams, "Hawthorne's Provincial
Tales," *NEQ*, XXX (1957), 39–57.

52. TO J. S. DIKE, STEUBENVILLE, OHIO

Salem, Septr 1st. 1830.

Dear John,

I thought it best not to answer your letter till after the trial of the Knapps, and I have since been prevented from writing by various causes. But first of all, I must congratulate you on your engagement.[1] I was heartily glad to hear of it, and was not very much surprised; for you may remember that we sometimes talked of the probability of such an event, when you were about leaving Salem. I have never seen your father more delighted, or more proud of his son, than he was on this occasion. You ask my advice respecting a young man's entering into matrimony, and I shall favour you with it, though I have not much experience in that holy state. With such fair prospects of competence and ultimate wealth as you possess, I do not see any wisdom in deferring your marriage longer than till the publishment is out (if folks are published in Ohio)—or at least, I would not wait a moment longer than may be necessary to satisfy the scruples of the lady. Courtship is said to be very pleasant business, but actual happiness is certainly far preferable to anxiety and expectation; and if I were in your situation, I should bring matters to a conclusion as speedily as I could, for fear of some undesirable accident. Besides, it is a good thing to be married young, before you or your bride have contracted any stubborn habits. I have heard it remarked that the marriages which take place before twenty five years of age generally turn out the best, because then the minds and dispositions of the husband and wife are more flexible, and they are able to form themselves according to each other's tastes and wishes. So I advise you to get married before cold weather comes on; and I should expect to be groomsman, if I were within any reasonable distance of you.

The town now begins to grow rather more quiet than it has been since the murder of Mr. White, but I suppose the excitement will revive at the execution of Frank Knapp, and at the next November term of the Court.[2] Frank Knapp's situation seems to make little or no impression on his mind. The night after his sentence, he joked and laughed with the men who watched him, with as much apparent gaiety as if he had been acquitted, instead of condemned. He says, however, that he would rather be hung than remain a year in prison. It is reported, also, that he declares that he will not go to the gallows, unless two women go with him. Who these women are, must be left to conjecture. Perhaps you have not heard that many people suspect Mrs. Bickford and her daughter, Joe Knapp's wife, of being privy to the whole affair before the murder was committed. I cannot say whether there are good grounds for these suspicions; but I know that it was daily expected, during the trial, that one or both of them would be arrested; and it is said that they were actually examined at the house of Mr. Brown the jailer. It is certain that Joseph Knapp's wife has twice attempted to hang herself. The first time was soon after her husband's arrest, and the second immediately after Frank was found guilty. Old Captain Knapp also made a similar attempt, a little while ago, and was cut down by his son Phippen. The poor old man is entirely broken in his mind and almost crazy; and it is no wonder that he should be so, when all sorts of trouble have come upon him at once. He and his son Phippen have injured their reputation for truth, by the testimony they gave at the trial; but I have little doubt that they believed what they said; and if not, they had as much excuse as there can possibly be for perjury. There seems to be an universal prejudice at

present against the whole family;—I am afraid Captain
Knapp himself meets with but little real pity, and I believe
every body is eager for the death of his two sons. For my part,
I wish Joe to be punished, but I should not be very sorry if
Frank were to escape. It is the general opinion, however,
that Joe will not live to be brought to trial. He contrives to
obtain spirituous liquors in his cell, and is in a state of intox-
ication almost all the time. He is utterly desperate, and will
not even wash and dress himself, and at one time he made a
resolution to starve himself to death. I do not wonder that he
feels unpleasantly, for he can have no hope of mercy, and it
is absolutely certain that he will not be alive at the end of six
months from this time.

Aunt Mary is at present in Raymond. We received a letter
from her, about a week ago, informing us that Uncle Richard
was in a very low state, and not expected to survive more
than two or three days.[3] Yesterday we had another letter, to
tell us the physicians did not apprehend any immediate danger, though he still keeps his bed, and continues very weak
and low. His constitution is so thoroughly broken that there
cannot be a rational hope of his ever regaining a comfortable
degree of health. Immediately on receiving the first letter,
your mother wrote to Mr. Ellingwood,[4] requesting him to go
to Raymond himself, or if that was impossible, to send some
other clergyman of his acquaintance. Aunt Mary does not say
anything about his arrival, though she mentions that several
ministers had been there.

Uncle Sam has been a journey this summer, and has returned in good health and spirits. Uncle Robert met with a
great misfortune the other day, by a strong easterly gale,
which shook down almost all the fruit in his garden, broke
the branches of the trees, and did an infinite deal of mischief.
He gave away whole wheelbarrow loads of unripe peaches.
You may judge that he did not bear this visitation very patiently, and his affliction was so much the more violent be-

cause he had scarcely any fruit last year, and the present season had been very promising till the time of this terrible accident. He has lately become a distinguished writer on horticultural subjects, in the New-England Farmer,[5] and he employs me to correct his contributions and to form them into pretty sentences. The Agricultural Society of this county have requested a long communication from him, to be read at their next anniversary, and afterwards to be published.[6] I believe he means to send them one.

I heard your father's voice down stairs, while I was writing the above. He is very well himself, and your mother enjoys as good health as usual; but they are both very apprehensive about you. It is two or three months since they have heard from you, and they think that nothing but sickness, or something worse, could induce you to delay writing so long.

The name of Theodore Morgan's wife was Sophia Frink. They arrived safely in South America. Nath. Carlile's wife has already been blest with a daughter, whom she calls Laura Prince Deland. Louisa says that the murder has put a stop to all engagements. She is very anxious to become acquainted with Miss Margueretta.—Do I spell the name right?—I should find a good deal more news to tell you, if I had room.

Your affectionate Cousin,
Nath: Hawthorne.

Write as often as you have leisure.

---

1. John was to marry Margaretta Woods, of Steubenville, originally of Bedford Springs, Pennsylvania.

2. On April 7, 1830, Captain Joseph White (b. 1747), a wealthy retired merchant, was brutally killed in his house. His money, however, was not taken. Rewards for information were offered, and public excitement was considerable. Eventually two brothers of good family, John Francis and Joseph Jenkins Knapp,

and a local criminal, Richard Crowninshield, were arrested; for their trial Daniel Webster was brought in as prosecuting attorney. The fact emerged that Joe Knapp had offered Crowninshield $1,000 to kill White. Knapp was married to Mary W. Beckford, whose mother was a niece of Captain White and had lived in his family as a housekeeper, and Knapp had burned White's will, believing that then Mrs. Beckford would inherit half of White's fortune. Frank Knapp was presumably present when the murder was committed, although his father and his brother Nathaniel Phippen tried to protect him by testifying that he had been at home at that time. Crowninshield hanged himself in jail on June 15 after Joe Knapp confessed to planning the crime. Frank Knapp was executed on September 28, and Joe, on December 31. See AN, p. 279.

3. Richard had suffered a ruptured bladder in January. Mary went to help in his household in Raymond in July and remained until his death in March 1831.

4. The Reverend John Wallace Ellingwood (1782–1860), of Bath, Maine, was the husband of the elder John Dike's sister Nancy.

5. An article by Robert Manning, "The Origin of the Bartlett Pear," had appeared in this journal, July 2.

6. NH's reference seems to be a mistake: the Massachusetts Horticultural Society, of which Manning was one of the founders, was to hold its second anniversary in Boston on September 10. There was no county society.

Canterbury (N.H.) August 17th. 1831

Dear Sister,

It is not much matter whether you are informed of our motions, but I have no better way of spending this lazy afternoon in a country tavern than in writing to you. Your Uncle Sam and I reached Concord[1] at noon of the second day, and before evening we both got into the State's Prison, and had the iron door of a cell barred upon us. However, you need say nothing about it, as we made our escape very speedily. One of Uncle Sam's old acquaintances keeps the tavern at Concord, so that it was like the seperation of soul and body to get him away. Moreover, he was surrounded by a whole troop of horse-dealers, who all seem to know him by instinct. He has already sent home two black mares and bought a gray one to drive tandem, and I should not wonder if we were to gallop into town, he at the head and I at the tail of a whole drove. The next day we set out for this place, which is about fourteen miles from Concord, meaning to inspect the Shaker village[2] in our way. Howbeit, your Uncle Sam kept on straight ahead, looking neither to the right nor left no more than if he had worn the horse's blinders, till we reached the tavern about two miles further on, where we now are.[3] The Shakers would have given us supper and lodging and have kept us over Sunday, and I was more anxious to stay than I have been about anything in the course of the ride. In the village we met some old acquaintances of yours, Jacob Stone and his wife and sister.[4] I bowed to him and Lois, but neither of them recognized me. The next morning I rode to the meeting with our Landlord and his daughter. I took a back seat at first, but a grave old Shaker soon came and marshalled me to a place of honour in the very front row, so that I had a perfect view of the whole business. There were thirty or forty Shaker ladies, some of them quite pretty, all dressed in very light gowns, with a muslin handkerchief crossed over the bosom and a stiff muslin cap, so that they looked pretty much as if they had just stept out of their coffins. There was nothing very remarkable in the men except their stupidity, and it did look queer to see these great boobies cutting all sorts of ridiculous capers with the gravest countenances imaginable. I was most tickled to see a man in a common frock coat and pantaloons between two little boys, and a very fat old lady in a black silk gown, rolling along in a stream of sweat between two young girls, and making ten thousand mistakes in the ceremonies. There were an Englishwoman and her son, recent proselytes, and not admitted to full communion. Every man and woman (except a few who sang) passed within a few inches of me in the course of the dance. Most of the females were above thirty, and the white muslin was very trying to all their complexions. There were two or three hundred or more of spectators present, and Jacob Stone and his womankind among them, they having spent the night in a Shaker house. I shook hands with him after the meeting was dismissed, spoke to Lois, and was introduced to Mrs. Stone. She is a remarkably plain woman, and I should suppose considerably older than her husband. They were to return to Concord that afternoon, and to Newburyport in due season. Your Uncle Sam took a great liking to our tavern, which is indeed an excellent one, so that he could hardly tear himself away after dinner, and the whole family assembled at the door when we rode off, as if we had been the oldest friends in the world. We reached Guilford, nine miles distant, that night. The next morning, the news of your Uncle Sam's arrival spread all over the country, and every man that had a horse mounted him and came galloping to the tavern door, hoping to make a trade or a swap; so that they fairly hunted us out of town, and we took refuge in the same tavern we had left the day before. Your Uncle Sam complains that his lungs are seriously injured by the immense deal of talking he was forced to do. I walked to the Shaker village yesterday, and was shown over the establishment, and dined there with a Squire and a doctor, also of the 'world's people.'[5] On my arrival, the first thing I saw was a jolly old shaker carrying an immense decanter, full of their superb cider, and as soon as I told my business, he turned out a tumbler full and gave me. It was as much as a common head could cleverly carry. Our dining room was well furnished, the dinner excellent, and the table was attended by a middle aged shaker lady, good-looking and cheerful, and not to be distinguished either in manners or conversation from other well-educated women in the country. This establishment is immensely rich. Their land extends two or three miles along the road, and there are streets of great houses, painted yellow and topt with red; they are now building a brick edifice for their public business, to cost seven or eight thousand dollars. On the whole, they lead a good and comfortable life, and if it were not for their ridiculous ceremonies, a man could not do a wiser thing than to join them. Those whom I conversed with were intelligent, and appeared happy. I spoke to them about becoming a member of the Society, but have come to no decision on that point.[6]

We have had a pleasant journey enough. The greatest difficulty has been a large bunch on the horse's back, which gives your Uncle Sam as much pain as if it was on his own. However, one of his persecutors came out from Guilford this morning and has sold him a gray mare which will ease the labour of the other. The people here are as different as possible from the sulky ruffians in Maine. I make innumerable acquaintances, and sit down, on the doorsteps in the midst ` of Squires, judges, generals, and all the potentates of the land, discoursing about the Salem Murder,[7] the cowskinning of Isaac Hill,[8] the price of hay, and the value of horseflesh. The country is very uneven and your Uncle Sam groans bitterly whenever we come to the foot of a long hill, though this ought to make me groan more than him, as I have to get out and trudge up every one of them. Your Uncle Sam begins to exhibit some symptoms of homesickness, and I am greatly mistaken if we see Canada this trip, or even get a mile nearer to it than we are at this moment. Mrs. Hill, our landlady, nurses him up, and feeds us both till we are ready to burst; but you need not be surprised if you see our tandem turning down the lane[9] on Tuesday, Wednesday, or Thursday at farthest.

This is not intended for a public letter, though it is truly a pity that the public should lose it. When John Steven's[10] epistles are published, this shall be inserted in the Appendix.

Nath: Hawthorne.

1. Concord, N.H.

2. The large and prosperous community eight miles from Canterbury had been organized in 1782. NH's tale "The Canterbury Pilgrims," in the 1833 *Token*, was inspired by this visit.

3. Hill's Tavern, Dudley Hill the landlord.

4. Jacob Stone, Jr. (1808–75), of Newburyport, was a bank official, lecturer, and writer. He had recently married Eliza Atkins, of Boston. Lois Stone (b. 1808), his sister, was a friend of Louisa.

5. Non-members of the community.

6. However playfully this statement is meant, NH's less favorable attitude toward the Shakers in the "Canterbury Pilgrims" and, especially, in "The Shaker Bridal" (published in the 1838 *Token* and the *TTT*, 1842) may be explained by his reading of Thomas Brown's *An Account of the People Called Shakers* (1812), which he borrowed from the Salem Athenaeum on August 27. See Seymour Gross, "Hawthorne and the Shakers," *AL*, XXIX (1958), 457–63. But compare also NH's "wayward fantasy" of return to Canterbury in "Monsieur du Miroir" (1837; *MOM*, p.165).

7. The murder of Captain White. See 52.2.

8. Hill (1789–1851) had been editor of the Concord, N.H., *Patriot* for twenty years, and was a leading supporter of President Jackson in the state. Timothy Upham, Whig candidate for governor, charged Hill with publishing forged documents, and with slander. Unable to obtain justice because of prejudiced courts and jurors, Upham publicly flogged ("cowskinned") Hill.

9. I.e., Dearborn Street, in the northern part of Salem, where the Hawthornes were now living.

10. John Stephen Dike.

Salem, September 9th. 1831.

Dear John,

I have been rather a negligent correspondent, but you must excuse me, as my time has been occupied with other affairs. I have had a good deal of writing to do on account of grand-mother's estate,[1] and have also been a journey into New Hampshire, besides various other engagements too numerous to mention. There is but little news at present. Perhaps you have not heard that your father has been for some time in a state of religious solicitude, and is now considered a hopeful convert. Messrs. Whipple & Lawrence[2] have also been under serious[3] impressions, but I believe the former has not attained a hope. There is now considerable religious excitement throughout this part of the country, owing to the great number of four-day meetings which have been held by the Calvinists, Baptists, Methodists &c. A clergyman from the south met with a sad accident, not long ago. He had been to Nahant, and had the misfortune to drink a little too much wine, and in returning through Marblehead, he overturned the chaise and broke some of his limbs. He was brought to Salem, and afterwards carried to Andover. Mr. Cleaveland, your minister,[4] would not at first believe this story, and went to Marblehead to investigate it; but he found sufficient evidence of the truth. I suppose it is no very uncommon thing for ministers to get drunk, at the southward. How do they behave in your part of the country? Mr. Cleaveland's wife[5] has brought herself into a great deal of trouble, and may possibly have to appear in open court and take her trial for a libel. She circulated a report among her acquaintances that William Ives,[6] one of the publishers of the Observer, had drank a blasphemous toast, to the health of the Holy Ghost. Mr. Ives is a member of Mr. Brazer's[7] church, and one of the steadiest men in town, and very religious in his own way. He traced this story up to Mrs. Cleaveland, who cannot give her authority for it. I believe he has concluded not to prosecute her, though he could undoubtedly recover damages. He attacked her in his newspaper, a week or two ago.[8] The trial of a minister's wife for slander would have caused nearly as great an excitement as the trial of the Knapps. The talk about Captain White's murder has almost entirely ceased. George Crowninshield[9] still lives at his father's, and seems not at all cast down by what has taken place. I saw him walk by our house, arm-in-arm with a girl, about a month since. Richard Stearns, who ran away with his brother's wife, has returned to Salem, and a reconciliation has taken place on all sides. The lady with whom he eloped left him at New-York, and took passage for Liverpool with an English gentleman. I suppose her husband thinks it a good riddance. Richard now lives with his own wife, but does not often make his appearance in public. Mrs. Knapp, Joseph Knapp's widow, is said to be engaged to a lawyer in Boston. She lives at Wenham with her mother, who is believed by every body to have had a hand in the murder. I cannot recollect any more news, and you must be careful how you report the above, for fear of bringing me into as great a difficulty as Mrs. Cleaveland's.

I suppose you have heard that Uncle Robert was brought very low by inflammation of the lungs, last spring. His health is now much improved, but not entirely re-established, and it is not probable that he will ever be so strong as he has been. He has not been able to pay much attention to his garden this summer, and it is now in very bad order, compared to what it was when you were here. Uncle Sam was also taken with bleeding at the lungs, while Uncle Robert was on the recovery, though his complaint was not quite so severe. He has been pretty comfortable of late, and is now gone on a journey. Aunt Mary returned from Raymond in April, not long after Uncle Richard's death. She boarded with us till within a week, but has now gone back to her own house,[10] where she occupies three or four chambers, and lets the rest to Mr. Winchester.[11] Mr. William Manning has hired old Nat. West's[12] house in Essex street, and I believe he means to open a tavern there.[13] You must recommend his establishment to any of your western friends, who may be travelling to this part of the country. I have not seen your father or mother since I returned from New-Hampshire. I met the former in the street, not long before I left Salem. He appeared well in health, but more serious than usual. I suppose your mind is so much engrossed by other feelings that you have no time to become religious. This may not be the case, however, as the unbelieving husband is sometimes brought over to the faith by the believing wife.

What is the reason that you say nothing about your engagement, in your last two letters? It is the most interesting subject which you could possibly write upon. I presume your marriage will take place very shortly, if it has not taken place already. If it were my case, I should feel very strangely, the moment after the knot was tied. I have some idea of joining the Shakers, as I had an opportunity of inspecting one of their villages, during my journey, and was much pleased with their manner of life. However, there will be time enough for that after I have tried how I can content myself in the married state.

I believe that your father and mother expect that you, and Mrs. J. S. Dike, whom we are all very impatient to see, will arrive in Salem very speedily. I know I shall laugh when I first meet you, and I beseech you to pardon me for it beforehand; for it seems very queer that you, who were little more than a lad when you departed, should so soon return transformed into a grave married man.

I do not know how to fill the remainder of the page, and am besides in a great hurry; so I remain,

Your affectionate cousin,
Nath. Hawthorne.

1. Miriam Lord Manning had died in 1826. The death of her eldest son, Richard, in March 1831, had made necessary the settling of her husband's and her own estates.

2. Henry Whipple (1789–1869) and Abel Lawrence, Jr. (b. 1786), were partners dealing in books, nautical charts, and stationery. Whipple was described by a contemporary as a "consistent supporter" of his "religious persuasion." See *EIHC*, XI (1872), 68.

3. Earnest about the things of religion: religious (*OED*).

4. John Payne Cleaveland (1799–1873) was pastor of the Congregational Tabernacle, Salem, 1827–34.

5. Susan Heard Dole Cleaveland (b. 1800).

6. (1794–1875), publisher of the Salem *Observer* with his brother Stephen, from 1823 to 1839. He was known as a strong proponent of temperance.

7. John Brazer (1789–1846), pastor of the North Church (Congregational), Salem, 1820–46.

8. Salem *Observer*, September 3, 1831, 2:3–4: "The Advantages of Slander."

9. A brother of Richard, who murdered Captain White; see 52.2. George was arrested for the murder but was acquitted. He was a nephew of John Crowninshield, husband of NH's aunt Sarah Hathorne.

10. The house on Herbert Street. See 47.2.

11. Possibly Jacob B. Winchester, a shipowner.

12. Nathaniel West (1756–1851), a shipmaster and merchant, grandfather of the sculptor Louisa Lander (see *FIN*, pp. 77, 740–42).

13. No record has been found that William ever operated a tavern.

Salem, Novr 4th. 1831

Dear L.

I send Susannah's[1] Gibraltars.[2] There were fourteen of them originally, but I doubt whether there will be quite a dozen when she gets them.—Susannah knows well enough that she was the debtor, instead of the creditor, in this business, and if she has any sort of conscience, she will send me back some sugar-plums.

I also send the bag of coins. I believe there is a silver three-pence among them, which you must take out and bring home, as I cannot put myself to the trouble of looking for it at present. It was a gift to me from the loveliest lady in the land, and it would break my heart to part with it.

I don't understand the hint about the smelling-bottle. I have made all possible enquiries, but neither mother nor Elizabeth recollect to have seen such a thing. I never make use of a smelling-bottle myself, and of course could have no motive for keeping it. I will speak to the town-crier tomorrow.

Mrs Ede's[3] wedding-cake will be very acceptable, and I wish she had brought it with her when she went through town. I am afraid there is little prospect of my repaying her in kind, but when I join the Shakers, I will send her a great slice of rye-and-indian bread.

Nath. Hawthorne.

P.S. You can't imagine how quiet and comfortable our house has been, since you went away.

1. Probably Susan Maria Lund (b. 1811), a distant cousin who lived in Newburyport.

2. Lemon flavored, rock-hard crystal candies, said to have been first made in Salem in 1826. NH thought in 1848–49 of writing a children's story about their manufacture; see *AN*, p. 284. See also *HSG*, pp. 35–36.

3. Lois Stone (53.4) had married the Reverend E. H. Edes, November 1, in Newburyport.

Salem (Mass.) Janu^y 27th. 1832

Gentlemen,

I am the author of some tales (My Kinsman Major Moli-
neaux, Roger Malvin's Burial, & the Gentle Boy) published
in the Token for the present year. I do not know whether
they attracted your notice; but the object of this letter is to
inquire whether you would choose to insert an article from
me in the next Souvenir?[1]—and if so, what number of
pages?—and whether there is any mode of transmitting the
manuscript to Philadelphia, except by mail?
I should not wish to be mentioned as the author of those
tales.

Very Respectfully
Nath. Hawthorne.

Messrs. Carey & Lea.

1. Henry C. Carey and Isaac Lea had published the first American giftbook
annual, the *Atlantic Souvenir* of 1826. The final volume, for 1832, had just
appeared; Samuel Goodrich was to buy the title and absorb it into the 1833 *Token
and Atlantic Souvenir,* published by Gray and Bowen, Boston. A cover note in an
unknown hand records, "Rec^d Feb 1st Ans^d Feb 2," but the reply is not known
to have survived.

Salem, June 28th. 1832.

Dear Mr. Speaker,

I sincerely congratulate you on all your public honours, in possession or in prospect.[2] If they continue to accumulate so rapidly, you will be at the summit of political eminence, by that time of life when men are usually just beginning to make a figure. I suppose there is hardly a limit to your expectations, at this moment; and I really cannot see why there should be any. If I were in your place, I should like to proceed by the following steps,—after a few years in Congress, to be chosen Governor, say at thirty years old,—next a Senator to Congress,—then minister to England,—then to be put at the head of one of the Departments (that of War would suit you, I should think)—and lastly—but it will be time enough to think of the next step, some years hence.[3] You cannot imagine how proud I feel, when I recollect that I myself was once in office with you, on the standing committee of the Athenaean Society.[4] That was my first and last appearance in public life.

I read the paper which you sent me from beginning to end, not forgetting Col. Pierce's neat and appropriate address.[5] I also perused John P. Hale's[6] speech in favour of grog-shops; he seems to have taken quite a characteristic and consistent course in this respect, and I presume he gives the retail dealers as much of his personal patronage as ever. I was rather surprised at not finding more of my acquaintances in your Legislature. Your own name and John P's were all that I recognized.

I was making preparations for a northern tour, when this accursed Cholera broke out in Canada.[7] It was my intention to go by way of New-York and Albany to Niagara, from thence to Montreal and Quebec, and home through Vermont and New-Hampshire. I am very desirous of making this journey on account of a book by which I intend to acquire an (undoubtedly) immense literary reputation, but which I cannot commence writing till I have visited Canada.[8] I still hope that the pestilence will disappear, so that it may be safe to go in a month or two. If my route brings me into the vicinity of Hillsboro', I shall certainly visit you. As to the Cholera, if it comes, I believe I shall face it here. By the by, I have been afflicted for two days past with one of the symptoms of it (viz. a diarrhoea) which has weakened me considerably, and makes me write rather a tremulous hand. I keep it secret, however, for fear of being sent to the Hospital.[9]

I suppose your election to Congress is absolutely certain. Of course, however, there will be an opposition, and I wish you would send me some of the newspapers containing articles either laudatory or abusive of you. I shall read them with great interest, be they what they may. It is a pity that I am not in a situation to exercise my pen in your behalf; though you seem not to need the assistance of newspaper scribblers.

I do not feel very well, and will close my letter here, especially as your many avocations would not permit you to read a longer one. I shall be happy to hear from you, as often as you can find leisure and inclination to write.

> Your friend
> Nath. Hawthorne,
> alias
> "Hath."

I observe that the paper styles you the "Hon. Franklin Pierce." Have you already an *official* claim to that title?

1. Pierce, NH's friend at Bowdoin, was now speaker of the New Hampshire legislature and, as the second paragraph indicates, an honorary colonel: he was the military aide of Governor Dinsmoor.

2. Pierce was elected to the U.S. Congress in March, 1833, on the Democratic ticket.

3. This prediction was realized, for Pierce became the fourteenth president of the United States in 1853, after being a senator. He did not hold the other offices mentioned.

4. Pierce was the committee chairman. See 38.2.

5. The *New Hampshire Patriot* of Concord had printed Pierce's acceptance speech after his reelection—by a vote of 205 against 3—as speaker in 1832.

6. Hale (1806–73), of Dover, N.H., another Bowdoin friend of NH, was a state legislator who was to be Pierce's opponent for the presidency in 1852, running for the Free Soil party.

7. The first recorded outbreak of Asiatic cholera in North America began in Montreal on June 6, spreading into New York state by June 14. The towns along the Erie Canal were especially affected. New York City suffered thousands of deaths before the disease subsided in late August. There was to be no epidemic in Boston or Salem. See Charles E. Rosenberg, *The Cholera Years: The United States in 1832, 1849, and 1866* (Chicago: University of Chicago Press, 1962), chapter 1.

8. The book was to be called "The Story Teller," its episodes being connected by the narration of a traveling storyteller. See Nelson F. Adkins, "The Early Projected Works of Nathaniel Hawthorne," *PBSA*, XXXIX (1945), 131–46; *Die Entwicklung*, pp. 145–63. The importance of the journey to Canada is not clear. See 58.2, and NH to W. D. Ticknor, June 7, 1854, and to Elizabeth Peabody, August 13, 1857 (MSS, Berg).

9. Earlier in June, President Jackson had publicly refused to declare a national fast day, in spite of the popular belief that epidemics were a punishment for sin. See Rosenberg, pp. 47–53. The onset of cholera is marked by diarrhea, acute spasmodic vomiting and abdominal cramps.

Burlington (Vt.) September 16th 1832

Dear Mother

I have arrived in health and safety at this place, and have so much to do and to see, that I cannot find time to tell you all my adventures. I passed through the White Hills and stayed two nights and part of three days in Ethan Crawford's house.[1] Moreover, I mounted what the people called a "plaguey high-lifed crittur" and rode with four gentlemen and a guide six miles to the foot of Mt. Washington. It was but four °clock A.M. when we started, and a showery morning, and we had to ride through the very worst road that ever was seen, mud and mire, and several rivers to be forded, and trees to be jumped over (fallen trees, I mean) through all which I galloped and trotted and tript and stumbled, and arrived without breaking my neck at last. The other particulars, how I climbed three miles into the air, and how it snowed all the way, and how, when I got up the mountain on one side, the wind carried me a great distance off my feet and almost blew me down the other, and how the thermometer stood at twelve degrees below the freezing point, I shall have time enough to tell you when I return.

I do not know exactly the course which I shall take from here.[2] I might be in Canada tomorrow if I thought proper, but I have no sort of intention of going there. I see that there have been five new cases of the Cholera in Boston,[3] and shall be impatient for further intelligence, which is very slow in getting to this part of the world.

Your affectionate Son
Nath. Hawthorne.

1. The Notch House, a hotel built in 1828 by Abel Crawford and his son Ethan Allen Crawford. Two of NH's "Sketches from Memory," "The Notch of the White Mountains" and "Our Evening Party among the Mountains," in the *New-England Magazine,* November, 1835, and collected in *MOM,* were inspired by this visit. In "The Story Teller" (see 57.7), the second of these was to introduce "The Great Carbuncle." Three miles from the hotel was the Willey House, where in August, 1826, the family was swept to death by an avalanche, an event that was to be the basis of "The Ambitious Guest," in the *New-England Magazine,* June, 1835, collected in the 1842 *TTT.* See B. Bernard Cohen, "The Sources of Hawthorne's 'The Ambitious Guest'," *BPLQ,* IV (1952), 221–24; Kenneth W. Cameron, "The Genesis of Hawthorne's 'The Ambitious Guest'," *Historiographer of the Episcopal Diocese of Connecticut,* XIV (1955), 2–36; John F. Sears, "Hawthorne's 'The Ambitious Guest' and the Significance of the Willey Disaster," *AL,* LIV (1982), 354–67.

2. There is no definite information about NH's itinerary, but it is known by a tourist's certification in the Pearson Collection, Yale, that he visited Niagara Falls on September 28. Other sketches likely derived from the journey were published in the *New-England* and *American Monthly* magazines in 1835–36: "The Canal-Boat" (collected in "Sketches from Memory," *MOM*), "Old Ticonderoga," "My Visit to Niagara," "The Inland Port," "Rochester," and "A Night Scene"—all in *SI.* An attributed sketch, "An Ontario Steamboat," appeared in the March, 1836, *American Magazine,* edited by NH.

3. Five deaths from cholera occurred September 10–11, apparently the first in Boston, the *Transcript* reported (September 12, 2:1). A few more deaths were reported in the next few weeks, but no general outbreak.

Boston, Janʸ 21, 1836.

Dear L.

I am so busy with agents, clerks, engravers, stereotype printers, devils—and the devil knows what all—that I have not much time to write.[1] I board at Thos. G. Fessenden's[2] (Editor of the Farmer) N° 53 Hancock St,[3] and am pleasantly situated. I mean to come down in a week or two if I can; for I had liever see one or other of you, once in a while, as not. If Ebe has concocted anything, let her send it.[4] I wish her to make extracts of whatever she thinks suitable; for I have merely the liberty of reading at the Atheneum, and am not allowed to take out books—so that I have but a narrow range of works to extract from.[5] I shall send my clothes soon; and when you return them, send my old coat. I can't write well without it—also my thermometer.[6]

Nath Hawthorne.

I was invited to a literary party last night; but did not go. It is holden weekly by two blue-stockings.[7] I shall go by and by. I want, among a thousand other things, some more handkerchiefs, and a cravat. If any letters have arrived send them; it will be as well to send by the stage, rather than mail.

1. After negotiations with George P. Morris, of the *New-York Mirror*, and Francis Preston Blair, of the Washington *Globe* (see *NHHW*, I, 133–35), NH

had taken the position of editor of the *American Magazine of Useful and Entertaining Knowledge*, published by the Bewick Company of Boston, which emphasized engraved illustrations accompanied by reprinted excerpts or explanation supplied by the editor. NH edited six issues, March–August, 1836.

2. Thomas Green Fessenden (1771–1837), a journalist and poet, had edited the *New England Farmer* (see 52.5) since 1822. NH wrote a notice of a new edition of Fessenden's poems in the *American Magazine*, June, 1836 (Turner, pp. 216–21); after his death in November, 1837, NH published a biographical sketch of Fessenden in Park Benjamin's *American Monthly*, January, 1838.

3. On Beacon Hill behind the Statehouse, between Mount Vernon and Cambridge streets.

4. Elizabeth Hawthorne assisted NH in preparing material for the magazine.

5. Elizabeth was free to borrow books from the Salem Athenaeum on NH's membership, but he was not accorded the same privilege at the Boston Athenaeum on Pearl Street by his employers. See Kesselring, p.7.

6. NH's personal effects were transported between Salem and Boston in a valise (see 61, 69, 70, 71) by the Manning stage line.

7. Probably Mary Elizabeth (1813–74) and Susan Margaret (1815–96), sisters of Park Benjamin, editor and proprietor of the *New-England Magazine*, to which NH had been a frequent contributor since November, 1834. The Benjamin home at 14 Temple Place "was famous as a social center for the younger literary circle of Boston and Cambridge"; among the guests were Charles Sumner, Oliver Wendell Holmes, and John Lothrop Motley, who was to marry Mary Benjamin in 1837. See Merle M. Hoover, *Park Benjamin* (New York: Columbia University Press, 1948), pp. 33–34.

Boston, Jan[y] 25th, 1836.

E——

Send these things back with the speed of light—at least, let me have them by Thursday noon, and sooner if may be. Also, the thermometer,—and the old coat, if it can be stowed away. Moreover, your concoctions, prose and poetical. I make nothing of writing a history or biography before dinner. Do you the same.

Daniel Webster drinks, and is notoriously immoral; he is enormously in debt (one man having indorsed $100,000 for him) and altogether a disreputable character;—so say the Whigs. His son takes after his father.[1]

My worshipful self is a very famous man in London—the Athenaeum having noticed all my articles in the last Token, with long extracts.[2]

I met Charles Andrew[3] in the State-house, the other day, and shook hands with him—this being our first acquaintance. He appears not to enjoy a very high reputation among his brother legislators. Those of them who visit at our house say that he speaks so much that nobody else can get in a word—and not greatly to the purpose either.

Pull Beelzebub's[4] tail for me; and so good bye.

Remember the direction—Thos. G. Fessenden, Esq. No. 53, Hancock St. I shall be too busy to come down at present. Concoct—concoct—concoct.

---

1. Daniel Webster (1782–1852), U.S. senator from Massachusetts, 1827–41, maintained law offices in Boston. His capacity for liquor was well known, as was

his reputation for sexual promiscuity, particularly in brothels. During the mid-1830s, he borrowed heavily to invest in midwestern land. He was a leader of the emerging Whig party, and had been nominated for president in January, 1835, by the Whig members of the Massachusetts legislature, but was to suffer a humiliating rebuff in the national election of 1836. His older son, Fletcher (1813–62), was a colorless person, but his younger, Edward (1820–48), had already incurred many infractions against discipline at Boston Latin School and Exeter Academy. See Irving H. Bartlett, *Daniel Webster* (New York: Norton, 1978), chapters 11, 15, 16.

2. Henry F. Chorley, in an anonymous review of the 1836 *Token* in the *Athenæum*, no. 419, November 7, 1835, 830–31, recommended "The Wedding-Knell" and "The Minister's Black Veil": "each of which has singularity enough to recommend it to the reader." He quoted four long extracts from "The May-Pole of Merry Mount." See Faust, pp. 19–20; *Critical Heritage*, p. 49.

3. Charles Andrew (1809–43), Salem lawyer and member of the Massachusetts legislature, was a grandson of Simon and Rachel Hathorne Forrester. His reputation for garrulity in the legislature is documented in Boston newspapers.

4. The family's cat, named from Milton's *Paradise Lost*.

Boston, Feby 5th 1836.

I ought to have more collars; nor would more shirts be amiss. Mother spoke about a small trunk that I might have;— it would be useful to put my shirts in. You may send it, if you have anything to fill it with. Send the clothes as soon as may be.[1] I have now, I believe, but three collars and two shirts, besides what are on. I can't come down, having now two orders of devils[2] in attendance on me—the Token[3] and the Magazine. My hands are cursed cold.

Let Ebe send further extracts—also concoctions. She can finish her life of Hamilton[4] by consulting some biographical dictionary—Allen's,[5] for instance. Perhaps I will get these infernal people to take off his head[6] for the next number. Her pen-and-ink sketch can't possibly be worse than their wood-scratching. I am ashamed of the whole concern.

I send the receipt.

Nath Hawthorne

P.S. I find I have four shirts; but only three collars./I wish some of the latter by Monday eve, at farthest—perhaps Tuesday might do, at noon. Send all on Monday, if possible. It would be better not to send the trunk and valise together.

1. NH sent his laundry home to Salem. He apparently included eight letters (61, 63–68, 70, 72) in the packages.

2. Apprentice workers, "printers' devils."

3. NH contributed eight tales and sketches to the 1837 *Token*, published by the American Stationers' Company. See *SI*, p. 486.

4. Eventually published as the leading article in May. NH's collaboration with Elizabeth in producing the article is analyzed by Turner, p.29, n. 20.

5. William Allen, *American Biographical and Historical Dictionary*, 1809, which NH had borrowed from the Salem Athenaeum in 1830 (Kesselring, p. 43). Allen had been president of Bowdoin during NH's college years.

6. To make a portrait of. The full-page engraving or vignette at the front of the May number, however, portrayed the full-length marble statue of Hamilton recently placed in the Exchange, New York.

Boston, Feby 10th, 1836.

E——

Uncle Robert cannot call on me anywhere but at Mr. Fessenden's; as I never stay at the Company's office, and do all my writing and other business at my own room—which is up nearer to Heaven than he is ever likely to climb. If he comes, he will have the pleasure of seeing Mrs. Fessenden and the gentleman and lady boarders; and that will doubtless be very agreeable. I have generally called at the stage-office on Saturdays, and shall continue to do so. Was he in Boston at the presentation of the plate?[1]

I don't know but I have *copy* (as the printers call it) enough to make up this number; but you may extract every thing good that you come across—provided always it be not too good; and even if it should be, perhaps it will not quite ruin the Magazine; my own selections being bad enough to satisfy any body. I can't help it. The Bewick Co. are a damned sneaking set, or they would have a share in Athenaeum for the use of the Editor *ex officio*. I have now the liberty of reading there but not taking out books. I have given the Puritan an enormous puff—knowing nothing in the world about it, except from those extracts.[2] Finish your life of Hamilton. I wish you would write a biography of Jefferson to fill about 4 magazine pages and be ready in a month or six weeks.—If you don't, I must; and it is not a subject that suits me.[3] Say whether you will or not. In regard to ordinary biographical subjects, my way is to take some old magazine and make an abstract—you can't think how easy it is.

Nath. Hawthorne.

1. Robert Manning had been presented a silver pitcher by the Massachusetts Horticultural Society, "for his meritorious exertions in advancing the cause of Pomological science, and for procuring and distributing new varieties of fruits from Europe." The honor was announced in Fessenden's *New England Farmer* on February 3. See also Albert Emerson Benson, *History of the Massachusetts Horticultural Society* (Boston: For the Society, 1929), pp. 54–55.

2. Elizabeth had sent three excerpts from John Oldburg [pseudonym for Leonard Withington], *The Puritan: A Series of Essays Critical, Moral, and Miscellaneous* (Boston: Perkins and Marvin, 1836). NH printed these in the March issue; his prefatory note is reprinted in Turner, p. 215.

3. No biography of Jefferson appeared.

Boston, Feby 15th, 1836

L——

For the Devil's sake, if you have any money, send me a little. It is now a month since I left Salem, and not a damned cent have I had, except five dollars that I borrowed of Uncle Robert—and out of that I paid my stage fare and other expenses. I came here trusting to Goodrich's positive promise to pay me 46 dollars as soon as I arrived; and he has kept promising from one day to another; till I do not see that he means to pay me at all. I have now broke off all intercourse with him, and never think of going near him.[1] In the first place, he had no business ever to have received the money. I never authorized Bowen[2] to pay it to him; and he must have got it by telling some lie. My mind is pretty much made up about this Goodrich. He is a good-natured sort of man enough; but rather an unscrupulous one in money matters, and not particularly trustworthy in anything. I don't feel at all obliged to him about this Editorship; for he is a stockholder and director in the Bewick Co; and of course it was his interest to get the best man he could; and I defy them to get another to do for a thousand dollars what I do for 500; and furthermore, I have no doubt that Goodrich was authorized to give me 600. He made the best bargain with me he could, and a hard bargain too. This world is as full of rogues as Beelzebub is of fleas.

I don't want but two or three dollars. Till I receive some of my own, I shall continue to live as I have done. It is well that I have enough to do; or I should have had the blues most damnably here; for of course I have no amusement. My present stock is precisely 34 cts. You must pay for the letter, as my pockets may be entirely empty when it comes. They made me pay for the trunk. Send also more extracts and concoctions. I shall come down when I am rich enough. All that I have spent in Boston, except for absolute necessaries has been 9 cents on the first day I came—6 for a glass of wine and three for a cigar. Don't send more than 2 or 3 dollars. Unless I receive a supply, I can send again.

Nath Hawthorne.

P.S. If Goodrich should not finally pay me, I shall still have a claim on Bowen, who is a fair man.

---

1. Within the next four days, Goodrich wrote two letters to NH: the first enclosed "$46 due on Token account" from the publisher Charles Bowen (1807–45), for NH's three contributions to the 1836 *Token*, and noted that Goodrich had been "hoping several days to see your face—but as I have been necessarily busy, & you do not make me a call, I have not had that pleasure" (see textual note, 70). The second letter requested that NH review Goodrich's *The Outcast and Other Poems* in the Boston *Daily Atlas* (MS, Bowdoin). NH's resentment toward Goodrich did not keep him from writing a prompt and favorable review. See Wayne Allen Jones, "Hawthorne's First Published Review," *AL*, XLVIII (1977), 492–500.

2. NH had known Charles Bowen as publisher of the *Token* since 1830. Payments were made to the authors of contributions after the cost of publication had been recovered.

[Boston] Feby 17th [1836]

The money is received. You need not send any more, unless I write for it. Tell Ebe to finish her life of Hamilton. I have set these wretches to work upon his head. Also Jefferson—each to fill about 4 pages, which will be 8 of hers. I received a letter from Mrs. Sigourney the other day.[1] Infernal woman! Send some new collars with the rest of the clothes.

---

1. Lydia Howard Huntley Sigourney (1791–1865), "the Sweet Singer of Hartford." She was a close friend of S. G. Goodrich (having encouraged his literary interests when he first came to Hartford about 1810), and a frequent contributor to *The Token*. Her poem, "The Mariner to the First-Seen Mountain, on Approaching His Native Coast," dated February 12 and noted as "original," was published in the March issue, p. 302. Compare *AN*, p. 16, written perhaps shortly before August 31, 1836.

[Boston] March 3ᵈ [1836]

I have but two clean shirts left. Where is that stock? Ebe should have sent me some original poetry—and other original concoctions.[1] Why dont Uncle Robert send those books? I suppose the Magazine will be out in a day or two; but I have concluded not to favour you with a copy. I shall be glad of the paper; for I have to give 25 cts. for what is not so good as that you used to buy. Concoct—concoct.

1. No poetry or other original writing by Elizabeth is detectable in the *American Magazine*.

[Boston, March 13, 1836][1]

Read this infernal Magazine and send me your criticisms.
To me it appears very dull and respectable—almost worthy
of Mr. Bradford[2] himself. The next number is within ten
pages, I should think, of being finished; and I have written
all but about half a page with my own pen; except what Ebe
sent. Let her send more; for I have worked my brain hard
enough for this month. Where the devil are my clothes? I
could not go to meeting to day, because I had but one clean
shirt, which I was afraid to expend till tomorrow; and so I
staid at home and wrote a dissertation on the Tower of Babel.[3] If you sent them Saturday, write immediately to say so.
Concoct—concoct.

1. The reference to "meeting," below, indicates that this note was written on
Sunday, and references in 69 date it after March 11.

2. Alden Bradford (1765–1843) preceded and succeeded NH as editor of the
magazine. He was a prolific though undistinguished writer of history, whose
books NH had borrowed from the Salem Athenaeum in 1826–27 (Kesselring, p.
45). See *DAB*.

3. In the May issue, p. 366; reprinted in Turner, pp. 123–25.

[Boston, ca. March 15, 1836]

The April No was made up before your last packet arrived, and there were one or two extracts remaining of the former batch—the whole being of my own concoction, except what you sent. You may continue to make extracts; for they will all come into play, sometime or other. I should be glad of some more when the shirts are returned. Also the Museums.[1] And what does that man mean by not sending those Natures & Arts?[2] See to it.

I have been applied to, to write a man's travels in Texas, Mexico, and the Devil knows where;[3] but declined on account of my numerous avocations.

---

1. Probably the *Museum of Foreign Literature, Science, and Art*, a monthly published in Philadelphia, 1822–42. There are, however, no extracts from this in the *American Magazine* during NH's editorship.

2. Probably the *American Journal of Science and Arts*, edited by the elder Benjamin Silliman since 1818. NH had quoted in the April *American Magazine* from current articles in it on "Preservation of the Dead" (pp. 314–15) and "Snakes" (p. 332). For May he was to use "Coinage," "Snoring" (both p. 365), and "Salt: Its Origins and Manufacture" (pp. 393–94); and in June and July, "Uses of Dead Animals" (p. 410), "Migration of Birds" (p. 450), and "Lime as a Manure" (p. 456).

3. Possibly Dr. Joseph E. Field, *Three Years in Texas, Including a View of the Texas Revolution* (Greenfield, Mass.: J. Jones; Boston: Abel Tompkins, 1836). The preface is dated September 2, Charlemont, Mass. The title page describes Field as "one of the few survivors of Fanning's command."

Boston March 17th, 1836.

Send up your life of Hamilton forthwith. I must have it tomorrow, as the engraving is to form the vignette of the May number.[1]—If not finished, send what you have written. Also, any other selections, or concoctions.

Nath Hawthorne.

1. See 61.6.

69. TO ELIZABETH M. HAWTHORNE, SALEM

Boston March 22ᵈ [23] 1836

You need proceed no further with Hamilton. As the press was in want of him, I have been compelled to finish his life myself, this forenoon. I did not receive the packet till last night (Tuesday.) I should have given you earlier notice; but did not know myself that the engraving was coming into this number. I seldom have more than a day or two's notice. I approve of your life; but have been obliged to correct some of your naughty notions about arbitrary government.[1] You should not make quotations; but put other people's thoughts into your own words, and amalgamate the whole into a mass. You may go on concocting and extracting and send me some more of both varieties, as soon as convenient. I shall probably send my valise the latter part of the week. I don't know that I shall need any extracts till then. Those ridiculous Gazette people were in such a hurry to puff me, that they puffed poor Mr. Bradford.[2] They could not possibly have seen the March number when that notice was inserted.

Nath Hawthorne

1. NH rewrote the opening paragraph. See Turner, p. 29 n. 20. Elizabeth always followed a political persuasion contrary to NH's; she now supported the Whigs.

2. The Salem *Gazette* of March 11 had commented favorably on the *American Magazine*. See 66.

[Boston, early April, 1836]

Send back the valise as soon as possible; for I am horribly in want of more extracts. Send all you can.

Hamilton has passed through the Devil's hands (I doubt whether the original will get clear of the Devil, so easily) and makes a splendid appearance. The April No. will not probably be out within ten days or more.

Boston, May 5th. 1836.

I am well enough, but was in a devil of a hurry when I sent the valise. The Magazine is not out; it will be, probably, in the course of next week. I saw Mr Goodrich yesterday, and he told me, that he was going to reply to Park Benjamin's criticism, in to-day's Courier. I looked at the Courier before breakfast this morning; and lo and behold! the ridiculous man had written a whole column against the Editor of the *American* Magazine.[1] I have a good mind to hit him a poke in my turn, to teach him not to commit such blunders in future. He wants me to undertake a Universal History,[2] to contain about as much matter as 50 or 60 pages of the Magazine. If you are willing to write any part of it (which I should think you might, now that it is warm weather) I shall agree to do it. If necessary, I will come home by-and bye, and concoct the plan of it with you. It need not be superiour, in profundity and polish, to the middling Magazine articles. Mean time, finish your life of Jefferson; and see that it contains nothing heterodox. I shall have nearly a dozen articles in the Token[3]—mostly quite short.

I do by no means consent that Beelzebub should be transmuted to Amber[4]; nor do I believe that it has been done with her good will.

Nath Hawthorne

Do not fail to send the shirts, or by all means the collars, this week.

1. See 59.7. Park Benjamin, whose *New-England Magazine* had now merged with the *American Monthly*, was coeditor of the magazine (which NH refers to without the "Monthly") and was to publish several of NH's tales and sketches in it. Benjamin's review of Goodrich's *The Outcast and Other Poems* in the *American Monthly*, n.s. I (May, 1836), 519–25, had ridiculed it. See Introduction. Replying in the Boston *Courier*, May 5, Goodrich referred to Benjamin's publication as "The American Magazine," a short title applied to the *American Magazine of Useful and Entertaining Knowledge*, which NH was editing.

2. *Peter Parley's Universal History on the Basis of Geography, for the Use of Families,* 2 vols. (Boston: American Stationers' Company, 1837). NH and Elizabeth finished the assignment by late September, 1836.

3. See 61.2.

4. Beelzebub (see 60.4) kept that name until her death; see NH's comment, Letter 268.

[Boston] May 12th. [1836]

I must have some black stockings to wear with shoes. I send three dollars to buy them with; being all I can spare. I did not receive a cent of money till last Saturday, and then only 20 dollars; and, as you may well suppose, I have undergone very grievous vexations. Unless they pay me the whole amount shortly, I shall return to Salem, and stay till they do. Otherwise, I cannot come at present, being in the midst of the July number. Our pay, as Historians of the Universe, will be 100 dollars the whole of which you may have.[1] It is a poor compensation; yet better than the Token; because the kind of writing is so much less difficult.

I cannot get along without at least 1/2 a dozen more collars. You need not send any thick stockings after this. I have not received the Magazine at this present writing, and don't know when it will be out. The life of Jefferson will come into the August number[2]; but it will be wanted soon. Return the things as soon as possible; and send extracts.

1. See 71.2.
2. See 62.3.

73. TO T. B. FESSENDEN, BOSTON

Salem, Feby 16th, 1837.

Dear Sir,

My book is at last out of the printer's hands, and will probably make its appearance in a few days.[1] I have written to request Mr. Russell[2] to give you a copy, and if he should neglect to do so, you must remind him of it. When received, I beg that you will make over your right and title in it to Mrs. Fessenden; as I can hardly hope that your more important studies will leave you time to read so idle a volume as mine. In fact, I am almost afraid to let it pass under the critical inspection of Dr. Caustic.[3]

I do not know when I shall have the pleasure of seeing you. I cannot plead business as an excuse for coming to Boston, at present; and it does not suit with a poor author's circumstances to be riding backwards and forwards, merely for the sake of visiting his friends. It would gratify me much to hear from you and Mrs. Fessenden.

Your affectionate friend,
Nath. Hawthorne.

1. *TTT* was published March 6, 1837, by the American Stationers' Company of Boston, an organization of writers (including S. G. Goodrich and Jared Sparks) interested in publishing their own books. They accepted NH's volume on the recommendation of Goodrich. See *TTT*, "Historical Commentary," p. 503 n.42.

2. John B. Russell, agent and editor for the American Stationers' Company. See letters from him to NH in *NHHW*, I, 146, 150–51.

3. A pseudonym frequently used by Fessenden.

Salem, March 7th, 1837

Dear Sir,

The agent of the American Stationers Company will send you a copy of a book entitled 'Twice-told Tales'—of which, as a classmate,[1] I venture to request your acceptance. We were not, it is true, so well acquainted at college, that I can plead an absolute right to inflict my 'twice-told' tediousness upon you;[2] but I have often regretted that we were not better known to each other, and have been glad of your success in literature, and in more important matters. I know not whether you are aware that I have made a good many idle attempts in the way of Magazine and Annual scribblings.[3] The present volume contains such articles as seemed best worth offering to the public a second time; and I should like to flatter myself that they would repay you some part of the pleasure which I have derived from your own Outre Mer.[4]

Your obedient servant
Nath. Hawthorne.

Prof. H. W. Longfellow.

---

1. NH and Longfellow were members of the Bowdoin class of 1825.

2. *King John*, III, iv, 108: "Life is as tedious as a twice-told tale."

3. In his answering letter of March 9, Longfellow noted his "lively recollection" of several tales by NH, and the "very great delight" he had received on reading them "in the Token, and the New England Magazine." He recalled in

particular "the Travelling Show-man" from "The Seven Vagabonds," and "the Shakers, who meet with the *world's* people at a fountain on a hill-side" in "The Canterbury Pilgrims," both in the 1833 *Token*. Also, "The Story Teller, No. II," in the *New-England Magazine*. December, 1834: "One of the most life-like things is that wandering Story-teller; and the contrast between his successful début and the poor clergiman's prayer-meeting in the dimly lighted school-house, is a most beautifully drawn picture." None of these was signed, and none appeared in *TTT*, 1837, but were deferred until *TTT*, 1842, *SI*, and *MOM*, 1854, respectively, the last as "The Village Theatre" in "Passages from a Relinquished Work." Longfellow's letter, which reached the Essex Institute collection in 1982, was first published by Peter Balakian in *NEQ*, LVI (September, 1983), 430–32.

4. *Outre-Mer: A Pilgrimage Beyond the Sea*, Longfellow's first literary book, had been published in Boston in 1833–34.

Salem, June 4th. 1837.

Dear Sir,

Not to burthen you with my correspondence, I have delayed a rejoinder to your very kind and cordial letter, until
now.[1] It gratifies me to find that you have occasionally felt an
interest in my situation; but your quotation from Jean Paul,
about the 'lark-nest,' makes me smile.[2] You would have been
much nearer the truth, if you had pictured me as dwelling in
an owl's nest;[3] for mine is about as dismal, and, like the owl,
I seldom venture abroad till after dusk. By some witchcraft
or other—for I really cannot assign any reasonable why and
wherefore—I have been carried apart from the main current
of life, and find it impossible to get back again. Since we last
met—which, I remember, was in Sawtell's[4] room, where you
read a farewell poem to the relics of the class—ever since
that time, I have secluded myself from society; and yet I
never meant any such thing, nor dreamed what sort of life I
was going to lead. I have made a captive of myself and put
me into a dungeon; and now I cannot find the key to let
myself out—and if the door were open, I should be almost
afraid to come out. You tell me that you have met with troubles and changes.[5] I know not what they may have been; but
I can assure you that trouble is the next best thing to enjoyment, and that there is no fate in this world so horrible as to
have no share in either its joys or sorrows. For the last ten
years, I have not lived, but only dreamed about living. It may
be true that there have been some unsubstantial pleasures
here in the shade, which I should have missed in the sunshine; but you cannot conceive how utterly devoid of satisfac-

tion all my retrospects are. I have laid up no treasure of pleasant remembrances, against old age; but there is some comfort in thinking that my future years can hardly fail to be more varied, and therefore more tolerable, than the past.

You give me more credit than I deserve, in supposing that I have led a studious life. I have, indeed, turned over a good many books, but in so desultory a way that it cannot be called study, nor has it left me the fruits of study. As to my literary efforts, I do not think much of them—neither is it worth while to be ashamed of them. They would have been better, I trust, if written under more favorable circumstances. I have had no external excitement—no consciousness that the public would like what I wrote, nor much hope nor a very passionate desire that they should do so. Nevertheless, having nothing else to be ambitious of, I have felt considerably interested in literature; and if my writings had made any decided impression, I should probably have been stimulated to greater exertions; but there has been no warmth of approbation, so that I have always written with benumbed fingers. I have another great difficulty, in the lack of materials; for I have seen so little of the world, that I have nothing but thin air to concoct my stories of, and it is not easy to give a lifelike semblance to such shadowy stuff. Sometimes, through a peep-hole, I have caught a glimpse of the real world; and the two or three articles, in which I have portrayed such glimpses, please me better than the others.

I have now, or soon shall have, one sharp spur to exertion, which I lacked at an earlier period;[6] for I see little prospect but that I must scribble for a living. But this troubles me much less than you would suppose. I can turn my pen to all sorts of drudgery, such as children's books &c, and by and bye, I shall get some editorship that will answer my purpose.[7] Frank Pierce, who was with us at college, offered me his influence to obtain an office in the Exploring Expedition;[8] but I believe that he was mistaken in supposing that a vacancy existed. If such a post were attainable, I should certainly accept it; for, though fixed so long to one spot, I have always had a desire to run round the world.

The copy of my Tales was sent to Mr. Owen's, the bookseller's in Cambridge.[9] I am glad to find that you had read and liked some of the stories. To be sure, you could not well help flattering me a little, but I value your praise too highly not to have faith in its sincerity. When I last heard from the publishers—which was not very recently—the book was doing pretty well. Six or seven hundred copies had been sold. I suppose, however, these awful times have now stopped the sale.[10]

I intend, in a week or two, to come out of my owl's nest, and not return to it till late in the summer—employing the interval in making a tour somewhere in New-England.[11] You, who have the dust of distant countries on your "sandal-shoon,"[12] cannot imagine how much enjoyment I shall have in this little excursion. Whenever I get abroad, I feel just as young as I did ten years ago. What a letter am I inflicting on you! I trust you will answer it.

Yours sincerely, Nath Hawthorne

1. Longfellow had begun his letter of March 9: "I had the pleasure of receiving your very friendly letter last evening and hasten to send you a reply as friendly" (MS, Essex).

2. Longfellow had written: "I have felt from time to time a lively curiosity to know something of your *environments*, as the Sartor would say; but I have never by any good luck met with any one who could tell me more, than that you were living a very quiet life—a retired and studious one. So that I have always thought of you, as of one who had realized Jean Paul's idea of happiness.—'to nestle yourself so snugly, so homewise in some furrow, that in looking out from your warm lark-nest you likewise can discover no wolf-dens, charnel-houses or thunder-rods, but only blades and ears, every one of which for the nest-bird is a tree, and a parasol and an umbrella.' Is it so? For your sake I hope it may be." Thomas Carlyle had used the then novel word *environment* in *Sartor Resartus* (first published as a book in Boston in 1836) to describe Teufelsdröckh's nurture in childhood and youth; see *OED*. Longfellow quotes Jean Paul Friedrich Richter (1763–

1825), "Letter to My Friends, Instead of Preface," *The Life of Quintus Fixlein* (1795), as translated by Carlyle in *German Romance* (1827), changing only Carlyle's "discern" to "discover," and "a sun-screen, and rain-screen" to "a parasol and an umbrella." In a letter to Samuel Ward, April 3, 1836, Longfellow had compared reading Jean Paul to "reveling like the lark" (*Letters*, I, 545).

3. NH was to use this phrase in the biographical sketch he gave to R. H. Stoddard for publication in the *National Magazine*, II (1853), 19: after publication of *TTT* in 1837, he was "compelled to come out of my owl's nest and lionize in a small way" (*NHHW*, I, 98). Compare also 337 below, where the Old Manse becomes "our old Owl's Nest at Concord." In his journal, March 16, 1838, Longfellow wrote: "Towards evening sallied forth from my owl's nest" (MS, Harvard) and in a letter of October 22, 1838, he described NH as "a strange owl" (*Letters*, II, 107). NH's use of the figure in *HSG*, *BR*, and *MF* is better known than Longfellow's in *Hyperion: A Romance* (1839), II, iii, "Owl-Towers."

4. Cullen Sawtelle (1805–87), of Norridgewock, Maine, who had become a lawyer, was to be a congressman in the 1840s.

5. Longfellow had written: "I have been somewhat parched with the heat and drenched with the rain of life; and have suffered more sorrowful changes, than I should be willing to tell you in a letter, or you to read. Fortunately, however, my heart has a *southern exposure*, as people say of houses; so that whenever there is any sunshine I bask therein."

6. Apparently a reference to the railroad between Salem and Boston, which would drive out of business the Manning family stage coach line, NH's principal source of income since his graduation from Bowdoin. See his mention in "Time's Portraiture," published in the Salem *Gazette*, January 1, 1838, of "the past season's" work on the railroad, which "promises to start the cars by the middle of next summer" (*SI*, pp. 334–35). See also Letter 77, which seems to indicate no large prospects from sale of family lands in Maine.

7. Longfellow had inquired "what other literary plans you may have in view," after asking: "By the way, why do you not write for the [North American] Review?" The recently completed *Peter Parley's Universal History* was NH's first effort to write for children. He had refused another such offer from Goodrich in December, 1836, but may have regretted his retirement from editorship of the *American Magazine;* see the ambiguous statement by Bridge in a letter of December 25: "I am sorry you didn't get the magazine" (*Recollections*, p. 72).

8. The U. S. Exploring Expedition of 1838–39 to the South Seas and Antarctica had announced appointments of participating scientists beginning in January, 1837. The unsuccessful efforts of Bridge and Pierce to have NH made the expedition's historian are recorded in *Recollections*, pp. 82–83, and in *NHHW*, I, 152–58, 161–64. Coverdale contemplates volunteering for the expedition in *BR;* see p. 140. See also William Stanton, *The Great United States Exploring Expedition of 1838–1842* (Berkeley: University of California Press, 1975).

9. Longfellow had written: "I am sorry, that the volume was not sent to me sooner; so that a Review might have made its appearance in the N. American for April." His review appeared in the July number (XLV, 59–73); rpt. *Critical Heritage*, pp. 55–59. John Owen (1805–72), originally from Portland, Maine, was a graduate of Bowdoin in 1827. He was to publish several books by Longfellow.

10. The economic depression following the Panic of 1837.

11. NH spent a month from early July into August with Bridge in Augusta, Maine. See *AN*, pp. 32-65.

12. *Hamlet*, IV, v, 26.

Salem, June 19th. 1837

Dear Longfellow,

I have to-day received, and read with huge delight, your review of 'Hawthorne's Twice-told Tales.'[1] I frankly own that I was not without hopes that you would do this kind office for the book; though I could not have anticipated how very kindly it would be done. Whether or no the public will agree to the praise which you bestow on me, there are at least five persons who think you the most sagacious critic on earth—viz. my mother and two sisters, my old maiden aunt,[2] and finally, the sturdiest believer of the whole five, my own self. If I doubt the sincerity and correctness of any of my critics, it shall be of those who censure me. Hard would be the lot of a poor scribbler, if he may not have this privilege.

I intend to set out on my travels early next week—probably on Monday or Tuesday—and as I must come first to Boston, I will, if possible, ride out to Cambridge; for I am anxious to hold a talk.[3]

Very sincerely yours,
Nath. Hawthorne.

1. See 75.9.
2. Mary Manning.
3. There is no record of a visit to Boston or to Longfellow; NH's journal entry begins with his arrival in Augusta, Maine.

77. TO ELIZABETH M. HAWTHORNE, SALEM[1]

Portland, July 1st. 1837.[2]

I have seen Mr Small.[3] He says that he received Miss Manning's letter, and had intended to answer it, but forgot it. He searched the records in my presence. There were no conveyances, except of the land sold by Mr. Adams,[4] on account of all the heirs of Richard Manning deceased. Miss Manning's suspicions are therefore entirely erroneous.[5]

I have sent Peter Staple's[6] letter by the Raymond driver.

N. H.

1. The recipient is uncertain; NH habitually began letters to his mother with a formal salutation, and to his sisters without one.

2. NH had stopped on his way to Augusta, where he arrived on the evening of July 3 (AN, p. 32).

3. Samuel Small, registrar of deeds and town clerk of Raymond.

4. Joseph Adams, a counselor of Portland, had held a power of attorney for the remaining heirs of the elder Richard Manning since the death of NH's uncle Richard in 1831. See 54.1.

5. Letters of Mary Manning beginning in 1835 indicate her mounting concern about her brother William's willingness to sell property in Salem and in Maine, apparently because of his difficulties in running the Salem & Boston Stage Company (MSS, Essex).

6. Peter Staples (1751–1846), a farmer in Raymond.

Salem, September 25th, 1837.

Mr. N. Hawthorne has recently been favored with a number of the Southern Rose, containing a very favorable notice of his 'Twice-told Tales.'[2] He feels far too much gratification in praise from such a source, not to maintain a sturdy faith in the correctness of the judgement there passed, although modesty might whisper him that the writer has been greatly more kind than critical. But the truth is, he has himself been so much delighted with certain productions from the pen, as he believes, of the Editor of the Rose, that he feels as if he might accept all the approbation that she can possibly bestow on him, and still leave her in his debt. He particularly remembers, in perusing the Recollections of a Housekeeper,[3] a year or two since, how hopelessly he compared his own writings with the nature and truth of that little work.

Mr. Hawthorne has delayed this acknowledgement, in the hope of being able to offer a tale or sketch for publication in the Rose; but anxieties of various kinds have kept his pen idle, and his fancy produces no flowers, nor hardly a weed that looks like one. In conclusion, he begs permission to express his high respect for the Editor, and for one whom the inhabitants of Salem are proud to claim as a native townsman.[4]

Editor of the Southern Rose.

---

1. Caroline Howard Gilman (1794–1888), born in Boston, had settled in Charleston after her marriage in 1819. She edited the Southern Rose as a magazine for children in 1832–33, and for adults, 1833–39. She was a prolific and

extremely popular author, especially for children. See *DAB*; William Stanley Hoole, "The Gilmans and the *Southern Rose*," *North Carolina Historical Review*, XI (1934), 116–28.

2. *Southern Rose*, V (July 8, 1837), 183. Reprinted in Wayne Allen Jones, "New Light on Hawthorne and the *Southern Rose*," *NHJ* 1974, pp. 36–37.

3. Mrs. Gilman's first book, published by Harper in New York, 1834, described humorously the little vicissitudes of early married life.

4. Samuel Gilman (1791–1858), Caroline's husband, was born in Gloucester and had spent his boyhood in Salem. He had been since 1819 the pastor of the Second Independent (Unitarian) Church of Charleston. See *DAB*. He later wrote for the *Southern Rose* VII (March 2, 16, 1839), "A Day of Disappointment in Salem. By an Admirer of 'Twice-told Tales'." See *NHJ* 1971, pp. 208–27.

Salem, Novr 7th. 1837

Dear Sir,

Your letter addressed to *Samuel* Hawthorne, lay some time in the Post-Office of this city, before I could feel myself justified in receiving it from the Postmaster. But as I know of no other person who spells the family name in the same manner, and as *Samuel* has somewhat of a scriptural affinity to *Nathaniel*,[1] I at length ventured to break the seal. Even now, I scarcely know whether to consider the letter as intended for myself, being too justly conscious of my slender pretensions to literary merit, to presume that my autograph would be a valuable item in your collection. But as I really happen to be the author of a volume entitled "Twice-told Tales," and may therefore claim at least a humble rank among American writers, I have deemed it no more than a proper courtesy to make this reply to your letter. Begging you to accept my thanks for your expressions of approbation, (if indeed I may appropriate them to myself,) and with my best wishes for your welfare,

I remain, Sir,
Respectfully,
Your obd't servt,
Nath. Hawthorne

Joseph B. Boyd, Esq
Cincinnati, Ohio

1. The name of Nathan the prophet first appears in 2 Samuel 7. The name Nathanael appears only in John 1 and 21. For NH's interest in the prophet Nathan, see *SL*, p. 126.

Salem, Jany 18th. 1838.

Dear Sir,

A variety of occupations must plead my apology for so long delaying to answer your letter of Novr 17th. I was likewise desirous of giving you some information relative to your inquiries, but have not succeeded in obtaining much. Governor Eustis was not a resident of Salem, but of Roxbury, in this State.[1] His son, I believe, is General Eustis of the army. Mr. Bancroft, the Historian, is now collector at Boston.[2] Permit me to suggest that the autograph of the Rev. Charles W. Upham of this city (if you have not already obtained it) would be worthy of a place in your contemplated volume. He is the author of the Life of Sir Henry Vane, in Mr. Sparkes' American Biography,[3] and of several other works, principally historical, which have been received with distinguished approbation here and in England. No collection of American autographs can be considered complete, without a specimen from him.

Very Sincerely Yours,
Nath. Hawthorne.

Joseph B. Boyd, Esq.
Cincinnati, Ohio.

---

1. William Eustis (1753–1825), governor of Massachusetts from 1823 to 1825, had resided in Roxbury. See *DAB*. His nephew Abraham (1786–1843) was a brigadier general in the U.S. Army.

2. George Bancroft (1800–1891) was appointed collector of the port of Boston in 1837. The first and second volumes of his *History of the United States* had appeared in 1834 and 1837.

3. Upham (see 44.4), *Sir Henry Vane* (Boston: Hilliard, Gray, 1835), in *The Library of American Biography*, ed. Jared Sparks, first series, volume 4.

Salem, February 8th. 1838.

Dear Bridge,

It is very long since I have written to you, or heard from you. My life, till latterly, has gone on in the same dull-[*excision*] It is my purpose to set out for Washington, in the course of a fortnight or thereabouts—but only to make a short visit. Would it be utterly impossible or extremely unadvisable, for you to come to Boston or this place, within that interval? Not that you can do me the least good; but it would be a satisfaction to me to hold a talk with the best friend I ever had or shall have (of the male sex)—and there may be cause for regret on your part, should we fail of a meeting. But I repeat that you cannot exercise the slightest favorable influence on my affairs—they being beyond your control, and hardly within my own. Perhaps you have been thinking of a visit to Boston, and this letter may merely hasten it. If so, I shall be glad. Do not come, if it will put you to serious inconvenience.[1]

God bless you and
Your friend, Nath.

Be mum![2]

1. There is no evidence that Bridge came to Boston or Salem until March 17, when Longfellow met him with NH on a Boston street (Longfellow journal, MS, Harvard; *Life*, I, 279). NH's reason for a trip to Washington, it has been ad-

vanced, was to see John L. O'Sullivan, the editor of the *United States Magazine and Democratic Review* and his rival for the affections of Mary Crowninshield Silsbee (1809–87), daughter of U.S. Senator Nathaniel Silsbee, of Salem. According to Bridge, who did not give the names, Mary "incited him to quarrel with one of his best friends," O'Sullivan. "He went to Washington for the purpose of challenging the gentleman, and it was only after ample explanations had been made, showing that his friend had behaved with entire honor, that [Franklin] Pierce and [Jonathan] Cilley, who were his advisers, could persuade him to be satisfied without a fight. The lady had appealed to him to redress her fancied wrongs, and he was too chivalrous to decline the service" (*Recollections*, pp. 5–6). Bridge is apparently in error in remembering a trip by NH to Washington; in 1853 NH wrote that his visit then was his first (*AN*, p. 552). See also 84, second paragraph. Julian Hawthorne included a similarly veiled account in *NHHW*, I, 167–73, based, he said, on the recollection of Elizabeth Peabody. See Norman Holmes Pearson, "Hawthorne's Duel," *EIHC*, XCIV (1958), 229–42.

2. The reference is to the excised passage, subject-matter unknown.

Salem, March 15th, 1838.

Sir,

I was a particular friend of the late lamented Mr. Cilley;[1] and the Editor of the Democratic Review has requested me to write a biographical sketch of him for that publication.[2] As it might appear indelicate in a stranger to intrude upon his family, I have been induced to apply to you, in the hope that you will have it in your power to favor me with a few facts respecting his life. In regard to his early life, I can obtain information from other sources, and will trouble you merely for a brief account of the incidents which occurred during his residence in Thomaston. The date of his marriage—his wife's name and parentage—his character and success as a lawyer—his entrance into political life &c—these are the principal topics on which information appears desirable.[3]

I trust you will excuse the liberty which I have taken; and, if convenient for you to comply with my request, please to hand this letter to some relative or friend of Mr. Cilley. As I have but a short time in which to prepare the biographical sketch, it will be necessary that any information should be sent me within two or three days after the receipt of this letter.

Your Ob[t] Servant,
Nath[l] Hawthorne.
Salem,
Mass.[4]

1. Jonathan Cilley (1802–38), born in New Hampshire and NH's classmate and friend at Bowdoin, was a lawyer, representative of Thomaston in the Maine legislature 1832–36, and speaker of the House in 1835–36. He was elected to the U.S. Congress in 1836 as a Democrat. On July 28, 1837, NH met him in Augusta for the first time since their graduation, and wrote a penetrating analysis of his character (see AN, pp. 61–63). A series of incidents in Washington, arising out of Cilley's proper refusal to receive a written note querying remarks he had made on the floor of the House, led to a duel in which on February 24, 1838, he was killed by William J. Graves (1805–48), a Whig congressman from Kentucky. See Horatio King, "History of the Duel between Jonathan Cilley and William Graves," *Collections and Proceedings of the Maine Historical Society*, III (1892), 127–48, 393–409.

2. "Biographical Sketch of Jonathan Cilley," *United States Magazine and Democratic Review*, III (September, 1838), 69–75. Publication was delayed, according to O'Sullivan's prefatory note, because of "difficulty in procuring a satisfactory accompanying drawing."

3. These questions are answered in NH's sketch.

4. In another hand follows: "Mr Fales you may ansor this if you pleas perhaps it wold be well so to do." Oliver Fales (1778–1858) was town clerk of Thomaston, 1822–27 and 1829–40.

83. TO H. W. LONGFELLOW, CAMBRIDGE

Salem, March 21st. 1838.

My dear Longfellow,

I was sorry that you did not come to dinner on Sunday;[1] for I wanted to hold a talk with you about that book of fairy tales, which you spoke of at a previous interview.[2] I think it a good idea, and am well inclined to do my part towards the execution of it—provided I have time—which seems more probable now than it did a few months since. Not but what I am terribly harassed with magazine scribbling, and moreover have had overtures from two different quarters, to perpetrate childrens' histories and other such iniquities.[3] But it seems to me that your book will be far more creditable, and perhaps quite as profitable; nor need it impede any other labors. Possibly we may make a great hit, and entirely revolutionize the whole system of juvenile literature. I wish you would shape out your plan distinctly, and write to me about it. Ought there not to be a slender thread of story running through the book, as a connecting medium for the other stories?[4] If so, you must prepare it. If I recollect right, it was your purpose to select some of the stories; but I should deem it preferable to have them all either original or translated—at least, for the first volume of the series. I would not have it a very bulky book—say two or three hundred 18mo pages, of large print; it being merely an experiment. You shall be the Editor, and I will figure merely as a contributor; for, as the conception and system of the work will be yours, I really should not think it honest to take an equal share of the fame which is to accrue. Seriously, I think that a very pleasant and peculiar kind of reputation may be acquired in this way—we will twine for ourselves a wreath of tender shoots and dewy buds, instead of such withered and dusty leaves as other people crown themselves with; and what is of more importance to me, though of none to a Cambridge Professor, we may perchance put money in our purses. Think about it, and write to me; and let us get our baby-house ready by October.

I am going to study German.[5] What dictionary had I better get? Perhaps you can procure me a second-hand one without trouble—which, as perhaps it is a large and costly work, would be quite a considerable favor. But it is no great matter; for I am somewhat doubtful of the stability of my resolution to pursue the study.

I mean to come to Boston, within a month, and will endeavor to see you.[6]

> Your friend,
> (in much of a hurry)
> Nath. Hawthorne.

P.S. If you have any reminiscences about Cilley, impart them to me. It has fallen to my lot to write a biographical sketch of him; and I fear it will be a thorny affair to handle.

1. In his journal for Saturday, March 17, Longfellow noted meeting NH and Bridge in the street in Boston, and "promised to dine with them tomorrow." Sunday brought a "tremendous snow-storm," and he was "shut up all day." The following Sunday he passed the afternoon in Salem with NH, "discussing literary matters. He is much of a lion here, sought after, fed and expected to roar. A man of genius and fine imagination. He is destined to soar high" (Journal, MS, Harvard).

2. A proposed collaboration of Longfellow and NH to be called "The Boys' Wonder-Horn" after *Des Knabens Wunderhorn* (1805–8), the famous collection of German folksongs by Ludwig Achim von Arnim and Clemens Brentano.

3. From the Boston bookseller and publisher Nahum Capen (1804–86), publisher of *Fanshawe* (whose "secret" existence he first confirmed in a letter to the Boston *Advertiser*, October 15, 1870), and from Horace Mann, secretary of the Massachusetts Board of Education, who was preparing to issue a series of books to be used as district school libraries. See Elizabeth Peabody's letter to Mann, March 3, 1838 (MS, MHS), in Wayne Allen Jones, "Sometimes Things Just Don't Work Out: Hawthorne's Income from *Twice-Told Tales* (1837), and Another 'Good Thing' for Hawthorne," *NHJ 1975*, pp. 10–26, which corrects Alexander C. Kern, "A Note on Hawthorne's Juveniles," *Philological Quarterly*, XXXIX (1960), 242–46, and Roy Harvey Pearce, "Historical Introduction," *TS*, pp. 290–91.

4. The device used in "The Story Teller" (see 57.7), and to be used in *Grandfather's Chair*, *WB* and *TT*.

5. Apparently NH was encouraged in this by Elizabeth Peabody. SH wrote to her, April 27: "Mary [Peabody] invited him to come with his sister on Saturday evening—& read German; but it seems to me he does not want to go on with the German & I do not believe he wants to come now you are gone" (MS, Berg; partly published, *NHHW*, I, 185). On July 23 SH wrote to Elizabeth that NH "could not take the trouble" to continue German, though his sister Elizabeth "went on famously" (MS, Berg).

6. Longfellow's journal, Sunday, May 6: "Afternoon with Bridge and Hawthorne. Tea at Hillard's; talked w[ith] Hedge there, and Miss Peabody" (MS, Harvard). This information helps understanding of the "puzzle" James Mellow found in NH's meeting with Elizabeth Peabody at the Tremont House in Boston—"probably innocent, but perhaps meaningful" (*Nathaniel Hawthorne in His Times* [Boston: Houghton Mifflin, 1980], pp. 144–45). SH's letters to Elizabeth of April 30 and May 10 show that Elizabeth came to Boston to see Frederick Henry Hedge, the Transcendentalist minister, coincidentally when NH was there to see Longfellow, Bridge, and Hillard (MSS, Berg).

84. TO MRS. LYDIA T. FESSENDEN[1] AND TO CATHARINE C. AINSWORTH,[2] BOSTON

Salem, April 12th. 1838.

Dear Mrs. Fessenden,

When I last saw you, you observed that you expected to give up house-keeping in May. It would be a great grief to me not to have an opportunity of paying you one more visit in your own house; so I hope you will give me timely notice before you migrate to any other part of the globe. I do not think that I shall be in Boston in less than three weeks, unless your intended removal should induce me to come sooner. My engagements here are very pressing.

I have almost entirely given up the idea of going to Washington.[3] What a pity that I did not hearken to your good counsel, and spend the winter in Boston! It has been a winter of much anxiety and of very little pleasure or profit. I intend to pass the summer somewhere in the country.

I have no news to tell you, except that my mother and sister Louisa are both unwell. They send their love to you— or doubtless they *would* have sent it, if they had known that I was going to write.

Your affectionate Friend,
Nath. Hawthorne.

Mrs. L. T. Fessenden.

Salem, April 12th, 1838.

Dear Catharine,

I owe you a postscript, but I have nothing in the world to pay it with. I am tired to death of pen, ink and paper, and would never touch either of the three again, if I were not a scribbler by profession. If I recollect right, you have relinquished your claim to a story for your own exclusive reading. I thank you for your generosity from the bottom of my heart—though I believe it was constrained rather than voluntary.

Is Miss Augusta still a wanderer in foreign parts?—not that I feel any interest in the question; only I think it time that the poor young lady should be restored to her friends. I have heard recently the interesting intelligence that I am engaged to two ladies in this city.[4] It was my first knowledge of the fact. I do trust that I shall not get married without my own privity and consent.

Excuse this nonsense, and answer it with some of your wisdom.

Your friend,
(in haste)
Nath. Hawthorne

(Do not leave Boston without letting me know.)

Miss C. C. Ainsworth.

1. Lydia Tuttle Fessenden (1785–1866), widow of Thomas Green Fessenden, who had died November 11, 1837. It was in their home that NH had worked at editing the *American Magazine;* see 62.

2. Catherine Calista Ainsworth (1812–93), niece of Mr. Fessenden, stayed with Mrs. Fessenden during the winter. She was, by family tradition, the model for Phoebe in *HSG:* "We always understood that [she] could have had [NH] for a husband if she had wanted such a queer person." See Porter Gale Perrin, *Thomas Green Fessenden* (Orono: University of Maine Press, 1925), p. 170.

3. Presumably with the U. S. Exploring Expedition, or some other government employment that Pierce and Bridge may have tried to arrange; see 75.5.

4. For three likely candidates—Mary Silsbee, Elizabeth Peabody, and Sophia Peabody—see Norman Holmes Pearson, "Hawthorne's Duel," *EIHC*, XCIV (1958), 237–39, and *Hawthorne's Two Engagements* (Northampton, Mass.: Smith College, 1963).

Salem, April 19th. 1838.

My Dear O'Sullivan,

This memoir[1] has been delayed by various causes—partly because I could not get all the information I wanted—partly because the task was so painful that I put it off as long as I could. I fear you will find it very coldly written; and you will perceive that some tact has been necessary, from the peculiar nature of Cilley's early political struggles.[2] I should like to have seen the report of the Com. of Investigation; but if there be anything to subjoin, you can put it in a note.[3] The value of the article may be applied as you suggested.

Miss Peabody desires me to ask you whether you would probably publish an article from her, "On the claims of the Beautiful Arts"—which she has written, and would copy and correct, if there were a chance of its coming before the public.[4] I have read the first part of the article, and thought it had a good deal of merit. She is somewhat too much of a theorist, but really possesses knowledge, feeling, eloquence, and imagination. I wish she had done herself more justice in the review of Nature—which was particularly poor.[5] Of course, you will not pledge yourself in the least to publish the article before seeing it; but if you will be gracious enough to look it over, say so.

I have not had the April Mag. What an article that was of yours—the Martyrdom of Cilley! Most eloquent and admirable; but I cannot altogether coincide with your view of the affair.[6]

Your friend, Nath. Hawthorne

1. Of Jonathan Cilley; see 82.2.

2. Cilley studied law with John Ruggles, who became his political mentor. But in 1832, when Cilley was elected to the legislature, NH wrote, "the friendly relations between Judge Ruggles and Mr. Cilley were broken off. The former gentleman, it appears, had imbibed the idea that his political aspirations (which were then directed towards a seat in the Senate of the United States) did not receive all the aid which he was disposed to claim from the influence of his late pupil."

3. *U.S. Congress. House Committee Appointed to Investigate the Causes Which Led to the Death of the Hon. Jonathan Cilley*, 182 pp. (25 Cong., 2d Sess., Report no. 825). Report made by Isaac Toucey. [Washington, 1838]. O'Sullivan's concluding note says that the "evidence confirmed, in the strongest manner, all that Cilley's warmest friends could have wished . . . " (*Democratic Review*, III [September, 1838], 76).

4. "Claims of the Beautiful Arts" was published anonymously in the *Democratic Review*, III (November, 1838), 253–68. NH received a letter from O'Sullivan about this article by July 23; see 86.2.

5. "Nature—a Prose Poem," *Democratic Review*, I (February, 1838), 319–29. This unsigned review of Emerson's *Nature* included a brief notice of "The American Scholar." NH apparently did not yet know of her review of *TTT* in the *New-Yorker*, V (March 24, 1838), 1–2: she found his writing Wordsworthian, even Emersonian. See Arlin Turner, "Elizabeth Peabody Reviews *Twice-Told Tales*," *NHJ 1974*, pp. 75–84; SH to Elizabeth Peabody, April 29, 1838 (MS, Berg).

6. "The Martyrdom of Cilley," *Democratic Review*, I (March, 1838), 493–508. O'Sullivan's view was much more political than NH's; he found the death of Cilley to be the result of evil tactics by the Whig party.

North Adams (Mass.) July 26th. 1838

Dear R.

I did not intend to write to any of my friends during my absence; but as it is possible that there may be some very important intelligence awaiting me, I am induced to break my resolution. If any letters have arrived for me, or if any should come to hand within ten days or a fortnight, I will thank you to direct them to this place.[1] If there should be a double letter from O'Sullivan, you need not send it, as it would probably contain only a letter for Miss Peabody.[2] Please also to write yourself, and tell me any news that may have transpired since my departure.

I am very pleasantly situated here, and think that I can content myself for two or three weeks—after which I intend to make a move into New-York, which lies close at hand. Do not tell anybody that you have heard from me, or that you know anything of my whereabout. You will see me again (God willing) in the course of six months.

Yours truly
(in a hurry)
Nath. Hawthorne.

1. NH had left Salem on July 23 and arrived in North Adams on the twenty-fifth. See AN, pp. 79–151. SH wrote to her sister Elizabeth on July 23 that NH "said he was not going to tell anyone where he was going to be the next three

months—that he thought he should change his name so that if he died no one would be able to find his grave stone. He should not even tell his Mother where he could be found—that he neither intended to write to anyone *nor be written to*" (MS, Berg).

2. Concerning her article for the November issue of the *Democratic Review*. See 85.3. SH in her letter of July 23 had told Elizabeth that O'Sullivan "was about writing to you & should enclose his letter to Mr Hawthorne's care or under cover to him. If it comes under cover, there seems to be no way of getting it" (MS, Berg). The reference "double letter" is to one of two sheets, with a doubled postage; see postscript, Letter 298.

Salem, Octr 12th 1838.

My Dear Professor,

It is a dreadful long while since we have collogued together. I have been rambling about since the middle of July, till within a week or two past; and have had such a pleasant time as seldom happens to a man of my age and experience. Meantime, how comes on the "Boy's WONDER-HORN?"[1] Have you blown your blast?—or will it turn out a broken-winded concern? I have not any breath to spare, just at present—yet I think it a pity that the echoes should not be awakened, far and wide, by such an admirable instrument. I suppose it would require only a short time to complete the volume, if we were to set about it in good earnest.

From Boston to Salem (as from the sublime to the ridiculous) it is but a step, now a days. Suppose you come down, shortly?—or I would meet you in Boston any pleasant day, next week.[2] Have you given up your plan of lecturing here? This, it seems to me, would be just the proper season; and if you say the word, I will set in motion all the machinery over which I have any control.[3] Our regular Lyceum lectures commence some time in November:—it would be well to begin in anticipation of them, unless you would like to have your course incorporated therewith. But there would be many objections—beside that, probably, it would not be half so profitable. But, by all means, favor us in one way or other; and I will puff—puff—puff—in the newspapers, till you shall blush as red as any rose.

Write forthwith.

Truly your friend
Nath. Hawthorne.

1. See 83.2.

2. Longfellow wrote to George Washington Greene on October 22, "I shall see Hawthorne tomorrow. He lives in Salem; and we are to meet and sup together tomorrow evening at Tremont house. . . . He is a strange owl; a very peculiar individual, with a dash of originality about him, very pleasant to behold" (*Letters,* II, 107). In his journal for October 24, Longfellow recorded of NH: "He had been in town, they told me at Tremont House, but had just gone back to Salem in the evening cars. He could not have received my letter" (MS, Harvard). See 93. The railroad from Boston to Salem, which opened August 27, 1838, reduced travel time from two hours to one. NH was to describe the effect in "The Sister Years" on January 1, 1839; see *TTT*, pp. 338–39.

3. The lecturers at the Salem Lyceum for 1838–39 did not include Longfellow. For a list of the lectures given, see Carl Bode, *The American Lyceum: Town Meeting of the Mind* (Carbondale: Southern Illinois University Press, 1956), p. 48. NH's connection with the Lyceum at this time is not known; he was to be corresponding secretary in 1848–49.

Salem, Novr 5th. 1838.

Dear O'S.

Yours of last Monday came duly to hand; and I read from it to Miss Peabody as much as concerned that lady. I hope you mean to have her for a constant correspondent.

As touching other matters—in accordance with your exhortations, I have seen our fair friend.[1] Her manner of receiving me was incomparably good—perfectly adapted to the circumstances—altogether beyond criticism. It might seem that I should have had the vantage-ground in such an interview—having been virtually invited to it by herself, after expressing a desire and determination to break off all intercourse—and having expressly stated, moreover, that any future intercourse should not be on the ground of friendship. But it was no such thing. All the glory was on her side; and no small glory it is, to have made a wronged man feel like an offender—and that, too, without permitting any direct allusion to the matter in dispute—and to have put on just so much dignity as to keep me precisely at the distance she chose, tempered with just so much kindness that I could not possibly quarrel with her.[2] She was dressed in better taste and looked more beautiful than ever I saw her before; and she, and her deportment and conversation, were all of a piece, and altogether constituted a perfect work of art— meaning the phrase in no bad sense.

Yet the interview has not produced the effect that she anticipated from it. I came away with, I think, the most dismal and doleful feeling that I ever experienced—a sense that all had been a mistake—that I never really loved—that there was no real sympathy between us—and that a union could only insure the misery of both. Surely, having this feeling, it is my duty to stop here, and to make her aware that I have no further aims.

It is fit that I do her all manner of justice, as respects her treatment of me. Looking back at her conduct, with the light that her last letter has given me, I am convinced that she has meant honorably and kindly by me,—that I have nothing to complain of in her motives, though her actions have not been altogether so well-judged. I now put a different interpretation on the "secret spring," which I was to discover "soon, or never." It cannot be her father's disapprobation; for I had reason to suppose that he knew something of the affair, and sanctioned it. That "spring" was within her own heart, and I was to discover it by reflecting on something that she had formerly revealed to me. I have reflected, and think that I have penetrated the mystery.

Yes—I will stop here. Nevertheless, do not you be one whit the less zealous to get me the Post-Office; for the salary may purchase other comforts as well as matrimonial ones. Do move Heaven and Earth. In the meantime, Mr. Bancroft has offered me the post of Inspector in the Custom-House, with a salary of $1100.[3] The office has many eligibilities, and I think I shall accept it.

Whenever my poor brains get into working order, the first use I make of them shall be to throw off an article or two. I hope to do so within a week or ten days.[4] There is a very kind review of my Tales in the Christian Examiner for this month.[5] It makes me smile to see what a mild, gentle, and holy personage the reviewer makes of me—living, one would think, in a heaven of peace and calm affection. I fear you would take rather a different view of me.

Most truly Your friend,

N. H.

1. Mary Silsbee.

2. According to Julian Hawthorne's report of Elizabeth Peabody's recollections, after the misunderstanding with O'Sullivan, Mary "managed to renew relations with [NH], and told him, (with no encouragement on his part) that she would marry him when he had an income of $3000. He said he never expected to have so much." See Norman Holmes Pearson, "Hawthorne's Duel," p. 232.

3. See 91.

4. This may be a reference to "Lady Eleanor's Mantle" and "Old Esther Dudley." See *TTT*, "Historical Commentary," p. 518.

5. A. P. P., "Hawthorne's *Twice-Told Tales*," *Christian Examiner*, XXV (November, 1838), 182–90; rpt. *Critical Heritage*, pp. 64–67. Andrew Preston Peabody (1811–93), minister of a Unitarian church in Portsmouth, preached occasionally in Salem, and was much appreciated by the Peabodys and their circle. He was later editor of the *North American Review* and Plummer Professor of Christian Morals at Harvard. See *DAB; TTT*, pp. 510–11.

Salem, Novr 7th, 1838.

Dear Sir,

I thank you for your proposition respecting the Twice-told Tales, and am willing to put them into your hands.[1] If I mistake not, however, the remaining copies, at 62 1/2 cts, would not balance my demand against the Stationers' Co. Instead of a power to settle all accounts, it will perhaps be better to give you merely an order to receive the books.

You have been misinformed in regard to my having a new work in preparation.[2] I have been advised by some of my friends to prepare another volume of Tales, but have as yet taken no steps towards it, nor given the matter any serious consideration.

Please to present my best respects to Mrs. F.[3] and Mrs. P. I shall call on the latter, as soon as I hear of her arrival in town.

Yours truly,
Nath. Hawthorne

1. The Boston *Advertiser* was to note on January 25, 1839, 3:5, that "the balance of the edition, being less than a hundred copies, are for sale by Weeks, Jordan & Co." The publisher, the American Stationers' Company, had collapsed; see 75.10.

2. Probably the "overtures" mentioned in 83.3. NH did submit *The Gentle Boy: A Thrice Told Tale* (with an illustration by SH) to Weeks, Jordan for publication as a pamphlet, issued in January, 1839. See *TTT*, pp. 566–68.

3. Possibly Lydia T. Fessenden.

90. TO MRS. C. H. GILMAN, CHARLESTON, S.C.

Salem, Decr. 27th. 1838.

Mr. Hawthorne regrets that he has not been able to send an earlier contribution to the Rose, and that, at last, he can repay the Editor's kind attention with nothing better than the above.[1] If this little tale may claim the praise of some degree of fancy and prettiness, it is all he can expect for it. Such as it is, he commends it to Mrs. Gilman's kind consideration, and will be proud to see it among her own beautiful productions, in the Southern Rose.

Some of the later numbers of the Rose have not reached him. He is grateful to the Editor for her long patience, and cannot wonder that it should have failed at last.

1. "The Lily's Quest" manuscript was sent with this note added on its final leaf. The note was later separated. The sketch appeared in the *Southern Rose*, VII (January 19, 1839), 161–64. It was reprinted in *The Picturesque Pocket Companion and Visitor's Guide through Mt. Auburn* (Boston: Otis, Broaders, 1839), and in Park Benjamin's *New-Yorker*, VI (February 16, 1839), 341–42, and was collected in *TTT*, 1842.

Salem, Jany 11th, 1839

Sir,

    After due reflection, I have determined to accept the office which you had the goodness to offer me, in the Inspector's department of the Custom-House.[1] On enquiry of Gen. McNeel and Mr. Jameson,[2] I find that the post vacated by Mr. Harris[3] is considered more laborious and responsible than an ordinary Inspectorship; and they were both of opinion that I should prefer the duties of the latter. From November to April, however, the Inspectorships are all on the same footing; so that it would not be necessary to decide immediately as to the eligibility of Mr Harris's post.

    I hope to be able to remove to Boston within a fortnight; and it would then be agreeable to me to enter upon office.[4]

With much obligation,
Very Respectfully Yours,
Nath. Hawthorne.

George Bancroft, Esq.
Boston.

---

    1. The office was apparently secured by Elizabeth Peabody's asking Orestes Brownson (1803–76), who had a similar appointment as steward of the Chelsea Marine Hospital, if NH might receive "an office like his—requiring very little time & work—& having abundant leisure and liberty—& in or about Boston—for I was afraid New England w'd otherwise lose him." Brownson replied that Bancroft would be "delighted to give him a place, but he had supposed he was a sort

of man who would by no means accept one" (Elizabeth Peabody to Elizabeth M. Hawthorne, October 17, 1838; MS, Essex); see Norman Holmes Pearson, "A 'Good Thing' for Hawthorne," *EIHC,* C (1964), 303–4. But in November Robert Rantoul, Jr., the prominent Democratic politician and lawyer, wrote to Bancroft, "I hear that N. Hawthorne declines the inspectorship" (MS, MHS). Apparently NH did not want so "laborious and responsible" a position. Another person influential in procuring an appointment for NH was Elizabeth Davis Bliss Bancroft (1799–1886), a close friend of Elizabeth Peabody and a widow who had married George Bancroft in August, 1838. She was also important in gaining NH the surveyorship at Salem in 1846. See Letters 299, 347.

2. John McNeil (1784–50) and Hugh Jameson, brothers-in-law of Franklin Pierce, had been surveyor and deputy surveyor, respectively, since 1829.

3. Jeremiah or John G. Harris. Mary Peabody wrote to SH on January 5 that after Elizabeth had told NH about the office, he *"felt very bad* when he found he actually got it" (MS, Essex). This seems to be the inspectorship that NH apparently declined.

4. NH, it turned out, replaced Paul R. George, a measurer, and William B. Pike of Salem, whom Rantoul had recommended, received the inspectorship on January 21. Bancroft wrote to Levi Woodbury, secretary of the treasury, on January 17 that he had appointed as measurer "Nathaniel Hawthorne of Salem (biographer of Cilley)" and requested approval. The salary was $1,500 per year. NH received his first quarterly payment of $304.17 on March 30, for the seventy-three days he had worked; see George Edwin Jepson, "Hawthorne in the Boston Custom House," *Bookman,* XIX (1904), 573–80.

[Salem, ca. January 11, 1839]

Dear Sir:

It will give me great pleasure to comply with your proposition in regard to contributions for the *Mirror,* so far as it may be in my power.[1] I think I can furnish the five articles within the year, at furthest—and perhaps much sooner. Just at the moment I am undergoing somewhat of a metamorphosis; for Mr. Bancroft has formed so high an opinion of my capacity for business as to offer me the post of Inspector in the Boston Custom House—and as I know nothing to the contrary of my suitableness for it (knowing nothing about the matter), I have determined to accept. I understand that I shall have a good deal of leisure time, the greater part of which I mean to employ in writing books for the series projected by the Board of Education,[2] which, I think, promises to be more profitable than any other line of literary labour. Still I shall not utterly lay by the story-telling trade, and shall be happy to come before the public through such a medium as the *Mirror.*[3] It rejoices me to hear of its high repute, under your management.

How is our friend Mr. Benjamin?[4]

Very truly yours,
Nathaniel Hawthorne

Geo. P. Morris

---

1. George Pope Morris (1802–64) published the *New-York Mirror,* a popular and well-regarded magazine, from 1823 to 1842. In letters of February and

October, 1836, Horatio Bridge had suggested that NH write for the *Mirror;* see *NHHW,* I, 134, 140.

2. See 83.3.

3. Although "The Gray Champion" was reprinted in the *Mirror,* February 23, 1839, no other contribution by NH seems to have appeared there.

4. Park Benjamin had formed a partnership with Horace Greeley at the beginning of 1838, and was now literary editor of the weekly *New-Yorker.*

Salem, Jany 12th. 1839

My dear Longfellow,

I was nowise to blame for going down the steps of the Tremont, almost at the moment that you were coming up; inasmuch as I did not receive your letter, appointing the rendezvous, till I reached Salem that evening.[1] Those little devils in your hollow teeth had made you oblivious,[2] and caused you to carry the epistle in your pocket at least a week, before putting it into the Post-Office. But never mind; for, please God, we will meet in future often enough to make up for lost time. It has pleased Mr. Bancroft (knowing that what little ability I have is altogether adapted for active life) to offer me the post of Inspector in the Boston Custom-House; and I am going to accept it, with as much confidence in my suitableness for it, as Sancho Panza had in his gubernatorial qualifications.[3] I have no reason to doubt my capacity to fulfil the duties; for I don't know what they are; but, as nearly as I can understand, I shall be a sort of Port-Admiral, and take command of vessels after they enter the harbor, and have control of their cargoes. Pray Heaven I may have opportunities to make defalcation! They tell me that a considerable portion of my time will be unoccupied; the which I mean to employ in sketches of my new experience, under some such titles as follow:—"Passages in the life of a Custom-House Officer"—"Scenes in Dock"—"Voyages at Anchor"—"Nibblings of a Wharf-Rat"—"Trials of a Tide-Waiter"—"Romance of the Revenue Service"—together with an ethical work in two volumes on the subject of Duties—the first volume to treat of moral and religious Duties; and the second, of the Duties imposed by the Revenue Laws, which I already begin to consider as much the most important class.

Thus you see I have abundance of literary labor in prospect; and this makes it more tolerable that you refuse to let me blow a blast upon the "Wonder-Horn."[4] Assuredly, you have a right to make all the music on your own instrument; but I should serve you right were I to set up an opposition— for instance, with a corn-stalk fiddle, or a pumpkin vine trumpet. Really I do mean to turn my attention to writing for children, either on my own hook, or for the series of works projected by the Board of Education—to which I have been requested to contribute. It appears to me that there is a very fair chance of profit.

I received a letter, the other day, from Bridge, dated at Rome, November 3[d]. He speaks of the Consul, Mr. Greene— "an old friend of Longfellow's."[5] Bridge seems to be leading a very happy life. I wish some one of the vessels, which are to be put under my command, would mutiny, and run away with the worshipful Inspector to the Mediterranean. Well— I have a presentiment that I shall be there one day.

I shall remove to Boston in the course of a fortnight; and, most sincerely, I do not know that I have any pleasanter anticipation than that of frequently meeting you. I saw Mr. Sparks[6] at Miss Silsbee's, some time since; and he said you were thinking of a literary paper.[7] Why not? Your name would go a great way towards insuring its success; and it is intolerable that there should not be a single belles-lettres journal in New-England. And whatever aid a Custom-House officer could afford, should always be forthcoming. By the way, "The Inspector" would be as good a title for a paper as "The Spectator."

If you mean to see me in Salem, you must come pretty quick.[8]

Yours truly,
Nath. Hawthorne.

1. On October 24; see 87.2.

2. In a letter of October 22 to George Washington Greene, Longfellow had confided: "I am suffering dismally, and have been for a fortnight past, with tooth-ache and a swollen jaw. I have had one great grinder out" (*Letters*, II, 109). See also his journal, October 17 (*Life*, I, 299), and *AN*, pp. 166, 593.

3. *Don Quixote*, part 2, chapter 33: "As I see it, in this matter of governments, everything depends on the kind of start you make; and it may be that after I've been governor for a couple of weeks, I'll have my hand in and will be better at the job than at work in the fields, which I was brought up to do" (Putnam trans.).

4. NH and Longfellow had apparently agreed that the latter would compile the book as he wished; see Lawrance Thompson, *Young Longfellow* (New York: Macmillan, 1938), p. 261. Longfellow continued to negotiate with his publisher, Samuel Colman (*Letters*, II, 148, 154), but eventually dropped the project.

5. Horatio Bridge had given up the practice of law in 1838 when he was appointed a paymaster in the U.S. Navy. George Washington Greene (1811–83), one of Longfellow's closest friends and most devoted correspondents, was U.S. consul at Rome from 1837 to 1845. See 273.6.

6. Jared Sparks (1789–1866), the editor and historian, had become in 1838 the McLean Professor of Ancient and Modern History at Harvard. On May 21, 1839, he was to marry Mary Silsbee.

7. The previous summer, Longfellow had considered establishing a literary newspaper in New York in collaboration with Sparks, Samuel Gray Ward, and Joseph Cogswell. When Cogswell was unable to become editor, Longfellow thought of moving the enterprise to Boston, but by January 5, 1839, had abandoned it. See *Young Longfellow*, pp. 288–90; *Letters*, II, 88–89, 93, 116–17; Arlin Turner, "Hawthorne and Longfellow: Abortive Plans for Collaboration," *NHJ 1971*, pp. 3–11.

8. There is no record of a visit by Longfellow at this time. The page of his MS journal at Harvard for the beginning of 1839 has been excised.

[Boston] Wednesday Afternoon, March 6th, 1839[1]

My dearest Sophie,

I had a parting glimpse of you, Monday forenoon, at your window[2]—and that image abides by me, looking pale, and not so quiet as is your wont. I have reproached myself many times since, because I did not show my face, and then we should both have smiled; and so our reminiscences would have been sunny instead of shadowy. But I believe I was so intent on seeing you, that I forgot all about the desirableness of being myself seen. Perhaps, after all, you did see me—at least you knew that I was there. I fear that you were not quite well that morning. Do grow better and better—physically I mean, for I protest against any spiritual improvement, until I am better able to keep pace with you—but do be strong, and full of life—earthly life—and let there be a glow in your cheeks. And sleep soundly the whole night long, and get up every morning with a feeling as if you were newly created; and I pray you to lay up a stock of fresh energy every day till we meet again; so that we may walk miles and miles, without your once needing to lean upon my arm. Not but what you *shall* lean upon it, as much as you choose—indeed, whether you choose or not—but I would feel as if you did it to lighten my footsteps, not to support your own. Am I requiring you to work a miracle within yourself? Perhaps so—yet not a greater one than I do really believe might be wrought by inward faith and outward aids. Try it, my Dove;[3] and be as lightsome on earth as your sister doves are in the air.

Tomorrow I shall expect a letter from you; but I am almost

in doubt whether to tell you that I expect it; because then your conscience will reproach you, if you should happen not to have written. I would leave you as free as you leave me. But I do wonder whether you were serious in your last letter, when you asked me whether you wrote too often, and seemed to think that you might thus interfere with my occupations. My dear Sophie, your letters are no small portion of my spiritual food, and help to keep my soul alive, when otherwise it might languish unto death, or else become hardened and earth-incrusted, as seems to be the case with almost all the souls with whom I am in daily intercourse. They never interfere with my worldly business—neither the reading nor the answering them—(I am speaking of your letters, not of those "earth-incrusted" souls)—for I keep them to be the treasure of my still and secret hours, such hours as pious people spend in prayer; and the communion which my spirit then holds with yours has something of religion in it. The charm of your letters does not depend upon their intellectual value, though that is great, but on the spirit of which they are the utterance, and which is a spirit of wonderful efficacy. No one, whom you would deem worthy of your friendship, could enjoy so large a share of it as I do, without feeling the influence of your character throughout his own—purifying his aims and desires, enabling him to realize that there is a truer world than this feverish one around us, and teaching him how to gain daily entrance into that better world. Such, so far as I have been able to profit by it, has been your ministration to me. Did you dream what an angelic guardianship was entrusted to you?

March 7th. Your letter did come. You had not the heart to disappoint me, as I did you, in not making a parting visit, and shall again, by keeping this letter to send by Mary.[4] But I disappoint you in these two instances, only that you may consider it a decree of Fate (or of Providence, which you please) that we shall not meet on the mornings of my departure, and that my letters shall not come oftener than on the alternate Saturday. If you will but believe this, you will be quiet. Otherwise I know that the Dove will flutter her wings, and often, by necessity, will flutter them in vain. Do forgive me, and let me have my own way, and believe (for it is true) that I never cause you the slightest disappointment without pain and remorse on my part. And yet, I know that when you wish me to do any particular thing, you will always tell me so, and that if my sins of omission or commission should ever wound your heart, you will by no means conceal it.

I did enjoy that walk infinitely—for certainly the enjoyment was not all finite. And what a heavenly pleasure we might have enjoyed this very day; the air was so delicious, that it seemed as if the dismal old Custom-House was situated in Paradise; and this afternoon, I sat with my window open, to temper the glow of a huge coal-fire. It almost seems to me, now, as if beautiful days were wasted and thrown away, when we do not feel their beauty and heavenliness through one another.

Your own friend,
N. H.

1. This letter is clearly not the first NH wrote to SH, but after his death she marked it "Letter I."

2. SH had been staying in Boston since the first of January with the Samuel Hooper family at 21 South Street, but had recently returned to Salem. NH had begun work at the Boston Custom House on January 17, and boarded at the house of Alma Louisa Livermore, 8 Somerset Place. SH's letter to her father, February 9–13, indicates that NH visited her at the Hoopers' almost every day, sometimes morning as well as evening. On February 9 he came to accompany her to Mary Benjamin Motley's, "but when we were on the way he said he did not want to see any body—& so we walked round the common & saw the sunset" (MS, Berg).

3. This first extant association of SH with the dove seems to derive from the beginnings of their courtship in Boston, and to be memorialized by the description in BR, p. 152, which invests the bird with a "slight, fantastic pathos."

Compare especially 118.4. Also suggestive is the description of the artistic young lovers of "The Seven Vagabonds" (1833) as "two doves that had flown into our ark" (*TTT*, p. 356).

4. Mary Peabody, SH's sister, had started a school for small children in Boston, and was contributing to Horace Mann's *Common School Journal*. She boarded in the home of Mrs. Susan Channing, 1 Chauncey Place. She went to visit her family in Salem on weekends, and carried some of NH's letters to SH. See 87.2.

Boston, April 2^d, 1839

Mine own Dove,

I have been sitting by my fireside ever since tea-time, till now it is past eight °clock; and have been musing and dreaming about a thousand things, with every one of which, I do believe, some nearer or remoter thought of you was intermingled. I should have begun this letter earlier in the evening, but was afraid that some intrusive idler would thrust himself between us, and so the sacredness of my letter would be partly lost;—for I feel as if my letters were sacred, because they are written from my spirit to your spirit. I wish it were possible to convey them to you by other than earthly messengers—to convey them directly into your heart, with the warmth of mine still lingering in them. When we shall be endowed with our spiritual bodies, I think they will be so constituted, that we may send thoughts and feelings any distance, in no time at all, and transfuse them warm and fresh into the consciousness of those whom we love. Oh what a bliss it would be, at this moment; if I could be conscious of some purer feeling, some more delicate sentiment, some lovelier fantasy, than could possibly have had its birth in my own nature, and therefore be aware that my Dove was thinking through my mind and feeling through my heart! Try—some evening when you are alone and happy, and when you are most conscious of loving me and being loved by me—and see if you do not possess this power already. But, after all, perhaps it is not wise to intermix fantastic ideas with the reality

of our affection. Let us content ourselves to be earthly creatures, and hold communion of spirit in such modes as are
ordained to us—by letters (dipping our pens as deep as may
be into our hearts) by heartfelt words, when they can be
audible; by glances—through which medium spirits do really
seem to talk in their own language—and by holy kisses,
which I do think have something supernatural in them.

And now good night, my beautiful Dove. I do not write
anymore at present, because there are three more whole days
before this letter will visit you; and I desire to talk with you,
each of those three days. Your letter did not come to-day.
Even if it should not come tomorrow, I shall not imagine that
you forget me or neglect me, but shall heave two or three
sighs, and measure salt and coal so much the more diligently.
Good night; and if I have any power, at this distance, over
your spirit, it shall be exerted to make you sleep like a little
baby, till the 'Harper of the golden Dawn' arouse you. Then
you must finish that ode.[1] But do, if you love me, sleep.

April 3ᵈ. No letter, my dearest; and if one comes tomorrow
I shall not receive it till Friday, nor perhaps then; because I
have a cargo of coal to measure in East Cambridge, and
cannot go to the Custom House till the job is finished. If you
had known this, I think you would have done your possible
to send me a letter to-day. Doubtless you had some good
reason for omitting it. I was invited to dine at Mr. Hooper's,[2]
with your sister Mary; and the notion came into my head,
that perhaps you would be there,—and though I knew that
it could not be so, yet I felt as if it might. But just as I was
going home from the Custom-House to dress, came an abominable person to say that a Measurer was wanted forthwith
at East-Cambridge; so over I hurried, and found that, after
all, nothing would be done till tomorrow morning at sunrise.
In the meantime, I had lost my dinner, and all other pleasures that had awaited me at Mr. Hooper's; so that I came
back in very ill-humor, and do not mean to be very good-

natured again, till my Dove shall nestle upon my heart again, either in her own sweet person, or by her image in a letter. But your image will be with me, long before the letter comes. It will flit around me while I am measuring coal, and will peep over my shoulder to see whether I keep a correct account, and will smile to hear my bickerings with the black-faced demons in the vessel's hold, (they look like the forgemen in Retsch's Fridolin)[3] and will soothe and mollify me amid all the pester and plague that is in store for me tomorrow. Not that I would avoid this pester and plague, even if it were in my power to do so. I need such training, and ought to have undergone it long ago. It will give my character a healthy hardness as regards the world; while it will leave my heart as soft—as fit for a Dove to rest upon—as it is now, or ever was. Good night again, gentle Dove. I must leave a little space for tomorrow's record; and moreover, it is almost time that I were asleep, being to get up in the dusky dawn. Did you yield to my conjurations, and sleep well, last night? Well then, I throw the same spell over you to-night.

April 4th. 1/2 past 9. P.M. I came home late in the afternoon, very tired, sun-burnt and sea-flushed, having walked or sat on the deck of a schooner ever since sunrise. Nevertheless, I purified myself from the sable stains of my profession—stains which I share in common with chimney-sweepers—and then hastened to the Custom-House to get your letter—for I *knew* there was one awaiting me. And now I thank you with my whole heart, and will straightway go to sleep. Do you the same. [*excision*]

April 5th

Your yesterday's letter is received, my beloved Sophie. I have no time to answer it; but, like all your communications, personal or written, it is the sunshine of my life. I have been busy all day, and am now going to see your sister Mary—and I hope, Elizabeth. Mr Pickens[4] is going with me.

1. This poem, of which the quoted phrase is probably a part, has been lost. An example of the verse SH included in her letters to NH is given by Rose Hawthorne Lathrop in *Memories*, p. 47.

2. Samuel Hooper (1808–75), a merchant from Marblehead, was now engaged in European and West Indian trade in Boston. He was a U.S. congressman from 1860 until his death. SH had visited the Hooper family at Marblehead the previous September.

3. Moritz Retzsch (1779–1857), *Eight Outlines to Schiller's Fridolin; or, An Errand to the Iron Foundry* (London: S. Prewett, 1824). "Fridolin" was a ballad, "Der Gang nach den Eisenhammer" (1798), by Schiller. SH's engraving for *The Gentle Boy: A Thrice Told Tale*, was "in the same style" as another work of Retzsch's published by Weeks, Jordan & Company, according to advertising in the Boston *Advertiser*, December 21, 1838, and the Boston *Transcript*, December 22. Park Benjamin, reviewing *The Gentle Boy* in the *New-Yorker*, January 26, 1839, said the illustration "has all the effect of one of Retzsch's." See Arlin Turner, "Park Benjamin on the Author and Illustrator of 'The Gentle Boy,'" *NHJ 1974*, p. 88; *Critical Heritage*, p. 69.

4. Apparently a friend of the Peabodys who had lived in Boston at least since the late 1820s. His "classical smile & eye" and "punditical" personality are mentioned in their letters of 1826–28. A James Pickens, merchant of 42 Bowdoin Street, is listed in the 1835 Boston *Directory*; by 1842 he was dead, leaving his widow, Charity, at the same address. The 1842 *Directory* also lists a John Pickens, at Walnut Street corner of Beacon.

[Boston] Wednesday April 17th. 1839—4 °clock P.M.

My Dearest,

If it were not for your sake, I should really be glad of this pitiless east-wind,[1] and should especially bless the pelting rain and intermingled snow-flakes. They have released me from the toils and cares of office, and given me license to betake myself to my own chamber; and here I sit by a good coal-fire, with at least six or seven comfortable hours to spend before bed-time. I feel pretty secure against intruders; for the bad weather will defend me from foreign invasion; and as to Cousin Haley,[2] he and I had a bitter political dispute last evening, at the close of which he went to bed in high dudgeon, and probably will not speak to me these three days. Thus you perceive that strife and wrangling, as well as east-winds and rain, are the methods of a kind Providence to promote my comfort—which could not have been so well secured in any other way. Six or seven hours of cheerful solitude! But I will not be alone. I invite your spirit to be with me—at any hour and as many hours as you please—but especially at the twilight hour, before I light my lamp. Are you conscious of my invitation? I bid you at that particular time, because I can see visions more vividly in the dusky glow of fire-light, than either by day-light or lamp-light. Come— and let me renew my spell against head-ache and other direful effects of the east-wind. How I wish I could give you a portion of my insensibility!—and yet I should be almost afraid of some radical transformation, were I to produce a change in that respect. GOD[3] made you so delicately, that it is especially unsafe to interfere with His workmanship. If my little Sophie—mine own Dove—cannot grow plump and rosy and tough and vigorous, without being changed into another nature, then I do think that, for this short life, she had better remain just what she is. Yes; but you always will be the same to me, because we have met in Eternity, and there our intimacy was formed. So get as well as you possibly can, and be as strong and rosy as you will; for I shall never doubt that you are the same Sophie who have so often leaned upon my arm, and needed its superfluous strength.

I *was* conscious, on those two evenings, of a peacefulness and contented repose such as I never enjoyed before. You could not have felt such quiet, unless I had felt it too—nor could I, unless you had. If either of our spirits had been troubled, they were then in such close communion that both must have felt the same grief and turmoil. I never, till now, had a friend who could give me repose;—all have disturbed me; and whether for pleasure or pain, it was still disturbance. But peace overflows from your heart into mine. Then I feel that there is a Now—and that Now must be always calm and happy—and that sorrow and evil are but phantoms that seem to flit across it.

You must never expect to see my sister E. in the day-time, unless by previous appointment, or when she goes to walk. So unaccustomed am I to daylight interviews, that I never imagine her in sunshine; and I really doubt whether her faculties of life and intellect begin to be exercised till dusk— unless on extraordinary occasions. Their noon is at midnight. I wish you could walk with her; but you must not, because she is indefatigable, and always wants to walk half round the world, when once she is out-of-doors.[4]

April 18th. My Dove—my hopes of a long evening of seclusion were not quite fulfilled; for, a little before nine °clock John Forrester[5] and Cousin Haley came in, both of whom I so fascinated with my delectable conversation, that they did not take leave till after eleven. Nevertheless, I had already secured no inconsiderable treasure of enjoyment, with all of which you were intermingled. There has been nothing to do at the Custom-House to-day; so I came home at two °clock, and—went to sleep! Pray Heaven you may have felt a sympathetic drowsiness, and have yielded to it. My nap has been a pretty long one; for—as nearly as I can judge by the position of the sun—it must be as much as five °clock. I think there will be a beautiful sunset; and perhaps, if we could walk out together, the wind would change and the air grow balmy at once. The Spring is not acquainted with my Dove and me, as the Winter was;—how then can we expect her to be kindly to us. We really must contrive to walk out and meet her, and make friends with her; then she will salute your cheek with her balmiest kiss, whenever she gets a chance. As to the East-Wind, if ever the imaginative portion of my brain recover from its torpor, I mean to personify it as a wicked, spiteful, blustering, treacherous—in short, altogether devilish sort of body, whose principle of life it is to make as much mischief as he can. The West wind—or whatever is the gentlest wind of Heaven—shall assume your aspect, and be humanized and angelicised with your traits of character. And the sweet West shall finally triumph over the fiendlike East, and rescue the world from his miserable tyranny; and if I tell the story well, I am sure my loving and beloved West Wind will kiss me for it.

When this week's first letter came, I held it a long time in my hand, marvelling at the superscription. How did you contrive to write it? Several times since, I have pored over it, to discover how much of yourself was mingled with my share of it; and certainly there is a grace flung over the facsimile, which was never seen in my harsh, uncouth autograph—and yet none of the strength is lost. You are wonderful. Imitate this.

Nath. Hawthorne.[6]

Friday

April 19th. Your Wednesday's letter has come, dearest.
Your letters delight me more than anything, save the sound
of your voice. And I love dearly to write to you—so be at
peace on that score. You *are* beautiful, my own heart's Dove.
Never doubt it again. I shall really and truly be very glad of
the extracts; and they will have a charm for me that could
not otherwise have been. I will imagine your voice repeating
them, tremulously, as when you are in my arms. The *spell*
which you laid upon my brow will retain its power till we
meet again—then it must be renewed.

Wh it a beautiful day—and I had a double enjoyment of it,
for your sake and my own. I have been to walk, this afternoon, to Bunker's Hill and the Navy-Yard, and am tired,
because I had not your arm to support me.

God keep you from East winds and every other evil.

Mine own Dove's own Friend,

N. H.

1/2 past 5 P. M.

1. The many references in the love letters to this phenomenon lead to its
appearance in NH's fiction, especially in *HSG*, where Hepzibah seems to be "in
her very person, only another phase of this gray and sullen spell of weather; the
East-Wind itself, grim and disconsolate" (p. 223), and *BR*, where Coverdale,
returning to Boston, finds the day "lowering, with occasional gusts of rain, and
an ugly-tempered east-wind, which seemed to come right off the chill and melancholy sea, hardly mitigated by sweeping over the roofs, and amalgamating itself
with the dusky element of city-smoke" (p. 145).

2. Thomas Haley Forrester Barstow (1816–71) was the son of Dr. Gideon
Barstow and Nancy Forrester Barstow, and grandson of Simon Forrester and
NH's aunt Rachel Hathorne Forrester. He graduated from Harvard in 1832. In
letters to her sister Elizabeth, SH had described "his intolerably pretty face &
little comfortable plump figure—& indifferent chitchat," and recorded that he
had called and "staid more than an hour! & was very agreeable but he is not
particularly profound" (May 1, May 14, 1838, MSS, Berg). Haley and John
Forrester (n.5) were evidently boarders in the house.

3. The spelling in capitals was a gesture to SH, who habitually used that form.

4. SH and her family were by now well aware of Elizabeth Hawthorne's distinctive habits, NH's "very remarkable sister who lives even more to herself than he has done" (Mary to George Peabody, November 16, 1837; MS, Berg). During the spring and summer of 1838, Elizabeth shared walks in Salem with Mary and Mrs. Peabody, and lent and borrowed books and magazines with them and SH. In her journal letters to Elizabeth Peabody, SH described on May 8 the return of a book to Elizabeth at Herbert Street, where she found Mrs. Hawthorne (whom she had never seen "in my life before") working in the garden: "She said she would inform" Elizabeth of SH's message, "& wished to know the very hour when I should come." On May 13 "Louisa came to the door & took me upstairs. As Elizabeth did not know I was coming, I thought that I should not, perhaps see her, yet I imagined that she might probably appear, as I was such a stranger to the house. It would be an unprecedented honor if she should come out to see me—for you know she never would see *you* except when she expected you in the evening. I asked for her immediately & Louisa went to enquire & came back with the astonishing intelligence that she would be there in a few moments! There now am I not a priviledged mortal? She received me very affectionately & seemed very glad to see me—& I all at once fell in love with her! . . . I staid in the house an hour—! I could not get away, she urged me to stay so much, as if she wanted me. . . . I believe it is extreme sensibility which makes her a hermitess." Later, when NH came on June 1 to ask Mary to walk with him and Elizabeth, SH commented: "Only think what a progress—to come & propose a walk at midday." Elizabeth then decided not to accompany them; Louisa told Mary "that E. was very sorry afterwards that she did not go" (MSS, Berg).

5. John Forrester (1813–41) was the son of John and Charlotte Story Forrester and a grandson of Simon Forrester.

6. The signature was boldly written as a model for her.

Boston, April 30th. 6. P.M. 1839.

My beloved,

Your sweetest of all letters found me at the Custom-House, where I had almost just arrived, having been engaged all the forenoon in measuring twenty chaldrons[1] of coal—which dull occupation was enlivened by frequent brawls and amicable discussions with a crew of funny little Frenchmen from Acadie.[2] I know not whether your letter was a surprise to me—it seems to me that I had a prophetic faith that the Dove would visit me—but at any rate, it was a joy, as it always is; for my spirit turns to you from all trouble and all pleasure. This forenoon I could not wait, as I generally do, to be in solitude before opening your letter; for I expected to be busy all the afternoon, and was already tired with working yesterday and to day; and my heart longed to drink your thoughts and feelings, as a parched throat for cold water. So I pressed the Dove to my lips (turning my head away, so that nobody saw me) and then broke the seal. I do think it is the dearest letter you have written; but I think so of each successive one; so you need not imagine that you have outdone yourself in this instance. How did I live before I knew you—before I possessed your affection! And my dearest, how can you speak as if there were no possibility of remaining best friends! I reckon upon your love as something that is to endure when everything that can perish has perished—though my trust is sometimes mingled with fear, because I feel myself unworthy of your love. But if I am worthy of it, you will always love me; and if there be anything good and pure in me, it will be proved by my always loving you.

After dinner, I had to journey over to East Cambridge, expecting to measure a cargo of Coal there; but the vessel had stuck in the mud on her way thither, so that nothing could be done till tomorrow morning. It must have been my guardian angel that steered her upon that mud-bank; for I really needed rest. Did you lead the vessel astray, my Dove? I did not stop to inquire into particulars, but returned home forthwith, and locked my door, and threw myself on the bed, with your letter in my hand. I read it over slowly and peacefully, and then folding it up, I rested my heart upon it, and fell fast asleep.

Friday, May 3^d. 5 P.M. My dearest, ten million occupations, and interruptions, and intrusions, have kept me from going on with my letter; but my spirit has visited you continually, and yours has come to me. I have had to be out a good deal in the east-winds; but your spell has proved sovereign against all harm, though sometimes I have shuddered and shivered for your sake. How have you borne it, my poor dear little Dove? Have you been able to flit abroad on to-day's west wind, and go to Marblehead, as you designed? You will not have seen Mrs. Hooper,[3] because she came up to Boston in the cars, on Monday morning. I had a brief talk with her, and we made mutual inquiries, she about you, and I about little Annie.[4] I will not attempt to tell you how it rejoices me that we are to spend a whole month together in the same city. Looking forward to it, it seems to me as if that month would never come to an end, because there will be so much of eternity in it.

I wish you had read that dream-letter through, and could remember its contents. I am very sure that it could not have been written by me, however, because I should not think of

addressing you as "My dear Sister"—nor should I like to have
you call me brother—nor ever should have liked it, from the
very first of our acquaintance. We are, I trust, kindred spirits, but not brother and sister. And then what a cold and dry
annunciation of that awful contingency—the "continuance
or not of our acquaintance." Mine own Dove, you are to
blame for dreaming such letters, or parts of letters, as coming
from me. It was you that wrote it—not I. Yet I will not
believe that it shows a want of faith in the steadfastness of
my affection, but only in the continuance of circumstances
prosperous to our earthly and external connection. Let us
trust in GOD for that. Pray to GOD for it, my Dove—for
you know how to pray better than I do. Pray, for my sake,
that no shadows of earth may ever come between us; because
my surest hope of being a good man, and my only hope of
being a happy man, depends upon the permanence of our
union. I have great comfort in such thoughts as those you
suggest—that our hearts have been drawn towards one another so naturally—that we have not cultivated our friendship, but let it grow,—that we have thrown ourselves upon
one another with such perfect trust;—and even the deficiency of worldly wisdom, that some people would ascribe to
us in following the guidance of our hearts so implicitly, is
proof to me that there is a deeper wisdom within us. Oh, let
us not think but that all will be well! And even if, to worldly
eyes, it should appear that our lot is not a fortunate one, still
we shall have glimpses, at least—and I trust a pervading
sunshine—of a happiness that we could never have found, if
we had unquietly struggled for it, and made our own selection of the means and species of it, instead of trusting all to
something diviner than our reason.

My Dove, there were a good many things that I meant to
have written in this letter; but I have continually lapsed into
fits of musing, and when I have written, the soul of my

thought has not readily assumed the earthly garments of language. It is now time to carry the letter to Mary.[5] I kiss you, dearest—did you feel it?

Your own friend
Nath. Hawthorne, Esqr.

Dear me! What an effect that Esquire gives to the whole letter!

1. A chaldron was a measure of 32 bushels.

2. French-speaking regions of the Maritime Provinces of Canada.

3. Anne Sturgis Hooper (1813–84), Mrs. Samuel Hooper.

4. Anne Maria (1835–1930), the Hoopers' daughter. In letters home, during visits to the Hoopers, SH described Annie's pronunciations with particular pleasure.

5. Mary had already departed her boardinghouse, so NH added on the cover address "Care of Dr. N. Peabody," and mailed the letter. Thereafter, NH often used that manner of addressing SH in Salem and later in Boston.

98. TO B. A. G. FULLER,[1] BRUNSWICK

Boston, May 15th, 1839

Dear Sir,

An absence of several days from the city has prevented my earlier acknowledgment of the letter, together with the Magazine[2] and Catalogue, which you had the kindness to send me. It gratifies me to find that the students of my Alma Mater consider my assistance desirable, in an undertaking which I am sure will prove creditable to the College. Just at the present juncture, my time is much taken up with occupations so alien from literature, that I find it impossible to fulfil several engagements which I have already contracted. But I earnestly hope that I may be able, at no very distant interval, to send you something suitable to your purpose. If you deem it important to insert my name in the list of probable contributors, you have my full permission to do so. I must beg, likewise, that you will consider me a subscriber to the Port-Folio.

I have revived many old and happy recollections, by looking over the Catalogue of the Athenaean Society, and rejoice in your account of its present prosperity.

Very truly Yours,
Nath. Hawthorne.

1. Benjamin Apthorp Gould Fuller (1818–85), of the Bowdoin class of 1839, practiced law in Augusta and later in Boston. In 1855 he was for a short time in

partnership with his nephew, Melville Weston Fuller, who later became chief justice of the U.S. Supreme Court.

2. The *Bowdoin Port-Folio*, a literary journal, first appeared in April, 1839. The second issue, in June, held an editorial announcement that NH and Longfellow "have kindly consented to contribute to our pages." Longfellow sent excerpts from his yet unpublished *Hyperion*, but NH sent nothing.

99. TO B. B. THATCHER,[1] BOSTON

Boston, May 15th, 1839.

Dear Sir,

I ought very long ago to have replied to your note, but have deferred so doing, partly because my present occupations, though not very irksome in themselves, entirely break me up as a literary man—and partly because I wished to obtain a copy of my Tales, whereof to ask your acceptance. If you will do me the kindness to call at Miss Livermore's, No. 8. Somerset Place, I will, if at home, deliver you the said Tales. Should you not find me, I will call at your office with them. Thus, in one way or other, I shall gain the pleasure of your personal acquaintance,—to which I may almost advance a claim, as we were two or three years contemporaries at Brunswick.

Very truly Yours,
Nath. Hawthorne.

1. Benjamin Bussey Thatcher (1809–40), of the Bowdoin class of 1826, had studied law and was admitted to the bar in Boston, but devoted himself to literature, and wrote for the *North American Review*. When he edited the 1837 *Boston Book*, he had invited SH to contribute an "allegory" (Bronson Alcott to SH, September 12, 1836; *The Letters of A. Bronson Alcott*, ed. Richard L. Herrnstadt [Ames: Iowa State University Press, 1969], p. 30). NH, in the *American Magazine*, II (April, 1836), 317, had mentioned Thatcher's lecture on the Boston Tea Party; see Turner, p. 91.

Boston, May 16th. 1839.

Dear Longfellow,

Why do you never come and see me, or at least make inquiry after me, either at the Custom-House, or at No. 8. Somerset Place?[1] I wanted to talk about a great many things, most of which are now past talking about—but nevertheless I should still be glad to see you. And I have done nothing yet about publishing a new volume of tales, and should like to take further counsel with you, on that matter.[2] If I write a preface, it will be to bid farewell to literature; for, as a literary man, my new occupations entirely break me up.

A friend of mine, the Rev. H. L. Conolly, an Episcopal clergyman, formerly of South Boston, is going South—to Washington and Virginia, with a view to establishing an Academy.[3] Can you give him any letters to people thereabouts, that would be useful to him? He is a good fellow and of superior acquirements.

If you come to Boston next Saturday, call on me. Very probably you may not find me, for Uncle Sam is rather despotic as to the disposal of my time; but I shall be grateful for your good-will.

Yours truly,
Nath. Hawthorne.

1. During March and April, Longfellow had been working on *Hyperion;* in May he suffered indisposition and exhaustion. His journal shows no visit to NH until October 10, 1839.

2. On May 20 Longfellow wrote to his New York publisher, Samuel Colman: "By the way, my friend Hawthorne wants to publish two vols of Tales in the same style with Hyperion; and would like the same terms you make with me. I think you would do well to take the work. Please write me a word on this subject in yr. next. Hawthorne is a great favorite with the public, as you know, and a man, who is in future to stand very, *very* high in our literature. You ought to be his publisher." Colman replied, May 27, inviting correspondence on the subject, but his bankruptcy in December made him unable to publish (*Letters*, II, 148).

3. Conolly's journey south led him to Philadelphia, where he organized St. Mark's Episcopal Church. He afterward returned to Salem. See Manning Hawthorne, "Hawthorne and 'the Man of God,'" *Colophon*, n.s. II (1937), 262–82.

Boston   May 19th, 1839.

Dear O'Sullivan,

A week or two since, the enclosed letter was sent me, to be transmitted to you, and as it may gratify you to know Miss Silsbee's very words, I here copy them:—"In examining many packages of letters I was about to burn, the enclosed is the only one I found left in Mr. O'Sullivan's handwriting. Judging that your kindness will do me the favor to direct and forward it to him—as I do not know where he may be found—I take the liberty of enclosing it to your care, the rest of my task being accomplished. Respectfully, M. C. Silsbee." By the "rest of her task," I suppose she means the destruction of my own letters, which I had requested her to burn. I hardly expected to be the medium of another communication between our fair friend and yourself, but now certainly the last knot of our entanglement is loosed. She is to be married, I believe, this week—an event which, I am almost sorry to think, will cause a throb in neither of our bosoms.[1] My visits to Salem have been so short and hurried, that I have found no time to call on her these three months; but I understand that I am still in good odor with her. As for me, I have neither resentment nor regrets, liking nor dislike—having fallen in love with somebody else.

I deeply regret your financial difficulties—not on my own account; for I find that you really do not owe me anything. You have paid me at different times, $25 in cash and $50 by a draft on Otis and Broaders, and $75 by a draft on John Ward & Co. of New York—$150 in all. I do not know how many pages I have contributed to the Magazine; but this sum may surely be considered a fair compensation. Consider it such, and let no more be said—unless, indeed, you think me overpaid, and demand fresh contributions to make up the debt. That I have not recently contributed, is owing to no disinclination thereto; but the fact is, I am quite done for and broken up as a literary man, so long as I retain this office. Nothing have I written since I held it, save two or three puffs of your own Magazine.[2] My duties have not been very laborious hitherto; but I have been cramped by a sense that I am no longer master of my own time and motions. Throughout the summer and autumn, I expect to be almost constantly employed from sunrise till sunset. The more business the better; for, by the omission of Congress to pass a certain regulation, I shall be entitled to the whole fees of my office, amounting possibly to $3000, instead of the paltry $1500.[3] If ever I come to be worth $5000, I will kick all business to the devil,—at least, till that be spent.

Miss Peabody wishes you to send back her article,[4] by some convenient opportunity. She likewise repeatedly requested me (suspecting something of your difficulties, though I entered into no particular explanation on that head) to assure you that you need not trouble yourself about paying for her "Beautiful Arts"—the article having been in a manner forced upon you. But I told her that I should do no such thing, nor that you would consent to such an arrangement. Nevertheless, it will make you easier to know that she is not in immediate want of the money. She is a good old soul, and would give away her only petticoat, I do believe, to anybody that she thought needed it more than herself.

The bearer of this letter is the Rev. H. L. Conolly, an Episcopal clergyman, formerly settled in Boston. He is going to Virginia, with the design of establishing a school or academy.[5] He is a man of talents and highly respectable attainments; and if you can do anything to forward his purposes, I beg that you will do so—he being a friend of mine. Perhaps you can give him letters to people in Richmond or thereabouts.

I mean to publish a new collection of Tales in the course of the summer.[6] I did not send you The Gentle Boy, because the engraving did no sort of justice to the original sketch.[7]

Pray write to me. Do not impute it to any diminished respect for you or concern for the welfare of the Democratic, that I have ceased to be a contributor. It was the absolute decree of fate. I think, too, that I am the less able to write, because a dozen editors of various periodicals, literary and political, are continually teazing me for articles. I have no refuge, save to declare myself no longer a literary man.

Yours truly,

N. H.

1. See 93.6.

2. One of these may be a long, one-and-a-half column notice in the Boston Morning Post, February 4, 1:6, of the Democratic Review for January, beginning, "This is the best number which has yet appeared of this very able periodical. It contains many articles which can but prove interesting to the politician, the scholar, and the general reader." The contents are described, including NH's "Old Esther Dudley": "Like all the other productions of its author, it is beautifully written, and is a story of much interest—just such an one as we like to read, or rather dream o'er, on a winter night." The review ends with congratulations to the Democratic party "on their having among the publications which advocate their cause, a periodical of such superior excellence." A short and lower-keyed notice of the February issue appeared in the Post on March 19, 2:1. NH may also refer to as "puffs" the reprintings, crediting the Democratic Review, of "Howe's Masquerade" and "Edward Randolph's Portrait" in the Boston Weekly Magazine, February 9 and 23, and "Old Esther Dudley" in the Salem Advertiser, February 13.

3. NH's sense of affluence encouraged O'Sullivan to borrow; in a note of September 30, 1839, he wrote: "Nathaniel Hawthorne Esq. Measurer, Custom House, Boston. Please pay to the order of Messrs. Prince Ward & King, Five Hundred & Fifty Dollars on account of J. L. O'Sullivan" (MS, Essex).

4. Unidentified.

5. See 100.3.

6. At this time twenty-one new tales and sketches by NH had appeared in periodicals since the 1837 publication of *TTT*. Sixteen of these were to appear in *TTT* of 1842, with five earlier pieces not collected in 1837. NH must have discussed with SH at this time collecting "The Haunted Mind" and "The Village Uncle" from the *Token* for 1835; see her letter to Elizabeth Peabody of June 23, in *Memories*, p. 29.

7. SH wrote to her father on January 9 that the engraver, Joseph Andrews, "had made a great many alterations of his own head, deliberately—in the faces!!! Did you ever hear of such unwarrantable liberties?" (MS, Berg).

Salem, May 26th. 1839

Mine own self,

I felt rather dismal yesterday—a sort of vague weight on my spirit—a sense that something was wanting to me here. What or who could it have been that I so missed? I thought it not best to go to your house last evening; so that I have not yet seen Elizabeth—but we shall probably attend the Hurley-Burley to-night.[1] Would that my Dove might be there! It seems really monstrous that here, in her own home—or what was her home, till she found another in my arms—she should no longer be.[2] Oh, my dearest, I yearn for you, and my heart heaves when I think of you—(and that is always, but sometimes a thought makes me know and feel you more vividly than at others, and *that* I call "thinking of you")—heaves and swells (my heart does) as sometimes you have felt it beneath you, when your head or your bosom was resting on it. At such moments it is stirred up from its depths. Then our two ocean-hearts mingle their floods.

I do not believe that this letter will extend to three pages. My feelings do not, of their own accord, assume words—at least, not a continued flow of words. I write a few lines, and then I fall a-musing about many things, which seem to have no connection among themselves, save that my Dove flits lightly through them all. I feel as if my being were dissolved, and the idea of you were diffused throughout it. Am I writing nonsense? That is for you to decide. You know what is

Truth—"what is what"—and I should not dare to say to you what I felt to be other than the Truth—other than the very "what." It is very singular (but I do not suppose I can express it) that, while I love you so dearly, and while I am so conscious of the deep embrace of our spirits, and while this is expressed by our every embrace of our hearts, still I have an awe of you that I never felt for anybody else. Awe is not the word, either; because it might imply something stern in you—whereas—but you must make it out for yourself. I do wish that I could put this into words—not so much for your satisfaction (because I believe you will understand) as for my own. I suppose I should have pretty much the same feeling if an angel were to come from Heaven and be my dearest friend—only the angel could not have the tenderest of human natures too, the sense of which is mingled with this sentiment. Perhaps it is because in meeting you, I really meet a spirit, whereas the obstructions of earth have prevented such a meeting in every other case. But I leave the mystery here. Sometime or other, it may be made plainer to me. But methinks it converts my love into religion. And then it is singular, too, that this awe (or whatever it be) does not prevent me from feeling that it is I who have the charge of you, and that my Dove is to follow my guidance and do my bidding. Am I not very bold to say this? And will not you rebel? Oh no; because I possess this power only so far as I love you. My love gives me the right, and your love consents to it.

Since writing the above, I have been asleep; and I dreamed that I had been sleeping a whole year in the open air; and that while I slept, the grass grew around me. It seemed, in my dream, that the very bed-clothes which actually covered me were spread beneath me, and when I awoke (in my dream) I snatched them up, and the earth under them looked black, as if it had been burnt—one square place, exactly the size of the bed clothes. Yet there was grass and herbage scattered over this burnt space, looking as fresh, and bright, and dewy, as if the summer rain and the summer sun had been cherishing them all the time. Interpret this for me, my Dove—but do not draw any sombre omens from it. What is signified by my nap of a whole year? (it made me grieve to think that I had lost so much of eternity)—and what was the fire that blasted the spot of earth which I occupied, while the grass flourished all around?—and what comfort am I to draw from the fresh herbage amid the burnt space? But it is a silly dream, and you cannot expound any sense out of it. Generally, I cannot remember what my dreams have been— only there is a confused sense of having passed through adventures, pleasurable or otherwise. I suspect that you mingle with my dreams, but take care to flit away just before I awake, leaving me but dimly and doubtfully conscious of your visits. [*excision*] Do you never start so suddenly from a dream that you are afraid to look round the room, lest your dream-personages (so strong and distinct seemed their existence, a moment before) should have thrust themselves out of dream-land into the midst of realities? I do, sometimes.

I wish I were to see you this evening. How many times have you thought of me to-day? All the time?—or not at all? Did you ever read such a foolish letter as this? Here I was interrupted, and have taken a stroll down on the Neck—a beautiful, beautiful, beautiful sunshine, and air, and sea. Would that my Dove had been with me. I fear that we shall perforce lose some of our mutual intimacy with Nature—we walk together so seldom that she will seem more like a stranger.

Would that I could write such sweet letters to mine own self, as mine own self writes to me. Good bye, dearest self. Direct yours to

Nath. Hawthorne, Esq.[3]
Custom-House, Boston

1. Macbeth, I. i. 3. Miss Susan Burley (1792–1850) sponsored a group that met regularly on Saturday or Sunday evenings for conversation and readings, at her house on Chestnut Street in Salem. See Caroline Howard King, *When I Lived in Salem, 1822–1866* (Brattleboro, Vt.: Stephen Daye, 1937), pp. 166–68; Marianne C. D. Silsbee, *A Half Century of Salem* (Boston: Houghton, Mifflin, 1887), p. 97. She continued to be a benefactor of NH and SH till her death. See 240, 364.

2. SH was staying at 4 Avon Place, Boston, with her cousin Theodore Dehon Parker, a merchant, his wife Caroline, and their children.

3. The signature is in a larger and heavier script, in reminder that SH should disguise her correspondence to him at the office.

Boston, July 3ᵈ. 1839.

Most beloved Amelia,

I shall call you so sometimes in playfulness, and so may
you; but it is not the name by which my soul recognizes you.[1]
It knows you as Sophie, but I doubt whether that is the
inwardly and intensely dearest epithet either. I believe that
"Dove" is the true word after all; and it never can be used
amiss, whether in sunniest gaiety or shadiest seriousness.
And yet it is a sacred word, and I should not love to have
anybody hear me use it, nor know that GOD has baptized
you so—the baptism being for yourself and me alone. By that
name, I think, I shall greet you, when we meet in Heaven.
Other dear ones may call you 'daughter,' 'sister,' 'Sophia';
but when, at your entrance into Heaven, or after you have
been a little while there, you hear a voice say 'Dove!' then
you will know that your kindred spirit has been admitted
(perhaps for your sake) to the mansions of rest. That word
will express his yearning for you—then to be forever satisfied; for we will melt into one another, and be close, close
together then. The name was inspired; it came without our
being aware that you were thenceforth to be my Dove, now
and through eternity. I do not remember how nor when it
alighted on you; the first I knew, it was in my heart to call
you so.

Good night now, my Dove. It is not yet nine °clock; but I
am somewhat aweary, and prefer to muse about you till bed-
time, rather than write.

July 5th. 1/2 past seven P.M. I must, somehow or other, finish this letter to-night, my dearest—or else it could not be sent tomorrow; and then I fear our head would ache, naughty head that it is. My heart yearns to communicate to you; but if it had any other means at hand, it certainly would not choose to communicate by the scratchings of an iron pen, which I am now compelled to use. This must and will inevitably be a dull letter. Oh how different from yours, which I received to day. You are absolutely inspired, my Dove; and it is not my poor stupid self that inspires you; for how could I give what is not in me. I wish I could write to you in the morning, before my toils begin; but that is impossible, unless I were to write before day-light. At eventide, my mind has quite lost its elasticity—my heart, even, is weary—and all that I seem capable of doing is to rest my head on its pillow, its own pillow, and there lay down the burthen of life. I do not mean to imply that I am unhappy or discontented; for this is not the case; my life is only a burthen, in the same way that it is so to every toilsome man, and mine is a healthy weariness, such as needs only a night's sleep to remove it. But from henceforth forever, I shall be entitled to call the sons of toil my brethren, and shall know how to sympathize with them, seeing that I, likewise, have risen at the dawn, and borne the fervor of the mid-day sun, nor turned my heavy footsteps homeward till eventide. Years hence, perhaps, the experience that my heart is acquiring now will flow out in truth and wisdom.

You ask me a good many questions, my Dove, and I will answer such of them as now occur to me, and the rest you may ask me again, when we meet. First as to your letters. My beloved, you must write whenever you will, in all confidence that I can never be otherwise than joyful to receive your letters. Do not get into the habit of trying to find out, by any method save your own intuition, what is pleasing and what displeasing to me. Whenever you need my counsel, or even my reproof, in any serious matter, you will not fail to receive it; but I wish my Dove to be as free as a Bird of Paradise. Now, as to this affair of the letters, I have sometimes been a little annoyed at the smiles of my brother measurers, who, notwithstanding the masculine fist of the direction, seem to know that such delicately sealed and folded epistles can come only from a lady's small and tender hand.[2] But this annoyance is not on my own account; but because it seems as if the letters were prophaned by being smiled at— but this is, after all, a mere fantasy, since the smilers know nothing about my Dove, not that I really have a Dove; nor can they be certain that the letters come from a lady, nor, especially, can they have the remotest imagination what heavenly letters they are. The sum and substance is, that they are smiling at nothing; and so it is no matter for their smiles. I would not give up one letter to avoid the "world's dread laugh,"[3]—much less to shun the good-natured raillery of three or four people who do not dream of giving pain. Why has my Dove made me waste so much of my letter in this talk about nothing?

My dearest, did you really think that I meant to express a doubt whether we should enjoy each other's society so much, if we could be together all the time. No, no; for I always feel, that our momentary and hurried interviews scarcely afford us time to taste the draught of affection that we drink from one another's hearts. There is a precious portion of our happiness wasted, because we are forced to enjoy it too greedily. But I thought, as you do, that there might be more communication of intellect, as well as communion of hearts, if we could be oftener together.

Your picture gallery of auxiliary verbs is an admirable fantasy.[4] You are certainly the first mortal to whom it was given to behold a verb; though, it seems as if they ought to be visible, being creatures whose office it is (if I remember my Grammar aright) "to be, to do, and to suffer."[5] Therein is comprehended all that we mortals are capable of. No; for, according to this definition, verbs do not feel, and cannot enjoy—they only exist, and act, and are miserable. My Dove and I are no verbs—or if so, we are passive verbs, and therefore happy ones. [*excision*]

1. This is the only known letter in which NH addressed SH as "Amelia."

2. SH was evidently now addressing letters in a heavier, "masculine" hand, to spare NH embarrassment. See 96.4.

3. James Thomson, *The Seasons: Autumn* (1730), lines 233–34: "For still the world prevailed, and its dread laugh, / Which scarce the firm philosopher can scorn."

4. For similar fantasies by NH, see AN, p. 30, for "the idea of an imaginary museum" (1836–37); p. 183, for "letters in the shape of figures of men, &c." (after January 4, 1839); p. 242, for "To personify If—But—And—Though—&c." (1842–44). He had perhaps just become acquainted with SH's illustrations of verbs; see *Memories*, p. 12, for Mary Peabody's account of Dr. Walter Channing's delight in them in 1833, and p. 31, for SH's continuing interest at this time.

5. Lindley Murray, *English Grammar, Adapted to the Different Classes of Learners*, "Etymology. of Verbs.": "A verb is a word which signifies to be, to do, or to suffer." Murray's grammar, first published in 1795, was used in the freshman course NH took at Bowdoin.

[Boston, ca. July 10, 1839]

I suppose I shall come home Saturday, and it will not be worth while to send the valise before—the pantaloons must be washed, above all things.[1]

I am very well—which is a wonder, considering how I am daily fried in the sun. I do really sizzle sometimes—but I guzzle more than I sizzle.

1. NH had resumed sending laundry home to Salem as he had done in 1836, but now the valise presumably went by train. See 61, 105.

Boston, July 13th. [1839]

I can't possibly come home tomorrow, as I must be here till after sunset, and on Monday morning at sunrise; and it would not be worth while to come for a few hours on Sunday—so I send my valise. Return it as soon as convenient; and put in some cake, if you choose; for I am often compelled to go to the uttermost parts of the Earth, where no dinners are to be had. I have received some wedding cake, but will not send it among my dirty shirts.

Hit Beelzebub a poke on my account.

Boston, Monday eve^g July 15th. [1839]

My blessed Dove,

Your letter was brought to me at East-Cambridge, this afternoon:—otherwise I know not when I should have received it; for I am so busy that I know not whether I shall have time to go to the Custom-House these two or three days. I put it in my pocket, and did not read it till just now, when I could be quiet in my own chamber—for I always feel as if your letters were too sacred to be read in the midst of people—and (you will smile) I never read them without first washing my hands!

And so my poor Dove is sick, and I cannot take her to my bosom.[1] I do really feel as if I could cure her, [excision] kiss that should [excision] inquire better into her bosom, more entirely than any kiss ever did before. Oh, my dearest, do let our love be powerful enough to make you well. I will have faith in its efficacy—not that it will work an immediate miracle—but it shall make you so well at heart that you cannot possibly be ill in the body. Partake of my health and strength, my beloved. Are they not your own, as well as mine? Yes—and your illness is mine as well as your's; and with all the pain it gives me, the whole world should not buy my right to share in it.

My dearest, I will not be much troubled, since you tell me (and your word is always truth) that there is no need. But, Oh, be careful of yourself—remembering how much earthly happiness depends on your health. Be tranquil—let me be your Peace, as you are mine. Do not write to me, unless your

heart be unquiet, and you think that you can quiet it by writing. [*excision verso*] God bless mine own Dove.
I have kissed those three last words. Do you kiss them too.

1. SH sent a note to Elizabeth Hawthorne on July 17: "I took cold last week & have been violently threatened with a fever—but today am quite recovered, excepting a slight languor" (MS, Berg).

[Boston] Wednesday eve^g. July 17th. [1839]

My Dearest,

I did not know but you would like another little note—and I think I feel a stronger impulse to write, now that the whole correspondence devolves on me. And I wrote my other note in such a hurry, that I quite forgot to give you the praise which you so deserved, for bearing up so stoutly against the terrible misfortune of my non-appearance. Indeed, I do think my Dove is the strongest little dove that ever was created— never did any creature live, who could feel so acutely, and yet endure so well.

This note must be a mere word, my beloved—and I wish I could make it the very tenderest word that ever was spoken or written. Imagine all that I cannot write.

God bless you, mine own Dove, and make you quite well against I take you to your home—which shall be on Saturday eve^g, without fail. Till then, dearest, spend your time in happy thoughts and happy dreams—and let my image be among them. Good bye, mine own Dove—I have kissed that holy word.

Your own, own, ownest—

My Dove must not look for another note.

Boston, July 24th, 1839—8 °clock. P.M.

Mine own,

I am tired this evening, as usual, with my long day's toil; and my head wants its pillow—and my soul yearns for the friend whom God has given it—whose soul He has married to my soul. Oh, my dearest, how that thought thrills me! We *are* married! I felt it long ago; and sometimes, when I was seeking for some fondest word, it has been on my lips to call you—'Wife'! I hardly know what restrained me from speaking it—unless a dread (for *that* would have been an infinite pang to me) of feeling you shrink back from my bosom, and thereby discovering that there was yet a deep place in your soul which did not know me. Mine own Dove, need I fear it now? Are we not married? God knows we are. Often, while holding you in my arms, I have silently given myself to you, and received you for my portion of human love and happiness, and have prayed Him to consecrate and bless the union. And any one of our innocent embraces—even when our lips did but touch for a moment, and then were withdrawn—dearest, was it not the symbol of a bond between our Souls, infinitely stronger than any external rite could twine around us? Yes— we are married; and as God Himself has joined us, we may trust never to be separated, neither in Heaven nor on Earth. We will wait patiently and quietly, and He will lead us onward hand in hand (as He has done all along) like little children, and will guide us to our perfect happiness—and will teach us when our union is to be revealed to the world. My beloved, why should we be silent to one another—why should our lips be silent—any longer on this subject? The world might, as yet, misjudge us; and therefore we will not speak to the world; but when I hold you in my arms, why should we not commune together about all our hopes of earthly and external, as well as our faith of inward and eternal union? Farewell for to-night, my dearest—my soul's bride! Oh, my heart is thirsty for your kisses; they are the dew which should restore its freshness every night, when the hot sunshiny day has parched it. Kiss me in your dreams; and perhaps my heart will feel it.

July 25th. 8 °clock. P.M. How does my Dove contrive to live and thrive, and keep her heart in cheerful trim, through a whole fortnight, with only one letter from me? It cannot be indifference; so it must be heroism—and how heroic! It does seem to me that my spirit would droop and wither like a plant that lacked rain and dew, if it were not for the frequent shower of your gentle and holy thoughts. But then there is such a difference in our situations. My Dove is at home— not, indeed, in her home of homes—but still in the midst of true affections; and she can live a spiritual life, spiritual and intellectual. Now, my intellect, and my heart and soul, have no share in my present mode of life—they find neither labor nor food in it; every thing that I do here might be better done by a machine. I *am* a machine, and am surrounded by hundreds of similar machines;—or rather, all of the business people are so many wheels of one great machine—and we have no more love or sympathy for one another than if we were made of wood, brass, or iron, like the wheels of other pieces of complicated machinery. Perchance—but do not be frightened, dearest—the soul would wither and die within me, leaving nothing but the busy machine, no germ for immortality, nothing that could taste of heaven, if it were not for the consciousness of your deep, deep love, which is renewed to me with every letter. Oh, my Dove, I have really thought sometimes, that God gave you to me to be the salvation of my soul.

Boston, July 30th. 8 (or thereabouts) P.M. [1839]

Beloved,

There was no letter from you to-day; and this circumstance, in connection with your mention of a headache on Sunday, made me apprehensive that my Dove is not well. Yet surely she would write, or cause to be written, intelligence of the fact (if fact it were) to the sharer of her well-being and ill-being. Do, dearest, give me the assurance that you will never be ill without letting me know, and then I shall always be at peace, and will not disquiet myself for the non-reception of a letter; for really, I would not have you crowd your other duties into too small a space, nor dispense with anything that it is desirable to do, for the sake of writing to me. If you were not to write for a whole year, I still should never doubt that you love me infinitely; and I doubt not that, in vision, dream, or reverie, our wedded souls would hold communion throughout all that time. Therefore I do not ask for letters while you are well, but leave all to your own heart and judgment; but if anything, bodily or mental, afflicts my Dove, her beloved *must* be told.

And why was my dearest wounded by that silly sentence of mine about "indifference"? It was not well that she should do anything but smile at it. I knew, just as certainly as your own heart knows, that my letters are very precious to you— had I been less certain of it, I never could have trifled upon the subject. Oh, my darling, let all your sensibilities be healthy;—never, never, be wounded by what ought not to wound. Our tenderness should make us mutually susceptible of happiness from every act of each other, but of pain from none; our mighty love should scorn all little annoyances, even from the object of that love. What misery (and what ridiculous misery too) would it be, if, because we love one another better than all the Universe besides, our only gain thereby were a more exquisite sensibility to pain from the beloved hand, and a more terrible power of inflicting it! Dearest, it never shall be so with us. We will have such an infinity of mutual faith, that even real offenses (should they ever occur) shall not wound, because we know that something external from yourself or myself must be guilty of the wrong, and never our essential selves. My beloved wife, there is no need of all this preachment now; but let us both meditate upon it, and talk to each other about it;—so shall there never come any cloud across our inward bliss—so shall one of our hearts never wound the other, and itself fester with the sore that it inflicts. And I speak now, when my Dove is not wounded nor sore, because it is easier than it might be hereafter, when some careless and wayward act or word of mine may have rubbed too roughly against her tenderest of hearts. Dearest, I beseech you grant me freedom to be careless and wayward—for I have had such freedom all my life. Oh, let me feel that I may even do you a little wrong without your avenging it (oh how cruelly) by being wounded.

[Boston] Custom-House, August 8th. 1839

Your letter, my beloved wife, was duly received into your husband's heart, yesterday. I found it impossible to keep it all day long, with unbroken seal, in my pocket; and so I opened and read it on board of a salt vessel, where I was at work, amid all sorts of bustle, and gabble of Irishmen, and other incommodities. Nevertheless its effect was very blessed, even as if, I had gazed upward from the deck of the vessel, and beheld my wife's sweet face looking down upon me from a sun-brightened cloud. Dearest, if your dove-wings will not carry you so far, I beseech you to alight upon such a cloud, sometimes, and let it bear you to me. True it is, that I never look heavenward without thinking of you, and I doubt whether it would much surprise me to catch a glimpse of you among those upper regions. Then would all that is spiritual within me so yearn towards you, that I should leave my earthy incumbrances behind, and float upward and embrace you in the heavenly sunshine. Yet methinks I shall be more content to spend a lifetime of earthly and heavenly happiness intermixed. So human am I, my beloved, that I would not give up the hope of loving and cherishing you by a fireside of our own, not for any unimaginable bliss of higher spheres. Your influence shall purify me and fit me for a better world— but it shall be by means of our happiness here below. In my present state of spiritual life, I cannot conceive my bliss without the privilege of pressing my lips to yours—of pillowing my head upon your bosom. Dearest wife, shall there be no holy kisses in the sky?—shall I not still hold you in my arms, when we are angels together?

Was such a rhapsody as the foregoing ever written in the Custom-House before? I have almost felt it a sin to write to my Dove here; because her image comes before me so vividly, and the place is not worthy of it. Nevertheless, I cast aside my scruples, because, having been awake ever since four °clock this morning (now thirteen hours) and abroad since sunrise, I shall feel more like holding intercourse in dreams than with my pen, when secluded in my room. I am not quite hopeless, now, of meeting you in dreams. Did you not know, beloved, that I dreamed of you, as it seemed to me, all night long, after that last blissful meeting? It is true, when I looked back upon the dream, it immediately became confused; but it had been vivid, and most happy, and left a sense of happiness in my heart. Come again, sweet wife! Force your way through the mists and vapors that envelope my slumbers— illumine me with a radiance that shall not vanish when I awake. I throw my heart as wide open to you as I can. Come and rest within it, my Dove. Where else should you rest at night, if not in your husband's arms—and quite securely in his heart.

Oh, how happy you make me by calling me your husband—by subscribing yourself my Wife. I kiss that word when I meet it in your letters; and I repeat over and over to myself, "she is my Wife—I am her Husband." Dearest, I could almost think that the institution of marriage was ordained, first of all, for you and me, and for you and me alone; it seems so fresh and new—so unlike anything that the people around us enjoy or are acquainted with. Nobody ever had a wife but me—nobody a husband, save my Dove. Would that the husband were worthier of his wife; but she loves him—and her wise and prophetic heart could never do so if he were utterly unworthy.

<u>At My own Room</u>. August 9th.—about 10. A.M. It is so rare a thing for your husband to find himself in his own room in the middle of the forenoon, that he cannot help advising his Dove of that remarkable fact. By some misunderstanding, I was sent on a fruitless errand to East-Cambridge, and have stopped here, on my return to the Custom-House, to rest and refresh myself—and what can so rest and refresh me as to hold intercourse with my darling wife? It must be but a word and a kiss, however—a written word and a shadowy kiss. Good bye, dearest. I must go now to hold controversy, I suppose, with some plaguy little Frenchman about a peck of coal more or less; but I will give my beloved another word and kiss, when the day's toil is over.

<u>About 8 °clock P.M.</u>—I received your letter, your sweet, sweet letter, my sweetest wife, on reaching the Custom-House. Now as to that swelled face of ours—it had begun to swell when we last met; but I did not tell you, because I knew that you would associate the idea of pain with it; whereas, it was attended with no pain at all. Very glad am I, that my Dove did not see me when one side of my face was swollen as big as two; for the image of such a monstrous one-sidedness, or double-sidedness, might have haunted her memory through the whole fortnight. Dearest, is it a weakness that your husband wishes to look tolerably comely always in your eyes?—and beautiful if he could!! My Dove is beautiful, and full of grace; she should not have an ugly mate. But to return to this "naughty swelling"—it began to subside on Tuesday, and has now, I think, entirely disappeared, leaving my visage in its former admirable proportion. Nothing is now the matter with me, save that my heart is as much swollen as my cheek was—swollen with love, with pent-up love, which I would fain mingle with the heart-flood of mine own sweet wife. Oh, dearest, how much I have to say to you!—how many fond thoughts die before their birth!

Dearest, I dare not give you permission to go out in the east-winds. The west-wind will come very often, I am sure, if it were only for the sake of my Dove. Have nothing to do with that hateful East-Wind, at least not till I can shelter you in my arms, and render you invulnerable with kisses. Oh, Dove, how I wish you were to rest this night in the bosom of your own, ownest husband!

Boston, August 21st. 1839

My dearest will be glad to know that her husband has not had to endure the heavy sunshine this afternoon;—he came home at three °clock or thereabouts, and locking the door, betook himself to sleep—first ensuring himself sweet slumber and blissful dreams (if any dreams should come) by reperusing his sweet wife's letter. His wife was with him at the moment of falling asleep, and at the moment of awaking; but she stole away from him during the interval. Naughty wife! In times to come, he will fold his arms around her so closely that he will be conscious of the beating of her heart all through his slumber. Nevertheless, he has slept and is refreshed—slept how long he does not know; but the sun has made a far progress downward, since he closed his eyes.

[*excision*] Oh, my wife, if it were possible that you should vanish from me, I feel and know that my soul would be solitary forever and ever. I almost think that there would be no 'forever' for me. I could not encounter such a desolate Eternity, were you to leave me. You are my first hope and my last. If you fail me (but there is no such *if*) I might toil onward through this life without much outward change; but I should sink down and die utterly upon the threshold of the dreary Future. Were *you* to find yourself deceived, you would betake yourself at once to God and Heaven, in the certainty of there finding a thousand-fold recompense for all earthly disappointment; but with me, it seems as if hope and happiness would be torn up by the roots, and could never bloom again, neither in this soil nor the soil of Paradise.

August 22ᵈ.—Five or six °clock. P.M.—I was interrupted

by the supper bell, while writing the foregoing sentence; and much that I might have added has now passed out of my mind—or passed into its depths. My beloved wife, let us make no question about our love, whether it be true and holy. Were it otherwise, God would not have left your heart to wreck itself utterly—His angels keep watch over you—they would have given you early and continued warning of the approach of Evil in my shape.

Two letters has my Dove blessed me with, since that of Monday—both beautiful—all three, indeed, most beautiful. There is a great deal in all of them that should be especially answered; but how may this be effected in one little sheet?— moreover, it is my pleasure to write in a more desultory fashion [*excision verso*] Nevertheless, propound as many questions as you see fit, in your letters, but, dearest, let it be without expectation of a set response.

When I first looked at that shadow of the Passing Hour, I thought her expression too sad; but the more I looked the sweeter and pleasanter it grew—and now I am inclined to think that few mortals are waited on by happier Hours than is my Dove, even in her pensive moods. My beloved, you make a Heaven roundabout you, and dwell in it continually; and as it is your Heaven, so is it mine. My heart has not been very heavy—not desperately heavy—any one time since I loved you; not even your illness and headaches, dearest wife, can make me desperately sad. My stock of sunshine is so infinitely increased by partaking of yours, that, even when a cloud flits by, I incomparably prefer its gloom to the sullen, leaden tinge, that used to overspread my sky. Were you to bring me, in outward appearance, nothing save a load of grief and pain, yet I do believe that happiness, in no stinted mea-sure, would somehow or other be smuggled into the dismal burthen. But you come to me with no grief—no pain—you come with flowers of Paradise; some in bloom, many in the bud, and all of them immortal.

August 23^d—Between 7 and 8 P.M. Dearest wife, when I think how soon this letter will greet you, it makes my heart yearn towards you so much the more. How much of life we waste! Oh, beloved, if we had but a cottage, somewhere beyond the sway of the East Wind, yet within the limits of New-England, where we could be always together, and have a place to *be* in—what could we desire more? Nothing—save daily bread, (or rather bread and milk; for I think I should adopt your diet) and clean white apparel every day for mine unspotted Dove. Then how happy I would be—and how good! I could not be other than good and happy, when your kiss would sanctify me at all my outgoings and incomings, and when I should rest nightly in your arms. And you should draw, and paint, and sculpture, and make music, and poetry too, and your husband would admire and criticize; and I, being pervaded with your spirit, would write beautifully, and make myself famous for your sake, because perhaps you would like to have the world acknowledge me—but if the whole world glorified me with one voice, it would be a meed of little value in comparison with my wife's smile and kiss. For I shall always read my manuscripts to you, in the summer afternoons or winter evenings; and if they please you I shall expect a smile and kiss as my reward—and if they do not please, I must have a smile and kiss to comfort me.

Good bye—sweet, sweet, dear, dear, sweetest, dearest Wife. I received the kiss you sent me and have treasured it up in my heart. Take one from your own Husband.

Boston, August 26th. 1839.

Dearest Wife,

I did not write yesterday, for several reasons—partly because I was interrupted by company; and also I had a difficult
letter to project and execute in behalf of an office-seeker; and
in the afternoon I fell asleep amid thoughts of my own Dove;
and when I awoke, I took up Miss Martineau's Deerbrook,[1]
and became interested in it—because, being myself a lover,
nothing that treats earnestly of Love can be indifferent to
me. Some truth in the book I recognized—but there seems to
be much of dismal fantasy.

Thus, one way or another, the Sabbath passed away without my pouring out my heart to my sweet wife on paper; but
I thought of you, dearest, all day long. Your letter came this
forenoon; and I opened it on board of a salt-ship, and
snatched portions of it in the intervals of keeping tally. Every
letter of your's is as fresh and new as if you had never written
a preceding one—each is like a strain of music unheard before, yet all are in sweet accordance—all of them introduce
me deeper and deeper into your being, yet there is no sense
of surprise at what I see, and feel, and know, therein. I am
familiar with your inner heart, as with my home; but yet
there is a sense of revelation—or perhaps of recovered intimacy with a dearest friend long hidden from me. Were you
not my wife in some past eternity?

Dearest, perhaps these speculations are not wise. We will
not cast dreamy glances too far behind us or before us, but
live our present life in simplicity; for methinks that is the

way to realize it most intensely. Good night, most beloved. Your husband is presently going to bed; for the bell has just rung (those bells are always interrupting us, whether for dinner, or supper, or bedtime) and he rose early this morning, and must be abroad at sunrise tomorrow. He is going to bed. Will not his wife come and rest in his bosom? Oh, blessed wife, how sweet would be my sleep, and how sweet my waking, when I should find your breathing self in my arms, as if my soul's most blissful dream had become a reality! What a happy and holy fashion it is that those who love one another should rest on the same pillow. I smile at this sentence, but I wrote it innocently, nevertheless. Good night, my wife. Receive your husband's kiss upon your eyelids.

August 27th. 1/2 past 7 °clock. Very dearest, your husband has been stationed all day at the end of Long Wharf; and I rather think that he had the most eligible situation of any body in Boston. I was aware that it must be intensely hot in the midst of the city; but there was only a very short space of uncomfortable heat in my region, halfway towards the centre of the harbour; and almost all the time there was a pure and delightful breeze, fluttering and palpitating, sometimes shyly kissing my brow, then dying away, and then rushing upon me in livelier sport, so that I was fain to settle my straw hat tighter upon my head. Late in the afternoon, there was a sunny shower, which came down so like a benediction, that it seemed ungrateful to take shelter in the cabin, or to put up an umbrella. Then there was a rainbow, or a large segment of one, so exceedingly brilliant, and of such long endurance, that I almost fancied it was stained into the sky, and would continue there permanently. And there were clouds floating all about, great clouds and small, of all glorious and lovely hues (save that imperial crimson, which never was revealed save to our united gaze) so glorious, indeed, and so lovely, that I had a fantasy of Heaven's being broken into fleecy fragments, and dispersed throughout space, with its blest inhabitants yet dwelling blissfully upon those scattered islands. Oh, how I do wish that my sweet wife and I could dwell upon a cloud, and follow the sunset round about the earth! Perhaps she might; but my nature is too earthy to permit me to dwell there with her—and I know well that she would not leave me here. Dearest, how I longed for you to be with me, both in the shower and the sunshine. I did but half see what was to be seen, nor but half feel the emotions which the scene ought to have produced. Had you been there, I do think that we should have numbered this among our most wondrously beautiful sunsets. And the sea was very beautiful too. Would it not be a pleasant life to—but I will not sketch out any more fantasies to-night.

Beloved, have not I been gone a great while? Truly it seems to me very long; and it is strange what an increase of apparent length is always added by two or three days of the second week. Do not you yearn to see me? I know you do, dearest. How do I know it? How should I, save by my own heart?

Dearest wife, I am tired now, and have scribbled this letter in such slovenly fashion, that I fear you will hardly be able to read it—nevertheless, I have been happy in writing it. But now, though it is so early yet, I shall throw aside my pen, especially as the paper is so nearly covered.

My sweet Dove,
Good night

1. Harriet Martineau, *Deerbrook, a Novel* (London: Moxon, 1839). Martineau was best known in America for her controversial account of travels here in 1834–36, and her sympathy for the cause of abolitionism in *Society in America* (1837) and *A Retrospect of Western Travel* (1838), which both SH and Elizabeth Hawthorne had read the previous summer.

Boston, [ca. August 30,] 1839

Your wisdom is not of the earth; it has passed through no other mind, but gushes fresh and pure from your own, and therefore I deem myself the safer when I receive your out-pourings as a revelation from Heaven. Not but what you have read, and tasted deeply, no doubt, of the thoughts of other minds; but the thoughts of other minds make no change in your essence, as they do in almost everybody else's essence. You are still sweet Sophie Hawthorne, and still your soul and intellect breathe forth an influence like that of wild-flowers, to which God, not man, gives all their sweet-ness. . . . [excision] of 'learned' and 'erudite,' to a creature whose [excision] soul translates into earthly language by those words? My dear, sweet, unlearned, inerudite, wild-flower [excision] you make on me is [excision]
If the whole world had been ransacked for a name, I do not think that another could have been found to suit you half so well. It is as sweet as a wildflower. You ought to have been born with that very name—only then I should have done you an irreparable injury by merging it in my own.

You are fitly expressed to my soul's apprehension by those two magic words—Sophia Hawthorne! I repeat them to my-self sometimes; and always they have a new charm. Beloved, I am afraid I do not write very clearly, having been pretty hard at work since sunrise. You are wiser than I, and will know what I have tried to say. [excision]

Boston, Sept. 6th. 1839—six °clock P.M.

[*excision*]

What a wonderful vision that is—the dream-angel. I do esteem it almost a miracle that your pencil should unconsciously have produced it; it is as much an apparition of an ethereal being, as if the heavenly face and form had been shadowed forth in the air, instead of upon paper. It seems to me that it is our guardian-angel, who kneels at the footstool of God, and is pointing to us upon earth, and asking earthly and heavenly blessings for us—entreating that we may not be much longer divided—that we may sit by our own fireside. [*excision*]

Beloved, I must bid you good-night [*excision*] it is yet very late. [*excision*] picturesquely. Yet my pen will run on. Now good night, sweetest wife of my bosom. Do, for pity's sake, glide into my dreams. Be with me all night long, if fate will permit such happiness;—or if that may not be, at least visit me in my latest morning dreams, that your visionary smile may bless me through the weary day. Dearest, I thank you for your care of my Dove, in resolving not to come to Boston tomorrow. I do not think it good for you to pay visits of merely a day, when there would be so [*excision*] I felt, as in this case. And [*excision*]

Boston, Septr 9th. 1/2 past 8 P.M. [1839]

[*excision*] in comparison with a fricaseed chicken. I was not at the end of Long Wharf to-day, but in a distant region;—my authority having been put in requisition to quell a rebellion of the Captain and 'gang' of shovellers aboard a coal-vessel. I would you could have beheld the awful sternness of my visage and demeanor in the execution of this momentous duty. Well—I have conquered the rebels, and proclaimed an amnesty; so tomorrow I shall return to that Paradise of Measurers, the end of Long Wharf—not to my former salt-ship, she being now discharged, but to another, which will probably employ me well nigh a fortnight longer. Sweetest Dove, fly thither sometimes, and alight in my bosom. I would not ask my white Dove to visit me on board a coal-vessel; but salt is white and pure—there is something holy in salt.

[*excision*] Or, rather, each of us will always have [*excision*] over our mutual self-direct [*excision*] because you are a woman—*the* woman; and because you are an immortal and pure spirit. May we not, without sin, so reverence a human immortality, as in some sort, to worship?—not as we do the Omnipotent, yet with a [*excision*] You are wiser, without being the lowlier—[*excision*] we always gain more than we give up—and that while we govern, we are sensible of a wholly unchained freedom in the governed. But, mine own immortal wife, the evening has worn away; and your husband must go to bed, ere he falls asleep amid these misty speculations. Oh, kiss me—come to my arms. I cannot express my yearning for you. I will not say good-night; for I mean to hold

you to my heart, close, close, till I fall asleep. Then, naughty
Dove, I know too well that [*excision*]
               ticular thing—she may paint,
               she may write; and everyth
               d with her angelic nature—
               she is—a woman, and an a
               stop to make out exactly
               l; for it is late, and I mu
               demurest, I feel the
               er, and happier, now,
               you a few moments
               rite to you—though
               ver I write it
               I meant to have spent
               in writing; but a friend
               in Chauncey place; so that
               ain, the moment I retur[1]

1. The Textual Note for 115 explains the trimming of the MS leaf.

Boston, September 23^d 1839. 1/2 past 6. P.M.

Belovedest little wife—sweetest Sophie Hawthorne—what a delicious walk that was, last Thursday! It seems to me, now, as if I could really remember every footstep of it. It is almost as distinct as the recollection of those walks, in which my earthly form did really tread beside your own, and my arm uphold you; and, indeed, it has the same character as those heavenly ramblings;—for did we tread on earth even then? Oh no—our souls went far away among the sunset clouds, and wherever there was ethereal beauty, there were we, our true selves; and it was there we grew into each other, and became a married pair. Dearest, I love to date our marriage as far back as possible; and I feel sure that the tie had been formed, and our union had become indissoluble, even before we sat down together on the steps of the 'house of spirits.' How beautiful and blessed those hours appear to me! True; we are far more conscious of our relation, and therefore infinitely happier, now, than we were then; but still those remembrances are among the most precious treasures of my soul. It is not past happiness; it makes a portion of our present bliss. And thus, doubtless, even amid the Joys of Heaven, we shall love to look back to our earthly bliss, and treasure it forever in the sum of our infinitely accumulating happiness. Perhaps not a single pressure of the hand, not a glance, not a sweet and tender tone, not one kiss, but will be repeated sometime or other in our memory.

[*excision*] Oh, dearest, blessedest Dove, I never felt sure of going to Heaven, till I knew that you loved me; but now I am conscious of God's love in your own. And now good bye for a

little while, mine own wife. I thought it was just on the verge
of supper-time when I began to write—and there is the bell
now. I was beginning to fear that it had rung unheard, while
I was communing with my Dove. Should we be the more
ethereal, if we did not eat? I have a most human and earthly
appetite.

Mine own wife, since supper I have been reading over
again (for the third time, the two first being aboard my salt-
ship—the Marcia Cleaves[1]—) your letter of yesterday—and
a dearest letter it is—and meeting with Sophie Hawthorne
twice, I took the liberty to kiss her very fervently. Will she
forgive me? Do know yourself by that name, dearest, and
think of yourself as Sophie Hawthorne. It thrills my heart to
write it, and still more, I think, to read it in the fairy letters
of your own hand. Oh, you are my wife, my dearest, truest,
tenderest, most beloved wife. I would not be disjoined from
you for a moment, for all the world. And how strong, while I
write, is the consciousness that I am truly your husband!
Dove, come to my bosom—it yearns for you as it never did
before. I shall fold my arms together, after I am in bed, and
try to imagine that you are close to my heart. Naughty wife,
what right have you to be anywhere else? How many sweet
words I should breathe into your ear, in the quiet night—
how many holy kisses would I press upon your lips—whenever I [*excision verso*] consciousness of my bliss. But I should
[*excision verso; excision*]

My little Dove, I have observed that butterflies—very
broad-winged and magnificent butterflies—frequently come
on board of the salt ships where I am at work. What have
these bright strangers to do on Long Wharf, where there are
no flowers nor any green thing—nothing but brick stores,
stone piers, black ships, and the bustle of toilsome men, who
neither look up to the blue sky, nor take notè of these wandering gems of air. I cannot account for them, unless,
dearest, they are the lovely fantasies of your mind, which you

send thither in search of me. There is the supper-bell. Good bye, darling.

Sept 25th. Morning.—Dove, I have but a single moment to embrace you. Tell Sophie Hawthorne I love her. Has she a partiality for your own, own,

Husband.

1. The *Marcia Cleaves*, based in Kennebunk, Maine, had crossed the Atlantic, leaving Liverpool August 5 and arriving in Boston on September 14. It was to clear for Mobile on October 26.

Boston, October 3^{d} 1839. 1/2 past 7. P.M.

Ownest Dove,

Did you get home safe and sound, and with a quiet and happy heart! How could you go without another press of lips? Providence acted lovingly towards us on Tuesday evening, allowing us to meet in the wide desert of this world, and mingle our spirits in a conjugal embrace. How strangely we should have felt, had we been compelled to meet and part without the pressure of one another's lips! It would have seemed all a vision then; now we have the symbol of its reality. You looked like a vision, beautifullest wife, with the width of the room between us—so spiritual that my human heart wanted to be assured that you had an earthly vesture on, and your warm kisses gave me that assurance. What beautiful white doves those were, on the border of the vase! Are they of mine own Dove's kindred? Do you remember a story of a cat who was changed into a lovely lady?—and on her bridal night, a mouse happened to run across the floor; and forthwith the cat-wife leaped out of bed to catch it.[1] What if mine own Dove, in some woeful hour for her poor husband, should remember her dove-instincts, and spread her wings upon the western breeze, and return to him no more! Then would he stretch out his arms, poor wingless biped,[2] not having the wherewithal to fly, and cry aloud— 'Come back, naughty Dove!—whither are you going?—come back, and fold your wings upon my heart again, or it will freeze!' And the Dove would flutter her wings, and pause a moment in the air, meditating whether or no she should come back; for in truth, as her conscience would tell her, this poor mortal had given her all he had to give—a resting-place on his bosom—a home in his deepest heart. But then she would say to herself—'my home is in the gladsome air—and if I need a resting place, I can find one on any of the sunset-clouds. He is unreasonable to call me back; but if he can follow me, he may!' Then would the poor deserted husband do his best to fly in pursuit of the faithless Dove; and for that purpose would ascend to the top-mast of a salt-ship, and leap desperately into the air, and fall down head-foremost upon the deck, and break his neck. And there should be engraven on his tombstone—"Mate not thyself with a Dove, unless thou hast wings to fly."

Now will my Dove scold at me for this foolish flight of fancy;—but the fact is, my goose-quill flew away with me. I do think that I have gotten a bunch of quills from the silliest flock of geese on earth. But the rest of the letter shall be very sensible. I saw Mr. Howes[3] in the reading-room of the Athenaeum, between one and two °clock to day; for I happened to have had leisure for an early dinner, and so was spending a half hour turning over the periodicals. He spoke of the long time since your husband had been at his house; and so I promised, on behalf of that respectable personage, that he would spend an evening there on his next visit to Salem. But if I had such a sweetest wife as your husband has, I doubt whether I could find in my heart to keep the engagement. Now good night, truest Dove in the world. You will never fly away from me; and it is only the infinite impossibility of it that enables me to sport with the idea. I want you very much in my arms to-night. I mean to dream of you with might and main. How sweet those kisses were, on Tuesday evening! Dearest, there was an illegible word in your yesterday's note. I have pored over it, but cannot make it out. Your words are too precious to be thus hidden under their own vesture. Good night, darlingest wife!

October 4th.—5 or thereabout. P.M.—Mine own Dove, I dreamed the queerest dreams last night, about being deserted, and all such nonsense—so you see how I was punished for that naughty romance of the Faithless Dove. It seems to me that my dreams are generally about fantasies, and very seldom about what I really think and feel. You did not appear visibly in my last night's dreams; but they were made up of desolation; and it was good to awake, and know that my spirit was forever and irrevocably linked with the soul of my truest and tenderest Dove. You have warmed my heart, mine own wife; and never again can I know what it is to be cold and desolate, save in dreams. You love me dearly—don't you?

And so my Dove has been in great peril since we parted. No—I do not believe she has; it was only a shadow of peril, not a reality. My spirit cannot anticipate any harm to you; and I trust you to God with securest faith. I know not whether I could endure actually to see you in danger; but when I hear of any risk—as for instance when your steed seemed on the point of dashing you to pieces (but I do quake a little at that thought) against a tree—my mind does not seize upon it as if it had any substance. Believe me, dearest, the tree would have stood aside to let you pass, had there been no other means of salvation. Nevertheless, do not drive your steed against trees wilfully. Mercy on us, what a peril that was of the fat woman, when she "smashed herself down" beside my Dove! Poor Dove! Did you not feel as if an avalanche had all but buried you. I can see my Dove at this moment, my slender, little delicatest white Dove, squeezed almost out of Christendom by that great mass of female flesh—that ton of woman—that beef-eater and beer guzzler, whose immense cloak, though broad as a ship's mainsail, could not be made to meet in front—that picture of an ale-wife—that triple, quadruple, dozen-fold old lady.

Will not my Dove confess that there is a little *nonsense* in this epistle? But be not wroth with me, darling wife;—my heart sports with you because it loves you.

If you happen to see Sophie Hawthorne, kiss her cheek for my sake. I love her full as well as I do mine own wife. Will that satisfy her, do you think? If not, she is a very unreasonable little person.

It is my chiefest pleasure to write to you, dearest.

Your ownest Husband.

1. The story of the cat, transformed to a maiden, that runs after a mouse, is catalogued as J1908.2 in Stith Thompson, *Motif-Index of Folk-Literature*, rev. ed. (Bloomington: Indiana University Press, 1966). In the same index the story of "marriage to dove-maiden" is B652.3.

2. Plato's definition of man in *The Statesman*, 266e.

3. Frederick Howes (1792–1855) was a Salem lawyer, president of the Salem Marine Insurance Company, and an officer of the Salem Athenaeum and the Essex Historical Society. He was the brother-in-law of Susan Burley (see 102.2).

Custom House, October 10th. 1839—1/2 past 2. P.M.

Belovedest, your two precious letters have arrived—the first yesterday forenoon, the second to day. In regard to the first, there was a little circumstance that affected me so pleasantly, that I cannot help telling my sweetest wife of it. I had read it over three times, I believe, and was reading it again, towards evening, in my room; when I discovered, in a remote region of the sheet, two or three lines which I had not before seen, and which Sophie Hawthorne had signed with her own name. It is the strangest thing in the world that I had not read them before—but certainly it was a happy accident; for, finding them so unexpectedly, when I supposed that I already had the whole letter by heart, it seemed as if there had been a sudden revelation of my Dove—as if she had stolen into my chamber, (as, in her last epistle, she dreams of doing) and made me sensible of her presence at that very moment. —Dearest, since writing the above, I have been interrupted by some official business; for I am at present filling the place of Colonel Hall[1] as head of the Measurer's department—which may account for my writing to you from the Custom-House. It is the most ungenial place in the whole world to write a love-letter in;—not but what my heart is full of love, here as elsewhere; but it closes up, and will not give forth its treasure now.

I do wish mine own Dove had been with me, on my last passage to Boston. We should assuredly have thought that a miracle had been wrought in our favor—that Providence had put angelic sentinels round about us, to insure us the quiet enjoyment of our affection—for, as far as Lynn, I was actually the sole occupant of the car in which I had seated myself. What a blissful solitude would that have been, had my whole self been there! Then would we have flown through space like two disembodied spirits—two or one. Are we singular or plural, dearest? Has not each of us a right to use the first person singular, when speaking in behalf of our united being? Does not "I," whether spoken by Sophie Hawthorne's lips or mine, express the one spirit of myself and that darlingest Sophie Hawthorne? But what a wilful little person she is! Does she still refuse my Dove's proffer to kiss her cheek? Well—I shall contrive some suitable punishment; and if my Dove cannot kiss her, I must undertake the task in person. What a painful duty it will be!

October 11th—1/2 past 4. P.M. Did my Dove fly in with me into my chamber, when I entered just now? If so, let her make herself manifest to me this very moment; for my heart needs her presence—You are not here dearest. I sit writing in the middle of the chamber, opposite the looking-glass; and as soon as I finish this sentence, I shall look therein—and really I have something like a shadowy notion, that I shall behold mine own white Dove peeping over my shoulder. One moment more—I defer the experiment as long as possible, because there is a pleasure in the slight tremor of the heart that this fantasy has awakened. Dearest, if you can make me sensible of your presence, do it now! —Oh, naughty, naughty Dove! I have looked, and saw nothing but my own dark face and beetle-brow. How could you disappoint me so? Or is it merely the defect of my own eyes, which cannot behold the spiritual? My inward eye can behold you, though but dimly. Perhaps, beloved wife, you did not come when I called, because you mistook the locality whence the call proceeded. You are to know, then, that I have removed from my old apartment, which was wanted as a parlor by Mr. and Mrs. Devens,[2]—and am now established in a back chamber—a pleasant enough and comfortable little room. The windows

have a better prospect than those of my former chamber; for
I can see the summit of the hill on which Gardner Greene's
estate[3] was situated; it is the highest point of the city, and
the boys at play on it are painted strongly against the sky. No
roof ascends so high as this—nothing but the steeple of the
Park-street Church, which points upward behind it. It is
singular that such a hill should have been suffered to remain
so long, in the very heart of the city; it affects me somewhat
as if a portion of the original forest were still growing here.
But they are fast digging it away now; and if they continue
their labors, I shall soon be able to see the Park-street steeple
as far downward as the dial. Moreover, in another direction,
I can see the top of the dome of the State-House; and if my
Dove were to take wing and alight there (the easiest thing in
the world for a Dove to do) she might look directly into my
window, and see me writing this letter. I glance thither as I
write, but can see no Dove there.[4] [*excision*]

1. Joseph Hall (1793–1859) had been appointed colonel in the Massachusetts
Militia during the War of 1812. He had been a sheriff and postmaster, and U.S.
representative from Maine, 1833–37, and was from 1838 to 1846 a measurer in
the Boston Custom House. A Democrat, he was to be a naval agent in Boston,
1846–49, and clerk in the custom house, 1857–59.

2. Probably Charles Devens (1791–1876) and Mary Lithgow Devens (1797–
1848). He was a hardware merchant in Charlestown, and had been town clerk
there. The couple had boarded at 3 Somerset Place with Mrs. Rebecca Clarke.
They were the parents of General Charles Devens (1820–91), a distinguished
soldier and jurist.

3. Gardner Greene (1753–1832), son-in-law of the painter John Singleton
Copley, had purchased the land on the east slope of Cotton Hill in 1803. "Joining
it with other properties that he had bought, he developed behind his house on
Tremont Street a hillside garden that was one of the wonders of the first third of
the nineteenth century, where terraces with ornamental trees, flowering shrubs,
Black Hamburg grape vines, peacocks and greenhouses led up to vantage points
where one had a splendid view in all directions" (Walter Muir Whitehill, *Boston:
A Topographical History* [Cambridge: Harvard University Press, 1959], pp. 106–
7). This locality later became Pemberton Square.

4. Compare *BR*, p. 152.

Boston, October 23^{d}. 1839—1/2 past 7.—P.M.

Dear little Dove,

Here sits your husband, comfortably established for the
evening in his own domicile, with a cheerful coal-fire making
the room a little too warm. I think I like to be a very little too
warm. And now if my Dove were here, she and that naughty
Sophie Hawthorne, how happy we all three—two—one—
(how many are there of us?)—how happy might we be!
Dearest, it will be a yet untasted bliss, when, for the first
time, I have you in a domicile of my own, whether it be in a
hut or a palace, a splendid suit of rooms or an attic chamber.
Then I shall feel as if I had brought my wife home at last.
Oh, beloved, if you were here now, I do not think I could
possibly let you go till morning—my arms should imprison
you—I would not be content, unless you nestled into my very
heart, and there slept a sweet sleep with your own husband.
My blessed Dove, how I long to hear your gentle breathing,
as you lie asleep in my arms. Which of us do you think will
fall asleep first? I hope it will be my Dove, because then she
will arrange a dream of pictorial magnificence and heavenly
love, and by and bye, her husband will enter beneath the
dusky veil of sleep and find himself in the midst of her enchantments. Shall Sophie Hawthorne be there too? Shall she
share our nuptial couch? Yes, mine own Dove, whether you
like it or no, that naughty little person must share our pillow.
You would wonder, were I to tell you how absolutely necessary she has contrived to render herself to your husband. His
heart stirs at her very name—even at the thought of her

unspoken name. She is his sunshine—she is a happy smile on the visage of his Destiny, causing that stern personage to look as benign as Heaven itself. And were Sophie Hawthorne a tear instead of a smile, still your foolish husband would hold out his heart to receive that tear within it, and doubtless would think it more precious than all the smiles and sunshine in the world. But Sophie Hawthorne has bewitched him— for there is great reason to suspect that she deals in magic. Sometimes, while your husband conceives himself to be hold- ing his Dove in his arms, lo and behold! there is the arch face of Sophie Hawthorne peeping up at him. And again, in the very midst of Sophie Hawthorne's airs, while he is meditating what sort of chastisement would suit her misdemeanors, all of a sudden he becomes conscious of his Dove, with her wings folded upon his heart to keep it warm. Methinks a woman, or angel (yet let it be a woman, because I deem a true woman holier than an angel)—methinks a woman, then, who should combine the characteristics of Sophie Hawthorne and my Dove would be the very perfection of her race. The heart would find all it yearns for, in such a woman, and so would the mind and the fancy;—when her husband was lightsome of spirit, her merry fantasies would dance hand in hand with his; and when he was overburthened with cares, he would rest them all upon her bosom—and his head, too. Oh, that my head were to rest upon such a bosom to-night!

Dearest, your husband was called on by Mr. Hillard[1] yes- terday, who said that he intended soon to take a house in Boston, and, in that case, would like to take your respectable spouse to lodge and breakfast. What thinks my Dove of this? Your husband is quite delighted, because he thinks matters may be managed so, that once in a while he may meet his own wife within his own premises. Might it not be so? Or would his wife—most preposterous idea!—deem it a sin against decorum to pay a visit to her husband? Oh, no, be- lovedest. Your unreserve, your out-gushing frankness, is one of the loveliest results of your purity, and innocence, and holiness. And now good night, wife worshipful and beloved. Amid many musings, nine °clock has surprised me at this stage of my epistle, and I have but time to give you the fondest imaginable kiss, and go to bed. Oh! will not you come, too?

October 24th.—1/2 past 6. P.M. Dearest Dove, your letter came to day; and I do think it the sweetest of all letters—but you must not therefore suppose that you have excelled yourself; for I think the same of each successive one. My dearest, what a delightful scene was that between Sophie Hawthorne and my Dove, when the former rebelled so stoutly against Destiny, and the latter, with such meek mournfulness, submitted. Which do I love the best, I wonder—my Dove, or my little Wild-Flower? I love each best, and both equally; and my heart would inevitably wither, and dry up, and perish utterly, if either of them were torn away from it. Yet, truly, I have reason to apprehend more trouble with Sophie Hawthorne than with my Dove [*excision*] that Sophie Hawthorne's patience will be worn quite threadbare, before his visit is at end. Sweetest wife, I fold you in my arms—can't you feel my heart throbbing against yours? Oh, kiss your husband.

---

1. George Stillman Hillard, on hearing of NH's appointment to the custom house, had immediately sent him an invitation to call (Mary Peabody to SH, January 5, 1839; MS, Essex).

Boston, Novr 13th—very late. [1839]

Dearest and best wife, I meant to have written you a long letter this evening; but an indispensable and unexpected engagement with Gen. McNiel[1] has prevented me. Belovedest, your yesterday's letter was received; and gave me infinite comfort. Yet, Oh, be prepared for the worst—if that may be called worst, which is in truth best for all—and more than all for George.[2] I cannot help trembling for you, dearest. God bless you and keep you.

I will write a full letter in a day or two. Meantime, as your husband is to rise with peep of day tomorrow, he must betake him to his mattress. Good night, dearest.

Your ownest.

1. John McNeil, surveyor at the custom house; see 91.2.

2. George Francis Peabody, SH's brother, had been long afflicted with tuberculosis of the spine. She nursed him during the autumn until his death on November 25.

[Boston] Custom-House, Novr 14th. [1839]

My dearest Wife,

May God sustain you under this affliction. I have long
dreaded it for your sake. Oh, let your heart be full of love for
me now, and realize how entirely my happiness depends on
your well-being. You are not your own, dearest—you must
not give way to grief. Were it possible, I would come to see
you now. When your head must have its pillow, send for me.
I will write again on Saturday.

Your own Husband.

My dearest, this note seems cold and lifeless to me, as if
there were no tenderness nor comfort in it. Think for yourself all that I cannot speak.

Boston, Novr 17th. 1839—6. P.M. or thereabouts.

I received no letter from my sweetest wife yesterday; and my heart is not quite at ease about her. Dearest, I pray to God for you—and I pray to yourself, too; for methinks there is within you a divine and miraculous power to counteract all sorts of harm. Oh be strong for the sake of your husband. Let all your love for me be so much added to the strength of your heart. Remember that your anguish must likewise be mine. Not that I would have it otherwise, mine own wife— your sorrows shall be as precious a possession to me as your joys.

Dearest, if you could steal in upon your husband now, you would see a comfortable sight. I wish you would make a sketch of me, here in our own parlour; and it might be done without trusting entirely to imagination, as you have seen the room and the furniture—and (though that would be the least important item of the picture) you have seen myself. I am writing now at my new bureau, which stands between the windows; there are two lamps before me, which show the polished shadings of the mahogany panels to great advantage. A coal fire is burning in the grate—not a very fervid one, but flickering up fitfully, once in a while, so as to remind me that I am by my own fireside. I am sitting in the cane-bottomed rocking-chair (wherein my Dove once sate, but which did not meet her approbation;) and another hair-cloth arm-chair, stands in front of the fire. Would that I could look round with the assurance of seeing mine own white Dove in it! Not that I want to see her apparition—nor to have her brought hither by miracle, but I want that full assurance of peace and joy, which I should have if my belovedest wife were near me in our own parlor, and with the door of our own sleeping apartment close at hand. Sophie Hawthorne, what a beautiful carpet did you choose for me![1] I admire it so much that I can hardly bear to tread upon it. It is fit only to be knelt upon; and I do kneel on it sometimes. As you saw it only in narrow strips, I doubt whether even you can imagine what an effect is produced by the tout ensemble, spreading its fantastic foliage, or whatever it is, all over the floor. Many times to-day have I found myself gazing at it; and I am almost tempted to call in people from the street to help me to admire it worthily. But perhaps they would not quite sympathise with my raptures. I am doubtless somewhat more alive to the merits of this carpet, because it was your choice, and is our mutual property. My Dove, there is an excellent place for a bust over the bookcase which surmounts my bureau; sometime or other, I shall behold a creation of your own upon it. At present, I have no work of art to adorn our parlour with, except an alumette-holder, on the mantel-piece, ornamented with drawings from Flaxman.[2] It was given me by Elizabeth; and, considerably to my vexation, one of the glasses has been broken, during the recent removal of my household gods.

My wife, I like sleeping on a mattress better than on a feather-bed. It is a pity, however, that a mattress looks so lean and lank;—it certainly does not suggest such ideas of comfort and downy repose as a well-filled feather-bed does; but my sleep, I think, is of better quality, though, indeed, there was nothing to complain of on that score, even while I reposed on feathers. You need not be afraid of my smothering in the little bed-room; for I always leave the door open, so that I have the benefit of the immense volumes of air in the spacious parlor.

Mrs. Hillard[3] takes excellent care of me, and feeds me with eggs and baked apples and other delectable dainties; and altogether I am as happily situated as a man can be, whose heart is wedded, while externally he is still a bachelor.

My wife, would you rather that I should come home next Saturday and stay till Monday, or that I should come to Thanksgiving and stay the rest of the week? Both I cannot do; but I will try to do the latter, if you wish it; and I think I shall finish the salt-ship which I am now engaged upon, about Thanksgiving time—unless foul weather intervene to retard our progress. How delightfully long the evenings are now! I do not get intolerably tired any longer; and my thoughts sometimes wander back to literature and I have momentary impulses to write stories. But this will not be, at present. The utmost that I can hope to do, will be to portray some of the characteristics of the life which I am now living, and of the people with whom I am brought into contact, for future use.[4] I doubt whether I shall write any more for the public, till I can have a daily or nightly opportunity of submitting my productions to the criticism of Sophie Hawthorne. I have a high opinion of that young lady's critical acumen, but a great dread of her severity—which, however, the Dove will not fail to temper with her sweetness.

Dearest, there is nothing at all in this letter; and perhaps it may come to you at a time when your heart needs the strongest, and tenderest, and most comfortable words that mine can speak to it. Yet what could I say, but to assure you that I love you, and partake whatever of good or evil God sends you—or rather, partake whatever good God sends you, whether it come in festal garments or mourning ones; for still it is good, whether arrayed in sable, or flower-crowned. God bless you belovedest,

Your ownest husband.

1. SH wrote to her brother George from Boston on November 3: "Yesterday morning . . . I bought the most beautiful carpet that ever was seen short of Brussels. Tell Mary [Peabody] that it cost not a cent more than the small-figured ugly one at which she & Mrs. Hillard looked. The ground is deepest garnet & looks exactly like velvet, & a faint fawn colored acanthus quirl is the superstructure going down one breadth and coming up the next, so that it has no appearance of formality like most kidderminsters. I wanted to buy the whole roll, it was so beautiful and uncommon. It is a carpet of a thousand" (MS. Berg).

2. John Flaxman (1755–1826), English sculptor and illustrator, whose neoclassical outline drawings for Homer, Aeschylus, Hesiod, Dante, and Milton were enormously popular, and frequently copied by, among others, SH.

3. Susan Tracy Howe Hillard (1808–79), daughter of Judge Samuel Howe, of Northampton, had been SH's friend since 1832. She married Hillard in 1835; he had taught in Northampton for George Bancroft at the Round Hill School in 1828–30.

4. NH kept a notebook while working at the Boston Custom House, but dated only he first entries, February 7–19, 1839 (AN, pp. 187–92). Later entries that can be dated refer to ships: the barque *Tiberius* (called a brig by NH) arrived in Boston from Liverpool on June 4, 1839, with "75 men and girls, for a manufactory in Springfield, Ms." (Boston *Advertiser*, June 5, 2:4; see AN, p. 194). The brig *Alfred Tyler* was in Boston harbor almost monthly through 1839, and for extended periods in 1840; see AN, pp. 194–95. It is therefore not likely that NH journalized much after the date of this letter.

Boston, Novr 19th.—6 P.M. [1839]

Belovedest Wife,

My heart bids me to send you a greeting; and therefore I do it, although I do not feel as if I had many thoughts and words at command to night, but only feelings and sympathies, which must find their way to you as well as they can. Dearest, I cannot bear to think of you sitting all day long in that chamber, and not a soul to commune with you. But I endeavor, and will still endeavor, to send my soul thither, from out of the toil and tedium of my daily life;—so think, beloved, whenever solitude and sad thoughts become intolerable, that, just at that moment I am near you, and trying to comfort you and make you sensible of my presence.

Beloved, it occurs to me, that my earnest entreaties to you to be calm and strong may produce an effect not altogether good. The behests of Nature may perhaps differ from mine, and be wiser. If she bids you shed tears, methinks it will be best to let them flow, and then your grief will melt quietly forth, instead of being pent up till it breaks out in a torrent. But I cannot speak my counsel to you, dearest, so decidedly as if I held you in my arms, for then my heart would know all the state of yours, and what it needed. But love me infinitely, my wife, and rest your heart with all its heaviness on mine. I know not what else to say;—but even that is saying something—is it not, dearest?

I rather think, beloved, that I shall come home on Saturday night, and take my chance of being able to come again on Thanksgiving-day. But then I shall not be able to remain the rest of the week. But you want me I know; and, dearest, my head and heart are weary with absence from you; so that it will be best to snatch the first chance that offers. Soon, mine own wife, I shall be able to spend much more time with you.

Your lovingest Husband.

Does Sophie Hawthorne keep up my Dove's spirits?

Boston, Novr 20th. 1/2 past 8. P.M. [1839]

Dearest, you know not how your blessed letter strengthens my heart on your account; for I know by it that God and the angels are supporting you. And, mine own wife, though I thought that I reverenced you infinitely before, yet never was so much of that feeling mingled with my love, as now. You are yourself one of the angels who minister to your departing brother—the more an angel, because you triumph over earthly weakness to perform those offices of affection. I feel, now, with what confidence I can rest upon your bosom in all my sorrows and troubles—as confident of your strength as of your love. Dearest, there is nothing in me worthy of you. My heart is weak in comparison with yours. Its strength, it is true, has never been tried; for I have never been called to minister at the dying bed of a dear friend; but I have often thought, that, in such a scene, I should need support from the dying, instead of being able to give it. I bless God that He has made Death so beautiful as he appears in the scene which you describe—that He has caused the light from 'the other side' to shine over and across the chasm of the grave.

My wife, my spirit has never yearned for communion with you so much as it does now. I long to hold you on my bosom—to hold you there silently—for I have no words to write my sympathy, and should have none to speak it. Sometimes, even after all that I have now learned of your divine fortitude, I feel as if I shall dread to meet you, lest I should find you quite worn down by this great trial. But, dearest, I will make up my mind to see you pale, and thinner than you were. Only do not be sick—do not give me too much to bear.

Novr 21st. 1/2 past 5. P.M. Mine own Dove, your fourth letter came to-day, and all the rest were duly received, and performed their heaven-appointed mission to my soul. The last has left a very cheering influence on my spirit. Dearest, I love that naughty Sophie Hawthorne with an unspeakable affection, and bless God for her every minute; for what my Dove could do without her, passes my comprehension. And, mine own wife, I have not been born in vain, but to an end worth living for, since you are able to rest your heart on me, and are thereby sustained in this sorrow, and enabled to be a help and comfort to your mother, and a ministering angel to George. Give my love to George. I regret that we have known each other so little in life; but there will be time enough here-after—in that pleasant region "on the other side."

Beloved, I shall come on Saturday, but probably not till the five °clock train, unless it should storm; so you must not expect me till seven or thereabouts. I never did yearn to have you in my arms so much as now. There is a feeling in me as if a great while had passed since we met. Is it so with you?

Mine own wife, what a cold night this is going to be! How I am to keep warm, unless you nestle close, close into my bosom, I do not by any means understand—not but what I have clothes enough on my mattress—but a husband cannot be comfortably warm without his wife. The days are cold now, too—the air eager and nipping—yet it suits my health amazingly. I feel as if I could run a hundred miles at a stretch, and jump over all the houses that happen to be in my way. Belovedest, I must bring this letter to a close now, for several reasons—partly that I may carry it to the Post-Office before it closes; for I hate to make your father pay the postage of my wife's letters. Also, I have another short letter of business to write;—and, moreover, I must go forth into the wide world to seek my supper. This life of mine is the perfection of a bachelor-life—so perfectly untrammelled as it is. Do you not fear, my wife, to trust me to live in such a way any longer?

Belovedest, still keep up your heart for your husband's sake. I pray to God for quiet sleeps for my Dove, and cheerful awakings—yes, cheerful; for Death comes with a sweet aspect into your household; and your brother passes away with him as with a friend. And now farewell, dearest of wives. You are the hope and joy of your husband's heart. Never, never forget how very precious you are to him. God bless you, dearest.

Your ownest husband.

Boston, Novr 25th 1839—6. P.M.

Belovedest Wife,

This very day I have held you in my arms; and yet, now that I find myself again in my solitary room, it seems as if a long while had already passed—long enough, as I trust my Dove will think, to excuse my troubling her with an epistle. I came off in the two °clock cars, through such a pouring rain, that doubtless Sophie Hawthorne set it down for certain that I should pass the day and night in Salem. And perhaps she and the Dove are now watching, with beating heart, to hear your husband lift the door latch. Alas, that they must be disappointed! Dearest, I feel that I ought to be with you now; for it grieves me to imagine you all alone in that chamber, where you "sit and *wait*"—as you said to me this morning. This, I trust, is the last of your sorrows, mine own wife, in which you will not have all the aid that your husband's bosom, and the profoundest sympathy that exists within it, can impart.

I found your letter in the Measurer's Desk; and though I knew perfectly well that it was there, and had thought of it repeatedly, yet it struck me with a sense of unexpectedness when I saw it. I put it in my breast-pocket, and did not open it till I found myself comfortably settled for the evening; for I took my supper of oysters on my way to my room, and have nothing to do with the busy world till sunrise tomorrow. Oh, mine own beloved, it seems to me the only thing worth living for that I have ever done, or been instrumental in, that God has made me the means of saving you from this heaviest anguish of your brother's loss. Ever, ever, dearest wife, keep my image, or rather my reality, between yourself and pain of every kind. Let me clothe you in my love as in an armour of proof—let me wrap my spirit round about your own, so that no earthly calamity may come in immediate contact with it, but be felt, if at all, through a softening medium. And it is a blessed privilege, and ever a happy one, to give such sympathy as my Dove requires—happy to give—and, dearest, is it not also happiness to receive it? Our happiness consists in our sense of the union of our hearts—and has not that union been far more deeply felt within us now, than if all our ties were those of joy and gladness? Thus may every sorrow still leave us happier than it found us, by causing our hearts to embrace more closely in the mutual effort to sustain it.

Dearest, I pray God that your strength may not fail you at the close of this scene. My heart is not quite at rest about you. It seems to me, on looking back, that there was a vague inquietude within me all through this last visit; and this it was, perhaps, that made me seem more sportive than usual. Yet I felt deep peace when my head was on your bosom—and also when my Dove's was on mine.

Did I tell my carefullest little wife that I had bought me a fur cap, wherewith my ears may bid defiance to the wintry blast—a poor image, by the way, to talk of *ears bidding* defiance. The nose might do it, because it is capable of emitting sounds like a trumpet—indeed, Sophie Hawthorne's nose bids defiance without any sound. But what nonsense this is. Also, (I have now been a married man long enough to feel these details perfectly natural, in writing to my wife) your husband, having a particular dislike to flannel, is resolved, every cold morning, to put on two shirts, and has already done so on one occasion, wonderfully to his comfort. Perhaps—but this I leave to Sophie Hawthorne's judgment—it might be well to add a daily shirt to my apparel as the winter advances, and to take them off again, one by one, with the approach of Spring. Dear me, what a puffed-out heap of cotton-bagging would your husband be, by the middle of January! His Dove would strive in vain to fold her wings around him.

My beloved, this is Thanksgiving week. Do you remember how we were employed, or what our state of feeling was, at this time, last year? I have forgotten how far we had advanced into each other's hearts—or rather, how conscious we had become that we were mutually within one another—but I am sure we were already dearest friends. But now our eyes are opened. Now we know that we have found all in each other— all that life has to give—and a foretaste of eternity. At every former Thanksgiving-day, I have been so ungrateful to Heaven as to feel that something was wanting, and that my life so far had been abortive; and therefore, I fear, there has often been repining instead of thankfulness in my heart. Now, I can thank God that He has given me my Dove, and all the world in her. I wish, dearest, that we could eat our Thanksgiving dinner together; and were it nothing but your bowl of bread and milk, we would both of us be therewith content. But I must sit at our mother's table. One of these days, sweetest wife, we will invite her to our own.

Will my Dove expect a letter from me so soon? I have written this evening, because I expect to be engaged tomorrow—moreover, my heart bade me write. God bless and keep you, dearest.

Your ownest Deodatus.[1]

---

1. "A gift of (or to) God," the Latin form of the more common Greek "Theodore" (see 214) and the Hebrew "Nathaniel." "Deodatus" was occasionally used in England; NH may be recalling the Puritan minister Deodat Lawson, whose sermon "Christ's Fidelity," given in Salem in 1692, was in pamphlet form in his own library. See B. Bernard Cohen, "Deodat Lawson's *Christ's Fidelity* and Hawthorne's 'Young Goodman Brown,'" *EIHC*, CIV (1965), 349–70.

Boston, Nov 29th. 1839.—6 or 7 P.M.

Blessedest wife,

Does our head ache this evening?—and has it ached all or any of the time to-day? I wish I knew, dearest, for it seems almost too great a blessing to expect, that my Dove should come quite safe through the trial which she has encountered. Do, mine own wife, resume all your usual occupations as soon as possible—your sculpture, your painting, your music (what a company of sister-arts is combined in the little person of my Dove!)—and above all, your riding and walking. Write often to your husband, and let your letters gush from a cheerful heart; so shall they refresh and gladden me, like draughts from a sparkling fountain, which leaps from some spot of earth where no grave has ever been dug. Dearest, for some little time to come, I pray you not to muse too much upon your brother, even though such musings should be untinged with gloom, and should appear to make you happier. In the eternity where he now dwells, it has doubtless become of no importance to himself whether he died yesterday, or a thousand years ago; he is already at home in the celestial city— more at home than ever he was in his mother's house. Then, my beloved, let us leave him there for the present; and if the shadows and images of this fleeting time should interpose between us and him, let us not seek to drive them away, for they are sent of God. By and bye, it will be good and profitable to commune with our brother's spirit; but so soon after his release from mortal infirmity, it seems even ungenerous towards himself to call him back by yearnings of the heart and too vivid picturings of what he was.

Little Dove, why did you shed tears the other day, when you supposed that your husband thought you to blame for regretting the irrevocable past? Dearest, I never think you to blame; for you positively have no faults. Not that you always act wisely, or judge wisely, or feel precisely what it would be wise to feel, in relation to this present world and state of being; but it is because you are too delicate and exquisitely wrought in heart, mind, and frame, to dwell in such a world—because, in short, you are fitter to be in Paradise than here. You needed, therefore, an interpreter between the world and yourself—one who should sometimes set you right, not in the abstract (for there you are never wrong) but relatively to human and earthly matters;—and such an interpreter is your husband, who can sympathise, though inadequately, with his wife's heavenly nature, and has likewise a portion of shrewd earthly sense, enough to guide us both through the labyrinth of time. Now, dearest, when I criticise any act, word, thought, or feeling of yours, you must not understand it as a reproof, or as imputing anything wrong, wherewith you are to burthen your conscience. Were an angel, however holy and wise, to come and dwell with mortals, he would need the guidance and instruction of some mortal; and so will you, my Dove, need mine—and precisely the same sort of guidance that the angel would. Then do not grieve, nor grieve your husband's spirit, when he essays to do his office; but remember that he does it reverently, and in the devout belief that you are, in immortal reality, both wiser and better than himself; though sometimes he may chance to interpret the flitting shadows around us more accurately than you. Hear what I say, dearest, in a cheerful spirit, and act upon it with cheerful strength. And do not give an undue weight to my judgment, nor imagine that there is no appeal from it, and that its decrees are not to be questioned. Rather, make it a rule always to question them and be satisfied of their correctness;—and so shall my Dove be improved and perfected in the gift of a human understanding, till she become even *earthly-wiselier* than her sagacious husband. Undine's husband gave her an immortal soul;[1] my beloved wife must be content with an humbler gift from me, being already provided with as high and pure a soul as ever was created.

God bless you, belovedest. I bestow three kisses on the air—they are intended for your eyelids and brow, to drive away the head-ache.—

Your ownest.

---

1. Friedrich de La Motte-Fouqué, *Undine* (1811). An edition translated by the Reverend Thomas Tracy was published in New York by Samuel Colman in 1839.

[Boston] Custom-House, Novr 30th. [1839]

Mine own Dove,

You will have received my letter, dearest, ere now; and I trust that it will have conveyed the peace of my own heart into yours; for my heart is too calm and peaceful in the sense of our mutual love, to be disturbed even by my sweetest wife's disquietude. Belovedest and blessedest, I cannot feel anything but comfort in you. Rest quietly on my deep, deep, deepest affection. You deserve it all, and infinitely more than all, were it only for the happiness you give me. I apprehended that this cup could not pass from you, without your tasting bitterness among its dregs. You have been too calm, my beloved—you have exhausted your strength. Let your soul lean upon my love, till we meet again—then all your trouble shall be hushed on your husband's bosom.

Your ownest, happiest,
Deodatus.

(How does Sophie Hawthorne do? Expect a letter on Tuesday. God bless my dearest.

Boston, December 1st. 1839. 6 or 7 P.M.

Very Dearest,

The day must not pass without my speaking a word or two
to my belovedest wife, of whom I have thought, with tender
anxieties mingled with comfortable hopes, all day long.
Dearest, is your heart at peace now? God grant it—and I
have faith that He will communicate the peace of my heart
to your's. Mine own wife, always when there is trouble
within you, let your husband know of it. Strive to fling your
burthen upon me; for there is strength enough in me to bear
it all, and love enough to make me happy in bearing it. I will
not give up any of my conjugal rights—and least of all this
most precious right of ministring to you in all sorrow. My
bosom was made, among other purposes, for mine ownest
wife to shed tears upon. This I have known, ever since we
were married—and I had yearnings to be your support and
comforter, even before I knew that God was uniting our
spirits in immortal wedlock. I used to think that it would be
happiness enough, food enough for my heart, if I could be
the life-long, familiar friend of your family, and be allowed
to see yourself every evening, and so watch around you to
keep harm away—though you might never know what an
interest I felt for you. And how infinitely more than this has
been granted me! Oh, never dream, blessedest wife, that you
can be other than a comfort to your husband—or that he can
be disappointed ! in you.— Mine own Dove, I hardly know
how it is, but nothing that you do or say ever surprises or
disappoints me; it must be that my spirit is so thoroughly and

intimately conscious of you, that there exists latent within me a prophetic knowledge of all your vicissitudes of joy or sorrow; so that, though I cannot foretell them beforehand, yet I recognize them when they come. Nothing disturbs the preconceived idea of you in my mind. Whether in bliss or agony, still you are mine own Dove—still my blessing—still my peace. Belovedest, since the foregoing sentence, I have been interrupted; so I will leave the rest of the sheet till tomorrow evening. Good night; and in writing those words, my soul has flown through the air to give you a fondest kiss. Did you not feel it?

Decr 2^d.—Your letter came to me at the Custom-House, very Dearest, at about eleven °clock; and I opened it with an assured hope of finding good news about my Dove; for I had trusted very much in Sophie Hawthorne's assistance. Well, I am afraid I shall never find in my heart to call that excellent little person 'naughty' again—no; and I have even serious thoughts of giving up all further designs upon her nose, since she hates so much to have it kissed. Yet the poor little nose!— would it not be quite depressed (I do not mean flattened) by my neglect, after becoming accustomed to such marked attention? And besides, I have a particular affection for that nose, insomuch that I intend, one of these days, to offer it an oblation of rich and delicate odours. But I suppose Sophie Hawthorne would apply her handkerchief, so that the poor nose should reap no pleasure nor profit from my incense. Naughty Sophie Hawthorne! There—I have called her 'naughty' already—and on a mere supposition, too.

Half a page of nonsense about Sophie Hawthorne's nose! And now have I anything to say to my little Dove? Yes—a reproof. My Dove is to understand, that she entirely exceeds her jurisdiction, in presuming to sit in judgment upon herself, and pass such severe censure as she did upon her Friday's letter—or indeed any censure at all. It was her bounden duty to write that letter; for it was the cry of her heart, which ought and must have reached her husband's ears, wherever in the world he might be. And yet you call it wicked. Was it Sophie Hawthorne or the Dove that called it so? Naughty Sophie Hawthorne—naughty Dove—for I believe they are both partakers of this naughtiness.

Dearest, I have never had the good luck to profit much, or indeed any, by attending lectures; so that I think the ticket had better be bestowed on somebody who can listen to Mr Emerson more worthily.[1] My evenings are very precious to me; and some of them are unavoidably thrown away in paying or receiving visits, or in writing letters of business; and therefore I prize the rest as if the sands of the hour-glass were gold or diamond dust. I have no other time to sit in my parlor (let me call it ours) and be happy by our own fireside—happy in reveries about a certain little wife of mine, who would fain have me spend my evenings in hearing lectures, lest I should incommode her with too frequent epistles.—

Good bye, dearest. I suppose I have left a dozen questions in your letter unanswered; but you shall ask them again when we meet. Do not you long to see me? Mercy on us—what a pen! It looks as if I had laid a strong emphasis on that sentence. God bless my Dove, and Sophie Hawthorne too.—So prays their ownest husband.

---

1. Emerson's course of ten lectures on "The Present Age," at the Masonic Temple, Boston, began December 4 and continued on successive Wednesday evenings, except Christmas, to February 12, 1840. See *The Early Lectures of Ralph Waldo Emerson*, ed. Robert E. Spiller and Wallace E. Williams (Cambridge: Harvard University Press, 1972), III, 175–315.

Boston, Decr 5th 1839—6 P.M.

Dearest wife,

I do wish that you would evince the power of your spirit over its outward manifestation, in some other way than by raising an inflammation over your eye. Do, belovedest, work another miracle forthwith, and cause this mountain—for I fancy it as of really mountainous bulk—cause it to be cast into the sea, or anywhere else;[1] so that both eyes may greet your husband, when he comes home. Otherwise, I know not but my eyes will have an inflammation too;—they certainly smarted in a very unwonted manner, last evening. "The naughty swelling!"—as my Dove (or Sophie Hawthorne) said of the swollen cheek that afflicted me last summer. Will kisses have any efficacy? No; I am afraid not; for if they were medicinal, my Dove's eyelids have been so imbued with them, that no ill could have come there. Nevertheless, though not a preventive, a kiss may chance to be a remedy. Can Sophie Hawthorne be prevailed upon to let me try it?

I went to see my wife's (and of course my own) sister Mary, on Tuesday evening. She appeared very well; and we had a great deal of good talk, wherein my Dove was not utterly forgotten—(now will Sophie Hawthorne, thinking the Dove slighted, pout her lip at that expression)—well then, my Dove was directly or indirectly concerned in all my thoughts, and most of my words. Mrs. Park[2] was not there, being gone, I believe, to some lecture. Mary and your husband talked with the utmost hopefulness and faith of my Dove's future health and well-being. Dearest, you *are* well (all but the naughty swelling) and you always will be well. I love Mary because she loves you so much;—our affections meet in you, and so we become kindred. But everybody loves my Dove—everybody that knows her—and those that know her not love her also, though unconsciously, whenever they image to themselves something sweeter, and tenderer, and nobler, than they ever met with on earth. It is the likeness of my Dove that has haunted the dreams of poets, ever since the world began. Happy me, to whom that dream has become the reality of all realities—whose bosom has been warmed, and is now forever warmed, with the close embrace of her who has flitted shadowlike away from all other mortals!— Dearest, I wish your husband had the gift of making rhymes; for methinks there is poetry in his head and heart, since he has been in love with you. You are a Poem, my Dove. Of what sort, then? Epic?—Mercy on me—no! A sonnet?—no; for that is too labored and artificial. My Dove is a sort of sweet, simple, gay, pathetic ballad, which Nature is singing, sometimes with tears, sometimes with smiles, and sometimes with intermingled smiles and tears.

I was invited to dine at Mr. Bancroft's, yesterday, with Miss Margaret Fuller; but Providence had given me some business to do; for which I was very thankful.[3] When my Dove and Sophie Hawthorne can go with me, I shall not be afraid to accept invitations to meet literary lions and lion-esses; because then I shall put the above-said redoubtable little personage in the front of the battle. What do you think, dearest, of the expediency of my making a caucus-speech? A great many people are very desirous of listening to your hus-band's eloquence; and that is considered the best method of making my debût. Now, probably, will Sophie Hawthorne utterly refuse to be kissed, unless I give up all notion of speechifying at a Caucus. Silly little Sophie!—I would not do it, even if thou thyself besought it of me.

Belovedest, I wish, before declining your ticket to Mr.

Emerson's lectures, that I had asked whether you wished me to attend them; for if you do, I should have more pleasure in going, than if the wish were originally my own.

[*excision*] Dearest wife, nobody can come within the circle of my loneliness, save you;— You are my only companion in the world;—at least, when I compare other intercourse with our intimate communion, it seems as if other people were the world's width asunder. And yet I love all the world better for my Dove's sake.

Good bye, belovedest. Drive away that "naughty swelling."

Your ownest Husband.

Do not expect me till seven °clock on Saturday—as I shall not leave Boston till sunset.

1. Compare Mark 11:23: "Have faith in God. For verily I say unto you, that whosoever shall say unto this mountain, 'Be thou removed, and be thou cast into the sea'; and shall not doubt in his heart, but shall believe that those things which he saith shall come to pass; he shall have whatsoever he saith."

2. Cornelia Romana Hall Park (b. 1807) was boarding, along with Mary Peabody, at 1 Chauncey Place, the home of Mrs. Susan Cleveland Higginson Channing (1788–1865), widow of Francis Dana Channing (1775–1810), the Reverend William Ellery Channing's brother. Connie Park, originally from Medford, Mass., had been SH's close friend since before her marriage to Thomas B. Park in 1830. In the early 1830s, the Parks had boarded with Mrs. Rebecca Hull Clarke at 3 Somerset Court, in company with Elizabeth and Mary Peabody, Horace Mann, and George Hillard. SH had spent several weeks with the Parks in Roxbury during the cholera scare of the summer of 1832. Thomas Park had left to seek his fortune in California in 1836, never to return.

3. Margaret Fuller (1810–50), author and journalist, whom NH and SH had met for the first time the previous October 28 at a party given by Connie Park; see SH to George Peabody, October 29, 1839 (MS, Berg). In 1868 SH published this sentence (out of context and without comment) in PAN.

Boston, Decr 11th. 1839—7 P.M.

Belovedest,

I am afraid you will expect a letter tomorrow—afraid, because I feel very sure that I shall not be able to fill this sheet
tonight. I am well, and happy, and I love you dearly, sweetest
wife;—nevertheless, it is next to impossibility for me to put
ideas into words. Even in writing these two or three lines, I
have fallen into several long fits of musing. I wish there was
something in the intellectual world analagous to the Daguer-
rotype (is that the name of it?)[1] in the visible—something
which should print off our deepest, and subtlest, and delicatest thoughts and feelings, as minutely and accurately as the
above-mentioned instrument paints the various aspects of
Nature. Then might my Dove and I interchange our reveries—but my Dove would get only lead in exchange for gold.
Dearest, your last letter brought the warmth of your very
heart to your husband.— Belovedest, I cannot possibly write
one word more, to-night. I want you in my arms. I want to
be close to your bosom—whereas this striving to talk on paper
does but remove you farther from me. It seems as if Sophie
Hawthorne fled away into infinite space, the moment I strive
to fix her image before me in order to inspire my pen;—
whereas, no sooner do I give myself up to reverie, than here
she is again, smiling lightsomely by my side. There will be
no writing of letters in Heaven; at least, I shall write none
there, though I think it would add considerably to my bliss to

receive them from my Dove. Never was I so stupid as to-night;—and yet it is not exactly stupidity either, for my fancy is bright enough, only it has, just at this time, no command of external symbols. Good night, dearest wife. Love your husband, and dream of him.

Decr 12th—6. P.M. Blessedest— Dove-ward and Sophie-Hawthorne-ward doth your husband acknowledge himself "very reprehensible," for leaving his poor wife destitute of news from him such an interminable time—one, two, three, four days, tomorrow noon. After seven years' absence, without communication, a marriage, if I mistake not, is deemed to be legally dissolved. Does it not appear at least seven years to my Dove, since we parted? It does to me. And will my Dove, or naughty Sophie Hawthorne, choose to take advantage of the law, and declare our marriage null and void? Oh, naughty, naughty, naughtiest Sophie Hawthorne, to suffer such an idea to come into your head! The Dove, I am sure, would not disown her husband, but would keep her heart warm with faith and love for a million of years; so that when he returned to her (as he surely would, at some period of Eternity, to spend the rest of eternal existence with her) he would seem to find in her bosom the warmth which his parting embrace had left there.

Very dearest, I do wish you could come to see me, this evening. If we could be together in this very parlour of ours, I think you, and both of us, would feel more completely at home than we ever have before in all our lives. Your chamber is but a room in your mother's house, where my Dove cannot claim an independent and separate right; she has a right, to be sure, but it is as a daughter. As a wife, it might be a question whether she has a right. Now this pleasant little room, where I sit, together with the bedroom in which I intend to dream to-night of my Dove, is my dwelling, my castle, mine own place wherein to be, which I have bought,

for the time being, with the profits of mine own labor. Then
is it not our home

1. Louis Jacques Mandé Daguerre (1787–1851) had recently discovered how
to fix chemically the image made by the camera obscura; his description of the
process, published in Paris in August 1839, reached America the following
month. During the next several weeks, the first American photographic experiments were reported with considerable excitement. See Beaumont Newhall, *The
Daguerreotype in America*, third ed. (New York: Dover, 1976).

Boston, Decr 18th. 1839—nearly 7 P.M.

Belovedest,

I wish you could see our parlour to night—how bright and cheerful it looks, with the blaze of the coal-fire throwing a ruddy tinge over the walls, in spite of the yellow gleam of two lamps. Now if my Dove were sitting in the easiest of our two easy chairs—(for sometimes I should choose to have her sit in a separate chair, in order to realize our individuality, as well as our unity)—then would the included space of these four walls, together with the little contiguous bed-room, seem indeed like home.— But the soul of home is wanting now. Oh, naughtiest, why are you not here to welcome your husband with a kiss, and a pressure in your arms against your warm bosom, when he comes in at eventide, chilled with his wintry day's toil? Why does he not find the table placed cosily in front of the fire, and a cup of tea steaming fragrantly—or else a bowl of warm bread and milk, such as his Dove feeds upon? A much-to-be-pitied husband am I, naughty wife—a homeless man—a wanderer in the desert of this great city; picking up a precarious subsistence wherever I happen to find a restaurateur or an oyster-shop—and returning at night to a lonely fireside and a lonely pillow. Dearest, have I brought the tears into your eyes? What an unwise little person is my Dove, to let the tears gather in her eyes for such nonsensical pathos as this! Yet not nonsensical neither, inasmuch as it is a sore trial to your husband to be estranged from that which makes life a reality to him and to be compelled to spend so many GOD-given days and nights

in a dream—in an outward show, which has nothing to satisfy the soul that has become acquainted with truth. But,
mine own wife, if you had not taught me what happiness is,
I should not have known that there is anything lacking to me
now. I am dissatisfied—not because, at any former period of
my life, I was ever a thousandth part so happy as now—but
because Hope feeds and grows strong on the happiness within
me. Good night, belovedest wife. I have a note to write to
Mr. Capen,[1] who torments me every now-and-then about a
book which he wants me to manufacture. Hereafter, I intend
that my Dove shall manage all my correspondence—indeed,
it is my purpose to throw all sorts of trouble upon my Dove's
shoulders. Good night now, dearest—and sleep in peace, before the trials and perplexities of connubial life disturb your
slumber.

December 20th—7. P.M. Blessedest wife—has not Sophie
Hawthorne been very impatient for this letter, one half of
which yet remains undeveloped in my brain and heart?
Would that she could enter those inward regions, and read
the letter there—together with so much that never can be
expressed in written or spoken words. And can she not do
this? The Dove can do it, even if Sophie Hawthorne fail.
Dearest, would it be unreasonable for me to ask you to manage my share of the correspondence, as well as your own?—
to throw yourself into my heart, and make it gush out with
more warmth and freedom than my own pen can avail to do?
How I should delight to see an epistle from myself to Sophie
Hawthorne, written by my Dove!—or to my Dove, Sophie
Hawthorne being the amanuensis! I doubt not, that truths
would then be spoken, which my heart would recognize as
existing within its depths, yet which can never be clothed in
words of my own. You know that we are one another's consciousness—then it is not from —My dearest, George Hillard
has come in upon me, in the midst of the foregoing sentence,
and I have utterly forgotten what I meant to say. But it is not

much matter. Even if I could convince you of the expediency of your writing my letters as well as your own, still, when you attempted to take the pen out of my hand, I believe I should resist very strenuously. For, belovedest, though not an epistolarian by nature, yet the instinct of communicating myself to you makes it a necessity and a joy to write.

Your husband has received an invitation, through Mr. Collector Bancroft, to go to Dr. Channing's to-night.[2] What is to be done? Anything, rather than to go. I never will venture into company, unless I can put myself under the protection of Sophie Hawthorne—she, I am sure, will take care that no harm comes to me. Or my Dove might take me "under her wing."

Dearest, you must not expect me too fervently on Christmas eve, because it is very uncertain whether Providence will bring us together then. If not, I shall take care to advise you thereof by letter—which, however, may chance not to come to hand till three °clock on Christmas day. And there will be my Dove, making herself nervous with waiting for me. Dearest, I wish I could be the source of nothing but happiness to you—and that disquietude, hope deferred, and disappointment, might not ever have aught to do with your affection. Does the joy compensate for the pain? Naughty Sophie Hawthorne—silly Dove—will you let that foolish question bring tears into your eyes?

My Dove's letter was duly received.

Your lovingest Husband

---

1. Nahum Capen, the publisher of "The School Library," had issued a prospectus in September, with the announcement that NH would contribute a volume, "New England Historical Sketches," to the Juvenile Series. See, e.g., *The Christian Examiner*, XXVII (September 1839), 132–35. See also 83.3.

2. William Ellery Channing (1780–1842), the eminent Unitarian minister, pastor of the Federal Street Church in Boston. Elizabeth Peabody had been his admirer and assistant since 1820. Bancroft's invitation to NH reads: "My Dear Sir, I am specially charged by Dr Channing, and by an authority which you must not slight, by Miss Channing herself, to have you bodily appear at Dr Channing's house this evening at eight o'clock. Fail not, bodily and spiritually. Yours truly, G. Bancroft" (MS, Huntington). Miss Mary Ruth Channing (1818–91) played the piano on social occasions at their home.

Boston, December 24th, 1839. 6 or 7. P.M.

My very dearest,

While I sit down disconsolately to write this letter, at this very moment is my Dove expecting to hear her husband's footstep upon the threshold. She fully believes, that, within the limits of the hour which is now passing, she will be clasped to my bosom, and will mingle her life with mine in a long holy kiss. Belovedest, I cannot bear to have you yearn for me so intensely. By and bye, when you find that I do not come, our head will begin to ache;—but still, being the "hopingest little person" in the world, you will not give me up, perhaps till eight °clock. But anon it will be bedtime—it will be deep night—and not a spoken word, not a written line, will have come to your heart from your naughtiest of all husbands. Sophie Hawthorne, at least, will deem him the naughtiest of husbands; but my Dove will keep her faith in him just as firmly and fervently, as if she were acquainted with the particular impossibilities which keep him from her bosom. Dearest wife, I did hope, till this afternoon, that I should be able to disburthen myself of the cargo of salt which has been resting on my weary shoulders for a week past; but it does seem as if Heaven's mercy were not meant for us miserable Custom-House officers. The holiest of holydays— the day that brought ransom to all other sinners—leaves us in slavery still.

Nevertheless, dearest, if I did not feel two disappointments in one—your own and mine—I should feel much more comfortable and resigned than I do. If I could have come to you to-night, I must inevitably have returned hither tomorrow evening. But now, in requital of my present heaviness of spirit, I am resolved that my next visit shall be at least one day longer than I could otherwise have ventured to make it. We cannot spend this Christmas eve together, mine own wife; but I have faith that you will be in my arms on the eve of the New-Year. Will not you be glad—when I come home to spend three whole days, or at least three whole nights— that I was kept away from you for a few brief hours on Christmas eve? For if I went now, I could not be with you then.

My blessedest, write and let me know that you have not been very much disturbed by my non-appearance. I pray you to have the feelings of a wife towards me, dearest—that is, you must feel that my whole life is yours, a life-time of long days and nights, and therefore it is no irreparable nor very grievous loss, though sometimes a few of those days and nights are wasted away from you. A wife should be calm and quiet, in the settled certainty of possessing her husband. Above all, dearest, bear these crosses with philosophy for my sake; for it makes me anxious and depressed, to imagine your anxiety and depression. Oh, that you could be very joyful when I come, and yet not sad when I fail to come! Is that impossible, my sweetest Dove?—is it impossible, my naughtiest Sophie Hawthorne?

Boston, Decr 26th. 1839

Dear Longfellow,

I was prevented from going to Salem yesterday, as I had intended, and therefore must needs be there on Saturday and Sunday—whereby I shall be prevented from spending next Saturday evening with you.[1] Look for me in a week from that time, unless it be inconvenient to you—in which case, g.ve me notice.

I read your poems over and over, and over again, and continue to read them at all my leisure hours—and they grow upon me at every re-perusal. Nothing equal to some of them was ever written in this world—this western world, I mean; and it would not hurt my conscience much to include the other hemisphere. I have not yet begun the review of the Poems and Hyperion.[2] My heart and brain are troubled and fevered now with ten thousand other matters; but soon I will set about it. God send you many a worthier reviewer!

Your friend,
Nath. Hawthorne

1. See 135.2.

2. Longfellow had published *Hyperion: A Romance* with Samuel Colman in New York in August, and *Voices of the Night* with J. Owen in Cambridge about December 10. Apparently NH did not write a review of them. Longfellow noted in his journal on January 11 "Hillard's laudatory notice of the Voices in the 'New World'" (MS, Harvard), Park Benjamin's New York weekly: see I (December 28, 1839), 2:8. There was a one-paragraph notice of *Voices* in the Salem *Gazette,* January 17, 2:1, very likely by the editor, Caleb Foote.

Boston Jany 1st. 1840. 6 °clock, P.M.

Belovedest wife

Your husband's heart was exceedingly touched by that little backhanded note, and likewise by the bundle of
allumettes[1]—half a dozen of which I have just been kissing
with great affection. Would that I might kiss that poor dear
finger of mine! Kiss it for my sake, sweetest Dove—and tell
naughty Sophie Hawthorne to kiss it too. Nurse it well,
dearest; for no small part of my comfort and cheeriness of
heart depends upon that beloved finger. If it be not well
enough to bear its part in writing me a letter within a few
days, do not be surprised if I send down the best surgeon in
Boston to effect its speedy cure. Nevertheless, darlingest
wife, restrain this good little finger, if it show any inclination
to recommence its labors too soon. If your finger be pained in
writing, your husband's heart ought to (and I hope would)
feel every twinge.

Belovedest, I have not yet wished you a Happy New Year!
And yet I have—many, many of them; as many, mine own
wife, as we can enjoy together—and when we can no more
enjoy them together, we shall no longer think of Happy New
Years on earth, but look longingly for the New-Year's Day of
eternity. What a year the last has been! Dearest, you make
the same exclamation; but my heart originates it too. It has
been the year of years—the year in which the flower of our
life has bloomed out—the flower of our life and of our love,
which we are to wear in our bosoms forever. Oh, how I love
you, blessedest wife!—and how I thank God that He has

made me capable to know and love you! Sometimes I feel, deep, deep down in my heart, how dearest above all things you are to me; and those are blissful moments. It is such a happiness to be conscious, at last, of something real! All my life hitherto, I have been walking in a dream, among shadows which could not be pressed to my bosom; but now, even in this dream of time, there is something that takes me out of it, and causes me to be a dreamer no more. Do you not feel, dearest, that we live above time and apart from time, even while we seem to be in the midst of time? Our affection diffuses eternity round about us.

My carefullest little wife will rejoice to know that I have been free to sit by a good fire all this bitter cold day—not but what I have a salt-ship on my hands, but she must have some ballast, before she can discharge any more salt; and ballast cannot be procured till the day after tomorrow. Are not these details very interesting? I have a mind, some day, to send my dearest a journal of all my doings and sufferings, my whole external life, from the time I awake at dawn, till I close my eyes at night. What a dry, dull history would it be! But then, apart from this, I would write another journal of my inward life throughout the self-same day—my fits of pleasant thought, and those likewise which are shadowed by passing clouds—the yearnings of my heart towards my Dove—my pictures of what we are to enjoy together. Nobody would think that the same man could live two such different lives simultaneously. But then, as I have said above, the grosser life is a dream, and the spiritual life a reality.

Very dearest, I wish you would make out a list of books that you would like to be in our library; for I intend, whenever the cash and the opportunity occur together, to buy enough to fill up our new bookcase; and I want to feel that I am buying them for both of us. When I next come to Salem, you shall read the list, and we will discuss it, volume by volume. I suppose the bookcase will hold about two hundred volumes; but you need not calculate upon making such a vast collection all at once. It shall be accomplished in small lots; and then we shall prize every volume, and receive a separate pleasure from the acquisition of it.

Does it seem a great while since I left you, dearest? Truly, it does to me. These separations lengthen our earthly lives by at least nine-tenths; but then, in our brief seasons of communion, there is the essence of a thousand years. Was it Thursday that I told my Dove would be the day of my next appearance?—or Friday? "Oh, Friday, certainly," says Sophie Hawthorne. Well; it must be as naughty Sophie says.

Oh, belovedest, I want you in my arms. My head desires very much to rest on your bosom. You have given me a new feeling, blessedest wife—a sense that, strong as I may have deemed myself, I am insufficient for my own support; and that there is a tender little Dove, without whose help I cannot get through this weary world at all. God bless you, ownest wife.

Your ownest husband.

1. One of the few surviving letters of SH to NH; see *NHHW*, I, 208–9. The allumettes SH made were twists of paper for lighting a taper or lamp with flame from the hearth.

Boston, Jany 3^d. 1840—3. P.M.

What a best of all possible husbands you have, sweetest wife, to be writing to you so soon again, although he has heard nothing from you since the latter part of the year 1839! What a weary length of time that naughty finger has been ill! Unless there are signs of speedy amendment, we must begin to think of 'rotation in office,' and the left hand must be nominated to the executive duties of which the right is no longer capable. Yet, dearest, do not imagine that I am impatient. I do indeed long to see your delicatest little penwomanship; (what an enormity it would be to call my Dove's most feminine of handwritings pen*man*ship!) but it would take away all the happiness of it, when I reflected that each individual letter had been a pain to you. Nay; I would not have you write, if you find that the impediments of this mode of utterance check the flow of your mind and heart.

But you tell me that the wounded finger will be no hindrance to your painting. Very glad am I, dearest; for you cannot think how much delight those pictures are going to give me. I shall sit and gaze at them whole hours together— and these will be my happiest hours, the fullest of you, though all are full of you. I never owned a picture in my life; yet pictures have always been among the earthly possessions (and they are spiritual possessions too) which I most coveted. I know not what value my Dove's pictures might bear at an auction-room; but to me, certainly, they will be incomparably more precious than all the productions of all the painters since Apelles.[1] When we live together in our own home, belovedest, we will paint pictures together—that is, our

minds and hearts shall unite to form the conception, to which
your hand shall give material existence. I have often felt as if
I could be a painter, only I am sure that I could never handle
a brush;—now my Dove will show me the images of my
inward eye, beautified and etherealized by the mixture of her
own spirit. Belovedest, I think I shall get these two pictures
put into mahogany frames, because they will harmonize better with the furniture of our parlor than gilt frames would.

While I was writing the foregoing paragraph, Mary has
sent to inquire whether I mean to go to Salem tomorrow,
intending, if I did, to send a letter by me. But, alas! I am not
going. The inquiry, however, has made me feel a great yearning to be there. But it is not possible, because I have an
engagement at Cambridge on Saturday evening;[2] and even if
it were otherwise, it would be better to wait till the middle
of the week, or a little later, when I hope to spend three or
four days with you. Oh, what happiness, when we shall be
able to look forward to an illimitable time in each other's
society—when a day or two of absence will be far more infre-
quent than the days which we spend together now. Then a
quiet will settle down upon us, a passionate quiet, which is
the consummation of happiness.

Dearest, I hope you have not found it impracticable to
walk, though the atmosphere be so wintry. Did we walk
together in any such cold weather, last winter. I believe we
did. How strange, that such a flower as our affection should
have blossomed amid snow and wintry winds—accompani-
ments which no poet or novelist, that I know of, has ever
introduced into a love-tale. Nothing like our story was ever
written—or ever will be—for we shall not feel inclined to
make the public our confidant; but if it could be told, methinks it would be such as the angels might take delight to
hear. If I mistake not, my Dove has expressed some such
idea as this, in one of her recent letters.

Well-a-day! I have strolled thus far through my letter,

without once making mention of naughty Sophie Hawthorne. Will she pardon the neglect? Present my profound respects to her beloved nose, and say that I still entreat her to allow my Dove to kiss her cheek. When she complies with this oft-repeated petition, I shall hope that her spirit is beginning to be tamed, and shall then meditate some other and more difficult trials of it. Nonsense! Do not believe me, dear little Sophie Hawthorne. I would not tame you for the whole Universe.

And now good bye, dearest wife. Keep yourself in good heart while I am absent, and grow round and plump and rosy;—eat a whole chicken every day;—go to bed at nine °clock or earlier, and sleep sound till sunrise. Come to me in dreams, beloved, for my pillow is very lonesome. What should I do in this weary world, without the idea of you, dearest! Give my love to your father and mother, and to Elizabeth. Kiss me, Dove, kiss me, naughty Sophie Hawthorne.

God bless you, darling.

Your ownest husband

1. Apelles, of the fourth century B.C., was the official portraitist of Alexander the Great and considered the greatest of all Greek painters.

2. Longfellow's journal for January 4 records: "Hawthorne came to pass the evening. Had a long conversation on Literature. He means to write a child's book. Told him of my Ballad ["The Wreck of the Hesperus," written December 30]; and that I meant to have it printed on a sheet, with a picture on top, like other ballads. He is delighted with idea and says he will distribute to every skipper of every craft he boards in his Custom House duties; so as to hear the criticisms thereon" (MS, Harvard; see Life, I, 343; Letters, II, 203–4).

[Boston, ca. January 21, 1840]

Have the Strophe and Antistrophe made up their quarrel yet?[1] There is an unaccountable fascination about that Sophie Hawthorne—whatever she chooses to do or say, whether reasonable or unreasonable, I am forced to love her the better for it. Not that I love her better than my Dove; but then it is right and natural that the Dove should awaken infinite tenderness, because she is a bird of Paradise, and has a perfect and angelic nature—so that love is her inalienable and unquestionable right. And yet my wayward heart will love this naughty Sophie Hawthorne;—yes, its affection for the Dove is doubled, because she is inseparably united with naughty Sophie. I have one love for them both, and it is infinitely intensified, because they share it together. But Sophie must remember that my Dove is the tenderest of creatures, and that it is her own appointed office to cheer and sustain her.

Dearest, I cannot yet tell how soon your husband will clasp you to his breast. Colonel Hall is not well yet, and does not feel able to come to the Custom-House every day. I wish—unless it involve too long a separation—to defer my coming until I can spend another week, or several days at least, with mine own wife. Perhaps I may come on Saturday—possibly not quite so soon. Do not, belovedest, delay to send the pictures, one moment after they are quite ready. I do yearn for them. Never were such precious pictures painted.

1. Perhaps a phonetic pun on "Sophie" and "Dove."

Boston, Jany 24th. 1840—4 P.M.

Ownest Dove,

Your letter came this forenoon, announcing the advent of the pictures; so I came home as soon as I possibly could—and there was the package! I actually trembled as I undid it, so eager was I to behold them. Dearissima, there never was anything so lovely and precious in this world. They are perfect. So soon as the dust and smoke of my fire had evaporated, I put them on the mantel-piece, and sat a long time before them with clasped hands, gazing, and gazing, and gazing, and painting a facsimile of them in my heart, in whose most sacred chamber they shall keep a place forever and ever. Belovedest, I was not long in finding out the Dove, in the Menaggio.[1] In fact, she was the very first object that my eyes rested on, when I uncovered the picture. She flew straightway into my heart—and yet she remains just where you placed her. Dearest, if it had not been for your strict injunctions that nobody nor anything should touch the pictures, I do believe that my lips would have touched that naughty Sophie Hawthorne, as she stands on the bridge. Do you think the perverse little damsel would have vanished beneath my kiss? What a misfortune would that have been to her poor lover!—to find that he kissed away his mistress. But, at worst, she would have remained on my lips. However, I shall refrain from all endearments, till you tell me that a kiss may be hazarded without fear of her taking it in ill part and absenting herself without leave.

Mine ownest, it is a very noble-looking cavalier with whom

Sophie is standing on the bridge. Are you quite sure that her own husband is the companion of her walk? Yet I need not ask—for there is the Dove to bear witness to his identity. That true and tender bird would never have alighted on another hand—never have rested so near another bosom. Yes; it must be my very self; and from henceforth it shall be held for an absolute and indisputable truth. It is not my picture, but the very I; and as my inner self belongs to you, there is no doubt that you have caused my soul to pervade the figure. There we are, unchangeable. Years cannot alter us, nor our relation to each other.

Ownest, we will talk about these pictures all our lives and longer; so there is no need that I should say all that I think and feel about them now; especially as I have yet only begun to understand and feel them. I have put them into my bedroom for the present, being afraid to trust them on the mantel-piece; but I cannot help going to feast my eyes upon them, every little while. I have determined not to hang them up till after I have been to Salem, for fear of the dust, and of the fingers of the chamber-maid and other visitants. Whenever I am away, they will be safely locked up, either in the bureau or in my closet. I shall want your express directions as to the height at which they ought to be hung, and the width of the space between them, and other minutest particulars. We will discuss these matters, when I come home to my wife.

Belovedest, there are several obstacles to my coming home immediately; but it shall not be long before I take you to my bosom. At present, two of the Measurers are employed, and another is detained at his home in Chelsea by the sickness of his family, and Colonel Hall continues too unwell to be at the Custom-House; so that I am the only one in attendance there; and moreover I have a coal vessel to discharge tomorrow. But this state of affairs will not continue long. I think I cannot fail to be at liberty by Tuesday or Wednesday at furthest; and at all events, next week shall not pass without our meeting; even if I should have barely time to press you in my arms, and say good-bye. But the probability is, that I shall come to spend a week.

Dearissima, be patient—Sophie Hawthorne as well as the Dove.

My carefullest little wife, I am of opinion that Elizabeth has been misinformed as to the increased prevalence of the small-pox. It could not be so generally diffused among the merchants and business-people without my being aware of it; nor do I hear of its committing such fearful ravages anywhere. The folks at the Custom-House know of no such matter; nor does George Hillard. In truth, I had supposed (till I heard otherwise from you) that all cause for alarm was past. Trust me, dearest, there is no need of heart-quake on my account. You have been in greater danger than your husband.

God be with you, blessedest and blessingest. I did [excision]

1. A landscape by SH of the resort of Menaggio on Lake Como in the north of Italy. It had been her practice for several years, encouraged by Sarah Clarke (see 163.2), to copy engravings of such scenes from illustrated books and portfolios. The other picture (called "Isola" in 138) is probably of the Isola Bella in Lake Maggiore, near Como. Both scenes would show steep hillsides above a lake, with luxuriant terraced gardens and intricate classical architecture. NH refers to them briefly in "The Old Manse" as "two pleasant little pictures of the Lake of Como" (*MOM,* p. 5). These pictures are apparently still in the possession of the Hawthorne family; see John J. McDonald, ed., "A Sophia Hawthorne Journal 1843–1844," *NHJ 1974,* p. 28 n. 42.

Boston, February 7th. 1840—1/2 past 3. P.M.

Ownest Dove,

Can you reckon the ages that have elapsed since our last embrace? It quite surpasses my powers of computation. I only know that, in some long by-gone time, I had a wife—and that now I am a widowed man, living not in the present, but in the past and future. My life would be empty indeed, if I could neither remember nor anticipate; but I can do both; and so my heart continues to keep itself full of light and warmth. Belovedest, let it be so likewise with you. You promised me—did you not?—to be happy during our separation; and really I must insist upon holding you to your word, even if it should involve a miracle.

Dearest, I have hung up the pictures—the Isola over the mantel-piece, and the Menaggio on the opposite wall. This arrangement pleased me better, on the whole, than the other which we contemplated; and I cannot perceive but that the light is equally favorable for them both. You cannot imagine how they glorify our parlor—and what a solace they are to its widowed inhabitant. I sit before them with something of the quiet and repose which your own beloved presence is wont to impart to me. I gaze at them by all sorts of light—daylight, twilight, and candle-light; and when the lamps are extinguished, and before getting into bed, I sit looking at these pictures, by the flickering fire-light. They are truly an infinite enjoyment. I take great care of them, and have hitherto hung the curtains before them every morning; and they remain covered till after I have kindled my fire in the afternoon. But I suppose this precaution need not be taken much longer. I think that this slight veil produces a not unpleasing effect, especially upon the Isola—a gentle and tender gloom, like the first approaches of twilight. Nevertheless, whenever I remove the curtains, I am always struck with new surprise at the beauty which then gleams forth. Mine ownest, you are a wonderful little Dove.

What beautiful weather this is—beautiful, at least, so far as sun, sky, and atmosphere are concerned; though a poor wingless biped, like my Dove's husband, is sometimes constrained to wish that he could raise himself a little above the earth. How much mud and mire, how many pools of unclean water, how many slippery footsteps and perchance heavy tumbles, might be avoided, if we could but tread six inches above the crust of this world. Physically, we cannot do this; our bodies cannot; but it seems to me that our hearts and minds may keep themselves above moral mud-puddles, and other discomforts of the soul's pathway; and so enjoy the sunshine.

I have added Coleridge's Poems, a very good edition in three volumes, [1] to our library. Dearest, dearest, what a joy it is to think of you, whenever I buy a book—to think that we shall read them aloud to one another, and that they are to be our mutual and familiar friends for life. I intended to have asked you again for that list which you shewed me; but it will do the next time I come. I mean to go to a book-auction this evening. [2] When our book-case is filled, my bibliomania will probably cease; for its shelves, I think, would hold about all the books that I should care to read—all, at least, that I should wish to possess as household friends.

What a reprehensible husband am I, not to have inquired, in the very first sentence of my letter, whether my belovedest has quite recovered from the varioloid! [3] But, in truth, it seemed so long since we parted, that none but chronic diseases can have subsisted from that time to this. I make no doubt, therefore, but that the afflicted arm is entirely recovered, and that only a slight scar remains—which shall be kissed, some time or other. And how are your eyes, my blessedest? Do not torture them by attempting to write, before they are quite well. If you inflict pain on them for such a purpose, your husband's eyes will be sensible of it, when he shall read your letters. Remember that we have now a common property in each other's eyes.

Dearest, I have not seen Colonel Hall since my return hither—he being gone to Maine. When he comes back, or shortly thereafter, I will try to prevail on your neglectful spouse to pay you a short visit. Methinks he is a very cold and loveless sort of person. I have been pestering him, ever since I began this letter, to send you some word of affectionate remembrance; but he utterly refuses to send anything, save a kiss apiece to the Dove's eyes and mouth, and to Sophie Hawthorne's nose and foot. Will you have the kindness to see that these valuable consignments arrive at their destination? Dearest wife, the letter-writer belies your ownest husband. He thinks of you and yearns for you all day long. [*excision*]

1. *The Poetical Works of Samuel Taylor Coleridge, including the Dramas of Wallenstein, Remorse, and Zapolya,* in three volumes, was first published by William Pickering (London, 1828; reprinted 1829); the 1834 edition acknowledged the editing of Henry Nelson Coleridge.

2. The Boston *Post* advertised the sale by F. Freeman, 36 Milk Street, of a "VALUABLE PRIVATE LIBRARY," including works of Byron, Coleridge, Shelley, Keats, Scott, Wordsworth, Fielding, Smollett, and Dickens.

3. A mild variety of smallpox occurring after vaccination.

Boston, Feb.ʸ 8th. 1840.

Dear Pike,

Letters have been received here by which it appears that no definite action has yet been had on the P.O. question.[1] I do not believe that it is yet too late to defeat the appointment of Woodbury.[2] Do you know whether Colonel Chase's[3] papers were forwarded to Washington?—and whose signatures had been obtained in his favor? If he means to transfer his interest to me, I should suppose that there ought to be no further delay in doing it.

Colonel Hall has not appeared at the Custom-House, since my return from Salem. The general belief is, that he is sick; but the Major[4] whispers me that he is gone to Maine.

Do write, if you have anything of interest to communicate, either with regard to your affairs or mine. I hear nothing about your appointment.

From certain circumstances, I suspect that communications have been held with Rantoul, relative to the impolicy of his pressing Woodbury's appointment.[5]

Yours truly,
Nath. Hawthorne.

1. NH was for several years anxious to be appointed postmaster of Salem. See 256, 265.

2. Charles W. Woodbury, editor of the Salem *Advertiser*, the Democratic news-

paper, was appointed postmaster on February 22 (Salem *Observer*, February 22, 3:1; *Advertiser*, February 22, 2:4).

3. Probably Cyrus Chase (b. 1796), a Democratic ward leader in Salem, and a sometime measurer at the custom house.

4. Major Joseph Grafton (1782–1861), a native of Salem, was an officer in the War of 1812, and since then a measurer at the Boston Custom House. See *AN*, p. 189.

5. Robert Rantoul, Jr. (1805–52), born in Beverly, had studied law in Salem with Leverett Saltonstall, and had defended the Knapps in the White murder trial; see 52. He kept close ties to Salem and Essex County, but now was a prominent Boston lawyer, a leading Democratic politician and social reformer, and a member of the Massachusetts Board of Education. He had married Jane Elizabeth Woodbury and was brother-in-law of Charles W. Woodbury. See *DAB*.

Boston, Feb^r 10th, 1840.

Dear Pike,

I was not more explicit in reference to those letters, because I did not know their precise purport, and because I
was requested not to mention the writer's name. The letters
were from the representative from Middlesex,[1] and were addressed to Ball[2] and Colonel Thomas.[3] I have seen Colonel
Thomas this afternoon; and he says that he has since received
another letter, dated the 6th. inst. which makes no mention
of the Post-Office affair. Ball's letter was dated the 3^d.

The result of my personal interview with Colonel Thomas
is that I consider the affair more desperate than when I wrote
you last. Its aspect is so discouraging that I should not wish
you to take any steps that may compromise yourself, and put
you on worse terms with Rantoul than you are already. It is
by no means clear to me that Woodbury's name has *not* been
sent to the Senate. The letters to Colonel Thomas are rather
negative than positive—he infers that the appointment is not
made, because the writer does not say so. The letter to Ball
is more positive; but (from a fact that has recently come to
my knowledge) I suspect that the writer might have reasons
for wishing to deceive him, and for inducing him to suppose
that he was earnest in my favor. If you draw any inferences

from this hint, keep them to yourself—but I don't believe that you will guess at the truth. On the whole, I conclude that we have lost the battle. Nevertheless, if Dr. Brown[4] feels inclined to come out against Woodbury, I would not do or say anything to prevent him. I impart to you my present gloomy view of the business, because you have a claim upon me to know the whole truth. I don't feel myself under much obligation to any body else; nor do I care how much they embroil themselves with the Rantoul faction.

What an astounding liar our venerated chief[5] turns out to be! I must confess, however, that I do not put implicit confidence in Palfray's[6] representation of the matter—his own conduct having been, in my opinion, not much more honorable than Bancroft's. So far as my personal gratification is concerned, I should like nothing better than to have you come out upon Bancroft in the way you propose; but for your own sake, I should advise you to consider well before taking such a step. It will render it impossible for him to offer, or for you to receive, any office hereafter; whereas, as the case now stands, it appears to me that you may sooner or later be forced upon him. Do not act hastily; it will never be too late to blow him up; and you will have other opportunities full as advantageous. As long as there is a possibility of his being of use to you, do not compel him to be your open enemy. I advise you, in the first place, to communicate with him in private. If you still resolve to open your battery upon him, be careful not to compromise Colonel Hall, from whom is derived most of our information as to his being favorable to my application for the Post-Office. As to myself, you may mention any thing that I have said to you with the single exception of what was said in reference to R's[7] ill opinion of you.

I don't know how soon I shall be in Salem. I wish you would come up here and hold a talk. There are some things that I should like to impart to you, but hardly feel myself at liberty—certainly not on paper. So I conclude with drinking your health in a glass of hot gin and water, and subscribe myself

Your friend,
Nath. Hawthorne

1. William Parmenter (1789–1866), U.S. representative from East Cambridge, served 1837–45.

2. Possibly Nahum Ball, measurer at the Boston Custom House.

3. Possibly Warren B. Thomas, inspector at the Salem Custom House. See 627.

4. Benjamin Frederick Browne (1793–1873), an apothecary in Salem (and therefore called "Doctor") and a leader in local Democratic politics, was a potential ally of NH in gaining the postmastership. Browne himself was postmaster, 1845–49.

5. George Bancroft.

6. Probably Edward Palfrey (1805–46), a printer and the former editor of the Salem *Advertiser*, surveyor of the Salem Custom House, 1838–41, and later an official at the Boston Custom House. He was also chairman of the Democratic Committee for Essex County.

7. Robert Rantoul, Jr.

Boston, Feby 11th. 1840—7. P.M.

Belovedest,

Your letter, with its assurance of your present convales-
cence, and its promise (to which I shall hold you fast) that you
will never be sick any more, cause me much joy.— Dearest,
George Hillard came in just as I had written the first sentence; so we will begin on a new score.

Your husband has been measuring coal all day, on board of
a black little British schooner, in a dismal dock at the north
end of the city. Most of the time, he paced the deck to keep
himself warm; for the wind (north-east, I believe it was) blew
up through the dock, as if it had been the pipe of a pair of
bellows. The vessel lying deep between two wharves, there
was no more delightful prospect, on the right hand and on
the left, than the posts and timbers, half immersed in the
water, and covered with ice, which the rising and falling of
successive tides had left upon them; so that they looked like
immense icicles. Across the water, however, not more than
half a mile off, appeared the Bunker Hill monument; and
what interested me considerably more, a church-steeple,
with the dial of a clock upon it, whereby I was enabled to
measure the march of the weary hours. Sometimes your husband descended into the dirty little cabin of the schooner,
and warmed himself by a red-hot stove, among biscuit-bar-
rels, pots and kettles, sea-chests, and innumerable lumber of
all sorts—his olfactories, meanwhile, being greatly refreshed
by the odour of a pipe, which the captain or some of his crew
were smoking. But at last came the sunset, with delicate

clouds, and a purple light upon the islands; and your husband blessed it, because it was the signal of his release; and so he came home to talk with his dearest wife. And now he bids her farewell, because he is tired and sleepy. God bless you, belovedest. Dream happy dreams of me to-night.

February 12th—Evening—All day long again, best wife, has your poor husband been engaged in a very black business—as black as a coal; and though his face and hands have undergone a thorough purification, he feels as if he were not altogether fit to hold communication with his white Dove. Methinks my profession is somewhat akin to that of a chimney-sweeper; but the latter has the advantage over me, because, after climbing up through the darksome flue of the chimney, he emerges into the midst of the golden air, and sings out his melodies far over the heads of the whole tribe of weary earth-plodders. My dearest, my toil to-day has been cold and dull enough; nevertheless your husband was neither cold nor dull; for he kept his heart warm and his spirit bright with thoughts of his belovedest wife. I had strong and happy yearnings for you to-day, ownest Dove—happy, even though it was such an eager longing, which I knew could not then be fulfilled, to clasp you to my bosom. And now here I am in our parlour, aweary—too tired, almost, to write—just tired enough to feel what bliss it would be could I throw myself on the sofa and rest my head on its own pillow. Blessedest, I want you to "help our sleep" to-night. That is your own idea. What a sweet one!

Well, dearest, my labors are over for the present. I cannot, however, come home just at present—three of the Measurers being now absent; but you shall see me very soon. Naughtiest, why do you say that you have scarcely seen your husband, this winter? Have there not, to say nothing of shorter visits, been two eternities of more than a week each, which were full of blessings for us? My Dove has quite forgotten these. Ah, well! If visits of a week long be not worth remembering, I shall alter my purpose of coming to Salem for another like space;—otherwise I might possibly have been there, by Saturday night, at furthest. Dear me, how sleepy I am! I can hardly write, as you will discover by the blottings and scratchings. So good-bye now, darlingest:—and I will finish in the freshness of the morning.

February 13th.—Past 8. A.M. Belovedest, how very soon this letter will be in your hands. It brings us much closer together, when the written words of one of us can come to the heart of the other, in the very same day that they flowed from the heart of the writer. I mean to come home to our parlour early to-day; so, when you receive this letter, you can imagine me there, sitting in front of the Isola. I have this moment interrupted myself to go and look at that precious production. How I wish that naughty Sophie Hawthorne could be induced to turn her face towards me! Nevertheless, the figure is her veritable self, and so would the face be, only that she deems it too beauteous to be thrown away on her husband's gaze. I have not dared to kiss her yet. Will she abide it?

My dearest, do not expect me very fervently till I come. I am glad you were so careful of your inestimable eyes as not to write to me yesterday. Mrs. Hillard says that Elizabeth[1] made her a call. Good-bye. I am very well to day, and unspeakably happy in the thought that I have a dearest little wife, who loves me pretty well. God bless her.

---

1. SH's sister Elizabeth was to move her family from Salem to 13 West Street, Boston, where she opened her famous bookshop on July 31, 1840. See 168.

Boston, March 11th. 1840—2 P.M.

Blessedest,

It seems as if I were looking back to a former state of existence, when I think of the precious hours which we have lived together.[1] And now we are in two different worlds—widowed, both of us—both of us deceased, and each lamenting the decease of the other. [*excision verso*]—it seems as if my spirit would be conscious of it.

Belovedest, almost my first glance, on entering our parlor after my return hither, was at the pictures—my very first glance, indeed, as soon as I had lighted the lamps. They have certainly grown more beautiful during my absence, and are still becoming more perfect, and perfecter, and perfectest. I fancied that Sophie Hawthorne, as she stands on the bridge, had slightly turned her head, so as to reveal somewhat more of her face; but if so, she has since turned it back again. I was much struck with the Menaggio this morning;—while I was gazing at it, the sunshine and the shade grew positively real, and I agreed with you, for the time, in thinking this a more superlative picture than the other. But when I came home about an hour ago, I bestowed my chiefest attention upon the Isola; and now I believe it has the first place in my affections, though without prejudice to a very fervent love for the other.

[*excision*]Dove. There is little prospect of one, indeed; but forgive me for telling you so, dearest—no prospect of my returning so soon as next Monday; but I have good hope to be again at liberty by the close of the week. Do be very good, my Dove—be as good as your nature will permit, naughty Sophie Hawthorne. As to myself, I shall take the liberty to torment myself as much as I please.

My dearest, I am very well, but exceedingly stupid and heavy; so the remainder of this letter shall be postponed till tomorrow. Has my Dove flown abroad, this cold, bright day? Would that the wind would snatch her up, and waft her to her husband.

[*excision*]How was it, dearest? And how do you do this morning? Is the wind east? The sun shone on the chimney-tops round about here, a few minutes ago; and I hoped that there would be a pleasant day for my Dove to take wing, and for Sophie Hawthorne to ride on horseback; but the sky seems to be growing sullen now. Do you wish to know how your husband will spend the day? First of the first—but there rings the bell for eight °clock; and I must go down to breakfast.

After Breakfast— First of the first, your husband will go to the Post-Office, like a dutiful husband as he is, to put in this letter for his belovedest wife. Thence he will proceed to the Custom House, and finding that there is no call for him on the wharves, he will sit down by the Measurer's fire, and read the Morning Post.[2] Next, at about half-past nine °clock, he will go to the Athenaeum, and turn over the Magazines and Reviews till eleven or twelve, when it will be time to return to the Custom-House to see whether there be a letter from Dove Hawthorne—and also (though this is of far less importance) to see whether there be any demand for his services as Measurer. At one °clock, or thereabouts, he will go to dinner—but first, perhaps, he will promenade the whole length of Washington street, to get himself an appetite. After dinner, he will take one more peep at the Custom-House; and it being by this time about two °clock, and no prospect of business to-day, he will feel at liberty to come home to our own parlor, there to remain till supper-time. At six °clock he will sally forth again, to get some oysters and read the evening papers, and returning between seven and eight, he will read and re-read his belovedest's letter—then take up a book—and go to bed at ten, with a blessing on his lips for the Dove and Sophie Hawthorne.

Thine ownest.

Don't expect another letter till Monday.

1. During his last stay in Salem. In 182 NH refers to "four weeks" with SH in Salem "last year," apparently because of reduced work at the custom house during the winter.

2. The Boston *Daily Morning Post*, a Democratic newspaper first published in 1831.

Boston, March 15th. 1840

Dear O'Sullivan,

Your letter came yesterday; and I have been thinking for the last twenty-four hours of the project which you therein communicate to me.[1] I have had no opportunity to consult with Pierce, because he is gone to Lowell, and probably will not be here for several days. My own impression is, that it would not be advisable for me to change my present situation, unless I were to cease to be an office-holder altogether— which I intend to do in a year hence, if not sooner. Nevertheless, there appear to be some desirable points about that same clerkship. Are you quite certain that I should be at liberty to absent myself from Washington during the whole of the intervals between the sessions of Congress, and that, during such absence, I should be in the receipt of my salary? It strikes me that there must be some mistake here.

My expenses would be so much higher at Washington than here, and the travel back and forth would amount to so much, and I should throw away so much more during the idle intervals, that I don't believe I should have a cent left, at the end of the twenty months. Whereas, if I continue a Measurer till a year from next May (which, if God will strengthen me to endure it, I mean to do) I shall receive in that time two thousand dollars, and am resolved to save at least half of it. Then I will retire on my fortune—that is to say, I will throw myself on fortune, and get my bread as I can. I ought not to be an office-holder. There is a most galling weight upon me—an intolerable sense of being hampered and degraded; and I am afraid I should feel it much more in the situation which you recommend, than in my present one. There I should be immediately under a master; whereas here, the Measurer's department is singularly independent of the general government of the Custom-House.

That Post-Office[2] would have suited me—at least, it would have been the next best thing to holding no office at all, which now appears to me the "summum bonum." When I next see you, I shall have some queer tales to tell about the faith and honor of politicians—of one politician at least.[3] Well—my first impression about him was the correct one; and hereafter I will always trust to first impressions.

When Pierce comes back, I will take counsel with him respecting this matter; and in the meantime, if you can cause the situation to be kept vacant, please to do so. And yet, perhaps, it would not be worth while that you should commit yourself at all in the affair; for I think there is hardly a chance of my taking any other view of the case.

I do wish you would come to Boston within a month or six weeks. Is it quite impossible? I am delightfully situated at No. 54 Pinckney-street, in the house of my friend George S. Hillard, where I have a little parlor and bed-room, and all sorts of bachelor-comforts. Do come.

Your friend,
Nath. Hawthorne.

1. O'Sullivan's letter has not been recovered.
2. At Salem. See 139.
3. George Bancroft. See 140.

Boston, March 15th, 1840—Forenoon.

Best-belovedest,

Thy letter by Elizabeth came, I believe, on Thursday, and the two which thou didst entrust to the post reached me not till yesterday—whereby I enjoyed a double blessing in recompense of the previous delay. Nevertheless, it were desirable that the new Salem postmaster be forthwith ejected, for taking upon himself to withold the outpourings of thy heart, at their due season. As for letters of business, which involve merely the gain or loss of a few thousand dollars, let him be as careless as he pleases; but when thou wouldst utter thyself to thy husband, dearest wife, there is doubtless a peculiar fitness of thy communications to that point and phase of our existence, at which they ought to be received. However, come when they will, they are sure to make sweetest music with my heartstrings.

Blessedest, what an ugly day is this!—and there thou sittest in thy own private chamber with a heart as heavy as thy husband's heart. And is his heart indeed heavy. Why no—it is not heaviness—not the heaviness, like a great lump of ice, which I used to feel when I was alone in the world—but—but—in short, dearest, where thou art not, there it is a sort of death. A death, however, in which there is still hope and assurance of a joyful life to come. Methinks, if my spirit were not conscious of thy spirit, this dreary snow-storm would chill me to torpor;—the warmth of my fireside would be quite powerless to counteract it. Most absolute little wife, didst thou expressly command me to go to Father Taylor's[1] church

this very Sabbath?—(Dinner, or luncheon rather, has inter-
vened since the last sentence). Now, belovedest, it would not
be an auspicious day for me to hear the aforesaid Son of
Thunder. Thou knowest not how difficult is thy husband to
be touched and moved, unless time, and circumstances, and
his own inward state, be in a "concatenation accordingly."[2]
A dreadful thing would it be, were Father Taylor to fail in
awaking a sympathy from my spirit to thine. Darlingest, pray
let me stay at home this afternoon. Some sunshiny Sunday,
when I am wide awake, and warm, and genial, I will go and
throw myself open to his blessed influences; but now, there
is but one thing (thou being absent) which I feel anywise
inclined to do—and that is, to go to sleep. May I go to sleep,
belovedest? Think what sweet dreams of thee may visit me—
think how I shall escape this snow-storm—think how my
heavy mood will change, as the mood of mind almost always
does, during the interval that withdraws me from the external world. Yes; thou bidst me sleep. Sleep thou too, my beloved—let us pass at one and the same moment into that
misty region, and embrace each other there.

Well, dearest, I have slept; but Sophie Hawthorne has
been naughty—she would not be dreamed about. And now
that I am awake again, here are the same snow-flakes in the
air, that were descending when I went to sleep. Would that
there were an art of making sunshine! Knowest thou any
such art? Truly thou dost, my blessedest, and hast often
thrown a heavenly sunshine around thy husband's spirit,
when all things else were full of gloom. What a woe—what
a cloud it is, to be away from thee! How would my Dove like
to have her husband continually with her, twelve or fourteen
months out of the next twenty? Would not that be real happiness?—in such long communion, should we not feel as if
separation were a dream, something that never had been a
reality, nor ever could be? Yes; but—for in all earthly happiness there is a but—but, during those twenty months, there

would be two intervals of three months each, when thy husband would be five hundred miles away—as far away as
Washington. That would be terrible. Would not Sophie
Hawthorne fight against it?—would not the Dove fold her
wings, not in the quietude of bliss, but of despair? Do not be
frightened, dearest—nor rejoiced either—for the thing will
not be. It might be, if I chose; but on multitudinous accounts, my present situation seems preferable; and I do pray,
that, in one year more, I may find some way of escaping from
this unblest Custom-House; for it is a very grievous thraldom. I do detest all offices—all, at least, that are held on a
political tenure. And I want nothing to do with politicians—
they are not men; they cease to be men, in becoming politicians. Their hearts wither away, and die out of their bodies.
Their consciences are turned to India-rubber—or to some
substance as black as that, and which will stretch as much.
One thing, if no more, I have gained by my Custom-House
experience—to know a politician. It is a knowledge which no
previous thought, or power of sympathy, could have taught
me, because the animal, or the machine rather, is not in
nature.

Oh my darlingest wife, thy husband's soul yearns to embrace thee! Thou art his hope—his joy—he desires nothing
but to be with thee, and to toil for thee, and to make thee a
happy wife, wherein would consist his own heavenliest happiness. Dost thou love him? Yes; he knoweth it. God bless
thee, most beloved.

Thine ownest Husband.

---

1. Edward Thompson Taylor (1793–1871), minister of the Seamen's Bethel in
North Square, Boston. His preaching, full of colorful nautical idiom, was widely
appreciated. He was the model for Melville's Father Mapple.

2. Goldsmith, *She Stoops to Conquer*, I, 2.

[Boston, March 17–18, 1840]

And now good night, best, beautifullest, belovedest, bless-ingest of wives. Notwithstanding what I have said of the fleeting and unsatisfying bliss of dreams, still, if thy husband's prayers and wishes can bring thee, or even a shadow of thee, into his sleep, thou or thy image will assuredly be there. Good night, ownest. I bid thee good night, although it is still early in the evening; because I must reserve the rest of the page to greet thee upon in the morning. [*excision*]

March 18th.— Past 8. My belovedest, is not this a beau-tiful morning; and I hope thou, like thy husband, feelest as if thou wert new made, so as not to be at odds with the new day. The sun shines into my soul. Oh, my sweetest wife, I do so long to be with thee. Hast thou been expecting me already, naughtiest? Perhaps that is the secret of thy not writing. Expect me not, impatientest Sophie Hawthorne, till the last cars on Saturday; and though I have full faith that God will bring me to thee by that time, yet I shall account it one of His especial favors. Colonel Hall is still detained at home by sickness—no joke to him, any more than to naugh-tiest Sophie Hawthorne. Another of the Measurers is about sending his son to the West, and so thinks it needful to spend all his time with him. Two more of our honorable body do not deem it necessary to make their appearance at the Cus-tom-House more than once a week; so that if thy husband were to be as careless of his duty as they, the commerce of the United States would undoubtedly go to wreck. Moreover, I have notice that a particular friend of mine[1] will be in the city in the course of this week. Were it not for all these hindrances, most dearest wife, I would have come home to thee tomorrow, to stay the rest of the week; but mourn not, mine ownest love, we will not lose anything by the delay. God bless thee forever and forever, Amen.

Thine ownest, innermostest friend,
and most lovingest Husband.

1. Probably Franklin Pierce. See 143.

Boston, March 19th. 1840.

Dear Pike,

I return Dr. Brown's Dartmoor manuscript, and beg you to express my acknowledgments to him for the perusal. It has afforded me much entertainment and instruction; and I should suppose that the work might easily be made very acceptable to the public.[1]

I have dunned Loring[2] on your account; and he promised to call immediately on Holman,[3] and pay him half the amount of the due-bill.

I intend to come to Salem on Saturday; and Colonel Hall has appointed to meet me at the Essex House there, at two °clock of that day. He wishes likewise to see you; and as it is possible that I may not be able to keep the appointment, I hope you will not fail to be there at the time aforesaid. If not fair weather, he probably will not come.

Yrs truly,
Nath. Hawthorne.

1. Benjamin Browne (see 140.4) had served as a young man on the privateering schooner *Frolic*, captured by the British; he was imprisoned for fifteen months, nine of them at Dartmoor, from August, 1814 to May, 1815. After NH brought his account to O'Sullivan's attention, it appeared anonymously in the *Democratic Review* in 1846. See 334.2.

2. William P. Loring had served as a measurer in the Boston Custom House from 1835 to 1838. He was listed in the Boston *Directory* from 1840 to 1843 as a

stable-keeper, and was reinstated as an inspector in the custom house in 1844. See 288, 298.

3. Possibly R. W. Holman & Co., proprietors of the United States Hotel at the corners of Lincoln, Beach, and Kingston Streets, where Pike may have lived while employed at the custom house.

Boston, March 26th. 1840—Afternoon.

Thou dearest wife,

Here is thy husband, yearning for thee with his whole heart—thou, meanwhile, being fast asleep, and perhaps hovering around him in thy dreams. Very dreary are the first few centuries which elapse after our separations, and before it is time to look forward hopefully to another meeting—these are the 'dark ages.' And hast thou been very good, my beloved? Dost thou dwell in the past and in the future, so that the gloomy present is quite swallowed up in sunshine? Do so, mine ownest, for the sake of thy husband, whose desire it is to make thy whole life as sunny as the scene beyond those high, dark rocks of the Menaggio.

Dearest, my thoughts will not flow at all—they are as sluggish as a stream of half-cold lava. Methinks I could sleep an hour or two—perhaps thou art calling to me, out of the midst of thy dream, to come and join thee there. I will take a book, and lie down awhile, and perhaps resume my pen in the evening. I will not say good-bye; for I am coming to thee now.

March 27th— Before breakfast.—Good morning, most belovedest. I felt so infinitely stupid, after my afternoon's nap, that I could not possibly write another word; and it has required a whole night's sleep to restore me the moderate share of intellect and vivacity that naturally belongs to me. Dearest, thou didst not come into my dreams, last night; but, on the contrary, I was engaged in assisting the escape of Louis XVI and Marie Antoinette from Paris, during the

French Revolution. And sometimes, by an unaccountable metamorphosis, it seemed as if my mother and sisters were in the place of the King and Queen. I think that fairies rule over our dreams—beings who have no true reason or true feeling, but mere fantaisies instead of those endowments.

Afternoon.— Blessedest, I do think that it is the doom laid upon me, of murdering so many of the brightest hours of the day at that unblest Custom-House, that makes such havoc with my wits; for here I am again, trying to write worthily to my etherealest, and intellectualest, and feelingest, and imaginativest wife, yet with a sense as if all the noblest part of man had been left out of my composition—or had decayed out of it, since my nature was given to my own keeping. Sweetest Dove, shouldst thou once venture within those precincts, the atmosphere would immediately be fatal to thee—thy wings would cease to flutter in a moment—scarcely wouldst thou have time to nestle into thy husband's bosom, ere thy pure spirit would leave what is mortal of thee there, and flit away to Heaven. Never comes any bird of Paradise into that dismal region. A salt, or even a coal ship is ten million times preferable; for there the sky is above me, and the fresh breeze around me, and my thoughts, having hardly anything to do with my occupation, are as free as air.

Nevertheless, belovedest, thou art not to fancy that the above paragraph gives thee a correct idea of thy husband's mental and spiritual state; for he is sometimes prone to the sin of exaggeration. It is only once in a while that the image and desire of a better and happier life makes him feel the iron of his chain; for after all, a human spirit may find no insufficiency of food fit for it, even in the Custom-House. And with such materials as these, I do think, and feel, and learn things that are worth knowing, and which I should not know unless I had learned them there; so that the present portion of my life shall not be quite left out of the sum of my real existence. Moreover, I live through my Dove's heart—I live an intellectual life in Sophie Hawthorne. Therefore ought those two in one to keep themselves happy and healthy in mind and feelings, inasmuch as they enjoy more blessed influences than their husband, and likewise have to provide happiness and moral health for him.

Very dearest, I feel a great deal better now—nay, nothing whatever is the matter. What a foolish husband hast thou, misfortunate little Dove, that he will grieve thee with such a long Jeremiad, and after all find out that there is not the slightest cause for lamentation. But so it must often be, dearest—this trouble hast thou entailed upon thyself, by yield ng to become my wife. Every cloud that broods beneath my sky, or that I even fancy is brooding there, must dim thy sunshine too. But here is no real cloud. It is good for me, on many accounts, that my life has had this passage in it. Thou canst not think how much more I know than I did a year ago—what a stronger sense I have of power to act as a man among men—what worldly wisdom I have gained, and wisdom also that is not altogether of this world. And when I quit this earthy cavern, where I am now buried, nothing will cling to me that ought to be left behind. Men will not perceive, I trust, by my look, or the tenor of my thoughts and feelings, that I have been a Custom-House officer.

Belovedest!—what an awful concussion was that of our two heads. It was as if two worlds had rushed together—as if the Moon (thou art my Moon, gentlest wife) had met in fierce encounter with the rude, rock-promontoried Earth. Dearest, art thou sure that thy delicatest brain has suffered no material harm? A maiden's heart, they say, is often bruised and broken by her lover's cruelty; it was reserved for naughtiest me to inflict those injuries on my mistress's head [*excision*]

March 28th.—Before breakfast. Dearest, good morning. How [*excision*] thy head were pil-[*excision*]

Boston, March 30th. 1840—5 or 6. P.M.

Infinitely belovedest,

Thy Thursday's letter came not till Saturday—so long was thy faithfullest husband defrauded of his rights! Thou mayst imagine how hungry was my heart, when at last it came. Thy yesterday's letter, for a wonder, arrived in its due season, this forenoon; and I could not refrain from opening it immediately; and then and there, in that 'earthy cavern' of the Custom-House, and surrounded by all those brawling slang-whangers,[1] I held sweet communion with my Dove. Dearest, I do not believe that any one of those miserable men received a letter which uttered a single word of love and faith—which addressed itself in any manner to the soul. No beautiful and holy woman's spirit came to visit any of them, save thy husband. How blest is he! Thou findest thy way to him in all dismallest and unloveliest places, and talkest with him there, nor can the loudest babble nor rudest clamor shut out thy gentle voice from his ear. Truly, he ought not to bemoan himself any more as in his last letter, but to esteem himself favored beyond all other mortals;—but truly he is a wayward and incalculable personage, and will not be prevailed with to know his own happiness. The lovelier thou art, mine ownest, the more doth thy unreasonable husband discontent himself to be away from thee, though thou continually sendest him all of thyself that can be breathed into written words. Oh, I want thee with me forever and ever!—at least, I would al-

ways have the feeling, amid the tumult and unsuitable associations of the day, that the night would bring me to my home
of peace and rest—to thee, my fore-ordained wife. Well,—
be patient, heart! The time will come. Meantime, foolishest
heart, be thankful for the much of happiness thou already
hast.

Dearest, thy husband was very reprehensible, yesterday.
Wilt thou again forgive him? He went not to hear Father
Taylor preach. In truth, his own private and quiet room did
have such a charm for him, after being mixed and tossed
together with discordant elements all the week, that he
thought his Dove would grant him indulgence for one more
Sabbath. Also, he fancied himself unfit to go out, on account
of a cold; though, as the disease has quite disappeared to-day,
I am afraid he conjured it up to serve his naughty purpose.
But, indeed, dearest, I feel somewhat afraid to hear this
divine Father Taylor, lest my sympathy with thy admiration
of him should be colder and feebler than thou lookest for.
Belovedest wife, our souls are in happiest unison; but we
must not disquiet ourselves if every tone be not re-echoed
from one to the other—if every slightest shade be not reflected in the alternate mirror. Our broad and general sympathy is enough to secure our bliss, without our following it
into minute details. Wilt thou promise not to be troubled,
should thy husband be unable to appreciate the excellence of
Father Taylor? Promise me this; and at some auspicious
hour, which I trust will soon arrive, Father Taylor shall have
an opportunity to make music with my soul. But I forewarn
thee, sweetest Dove, that thy husband is a most unmalleable
man;—thou art not to suppose, because his spirit answers to
every touch of thine, that therefore every breeze, or even
every whirlwind, can upturn him from his depths. Well,
dearest, I have said my say, on this matter.

What a rain is this, my poor little Dove! Yet, as the wind
comes from some other quarter than the East, I trust that

thou hast found it genial. Good bye, belovedest, till tomorrow evening. Meantime, love me, and dream of me.

March 31st.—Evening.— Best Wife, it is scarcely dark yet; but thy husband has just lighted his lamps, and sits down to talk to thee. Would that he could hear an answer in thine own sweet voice; for his spirit needs to be cheered by that dearest of all harmonies, after a long, listless, weary day. Belovedest, thou knowest not how I am famished for a kiss, tonight at this moment, it does seem as if life could not go on without it. What is to be done?

Dearest, if Elizabeth Hoare[2] is to be with you on Saturday, it would be quite a calamity to thee and thy household, for me to come at the same time. Now will Sophie Hawthorne scold, and the Dove's eyes be suffused, at my supposing that their husband's visit could be a calamity at any time. Well; at least, we should be obliged to give up many hours of happiness, and it would not even be certain that I could have the privilege of seeing mine own wife in private, at all. Wherefore, considering these things, I have resolved, and do hereby make it a decree of fate, that my present widowhood shall continue one week longer. And my sweetest Dove—yes, and naughtiest Sophie Hawthorne too—will both concur in the fitness of this resolution, and will help me to execute it with what of resignation is attainable by mortal man, by writing me a letter full of strength and comfort. And I, infinitely dear wife, will write to thee again; so that, though my earthly part will not be with thee on Saturday, yet thou shalt have my heart and soul in a letter. Will not this be right, and for the best? 'Yes, dearest husband,' saith my meekest little Dove; and Sophie Hawthorne cannot gainsay her.

My unspeakably ownest, dost thou love me a million of times as much as thou didst a week ago? As for me, my heart grows deeper and wider every moment, and still thou fillest it in all its depths and boundlessness. Wilt thou never be satisfied with making me love thee? To what use canst thou put so much love as thou continually receivest from me? Dost thou hoard it up, as misers do their treasure?

Thine own blessedest husband.

April 1st. Before breakfast.— Good morning, entirely belovedest.

Sophie Hawthorne, I have enclosed something for thee in this letter. If thou findest it not, then tell me what thou art.[3]

1. Noisy or abusive talkers, in the sense of "slang" as impertinence or abuse. "Slangwhanger" also described violently partisan newspaper editors and haranguing political orators (*OED*). Compare 409.

2. Elizabeth Sherman Hoar (1814–78), daughter of the prominent Concord attorney Samuel Hoar. The visit concerned the medallion SH was making of Charles Emerson. See 151.

3. Each of the paragraphs of this postscript is in a small hand in a corner of the cover.

Boston, April 3ᵈ 1840.—Evening

Blessedest wife, thy husband has been busy all day, from early breakfast-time till late in the afternoon; and old Father Time has gone onward somewhat less heavily, than is his wont when I am imprisoned within the walls of the Custom-House. It has been a brisk, breezy day, as thou knowest—an effervescent atmosphere; and I have enjoyed it in all its freshness, breathing air which has not been breathed in advance by the hundred thousand pairs of lungs which have common and indivisible property in the atmosphere of this great city. My breath had never belonged to anybody but me. It came fresh from the wilderness of ocean. My Dove ought to have shared it with me, and so have made it infinitely sweeter— save her, I would wish to have an atmosphere all to myself. And, dearest, it was exhilarating to see the vessels, how they bounded over the waves, while a sheet of foam broke out around them. I found a good deal of enjoyment, too, in the busy scene around me; for several vessels were disgorging themselves (what an unseemly figure is this—'disgorge,' quotha, as if the vessels were sick at their stomachs) on the wharf; and everybody seemed to be working with might and main. It pleased thy husband to think that he also had a part to act in the material and tangible business of this life, and that a part of all this industry could not have gone on without his presence. Nevertheless, my belovedest, pride not thyself too much on thy husband's activity and utilitarianism;[1] he is naturally an idler, and doubtless will soon be pestering thee with his bewailments at being compelled to earn his bread by taking some little share in the toils of mortal man.

Most beloved, when I went to the Custom-House, at one °clock, Colonel Hall held up a letter, turning the seal towards me; and he seemed to be quite as well aware as myself, that the long-legged little fowl thereon impressed was a messenger from my Dove. And so, naughtiest, thou art not patient. Well; it will do no good to scold thee. I know Sophie Hawthorne of old—yea, of very old time do I know her; or rather, of very old eternity. There was an image of such a being, deep within my soul, before we met in this dim world; and therefore nothing that she does, or says, or thinks, or feels, ever surprises me. Her naughtiness is as familiar to me as if it were my own. But, dearest, do be patient; because thou seest that the busy days are coming again; and how is thy husband to bear his toil lightsomely, if he knows that thou art impatient and disquieted. By and bye, as soon as God will open a way to us, we will help one another every night to bear the burthen of the day, whatever it may be.

My little Dove, the excellent Colonel Hall, conceiving, I suppose, that our correspondence must necessarily involve a great expenditure of paper, has imparted to thy husband a quire or two of superfine gilt-edged, which he brought from Congress.[2] The sheet on which I am now writing is a specimen; and he charged me to give thee a portion of it, which I promised to do—but whether I shall convey it to thee in the mass, or sheet by sheet, after spoiling it with my uncouth scribble, is yet undetermined. Which wouldst thou prefer? Likewise three sticks of sealing-wax did the good Colonel bestow; but unfortunately it is all red. Yet I think it proper enough that a gentleman should seal all his letters with red sealing-wax; though it is sweet and graceful in my Dove to use fancy-colored. Dearest, the paper thou shalt have, every sheet of it, sooner or later; and only that it is so burthensome to thy foolish husband to carry anything in his hand, I would bring it to thee. Meantime, till I hit upon some other method, I will send it sheet by sheet.

[*excision*]

1. "Utilitarian" was a rather new word, one which John Stuart Mill claimed to have first used in self-description in 1822–23, to indicate his allegiance to Jeremy Bentham's philosophy. Mill recalled that it "got into rather common use just about the time when those who had originally assumed it, laid down that along with other sectarian characteristics" (*Autobiography* [1873], Oxford World's Classics, p. 67).

2. Hall had been a congressman for Maine, 1833–37; see 118.1.

[Boston] Custom-House, April 6th. 1840. 5. P.M.

How long it is, belovedest, since I have written thee a letter from this darksome region. Never did I write thee a word from hence that was worth reading, nor shall I now; but perhaps thou wouldst get no word at all, these two or three days, unless I write it here. This evening, dearest, I am to have a visitor—the illustrious Colonel Hall himself; and I have even promised him a bed on my parlor floor—so that, as thou seest, the duties of hospitality will keep me from communion with the best little wife in the world. [*excision*] out for thee; for, foolish heart that it is, it cannot be made to understand why it was not pressed to thine, last night and the night before and these many nights past. Hearts never do understand the mystery of separation—that is the business of the head. My sweetest, dearest, purest, holiest, noblest, faithfullest wife, dost thou know what a loving husband thou hast? Dost thou love him most immensely?—beyond conception; and dost thou feel, as he does, that every new throb of love is worth all other happiness in this world.

Dearest, my soul drank thy letter this forenoon, and has been conscious of it ever since, in the midst of business and noise, and all sorts of wearisome babble. How dreamlike it makes all my external life, this continual thought and deepest, inmostest musing upon thee! I live only within myself; for thou art always there. Thou makest me a disembodied spirit; and with the eye of a spirit, I look on all worldly things—and this it is that separates thy husband from those who seem to be his fellows—therefore is he "among them, but not of them."[1] Thou art transfused into his heart, and spread all round about it; and it is only once in a while that he himself is even imperfectly conscious of what a miracle has been wrought upon him.

Well, dearest, were ever such words as these written in a Custom-House before! Oh, and what a mighty heave my heart has given, this very moment! Thou art most assuredly thinking of me now, wife of my inmost bosom. Never did I know what love was before—I did not even know it when I began this letter. Ah; but I ought not to say that; it would make me sad to believe that I had not always loved thee. Farewell now, dearest; or [*excision verso*] husband's secret heart, and lie [*excision verso*] interrupted, and must cease, for the present, to worship thee in written words. Be quiet, my Dove; lest my heart be made to flutter by the fluttering of thy wings.

April 7th. 6. P.M. My tenderest Dove, how hast thou lived through the polar winter of to-day; for it does appear to me to have been the most uncomfortable day that ever was inflicted on poor mortals. Thy husband has had to face it in all its terrors; and the cold has penetrated through his cloak, through his beaver-cloth coat and vest, and was neutralized no where but in the region round about his heart—and that it did not chill him even there, he owes to thee. I know not whether I should not have jumped overboard in despair to-day, if I had not sustained my spirits by the thought of thee, most beloved wife; for, besides the bleak, unkindly air, I have been plagued by *two* vessels of coal-shovellers at the same time, and have had to keep two separate tallies simultaneously. But, dearest, I was conscious that all this was merely a vision and a phantasy, and that, in reality, I was not half-frozen by the bitter blast, nor plagued to death by these grimy coal-heavers, but that I was basking quietly in the sunshine of eternity, with mine own Dove. Any sort of bodily and earthly torment may serve to make us sensible that we have a soul that is not within the jurisdiction of such shadowy demons—it separates the immortal within us from the mortal. But the wind has blown my brain into such confusion that I cannot philosophize now.

Blessingest wife, what a habit have I contracted of late, of telling thee all my grievances and annoyances, as if such trifles were worth telling—or as if, supposing them to be so, they would be the most agreeable gossip in the world to thee. Thou makest me behave like a child, naughtiest. Why dost thou not frown at my nonsensical complaints, and utterly refuse thy sympathy? But I speak to thee of the miseries of a cold day, and blustering wind, and intractable coal-shovellers, with just the same certainty that thou wilt listen lovingly and sympathizingly, as if I were speaking of the momentous and permanent concerns of life.

Dearest, [excision] I do not think that I can come on Friday—there is hardly any likelihood of it; for one of the Measurers is indisposed, which throws additional duty on the efficient members of our honorable body. But there is no expressing how I do yearn for thee! The strength of the feeling seems to make my words cold and tame. Dearest, this is but a poor epistle, yet is written in very great love and worship of thee—so, for the writer's sake, thou wilt receive it into thy heart of hearts. God keep thee—and me also for thy sake.

Thine ownest.

1. Byron, *Childe Harold's Pilgrimage*, Canto 3, stanza 113.

Boston, April 15th. 1840   Afternoon.

Belovedest—since writing this word, I have made a considerable pause; for, dearest, my mind has no activity to-day. I
would fain sit still, and let thoughts, feelings, and images of
thee, pass before me and through me, without my putting
them into words, or taking any other trouble about the matter. It must be that thou dost not especially and exceedingly
need a letter from me; else I should feel an impulse and
necessity to write. I do wish, most beloved wife, that there
were some other method of communing with thee at a distance; for really this is not a natural one to thy husband. In
truth, I never use words, either with the tongue or pen,
when I can possibly express myself in any other way;—and
how much, dearest, may be expressed without the utterance
of a word! Is there not a volume in [*excision*] many of our
glances?—even in a pressure of the hand? And when I write
to thee, I do but painfully endeavor to shadow into words
what has already been expressed in those realities. In
heaven, I am very sure, there will be no occasion for
words;—our minds will enter into each other, and silently
possess themselves of their mutual riches. Even in this
world, I think, such a process is not altogether impossible—
we ourselves have experienced it—but words come like an
earthy wall betwixt us. Then our minds are compelled to
stand apart, and make signals of our meaning, instead of
rushing into one another, and holding converse in an infinite
and eternal language. Oh, dearest, have not the moments of
our oneness been those in which we were most silent? It is
our instinct to be silent then, because words could not ade-

quately express the perfect concord of our hearts, and therefore would infringe upon it. Well, ownest, good bye till
tomorrow; when perhaps thy husband will feel a necessity to
use even such a wretched medium as words, to tell thee how
he loves thee. No words can tell it now.

April 16th. Afternoon— Most dear wife, never was thy
husband gladder to receive a letter from thee than to-day.
And so thou didst perceive that I was rather out of spirits on
Monday. Foolish and faithless husband that I was, I supposed that thou wouldst not take any notice of it; but the
simple fact was, that I did not feel quite so well as usual; and
said nothing about it to thee, because I knew thou wouldst
desire me to put off my departure, which (for such a trifle) I
felt it not right to do—and likewise, because my Dove would
have been naughty, and so perhaps have made herself ten
times as ill as her husband. Dearest, I am quite well now—
only very hungry; for I have thought fit to eat very little for
two days past; and I think starvation is a remedy for almost
all physical evils. You will love Colonel Hall, when I tell you
that he has not let me do a [excision verso] return; and even
to-day he has sent me home to my room, although I assured
him that I was perfectly able to work. Now, dearest, if thou
givest thyself any trouble and torment about this past indisposition of mine, I shall never dare to tell thee about my
future incommodities; but if I were sure thou wouldst estimate them at no more than they are worth, thou shouldst
know them all, even to the slightest prick of my finger. It is
my impulse to complain to thee in all griefs, great and small;
and I will not check that impulse, if thou wilt sympathize
reasonably, as well as most lovingly. And now, ownest wife,
believe that thy husband is well;—better, I fear, than thou,
who art tired to death, and hast even had the headache.
Naughtiest, dost thou think that all the busts in the world,
and all the medallions and other forms of sculpture, would
be worth creating, at the expence of such weariness and

headache to thee. I would rather that thy art should be an-
nihilated, than that thou shouldst always pay this price for
its exercise. But perhaps, when thou hast my bosom to repose
upon, thou wilt no longer feel such overwhelming weariness.
I am given thee to repose upon, that so my most tender and
sensitivest little Dove may be able to do great works.

And dearest, I do by no means undervalue thy works,
though I cannot estimate all thou hast ever done at the price
of a single throb of anguish to thy belovedest head. But thou
hast achieved mighty things. Thou hast called up a face
which was hidden in the grave—hast re-created it, after it
was resolved to dust—and so hast snatched from Death his
victory.[1] I wonder at thee, my beloved. Thou art a miracle
thyself, and workest miracles. I could not have believed it
possible to do what thou hast done, to restore the lineaments
of the dead so perfectly that even she who loved him so well[2]
can require nothing more;—and this too, when thou hadst
hardly known his living face.[3] Thou couldst not have done it,
unless God had helped thee. This surely was inspiration, and
of the holiest kind, and for one of the holiest purposes.

Dearest, I shall long to see thee exceedingly next Saturday;
but having been absent from duty for two or three days past
it will not be right for me to ask any more time so soon. Dost
thou think it would?

How naughty was thy husband to waste the first page of
this letter in declaiming against this blessed art of writing! I
do not see how I could live without it;—thy letters are my
heart's food; and oftentimes my heart absolutely insists upon
pouring itself out on paper, for thy perusal. In truth, if the
heart could do all the work, I should probably write to thee
the whole time of my absence; but thou knowest that the co-
operation of the hand and head are indispensable; and they,
not being able to comprehend the infinite necessity of the
heart's finding an utterance, are sometimes sluggish.

April 17th.—Before breakfast.—Ownest, I am perfectly

well this morning, and want to give thee ten thousand kisses. Dost thou love me? Dearest, expect not another letter till Tuesday. Is thy weariness quite gone?

Thine ownest, ownest husband.

1. Charles Chauncy Emerson (1808–36), brother of Ralph Waldo and fiancé of Elizabeth Hoar, died of tuberculosis. SH had modeled in clay a bas-relief medallion of him similar to one she had made of her brother George shortly before his death. Emerson had seen the model when he visited SH on February 26, the occasion of a lecture he gave at the Salem Lyceum. See Emerson, *Letters*, II, 257.

2. Elizabeth Hoar never married: she remained constant to Charles after his death. She had come to Salem in early April to see the medallion; see 148.2; Emerson, *Letters*, II, 274, 284. She was to become SH's close friend when the Hawthornes lived in Concord.

3. Emerson wrote to Margaret Fuller on this date: "Sophia Peabody's medallion is a likeness; a fine head; & in the circumstances of its execution, wonderful. She never saw Charles E. but once & had only for her guide a pencil sketch taken by herself at that time, but *not like*, & a profile-shadow taken at Plymouth. Elizabeth is greatly contented" (*Letters*, II, 281–82).

Boston, April 19th. 1840—Forenoon.

Dearest, there came no letter from thee yesterday; and I have been a little disquieted with fears that thou art not well, and art naughty enough to conceal it from thy husband. But this is a misdemeanor of which my Dove ought not to be lightly suspected. Or perhaps, ownest wife, thou didst imagine that I might mean to surprise thee by a visit, last evening, and therefore, instead of writing, didst hope to commune with me in living words and sweetest kisses. But, belovedest, if I could have come, I would have given thee notice beforehand; for I love not surprises, even joyful ones—or at least, I would rather that joy should come quietly, and as a matter of course, and warning us of its approach by casting a placid gleam before it. Mine own wife, art thou very well? Thy husband is so, only love-sick—a disease only to be cured by [obliteration] and the pressure of a certain heart to his own heart.

Belovedest, what a beautiful day was yesterday. Wert thou abroad in the sky and air? Thy husband's spirit did rebel against being confined in his darksome dungeon, at the Custom-House; it seemed a sin—a murder of the joyful young day—a quenching of the sunshine. Nevertheless, there he was kept a prisoner, till it was too late to fling himself on a gentle wind and be blown away into the country. I foresee, dearest, that thou wilt, now that the pleasant days of May and June are coming, be tormented quite beyond thine infinite patience, with my groans and lamentations at being compelled to lose so much of life's scanty summertime. But thou must enjoy for both of us. Thou must listen to the notes of the birds, because the rumbling of wheels will be always in my ears—thou must fill thyself with the fragrance of wild flowers, because I must breathe in the dust of the city—thy spirit must enjoy a double share of freedom, because thy husband is doomed to be a captive. It is thine office now, most sweet wife, to make all the additions that may be made to our common stock of enjoyment. By and bye, there shall not be so heavy a burthen imposed upon thee. When I shall be again free, I will enjoy all things with the fresh simplicity of a child of five years old; thou shalt find thine husband grown young again, made over all anew—he will go forth and stand in a summer-shower, and all the worldly dust that has collected on him shall be washed away at once. Then, dearest, he will be fit to be taken into thine arms, and to rest on thy bosom; and whenever thou art aweary, thou shalt lie down upon his heart as upon a bank of fresh flowers.

Nearly 6—P.M. Thy husband went out to walk, dearest, about an hour ago; and found it very pleasant, though there was a somewhat cool wind. I went round and across the common, and stood on the highest point of it, whence I could see miles and miles into the country. Blessed be God for this green tract, and the view which it affords; whereby we poor citizens may be put in mind, sometimes, that all God's earth is not composed of brick blocks of houses, and of stone or wooden pavements. Blessed be God for the sky too; though the smoke of the city may somewhat change its aspect—but still it is better than if each street were covered over with a roof. There were a good many people walking on the mall, mechanicks, apparently, and shopkeeper's clerks, with their wives and sweethearts; and boys were rolling on the grass— and thy husband would have liked to lie down and roll too. Wouldst thou not have been ashamed of him? And, Oh, dearest, thou shouldst have been there, to help me to enjoy the green grass, and the far-off hills and fields—to teach me how to enjoy them; for when I view Nature without thee, I feel that I lack a sense. When we are together, thy whole mind and fancy, as well as thy whole heart, is mine; so that all thy impressions from earth, sea, and sky, are added to all mine. How necessary hast thou made thyself to thy husband, my little Dove! When he is weary and out of spirits, his heart yearneth for thee; and when he is among pleasant scenes, he requireth thee so much the more.

My dearest, why didst thou not write to me, yesterday?— It were always advisable, methinks, to arrange matters so that a letter may be sent on each Saturday, when I am not coming home; because Sunday leaves me free to muse upon thee, and to imagine the state and circumstances in which thou art—and this present Sunday I have been troubled with fancies that thou art ill of body or ill at ease in mind. Do not thou have any such foolish fancies about me, mine ownest. Oh, how we find, at every moment of our lives, that we ought always to be together! Then there would be none of these needless heart-quakes; but now how can they be avoided, when we mutually feel that one half our being is wandering away by itself, without the guidance and guard of the other half! Well; it will not be so always. Doubtless, God has planned how to make us happy; but thy husband, being of a distrustful and rebellious nature, cannot help wishing sometimes that our Father would let him into His plans.
[*excision*]

[Boston, April 20, 1840]

I had learned from the papers the destruction of Langtrie's[1] establishment by fire, and apprehended that you must be a sufferer; but I had not considered the event with any reference to myself. I never should have thought of requiring any additional security on this account and, in fact, never should have bestowed any thought on the matter, had you not written. I am in no present need of the money nor shall I be, so long as I continue in office, so that your proposed arrangement will be perfectly satisfactory to me, and if a more distant date of payment will accommodate you better, I entreat you to take your own time. As to interest, it sounds queer between you and me. If it will be any easement to your mind, it is not worth while for me to object, but it quite deprives me of the pleasant feeling of having done you a kindness.[2]

The draft on Messrs. Otis & Broaders,[3] for $50, was not available, they having paid a draft to that amount before I presented mine.

Unless Congress puts that accursed restriction on the fee offices of the Custom-House, I shall soon have a good deal of cash coming in, and should there be any occasion, I beg you to make use of it, as if it were your own.[4] I will not lend you any money on interest because then I should lose the security of your faith and honor, and make a mere commercial speculation of it, and put myself in the same category as other usurers. But if you will borrow it as a friend you may command every cent that I can spare.

I should rejoice that there might be a possibility of my

spending any part of the summer in Stockbridge, but I can see none.[5] Last summer was no summer at all to me, every golden day of it having been spent in one filthy dock or other, and so it must continue to be, as long as I remain in the Custom-House. What a miserable sort of thrift it is, to give up a whole summer of this brief life for a paltry thousand or two thousand dollars! I am a fool.

But I will not give up the hope of your paying a short visit to Boston. Did I tell you in my last that our friend, Mrs. S.[6] has had a miscarriage? Such seems to be her fate, in her life as a whole, and in all details.

1. Samuel Daly Langtree, O'Sullivan's brother-in-law, and Thomas Allen were the publishers of the *Democratic Review*. Their building in Washington was destroyed by fire on April 11; the loss, estimated at $18,000, was covered only by $6,000 insurance. At this time O'Sullivan was practicing law at 4 Wall Street in New York, having given up the editorship of the review.

2. According to Thomas F. Madigan, who first printed this letter in *Word Shadows of the Great* (New York: Frederick A. Stokes, 1930), pp. 193–94, O'Sullivan had borrowed money from NH and now "hastened to assure the novelist that while the loss might compel him to ask for an extension of time on the debt, it had by no means ruined him." NH had paid $550 for an account of O'Sullivan, on September 30, 1839 (MS, Essex).

3. James A. G. Otis and E. R. Broaders & Co., booksellers, 120 Washington Street, Boston. This may refer to the $50 mentioned in 101.

4. See 101.

5. Probably O'Sullivan planned to visit his close friends the Sedgwick family in Stockbridge, Mass.

6. Presumably Mary Silsbee Sparks.

Boston, April 21st. 1840.—Custom-House

I do trust, my dearest, that thou hast been enjoying this bright day for both of us; for thy husband has spent it in his dungeon—and the only ray of light that broke upon him, was when he opened thy letter. Belovedest, I have folded it to my heart, and ever and anon it sends a thrill through me; for thou hast steeped it with thy love—it seems as if thy head were leaning against my breast. I long to get home, that I may read it again and again; for in this uncongenial region, I can but half comprehend it—at least, I feel that there is a richness and sweetness in it, too sacred to be enjoyed, save in privacy. Dearest wife, thy poor husband is sometimes driven to wish that thou and he could mount upon a cloud (as we used to fancy in those heavenly walks of ours) and be borne quite out of sight and hearing of all this world;—then, at last, our souls might melt into each other; but now, all the people in the world seem to come between us. How happy were Adam and Eve! There was no third person to come between them, and all the infinity around them only served to press their hearts closer together. We love one another as well as they; but there is no silent and lovely garden of Eden for us. Mine own, wilt thou sail away with me to discover some summer island?[1]—dost thou not think that God has reserved one for us, ever since the beginning of the world? Ah, foolish husband that I am, to raise a question of it, when we have found such an Eden, such an island sacred to us two, whenever, whether in Mrs. Quincy's[2] boudoir, or any-where else, we have been clasped in one another's arms! That holy circle shuts out all the world—then we are the Adam and Eve of a virgin earth. Now good-bye dearest; for voices are babbling around me, and I should not wonder if thou wert to hear the echo of them, while thou readest this letter.

April 22^d— 6 °clock P.M. To-day, dearest, I have been measuring salt, on Long-Wharf; and though considerably weary, I feel better satisfied than if I had been murdering the blessed day at the Custom-House. Mine own wife, how very good wast thou, to take me with thee on that sweet walk, last Monday! And how kind-hearted was that sensible old stump! Thou enquirest whether I ever heard a stump speak before. No, indeed; but "stump-speeches" (as thou mayst learn in the newspapers) are very common in the western country. Belovedest, I have met with an immense misfortune. Dost thou sympathize from the bottom of thy heart? Wouldst thou take it upon thyself, if possible? Yea; I know thou wouldst, even without asking the nature of it; and truth to tell, I could be selfish enough to wish that thou mightest share it with me. Now art thou all in a fever of anxiety! I feel the fluttering of thy foolish little heart. Shall I tell thee? No. —Yes; I will. I have received an invitation to a party at General McNeil's,[3] next Friday evening. Why will not people let your poor persecuted husband alone? What possible good can it do for me to thrust my coal-begrimed visage and salt-befrosted locks into good society? What claim have I to be there—a humble Measurer, a subordinate Custom-House officer, as I am? I cannot go. I will not go. I intend to pass that evening with my wife—that is to say, in musings and dreams of her—and moreover, it was an exceeding breach of etiquette, that this belovedest wife was not included in the invitation.

[*excision*] My duties began at sunrise, after a somewhat scanty night's rest; for George Hillard and his brother, from London,[4] came to see me, when I was preparing to go to bed; and I was kept up pretty late. But I came home at about four °clock, and straightway went to bed! What a sinful way was that of misusing this summer afternoon! I trust, most dear wife, that the better half of my being has drawn from the sweet day all the honey that it contained. I feel as if it were not so much matter, now, whether my days pass pleasantly or irksomely, since thou canst be living a golden life for both of us. Sometime or other, we will contribute each an equal share of enjoyment.

Dearest, thou knowest not how I have yearned for thee. And now there is but one day more of widowhood! Sophie Hawthorne must not expect me any more on Fridays, till the busy season is over. If I can always come on the appointed Saturday, it will be a great mercy of Heaven; but I trust in Heaven's goodness, and the instrumentality of Colonel Hall. Now God bless thee, ownest wife. [excision]

God bless us

1. Compare "The Old Manse": "The idea of an infinite generosity and exhaustless bounty . . . can be enjoyed in perfection only by the natives of the summer islands, where the bread-fruit, the cocoa, the palm, and the orange, grow spontaneously, and hold forth the ever-ready meal"(MOM, p. 13).

2. Mary Jane Miller Quincy (1806–74), wife of Josiah Quincy, Jr. (1802–82), a lawyer who was to be mayor of Boston, 1845–49. Mary Peabody had been teaching her three children in the Quincy house since 1838. See Tharp, Until Victory, pp. 182–83. For NH's acquaintance with Mr. Quincy's sister Eliza, see 235, 245.

3. John McNeil; see 91.2.

4. John Hillard, who was associated with Coates & Co., 13 Bread St., London.

[Boston] April 28 1840

Sweetest, do not say nor ever think again that I must have thought thee "absurd" or that I can have had any thought of thee, save that thou are all that is good and holy and beautiful—yes—and wise and strong hearted. Nothing can shake this Faith in me;—nothing can take away the comfort which I feel in it—nor the perfect trust which fills my heart that thou wilt ever be as thou now art, my peace and happiness. Dearest, I know how sensitive is thy nature—how easily thy heart might be broken—how soon thou wouldst vanish away from the earth, were thy soul to be wronged or violated in any manner; and yet I feel that if thou shouldst not be happy, and shouldst fail to make me so, the fault would be my own. But thou wilt be happy—we will both be happy. God, since He has intrusted thee to me, will make me wise to comprehend thy celestial nature, and whatever is in me of heavenly origin will guard and minister unto thee.

Blessedest, dost thou think it strange that thou shouldst be depressed at our separation? Did not my heart sink too? dost thou believe that I am never unreasonably sad? Oh, I am not so wise as thou supposest. x x x God hath married us, and in Heaven this will be all in all; but to our perfect peace and fulness of security on earth, it is necessary that man should marry us too. It will be an external pledge of our eternal and infinite union.

Boston, April 30th. 1840.—8 °clock. P.M.

Ownest Dove, thy letter was brought to me by Colonel Hall, on board of my salt-ship, this afternoon; and I opened it with the fullest faith that thou wert comforted and happy; for there was already an assurance within me that sunshine was restored to thy soul. I knew, dearest, that I could comfort thee. This one divine gift thy husband is conscious of— an instinct to know what thy heart needs. Other gifts worthy of thee he doth not pretend to have. But with this, God has endowed him for [*excision verso*]

Dearest, I arose this morning, feeling more elastic than I have throughout the winter; for the breathing of the ocean air has wrought a very beneficial effect; and who can tell, moreover, what weight thy lightened spirits had removed from mine? What a beautiful, beautifullest afternoon this has been! It was a real happiness to live;—if I had been merely a vegetable—a hawthorn-bush, for instance—I must have been happy in such an air and sunshine; but having a mind and a soul, and being married in mind and soul to thee, dost thou not think I enjoyed somewhat more than mere vegetable happiness? Belovedest, I wish thou couldst spend such an afternoon with me. I should see a thousand beautiful things that are hidden from me now. Wilt thou go a-Maying with me tomorrow morning?—for the footsteps of May can be traced upon the islands in the harbor; and I have been watching the tints of green upon them, gradually deepening, till now they are almost as beautiful as they ever can be. Dearest wife, good night; for thy husband is tired. Doctor Channing sent me a message, while I was in the midst of the first sentence of this letter, desiring me to come and spend the evening with him; but I made answer that I was writing to my wife, and could not possibly come. The above is all true, except that I did not actually specify my dearest little wife as the person who deprived him of my company. Dearest, have no compunctions on account of thy keeping me away from the Doctor; for nothing could have induced me to go, with such a burthen of weary mind and body, as a long day's toil has heaped upon me. [*excision*]

May 1st.—4. P.M. Sweetest wife, this has been rather a weary day to thy husband—a provoking day; for he has been imprisoned either in the Custom-House or on board the salt ship, and yet has brought nothing to pass. The frequent showers have continually interrupted our labours; so that I have not the satisfaction of having done a great day's work. And now, when I have come home and put on my slippers, and resolved not to leave our own domicile till tomorrow morning, the sun comes out and strives to entice me forth again. But I will not go. Oh, what a beautiful sunset walk we might have, dearest! I trust that thou wilt bathe thyself in a flood of pleasant sunshine—I did hope so, at least; but at this moment a gloom spreads itself through our parlor— for lo! the sun has hidden himself again. Well, belovedest, my thoughts do not flow with any freedom, just now; so I will break off till the evening, and read some book that will re- quire not much attention. Such a book will suit me best; for between every word, and interwoven throughout all the sen- tences, there will be musings about a certain Dove. And how does the said Dove do to-day? Has she been good?—that is to say, has she been happy? Dearest, dost thou really think that I impute it as a sin or a fault to thee, when thou art not happy? Never; it is only a foolish form of speech of thy hus- band's; yet, if I could make it a matter of conscience with thee to be happy, it would please me well. But I would not for the world have thee torment thyself with remorse, when thy soul is suffering from any cause, whether known or inscrutable; for a cause, I am very sure, there always is, though neither thou nor I may be able to search it out. Dearest, I think thou, whom God has made so sensitive, hast a right to be miserable for causes that would not at all disturb the peace of other people; and yet how sunny is thy heart, almost all the time. [*excision*]

157. FRAGMENT?, TO HORACE CONOLLY, PHILA-DELPHIA

[Boston] May, 1840

The day after the great storm in March,[1] I went with David Roberts to make a call on the Duchess[2] at the old house in Turner Street, to learn how she weathered the gale. I had a more than ordinary pleasant visit, and among other things, in speaking of the old house, she said it has had in the history of its changes and alterations Seven Gables.[3] The expression was new and struck me very forcibly; I think I shall make something of it. I expressed a wish to go all over the house; she assented and I repaired to the Attic, and there was no corner or dark hole I did not peep into. I could readily make out five gables, and on returning to the parlour, I inquired where the two remaining gables were placed. The information I received was that the remaining gables were on the north side, and that when Col. Turner[4] became the owner of the house, he removed the 'lean to' on which were the missing gables, and made amends by placing three gables on the L or addition which he made on the south side of the house; the mark of beams still remains in the studding to show precisely where they were. On my return after the exploration I had made of the old structure, the Duchess said to me, "Why don't you write something?"

"I have no subject to write about."

"Oh, there are subjects enough,—write about that old chair in the room; it is an old Puritan relict and you can make a biographical sketch of each old Puritan who became in succession the owner of the chair."

It was a good suggestion and I have made use of it under the name "Grandfather's Chair," finished and ready for the

printer.[5] It will be a child's book, and I have nearly completed
it, as you may see when you come from Philadelphia.[6]

1. Tuesday, March 24.

2. NH's nickname for Susan Ingersoll; see 86, 100.

3. This is the apparent genesis of NH's romance of 1851.

4. Colonel John Turner (1671–1742), a wealthy Salem merchant and shipowner, inherited the home from his father, and remodeled it to accord with his
heightened status. See Gilbert L. Streeter, "Some Historic Streets and Colonial
Houses of Salem," *EIHC*, XXXVI (1900), 205–13; J. D. Phillips, *Salem in the
Eighteenth Century* (Boston: Houghton Mifflin, 1937), pp. 35–36.

5. The book was published by Elizabeth Peabody and Wiley & Putnam in
December 1840 (dated 1841). According to Conolly's letter to William N. Nor-
thend, from which this text of NH's letter is taken, the writing was finished by
June. See Streeter, *EIHC*, XXXVI (1900), 211, and *TS*, "Historical Introduction," pp. 292–93.

6. Where Conolly had been pastor of St. Mark's Episcopal Church.

Boston May 15th. 1840

Darlingest,

I did not reach home last night till candle-light; and then I was beyond expression weary and spiritless; and I could as soon have climbed into Heaven without a ladder, as to come to see thee at Mrs Park's. So, instead of dressing to pay a visit, I undressed and went to bed; but yet I doubt whether I ought not to have gone, for I was restless and wakeful a great part of the night; and it seemed as if I had scarcely fallen asleep, when I awoke with a start, and found the gray dawn creeping over the roofs of the houses. So then it was necessary for thy poor husband to leave his pillow, without enjoying that half-dreaming interval which I so delight to devote to thee. However the fresh morning air made a new creature of me; and all day I have felt tolerably lively and cheerful— as much so as is anywise consistent with this intolerable position of near distance, or distant nearness, in which we now find ourselves. Truly Providence does not seem to have smiled on this visit of thine, my dearest. The dispensation is somewhat hard to bear. There is a weight and a gnawing at my heart; but, belovedest, do let thy heart be cheerful, for thy husband's sake.

Very reviving to me was thy letter, mine ownest. Colonel Hall brought it at noon to the eating-house where we had agreed to dine together; and I forthwith opened and read it while my beef-steak was broiling. It refreshed me much more than my dinner—which is a great deal for a hungry man to say. Dearest, I am in admirable health; it is not the nature of my present mode of life to make me sick; and my nightly weariness does not betoken anything of that kind. Each day, it is true, exhausts all the life and animation that there is in me; but each night restores as much as will be required for the expenditure of the next day. I think this week has been about as tough as any that I ever experienced. I feel the burthen of such constant occupation the more sensibly, from having had so many idle intervals of late.

Oh, dearest, do not thou tire thyself to death. Whenever thou feelest weary, then oughtest thou to glide away from all the world; and go to sleep with the thought of thy husband in thy heart. Why do not people know better what is requisite for a Dove, than thus to keep her wings fluttering all day long, never allowing her a moment to fold them in peace and quietness? I am anxious for thee, mine ownest wife. When I have the sole charge of thee, these things shall not be.

Belovedest, didst thou not bless this shower? It caused thy husband's labors to cease for the day, though it confined him in the cabin of the salt-ship till it was over; but when the drops came few and far between, I journeyed hither to our parlor, and began this scribble. Really I did not think my ideas would be alert enough to write half so much; but I have scrawled one line after another; and now I feel much revived, and soothed and cheered in mind. I shall sleep the more quietly, sweetest wife, for having had this talk with thee— thou wilt bless my sleep. I wish that thou couldst receive the letter to-night, because I am sure thou needest it [excision]

Let me know, mine ownest, what time thou intendest to go to Salem; and if it be possible, I will come to the Depôt to see thee. But do not expect me too fervently, because there are many chances that it will not be in my power. What a time this has been for my Dove and me! Never, since we were married, have the fates been so perverse. And now farewell, my dearest, dearest wife, on whom I repose, in whom I am blest—whom I love with all the heart that is in me, and will love more and more forever, as I grow more worthy to love thee. Be happy, dearest; for my happiness must come through thee.

God bless thee, and let me feel his blessing through thy heart.

Thy lovingest Husband,
de l'Aubepine.[1]

1. French for "Hawthorne," first suggested in 1837 by Monsieur Schaeffer, the Frenchman who boarded with Horatio Bridge in Augusta, Maine; see *AN*, p. 46. Compare the reference to himself as a hawthorn bush in 156. NH was to sign other letters with the pseudonym, and to use it in a prefatory passage of "Rappaccini's Daughter," titled "Writings of Aubépine" (*MOM*, pp. 91, 573).

Boston, May 19th 1840

My dearest,

Where in the world art thou?—or hast thou flown away to Paradise, naughtiest Dove, without bidding thy husband farewell? I know not whereabouts this letter will find thee; but I throw it upon the winds, in the confidence that some breeze of Heaven will bear it to thee; for I suppose heart never spoke to heart, without being heard, and sooner or later finding a response.[1] Perhaps some hearts that speak to other hearts here on earth, may find no response till they have passed far into Eternity; but our hearts catch each other's whispers even here. Happy we! But, belovedest, how is it that thou hast sent me no token of thy existence, since we parted on Mr. Hooper's doorstep, when thou didst press my hand without a word? It seems an age since then. Thou saidst, on Sunday, that thou shouldst probably return to Salem to-day; but surely thou hast not gone. I feel lonely and not cheerful—my spirit knows not whereabout to seek thee, and so it shivers as if there were no *Thou* at all—as if my Dove had been only a dream and a vision, and now had vanished into unlocality[2] and nothingness.

But tomorrow I shall surely hear from thee; and even should it be otherwise, I shall yet know, with everlasting faith, that my Dove's heart has been striving to make me sensible of its embraces all this time. My dearest, was not that a sweet time—that Sabbath afternoon and eve? But why didst thou look up in my face, as we walked, and ask why I was so grave? If I was grave, I know no cause for it, beloved.

Lights and shadows are continually flitting across my inward sky, and I know neither whence they come nor whither they go; nor do I inquire too closely into them. It is dangerous to look too minutely at such phenomena. It is apt to create a substance, where at first there was a mere shadow. If at any time, dearest wife, there should seem—though to me there never does—but if there should ever seem to be an expression unintelligible from one of our souls to another, we will not strive to interpret it into earthly language, but wait for the soul to make itself understood; and were we to wait a thousand years, we need deem it no more time than we can spare. I speak only in reference to such dim and untangible matters as that which suggested this passage of my letter. It is not that I have any love for mystery; but because I abhor it—and because I have felt, a thousand times, that words may be a thick and darksome veil of mystery between the soul and the truth which it seeks. Wretched were we, indeed, if we had no better means of communicating ourselves, no fairer garb in which to array our essential selves, than these poor rags and tatters of Babel. Yet words are not without their use, even for purposes of explanation,—but merely for explaining outward acts, and all sorts of external things, leaving the soul's life and action to explain itself in its own way.

My belovedest, what a misty disquisition have I scribbled! I would not read it over for sixpence. Think not that I supposed it necessary to sermonize thee so; but the sermon created itself from sentence to sentence; and being written, thou knowest that it belongs to thee, and I have no right to keep it back. Dearest, I was up very early this morning, and have had a good deal to do, especially this afternoon. Let me plead this in excuse for my dulness and mistiness. I suspect that, hereafter, my little Dove will know how to estimate the difficulty of pouring one's self out in a soul-written letter, amid the distractions of business and society—she herself having experienced these checks upon her outpourings.

Now good bye, mine ownest wife. God bless us both—or may God bless either of us, and that one will bless the other. Dost thou sleep well now-a-nights, belovedest? Of whom dost thou dream? Thy husband's long days and short nights hardly leave him time to dream.

Thine ownest.

Dearest, just as I was folding this letter, came thy note. Do thou be at the Depôt as soon as possible after eleven; and I will move Heaven and Earth to meet thee there. Perhaps a little before eleven.

1. The letter is addressed to "South Street," after NH had learned by the note mentioned in the postscript her presence at the home of her friends, the Hoopers; see 94.2.

2. "Locality" was one of the thirty-seven phrenological "faculties," that of recognizing and remembering places. See *OED*.

Boston, May 29th 1840—6.P.M.

My dearest,

Rejoice with thy husband; for he is free from a load of coal, which has been pressing upon his shoulders throughout all this hot weather. I am convinced that Christian's burthen consisted of coal; and no wonder he felt so much relieved when it fell off and rolled into the sepulchre.[1] His load, however, at the utmost, could not have been more than a few bushels; whereas mine was exactly one hundred and thirty-five chaldrons and seven tubs. [*excision verso*] all well; for thou hast been sun-stricken. Oh, my dearest, I feel the stroke upon mine own head. Except through thee, I can never feel any torment of that nature; for all these burning suns have blazed upon my head, unprotected except by a black hat, and yet I have felt no more inconvenience than if I had been sitting in the pleasant gloom of a dewy grot. Belovedest, be a great deal more careful of thyself. Remember always that thou art not thine own, but that Providence has entrusted to thy keeping a most delicate physical frame, which belongs wholly to me, and which therefore thou must keep with infinitely more care than thou wouldst the most precious jewel. And yet I would not have thee anxious and watchful like an invalid; but thou shouldst consider that thou wert created to dwell nowhere but in the clime of Paradise, and wast only placed upon this earth, because thy husband is here and cannot do without thee—and that east-winds and fierce suns are evil unknown in thy native region, and there-fore thy frame was not so constructed as to resist them;

wherefore thine own wise precautions must be thy safeguard. Blessedest, I kiss thy brow,—at least, I kiss the air thrice; and if none of the three kisses reach thee, then three very precious things will have gone forth from my heart in vain. But if any of thy headache and bewilderment have remained hitherto, and now thou feelest somewhat like a breath of Heaven on thy brow, we will take it for granted that my kisses have found thee out. Good bye now, dearest wife; for I am weary and stupid; and as I need not be at the Custom-House before eight or nine °clock tomorrow, thou shalt have the rest of the letter freshly written in the morning. My spirit [*excision*]

May 30 [*excision*] now it will be lucky for thee if thou gettest the last page of this letter entirely full. Dearest, thy last letter had the fragrance of a bank of violets—yea, of all sorts of sweet smelling flowers and perfumed shrubs. I can lie down and repose upon it, as upon a bed of roses. It rejoices me to think that my whole being is not enveloped with coal-dust, but that its better half is breathing the breath of flowers. Oh, do be very happy, mine ownest wife, and fill thyself with all gentle pleasures that lie within thy reach; because at present thou hast a double duty to perform in this respect; since, so far as my enjoyments depend on external things, I can contribute nothing to the common stock of happiness. And yet dearest, nothing that I ever enjoyed before can come into the remotest comparison with my continual enjoyment of thy love—with the deep, satisfied respose which that consciousness brings to me; a repose subsisting, and ever to subsist, in the midst of all anxieties, troubles, and agitations.

Belovedest, I sometimes wish that thou couldst be with me on board my salt-vessels and colliers; because there are many things of which thou mightst make such pretty descriptions; and in future years, when thy husband is again busy at the loom of fiction, he would weave in these little pictures. My fancy is rendered so torpid by my ungenial way of life, that I cannot sketch off the scenes and portraits that interest me; and I am forced to trust them to my memory, with the hope of recalling them at some more favorable period. For three or four days past, I have been observing a little Mediterranean boy, from Malaga, not more than ten or eleven years old, but who is already a citizen of the world, and seems to be just as gay and contented on the deck of a Yankee coal-vessel, as he could be while playing beside his mother's door. It is really touching to see how free and happy he is—how the little fellow takes this whole wide world for his home, and all mankind for his family. He talks Spanish—at least, that is his native tongue; but he is also very intelligible in English, and perhaps he likewise has smatterings of the speech of other countries, whither the winds may have wafted this little sea-bird. He is a Catholic; and yesterday, being Friday, he caught some fish and fried them for his dinner, in sweet oil; and really they looked so delicate that I almost wished he would invite me to partake. Every once in a while, he undresses himself and leaps overboard, plunging down beneath the waves, as if the sea were as native to him as the earth; then he runs up the rigging of the vessel, as if he meant to fly away through the air. Do thou remember this little boy, dearest, and tell me of him one of these days; and perhaps I may make something more beautiful of him than thou wouldst think from these rough and imperfect touches.

Belovedest, is thy head quite well? Art thou very beautiful now? Dost thou love me infinitely? [*excision*]

1. "So I saw in my Dream that just as *Christian* came up with the *Cross*, his burden loosed from off his Shoulders, and fell from off his back; and began to tumble; and so continued to do, till it came to the mouth of the Sepulcre, where it fell in, and I saw it no more." Bunyan, *Pilgrim's Progress*, ed. James Blanton Wharey, 2nd ed. rev. Roger Sharrock (Oxford: Clarendon Press, 1960), p. 38.

Salem (Mass) May 31st, 1840.

Sir,

I have been requested to appeal to you[2] in behalf of a young man, James Cook[3] by name, who is now serving as a common seaman in the navy. Mr. Cook had been one of the publishers of the Salem Advertiser (the leading Democratic paper in Essex county) from the time of its establishment till its transfer to other hands—a space of four or five years. My own acquaintance with him was but slight; but I know him to have been a man of education and ability, and much respected for his exemplary conduct. Some six or eight months since, he disappeared from home; and as his friends could gain no intelligence of him, he was generally supposed to have committed suicide in a fit of insanity—an idea which was strengthened by the singularity of his deportment, when last seen. Nothing had since been heard of him until very recently, when a letter was received by his parents, informing them of his enlistment in the navy, and that he is now at the Norfolk station, on board of the ship Delaware. There can be no doubt that he took this step under the influence of insanity, both because his previous demeanor indicated mental derangement, and because no reasonable motive is discoverable or imaginable; inasmuch as he thereby sacrificed very fair prospects, and gave up all the advantages of prosperous circumstances and an unstained character. If, on consideration of the facts, you should judge this a case where the rigid rule of the service may be relaxed, you would comfort the hearts of his aged parents, who are awaiting your decision with anxious hopes. I know not whether it be worth while to mention—yet perhaps I may say it to Mr. Paulding, if not to the Secretary of the Navy—that there is a young lady to whom Cook was engaged to be married, and who has kept both her faith and her hopes throughout the period of his absence.[4]

It is with reluctance, Sir, that I have taken this liberty, as being unknown to you personally, nor perhaps by reputation; and yet, apart from your official character, I cannot but feel it one of my birth-rights to address Mr. Paulding, who has made himself the admired and familiar friend of every reader in the land.

Respectfully,
Your obedient serv[t]
Nathaniel Hawthorne.

Hon. J. K. Paulding,
Sec[y] of the Navy.

1. James Kirke Paulding (1778–1860), secretary of the navy from 1838 to 1841, author, and collaborator with Washington Irving. See *DAB*.

2. By William B. Pike; see 166. See also Ralph M. Aderman, "The Case of James Cook: A Study of Political Influence in 1840," *EIHC*, XCII (1956), 59–67.

3. James Kennedy Cook (1809–84), a printer, had begun the Salem *Commercial Advertiser* in 1832. This Democratic semiweekly was sold in 1837 to Charles W. Woodbury, and became the Salem *Advertiser*.

4. Cook married Catherine P. Ware of Marblehead, but not until 1846.

Boston, June 2^{d} 1840—Before breakfast.

My dearest,

Thy Friday's letter came in due season to the Custom-House; but Colonel Hall could not find time to bring it to the remote region of the earth, where I was then an exile; so that it awaited me till the next morning. At noon, came thy next letter, at an interval of several hours from the receipt of the former—a space quite long enough to be interposed between thy missives. And yesterday arrived thy letter of the Sabbath—and all three are very precious to thy husband; and the oftener they come, the more he needs them. Now I must go down to breakfast. Dost thou not wonder at finding me scribbling between seven and eight °clock in the morning? I do believe, naughtiest, that thou hast been praying for the nonarrival of salt and coal—not considering that, if thy petitions are heard, the poor Measurers will not earn a sixpence.

Belovedest, I know not what counsel to give thee about calling on my sisters; and therefore must leave the matter to thine own exquisite sense of what is right and delicate. We will talk it over at an early opportunity. I think I can partly understand why they appear cool towards thee; but it is for nothing in thyself personally, nor for any unkindness towards my Dove, whom every body must feel to be the loveablest being in the world.[1] But there are some untoward circumstances. Nevertheless, I have faith that all will be well, and that they will receive Sophie Hawthorne and the Dove into their heart of hearts; so let us wait patiently on Providence, as we always have, and see what time will bring forth. And, my dearest, whenever thou feelest disquieted about things of this sort—if ever that be the case—do thou speak freely to thy husband; for these are matters in which words may be of use, because they concern the relations between ourselves and others. Now, good bye, belovedest, till night. I perceive that the sun is shining dimly; but I fear there is still an east wind to keep my Dove in her dove-cote. I give thee a kiss which must last thee all day long.

Towards night— Ownest wife, this day has been spent without much pleasure or profit—a part of the time at the Custom-House, waiting there for the chance of work,— partly at the Athenaeum, and partly at a bookstore, looking for something suitable for our library. Among other recent purchases, I have bought a very good edition of Milton (his poetry) in two octavo volumes;[2] and I saw a huge new London volume of his prose works, but it seemed to me that there was but a small portion of it that thou and I should ever care about reading—so I left it on the shelf.[3] Dearest, I have bought some lithographic prints at auction, which I mean to send thee, that thou mayst show them to thy husband, the next afternoon that thou permittest him to spend with thee. Thou art not to expect anything very splendid; for I did not enter the auction-room till a large part of the collection was sold; so that my choice was limited. Perhaps there are one or two not altogether unworthy to be put on the walls of our sanctuary; but this I leave to thy finer judgment.[4] I would thou couldst peep into my room and see thine own pictures, from which I have removed the black veils; and there is no telling how much brighter and cheerfuller the parlor looks now, whenever I enter it.

Belovedest, I love thee very especially much to day, and desire exceedingly to cherish thee in my bosom, which I know thou needest, because the wind is east. But then that naughty Sophie Hawthorne—it would be out of the question to treat her with smiling tenderness. Nothing shall she get from me, at my next visit, save a kiss upon her nose; and I should not wonder if she were to return the favor with a cuff upon my ear. Mine own Dove, how unhappy art thou to be linked with such a mate!—to be bound up in the same volume with her!—and me unhappy, too, to be forced to keep such a turbulent little rebel in my inmost heart! Dost thou not think she might be persuaded to withdraw herself, quietly, and take up her residence somewhere else? Oh, what an idea. It makes my heart close its valves and embrace her the more closely—[*excision*]

Well, dearest, it is breakfast time, and thy husband hath an appetite. What dost thou eat for breakfast?—but I know well enough that thou never eatest anything but bread and milk and chickens. Dost thou love pigeons in a pie? I am fonder of Dove than anything else—it is my heart's food and sole sustenance.

God bless us.

Thine own Husband.

1. NH's mother and sisters were apparently no longer socially active with the Peabodys, if the lack of mention in surviving letters is an accurate indication.

2. *The Poetical Works of John Milton, with Notes, and a Life of the Author by the Rev. John Mitford* (Boston: Hilliard, Gray, 1838). NH's copy of Vol. I is in the Berg Collection. For NH reading aloud *Paradise Lost* at the Old Manse, see 260, 262.

3. *The Prose Works of John Milton, with an Introductory Review by Robert Fletcher* (London: Westley and Davis, 1833; rpt. W. Ball, 1838).

4. The Boston firm of Clark and Hatch had advertised in the *Post* and the *Advertiser* for Monday June 1 a sale of "a splendid collection of about 1700 colored and lithographic engravings . . . scenes from sacred and profane history, ancient and modern—portraits of celebrated men and women—interesting views from nature and fabulous designs—the principles of drawing—allegorical pieces . . . views of France, Sicily and Switzerland perfectly beautiful, among which are a great number richly colored by celebrated artists."

Boston, June 11th. 1840—5 or 6. P.M.

My blessedest,

Thou hast strayed quite out of the sphere of my imagination, and I know not how to represent thy whereabout, anymore than if thou hadst gone on pilgrimage beyond sea, or to the moon. Dost thou still love me, in all thy wanderings? Are there any East-winds there? Truly, now that thou hast escaped beyond its jurisdiction, I could wish that the east wind would blow every day, from ten °clock till five; for there is great refreshment in it to us poor mortals that toil beneath the sun. Dearest, thou must not think too unkindly even of the east-wind. It is not, perhaps, a wind to be loved, even in its benignest moods; but there are seasons when I delight to feel its breath upon my cheek, though it be never advisable to throw open my bosom and take it into my heart, as I would its gentle sisters of the South and West. To-day, if I had been on the wharves, the slight chill of an east wind would have been a blessing, like the chill of death to a world-weary man. But, dearest, thou wilt rejoice to hear that this has been one of the very idlest days that I ever spent in Boston. Oh, hadst thou been here! In the morning, soon after breakfast, I went to the Athenaeum Gallery;[1] and during the hour or two that I stayed, not a single visiter came in. Some people were putting up paintings in one division of the room; but we might have had the other all to ourselves—thy husband had it all to himself—or rather, he did not have it, nor possess it in fulness and reality, because thou wast not there. I cannot see pictures without thee; so thou must not expect me to criticize this exhibition. There are two pictures there by our friend (thy friend—and is it not the same thing?) Sarah Clark—scenes in Kentucky.[2] Doubtless I shall find them very admirable, when we have looked at them together. The gallery of sculpture I shall not visit, unless I can be there with thee.

From the picture-gallery I went to the reading-room of the Athenaeum, and there read the magazines till nearly twelve—thence to the Custom-House, and soon afterwards to dinner with Colonel Hall—then back to the Custom-House, but only for a little while. There was nothing in the world to do; and so, at two °clock, I came home and lay down on the bed, with the Faery Queen[3] in my hand, and my Dove in my heart. Soon a pleasant slumber came over me; it was not a deep, sound sleep, but a slumbrous withdrawing of myself from the external world. Whether thou camest to me in a dream, I cannot tell; but thou didst peep at me through all the interstices of sleep. After I awoke, I did not take up the Faery Queen again, but lay thinking of thee, and at last bestirred myself and got up to write this letter. My belovedest wife, does it not make thee happy to think that thy husband has escaped, for one whole summer day, from his burthen of salt and coal, and has been almost as idle as ever his idle nature could desire?—and this, too, on one of the longest days of all the year! Oh, could I have spent it in some shady nook, with mine own wife! Now good-bye, blessedest. So indolent is thy husband, that he intends now to relieve himself even from the sweet toil of shaping his thoughts of thee into written words; moreover, there is no present need of it, because I am not to be at the Custom-House very early, and can finish the letter tomorrow morning. Good bye, dearest; and keep a quiet heart.

June 12th. 1/2 past 7. A.M. Belovedest, art thou not going to be very happy to-day? I hope so, and believe so; and, dearest, if thou findest thyself comfortable at Concord—and if

the Emersonians love thee and admire thee as they ought—
do not thou too stubbornly refuse to stay a week longer than
the term first assigned.[4] I do think (yet always with submission to thy better judgment

1. The fourteenth annual Boston Athenaeum Exhibition opened on June 10.
Newspaper notices mentioned paintings and "a Gallery of Statuary, comprising
over an hundred pieces of much merit."

2. Sarah Anne Clarke (1808–96). Elizabeth and Mary Peabody had lived at
her widowed mother's boarding house in Somerset Court, Boston, in the early
1830s, and she had become SH's close friend. A disciple of Washington Allston,
who encouraged her to become a landscape painter, Sarah had taught art at
Bronson Alcott's Temple School. She had visited her brother James Freeman
Clarke, minister of the Unitarian Church in Louisville, Kentucky, for six months
in 1836–37. Although not mentioned in NH's letters again until 1848, Sarah
remained a close friend of SH; she was present at the wedding, at which her
brother officiated, and she visited the Old Manse with Margaret Fuller in July
1844; see 296, 297.

3. George Hillard had recently edited the first American edition of *The Poetical
Works of Edmund Spenser, in five volumes, with Introductory Observations on the
Faerie Queene, and Notes by the Editor* (Boston: Little and Brown, 1839).

4. Emerson had invited SH to Concord for the second week of June "to hear
what we have to say of" the medallion of Charles Emerson, which he characterized as "a beautiful possession; the gift of a Muse, and not the less valuable that
it was so unexpected." See *Memories*, pp. 183–84, and 151.1.

Boston, June 22^d (Monday) 1/2 past 4. [1840]

Ownest, Colonel Hall put thy letter into my hand at our eating-house; so that its reception was timed very like that of mine to thee; but thy husband cared not for ceremony, nor for the presence of fifty people, but straightway broke the 'long-legged little fowl'[1] asunder, and began to read. Beloved-est, what a letter! Never was so much beauty poured out of any heart before; and to read it over and over is like bathing my brow in a fresh fountain, and drinking draughts that renew the life within me. Nature is kind and motherly to thee, and taketh thee into her inmost heart and cherisheth thee there, because thou lookest on her with holy and loving eyes. My dearest, how canst thou say that I have ever written anything beautiful, being thyself so potent to reproduce whatever is loveliest? If I did not know that thou lovest me, I should even be ashamed before thee. Sweetest wife, it glad-dens me likewise that thou meetest with such sympathy there, and that thy friends have faith that thy husband is worthy of thee, because they see that thy wise heart could not have gone astray.[2] Worthy of thee I am not; but thou wilt make me so; for there will be time, or eternity enough, for thy blessed influence to work upon me. Would that we could build our cottage this very now, this very summer, amid the scenes which thou describest.[3] My heart thirsts and lan-guishes to be there, away from the hot sun and the coal-dust, and the steaming docks, and the thick-pated, stubborn, con-tentious men, with whom I brawl from morning till night, and all the weary toil which quite engrosses me, and yet occupies only a part of my being which I did not know existed before I became a Measurer. I do think that I should sink down quite disheartened and inanimate, if thou wert not happy, and gathering from earth and sky enjoyment for both of us; but this makes me feel that my real, innermost soul is apart from all these unlovely circumstances,—and that it has not ceased to exist, as I might sometimes suspect, but is nourished and kept alive through thee. Belovedest, if thou findest it good to be there, why wilt thou not stay even a little longer than this week? Thou knowest not what comfort I have in thinking of thee amid those beautiful scenes, where the east wind cometh not, and amid those sympathizing hearts, which perhaps thou wilt not find elsewhere—at least not everywhere. I feel as if thou hadst found a haven of peace and rest, where I can trust thee without disquiet, and feel that thou art safe even when not within my arms. I yearn to embrace thee, dearest; but if thou art well and happy, if thy cheek is becoming rosier, if thy step is light and joyous there, and if thy heart makes pleasant music, then is it not better for thee to stay a little longer? And if better for thee, it is so for thy husband likewise. Now, ownest wife, I do not press thee to stay, but leave it all to thy wisdom; and if thou feelest that it is now time to come home to thy husband's bosom, most gladly will he welcome thee.

Dearest, I meant to have written to thee yesterday afternoon, so that thou shouldst have received the letter to-day; but Mrs Hillard pressed her husband and myself to take a walk into the country, because his health needed such an excursion. So, after taking a nap, we set forth over the western avenue—a dreary, treeless, fierce-sunshiny, irksome road; but after journeying three or four or five miles, we came to some of the loveliest rural scenery—yes, the very loveliest—that ever I saw in my life. The first part of our road was like the life of toil and weariness that I am now leading; the latter part was like the life that we will lead hereafter. Would that I had thy pen, and I would give thee pictures of beauty to match thine own; but I should only mar my remembrance of them by the attempt. Not a beautiful scene did I behold, but I imaged thee in the midst of it—thou wast with me in all the walk, and when I sighed it was for thee, and when I smiled it was for thee, and when I trusted in future happiness, it was for thee; and if I did not doubt and fear, it was altogether because of thee. What else than happiness can God intend for thee?—and if thy happiness, then mine also. On our return, we stopped at Braman's baths, and plunged in, and washed away all stains of earth, and became new creatures.[4] Dearest, I sympathize with thee in thy love of the bath, and conveniences for it must not be forgotten in our domestic arrangements. Yet I am not entirely satisfied with any more contracted bath than the illimitable ocean; and to plunge into it is the next thing to soaring into the sky.

This morning I rose early to finish measuring a load of coal; which being accomplished in the forenoon, and there being little prospect of anything more to do, Colonel Hall, who perceived that thy husband's energies were somewhat exhausted by the heat, and by much brawling with the coal-people, did send me home immediately after dinner. So then I took a nap, with a volume of Spenser in my hand; and awaking at four, I re-re-reperused thy last letter, and sat down to pour myself out to thee; and in so doing, dearest wife, I have had great comfort. And now the afternoon is beautiful in its decline; but my feet are somewhat afflicted with yesterday's excursion; so that I am in doubt whether to go out again, although I should like a bath.

Belovedest, I must not forget to thank Mr. Emerson for his invitation to Concord; but really it will not be in my power to accept it. Do thou say this in the way it ought to be said, and let him know what a business-machine thy husband is. Now, good-bye. Art thou very happy? I trust so, dearest.

Thou hast our whole treasure of happiness in thy keeping. Keep it safe, ownest wife, and add to it continually. God bless thee [*excision*]

1. The device on SH's seal; see 149, second paragraph.

2. SH had revealed their engagement to friends in Concord. Emerson wrote to his brother William on June 30 concerning a commission to George Henry Calvert to purchase in Italy for SH some engravings of works by Michelangelo and Raphael: "If Mr C. reads Twice Told Tales, you shall tell him that the fair artist whom we wish to please is engaged to Mr Hawthorne the tale-writer" (*Letters*, II, 308).

3. This is apparently the first record of the Hawthornes' intention to live in Concord after their marriage. In the following paragraph, NH's description of the scenery west of Boston, possibly in West Roxbury, may anticipate his joining the Brook Farm community.

4. Boston newspapers in mid-May began to advertise Jarvis Braman's "New Swimming School and Bathing House, at the foot of Chestnut Street . . . now open for bathers, and those who wish to learn to swim."

Boston, June 24th.— past 8 °clock P.M. [1840]

Mine ownest,

I have just received thy letter, and rejoice unspeakably at the news which thou tellest me. Dearest, thou knowest not how I have yearned for thee during thy absence; and yet thou didst seem so well and happy there, that I sent thee a letter, yesterday morning, submitting it to thy wisdom whether thou hadst not better stay another week.[1] But thou hast done more wisely to come; for my heart is faint with hunger for thee. I have been quite sad and dolorous at thy absence. And, Oh, what joy to think that henceforth there shall be no long separations for us.[2] It has taken me so by surprise that I know not what to say upon the subject; but my heart throbs mightily.

Dearest, thou canst not have a long letter to-night, because thy husband is weary, and moreover he wants to think about thee, and embrace thee a thousand million times deep within himself. Art thou quite well? Most beloved, I beseech thee not to agitate thyself in this removal of the household gods. I shall come on Saturday, but perhaps not till late. God bless and keep thee.

Thine ownest,
lovingest husband
D'l'Aubepine.

1. NH's letter of June 22 was mailed from Boston on June 23, and forwarded from Concord to SH at Salem on June 24. See Textual Note, 164.

2. SH and the rest of the Peabody family were to join Elizabeth at West Street, Boston, in August.

Salem June 28th. 1840

Dear Pike,

I have received a letter from the Navy Department, in answer to the one which you requested me to write. Mr. Paulding says—"The Department has already referred an application, made by the Hon. Mr. Parmenter in behalf of the same person, to Com. Warrington for a report; and I hope when that is received, it will be such as will enable me to accede to your wishes by directing Cook's discharge."[1]

Yours truly,
Nath. Hawthorne.

1. Commodore Lewis Warrington (1800–1851), then of the U.S. Naval Yard at Gosport, where James Cook was stationed. Warrington reported to Paulding on July 23 that Cook had been discharged (MS, Office of Naval Records, Washington).

Boston, July 10th. 1840—Morning.

Belovedest,

Doubtless thou didst expect a letter from me yesterday; but my days have been so busy, and my evenings so invaded with visitants, that I have not had a moment's time to talk with thee. Scarcely, till this morning, have I been able to read thy letter quietly. Night before last, came Mr. Jones Very;[1] and thou knowest that he is somewhat unconscionable as to the length of his calls. Yesterday I came home early; and had the fates been propitious, thou shouldst have had a long letter; but in the afternoon came M[r] Hillard's London brother, and wasted my precious hours with a dull talk of nothing; and in the evening I was sorely tried with Mr. Conolly,[2] and a Cambridge law-student, who came to do homage to thy husband's literary renown. So my sweetest wife was put aside for these idle people. I do wish the blockheads, and all other blockheads in this world, could comprehend how inestimable are the quiet hours of a busy man— especially when that man has no native impulse to keep him busy, but is continually forced to battle with his own nature, which yearns for seclusion (the solitude of a united two, my belovedest) and freedom to think, and dream, and feel.

Well, dearest, thy husband is in perfect health this morning, and good spirits; and much doth he rejoice that thou art so soon to be near him. No tongue can tell—no pen can write—what I feel. Belovedest, do not thou make thyself sick in the bustle of removing; for I think that there is nothing more trying, even to a robust frame and rugged spirit, than the disturbance of such an occasion. Now, good-bye; for I must hurry to the Custom-House to see Colonel Hall, who is going out of town for two days, and will probably leave the administration of our department in my hands.

God bless thee, belovedest;—perhaps thou wilt receive another letter before thy advent, but do not thou count upon it.

Thine ownest Husband,
De l'Aubepine

1. Jones Very (1813–80), son of a Salem captain, had graduated from Harvard in 1836 and had taught Greek there until his sudden aggressive and mentally unbalanced expression of religious enthusiasm forced his resignation and return to Salem in 1838. Elizabeth Peabody, recognizing his poetic genius in 1837, had introduced him to NH and, at about the same time, to Emerson, who befriended Very and edited his *Essays and Poems* for publication, in August 1839. For letters about the Hawthornes' acquaintance with Very, see *Memories* pp. 23–30, and William Bartlett Irving, *Jones Very: Emerson's 'Brave Saint'* (Durham: Duke University Press, 1942), pp. 108–12. Mary Peabody had written to SH on January 5, 1839, that NH "says Very wants a brother and is trying to convert him and goes there very often. 'What shall I do?' says he" (MS, Berg). According to Elizabeth Peabody's later recollection, for NH Very "more than realized the conception of entire subjectiveness he had tried to describe in the preacher of 'the Story Teller' " ("A Fellow-Traveller," *MOM*, pp. 411–17). See Edwin Gittleman, *Jones Very: The Effective Years, 1833–1840* (New York: Columbia University Press, 1967), pp. 161–62, 282–85. NH mentioned Very in "A Virtuoso's Collection" and in "The Hall of Fantasy" (*MOM*, pp. 491, 638).

2. Conolly was at this time studying law at Harvard.

[Boston] 54 Pinckney St. August 9th. [1840]

Ownest Dove,

I have almost forgotten how to write letters—not having put pen to paper for that purpose (or any other, indeed) since my last to thee; but I cannot help writing thee a few lines, now when I had hoped to be listening to thy sweetest voice, and ever and anon giving thee a kiss, as my share of our conversation. Dearest, what a length of time it is since I held thee in my arms! Art thou much changed in this intervening time? Is thy hair grown gray? Art thou an old woman? Truly, it does appear very, very long to thy husband—an incomputable period. Belovedest, I had been out this forenoon; and when I returned, there was thy letter, lying on the threshold of my chamber-door. I had a presage of calamity, as soon as I saw it. Had I known of this visit of thine aunt, I would have taken the opportunity to go to Salem, and so we would have had next Sunday to ourselves. Does thine aunt say that thou lookest in magnificent health?—and that thou art very beautiful? If she has not yet said so, thou shouldst ask her opinion on that point. [*excision verso*] husband did put thy [*excision verso*]

Belovedest, even if thine aunt Curtis[1] should stay a week, do not thou incommode thy mother and sisters by trying to arrange a meeting.[2] It is very painful to me to disturb and derange anybody in the world.

Thou dost not say whether thou art very well to-day—and whether thou art light of heart. I beseech thee never to write me even the shortest note, without giving me a glimpse of thyself in the very moment of writing;—and yet, I leave it all to thee, and withdraw this last petition. Thou knowest best what to write; for thou art an inspired little penwoman.

Thy husband is to measure salt at the end of Long-Wharf tomorrow, and the next day, and probably the next, and the next. It is as desirable a place and employment as a Measurer can expect; so let thy visions of me be rather pleasurable than otherwise. I am in particularly good health; but my heart hungers for thee—nevertheless, I mean to be cheerful and content. Do thou be so likewise, little Dove—and naughty Sophie Hawthorne too. Now, good-bye. This is a very empty letter—at least, it would be so, if it had not an infinite love in it. God bless thee [excision]

1. Amelia Palmer Curtis (1784–1854), sister of SH's mother, was the widow of Abel Winslow Curtis (d. 1816), a Salem schoolteacher. She had kept a school in Salem that NH's sisters had attended. See 18, and A. P. Curtis to Mrs. Elizabeth Hathorne, n.d. (MS, Morgan); Mary Palmer Tyler, *Grandmother Tyler's Book* (New York: G. P. Putnam, 1925), p. 151. See 170.

2. After George's death the Peabodys moved from Salem to 13 West Street, Boston.

[Boston, August 21, 1840]

August 21.— Last night I slept like a child of five years old, and had no dreams at all,—unless just before it was time to rise, and I have forgotten what those dreams were. After I was fairly awake this morning I felt very bright and airy, and was glad that I had been compelled to snatch two additional hours of existence from annihilation. The sun's disc was but half above the ocean's verge when I ascended the ship's side. These early morning hours are very lightsome and quiet. Almost the whole day I have been in the shade, reclining on a pile of sails, so that the life and spirit are not entirely worn out of me. . . . The wind has been east this afternoon,— perhaps in the forenoon too,—and I could not help feeling refreshed when the gentle chill of its breath stole over my cheek. I would fain abominate the east wind, . . . but it persists in doing me kindly offices now and then. What a perverse wind it is! Its refreshment is but another mode of torment.

54 Pinckney St., [Boston]
August 24th. 1/4 past 6 P. M. [1840]

Own belovedest,

I had a presentiment of a letter from thee this morning; and so was not at all surprised when I saw thy father in the long, low, darksome room where thy husband was in durance. But I had not the least anticipation of the intelligence which thou didst send me; and it is the harder to be borne, because—(do not be naughty, ownest Dove)—I have an indispensable engagement at Cambridge tomorrow afternoon and evening;[1]—whereby our meeting must be delayed yet another day. Dearest, do set me a lofty example of patience. Be very good and very quiet, and enjoy thy Aunt Curtis's society to the utmost, and press her to stay with thee till Wednesday at six °clock. But not an hour longer! Thou must absolutely eject her with thine own tender little hands, if she propose to tarry that night also.

Belovedest, I went to the Hurley Burley last evening; and considering that it was the first time I had been there without thee since we were married, I enjoyed it very well. We had a good deal of talk; but I missed thy gentle voice, which is surely the sweetest sound that was ever heard anywhere save in Paradise. Thy husband talked somewhat more than is his wont, but said nothing that is at all worth repeating; and I think he might as well have dispensed with saying anything. He shows his wisdom and policy much more in his general silence than in his occasional loquacity. Dearest, if I had not so high a respect for thy judgment, I should pronounce thy husband but a tolerable person, at best; but as thou hast been impelled to give thy precious self to such a man, there must be more in him than ordinary eyes can perceive. Miss Burley proposed to me to write an address of some kind for the Bunker-Hill fair;[2] but I manifested no readiness to comply— neither do I feel any. Has my Dove contributed anything?

I went home in the midst of that beautiful rain, and sat up two hours with Elizabeth and Louisa, and then withdrew myself to my couch and to thee. Dearest, my heart yearns for thee mightily, but it is a joyful yearning that I feel—not only then, but now and continually. My desire is full of warmth and hope; and though now I press my arms to my bosom and find thee not within them, yet I know that thou art destined there to be, and there to have thy abiding place.

This has not been a toilsome day, my wife. Indeed, I have had nothing to do; nor is it certain that I shall be employed tomorrow morning. Quite unexpected is this lull amid the tempest of business.—I left the Custom-House at about four °clock, and went to the bath, where I spent half an hour very deliciously. Dearest, we must have all sorts of bathing conveniences in our establishment. Thou art a water-spirit, like Undine. And thy spirit is to mine a pure fountain, in which I bathe my brow and heart; and immediately all the fever of the world departs. Thou art—but I cannot quite get hold of the idea that I meant to express; and as I want to leave a part of the page till tomorrow morning, I will stop here. God bless thee. I think I shall dream of thee to night; for I never loved thee so much. [*excision*]

---

1. Presumably with Longfellow. See 171. There are no entries in Longfellow's journal (MS, Harvard) between July 7, 1840, and November 8, 1841.

2. An event to raise money for the completion of the Bunker Hill Monument, held in Boston from September 8 to 15, drawing large crowds from throughout Massachusetts. Salem and other cities were represented by tables at which home-made articles were for sale. NH's lack of enthusiasm may have been caused in part by the connection of the fair with a large Whig rally on September 10.

Boston, August 31st. 1840.

Dear Sir,

Professor Longfellow and myself contemplate establishing a paper in Boston;[2] and we are desirous of gaining some lights upon the subject, from your experience. Our plans are yet in embryo; but we think of a daily evening paper upon the cash principle, together with a weekly sheet. Will you be kind enough to give us an estimate of the cost of such a paper— say of the size of the Transcript?[3] We should likewise be glad of your advice, whether to confide the printing, distributing, and other business of the paper, to a publisher, or to keep that department in our own hands. In short, no advice in the premises can come amiss.

I will endeavor to see you at my next visit to Salem, but, in the meantime, should feel obliged by a few lines from you.

Very truly Yours,
Nath. Hawthorne

Hon. Caleb Foote,
Salem.

1. (1803–94), editor of the Salem *Gazette*, a Whig paper, and proprietor of the Bible and Book Shop. He had been with the *Gazette* since 1825, and had published "The Hollow of the Three Hills" in 1830, and eighteen subsequent tales and sketches by NH. In 1835 he had married Mary Wilder White (1810–57), a close friend of the Peabody sisters. See Mary Wilder Tileston, ed., *Caleb and Mary Wilder Foote: Reminiscences and Letters* (Boston: Houghton Mifflin, 1918).

2. See Arlin Turner, "Hawthorne and Longfellow: Abortive Plans for Collaboration," *NHJ 1971*, pp. 6–7. No evidence of further planning has been found.

3. The Boston *Evening Transcript*, at this time a Whig newspaper.

[Boston] 54 Pinckney St.
Sept. 18th. 1840. 8 °clock P.M.

Sweetest Dove,

Thy father, apparently, did not see fit to carry thy letter to the Custom-House; and yet I think my intuition informed me that a letter was written; for I looked into the Desk very eagerly, although Colonel Hall neither pointed with his finger nor glanced with his eye, as is his custom when anything very precious is in store. It reached me here in mine own tabernacle, about half an hour since, while I sat resting myself from the toils of the day, and thinking of thee, my Dove, and longing to press thee to my heart this very night. Thou didst make me happier, last evening, than I ever hoped to be, save in Heaven—and still that same happiness is around me and within me. I am the happier for everything thou dost and sayest—thou canst not possibly act so that I will not love thee better and be the happier for that very individual action.

Dearest, it was necessary that I should speak to thee to-night; but thou must not look for such a golden letter as thou didst write this morning; for thy husband is tolerably weary, and has very few thoughts in his mind, though much love in his heart. Oh that thou wert in my bosom this very now! I cannot do without thy voice—thou knowest not what a sweet influence it has upon me, even apart from the honied wisdom which thou utterest. If thou shouldst talk in an unknown tongue, I should listen with infinite satisfaction, and be much edified in spirit at least, if not in intellect. When thou speakest to me, there is mingled with those earthly words, which are mortal inventions, a far diviner language, which thy soul utters and my soul understands.

Ownest Dove, I did not choose to go to Malden this evening, to hear the political lecture which I told thee of;[1] for, indeed, after toiling all day, it is rather too hard to be bothered with such nonsense at night. I have no desire to go anywhither, after sunset, save to see mine own wife; and as to lectures, I love none but 'curtain lectures';[2]—for such I suppose thine may be termed, although our beloved sofa hath no curtains. Dearest, when we live together, thou wilt find me a most tediously stay-at-home husband. Thou wilt be compelled to rebuke and objurgate me, in order to gain the privilege of spending one or two evenings in a month by a solitary fire-side.

Sweetest wife, I must bid thee farewell now, exhorting thee to be as happy as the angels; for thou art as good and holy as they, and have more merit in thy goodness than they have; because the angels have always dwelt in sinless heaven; whereas thy pilgrimage has been on earth, where many sin and go astray. I am ashamed of this letter; there is nothing in it, worthy of being offered to my Dove; but yet I shall send it; for a letter to one's beloved wife ought not to be kept back for any dimness of thought or feebleness of expression, any more than a prayer should be stifled in the soul, because the tongue of man cannot breathe it eloquently to the Deity. Love has its own omniscience; and what Love speaks to Love is comprehended in the same way that prayers are.

Ownest, dost thou not long very earnestly to see thy husband? Well—thou shalt see him on Monday night; and this very night he will come into thy dreams, if thou wilt admit him there.

Thy very lovingest,
and very sleepiest
Husband.

1. The Boston *Post* of Thursday, September 17, announced: "Mr. William B. Pike, of Salem, will deliver a lecture before the democrats of Malden, on Friday evening next." The *Post* reported on September 26: "For two hours, Mr. Pike poured forth a strain of argumentation and nervous eloquence," apparently seeking to counter the effects of the Whig rally of September 10; see 170.2.

2. "A reproof given by a wife to her husband in bed" (Johnson; see *OED*).

Salem, October 4th 1840—1/2 past 10. A.M.

Mine ownest,

Here sits thy husband in his old accustomed chamber, where he used to sit in years gone by, before his soul became acquainted with thine. Here I have written many tales—many that have been burned to ashes—many that doubtless deserved the same fate. This deserves to be called a haunted chamber; for thousands upon thousands of visions have appeared to me in it; and some few of them have become visible to the world. If ever I should have a biographer, he ought to make great mention of this chamber in my memoirs, because so much of my lonely youth was wasted here; and here my mind and character were formed; and here I have been glad and hopeful, and here I have been despondent; and here I sat a long, long time, waiting patiently for the world to know me, and sometimes wondering why it did not know me sooner, or whether it would ever know me at all—at least, till I were in my grave. And sometimes (for I had no wife then to keep my heart warm) it seemed as if I were already in the grave, with only life enough to be chilled and benumbed. But oftener I was happy—at least, as happy as I then knew how to be, or was aware of the possibility of being. By and bye, the world found me out in my lonely chamber, and called me forth—not, indeed, with a loud roar of acclamation, but rather with a still, small voice;[1] and forth I went, but found nothing in the world that I thought preferable to my old solitude, till at length a certain Dove was revealed to me, in the shadow of a seclusion as deep as my own had been.

And I drew nearer and nearer to the Dove, and opened my bosom to her, and she flitted into it, and closed her wings there—and there she nestles now and forever, keeping my heart warm, and renewing my life with her own. So now I begin to understand why I was imprisoned so many years in this lonely chamber, and why I could never break through the viewless bolts and bars; for if I had sooner made my escape into the world, I should have grown hard and rough, and been covered with earthly dust, and my heart would have become callous by rude encounters with the multitude; so that I should have been all unfit to shelter a heavenly Dove in my arms. But living in solitude till the fulness of time was come, I still kept the dew of my youth and the freshness of my heart, and had these to offer to my Dove.

Well, dearest, I had no notion what I was going to write, when I began; and indeed I doubted whether I should write anything at all; for after such intimate communion as that of our last blissful evening, it seems as if a sheet of paper could only be a veil betwixt us. Ownest, in the times that I have been speaking of, I used to think that I could imagine all passions, all feelings, all states of the heart and mind; but how little did I know what it is to be mingled with another's being! Thou only hast taught me that I have a heart—thou only hast thrown a light deep downward, and upward, into my soul. Thou only hast revealed me to myself; for without thy aid, my best knowledge of myself would have been merely to know my own shadow—to watch it flickering on the wall, and mistake its fantasies for my own real actions. Indeed, we are but shadows—we are not endowed with real life, and all that seems most real about us is but the thinnest substance of a dream—till the heart is touched. That touch creates us—then we begin to be—thereby we are beings of reality, and inheritors of eternity. Now, dearest, dost thou comprehend what thou hast done for me? And is it not a somewhat fearful thought, that a few slight circumstances might have prevented us from meeting, and then I should have returned to my solitude, sooner or later (probably now, when I have thrown down my burthen of coal and salt) and never should have been created at all! But this is an idle speculation. If the whole world had stood between us, we must have met— if we had been born in different ages, we could not have been sundered.

Belovedest, how dost thou do? If I mistake not, it was a southern rain yesterday, and, next to the sunshine of Paradise, *that* seems to be thy element. [*excision*]

1. I Kings 19:11.

Boston, October 12th. 1840

Dear Longfellow,

I forget which you told me were your leisure days; but I wish you would come and dine with me on Wednesday. If not then, come any other day, Saturday excepted. I will wait for you on Wednesday, at my room, till two °clock—or three, perhaps. I have broken my chain and escaped from the Custom-House.

I have bought some cigars for you.[1]

Yours truly,
Nath. Hawthorne.

1. See 177 and 178.

Boston, Oct 24th. 1840

Dear Pike,

I have discussed the subject of your letter with the Colonel; and with some difficulty, he has been led to perceive that there is an amount due you from the Department.[1] The following appears to be the view of the case which strikes him. When you came into the Department, in February, the other officers had received about 625 dollars which became a debt due by us to the Government. You could not justly be made liable for any part of this debt, having received none of the money; yet you labored equally with us to discharge it. Some fees, however, accrued in the month of January, before you came into office. Those must be subtracted from the above $625; and a fifth part of the remainder will be due to you.

The Colonel says he will pay you his proportion of whatever may be found due; but I doubt whether you will ever collect anything from Green[2] or Grafton.[3] I am liable for no part of it—having myself a claim of a similar nature, though smaller amount. The Colonel will not be brought to pay anything out of the funds of the Department; but he says that, if you will come to Boston after the election, and spend a part of your time here, he does not doubt that he shall find some method to give you a share of the spoils. I think it may be arranged that you shall receive a hundred or two of dollars, without giving yourself much trouble.

Yours truly,
N Hawthorne.

P.S. You will almost always find me in my room, except between 12 °clock and 3. P.M.

1. The Treasury Department.
2. Andrew Green, a measurer at the Boston Custom House.
3. See 139.4.

Boston, Novr 14th. 1840.

Dear Pike,

I met Rantoul and Woodbury this morning, on their way
to see Bancroft, in order to intercede on Hill's[1] behalf, for
my place.[2] I have understood (but this is a profound secret)
that the permanent office has been promised to Seaver.[3] If
this be the case, is there not some danger that Hill will have
the temporary office,[4] which was promised to you?
I do not know what success R. & W. met with.

Yours truly,
N Hawthorne.

---

1. Possibly Increase S. Hill (see 357) or Charles L. Hill, an inspector at the
Boston Custom House who may have wished to change his appointment.

2. NH's position in the Boston Custom House. His resignation would be effective January 1, 1841; see 178. See George Edwin Jepson, "Hawthorne in the
Boston Custom House," *The Bookman*, XIX (1904), 579.

3. Possibly the Hon. Ebenezer Seaver, of Roxbury.

4. An office that would be filled eventually by the incoming Whig collector.

Boston, Novr 15th 1840

Dear R.

Longfellow is highly delighted with those cigars, and wants another thousand of them. I wish you would take the trouble to bespeak them—of course, being careful to ascertain that they are of the right quality. If you will pay for them, I will reimburse you at our next meeting—or Smith[1] may give credit till then. Longfellow is terribly afraid that the whole lot will be gone.

The Custom House officers begin to suspect that Harrison[2] will be the next President. Poor devils, they are in a miserable condition. I have sent in my resignation, and adhere to it, though Bancroft requested me to take it back.

I shall be in Salem about Thanksgiving-time. Shan't you come to Boston before then?

[*MS torn*]

1. James Smith, cigar maker, of Essex Street, Salem.
2. William Henry Harrison (1773–1841), the Whig candidate, was elected ninth president of the United States. He died soon after taking office, in March 1841.

Boston, Novr 20th. 1840.

Dear Longfellow,

I have suspended my thermometer outside of the window; and looking at it a moment ago, I perceive that it is polar weather, out-of-doors. Really, an expedition into the country is not to be thought of, in this first fierceness of the winter. So pray do not expect me tomorrow. By occupying Grandfather's Chair,[1] for a month past, I really believe I have grown an old man prematurely—and not very prematurely either. My youthful ardor and adventurous spirit have left me, and I love to keep my feet on the hearth, and dread many shapeless perils, when I contemplate such a journey as from here to Cambridge, with the prospect of spending a night (or perhaps two) away from my own roof. Such is always the case with aged men.

But the truth is, I cannot so conveniently come now, as a week or two hence—being very busy, both with my book in the press, and my book in the brain;[2] and I shall have to spend the greater part of next week in Salem.

I wrote to Salem about those cigars, and find that the man has none of the lot remaining; but he thinks that he can procure some of the same, which he sent to be sold on commission, here in Boston. If so, I will secure them; but it does appear to me that you are a most voluminous smoker.

I am a Custom-House officer still. Bancroft represented to me, that, by resigning before the close of the year, I should make him a great deal of trouble; and so my good nature was wrought upon to hold the office a-while longer. However, my duties are merely nominal, as well as my emoluments. In fact, it is an office of honor now!

Whenever you come into the city in season to find me at my room, I shall be most happy to have you take a humble dinner with me. I generally walk out at about 12, and return before three—dining in the interim.

Your friend
Nath. Hawthorne.

1. The first of NH's children's books, *Grandfather's Chair*, was to be published in December. See 157.5.

2. The second book in the *Grandfather's Chair* format was *Famous Old People*, finished in December and published by Elizabeth Peabody in January, 1841. It was followed by *Liberty Tree*, finished in February and published by Elizabeth Peabody in March.

Salem, Novr 27th—Friday. [1840]

Dearest Wife,

Never was a wife so yearned for as thou art. I wonder how I could have resolved to be absent from thee so long—it is far too long a time to be wasted in a suspension of life. My heart is sometimes faint for want of thee—and sometimes it is violent and tumultuous for the same cause. How is it with thine, mine ownest? Dost thou not feel, when thou goest to bed, that the day is utterly incomplete?—that it has not the stamp of reality upon it?—that it has been an unsatisfactory dream, wherein the soul groped wearily for something that it could not obtain? Thus it is with thy husband. But I have dreamed of being with thee, and that dream of my sleep was more real that my waking dream of absence.   ·

What a history wilt thou have to tell me, when I come back! We shall be a week in getting through it. Poor little Dove, I pity thee now; for I apprehend that, by this time, thou hast got thy husband's dullest of all books to read.[1] And how many pages canst thou read, without falling asleep? Well is it for thee, that thou hast adopted the practice of extending thyself on the sopha, while at thy studies; for now I need be under no apprehension of thy sinking out of a chair. I would, for thy sake, that thou couldst find anything laudable in this awful little volume; because thou wouldst like to tell thy husband that he has done well.

Oh, this weather!—how dismal it is. A sullen sky above, and mud and 'slosh' below! Thy husband needs thy sunshine, thou cheerfullest little wife; for he is quite pervaded and imbued with the sullenness of all nature. Thou knowest that his disposition is never the most gracious in the world; but now he is absolutely intolerable. The days should be all sunshine when he is away from thee; because, if there were twenty suns in the unclouded sky, yet his most essential sunshine would be wanting. Well; there is one good in absence; it makes me realize more adequately how much I love thee—and what an infinite portion of me thou art. It makes me happy even to yearn and sigh for thee as I do; because I love to be conscious of our deep, indissoluble union—and of the impossibility of living without thee. There is something good in me, else thou couldst not have become one with me, thou holy wife. I shall be happy, because God has made my happiness necessary to that of one whom He loves. Thus is it that I reason with myself; and therefore my soul rejoices to feel the intermingling of our beings, even when it is felt in this longing desire for thee.

Dearest, amongst my other reasons for wishing to be in Boston, wouldst thou believe that I am eager to behold thy alabaster vase—and the little flower vase—and thy two precious pictures? Even so it is. Thou, who art the loadstone of my soul, hast magnetized them; therefore they attract me.

I met Frederic Howes last evening, and promised to go there to-night; although he seemed to think that Miss Burley will be in Boston. Perhaps thou wilt see her there. I wonder if she will not come and settle with us in Mr. Ripley's Utopia.[2] And this reminds me to ask whether thou hast drawn those caricatures—especially the one of thy husband, staggering, and puffing, and toiling onward to the gate of the farm, burthened with the unsaleable remnant of Grandfather's Chair. Dear us, what a ponderous, leaden load it will be!

Dearest, I am utterly ashamed of my handwriting. I wonder how thou canst anywise tolerate what is so ungraceful, being thyself all grace. But I think I seldom write so shamefully as in this epistle. It is a toil and torment to write upon this sheet of paper; for it seems to be greasy, and feels very unpleasantly to the pen. Moreover the pen itself is very culpable. Yet thou wouldst make the fairest, delicatest strokes upon the same paper, with the same pen. Thou art beautiful throughout, even in the minutest thing. [*excision*]

1. *Grandfather's Chair.*

2. Brook Farm, in West Roxbury, Mass. There is no record of Miss Burley's association. George Ripley (1802–80), a Unitarian minister, organizer of the Transcendental Club, had been living on the farm since the previous summer. The first surviving mention of his plan for establishing a community there is in Emerson's journal for October 17, 1840: "Yesterday George & Sophia Ripley, Margaret Fuller & Alcott discussed here the new social plans" (*JMN*, VII, 407). Ripley wrote to Emerson on November 9: "Our proposal now is for three or four families to take possession on the first of April next, to attend to the cultivation of the farm and the erection of buildings, to prepare for the coming of as many more in the autumn . . . " (O. B. Frothingham, *George Ripley* [Boston: Houghton, Mifflin, 1881], p. 308). For a convenient gathering of primary source materials, see Henry W. Sams., ed., *Autobiography of Brook Farm* (Englewood Cliffs, N.J.: Prentice-Hall, 1958).

[Boston] 54 Pinckney St. Jany 1st. [1841]

Very dearest,

I would gladly go to Salem immediately if I could, but am detained here by some ceremonies, which are needful to be gone through, previous to my final deliverance from the Custom House. As Mr. Bancroft is not expected back from Washington for some days, I shall probably remain till nearly the close of next week. Meantime, I must be near at hand, because my presence may be required at any moment.

Naughtiest, thou shouldst not put thy little white hands into cold clay. Canst thou not use warm water? How canst thou hope for any warmth of conception and execution, when thou art working with material as cold as ice?

As to the proof-sheets,[1] I think we need not trouble

---

1. Of *Famous Old People*.

Boston, Jany 8th. 1841.

Dear Sir,

I know not whether you will think it necessary for me again to express my wish to retire from the Custom House. But as I have not yet been informed of my removal, I would respectfully request that it may now take place.

I regret that my former movement should have caused you any disturbance or displeasure. I contemplated nothing of the kind; for I supposed that the payment of the whole year's emolument, so soon as earned, took place in the common course of things, and with the knowledge and consent both of yourself and the Secretary of the Treasury. And, as I had received no more than the amount legally due me, and as it came to me through the regular channel, and was obtained by no deception on my part—and, moreover, as I was willing that the correctness of my position should be tested by law— it struck me as a very singular proposition that I was bound in honor to pay back any part of the money, or to serve a longer term for what was already my own. Still, I felt myself under a moral obligation, arising from your past kindness, not to do what you seemed to suppose might compromise you with the Secretary or the public.

I understand that Mr. Frothingham[1] considers himself much aggrieved by my conduct—but surely without reason; for it never occurred to me that he would take the responsi- bility of paying large sums of money without your knowledge, or against your positive orders. Nor, in making up my mind on the course to be pursued, did I once think of Mr. Frothingham, any more than of the desk on which he counted out the money. I trust, therefore, that he will revise his opinion (not expressed to myself, but whispered to others) as to the dishonorableness of my proceedings.

In conclusion, my dear Sir, I beg to renew my thanks for favors past, and am,

Very Respectfully Yours,
Nath. Hawthorne.

George Bancroft, Esq,
Boston.

1. Ephraim L. Frothingham, cashier at the Boston Custom House.

[Salem, January 11, 1841][1]

And how does thy head, thou much enduring Dove? Has sister Sarah hit it another great knock? Dearest, I still bear malice against her; and I beseech thee to tell her what an enormity she was guilty of. I shall not forgive her, till she has done penance.

Darling, it is my belief that I shall deem it advisable and needful to remain here a whole week from to-day! This is probably the longest visit that I shall ever make to my mother's house, until I bring mine ownest wife with me. Was it in this month, or February, last year, that I spent four weeks with thee? How happy we thought ourselves, then, in the possession of those four weeks![2] Now, I cannot imagine how we lived, when our life was months of separation, intermixed with only weeks and days of union. How strange it is, thou tender and fragile little Dove, that the shelter of thine arms should have become absolutely necessary to such a great, rough, burly, broad-shouldered personage as thy husband! He needs thy support as much as thou dost his.

What ugly, hideous handwriting is this, to present to thy beauty-loving eyes! But the paper, pen, and ink, are all more in fault than I.

1. Postmark, Salem, January 11.
2. See 141, 142, marking a month's gap in NH's 1840 correspondence to SH.

Salem Jan.ʸ 13th 1841

Infinitely dearest, I went to the Post Office yesterday, after dinner, and inquiring for a letter, thy "visible silence" was put into my hands. Canst thou remotely imagine how glad I was? Hast thou also been gladdened by an uncouth scribbling, which thy husband dispatched to thee on Monday? Oh, belovedest, no words can tell how thirsty my spirit is for thine! Surely I was very reprehensible to conceive the idea of spending a whole week and more away from thee. Why didst thou not scold me? Why didst thou not enforce thy conjugal privileges, and cling to my bosom, and nestle within it, and go with me wherever I went? Without thee, I have but the semblance of life. All the world hereabouts seems dull and drowsy—a vision, but without any spirituality—and I, likewise an unspiritual shadow, struggle vainly to catch hold of something real. Thou art my reality; and nothing else is real for me, unless thou give it that golden quality by thy touch.

Dearest, how camest thou by the head-ache? Thou shouldst have dreamed of thy husband's breast, instead of that Arabian execution; and then thou wouldst have awaked with a very delicious thrill in thy heart, and no pain in thy head. And what wilt thou do to-day, persecuted little Dove, when thy abiding-place will be a Babel of talkers?[1] Would that Miss Margaret Fuller might lose her tongue!—or my Dove her ears, and so be left wholly to her husband's golden silence! Dearest wife, I truly think that we could dispense with audible speech, and yet never feel the want of an interpreter between our spirits. We have soared into a region where we talk together in a language that can have no earthly echo. Articulate words are a harsh clamor and dissonance. When man arrives at his highest perfection, he will again be dumb!—for I suppose he was dumb at the Creation, and must perform an entire circle in order to return to that blessed state. Cousin Cristopher, by thy account, seems to be of the same opinion, and is gradually learning to talk without the use of his voice.[2]

Jany 15th. Friday.— Oh, belovedest, what a weary week is this! Never did I experience the like. I went to bed last night, positively dismal and comfortless for want of thee. It is an immemorial age since I held thee in my arms. Wilt thou know thy husband's face, when we meet again? Art thou much changed by the flight of years, my poor little wife? Is thy hair turned gray? Dost thou wear a day-cap, as well as a night cap? How long since didst thou begin to use spectacles? Perhaps thou wilt not like to have me see thee, now that Time has done his worst to mar thy beauty; but fear thou not, sweetest Dove, for what I have loved and admired in thee is eternal. I shall look through the envious mist of age, and discern thy immortal grace as perfectly as in the light of Paradise. As for thy husband, he is grown quite bald and gray, and has very deep wrinkles across his brow, and crows-feet and furrows all over his face. His eyesight fails him, so that he can only read the largest print in the broadest day-light; but it is a singular circumstance, that he makes out to decypher the pigmy characters of thy epistles, even by the faintest twilight. The secret is, that they are characters of light to him, so that he could doubtless read them in midnight darkness. Art thou not glad, belovedest, that thou wast ordained to be a heavenly light to thy husband, amid the dreary twilight of age?

Grandfather is very anxious to know what has become of his chair, and the Famous Old People[3] who sat in it. I tell him that it will probably arrive in the course of to-day; and that he need not be so impatient; for the public will be very well content to wait, even were it till Doomsday. He acquiesces, but scolds, nevertheless.

I saw thy cousin Mary Toppan[4] yesterday, and felt the better for it, because she is connected with thee in my mind. Dearest, I love thee very much!!!! Art thou not astonished? I wish to ask thee a question, but will reserve it for the extreme end of this letter. [*excision*] received, during the whole week. I trust that thou art quite well, belovedest. That head-ache took a very unfair advantage, in attacking thee while thou wast away from thy husband's bosom. It is his province to guard thee both from head-ache and heart-ache; and thou performest the same blessed office for him, so far as regards the heart-ache—as to the head-ache, he knows it not, probably because his head is like a block of wood.

Now good bye, dearest, sweetest, loveliest, holiest, truest, suitablest little wife. I worship thee. Thou art my type of womanly perfection. Thou keepest my heart pure, and elevatest me above the world. Thou enablest me to interpret the riddle of life, and fillest me with faith in the unseen and better land, because thou leadest me thither continually. God bless thee forever.

Dost thou love me?

1. The second year of Margaret Fuller's "conversations" with the educated women of Boston had begun November 4, 1840, at the Peabody house on West Street; see Emerson, *Letters*, II, 354, 359, 361. (Higginson's and later biographers' claim that the first "conversation," on November 6, 1839, was "at Miss Peabody's rooms in West Street" seems in error, since Elizabeth did not move there until July 1840; see Thomas Wentworth Higginson, *Margaret Fuller Ossoli* [Boston: Houghton, Mifflin, 1884], pp. 113–14.)

2. Probably Christopher Pearse Cranch (1813–92), the poet, painter, and Unitarian minister, whose great-grandfather was a brother of SH's grandmother, Mary Cranch Palmer. NH may refer to Cranch's first efforts at landscape painting in oils, or to cartoons he had drawn to satirize the early issues of the *Dial*, caricaturing, among others, Fuller. See F. DeWolfe Miller, *Christopher Pearse*

JANUARY, 1841

Cranch and his Caricatures of New England Transcendentalism (Cambridge: Harvard University Press, 1951), pp. 60–62.

3. *Famous Old People* was advertised for sale in Boston on January 18.

4. Mary Toppan Pickman (1816–78), daughter of SH's aunt Sophia Palmer Pickman and Dr. Thomas Pickman.

[Boston] 54 Pinckney St,
Jany 26th. 1841

Sir,

Mr. Pike called on me, on Sunday afternoon, and read me the copy of a letter, addressed to you, and which he informed me had already been left at your door. Greatly to my surprise, I found that much of the subject-matter of the letter related to transactions with which I was connected; but, I presume, you will not suppose that I had any thing whatever to do with the concoction of this document.

I am now on the point of leaving the city, to spend a few days in Salem; but before doing so, I think it right to inform you that I have reason to believe, that Mr. Pike is taking measures to bring this letter before the public.

Very respectfully,
Nath. Hawthorne.

George Bancroft, Esq.
Custom-House.

Salem, Jany 27th. 1841.—1/2 past 2. P.M.

Very dearest, what a dismal sky is this that hangs over us!
Thy husband doth but half live to-day—his soul lies asleep,
or rather torpid. As for thee, thou hast been prating at a great
rate, and hast spoken many wonderful truths in to-day's conversation; and, now, I trust, thou art lain down to a quiet
slumber, either on our sofa, or in thy bed—which is *our* bed
likewise. Wouldst thou be the worse for resting thy head a
moment on thy husband's breast? Would a kiss make thee
turn aside thy face in huge displeasure and absolute discom-
fiture? Wouldst thou prefer the most uncomfortable chair or
stool that ever was made, to a seat in thy husband's lap?
Wouldst thou inexorably forbid him to touch his lips even to
the extreme tip of thy nose? Oh, naughtiest, thou well knowest that thou wouldst! Poor unbeloved husband that he is?
Well, he deserves no better.

Belovedest, thou wast very sweet and lovely in our walk,
yesterday morning; and it gladdens me much that Providence
brought us together. Dost thou not think that there is always
some especial blessing granted us, when we are to be divided
for any length of time? Thou rememberest what a blissful
evening came down from Heaven to us, before our last separation; insomuch that our hearts glowed with its influence,
all through the ensuing week. And yesterday there came a
heavenly morning, and thou camest with it like a rosy vision,
which still lingers with me, and will not quite fade away, till
it be time for it to brighten into reality. Surely, thou art
beloved of Heaven, and all these blessings are vouchsafed for
thy sake; for I do not remember that such things used to

happen to me, while I was a solitary sinner. Thou bringest a
rich portion to thy husband, dearest—even the blessing of
thy Heavenly Father.

Whenever I return to Salem, I feel how dark my life would
be, without the light that thou shedst upon it—how cold,
without the warmth of thy love. Sitting in this chamber,
where my youth wasted itself in vain, I can partly estimate
the change that has been wrought. It seems as if the better
part of me had been born, since then. I had walked those
many years in darkness, and might so have walked through
life, with only a dreamy notion that there was any light in
the universe, if thou hadst not kissed mine eye-lids, and
given me to see. Thou, belovedest, hast always been positively happy. Not so thy husband—he has only not been
miserable. Then which of us has gained the most? Thy husband, assuredly. When a beam of heavenly sunshine incor-
porates itself with a dark cloud, is not the cloud benefitted
more than the sunshine? What a happy image is this!—my
soul is the cloud, and thine the sunshine—but a gentler,
sweeter sunshine than ever melted into any other cloud.

Dearest wife, nothing at all has happened to me, since I
left thee. It puzzles me to conceive how thou meetest with so
many more events than thy husband. Thou wilt have a volume to tell me, when we meet, and wilt pour thy beloved
voice into mine ears, in a stream of two hours' long. At length
thou wilt pause, and say—"But what has *thy* life been?"—
and then will thy stupid husband look back upon what he
calls his life, for three or four days past, and behold a blank!
Thou livest ten times as much as he; because thy spirit takes
so much more note of things.

I met our friend Mr Howes in the street, yesterday, and
held a brief confabulation. He did not inquire how my wife's
health is. Was not this a sin against etiquette? Dearest, thy
husband's stupid book seems to meet more approbation here,
than the former volume did—though *that* was greeted more

favorably than it deserved.[1] There is a superfluity of newspaper puffs here, and a deficiency in Boston, where they are much needed. I ought to love Salem better than I do; for the people have always had a pretty generous faith in me, ever since they knew me at all. I fear I must be undeserving of their praise, else I should never get it. What an ungrateful blockhead thy husband is![2]

[excision]

1. *Grandfather's Chair* had been published on December 8, and *Famous Old People* on January 18. On the first occasion, the Salem *Gazette* ran advertisements by three bookstores, headed in large type "HAWTHORNE'S NEW BOOK," "BY NATHANIEL HAWTHORNE," and "GRANDFATHER'S CHAIR." For *Famous Old People* the same paper on January 22 ran an advertisement headed "HAWTHORNE'S NEW WORK," and a notice describing the book as written in an "exquisite style," and "full of valuable information, conveyed in the attractive manner which will win for all the facts which are interwoven with the charming stories an abiding place in the memories of children, and make all the older people wish that they too could have been so ministered to in the days of their childhood." There were no such notices in Boston papers, and advertisements there were much less frequent and prominent.

2. On the cover of this letter, SH wrote "especial."

Boston, Monday. March 8th. [1841]

Dear Longfellow,

I did not receive your note till this morning. We will come at the hour appointed—at least, I will, and no doubt the parson,[1] whom I expect from Salem to-day.

By the bye, if it should storm most infernally, I doubt whether we do come.

Yours truly,
Nath H.

1. Horace Conolly. This was probably the occasion of Longfellow's asking Conolly to retell the story of Evangeline, after he had read NH's "The Acadian Exiles" in *Famous Old People.* See *TS*, pp. 125–29. See Manning Hawthorne and Henry Wadsworth Longfellow Dana, "The Origin of Longfellow's 'Evangeline,'" *PBSA*, XLI (1947), 174–75.

Boston, March 17th. 1841.

My dear Sir,

I intended to call on you, either on Thursday or Saturday evening of the present week; but I find it necessary to go to Salem. Next week, I trust, there will be no obstacle to the accomplishment of this long projected visit.

Yours very truly,
Nath. Hawthorne.

Rev. R. C. Waterston,
Boston.

1. Robert Cassie Waterston (1812–93), whom NH had known since 1837 (see AN, p. 70), was a Unitarian minister, at this time at the Pitts Street Chapel, Boston. Waterston may have been proposing the reprinting of NH's work for church use; see 251. It is also possible that NH had asked him to marry SH and himself before she joined him at Brook Farm soon after he moved there. If they had such plans, they abandoned them as soon as NH appreciated the style of life there.

Salem, March 18th 1841

Dearest wife, here is thy poor husband, enduring his banishment as best he may. Methinks all enormous sinners should be sent on pilgrimage to Salem, and compelled to spend a length of time there, proportioned to the enormity of their offences. Such a punishment would be suited to crimes that do not quite deserve hanging, yet are too aggravated for the States-Prison. Oh, thy naughty husband! If it be a punishment, he well deserves to suffer a life-long infliction of it, were it only for slandering his native town so vilely. Thou must scold him well. But, belovedest, any place is strange and irksome to me, where thou art not; and where thou art, any place will be home. Here I have made a great blot, as thou seest; but, sweetest, there is, at this moment, a portrait of myself in the mirror of that ink-spot. Is not that queer to think of? When it reaches thee, it will be nothing but a dull black spot; but now, when I bend over it, there I see myself, as at the bottom of a pool. Thou must not kiss the blot, for the sake of the image which it now reflects; though, if thou shouldst, it will be a talisman to call me back thither again.

Thy husband writes thee nonsense, as his custom is. I wonder how thou managest to retain any respect for him. Trust me, he is not worthy of thee—not worthy to kiss the sole of thy shoe, and yet how often has he tasted the sweetness of thy lips! For the future, thou perfectest Dove, let thy greatest condescension towards him, be merely an extension of the tip of thy forefinger, or of thy delicate little foot in its stocking. Nor let him dare to touch it without kneeling—which he will be very ready to do, because he devoutly worships thee; which is the only thing that can be said in his favor. But, think of his arrogance! At this very moment,—

March 19th. Forenoon.— Dearest soul, thou hast irrecoverably lost the conclusion of this sentence; for I was interrupted by a visitor, and have now forgotten what I meant to say. No matter; thou wilt not care for the loss; for, now I think of it, it does not please thee to hear thy husband spoken slightingly of. Well; then thou shouldst not have married such a vulnerable person. But, to thy comfort be it said, some people have a much more exalted opinion of him than I have. The Rev. Mr. Gannet[1] delivered a lecture at the Lyceum here, the other evening, in which he introduced an enormous eulogium on whom dost thou think? Why, on thy respectable husband! Thereupon all the audience gave a loud hiss. Now is my mild little Dove exceedingly enraged, and will plot some mischief and all-involving calamity against the Salem people. Well, belovedest, they did not actually hiss at the praises bestowed on thy husband—the more fools they!

Ownest wife, what dost thou think I received, just before I re-commenced this scribble? Thy letter! Dearest, I felt as thou didst about our meeting, at Mrs. Hillard's. It is an inexpressible torment! Thy letter is very sweet and beautiful—an expression of thyself. But I do trust thou hast given Mr. Ripley a downright scolding for doubting either my will or ability to work. He ought to be ashamed of himself, to try to take away the good name of a laboring man, who must earn his bread (and thy bread too) by the sweat of his brow.

Sweetest, I have some business up in town; and so must close this letter—which has been written in a great hurry, and is not fit to be sent thee. Say what thou wilt, thy husband is not a good letter-writer; he never writes, unless compelled by an internal or external necessity; and most glad would he be to think that there would never, henceforth, be occasion for his addressing a letter to thee. For would not that imply that thou wouldst always hereafter be close to his bosom?

Dearest love, expect me Monday evening. Didst thou expect me sooner? It may not be; but if longing desires could bear me to thee, thou wouldst straightway behold my shape in the great easy chair, with arms opened to receive thee. God bless thee, thou sinless Eve—thou dearest, sweetest, purest, perfectest wife.

Thine ownest.

1. Ezra Stiles Gannett (1801–71), Channing's assistant and soon-to-be successor in the pastorate of the Federal Street Congregational Church in Boston; one of the most important of the Unitarian clergy (see *DAB*). The lecture, given on March 17, was titled "Excitability of the American Character." No account of it is given in local newspaper reports.

[Boston] Pinckney St. April 4th. [1841]

Very dearest-est,

I have hitherto delayed to send these stories, because Howe's Masquerade was destroyed by the printers; and I have been in hopes to procure it elsewhere. But my own copy of the Magazine, in Salem, is likewise lost; so that I must buy the Boston Book, and request Mary's acceptance of it.[1]

Belovedest, how dost thou do this morning? I am very well; and surely Heaven is one with earth, this beautiful day. I met Miss Burley in the street, yesterday, and her face seemed actually to beam and radiate with kindness and goodness; insomuch that my own face involuntarily brightens, every time I think of her. I thought she looked really beautiful.

Oh, dearest, how I wish to see thee! I would thou hadst my miniature to wear in thy bosom; and then I should feel sure that now and then thou wouldst think of me—of which now, thou art aware, there can be no certainty. Sweetest, I feel that I shall need great comfort from thee, when the time of my journey to the far wilderness[2] actually comes. But we will be hopeful—thou shalt fill thy husband with thy hopefulness, and so his toil shall seem light, and he shall sing (though I fear it would be a most unlovely sort of screech) as he drives the plough.

Now, belovedest, good bye. My visit to Salem will be so brief, that a letter would hardly reach thee, before I myself shall return; so it will not be best for me to write. God bless thee and keep thee; which He will do without my prayers, because the good and pure, of which class my Dove is the

best and purest, always dwell within the walls of Heaven. I
am in great haste, most beloved; so, embracing thee,

I remain thy
lovingest Husband,
Nath. Hawthorne

1. "Howe's Masquerade" had been published in the *Democratic Review*, II
(May, 1838), 129–40, as No. 1 of "Tales of the Province House." It was reprinted in *The Boston Book* for 1841, pp. 168–89; the volume was edited by
George Hillard and published by George W. Light. The tale was to be collected
also in the 1842 *TTT*. NH had dined with Hillard and C. C. Felton at Longfellow's the day before (Hillard to H. R. Cleveland, April 6, 1841; MS, Berg).

2. Brook Farm.

Oak Hill,[1] April 13th. 1841

Ownest love,

Here is thy poor husband in a polar Paradise![2] I know not how to interpret this aspect of Nature—whether it be of good or evil omen to our enterprise. But I reflect that the Plymouth pilgrims arrived in the midst of storm and stept ashore upon mountain snow-drifts; and nevertheless they prospered, and became a great people—and doubtless it will be the same with us.[3] I laud my stars, however, that thou wilt not have thy first impressions of our future home from such a day as this. Thou wouldst shiver all thy life afterwards, and never realize that there could be bright skies, and green hills and meadows, and trees heavy with foliage, where now the whole scene is a great snow-bank, and the sky full of snow likewise. Through faith, I persist in believing that spring and summer will come in their due season; but the unregenerated man shivers within me, and suggests a doubt whether I may not have wandered within the precincts of the Arctic circle, and chosen my heritage among everlasting snows. Dearest, provide thyself with a good stock of furs; and if thou canst obtain the skin of a polar bear, thou wilt find it a very suitable summer dress for this region. Thou must not hope ever to walk abroad, except upon snow-shoes, nor to find any warmth, save in thy husband's heart.

Belovedest, I have not yet taken my first lesson in agriculture, as thou mayst well suppose—except that I went to see our cows foddered, yesterday afternoon. We have eight of our own; and the number is now increased by a transcendental heifer, belonging to Miss Margaret Fuller. She is very fractious, I believe, and apt to kick over the milk pail.[4] Thou knowest best, whether, in these traits of character, she resembles her mistress. Thy husband intends to convert himself into a milk-maid, this evening; but I pray heaven that Mr. Ripley may be moved to assign him the kindliest cow in the herd—otherwise he will perform his duty with fear and trembling.

Ownest wife, I like my brethren in affliction very well; and couldst thou see us sitting round our table, at meal-times, before the great kitchen-fire, thou wouldst call it a cheerful sight.[5] Mrs. Barker[6] is a most comfortable woman to behold; she looks as if her ample person were stuffed full of tenderness—indeed, as if she were all one great, kind heart. Wert thou but here, I should ask for nothing more—not even for sunshine and summer weather; for thou wouldst be both, to thy husband. And how is that cough of thine, my belovedest? Hast thou thought of me, in my perils and wanderings? Thou must not think how I longed for thee, when I crept into my cold bed last night,—my bosom remembered thee,—and refused to be comforted without thy caresses. I trust that thou dost muse upon me with hope and joy, not with repining. Think that I am gone before, to prepare a home for my Dove, and will return for her, all in good time.

Thy husband has the best chamber in the house, I believe; and though not quite so good as the apartment I have left, it will do very well.[7] I have hung up thy two pictures;[8] and they give me a glimpse of summer and of thee. The vase I intended to have brought in my arms, but could not very conveniently do it yesterday; so that it still remains at Mrs. Hillards, together with my carpet. I shall bring them the next opportunity.

Now farewell, for the present, most beloved. I have been writing this in my chamber; but the fire is getting low, and the house is old and cold; so that the warmth of my whole person has retreated to my heart, which burns with love for thee. I must run down to the kitchen or parlor hearth, where thy image shall sit beside me—yea be pressed to my breast. At bed-time, thou shalt have a few lines more. Now I think of it, dearest, wilt thou give Mrs. Ripley[9] a copy of Grandfather's Chair and Liberty Tree;[10] she wants them for some boys here. I have several vols of Famous Old People.

April 14th. 10.A.M. Sweetest, I did not milk the cows last night, because Mr. Ripley was afraid to trust them to my hands, or me to their horns—I know not which. But this morning, I have done wonders. Before breakfast, I went out to the barn, and began to chop hay for the cattle; and with such "righteous vehemence" (as Mr. Ripley says) did I labor, that, in the space of ten minutes, I broke the machine.[11] Then I brought wood and replenished the fires; and finally sat down to breakfast and ate up a huge mound of buckwheat cakes. After breakfast, Mr. Ripley put a four-pronged instrument into my hands, which he gave me to understand was called a pitch-fork; and he and Mr. Farley[12] being armed with similar weapons, we all three commenced a gallant attack upon a heap of manure. This affair being concluded, and thy husband having purified himself, he sits down to finish this letter to his most beloved wife. Dearest, I will never consent that thou come within half a mile of me, after such an encounter as that of this morning. Pray Heaven that this letter retain none of the fragrance with which the writer was imbued. As for thy husband himself, he is peculiarly partial to the odor; but that whimsical little nose of thine might chance to quarrel with it.

Belovedest, Miss Fuller's cow hooks the other cows, and has made herself ruler of the herd, and behaves in a very tyrannical manner. Sweetest, I know not when I shall see thee; but I trust it will not be longer than till the end of next week. I love thee! I love thee! I would thou wert with me; for then would my labor be joyful—and even now, it is not sorrowful. Dearest, I shall make an excellent husbandman. I feel the original Adam reviving within me.

1. A location in West Roxbury, near the site of Brook Farm, where NH is actually writing .

2. Compare *BR*, pp. 9–13.

3. Compare *BR*, p. 13.

4. Compare *BR*, p. 65.

5. Compare *BR*, p. 12.

6. Elise Barker, apparently a neighbor to Brook Farm (from "over the hill"), who later brought her family to live there. See Zoltan Haraszti, *The Idyll of Brook Farm* (Boston: Boston Public Library, 1937), p. 14; Katherine Burton, *Paradise Planters* (New York: Longmans, Green, 1939), p. 43. Compare Mrs. Foster in *BR*, p. 13.

7. Compare *BR*, p. 40.

8. Of Menaggio and Isola.

9. Sophia Willard Dana Ripley (1803–61), daughter of Francis Dana of Cambridge, had married George Ripley in 1827.

10. The third volume of the Grandfather's Chair series, published in March.

11. Compare *BR*, p. 65.

12. Francis D. Farley, described in a letter of William Brockway Allen to his fiancée, Sylvia Farrar, May 3, 1841, as "about thirty, short and not very thick set rather dark with black hair and eyes, he is naturally active and wity, can suit himself to almost any sort of company and can entertain them with novel stories and wity sayings. . . . " See Edith Roelker Curtis, *A Season in Utopia* (New York: Thomas Nelson, 1961), p. 58.

Oak Hill, April 16th. 1/2 past 6. A.M. [1841]

Most beloved, I have a few moments to spare before break-fast; and perhaps thou wilt let me spend them in talking to thee. Thy two letters blessed me yesterday, having been brought by some private messenger of Mrs. Ripley's. Very joyful was I to hear from my Dove, and my heart gave a mighty heave and swell as thou hast sometimes felt it do while thou was resting upon it. That cough of thine—I do wish it would take its departure; for I cannot bear to think of thy tender little frame being shaken with it all night long. Thou dost need to be kissed, little Dove, every hour of thy life—that would be a sovereign remedy.

Dearest, since I last wrote thee, there has been an addition to our community of four gentlemen in sables, who promise to be among our most useful and respectable members. They arrived yesterday, about noon. Mr. Ripley had proposed to them to join us, no longer ago than that very morning. I had some conversation with them in the afternoon, and was glad to hear them express much satisfaction with their new abode, and all the arrangements. They do not appear to be very communicative, however—or perhaps it may be merely an external reserve, like that of thy husband, to shield their delicacy. Several of their prominent characteristics, as well as their black attire, lead me to believe that they are members of the clerical profession; but I have not yet ascertained, from their own lips, what has been the nature of their past lives. I trust to have much pleasure in their society, and, sooner or later, that we shall all of us derive great strength from our intercourse with them. I cannot too highly applaud the readiness with which these four gentlemen in black have thrown aside all the fopperies and flummeries, which have their origin in a false state of society. When I last saw them, they looked as heroically regardless of the stains and soils incident to our profession, as thy husband did when he emerged from the gold mine.[1]

Ownest wife, thy husband has milked a cow!!!

Belovedest, the herd have rebelled against the usurpation of Miss Fuller's cow; and whenever they are turned out of the barn, she is compelled to take refuge under our protection. So much did she impede thy husband's labors, by keeping close to him, that he found it necessary to give her two or three gentle pats with a shovel; but still she preferred to trust herself to my tender mercies, rather than venture among the horns of the herd. She is not an amiable cow; but she has a very intelligent face, and seems to be of a reflective cast of character. I doubt not that she will soon perceive the expediency of being on good terms with the rest of the sisterhood.

I have not yet been twenty yards from our house and barn; but I begin to perceive that this is a beautiful place. The scenery is of a mild and placid character, with nothing bold in its character; but I think its beauties will grow upon us, and make us love it the more, the longer we live here. There is a brook, so near the house that we shall be able to hear its ripple, in the summer evenings; and whenever we lie awake in the summer nights; but, for agricultural purposes, it has been made to flow in a straight and rectangular fashion, which does it infinite damage, as a picturesque object.

Naughtiest, it was a moment or two before I could think whom thou didst mean by Mr. Dismal View.[2] Why, he is one of the best of the brotherhood, so far as cheerfulness goes; for, if he do not laugh himself, he makes the rest of us laugh continually. He is the quaintest and queerest personage thou didst ever see—full of dry jokes, the humor of which is so incorporated with the strange twistifications of his physiognomy, that his sayings ought to be written down, accompanied with illustrations by Cruikshank.[3] Then he keeps quoting innumerable scraps of Latin, and makes classical allusions, while we are turning over the gold mine; and the contrast between the nature of his employment and the character of his thoughts is irresistibly ludicrous.

Sweetest, I have written this epistle in the parlor, while Farmer Ripley, and Farmer Farley, and Farmer Dismal View, are talking about their agricultural concerns, around the fire. So thou wilt not wonder if it is not a classical piece of composition, either in point of thought or expression. I shall have just time, before breakfast is ready—the boy has just come to call us now—but still I will tell thee that I love thee infinitely; and that I long for thee unspeakably, but yet with a happy longing. The rest of them have gone into the breakfast room; [excision]

---

1. "The gold mine" was George Ripley's name for the manure pile. See George P. Bradford, "Reminiscences of Brook Farm by a Member of the Community," *Century*, XLV (1892), 142. SH published this letter in part, in *PAN*, with the concluding unacknowledged editorial addition, "Mr. Ripley has bought four black pigs" (p. 290). See also *AN*, pp. 203–5, *BR*, pp. 20, 143–44.

2. Probably Warren Burton (1800–1866), a Unitarian and Swedenborgian clergyman who served various congregations in and near Boston intermittently while identifying himself with a series of reform movements. See *DAB*.

3. George Cruikshank (1792–1878), English illustrator and caricaturist, had illustrated Dickens's *Sketches by Boz* (1836–37), *Oliver Twist* (1837–39), and other works published serially in *Bentley's Miscellany*, which was edited by Dickens.

[Brook Farm] April 22d [1841]

What an abominable hand do I scribble! but I have been chopping wood, and turning a grindstone all the forenoon; and such occupations are apt to disturb the equilibrium of the muscles and sinews. It is an endless surprise to me how much work there is to be done in the world; but, thank God, I am able to do my share of it,—and my ability increases daily.[1] What a great, broad-shouldered, elephantine personage I shall become by and by!

I milked two cows this morning, and would send you some of the milk, only that it is mingled with that which was drawn forth by Mr. Dismal View and the rest of the brethren.

1. Elizabeth Peabody wrote to John S. Dwight on April 26 that NH had "taken hold with the greatest spirit" at Brook Farm (MS, Boston Public Library). Compare *BR*, p. 64.

Brook Farm, April 28th. 1841—7. A.M.

Mine ownest, what a beautiful bright morning is this! I do trust that thou hast not suffered so much from the late tremendous weather, as to be unable now to go abroad in the sunshine. I tremble, almost, to think how thy tender frame has been shaken by that continual cough, which cannot but have grown more inveterate throughout these interminable ages of east wind. At times, dearest, it has seemed an absolute necessity for me to see thee, and hold thee in my arms, and find out for a certain truth whether thou wert well or ill. Even hadst thou been here, thou wouldst have been penetrated to the core with the chill blast. Then how must thou have been afflicted, where it comes directly from the sea. I am afraid thou hast needed my kisses very much.

Belovedest, thy husband was caught by a cold, during his visit to Boston.[1] It has not affected his whole frame, but took entire possession of his head, as being the weakest and most vulnerable part. Never didst thou hear anybody sneeze with such vehemence and frequency; and his poor brain has been in a thick fog—or rather, it seemed as if his head were stuffed with coarse wool. I know not when I have been so pestered before; and sometimes I wanted to wrench off my head, and give it a great kick, like a foot-ball. This annoyance has made me endure the bad weather with even less than ordinary patience; and my faith was so far exhausted, that when they told me yesterday that the sun was setting clear, I would not even turn my eyes towards the west. But, this morning, I am made all over anew, and have no greater remnant of my cold, than will serve as an excuse for doing no work to-day.[2] Dearest, do not let Mrs. Ripley frighten thee with apocryphal accounts of my indisposition. I have told thee the whole truth. I do believe that she delights to disquiet people with doubts and fears about their absent friends; for, once or twice, she has made thy cough a bugbear to thy husband. Nevertheless, I will not judge too harshly of the good lady, because I like her very well, in many respects.

The family has been dismal and dolorous, throughout the storm. The night before last, William Allen[3] was stung by a wasp, on the eye-lid; whereupon, the whole side of his face swelled to an enormous magnitude; so that, at the breakfast table, one half of him looked like a blind giant (the eye being closed) and the other half had such a sorrowful and ludicrous aspect, that thy husband was constrained to laugh out of sheer pity. The same day, a colony of wasps was discovered in thy husband's chamber, where they had remained throughout the winter, and were now just bestirring themselves, doubtless with the intention of stinging me from head to foot. Thou wilt readily believe, that not one of the accursed crew escaped my righteous vengeance. A similar discovery was made in Mr. Farley's room. In short, we seem to have taken up our abode in a wasp's nest. Thus thou seest, belovedest, that a rural life is not one of unbroken quiet and serenity.

If the middle of the day prove warm and pleasant, thy husband promises himself to take a walk, in every step of which thou shalt be his companion. Oh, how I long for thee to stray with me, in reality, among the hills, and dales, and woods, of our home. I have taken one walk, with Mr. Farley; and I could not have believed that there was such seclusion, at so short a distance from a great city. Many spots seem hardly to have been visited for ages—not since John Eliot[4] preached to the Indians here. If we were to travel a thousand miles, we could not escape the world more completely than we can here.

Sweetest, I long unspeakably to see thee—it is only the thought of thee that draws my spirit out of this solitude. Otherwise, I care nothing for the world nor its affairs. I read no newspapers, and hardly remember who is President, and feel as if I had no more concern with what other people trouble themselves about, than if I dwelt in another planet. But, still, thou drawest me to thee continually; and so I can realize how a departed spirit feels, while looking back from another world to the beloved ones of this. All other interests appear like shadows and trifles; but love is a reality, which makes the spirit still an inhabitant of the world which it has quitted.

Ownest wife, if Mr. Ripley comes into Boston on Sunday, it is my purpose to accompany him. Otherwise, thou mayst look for me some time during the ensuing week. Be happy, dearest; and above all, do shake off that tremendous cough. Take great care of thyself, and never venture out when there is the least breath of east-wind; but spread thy wings in the sunshine, and be joyous as itself.

God bless thee.

Thine ownest.

Will thy father have the goodness to leave the letter for Colonel Hall[5] at the Post Office?

1. Compare *BR*, pp. 37–38.

2. Compare *BR*, p. 61.

3. William Brockway Allen, from New Hampshire, was head farmer and holder of three shares in the Brook Farm Institute of Agriculture and Education. He had recently managed Theodore Parker's farm in West Roxbury. See Curtis, *Utopia*, p. 54.

4. John Eliot (1604–90), the missionary to the Indians. A graduate of Cambridge, he emigrated to Boston in 1631, and was pastor of the church in Roxbury for almost sixty years. He began preaching to the Indians in 1646, and translated the Bible into their language. See *DAB*. NH quoted from Converse Francis's *Life of Eliot* in the *American Magazine*, II (August, 1836), 495–96, and wrote a sketch of his life in *TS*, pp. 43–50. See also *BR*, chapter 14, "Eliot's Pulpit," especially p. 118.

5. Unrecovered.

[Brook Farm] May 1st [1841]

Every day of my life makes me feel more and more how seldom a fact is accurately stated; how, almost invariably, when a story has passed through the mind of a third person, it becomes, so far as regards the impression that it makes in further repetitions, little better than a falsehood, and this, too, though the narrator be the most truth-seeking person in existence. How marvellous the tendency is! . . . Is truth a fantasy which we are to pursue forever and never grasp? . . .

My cold has almost entirely departed. Were it a sunny day, I should consider myself quite fit for labor out of doors; but as the ground is so damp, and the atmosphere so chill, and the sky so sullen, I intend to keep myself on the sick-list this one day longer, more especially as I wish to read Carlyle on Heroes.[1] . . .

There has been but one flower found in this vicinity,— and that was an anemone, a poor, pale, shivering little flower, that had crept under a stone wall for shelter. Mr. Farley found it, while taking a walk with me. . . .

This is May-day! Alas, what a difference between the ideal and the real![2]

---

1. Thomas Carlyle, *On Heroes, Hero-Worship, & the Heroic in History* (London: James Fraser, 1841).

2. Compare *BR*, p. 58.

Brook Farm, West Roxbury,
May 3^d, 1841

As the weather precludes all possibility of ploughing,
hoeing, sowing, and other such operations, I bethink me that
you may have no objection to hear something of my whereabout and whatabout. You are to know then, that I took up
my abode here on the 12th ultimo, in the midst of a snowstorm, which kept us all idle for a day or two. At the first
glimpse of fair weather, Mr. Ripley summoned us into the
cow-yard, and introduced me to an instrument with four
prongs, commonly called a dung-fork. With this tool, I have
already assisted to load twenty or thirty carts of manure, and
shall take part in loading nearly three hundred more. Besides, I have planted potatoes and pease, cut straw and hay
for the cattle, and done various other mighty works. This
very morning, I milked three cows; and I milk two or three
every night and morning. The weather has been so unfavorable, that we have worked comparatively little in the fields;
but, nevertheless, I have gained strength wonderfully—
grown quite a giant, in fact—and can do a day's work without
the slightest inconvenience. In short, I am transformed into
a complete farmer.

This is one of the most beautiful places I ever saw in my
life, and as secluded as if it were a hundred miles from any
city or village. There are woods, in which we can ramble all
day, without meeting anybody, or scarcely seeing a house.
Our house stands apart from the main road; so that we are
not troubled even with passengers looking at us. Once in a
while, we have a transcendental visitor, such as Mr. Alcott;[1]
but, generally, we pass whole days without seeing a single
face, save those of the brethren. At this present time, our

effective force consists of Mr. Ripley, Mr. Farley, (a farmer from the far west,) Rev. Warren Burton (author of various celebrated works)[2] three young men and boys, who are under Mr. Ripley's care, and William Allen, his hired man, who has the chief direction of our agricultural labors. In the female part of the establishment there is Mrs Ripley, and two women folks.[3] The whole fraternity eat together; and such a delectable way of life has never been seen on earth, since the days of the early Christians. We get up at half-past four, breakfast at half past six, dine at half past twelve, and go to bed at nine.

The thin frock, which you made for me, is considered a most splendid article; and I should not wonder if it were to become the summer uniform of the community. I have a thick frock, likewise; but it is rather deficient in grace, though extremely warm and comfortable. I wear a tremendous pair of cow-hide boots, with soles two inches thick. Of course, when I come to see you, I shall wear my farmer's dress.

We shall be very much occupied during most of this month, ploughing and planting; so that I doubt whether you will see me for two or three weeks. You have the portrait by this time, I suppose; so you can very well dispense with the original.[4] When you write to me (which I beg you will do soon) direct your letter to West Roxbury, as there are two Post Offices in the town. I would write more; but William Allen is going to the village, and must have this letter; so good bye.

Nath. Hawthorne,
Ploughman.

1. A. Bronson Alcott (1799–1888) had participated in the first planning of Brook Farm (see 179.2), but George Ripley could not convince him to join. He

found the community insufficiently "ideal" because based on "intolerably arithmetical" planning. See Odell Shepard, *Pedlar's Progress: The Life of Bronson Alcott* (Boston: Little, Brown, 1937), pp. 268, 289, 293, 297; Swift, pp. 233–37.

2. *My Religious Experience at my Native Home* (1829), *Cheering Views of Man and Providence* (1832), *The District School as It Was* (1833), *An Essay on the Divine Agency in the Material Universe* (1834).

3. Perhaps Mrs. Elise Barker and Mrs. Farley.

4. A portrait of NH in 1840 by the Salem artist Charles Osgood (1809–90). See *Catalogue of Portraits in the Essex Institute* (Salem: Essex Institute, 1936), No. 123; Gollin, pp. 19–22. Louisa wrote to NH from Salem on May 10 that "the portrait came home a fortnight ago, and gives great delight" (*NHHW*, I, 229).

Brook Farm, May 4th. 1841. 1/2 past 1 PM

Belovedest, as Mrs. Ripley is going to the city this afternoon, I cannot but write to thee, though I have but little
time; for the cornfield will need me very soon. My cold no
longer troubles me; and all the morning, I have been at work
under the clear blue sky, on a hill side. Sometimes it almost
seemed as if I were at work in the sky itself; though the
material in which I wrought was the ore from our gold mine.[1]
Nevertheless, there is nothing so unseemly and disagreeable
in this sort of toil, as thou wouldst think. It defiles the hands,
indeed, but not the soul. This gold ore is a pure and whole-
some substance; else our Mother Nature would not devour it
so readily, and derive so much nourishment from it, and
return such a rich abundance of good grain and roots in
requital of it.

The farm is growing very beautiful now—not that we yet
see anything of the pease or potatoes, which we have planted;
but the grass blushes green on the slopes and hollows. I wrote
that word blush almost unconsciously; so we will let it go as
an inspired utterance. When I go forth afield, I think of my
Dove, and look beneath the stone walls, where the verdure
is richest, in hopes that a little company of violets, or some
solitary bud, prophetic of the summer, may be there; to
which I should award the blissful fate of being treasured for
a time in thy bosom; for I doubt not, dearest, that thou
wouldst admit any flower of thy husband's gathering into that
sweetest place. But not a wild flower have I yet found. One
of the boys gathered some yellow cowslips, last Sunday; but I
am well content not to have found them; for they are not
precisely what I should like to send my Dove, though they

deserve honor and praise, because they come to us when no others will. We have our parlor here dressed in evergreen, as at Christmas. That beautifullest little flower vase of thine stands on Mr. Ripley's study table, at which I am now writing. It contains some daffodils and some willow blossoms. I brought it here, rather than kept it in my chamber; because I never sit there; and it gives me many pleasant emotions to look round and be surprised (for it is often a surprise, though I well know that it is there) by something which is connected with the idea of thee.

Most dear wife, I cannot hope that thou art yet entirely recovered from that terrible influenza; but if thou art not almost well, I know not how thy husband will endure it. And that cough too. It is the only one of thy utterances, so far as I have heard them, which I do not love. Wilt thou not be very well, and very lightsome, at our next meeting. I promise myself to be with thee next Thursday, the day after tomorrow. It is an eternity since we met; and I can nowise account for my enduring this lengthened absence so well. I do not believe that I could suffer it, if I were not engaged in a righteous and heaven-blessed way of life. When I was in the Custom House, and thou at Salem, I was not half so patient; though my love and desire of thee has grown infinitely since then.

We had some tableaux last evening, the principal characters being sustained by Mr. Farley and Miss Ellen Slade.[2] They went off very well. I would like to see a tableaux, arranged by my Dove.

Dearest, I fear it is time for thy clod-compelling[3] husband to take the field again. Good bye. Oh, how I do [*excision*]

1. Compare *BR*, pp. 65–66; *FIN*, p. 446.

2. A girl about sixteen years old who lived at Brook Farm. See Haraszti, *The Idyll of Brook Farm*, pp. 17–18; *AN*, p. 202.

3. A pun on Homer's epithet for Zeus, *nephelegeretes*, "cloud-compelling" or "cloud-gathering."

[Brook Farm] May 11th [1841]

. . . This morning I arose at milking-time in good trim for work; and we have been employed partly in an augean labor of clearing out a wood-shed, and partly in carting loads of oak. This afternoon I hope to have something to do in the field, for these jobs about the house are not at all to my taste.

Brook Farm, June 1st. 1841—nearly 6 A.M.

Very dearest,

I have been too busy to write thee a long letter by this opportunity; for I think this present life of mine gives me an antipathy to pen and ink, even more than my Custom House experience did. I could not live without the idea of thee, nor without spiritual communion with thee; but, in the midst of toil, or after a hard day's work in the gold mine, my soul obstinately refuses to be poured out on paper. That abominable gold mine! Thank God, we anticipate getting rid of its treasurers, in the course of two or three days. Of all hateful places, that is the worst; and I shall never comfort myself for having spent so many days of blessed sunshine there. It is my opinion, dearest, that a man's soul may be buried and perish under a dung-heap or in a furrow of the field, just as well as under a pile of money.[1] Well; that giant, Mr. George Bradford,[2] will probably be here to-day; so that there will be no danger of thy husband being under the necessity of laboring more than he likes, hereafter. Meantime, my health is perfect, and my spirits buoyant, even in the gold mine.

And how art thou belovedest? Two or three centuries have passed since I saw thee; and then thou wast pale and languid. Thou didst comfort me in that little note of thine;[3] but still I cannot help longing to be informed of thy present welfare. Thou art not a prudent little Dove, and wast naughty to come on such a day as thou didst; and it seems to me that Mrs. Ripley does not know how to take care of thee at all. Art thou quite well now.

Dearest wife, I intend to come and see thee either on Thursday or Friday—perhaps my visit may be deferred till Saturday, if the gold mine should hold out so long. I yearn for thee unspeakably. Good bye now; for the breakfast horn has sounded, sometime since. God bless thee, ownest.

Thy lovingest husband.

1. Compare *BR*, p. 66.

2. George Partridge Bradford (1807–90), head of the "department of belles-lettres" at Brook Farm. He was a graduate of Harvard and its Divinity School, and brother-in-law of Samuel Ripley, from whom the Hawthornes were to rent the Old Manse. He never held a regular parish, but delivered occasional sermons, and taught school in various places. See Swift, pp. 74, 187–94. In a letter of June 15, Bradford described NH as "a very handsome finely formed man, but very silent & diffident or reserved, however I have become somewhat acquainted with him in the course of our hoeing, shovelling & milking together and find something very pleasing in him." See James W. Mathews, "An Early Brook Farm Letter," *NEQ*, LIII (1980), 228.

3. Apparently an unrecovered note previous to her letter to him of May 30–31 (MS, Berg).

Mr. Hawthorne requests that Miss Peabody will cause the accompanying note to be conveyed to Mr. Munroe.[1] It is such a conditional acceptance as she suggested.

Mr. Hawthorne particularly desires that the bargain with Mr. Munroe, in respect to the remaining copies of Grandfathers Chair &c. may be concluded on such terms as Miss Peabody thinks best, without further reference to himself. Being wholly ignorant of the value of the books, he could do no other than consent to any arrangement that she might propose.[2]

West Roxbury, June 23^{d}, 1841

1. James Munroe (1808–61), the Boston publisher, who was to bring out a second, two-volume edition of TTT in December.

2. Elizabeth had published *Grandfather's Chair, Famous Old People,* and *Liberty Tree* at her own press at the West Street bookshop. She was preparing to move in the autumn to 109 Washington Street, and now apparently wished to rid herself of the remainder of the first editions. No satisfactory arrangements were made, and she eventually was to advertise that *Famous Old People* and *Liberty Tree* were for sale at her new location (Boston *Advertiser,* November 6, 1841; 3:5). NH was also perhaps considering to ask Munroe to reprint the books and continue the series. See *TS,* "Historical Introduction," p. 294; *TTT,* "Historical Commentary," p. 522 n.85.

Brook Farm, Friday, July 9th. 1/2 past 5 PM [1841]

Oh, unutterably ownest wife, no pen can write how I have longed for thee, or for any the slightest word from thee; for thy Sunday's letter did not reach me till noon of this very day! Never was such a thirst of the spirit as I have felt. I began to wonder whether my Dove did really exist, or was only a vision; and canst thou imagine what a desolate feeling that was. Oh, I need thee, my wife, every day, and every hour, and every minute, and every minutest particle of forever and forever.

Belovedest, the robe reached me in due season; and on Sabbath day, I put it on; and truly it imparted such a noble and stately aspect to thy husband, that thou couldst not possibly have known him. He did really look tolerably personable! And, moreover, he felt as if thou wert embracing him, all the time that he was wrapt in the folds of this precious robe. Hast thou made it of such immortal stuff as the robes of Bunyan's Pilgrim were made of?—else it would grieve my very heart to subject it to the wear and tear of this world.[1]

Belovedest, when dost thou mean to come home?[2] It is a whole eternity since I saw thee. If thou art at home on a Sunday, I must and will spend it, and the night, likewise, with mine ownest wife. Oh, how my heart leaps at the thought.

God bless thee, thou belovedest woman-angel—I cannot write a single word more; for I have stolen the time to write this from the labors of the field. I ought to be raking hay, like my brethren, who will have to labor the longer and later, on account of these few moments which I have given to thee.

Now that we are in the midst of haying, we return to our toil, after an early supper. I think I never felt so vigorous as now; but, Oh, I cannot be well without thee. Farewell, I kiss thee a million of times.

Thine ownest.

1. Bunyan, *Pilgrim's Progress*, ed. James Blanton Wharey, 2nd ed. rev. Roger Sharrock (Oxford: Clarendon Press, 1960), p. 41: "And as for this Coat that is on my back, it was given me by the Lord of the place whither I go."

2. Probably from Milton Hill, outside Boston, where SH had written to him on June 12 from the summer home of her friends John Murray Forbes (1813–98) and Sarah Hathaway Forbes (MS, Berg). Sarah had been a student at Elizabeth's school in New Bedford; see Forbes's *Letters and Recollections* (Boston: Houghton, Mifflin, 1899), I, 65. SH was still at Milton Hill on July 4, when she wrote to her mother (MS, Berg).

Brook Farm, July 16th. 1841.

Dear Hillard,

I have not written that infernal story.[1] The thought of it has tormented me ever since I came here, and has deprived me of all the comfort I might otherwise have had, in my few moments of leisure. Thank God, it is now too late—so I disburthen my mind of it, now and forever.

You cannot think how exceedingly I regret the necessity of disappointing you; but what could be done? An engagement to write a story must in its nature be conditional; because stories grow like vegetables, and are not manufactured, like a pine table. My former stories all sprung up of their own accord, out of a quiet life. Now, I have no quiet at all; for when my outward man is at rest—which is seldom, and for short intervals—my mind is bothered with a sort of dull excitement, which makes it impossible to think continuously of any subject. You cannot make a silk purse out of a sow's ear; nor must you expect pretty stories from a man who feeds pigs.

My hands are covered with a new crop of blisters—the effect of raking hay; so excuse this scrawl.

Yours truly,
Nath. Hawthorne

1. For the 1842 *Token*, edited by Hillard, and scheduled to be printed in the autumn of 1841. See *TTT*, "Historical Commentary," pp. 518–19. This is prob-

ably the "annual to be published in Boston, and 'which is to be a fair specimen of the arts of this country,' . . . edited (*sub rosa*) by Longfellow, Felton, Hillard and that set," of which J. R. Lowell wrote to G. B. Loring February 18, 1841. Lowell wrote that he had been asked to contribute: "Hawthorne and Emerson are writing for it, and Bryant and Halleck have promised to write." See Horace E. Scudder, *James Russell Lowell: A Biography* (Boston: Houghton, Mifflin, 1901), I, 93.

Boston, July 18th, 1841.

My dear Sir,

Your letter has this moment been put into my hands. I truly thank you for it, and wish to lose no time in correcting some misapprehensions which have been caused by your judging of my feelings through the medium of third persons—and partly from my brief and imperfect communications to you, last Sunday.

I have never felt that I was called upon by *Mr. Ripley* to devote so much of my time to manual labor, as has been done since my residence at Brook Farm; nor do I believe that others have felt constraint of that kind, from him personally. We have never looked upon him as a master, or an employer, but as a fellow laborer on the same terms as ourselves, with no more right to bid us perform any one act of labor, than we have to bid him. Our constraint has been merely that of circumstances, which were as much beyond his control as our own; and there was no way of escaping this constraint, except by leaving the farm at once; and this step none of us were prepared to take, because (though attributing less importance to the success of this immediate enterprise than Mr. Ripley does) we still felt that its failure would be very inauspicious to the prospects of the community. For my own part, there are private and personal motives which, without the influence of those shared by us all, would still make me wish to bear all the drudgery of this one summer's labor, were it much more onerous than I have found it. It is true that I not

infrequently regret that the summer is passing with so little
enjoyment of nature and my own thoughts, and with the
sacrifice of some objects that I had hoped to accomplish. Such
were the regrets to which I alluded, last Sunday; but Mr.
Ripley cannot be held responsible for the disagreeable circumstances which cause them.

I recollect speaking very despondingly, or perhaps despair-
ingly, of the prospects of the institution. My views in this
respect vary somewhat with the state of my spirits; but I
confess that, of late, my hopes are never very sanguine. I
form my judgment, however, not from anything that has
passed within the precincts of Brook Farm, but from external
circumstances—from the improbability that adequate funds
will be raised, or that any feasible plan can be suggested, for
proceeding without a very considerable capital. I likewise
perceive that there would be some very knotty points to be
discussed, even had we capital enough to buy an estate.
These considerations have somewhat lessened the heartiness
and cheerfulness with which I formerly went forth to the
fields, and perhaps have interposed a medium of misunderstanding between Mr. Ripley and us all. His zeal will not
permit him to doubt of eventual success; and he perceives, or
imagines, a more intimate connection between our present
farming operations and our ultimate enterprise, than is visible to my perceptions. But, as I said before, the two things
are sufficiently connected, to make me desirous of giving my
best efforts to the promotion of the former.

You will see, I think, from what I have now stated, that
there was no pressing necessity for me, or my fellow laborers,
to dishearten Mr. Ripley, by expressing dissatisfaction with
our present mode of life. It is our wish to give his experiment
a full and fair trial; and if his many hopes are to be frustrated,
we should be loth to give him reason to attribute the failure
to lack of energy and perseverance in his associates. Never-

theless, we did, several days since (he and myself, I mean) have a conversation on the subject; and he is now fully possessed of my feelings, in respect to personal labor.

Probably you have not yet heard of Mr. Burton's departure from Brook Farm.[2] It occurred the night before last. It is an unfortunate event, in all its aspects. You will probably learn some of the circumstances which led to it, from Mr. Ripley, who, I doubt not, will render all justice to Mr. Burton, so far as his position may enable him to form a correct judgment. It is a subject not easily to be discussed in a letter; but I hope, at some future time, to communicate my view of the matter *viva voce*.

I have written this letter in great haste; so that, very probably, it may fail to satisfy your mind on the subjects involved. I shall be happy, whenever an opportunity occurs, to talk at large, and with all frankness, about the interests which we have in common. This, however, cannot be done for a week or two, as I am about to accompany Mr. Farley to the seashore, at his own and Mr. Ripley's request. His health is such, that this step is deemed essential. [*excision*]

1. David Mack (1804–78), born in Amherst, Massachusetts, had attended Williams College and had graduated from Yale in 1823. He then studied law with his uncle Elisha Mack in Salem, and may have practiced for two or three years. He became a private tutor in New Bedford and Cambridge. On September 29, 1841, he signed the articles of agreement for Brook Farm, but did not join the Association. In 1842 he joined the Northampton community. See Swift, p. 18; Manning Hawthorne, "Hawthorne and Utopian Socialism," *NEQ*, XII (1939), 726–30; Alice Eaton McBee, 2nd, *From Utopia to Florence: The Story of a Transcendentalist Community in Northampton, Mass. 1830–1852* (Philadelphia: Porcupine Press, 1975; orig. Northampton: Smith College Studies in History, XXXII, 1947), pp. 32–33.

2. Mrs. Ripley had written in a letter of May 6: "Mr. Burton does well and (entre nous) if he does not add to the charms of our social circle, does not interfere with them." He apparently rejoined the community later. See Manning Hawthorne, "Hawthorne and Utopian Socialism," p. 728 n.4.

West Roxbury, Aug 3ᵈ. 1841

Dear Louze,

I have been to Monument Point, about seven miles from Plymouth, for nearly a fortnight past, fishing and otherwise enjoying myself after the arduous labors of the summer.[1] I got back hither only this forenoon.

Furthermore, I have made an engagement with J. Munroe & Co. to write and edit a series of juvenile books, partly original and partly English books, to be adapted to our market. The first number is to be a new edition of Grandfather's Chair.[2] We expect to make a great deal of money. I wish Elizabeth would write a book for the series. She surely knows as much about children as I do, and ought to succeed as well. I do hope she will think of a subject—whether historical, scientific, moral, religious, or fanciful—and set to work. It will be a good amusement to her, and profitable to us all.

After the first of September, I shall cease laboring for my board, and begin to write. I doubt whether you see me before that period; but I intend then to pay you a visit of a week or two.[3] By the bye, you seem quite to have forgotten my existence. Why do you never write?

It is nearly milking time. Good bye.

Nath. Hawthorne.

Cannot your mother write a book?[4]

---

1. Louisa had written scolding letters on May 10 and June 11; she, Elizabeth, and Mrs. Hawthorne "do most seriously object to your staying away from home

so long." He had come home in late June, but only briefly. Louisa wrote on June 11: "I am sure it cannot be for your health to work from half-past four till seven, and I cannot bear to think that this hot sun is beating upon your head. . . What is the use of burning your brains out in the sun, when you can do anything better with them?" (MS, Berg). See James R. Mellow, *Nathaniel Hawthorne in His Times* (Boston: Houghton Mifflin, 1980), p. 185.

2. *Biographical Stories for Children*, published in April, 1842, but by Tappan and Dennet of Boston, not Munroe, was the only writing by NH resulting from this initiative.

3. He would leave formal membership in the Brook Farm community. During his later residence there, he would become a paying boarder (at $4 per week) with no obligation to work or teach. Compare *BR*, pp. 62, 140–41.

4. Louisa had last written, "Mother apostrophizes your picture [by Charles Osgood] because you do not come home." See Mellow, p. 186.

Brook Farm, Aug. 12th. 1841.

Dearest unutterably, Mrs. Ripley is going to Boston this morning, to Miss Slade's[1] wedding; so I sit down to write a word to thee, not knowing whither to direct it.[2] My heart searches for thee, but wanders about vaguely, and is strangely dissatisfied. Where art thou? I fear that thou didst spend yesterday in the unmitigated east-wind of the sea-coast. Perhaps thou art shivering, at this moment, and yearning for the warmth of thy husband's breast.

Dearest, I would that I were with thee. It seems as if all evil things had more power over thee, when I am away. Then thou art exposed to noxious winds, and to pestilence, and to deathlike weariness; and, moreover, nobody knows how to take care of thee but thy husband. Everybody else thinks it of importance that thou shouldst paint and sculpture; but it would be no trouble to me, if thou shouldst never touch clay or canvass again. It is not what thou dost, but what thou art, that I concern myself about. And if thy mighty works are to be wrought only by the anguish of thy head, and weariness of thy frame, and sinking of thy heart, then do I never desire to see another. And this should be the feeling of all thy friends. Especially ought it to be thine, for thy husband's sake.

Belovedest, I am very well, and not at all weary; for yesterday's rain gave us a holyday; and moreover the labors of the farm are not so pressing as they have been. And—joyful thought!—in a little more than a fortnight, thy husband will be free from his bondage—free to think of his Dove—free to enjoy Nature—free to think and feel! I do think that a greater weight will then be removed from me, than when Christian's burthen fell off at the foot of the cross.[3] Even my Custom House experience was not such a thraldom and weariness; my mind and heart were freer. Oh; belovedest, labor is the curse of this world, and nobody can meddle with it, without becoming proportionably brutified. Dost thou think it a praiseworthy matter, that I have spent five golden months in providing food for cows and horses? Dearest, it is not so. Thank God, my soul is not utterly buried under a dung-heap. I shall yet rescue it, somewhat defiled, to be sure, but not utterly unsusceptible of purification.

Farewell now, truest wife. It is time this letter were sealed. Love me; for I love thee infinitely, and pray for thee, and rejoice in thee, and am troubled for thee—for I know not where thou art, nor how thou dost.

Wilt thou accept a thousand of kisses?

Thine ownest.

1. Elizabeth Bromfield Slade, a sister of Ellen (see 196), and a member of Brook Farm, married Henry Schmidt, according to the Boston *Advertiser,* August 16 (2:3).

2. The letter was addressed in care of Daniel Newhall of Lynn, who was probably the father of Mary Bailey Newhall (b. 1818), SH's friend and former student.

3. See 160.1.

Brook Farm 16th. Aug. 1841 1/2 12 P.M.

Belovedest, Mrs. Ripley met me at the door, as I came
home from work, and told me that Mary was at Mrs. Park's,[1]
and that I might have an opportunity to send a message to
thee. Whether thou hast written I do not know. At all
events, Mrs. Ripley has not yet given me the letter; nor have
I had a chance to ask her what she has heard about thee;
such a number of troublesome and intrusive people are there
in this thronged household of ours. Dearest, if thou hast not
written, thou art very sick—one or the other is certain. That
wretched and foolish woman! Why could not she have put
the letter on my table, so that I might have been greeted by
it immediately on entering my room? She is not fit to live.

Dearest, I am very well; only somewhat tired with walking
half a dozen miles immediately after breakfast, and raking
hay ever since. We shall quite finish haying this week; and
then there will be no more very hard or constant labor, during the one other week that I shall remain a slave. Most
beloved, I received thy Lynn letter on Saturday, and thy
Boston letter yesterday. Then thou didst aver that thou wast
very well—but thou didst not call thyself magnificent. Why
art thou not magnificent? In thy former letter, thou sayest
that thou hast not been so well for two months past. Naughtiest wife, hast thou been unwell for two months?

Ownest, since writing the above, I have been to dinner;
and still Mrs. Ripley has given no sign of having a letter for
me; nor was it possible for me to ask her—nor do I know
when I can see her alone, to inquire about thee. Surely thou
canst not have let Mary come without a letter. And if thou

art sick, why did she come at all? Belovedest, the best way is always to send thy letters by the mail; and then I shall know where to find them.

Aug. 17th.— After breakfast.— Dearest, thou didst not write—that seems very evident. I have not, even yet, had an opportunity to ask Mrs. Ripley about thee; for she was gone out last evening; and when she came back, Miss Ripley[2] and another lady were with her. She mentioned, however, that thy sister Mary looked very bright and happy; so I suppose thou couldst not be very intensely and dangerously sick. I might have asked Mrs. Ripley how thou didst, even in the presence of those two women, but I have an inexpressible and unconquerable reluctance to speak of thee to almost anybody. It seems a sin. Well; I do not feel so apprehensive about thy health as I did yesterday; but, sweetest, if thou hadst sent some distinct message, even though not a letter, it would have saved thy husband some disquietude. Now farewell for the present. I do long to see thee, but know not how to get to thee. Dost thou love me at all? It is a great while since thou hast told me so.

Ownest wife, I meant to have finished my letter this afternoon, and to have sent it by William Allen in the morning; but I have just learnt that Mrs. Ripley is about to start for Boston; so I conclude suddenly. God bless thee, and make thee magnificent, and keep thee so forever and ever. I love thee. I love thee. Mine ownest. Do not write to me, if thou art not well.

1. Cornelia Hall "boarded for periods of varying length" at Brook Farm, where she assumed the nickname "Camilla" (Swift, p. 59). She used her maiden name (see 129) apparently because her husband Thomas Park had not returned from California and she had heard nothing from him. By the fall of 1842, she had divorced Park, and then lived at the Northampton community. See Mary Peabody to SH, [November?] 1842 (MS, Berg).

2. Marianne Ripley (d. 1868), George's sister, was in charge of the school,

called the Nest, where some of the teachers and pupils lodged. She was described by Georgianna Bruce Kirby, *Years of Experience: An Autobiographical Narrative* (New York: G. P. Putnam, 1887), p. 94, as "a lady between forty and fifty, tall, straight, large-featured; exact, formal, unattractive, but well-meaning and conscientious."

Brook Farm, Aug. 22^d. 1841.

Most dear wife, it seems a long time since I have written to thee. Dost thou love me at all? I should have been reprehensible in not writing, the last time Mr. and Mrs. Ripley went to town; but I had an indispensible engagement in the bean-field—whither, indeed, I was glad to betake myself, in order to escape a parting scene with poor Mr. Farley. He was quite out of his wits, the night before, and thy husband sat up with him till long past midnight. The farm is pleasanter now that he is gone; for his unappeasable wretchedness threw a gloom over everything. Since I last wrote to thee, we have done haying; and the remainder of my bondage will probably be light. It will be a long time, however, before I shall know how to make a good use of leisure, either as regards enjoyment or literary occupation.

Belovedest, my bosom yearns for thee. Methinks it is an age since thou hast been in my arms. When am I to see thee again? The first of September comes a week from Tuesday next; but I think I shall ante-date the month, and compel it to begin on Sunday. Wilt thou consent? Then, on Saturday afternoon, (for I will pray Mr. Ripley to give me up so much time, for the sake of my past diligence) I will come to thee, dearest wife, and remain in the city till Monday evening. Thence I shall go to Salem, and spend a week there, longer or shorter according to the intensity of the occasion for my presence. I do long to see our mother and sisters; and I should not wonder if they felt some slight desire to see me. I received a letter from Louisa, a week or two since, scolding me most pathetically for my long absence.[1] Indeed, I have been rather naughty in this respect; but I knew that it would be unsatisfactory to them and myself, if I came only for a single day—and that has been the longest space that I could command.

Dearest wife, it is extremely doubtful whether Mr. Ripley will succeed in locating his community on this farm. He can bring Mr. Ellis to no terms; and the more they talk about the matter, the farther they appear to be from a settlement.[2] Thou and I must form other plans for ourselves; for I can see few or no signs that Providence purposes to give us a home here. I am weary, weary, thrice weary of waiting so many ages. Yet what can be done? Whatever may be thy husband's gifts, he has not hitherto shown a single one that may avail to gather gold. I confess that I have strong hopes of good from this arrangement with Munroe;[3] but when I look at the scanty avails of my past literary efforts, I do not feel authorized to expect much from the future. Well; we shall see. Other persons have bought large estates and built splendid mansions with such little books as I mean to write; so perhaps it is not unreasonable to hope that mine may enable me to build a little cottage—or, at least, to buy or hire one. But I am becoming more and more convinced, that we must not lean upon the community. What ever is to be done, must be done by thy husband's own individual strength. Most beloved, I shall not remain here through the winter, unless with an absolute certainty that there will be a home ready for us in the spring. Otherwise I shall return to Boston,—still, however, considering myself an associate of the community; so that we may take advantage of any more favorable aspect of affairs. Dearest, how much depends on those little books! Methinks, if anything could draw out my whole strength, it should be the motives that now press upon me. Yet, after all, I must keep these considerations out of my mind, because an external pressure always disturbs, instead of assisting me.

Dearest, I have written the above in not so good spirits as sometimes; but now that I have so ungenerously thrown my despondency on thee, my heart begins to throb more lightly. I doubt not that God has great good in store for us; for He would not have given us so much, unless He were preparing to give a great deal more. I love thee! Thou lovest me! What present bliss! What sure and certain hope!

Thine ownest husband.

1. See *NHHW*, I, 234–35; Mellow, *Nathaniel Hawthorne in His Times*, pp. 185–86.

2. The purchase of the farm from Charles and Maria M. Ellis was made on October 11, 1841, according to the deed. See Swift, p. 19.

3. *Biographical Stories for Children*. NH was perhaps also thinking of the two-volume *TTT*, for which he was negotiating with Munroe. See 212 for his subsequent doubts of Munroe's probity.

Salem Sept 3^{d} 1841—4 °clock P.M.

Most beloved.— Thou dost not expect a letter from thy husband; and yet, perhaps, thou wilt not be absolutely displeased should one come to thee tomorrow. At all events, I feel moved to write; though the haze and sleepiness, which always settles upon me here, will certainly be perceptible in every line. But what a letter didst thou write to me! Thou lovest like a celestial being, (as truly thou art) and dost express thy love in heavenly language;—it is like one angel writing to another angel; but alas! the letter has miscarried, and has been delivered to a most unworthy mortal. Now wilt thou exclaim against thy husband's naughtiness! And truly he is very naughty. Well then; the letter was meant for him, and could not possibly belong to any other being, mortal or immortal. I will trust that thy idea of me is truer than my own consciousness of myself.

Dearest, I have been out only once, in the day time, since my arrival. How immediately and irrecoverably (if thou didst not keep me out of the abyss) should I relapse into the way of life in which I spent my youth! If it were not for my Dove, this present world would see no more of me forever. The sunshine would never fall on me, no more than on a ghost. Once in a while, people might discern my figure gliding stealthily through the dim evening—that would be all. I should be only a shadow of the night; it is thou that givest me reality, and makest all things real for me. If, in the interval since I quitted this lonely old chamber, I had found no woman (and thou wast the only possible one) to impart reality and significance to life, I should have come back hither ere now, with the feeling that all was a dream and a mockery. Dost thou rejoice that thou hast saved me from such a fate? Yes; it is a miracle worthy even of thee, to have converted a life of shadows into the deepest truth, by thy magic touch.

Belovedest, I have not yet made acquaintance with Miss Polly Metis. Mr. Foote was not in his office when I called there; so that my introduction to the erudite Polly was unavoidably deferred.[1] I went to the Athenaeum this forenoon, and turned over a good many dusty books. When we dwell together, I intend that my Dove shall do all the reading that may be necessary, in the concoction of my various histories; and she shall repeat the substance of her researches to me, when our heads are on the pillow. Thus will knowledge fall upon me like heavenly dew.

Sweetest, it seems very long already since I saw thee; but thou hast been all the time in my thoughts; so that my being has been continuous. Therefore, in one sense, it does not seem as if we had parted at all. But really I should judge it to be twenty years since I left Brook Farm; and I take this to be one proof that my life there was an unnatural and unsuitable, and therefore an unreal one. It already looks like a dream behind me. The real Me was never an associate of the community; there has been a spectral Appearance there, sounding the horn at day-break, and milking the cows, and hoeing potatoes, and raking hay, toiling and sweating in the sun, and doing me the honor to assume my name. But be not thou deceived, Dove of my heart. This Spectre was not thy husband.[2] Nevertheless, it is somewhat remarkable that thy husband's hands have, during this past summer, grown very brown and rough; insomuch that many people persist in believing that he, after all, was the aforesaid spectral horn-sounder, cow-milker, potatoe-hoer, and hay-raker. But such a people do not know a reality from a shadow.

Enough of nonsense. Belovedest, I know not exactly how

soon I shall return to the Farm. Perhaps not sooner than a fortnight from tomorrow; but, in that case, I shall pay thee an intermediate visit of one day. Wilt thou expect me on Friday or Saturday next, from ten to twelve °clock on each day,—not earlier nor later.

[*excision*]

1. A jesting private reference to a Salem lady known to Caleb Foote and to whom NH applied the epithet *polymetis*, "of many councils or devices," used by Homer to characterize Odysseus. Compare *AN*, p. 236: "Miss Polly Syllable—a schoolmistress."

2. Compare *BR*, pp. 145–46.

Salem, Septr 9th. 1841.—A.M.

Ownest love,

In my last letter, I left it uncertain whether I should come Friday or Saturday, because I deemed it good to allow myself the freedom of choosing the day that should be most vacant from all earthly care and inconvenience, so that thou mightest be sure to meet the whole of me; and, likewise, I desired to have a brightest and sunniest day, because our meetings have so often been in clouds and drizzle. Also, I thought it well that thy expectation of seeing thy husband should be diffused over two days, so that the disappointment might be lessened, if it were impossible for me to come on the very day appointed. But these reasons are of no moment, since thou so earnestly desirest to know exactly the day and hour.[1] Unless the sky fall, belovedest, I will come tomorrow. I know of no obstacle; and if there were a million, it would be no matter. When once we are together, our own world is round about us, and all things else cease to exist.

Belovedest, thy letter of a week from Thursday reached me not till Tuesday! It had got into the hands of the penny-post. Farewell, ownest. I love thee with infinite intensity, and think of thee continually, and desire thee as never before.

Thine ownest Husband.

1. Compare Matthew 24:35–36: "Heaven and earth shall pass away, but my words shall not pass away. But of that day and hour knoweth no man, no, not the angels of heaven, but my Father only."

Salem, September 14th. 1841—A.M.

Ownest beloved, I know not whether thou dost expect a letter from thy husband; but I have a comfortable faith that it will not be altogether unwelcome; so I boldly sit down to scribble. I love thee transcendantly; and nothing makes me more sensible of the fact, than that I write thee voluntary letters, without any external necessity. It is as if intense love should make a dumb man speak. (Alas! I hear a knocking at the door, and suspect that some untimely person is about to call me away from my Dove.)

Afternoon— Dearest, it was even as I suspected. How sad it is, that we cannot be sure of one moment's uninterrupted communication, even when we are talking together in that same old chamber, where I have spent so many quiet years! Well; thou must be content to lose some very sweet outpourings wherewith my heart would probably have covered the first, and perhaps the second, page of this sheet. The amount of all would have been, that I am somewhat partial to thee— and thou hast a suspicion of that fact, already.

Belovedest, Master Cheever is a very good subject for a sketch—especially if thou doest portray him in the very act of executing judgment on an evil-doer.[1] The little urchin may be laid across his knee, and his arms and legs (and whole person, indeed) should be flying all abroad, in an agony of nervous excitement and corporeal smart. The Master, on the other hand, must be calm, rigid, without anger or pity, the very personification of that immitigable law, whereby suffering follows sin. Meantime, the lion's head should have a sort of sly twist of one side of its mouth, and wink of one eye, in order to give the impression, that, after all, the crime and the punishment are neither of them the most serious things in the world. I would draw this sketch myself, if I had but the use of thy magic fingers. Why dost thou—being one and the same person with thy husband—unjustly keep those delicate little instruments (thy fingers, to wit) all to thyself?

Then, dearest, the Acadians will do very well for the second sketch. Wilt thou represent them as just landing on the wharf?—or as presenting themselves before Governor Shirley, seated in the great chair?[2] Another subject (if this do not altogether suit thee) might be old Cotton Mather, venerable in a three cornered hat and other antique attire, walking the streets of Boston, and lifting up his hands to bless the people, while they all revile him. An old dame should be seen flinging water or emptying some vials of medicine on his head, from the latticed window of an old-fashioned house; and all around must be tokens of pestilence and mourning—as a coffin borne along, a woman or children weeping on a door-step.[3] Canst thou paint the tolling of the Old South bell?

If thou likest not this subject, thou canst take the military council, holden at Boston by the Earl of Loudoun, and other captains and governors—his lordship in the great chair, an old-fashioned military figure, with a star on his breast.[4] Some of Louis XV's commanders will give thee the costume. On the table and scattered about the room must be symbols of warfare, swords, pistols, plumed hats, a drum, trumpet, and rolled up banner, in one heap. It were not amiss that thou introduce the armed figure of an Indian Chief, as taking part in the council—or standing apart from the English, erect and stern.

Now for Liberty-tree—there is an engraving of that famous vegetable in Snow's History of Boston;[5] but thou wilt draw a better one out of thine own head. If thou dost represent it, I see not what scene can be beneath it, save poor Mr. Oliver taking the oath.[6] Thou must represent him with a bag

wig, ruffled sleeves, embroidered coat, and all such ornaments, because he is the representative of aristocracy and
artificial system. The people may be as rough and wild as thy
sweetest fancy can make them;—nevertheless, there must be
one or two grave, puritanical figures in the midst. Such an
one might sit in the great chair, and be an emblem of that
stern, considerate spirit, which brought about the revolution.
But thou wilt find this a hard subject.

But what a dolt is thy husband, thus to obtrude his counsel
in the place of thine own inspiration! Belovedest, I want room
to tell thee how I love thee. Thou must not expect me till
Saturday afternoon. I yearn infinitely to see thee. Heaven
bless thee forever and forever.

Thine ownest.

1. *Famous Old People*, III; *TS*, p. 84. For the lion's head (carved on Grandfather's chair), see *TS*, p. 10.

2. *Famous Old People*, IX; *TS*, pp. 127–28.

3. *Famous Old People*, VI; *TS*, p. 103.

4. *Famous Old People*, XI; *TS*, pp. 136–37.

5. Caleb Hopkins Snow, *A History of Boston, the Metropolis of Massachusetts,
from its origin to the present period; with some account of the environs* (Boston: A.
Bowen, 1825). NH had borrowed it twice from the Salem Athenaeum, in 1827
and 1829 (Kesselring, p. 61). For its importance to NH, see Charles Ryskamp,
"The New England Sources of *The Scarlet Letter*," AL, XXXI (1959), 257–72;
and Robert C. Grayson, "The New England Sources of 'My Kinsman, Major
Molineux,'" AL, LIV (1982), 545–59.

6. *Liberty Tree*, III; *TS*, pp. 159–60.

Salem, Septr 16th. 1841—A.M.

Most dear wife, thou canst not imagine how strange it seems to me that thou shouldst ever suffer any bodily harm. I cannot conceive of it—the idea will not take the aspect of reality. Thou art to me a spirit gliding about our familiar paths; and I always feel as if thou wert beyond the reach of mortal accident—nor am I convinced to the contrary even by thy continual gashings of thy dearest fingers and sprainings of thy ancle. I love thee into the next state of existence, and therefore do not realize that thou art here as subject to corporeal harm as is thy husband himself—nay, ten times more so, because thy earthly manifestation is refined almost into spirit.

But, dearest, thy accident did make thy husband's heart flutter very riotously. I wanted to hold thee in mine arms; for I had a foolish notion that then thou wouldst be much better—perhaps quite well! I cannot tell thee all I felt; but still I had not the horrible feelings that I should expect, because there was a shadowiness interposed between me and the fact, so that it did not strike my heart, as the beam did thy head. Let me not speak of it any more, lest it become too real.

Sweetest, thou dost please me much by criticizing thy husband's stories, and finding fault with them. I do not very well recollect Monsieur du Miroir; but as to Mrs. Bullfrog, I give her up to thy severest reprehension.[1] The story was written as a mere experiment in that style; it did not come from any depth within me—neither my heart nor mind had anything to do with it. I recollect that the Man of Adamant[2] seemed a fine idea to me, when I looked at it prophetically; but I failed in giving shape and substance to the vision which I saw. I don't think it can be very good.

Ownest wife, I cannot believe all these stories about Munroe, because such an abominable rascal never would be sustained and countenanced by respectable men. I take him to be neither better nor worse than the average of his tribe. However, I intend to have all my copy-rights taken out in my own name;[3] and if he cheats me once, I will have nothing more to do with him, but will straightway be cheated by some other publisher—that being, of course, the only alternative.

Dearest love, what dost thou think of taking Governor Shirley's young French wife as the subject of one of the cuts.[4] Thou shouldst represent her in the great chair, perhaps with a dressing glass before her, and arrayed in all manner of fantastic finery, and with an outré French air; while the old Governor is leaning fondly over her, and a Puritanic counsellor or two are manifesting their disgust, in the back ground. A negro footman and French waiting maid might be in attendance. Do not think that I expect thee to adopt my foolish fancies about these things. Whatever thou mayst do, it will be better than I can think. In Liberty Tree, thou mightest have a vignette, representing the chair in a very shattered, battered, and forlorn condition, after it had been ejected from Hutchinson's house.[5] This would serve to impress the reader with the woeful vicissitude of sublunary things. Many other subjects could thy husband suggest, but he is terribly afraid that thou wouldst take one of them, instead of working out thine own inspirations.

Belovedest, I long to see thee. Do be magnificently well by Saturday—yet not on my account, but thine own. Meantime, take care of thy dearest head. Thou art not fit to be trusted away from thy husband's guidance, one moment.

Dear little wife, didst thou ever behold such an awful

scribble as thy husband writes, since he became a farmer? His chirography always was abominable; but now it is outrageous.

God bless thee, dearest, and may His hand be continually outstretched over thy head. Expect me on Saturday afternoon.

Thine ownest husband.

1. Two tales published anonymously by NH in the *Token* for 1837, pp. 49–64, 66–75. NH was apparently considering them for the new, second edition of *TTT*. They were, however, not collected until *MOM*, 1846. For the deletions SH provoked (concerning "pot-houses," "even more disreputable haunts," and habits of worship) from "Monsieur du Miroir," see Arlin Turner, "A Note on Hawthorne's Revisions," *Modern Language Notes*, LI (1936), 426–28; *MOM*, pp. 518, 633–34. That "The New Adam and Eve," one of the first tales NH wrote at the Old Manse, is "an act of penance" to SH for the cynical view of marriage in "Mrs. Bullfrog," is suggested by John M. Solensten, "Hawthorne's Ribald Classic: 'Mrs. Bullfrog' and the Folktale," *Journal of Popular Culture*, VII (1973), 587.

2. Also published anonymously in the 1837 *Token*, pp. 119–28. Collected in *SI*. See *TTT*, "Historical Commentary," p. 521.

3. NH held copyright in the second edition of *TTT*, 1842, but the American Stationers' Company retained rights to the first edition.

4. *Famous Old People*, IX; *TS*, p. 123.

5. *Liberty Tree*, IV; *TS*, p. 161.

Brook Farm, Septr 22^d 1841—P.M.

Dearest love, here is thy husband again, slowly adapting himself to the life of this queer community, whence he seems to have been absent half a life time—so utterly has he grown apart from the spirit and manners of the place.[1] Thou knowest not how much I wanted thee, to give me a home-feeling in the spot—to keep a feeling of coldness and strangeness from creeping into my heart and making me shiver. Nevertheless, I was most kindly received; and the fields and woods looked very pleasant, in the bright sunshine of the day before yesterday. I had a friendlier disposition towards the farm, now that I am no longer obliged to toil in its stubborn furrows. Yesterday and to-day, however, the weather has been intolerable—cold, chill, sullen, so that it is impossible to be on kindly terms with mother Nature. Would I were with thee, mine own warmest and truest-hearted wife! I never shiver, while encircled in thine arms.

Belovedest, I doubt whether I shall succeed in writing another volume of Grandfather's Library,[2] while I remain at the farm. I have not the sense of perfect seclusion, which has always been essential to my power of producing anything. It is true, nobody intrudes into my room; but still I cannot be quiet. Nothing here is settled—everything is but beginning to arrange itself—and though thy husband would seem to have little to do with aught beside his own thoughts, still he cannot but partake of the ferment around him. My mind will not be abstracted. I must observe, and think, and feel, and content myself with catching glimpses of things which may be wrought out hereafter. Perhaps it will be quite as well that I find myself unable to set seriously about literary occupation for the present. It will be good to have a longer interval between my labor of the body and that of the mind. I shall work to the better purpose, after the beginning of November.[3] Meantime, I shall see these people and their enterprise under a new point of view, and perhaps be able to determine whether thou and I have any call to cast in our lot among them.

Sweetest, our letters have not yet been brought from the Post Office; so that I have known nothing of thee since our parting kiss. Surely we were very happy—and never had I so much peace and joy as in brooding over thine image, as thou wast revealed to me in our last interview. I love thee with all the heart I have—and more. Now farewell, most dear. Mrs. Ripley is to be the bearer of this letter; and I reserve the last page for tomorrow morning. Perhaps I shall have a blessed word from thee, ere then.

Septr 23^d— Before breakfast— Sweetest wife, thou hast not written to me. Nevertheless, I do not conclude thee to be sick, but will believe that thou hast been busy in creating Laura Bridgman.[4] What a faithful and attentive husband thou hast! For once he has anticipated thee in writing.

Belovedest, I do wish the weather would put off this sulky mood. Had it not been for the warmth and brightness of Monday, when I arrived here, I should have supposed that all sunshine had left Brook Farm forever. I have no disposition to take long walks, in such a state of the sky; nor have I any buoyancy of spirit. Thy husband is a very dull person, just at this time. I suspect he wants thee. It is his purpose, I believe, either to walk or ride to Boston, about the end of next week, and give thee a kiss—after which he will return quietly and contentedly to the farm. Oh what joy, when he will again see thee every day!

We had some tableaux last night.[5] They were very stupid, (as, indeed, was the case with all I have ever seen) but do not thou tell Mrs. Ripley so. She is a good woman, and I like her better than I did—her husband keeps his old place in my judgment. Farewell, thou gentlest Dove—thou perfectest woman—thou desirablest wife.

Thine ownest Husband.

1. See 202A.3.

2. *Biographical Stories for Children,* to be published April 12, 1842, in Boston by Tappan and Dennet. See *TS,* pp. 294–95.

3. Apparently the time NH had set for departure from Brook Farm.

4. A bust, about eighteen inches high, of Laura Dewey Bridgman (1829–89), a remarkable blind deaf-mute, from 1837 the pupil of Samuel Gridley Howe at the Perkins Institution in Boston. She became the first person with her disabilities to be successfully educated. See *DAB.* By the following autumn Elizabeth Peabody was trying unsuccessfully to persuade NH to write a memoir of Laura (see Mary Peabody to SH, October [5?], 1842; MS, Berg).

5. Compare *BR,* p. 106.

Brook Farm, Septr 25th. 1841.—1/2 past 7.A.M.

Ownest Dove, it was but just now that I thought of sending thee a few lines by Mr. Ripley; for this penning of epistles is but a wretched resource, when I want thee on my very bosom. What shall I do? What shall I do? To talk to thee in this way does not bring thee nearer; it only compels me to separate myself from thee, and put thee at a distance. Of all humbugs, pretending to alleviate mortal woes, writing is the greatest.

Yet thy two letters were a great comfort to me—so great, that they could not possibly have been dispensed with. Dearest, I did not write thee what Mr. and Mrs. Ripley said to me, because they have said nothing which I did not know before. The ground, upon which I must judge of the expediency of our abiding here, is not what they may say, but what actually is, or is likely to be; and of this I doubt whether either of them is capable of forming a correct opinion. Would that thou couldst be here—or could have been here all summer—in order to help me think what is to be done. But one thing is certain—I cannot and will not spend the winter here. The time would be absolutely thrown away, so far as regards any literary labor to be performed,—and then to suffer this famished yearning for thee, all winter long! It is impossible.

Dearest, do not thou wear thyself out with working upon that bust. If it cause thee so much as a single head-ache, I shall wish that Laura Bridgman were at Jericho.[1] Even if thou shouldst not feel thyself wearied at the time, I fear that the whole burthen of toil will fall upon thee when all is accomplished. It is no matter if Laura should go home without being sculptured—no matter if she goes to her grave without it. I dread to have thee feel an outward necessity for such a task; for this intrusion of an outward necessity into labors of the imagination and intellect is, to me, very painful.

Oh, what weather! It seems to me as if every place were sunny, save Brook Farm. Nevertheless, I had rather a pleasant walk to a distant meadow, a day or two ago; and we found white and purple grapes, in great abundance, ripe, and gushing with rich juice when the hand pressed their clusters.[2] Didst thou know what treasures of wild grapes there are in this land. If we dwell here, we will make our own wine—of which, I know, my Dove will want a great quantity.

Good bye, sweetest. If thou canst contrive to send me a glimpse of sunshine, I will be the gratefullest husband on earth. I love thee inextinguishably. Thou hast no place to put all the love that I feel for thee.

Thine ownest husband.

1. In hell (Partridge, *Dictionary of Slang*).
2. Compare *BR*, p. 208.

Brook Farm, Septr 27th. 1841 7 1/2 A.M.

Dearest love,

Thy two letters of business came both together, Saturday evening! What an acute and energetic personage is my little Dove! I say it not in jest (though with a smile) but in good earnest, and with a comfortable purpose to commit all my business transactions to thee, when we dwell together. And why dost thou seem to apprehend that thou mayst possibly offend me. Thou canst do so never, but only make me love thee more and more.

Now as to this affair with Munroe. I fully confide in thy opinion that he intends to make an unequal bargain with thy poor simple and innocent husband—never having doubted this, myself. But how is he to accomplish it? I am not, nor shall be, in the least degree in his power; whereas, he is, to a certain extent, in mine. He might announce his projected library, with me for the editor, in all the newspapers in the universe; but still I could not be bound to become the editor, unless by my own act; nor should I have the slightest scruple in refusing to be so, at the last moment, if he persisted in treating me with injustice. Then, as for his printing Grand-father's Chair, I have the copyright in my own hands, and could and would prevent the sale, or make him account to me for the profits, in case of need. Meantime, he is making arrangement for publishing this library, contracting with other booksellers, and with printers and engravers, and, with every step, making it more difficult for himself to draw back. I, on the other hand, do nothing which I should not do, if the affair with Munroe were at an end; for if I write a book,[1] it will be just as available for some other publisher as for him. My dearest, instead of getting me within his power by this delay, he has trusted to my ignorance and simplicity, and has put *himself* in *my* power. Show the contrary, if thou canst.

He is not insensible of this. At our last interview, he himself introduced the subject of the bargain, and appeared desirous to close it. But thy husband was not prepared, among other reasons, because I do not yet see what materials I shall have for the republications in the library; the works that he had shown me being ill-adapted for that purpose; and I wish first to see some French and German books, which he has sent for to New York. And, belovedest, before concluding the bargain, I have promised George Hillard to consult him and let him do the business. Is not this consummate discretion? And is not thy husband perfectly safe? Then why does my Dove put herself into a fever? Rather, let her look at the matter with the same perfect composure that I do, who see all round my own position, and know that it is impregnable.

Most sweet wife, I cannot write thee any more at present, as Mr. Ripley is going away instantaneously; but we will talk at large on Saturday, when God means to send me to thy arms. I love thee infinitely, and admire thee beyond measure, and trust thee in all things, and will never transact any business without consulting thee—though on some rare occasions, it may happen that I will have my own way, after all. I feel inclined to break off this engagement with Munroe, as thou advisest, though not for precisely the reasons thou urgest; but of this hereafter.

Thy most own husband.

1. *Biographical Stories.*

Brook Farm, Septr 29th. [30] 1841.—A.M.

Ownest wife, I love thee most exceedingly—never so much before; though I am sure I have loved thee through a past eternity. How dost thou do? Dost thou remember that, the day after tomorrow, thou art to meet thy husband? Does thy heart thrill at the thought?

Dearest love, thy husband was elected to two high offices, last night—viz., to be a Trustee of the Brook Farm estate, and Chairman of the Committee of Finance!!!!^{1} Now dost thou not blush to have formed so much lower an opinion of my business talents, than is entertained by other discerning people? From the nature of my office, I shall have the chief direction of all the money affairs of the community—the making of bargains—the supervision of receipts and expenditures &c. &c &c. Thou didst not think of this, when thou didst pronounce me unfit to make a bargain with that petty knave of a publisher. A prophet has no honor among them of his own kindred,^{2} nor a financier in the judgment of his wife.

Belovedest, my accession to these august offices does not at all decide the question of my remaining here permanently. I told Mr. Ripley, that I could not spend the winter at the farm, and that it was quite uncertain whether I returned in the spring.

Now, farewell, most dear and sweet wife. Of course, thou canst not expect that a man in eminent public station will have much time to devote to correspondence with a Dove. I will remember thee in the intervals of business, and love thee in all my leisure moments. Will not this satisfy thee?

God bless thee, mine ownest—my treasure—thou gold and

diamond of my soul!—my only desirablest—my possession forever—my enough and to spare, yet never, never to be spared! Sweetest, if it should be very stormy on Saturday, expect me not—but the first fair day thereafter.

I put all my love into one kiss, and have twice as much left as before.

Thy truest husband.

1. "At a meeting of the Brook Farm Institute of Agriculture and Education, held on Wednesday, September 29, 1841, the following persons were appointed to office as follows: . . . *Direction of Finance*. Nath. Hawthorne." At this meeting NH purchased two shares, worth $1,000, and became one of four trustees elected annually by the subscribers to hold their property. See O. B. Frothingham, *George Ripley* (Boston: Houghton, Mifflin, 1883), pp. 112–17; rpt. Sams, *Autobiography of Brook Farm*, pp. 44–47. NH's investment, later a matter of controversy, was intended, Ripley wrote, "toward building one of our houses, which was undertaken & planned with a view to his living in it himself" (George Ripley to R. H. Dana, Jr., December 8, 1845; MS, MHS).

2. Matthew 13:57. See 252.

[Boston] 54 Pinckney St. 12 °clock A.M. Monday.
[October 4, 1841?]

Truest Heart,

I cannot come to thee this evening, because my friend Bridge is in town, whom I hardly have seen for years past.[1] Alas! I know not whether I am a very faithful friend to him; for I cannot rejoice that he is here, since it will keep me from my Dove. Thou art my only reality—all other people are but shadows to me; all events and actions, in which thou dost not mingle, are but dreams.

Do thou be good, dearest love, and when I come, tomorrow night, let me find thee magnificent. Thou didst make me very happy, yesterday forenoon—thou wast a south-west wind— or the sweetest and wholesomest wind that blows, whichever it may be. I love thee more than I can estimate; and last night I dreamed of thee. I know not exactly what; but we were happy.

God bless thee,
Thine ownest husband,
Theodore de L'Aubepine.[2]

A Madame,
Madame Sophie Amelie de L'Aubepine,
Rue d'Ouest,
à Boston.

---

1. In *Recollections*, pp. 84–85, Bridge mentions seeing NH both at Brook Farm and in Boston during NH's residence at the farm.

2. An adaptation of two pseudonyms NH had already used (see 125, 158). "Theodore" is the "soft and pretty name (such as we, of the literary sisterhood, invariably bestow upon our heroes)" of "Zenobia's Legend"; see *BR*, p. 109. After Julian was born in June, 1846, SH apparently proposed that he be named Theodore, but NH "does not like it, & it is rather hard to pronounce" (SH to her mother, February 5, 1847; MS, Berg).

Brook Farm, Octr 9th.— Before breakfast [1841]

Most dear,

Here is thy husband trying to write to thee, while it is so dark that he can hardly see his own scribble—not that it is very early; for the sun is up long ago, and ought to be shining into my window. But this dismal gloom! I positively cannot submit to have this precious month all darkened with cloud and sullied with drizzle.

Dearest, I return the manuscript tale. It is pretty enough; but I doubt whether it be particularly suited to the American public; and, if intended for publication, I trust it will undergo a *very* severe revision. It will need it. I speak frankly about this matter; but I should do the same (only more frankly still) if the translation were my Dove's own.[1]

I wonder whether Munroe has yet returned Grandfather's Chair to Elizabeth.[2] I send back his books to-day.[3]

Belovedest, I think thou wilt see me in the latter half of next week. Thou needest not to give up any visit to South Boston on this account; for I cannot get to thee before twelve °clock. It will be but an hour or so's visit.

Thine with deepest and keenest love,
Theodore De L'Aubepine

1. Possibly a translation by SH's mother, who at this time was translating Goethe's *Hermann und Dorothea*.

2. Munroe did not publish *Grandfather's Chair*; in December a new edition was published by Tappan & Dennet.

3. The French and German books mentioned in 212. Whatever Munroe's plans for a "library" (see 212), he seems to have abandoned the idea of NH's editorship by this time. On October 11 the author and publisher signed an agreement for the publication in two volumes of "one edition not exceeding fifteen hundred copies" of *TTT*, for which NH was to receive a 10% royalty of the price, $2.25. See *TTT*, "Historical Commentary," pp. 520–23; *TS*, "Historical Introduction," p. 294; *TTT*, "Bibliographical Information," p. 552.

Brook Farm, October 18th [16]. Saturday. [1841]

Most dear wife, I received thy letters and note, last night, and was much gladdened by them; for never has my soul so yearned for thee as now. But, belovedest, my spirit is moved to talk with thee to-day about these magnetic miracles, and to beseech thee to take no part in them.[1] I am unwilling that a power should be exercised on thee, of which we know neither the origin nor consequence, and the phenomena of which seem rather calculated to bewilder us, than to teach us any truths about the present or future state of being. If I possessed such a power over thee, I should not dare to exercise it; nor can I consent to its being exercised by another. Supposing that this power arises from the transfusion of one spirit into another, it seems to me that the sacredness of an individual is violated by it; there would be an intrusion into thy holy of holies—and the intruder would not be thy husband! Canst thou think, without a shrinking of thy soul, of any human being coming into closer communion with thee than I may?—than either nature or my own sense of right would permit me? *I* cannot. And, dearest, thou must remember, too, that thou art now a part of me, and that by surrendering thyself to the influence of this magnetic lady, thou surrenderest more than thine own moral and spiritual being—allowing that the influence *is* a moral and spiritual one. And, sweetest, I really do not like the idea of being brought, through thy medium, into such an intimate relation with Mrs. Park![2]

Now, ownest wife, I have no faith whatever that people

are raised to the seventh heaven, or to any heaven at all, or
that they gain any insight into the mysteries of life beyond
death, by means of this strange science. Without distrusting
that the phenomena which thou tellest me of, and others as
remarkable, have really occurred, I think that they are to be
accounted for as the result of a physical and material, not of
a spiritual, influence. *Opium* has produced many a brighter
vision of heaven (and just as susceptible of proof) than those
which thou recountest. They are dreams, my love—and such
dreams as thy sweetest fancy, either waking or sleeping,
could vastly improve upon. And what delusion can be more
lamentable and mischievous, than to mistake the physical
and material for the spiritual? What so miserable as to lose
the soul's true, though hidden, knowledge and consciousness
of heaven, in the mist of an earth-born vision? Thou shalt
not do this. If thou wouldst know what heaven is, before
thou comest thither hand in hand with thy husband, then
retire into the depths of thine own spirit, and thou wilt find
it there among holy thoughts and feelings; but do not degrade
high Heaven and its inhabitants into any such symbols and
forms as those which Miss Larned[3] describes—do not let an
earthy effluence from Mrs. Park's corporeal system bewilder
thee, and perhaps contaminate something spiritual and sacred. I should as soon think of seeking revelations of the
future state in the rottenness of the grave—where so many
do seek it.

Belovedest wife, I am sensible that these arguments of
mine may appear to have little real weight; indeed, what I
write does no sort of justice to what I think. But I care the
less for this, because I know that my deep and earnest feeling
upon the subject will weigh more with thee than all the
arguments in the world. And thou wilt know that the view
which I take of this matter is caused by no want of faith in
mysteries, but from a deep reverence of the soul, and of the

mysteries which it knows within itself, but never transmits to the earthly eye or ear. Keep thy imagination sane—that is one of the truest conditions of communion with Heaven.

Dearest, after these grave considerations, it seems hardly worth while to submit a merely external one; but as it occurs to me, I will write it. I cannot think, without invincible repugnance, of thy holy name being bruited abroad in connection with these magnetic phenomena. Some (horrible thought!) would pronounce my Dove an impostor; the great majority would deem thee crazed; and even the few believers would feel a sort of interest in thee, which it would be anything but pleasant to excite. And what adequate motive can there be for exposing thyself to all this misconception? Thou wilt say, perhaps, that thy visions and experiences would never be known. But Miss Larned's are known to all who choose to listen. Thy sister Elizabeth would like nothing so much as to proclaim thy spiritual experiences, by sound of trumpet.

October 19th [18]. Monday.—Most beloved, what a preachment have I made to thee! I love thee, I love thee, I love thee, most infinitely. Love is the true magnetism. What carest thou for any other? Belovedest, it is probable that thou wilt see thy husband tomorrow. Art thou magnificent. God bless thee. What a bright day is here, but the woods are fading now. It is time I were in the city, for the winter.

Thine ownest.

1. See Taylor Stoehr, *Hawthorne's Mad Scientists: Pseudoscience and Social Science in Nineteenth-Century Life and Letters* (Hamden, Conn.: Archon, 1978), pp. 41–46, for an analysis of this letter and its relation to *BR*, esp. chapter 23, "A Village-Hall."

2. Mrs. Park, "Cornelia Hall," as she was known at Brook Farm, "used to give

remarkable dramatic readings, which attracted attention from the outside world" (Swift, p. 59; see Kirby, *Years of Experience*, pp. 144–45). According to Kirby, p. 161, "Cornelia H. had found that she possessed the genuine magnetic power. . . . Cornelia had the greatest desire to induce clairvoyance in me, believing that in that state I should see denizens of the other world; and since I had a passion for analyzing character, could describe them so accurately that they would be recognized by their friends."

3. Georgianna Bruce Kirby said that Cornelia used her magnetic power "with entire success in the case of a young friend who was supposed to be far gone in consumption. With her superb physique she could afford to dispense a little vitality. The young lady slept peacefully for any desired length of time, gained recuperative strength from her friend, and recovered her health perfectly" (*Years of Experience*, p. 161). SH's letters of 1839 mention several times a Mr. Larned, a friend of Cornelia Hall Park. On one occasion, when he was "one of the party" with NH, SH and Mary Peabody, Mary wrote to her brother George that the atmosphere was therefore "not quite so cosey as it would otherwise have been" (October 27, 1839; MS, Berg).

Brook Farm, October 21st. 1841.—Noon.

Ownest beloved, I know thou dost not care in the least about receiving a word from thy husband—thou lovest me not—in fact thou has quite forgotten that such a person exists. I do love thee so much, that I really think all the love is on my side;—there is no room for any more in the whole universe.

Sweetest, I have nothing at all to say to thee—nothing, I mean, that regards this external world; and as to matters of the heart and soul, they are not to be written about. What atrocious weather! In all this month, we have not had a single truly October day; it has been a real November month, and of the most disagreeable kind. I came to this place in one snow-storm, and shall probably leave it in another; so that my reminiscences of Brook Farm are like to be the coldest and dreariest imaginable. But next month, thou, belovedest, will be my sunshine and my summer. No matter what weather it may be then.

Dearest, good bye. Dost thou love me, after all? Art thou magnificently well? God bless thee. Thou didst make me infinitely happiest, at our last meeting. Was it a pleasant season likewise to thee?

Thine Ownest,
Theodore de l'Aubepine

[Boston] 54 Pinckney St. Monday 11 °clock A.M.
[November 1, 1841]

Most dear love,

I have been caught by a personage who has been in search
of me for two or three days, and shall be compelled to devote
this unfortunate evening to him, instead of to my Dove. Dost
thou regret it?—so does thy poor husband, who loves thee
infinitely, and needs thee continually. Art thou well to-day,
very dearest? How naughty was I, last night, to contend
against thy magnetic influence, and turn it against thyself! I
will not do so again. My head has been in pain for thine—at
least my heart has. Thou wast very sweet and lovely, last
night;—so art thou always.

Belovedest, thou knowest not how I yearn for thee—how I
long and pray for the time when we may be together without
disturbance—when absence shall be a rare exception to our
daily life. My heart will blossom like a rose,[1] when it can be
always under thy daily influence—when the dew of thy love
will be falling upon it, every moment.

Most sweet, lest I should not be able to avoid another
engagement for tomorrow evening, I think it best for me to
come in the afternoon—shortly after two °clock, on Tuesday.
Canst thou devote so much of thy precious day to my unworthiness? Unless I hear from thee, I shall come. I love thee. I
love thee.

Dearest I kiss thee with my whole spirit.

Thy Husband,
Theodore de l'Aubepine

1. Isaiah 35:1: "The desert shall rejoice, and blossom as the rose."

Boston, Nov[r] 15th. 1841.

Dear Sir,

I have but just received your note. Messrs. Munroe & Co. have a second edition of Twice-told Tales in press, and likewise another volume.[2]

Respectfully Yrs,
Nath. Hawthorne.

Jno. R. Willis, Esqr.

1. Unidentified.
2. The second edition of the first volume, and a new collection making up the second volume in its first edition.

Salem, Novr 27th. 1841.

Dearest soul,

I know not whether thou wilt have premonitions of a letter from thy husband; but I feel absolutely constrained to write thee a few lines this morning, before I go up in town. I love thee—I love thee—and I have no real existence but in thee. Never before did my bosom so yearn for the want of thee— so thrill at the thought of thee. Thou art a mighty enchantress, my little Dove, and hast quite subdued a strong man, who deemed himself independent of all the world. I am a captive under thy little foot, and look to thee for life. Stoop down and kiss me—or I die!

Dearest, I am intolerably weary of this old town; and I would that my visits might not be oftener than once in ten years, instead of a fortnight. Dost thou not think it really the most hateful place in all the world? My mind becomes heavy and nerveless, the moment I set my foot within its precincts. Nothing makes me wonder more than that I found it possible to write all my tales in this same region of sleepy-head and stupidity. But I suppose the characteristics of the place are reproduced in the tales; and that accounts for the overpowering disposition to slumber which so many people experience, in reading thy husband's productions.

Belovedest, according to thy instructions, I have been very careful in respect to mince-pies and other thanksgiving-dainties; and so have passed pretty well through the perils of the Carnival season. Thou art a dearest little wife, and I would live on bread and water to please thee, even if such temperate regimen should produce no other good. But truly thou art very wise in thy dietetic rules; and it is well that I have such a wife to take care of me; inasmuch as I am accustomed to eat whatever is given me, with an appetite as indiscriminate, though not quite so enormous, as that of an ostrich. Setting aside fat pork, I refuse no other Christian meat.

Dearest, I write of nothing; for I had nothing to write when I began, save to make thee aware that I loved thee infinitely; and now that thou knowest it, there is no need of saying a word more. On Monday evening, please God, I shall see thee. How could I have borne it, if thy visit to Ida Russel[1] were to commence before my return to thine arms!

God bless thee, mine ownest.

Thy truest husband.

---

1. Ida Russell (1818–55), daughter of Jonathan (1771–1832) and Lydia Smith Russell (1789–1859), of Milton, Massachusetts. Her father had been a diplomat during the War of 1812, and was later a congressman. She was a cousin of Richard Henry Dana, Jr., and a friend of Herman Melville. She was to be at Brook Farm with her half-sister Amelia (b. 1798, who wrote a memoir of the community for the *Atlantic* in 1878) during the summers of 1842–44. See Curtis, *A Season in Utopia*, pp. 103, 147, 204.

[Boston] 54 Pinckney St.
Dec[r] 6th, 1841.

My dear Sir,

I ought before now to have made my acknowledgements for the Magazine, which you were kind enough to send me. I have read it with great pleasure, and like it very much indeed, both as to its external and material aspect, and its intellectual and spiritual being. I hope it will succeed, and see no cause to doubt it.

As I have returned to Boston for the winter, I should be glad to see you here; and beg that (if you feel inclined to call) you will not await the ceremony of an introduction.

Respectfully Yours,
Nath. Hawthorne.

Nathan Hale, Jr. Esqr.

---

1. Hale (1818–71), son of the editor of the Boston *Daily Advertiser*, had undertaken to publish the *Boston Miscellany of Literature and Fashion*. The first issue, which he had sent to NH, was dated January, 1842. A favorable review of the 1842 *TTT* was to appear in the February issue, and NH's signed sketch, "A Virtuoso's Collection," was to lead the May number.

Boston, Decr 22^d, 1841.
54 Pinckney St.

Gentlemen,

Your letter of the 16th. inst. has reached me only to-day. For about six months past, I have been meditating a letter to Arcturus, expressive of my very deep gratitude for the article in the May number,[1] and likewise for several other kind words, each and all of which are treasured up as among the most valuable recompenses of my literary toils. You would have heard from me long ago; but during the summer, my fingers were so stiff with exercising the hoe and other agricultural tools, that positively I could not write legibly. Latterly, I have deferred my letter of thanks, until I could accompany it with a new volume of Twice-told Tales, which Mr. Munroe has in press.

I do not think it possible that any praise can be in store for me, which will give me so much pleasure as your article about my writings. Perhaps it would be decorous in me to decline some considerable part of the approbation there bestowed, as being quite beyond my deserts; but I cannot find in my heart to do it. It is true, the public will never ratify it; but at least, the writer felt what he expressed; and therefore I have a right to receive it as genuine testimony to the impression which I have produced. And, certainly, I would far rather receive earnest praise from a single individual, than to be deemed a tolerably pleasant writer by a thousand, or a million.

I have mentioned that Mr. Munroe has a new volume of my tales in press—and also a second edition of the former volume. I fear, therefore, that the tales will not be of any value to you, as they will be offered to the public in another form. They are at your disposal. Several (which, for aught I know, are as good as the rest) will be left out of the new collection[2]. In the Token for 1832 are some of the first stories which I wrote—"The Wives of the Dead"—"Major Molineux"—"Roger Malvin's Burial."—in that for 1833, "The Canterbury Pilgrims"—for 1837, "the Man of Adamant," and "Monsieur du Miroir"—for 1838, "Sylph Etherege." In the New England Magazine is "Young Goodman Brown."[3] I have burnt whole quires of manuscript stories, in past times—which, if I had them now, should be at your service. I do not believe that I shall ever write any more—at least, not like my past productions; for they grew out of the quietude and seclusion of my former life; and there is little probability that I shall ever be so quiet and secluded again. During the last three or four years, the world has sucked me within its vortex; and I could not get back to my solitude again, even if I would.

I shall not expect to be remunerated for any use that you may make of my articles. It would give me great pleasure to see them in a Magazine which I like so much as Arcturus— I will not say how much I like it, because I cannot praise you gracefully, after you have praised me so much.

If either of you should visit Boston this winter, it would make me very happy to see you. Mr. Duyckinck and myself are already personally known to each other;[4] and I wish I could say the same of Mr. Mathews.[5]

Very truly Yours,
Nath. Hawthorne.

1. *Arcturus,* I (May, 1841), 330–37, by Evert Duyckinck. See Faust, pp. 38–40; *Critical Heritage,* pp. 74–78.

2. Duyckinck's *Arcturus* reprinted four pieces by NH, only the first of which was collected in the 1842 *TTT*: in January, 1842, "The Old Maid in the Winding-Sheet" ("The White Old Maid"); in February, "The Man of Adamant"; in March, "The Canterbury Pilgrims"; and in April, "Sir William Pepperell." In April, apparently responding to NH's statement here, Duyckinck wrote of the newly published second volume of *TTT*, "to these, the series we are at present publishing in Arcturus, will, we trust, be added and form a third" (III, 394). The April number was the last of *Arcturus* to be published.

3. "Young Goodman Brown," in the *New-England Magazine* in 1835, was collected in *MOM*, 1846, as were "Monsieur du Miroir" and "Roger Malvin's Burial" (which was reprinted in the *Democratic Review* in 1843). On Duyckinck's subsequent notice of "Young Goodman Brown," see Introduction. The five other stories were not collected until *SI*, 1851.

4. NH had met Duyckinck, with his brother George (1823–63) and friend James William Beekman (1815–77), when they visited Salem in June and July, 1838, after receiving a letter of introduction from Longfellow. NH had shown them around, including the Town Pump, Witches' House, Gallows Hill, and East India Museum. See Leland Schubert, "A Boy's Journal of a Trip into New England in 1838," *EIHC*, LXXXVI (1950), 97–105; Longfellow, *Letters*, II, 84.

5. Cornelius Mathews (1817–89), a New York lawyer who had turned early to literary production and editorial work, founded and edited *Arcturus* with Evert Duyckinck. NH apparently did not meet him until August, 1850, at David Dudley Field's memorable picnic in Stockbridge (see *AN*, p. 295).

[Boston, January 1842]

Gentlemen,

I cannot, at this moment, think of all the Editors to whom it may be advisable to send copies.[1] The Editors of all the Salem papers will notice it favorably.[2] I should like to have one sent to Arcturus; and to the Democratic Review. Also, to the Dial—and to the Magazines generally.[3] The Editor of the Nantucket Islander will do the needful for it, in that quarter.[4]

I leave it for you to decide, as to the rest.

I should like to have a copy transmitted to Rev. Andrew Peabody of Portsmouth.[5]

Yours truly,
Nath. Hawthorne.

Mr. Brownson, of the Boston Quarterly, should have a copy.[6]

1. Review copies of the two-volume edition of *TTT*, first advertised for sale in the Boston newspapers on January 13.

2. The Salem *Gazette* of January 25 noticed the publication of "a third edition of 'Twice-Told Tales,'" and quoted extensively from "Fancy's Show Box."

3. An unsigned review by Evert Duyckinck appeared in *Arcturus*, III (April, 1842), 394; an unsigned review, probably by J. L. O'Sullivan, in *Democratic Review*, X (February, 1842), 197–98; and an unsigned review by Margaret Fuller, in *Dial*, III (July, 1842), 130–31, followed by a brief notice of *Biographical Stories for Children*. Other reviewers included Hillard in *North American Review*,

Edgar Allan Poe in *Graham's Magazine,* and Lewis Gaylord Clark in *Knickerbocker Magazine;* see Faust, pp. 40–48, 148–49.

4. Charles Creighton Hazewell (1814–83) edited the *Islander,* a Democratic paper, 1840–43. He had been a printer and editor of the Boston *Advocate* and *Post.* In 1852 NH was to write to Franklin Pierce that he was not personally acquainted with Hazewell. See 548.

5. Andrew Preston Peabody, who had favorably reviewed *TTT* in 1837. See 88.5.

6. Orestes Brownson's review, in the *Boston Quarterly Review,* V (April, 1842), 251–52, is reprinted in part in *Critical Heritage,* pp. 86–87.

Boston, Jany 17th 1842.

My dear Sir,

I shall be in Salem on Wednesday or Thursday; and then, if convenient to you, I should like to receive the remainder of your note. The amount now due is $500.[1]

Very truly Yours,
Nath. Hawthorne.

Hon. C. Foote,
Salem.

1. Presumably the remainder of a loan that NH made during his employment at the Boston Custom House.

Salem, Jany 20th, 1842—11 °clock A.M.

Truest Heart,

Here is thy husband in his old chamber, where he produced those stupendous works of fiction, which have since
impressed the Universe with wonderment and awe! To this
chamber, doubtless, in all succeeding ages, pilgrims will
come to pay their tribute of reverence;—they will put off
their shoes at the threshold, for fear of desecrating the tattered old carpet. "There," they will exclaim, "is the very bed
in which he slumbered, and where he was visited by those
ethereal visions, which he afterwards fixed forever in glowing
words! There is the wash-stand, at which this exalted personage cleansed himself from the stains of earth, and rendered his outward man a fitting exponent of the pure soul
within. There, in its mahogany frame, is the dressing-glass,
which often reflected that noble brow, those hyacinthine
locks, that mouth, bright with smiles, or tremulous with
feeling, that flashing or melting eye, that—in short, every
item of the magnanimous phiz of this unexampled man!
There is the pine table—there the old flag-bottomed chair—
in which he sat, and at which he scribbled, during his agon-
ies of inspiration! There is the old chest of drawers, in which
he kept what shirts a poor author may be supposed to have
possessed! There is the closet, in which was reposited his
threadbare suit of black! There is the worn-out shoe-brush
with which this polished writer polished his boots. There
is—" but I believe this will be pretty much all;—so here I
close the catalogue.[1]

Most dear, I love thee beyond all limits, and write to thee

because I cannot help it;—nevertheless writing grows more and more an inadequate and unsatisfactory mode of revealing myself to thee. I no longer think of saying anything deep, because I feel that the deepest and truest must remain unsaid. We have left expression—at least, such expression as can be achieved with pen and ink—far behind us. Even the spoken word has long been inadequate. Looks—pressures of the lips and hands, and the touch of bosom to bosom—these are a better language; but, bye-and-bye, our spirits will demand some more adequate expression even than these. And thus it will go on; until we shall be divested of these earthly forms, which are at once our medium of expression, and the impediments to full communion. Then we shall melt into another, and all be expressed, once and continually, without a word—without an effort.

Belovedest, my cold is very comfortable now. Mrs. Hillard gave me some homo—I don't know how to spell it—homeopathic medicine, of which I took a dose last night; and shall not need another. Art thou likewise well? Didst thou weary thy poor little self to death, yesterday? I do not think that I could possibly undergo the fatigue and distraction of mind which thou dost. Thou art ten times as powerful as I, because thou art so much more etherereal.[2]

Sweetest, thy husband has recently been both lectured about and preached about, here in his native city. The preacher was Rev. Mr. Fox of Newburyport; but how he contrived to hook me into a sermon, I know not.[3] I trust he took for his text that which was spoken of my namesake of old—"Behold an Israelite indeed, in whom there is no guile."[4] Belovedest, if ever thou shouldst happen to hear me lauded on any public occasion, I shall expect thee to rise, and make thine own and my acknowledgments, in a neat and appropriate speech. Wilt thou not? Surely thou wilt—inasmuch as I care little for applause, save as it shall please thee; so it is rather thy concern than mine.

Mine ownest, it is by no means comfortable to be separated from thee three whole days at a time. It is too great a gap in life. There is no sunshine in the days in which thou dost not shine on me. And speaking of sunshine, what a beautifullest day (to the outward eye, I mean) was yesterday; and to-day seems equally bright and *gladsome,* although I have not yet tasted the fresh air. I trust that thou hast flown abroad, and soared upward to the seventh heaven. But do not stay there, sweetest Dove! Come back for me; for I shall never get there, unless by the aid of thy wings.

Now God bless thee, and make thee happy and joyful, until Saturday evening, when thou must needs bear the infliction of

Thine ownest Husband.

1. This seems a parody of the travel writing exemplified by Nathaniel Parker Willis's account of his visit to Sir Walter Scott's Abbotsford in *Pencillings by the Way* (1835), Letter CXXXVII: "It really is a pity that this sacred place, with its thousand valuable and irreplaceable curiosities, should be so carelessly neglected. . . . Why does not *Scotland* buy Abbotsford, and secure to herself, while it is still perfect, the home of her great magician, and the spot that to after ages would be, if preserved in its curious details, the most interesting in Great Britain? After showing us the principal rooms, the woman opened a small closet adjoining the study, in which hung the last clothes that Sir Walter had worn. There was the broad-skirted blue coat with large buttons, the plaid trousers, the heavy shoes, the broad-rimmed hat and stout walking-stick. . . . There was a character in the hat and shoes. The coat was an honest and hearty coat. The stout, rough walking-stick, seemed as if it could have belonged to no other man. . . . " Compare NH's own comment on how "almost all forms of popular superstition do clothe the ethereal with earthly attributes" on his first visit to Abbotsford in 1856 (*EN*, p. 342). NH's description of his "magnanimous phiz" here resembles that of the Master Genius in "A Select Party" (1844; *MOM,* p. 65–66).

2. NH's invention to combine "ethereal" and "real."

3. Thomas Bayley Fox (1808–76), pastor of the First Religious Society (Congregational) of Newburyport, 1831–46. No account of the sermon is given in Salem newspapers.

4. John 1:47. See 79.1.

Boston, Jan[y] 23[d], 1842.

Gentlemen,

I thank you for the honor conferred on me by your invitation to the dinner, to be given to Mr. Dickens; and shall have great pleasure in complying with it.[2]

Very Respectfully Yours,
Nath. Hawthorne.

George Tyler Bigelow ⎫
Nathan Hale, Jr.   ⎪
J. F. Barrett,   ⎬ Esqr.
F. W. Crocker,   ⎪
W. W. Story   ⎭

1. The recipients were the invitation committee of the "Young Men of Boston." Bigelow (1810–78) became judge of the Massachusetts Court of Common Pleas, 1847–50, justice of the Massachusetts Supreme Court, 1850–60, and chief justice, 1860–68. For Hale, see 221.1. Jonathan Fay Barrett (1817–85), from Concord, was a counsellor at 20 Court Street, and Frederick W. Crocker was partner of a bookshop at 107 Washington Street. William Wetmore Story (1819–95) was a member of George Hillard's law firm (see also 468).

2. It is doubtful that NH attended the dinner at Papanti's Hall on February 1, where Dickens made an earnest argument for international copyright agreements. NH's friend and landlord George Hillard was a vice-president of the event. See William Glyde Wilkins, *Charles Dickens in America* (New York: Charles Scribner's Sons, 1911), pp. 19–87.

[Boston] 54 Pinckney St. Feb^r 19th. 1842

Mr. Hawthorne has been somewhat misunderstood.[1] He did not mean to say, that Messrs. Tappan and Dennet affirmed that they had offered to take the remnant of the books at any particular price.[2] He did understand, however, that they had entered, or proposed to enter, into a negotiation upon the subject; and as no such transfer of the books took place, he naturally supposed that it was because Miss Peabody did not think fit to accede to their terms. Mr. Hawthorne will seek an explanation with Messrs. Tappan and Dennet on this matter; and it will depend upon the result of that explanation, whether he will feel himself justified in attempting to *force* the books upon those gentlemen.

If Mr. Hawthorne had felt himself solely, or chiefly, interested, he would have advised the sale of the first edition of these books, long since, at any price that could have been obtained for them. But, as he hoped that Miss Peabody would see the justice, to both parties, of taking to herself the publisher's share of the profits, he did not feel himself authorized to speak so strongly as he otherwise might. He *now* recommends that they should be got rid of on *any* terms.

Mr. Hawthorne will take the liberty to communicate to Miss Peabody anything that it may be necessary for her to know, in regard to his explanation with Messrs. Tappan and Dennet.

1. At the foot is an endorsement by Elizabeth Peabody: "The above formal letter was written during a very temporary quarrel there was between us because

I did not want to take my percentage on Grandfathers Chair. [¶] It was before he became my brother in law."

2. Elizabeth had been unable to dispose of the first editions of NH's three biographical books for children to James Munroe & Co.; see 199. She apparently also failed to make similar arrangements with the new publishers of these books, Tappan & Dennet. When she reorganized her business in the spring of 1842, planning to let her office on Washington Street, she advertised "remnants of *Famous Old People* and *Liberty Tree*, first editions at 1/2 price" (Boston *Advertiser*, April 7, 3:5). She still held 250 or more copies of *Liberty Tree* when *TS* (containing *Liberty Tree*) was published by Ticknor in 1851. Margaret Corliss wrote to her on April 24, 1851, of the Philadelphia bookseller W. P. Hazards' reluctance to sell them in conflict with Ticknor's interest (MS, Virginia). The remainder was finally bought for an unknown sum by George Briggs and put on sale at the Liberty Tree Bookstore, Boston. See *TS*, "Historical Introduction," p. 295, and "Textual Introduction," p. 321.

Salem, Feby 27th. 1842—Forenoon.

Thou dearest Heart,

As it is uncertain whether I shall return to Boston tomorrow, I write thee a letter; for I need to commune with thee; and even if I should bring the scroll of my thoughts and feelings with me, perhaps thou wilt not refuse to receive it. It is awful, almost (and yet I would not have it otherwise, for the world) to feel how necessary thou hast become to my well-being, and how my spirit is disturbed at a separation from thee, and stretches itself out through the dimness and distance to embrace its other self. Thou art my quiet and satisfaction—not only my chiefest joy, but the condition of all other enjoyments. When thou art away, vague fears and misgivings sometimes steal upon me; there are heart-quakes and spirit-sinkings for no real cause, and which never trouble me when thou art pressed close to my breast.

Belovedest, I have thought much of thy parting injunction to tell my mother and sisters that thou art her daughter and their sister. I do not think thou canst estimate what a difficult task thou didst propose to me—not that any awful and tremendous effect would be produced by the disclosure; but because of the strange reserve, in regard to matters of feeling, that has always existed among us. We are conscious of one another's feelings, always; but there seems to be a tacit law, that our deepest heart-concernments are not to be spoken of. I cannot gush out in their presence—I cannot take my heart in my hand, and show it to them. There is a feeling within me (though I know it is a foolish one) as if it would be as indecorous to do so, as to display to them the naked breast, on which God is well pleased that thou shouldst lay thy head. And they are in the same state as myself. None, I think, but delicate and sensitive persons could have got into such a position; but doubtless this incapacity of free communion, in the hour of especial need, is meant by Providence as a retribution for something wrong in our early intercourse.

Then it is so hard to speak of thee—*really* of thee—to any body! I doubt whether I ever have *really* spoken of thee, to any person. I have spoken the name of Sophia, it is true; but the idea in my mind was apart from thee—it embraced nothing of thine inner and essential self; it was an outward and faintly-traced shadow that I summoned up, to perform thy part, and which I placed in the midst of thy circumstances; so that thy sister Mary, or Mrs. Ripley, or even Margaret,[1] were deceived, and fancied that I was talking about thee. But there didst thou lie, thy real self, in my deepest, deepest heart, while far above, at the surface, this distant image of thee was the subject of talk. And it was not without an effort which few are capable of making, that I could even do so much; and even then I felt as if it were profane. Yet I spoke to persons from whom, if from any, I might expect true sympathy in regard to thee.

I tell thee these things, in order that my Dove, into whose infinite depths the sunshine falls continually, may perceive what a cloudy veil stretches over the abyss of my nature. Thou wilt not think that it is caprice or stubbornness that has made me hitherto resist thy wishes. Neither, I think, is it a love of secrecy and darkness. I am glad to think that God sees through my heart; and if any angel has power to penetrate into it, he is welcome to know everything that is there. Yes; and so may any mortal, who is capable of full sympathy, and therefore worthy to come into my depths. But he must find his own way there. I can neither guide him nor enlighten him. It is this involuntary reserve, I suppose, that has given the objectivity to my writings. And when people think that I am pouring myself out in a tale or essay, I am merely telling what is common to human nature, not what is peculiar to myself. I sympathize with them—not they with me.[2]

Feb^r 28th— Forenoon.—Sweetest, thou shalt have this letter instead of thy husband, to-night. Dost thou love me? I shall not find any letter from thee at the Post Office, because thou dost expect to hear my footstep on thy staircase, at six °clock this evening. Oh, but another day will quickly pass; and then this yearning of the soul will be appeased, for a little while at least. I wonder, I wonder, I wonder, where on earth we are to set up our Tabernacle. God knows;—but I want to know too.

Dearest love, I am very well, and comfortable as I desire to be, in thy absence. After all, it is a happiness to need thee, to sigh for thee, to feel the nothingness of all things without thee. But do not thou think so—thou must be happy always, not independently of thy husband, but with a bliss equally pervading presence and absence.

Belovedest, I have employed much of my time here in collecting curiosities, and have so many on my hands that I begin to fear it will require a volume to contain the catalogue.[3] I would we had such a museum in reality. And now good-bye, most true Heart. Methinks this is the longest letter that I have written thee for a great while. Shalt thou expect me to write during my journey to New York?[4]—or, were it not better to allow thee to forget me entirely, during that interval of a week? God bless thee, thou unforgettablest and unforgettingest.

Thine ownest husband.

1. Fuller.
2. Compare *MOM*, pp. 32–33.

3. Material for "A Virtuoso's Collection"; see 233. The idea for the catalogue came from NH's visits to a Salem museum; see Charles E. Goodspeed, "Nathaniel Hawthorne and the Museum of the East India Marine Society," *American Neptune*, V (1945), 266–85.

4. See 231.

Boston, March 2[d]. 1842

My dear Sir:

I have read your "Summer Hours" with great pleasure. The pieces entitled the "Poet's Pilgrimage," and an "Evening in the City," struck me particularly; but I find that I like each article as I read it.

It gratifies me to know that I am indebted, for this beautiful little book, to the interest which you so kindly express in my own writings. Please to accept my best thanks, and believe me

Very truly yours,
Nath. Hawthorne.

Charles Lanman, Esqr.,
Norwich.

1. (1819–95), a writer, artist and amateur explorer, Park Benjamin's cousin, published *Essays for Summer Hours* with Hilliard and Gray in Boston in 1841, the first of his more than thirty books. In his autobiography, *Haphazard Personalities; Chiefly of Noted Americans* (Boston: Lee & Shepard, 1886), p. 28, he wrote that he had sent copies of his "maiden volume" to "the men of my literary idolatry . . . Hawthorne (then without fame), Dana, and Longfellow." See *DAB*.

New-York, March 4th. 1842.

Dearest, I can find only this torn sheet of paper, on which to scribble thee a bulletin. We arrived safely; but I am very homesick for thee—otherwise well and in good spirits. I love thee infinitely much. Belovedest, I know not whether the Colonel[1] and I will leave this city on Monday or Tuesday; but if thou hast not already written, it will be too late to direct a letter hither. In that case, best wife, write to Albany— whence I shall write to thee. The steam-engine kept me awake last night; but I cared not, for I was thinking about thee.

I am exceedingly well.

Dost thou love me.

Thine ownest Husband.

1. Joseph Hall, NH's co-worker in the Boston Custom House.

Albany, March 10th. 1842.

Mine own Heart, I arrived here early this morning, by the Steam-boat; and thou mayst be well assured that I lost no time in going to the Post-Office; and never did ever a letter from thee so thrill my heart as this. There is no expressing what I feel; and so I will not try—especially now, when I am compelled to write in a bar-room, with people talking an l drinking around me. But I love thee a thousand infinities more than ever.

Most dear, I have come hither to see Mr. O'Sullivan,[1] with whom I have relations of business as well as friendship, all which thou shalt know, if thou thinkest them worth enquiring about. The good colonel is with me; but is going about a hundred miles into the interior, tomorrow. In the meantime I shall remain here; but thou wilt see me again on Tuesday evening. How is it possible to wait so long. It is not possible— yet I have much to talk of with O'Sullivan; and this will be the longest absence that we shall be compelled to endure, before the time when thou shalt be the companion of all my journeys.

Truest wife, it is possible that the cars may not arrive in Boston till late in the evening; but I have good hope to be with thee by six °clock, or a little after, on Tuesday. God bless us.

Thine ownest.

---

1. John L. O'Sullivan was elected to the New York legislature for 1841–42. He had resumed editorship of the *Democratic Review* with the July, 1841, number, after withdrawing at the end of 1839 to practice law in New York.

[Boston] 54 Pinckney St.
March 12th [13]—Sunday. [1842]

My Life,

I have come back to thee! Thy heart gives thee no warning
of my presence; yet I am here—embracing thee with all the
might of my soul. Ah, forgetful Dove! How is it that thou
hast had no spiritual intelligence of my advent? I am sure
that if yearnings and strivings could have brought my spirit
into communion with thine, thou wouldst have felt me
within thy bosom.

Thou truest Heart, thou art conscious of me, as much as
a heavenly spirit can be, through the veil of mortality. Thou
hast not forgotten me for a moment. I have felt thee drawing
me towards thee, when I was hundreds of miles away. The
farther I went, the more was I conscious of both our loves. I
cannot write how much I love thee, and what deepest trust I
have in thee.

Dearest, expect me at six °clock this afternoon. I have not
the watch, as thou knowest; and so it may be a few moments
before or after six. Oh, I need thee this very, very moment—
my heart throbs—and so does my hand, as thou mayst see by
this scribble. God bless thee! I am very well.

Thine ownest husband.

[Boston] 54 Pinckney St. March 28th. [1842]

Dear Sir,

I hand you an article[1] for your Magazine—very absurd, to be sure; but perhaps somewhat amusing. Should you deem it too long, or otherwise unfit for your purpose, I shall be entirely willing to receive it back. Pray do not hesitate to return it, if so inclined.

I should be glad to look over the proof-sheets myself.

Yours truly,
Nath. Hawthorne.

1. "A Virtuoso's Collection," *Boston Miscellany,* I (May, 1842), 193–200. See 228.3.

Salem, Wednesday, April 6th. 1842.

My Dear,

It was thy husband's intention to spend all his leisure time, here at home, in sketching out a tale; but my spirit demands communion with thine so earnestly, that I must needs write to thee, if all the affairs in the world were pressing upon me at once. My breast is full of thee; thou art throbbing throughout all my veins. Never, it seems to me, did I know what love was, before. And yet I am not satisfied to let that sentence pass; for it would do wrong to the blissful and holy time that we have already enjoyed together. But our hearts are new-created for one another, daily; and they enter upon existence with such up-springing rapture as if nothing had ever existed before—as if, at this very *now*, the physical and spiritual world were but just discovered, and by ourselves only. This is Eternity—thus will every moment of forever-and-ever be the first moment of life, and no weariness can gather upon us from the past.

[*excision*] It is a bliss which I never wish to enjoy, when I can attain that of thy presence; but it is nevertheless a fact, that there is a bliss even in being absent from thee. This yearning that disturbs my very breath—this earnest stretching out of my soul towards thee—this voice of my heart, calling for thee out of its depths, and complaining that thou art not instantly given to it—all these are a joy; for they make me know how entirely our beings have blended into one another. After all, these pangs are but symptoms of the completeness of our spiritual union—the effort of the outward to respond to the inward. Dearest, I do not express myself clearly on this matter; but what need?—wilt not thou know better what I mean than words could tell thee? Dost not thou too rejoice in everything that gives thee a more vivid consciousness that we are one?—even if it have somewhat like pain in it. The desire of my soul is to know thee continually, and to know that thou art mine; and absence, as well as presence, gives me this knowledge—and as long as I have it, I live. It is, indeed, impossible for us ever to be really absent from one another; the only absence, for those who love, is estrangement or forgetfulness—and we can never know what those words mean. Oh, dear me, my mind writes nonsense, because it is an insufficient interpreter for my heart.

Sweetest love, I did not think of writing thee more [*excision verso*] here we are, beyond the mid-[*excision verso*] to Adam and Eve in their [*excision verso*]

Most beloved, I am thinking at this moment of thy dearest nose! Thou canst not think how infinitely better I know and love Sophie Hawthorne, since, in moments of our deepest tenderness, she has yielded up that fortress. And, in requital, I yield my whole self up to her, and kiss her beloved foot, and acknowledge her for my queen and liege-lady forever more. Come into my heart, dearest; for I am about to close my letter. Hitherto, I have kept thee at arms' length; because the very act of writing necessarily supposes that thou art apart from me; but now I throw down the pen, in order that thou mayst be the closer to me.

Thine ownest Husband,
Nath. Hawthorne.

[Boston] 54 Pinckney St.—May 16th. [1842]

Mr. Hawthorne regrets that he cannot have the pleasure of calling on Miss Quincy, during the present week. He is under the necessity of going to Concord to-day,[2] and has made arrangements to spend the remainder of the week in Salem. He hopes, however, to return the manuscripts with which Miss Quincy favored him, very soon, and (since she is kind enough to desire it) in person.

Miss Quincy will please to accept his thanks for the memoir of her celebrated ancestor.[3]

1. Eliza Susan Quincy (1798–1884), daughter of Josiah Quincy (1772–1864), president of Harvard. For her early journal, see M. A. DeWolfe Howe, *The Articulate Sisters* (Cambridge: Harvard University Press, 1946), pp. 9–46.

2. NH and SH had gone to Concord on Saturday, May 7, "to look at Dr [Ezra] Ripley's house with a view to rent it" (Emerson, *Letters*, III, 52). On May 11 SH wrote to Margaret Fuller that they had decided, the day before, to do so (MS, Harvard).

3. Presumably her "Memoir of Edmund Quincy (1681–1738) of Braintree, Massachusetts bay," which was published after her death in the *New England Historical and Genealogical Register*, April, 1884.

[Boston] 54 Pinckney St. May 19th. [1842]

My Dearest,

Mr. Hillard, this morning, put into my hands the enclosed paragraph from the Philadelphia Saturday Courier.[1] It is to be hoped that the penny papers of this city will copy an item of so much public importance.

Canst thou tell me whether the "Miss Peabody," here mentioned, is Miss Mary, or Miss Elizabeth Peabody?

Thine ownest.

P.S. Please to present my congratulations to the "accomplished Miss Peabody." But I shall call, this evening, and present them in person.

---

1. Unidentified. This paper had recently reprinted NH's "The Shaker Bridal," and poems by Park Benjamin and James Russell Lowell.

237. TO DAVID MACK, NORTHAMPTON

Boston, May 25th, 1842.

My dear Sir,

When I last met you, I expressed my purpose of coming to Northampton, in the course of the present month, in order to gain information as to the situation and prospects of your community.[1] Since our interview, however, circumstances of various kinds have induced me to give up the design of offering myself as a member. As a matter of conscience, with my present impressions, I should hardly feel myself justified in taking such a step; for, though I have much faith in the general good tendency of institutions on this principle, yet I am troubled with many doubts (after my experience of last year) whether I, as an individual, am a proper subject for those beneficial influences. In an economical point of view, undoubtedly, I could not do so well anywhere else; but I feel that this ought not to be the primary consideration. A more important question is, how my intellectual and moral condition, and my ability to be useful, would be affected by merging myself in a community. I confess to you, my dear Sir, it is my present belief that I can best attain the higher ends of life, by retaining the ordinary relation to society.

With my best wishes for your prosperity and happiness,

I remain Yours sincerely,
Nath. Hawthorne.

1. They "last met" apparently well after NH's departure from Brook Farm; there is no such interest in the Northampton community in 202. Mack, with his

wife and two children, had joined the Northampton Association of Education and Industry in May, the community having begun operation on April 8. He was to be president briefly in 1843, and then secretary and director of the educational department. By September 1845 the strain of his many responsibilities broke Mack's health; he withdrew and returned to Belmont, Mass. See McBee, *From Utopia to Florence* (cited 202.1), Appendix C, pp. 24, 46, 53, 63.

[Boston] 54 Pinckney St. May 27th. 1842

Dearest Heart,

Thy letter to my sisters was most beautiful—sweet, gentle, and magnanimous; such as no angel, save my Dove, could have written.[1] If they do not love thee, it must be because they have no hearts to love with;—and even if this were the case, I should not despair of thy planting the seeds of hearts in their bosoms. They will love thee, all in good time, dearest; and we will be very happy. I am so, at this moment, while my breast heaves with the consciousness of what a treasure God has given me—in whom I see more to worship, and admire, and love, every day of my life; and shall see more and more as long as I live; else, it will be because my own nature retrogrades, instead of advancing. But thou wilt make me better and better, till I am even worthy to be thy husband.

Oh, truest wife, what a long widowhood is this! Three evenings without a glimpse of thee! And I know not whether I am to come at six or seven °clock tomorrow evening—or scarcely, indeed, whether I am to come at all. But, unless thou orderest me to the contrary, I shall [*obliteration*] at seven °clock.

I saw Mr. Emerson at the Athenaeum, yesterday. He tells me that our garden, &c, makes fine progress. Would that we were there. God bless us.

Thine ownest.

1. SH's letter has not been recovered. Elizabeth Hawthorne had written on May 23: "My dear Sophia, [¶] Your approaching union with my brother makes it

incumbent upon me to offer you the assurances of my sincere desire for your mutual happiness. With regard to my sister and myself, I hope nothing will ever occur to render your future intercourse with us other than agreeable, particularly as it need not be so frequent or so close as to require more than reciprocal good will, if we do not happen to suit each other in our new relationship. I write thus plainly, because my brother has desired me to say only what was true; though I do not recognise his right to speak of truth, after keeping us so long in ignorance of this affair. But I believe him when he says that this was not in accordance with your wishes, for such concealment must naturally be unpleasant, and besides, what I know of your amiable disposition convinces me that you would not give us unnecessary pain. It was especially due to my mother that she should long ago have been made acquainted with the engagement of her only son; it is much more difficult to inform her of it at this late period, with but a few weeks to prepare her feelings for his marriage. [¶] I anticipate with pleasure the renewal of our acquaintance, with the opportunity of becoming better known to each other. In the meantime, accept my best wishes, with those of my sister, for the continuance of your health, and the accomplishment of your hopes of happiness, and believe me to be / yours, / with regard, / E. M. Hawthorne" (MS, Berg). After receiving SH's letter, Elizabeth responded, on June 15: "My dear Sophia, [¶] I am sorry to be so soon obliged to begin a note to you with an apology; but so it must be,—for not immediately replying to your very kind letter. Indeed, a *note* in itself requires an apology; it ought to be an epistle of proper form and length; but I have an aversion to letter-writing which I trust you will take into consideration upon this and all future occasions. [¶] We are all very desirous of seeing you, dear Sophia, but my brother gives us no hopes of enjoying that pleasure at present. My mother desires me to beg that you will both visit us this summer, even if you cannot come before your marriage. I dare say we shall, and must seem very cold and even apathetic to you; but after you have known us a little while it may be that you will discover more warmth and sympathy than is at first apparent. My mother, indeed, in disposition resembles her son; and you need not doubt that she is prepared to receive and love you as a daughter. Neither are my sister and myself wanting in that sisterly affection to which we feel that you are entitled, and which it will be a source of great happiness to us to find returned. I deeply regret that I said any thing in my note to give you pain; if w ; can all forget the past, and look forward to the future, it will be better. The future seems to promise much of happiness to you, for certainly I think your disposition and my brother's well suited to each other; but have you no dread of the cares and vexations inevitable in married life, and in *all* life, I allow, only in some situations we have in a great degree the power to withdraw from and forget them? I confess I should not have courage to incur any responsibility not forced upon me by circumstances beyond my control. I should not like to feel as if much depended upon me. In this however, I am aware how much I differ from almost every one else, and how strange it must appear to you, especially just now. And this reminds me of the innumerable engagements that must press upon you and so occupy your time that you can have no more to spare for me; so I will no longer detain you. My mother and sister send their love to you, and I am / yours affectionately / E. M. Hawthorne" (MS, Berg).

Salem, June 9th, 1842.—Afternoon.

Dearest Wife,

I love thee beyond all hope of expression—so do thou measure it by thine own love for me; if indeed thou canst continue to love me, after our kiss-less parting. But never did I love thee better than then; and I am even glad that this vapor of tobacco smoke did, for once, roll thus darkly and densely between us, because it helps me to hate the practice forevermore. Thou wast very sweet not to scold me fiercely, for allowing myself to be so impregnated.

Sweetest, scarcely had I arrived here, when our mother came out of her chamber, looking better and more cheerful than I have seen her this some time, and enquired about the health and well-being of my Dove! Very kindly, too. Then was thy husband's heart much lightened; for I know that almost every agitating circumstance of her life had hitherto cost her a fit of sickness; and I knew not but it might be so now. Foolish me, to doubt that my mother's love would be wise, like all other genuine love! And foolish again, to have doubted my Dove's instinct—whom, henceforth—(if never before)—I take for my unerring guide and counsellor in all matters of the heart and soul. Yet if, sometimes, I should perversely follow mine own follies, do not thou be discouraged. I shall always acknowledge thy superior wisdom in the end; and, I trust, not too late for it to exert its good influence. Now I am very happy—happier than my naughtiness deserves. It seems that our mother had seen how things were, a long time ago. At first, her heart was troubled, because she knew that much of outward as well as inward fitness was requisite to secure thy foolish husband's peace; but, gradually and quietly, God has taught her that all is good; and so, thou dearest wife, we shall have her fullest blessing and concurrence. My sisters, too, begin to sympathize as they ought; and all is well. God be praised! I thank Him on my knees, and pray him to make me worthy of thee, and of the happiness thou bringest me.

Mine ownest, I long for thee, yet bear our separation patiently, because time and space, and all other finite obstructions, are so fast flitting away from between us. We can already measure the interval by days and hours. What bliss!—and what awe is intermingled with it!—no fear nor doubt, but a holy awe, as when an immortal spirit is drawing near to the gate of Heaven. I cannot tell what I feel; but thou knowest it all.

Sweetest, it is my purpose to remain here till Friday, when, unless thou forbiddest me, I shall be with thee at seven °clock. God bless thee! I have no more words, but a heart full of love.

Thine ownest husband.

Salem, June 20th, 1842.—A.M. 11°clock.

True and Honorable Wife,

Thou hast not been out of my mind a moment since I saw thee last,—and never wilt thou be, so long as we exist. Canst thou say as much? Dearest, dost thou know that there are but ten days more in this blessed month of June? And dost thou remember what is to happen within those ten days? Poor little Dove! Now dost thou tremble, and shrink back, and beginnest to fear that thou hast acted too rashly in this matter. Now dost thou say to thyself—"Oh, that I could prevail upon this wretched person to allow me a month or two longer to make up my mind; for, after all, he is but an acquaintance of yesterday; and unwise am I, to give up father, mother, and sisters, for the sake of such a questionable stranger!" Ah, foolish virgin! It is too late; nothing can part us now; for God Himself hath ordained that we shall be one. So nothing remains, but to reconcile thyself to thy destiny. Year by year, thou must come closer and closer to me; and a thousand ages hence, we shall be only in the honeymoon of our marriage. Poor little Dove!

Sweetest wife, I cannot write to thee. The time for that species of communion is past. Hereafter, I cannot write my feelings, but only external things, business, facts, details, matters which do not relate to the heart and soul, but merely to our earthly condition. I have long had such a feeling, whenever I took up my pen—and now more than ever.

Would that I knew when the priest is to thrust himself between us![1] Dearest, the last day of the month, if I mistake not, is Thursday of next week. Unless thou desirest my presence sooner, I shall return to Boston probably on Sunday evening. Then will the days lag heavily, till we can flee away and be at rest. And, I pray thee, let our flight be in the morning; for it would be strange and wearisome to live half a day of ordinary life, at such an epoch. I should be like a body walking about the city without a soul—being therein the reverse of good old Dr. Harris,[2] whose soul walks about without the body. And this reminds me, that he has not made himself visible of late. Foolish me, not to have accosted him; for perhaps he wished to give us some good advice on our entrance into connubial life—or possibly, he intended to disclose the hiding-place of some ancient hoard of gold, which would have freed us forever from all pecuniary cares. I think we shall not need his counsel on the former point; but on the latter, it would have been peculiarly acceptable.[3]

Ownest, would there be anything amiss in exchanging that copy of Southey's Poems for some other book?[4] We should still have Campbell's English Poets[5] as an immediate keepsake from Miss Burley;[6] and whatever book we might procure would be none the less a gift from her. My copy of Southey went to the Manse with my furniture; else I should have brought it hither, and given it to Elizabeth—who, however, does not especially admire Southey.

Now good bye, dearest love. I fear thou wilt make thyself sick with much care and toil. God bless thee! Our mother and sisters would send their love, if they knew that I am writing to thee. They love thee, and link us together in their thoughts. God bless them, and us, and everybody. Dost thou perceive how love widens my heart?

Thine ownest husband.

1. SH wrote to Margaret Fuller on May 11, "We shall be married in June, the month of roses & of perfect bloom" (MS, Harvard), and to Mary Wilder Foote on

June 19, "The ceremony is nothing, our true marriage was three years ago" (MS, Berg).

2. Dr. Thaddeus Mason Harris (1768–April 3, 1842), pastor of the Unitarian church in Dorchester from 1793 to 1836. See *DAB*. NH's account of seeing his ghost was written in England in 1856, and first published in the *Nineteenth Century*, XLVII (1900), 88–93. See *EN*, pp. 106, 634 n. 148; *FIN*, pp. 419, 745, 842.

3. NH recorded in his journal an anecdote of Doctor Harris's fabulous luck in finding a gold ring, taking the account from a sermon given at his funeral; see *AN*, pp. 229, 609.

4. *The Poetical Works of Robert Southey, Collected by Himself* (New York: D. Appleton, 1839). NH's signed copy is in the Bowdoin College Library.

5. Probably Thomas Campbell, *Specimens of the British Poets*, ed. Peter Cunningham, in one volume (London: John Murray, 1841). Originally published in seven volumes in 1819.

6. Susan Burley now lived in Boston at 11 Chestnut Street.

[Boston] 54 Pinckney St.
June 27th.— 7 °clock P.M. [1842]

Most Dear,

I have just arrived from Salem, and find thy note, in which thou tellest me of thy illness.[1] Oh, my poor little Dove, thou dost need a husband with a strong will to take care of thee; and when I have the charge of thee, thou wilt find thyself under much stricter discipline than ever before. How couldst thou be so imprudent! Yet I will not scold thee till thou art quite well. Then thou must look for scoldings and chastisement too.

Ownest, I shall not say a single word to induce thee to go through the ceremony on Monday;[2]— nay I do not know that I will consent to its taking place then. This we will determine upon tomorrow evening. If thou art not very well indeed, I shall be afraid to take thee from under thy mother's care. And, belovedest, do not fear but that I will bear patiently any necessary delay—and I know that thou wilt recover as soon as possible, for my sake.

Dearest, God bless thee. Keep thy heart quiet; and tomorrow evening we will meet, in hope and joy.

Thy lovingest Husband

1. Apparently a nervous illness.
2. July 4th, and NH's birthday.

[Boston] 54 Pinckney St.—June 30th.—morning. [1842]

Dearest Love,

Thy sister Mary, after I left thee, told me that it was her opinion that we should not be married for a week longer. I had hoped, as thou knowest, for an earlier day; but I cannot help feeling that Mary is on the safe and reasonable side. Shouldst thou feel that this postponement is advisable, thou wilt find me patient beyond what thou thinkest me capable of. I will even be happy, if thou wilt only keep thy mind and heart in peace.

Belovedest, didst thou sleep well, last night? My pillow was haunted with ghastly dreams, the details whereof have flitted away like vapors, but a strong impression remains about thy being magnetized. God save me from any more such![1] I awoke in an absolute quake. Dearest, I cannot oppose thy submitting to so much of this influence as will relieve thy headache; but, as thou lovest me, do not suffer thyself to be put to sleep. My feeling on this point is so strong, that it would be wronging us both to conceal it from thee.

Mine ownest, if it will at all reconcile thee to the postponement of the ceremony, I will go to Concord, tomorrow or next day, and see about our affairs there. I would even go there and live alone, if thou didst bid me; though I shall be much happier in lingering here, and visiting thy couch every evening, and hearing thee say that thou art better than the night before.

What a sweet morning is this; it makes me feel bright and hopeful, after the troubles of the night.

Thine ownest husband.

P.S. I enclose an order for a case of wine, which is to be given to the baggage-wagoner, when he comes for the furniture. He can present it, and receive the case.

P.S. 2^d— I love thee! I love thee! I love thee.

P.S. 3^d— Dost thou love me at all?

1. See 216. Cornelia Park was an attendant at the wedding. See 244.2.

Boston July 1, 1842

Dear Louiza,

I suppose you are looking in the papers for the notice of the execution: the fact is, Sophia refuses to let matters proceed, till next week. She is tired with two months' labor in making preparations, and not so well as usual, though not seriously unwell. I will not be married on Monday, because I wish to see the fireworks here, in the evening: so I suppose the affair will come off by Tuesday or Wednesday. I shall not visit Salem again till I am haltered—unless my shirts and collars fall short.

Yours truly,
N H

[Boston] 54 Pinckney St. Friday, July 8th. 1842.

My dear Sir,

Though personally a stranger to you, I am about to request of you the greatest favor which I can receive from any man. I am to be married to Miss Sophia Peabody tomorrow; and it is our mutual desire that you should perform the ceremony. Unless it should be decidedly a rainy day, a carriage will call for you at half past eleven °clock, in the forenoon.[2]

Very Respectfully
Yours,
Nath. Hawthorne.

Rev. James F. Clarke,
Chesnut St.

1. James Freeman Clarke (1810–88), Unitarian minister and participant in the Transcendentalist movement, brother of SH's close friend Sarah Clarke. He was minister of the Church of the Disciples, Boston, from 1840 until his death, and a frequent contributor to the *Dial*, the *Christian Examiner*, and the *North American Review*.

2. The wedding took place at the Peabody home on West Street. "There were present beside the family Cornelia [Hall Park] and Sarah [Clarke] and the cook Bridget" (SH diary, August 10, 1842; MS, Morgan).

[Boston] 54 Pinckney St. July 8th. 1842.

I trust that Miss Quincy will be charitable enough to believe me ashamed of having kept these letters[1] so long—and not less ashamed to return them now, without making my apologies in person. But the truth is, I have been absent from Boston a great part of the time since I received them, and have had many and unavoidable occupations, while here. Moreover, Miss Peabody has been almost constantly engaged, and latterly has been much indisposed; so that I could not have the pleasure of bringing her with me. I hope that, hereafter, we shall both have an opportunity of acknowledging Miss Quincy's kindness; and we flatter ourselves with the idea that we may receive her under our own roof, in Concord.

Very Respectfully,
Nath. Hawthorne

Miss Quincy,
Cambridge.

1. "These" may relate to Miss Quincy's memoir of Edmund Quincy (see 235) but may be those by George Washington, Benjamin Franklin, and John Adams to her grandfather Josiah Quincy, Jr. (1744–75), "The Patriot," of whom she published a memoir under her father's name. See Howe, *The Articulate Sisters*, p. 45.

Concord, July 10th, 1842.

Dear Louze,[1]

The execution took place yesterday. We made a christian end, and came straight to Paradise, where we abide at this present writing. We are as happy as people can be, without making themselves ridiculous, and might be even happier; but, as a matter of taste, we choose to stop short at this point. Sophia is very well, and sends her love. We intend that you shall be our first guest (unless there should be a chance visiter) and shall beseech the honor and felicity of your presence, sometime in August. New married people, I believe, are not considered fit to be seen, in less time than several weeks.

I know you will be delighted with our home and the neighboring scenery; and I have a confident hope that you will be delighted with ourselves likewise. I intend to improve vastly by marriage—that is, if I can find any room for improvement. But all this remains to be seen. Meantime, I promise myself few greater pleasures than that of receiving you here; for, in taking to myself a wife, I have neither given up my own relatives, nor adopted others. Give my love to mother and Ebe.

Yours affectionately,

N. H.

P.S. We have not got a kitten—yet.[2]

1. NH's nickname for Louisa.
2. The Manse acquired a female kitten named "Megara, after one of the

furies," SH wrote to her mother September 3; by September 20 it had been renamed "Moloch," she reported (MSS, Berg). The same cat became "Pigwiggen"; see 260.

Concord, August 2ᵈ, 1842.

Dear Hillard,

Concluding that you have by this time returned from your tour,[1] I write to request that Mrs. Hillard and yourself will spend either the coming Sunday, or the next afterwards, at our house.[2] We expect my sister from Salem, to stay a week or two, about the middle of the month; and unless you come before her visit, we could not give you a night's lodging until the beginning of September. Pray do not put it off so long; for we are very desirous of seeing you both. We shall expect you on one of the two ensuing Saturdays.

Remember me kindly to Susan,[3] and say that her lamps light us to bed every night, and that her holders were just the articles that we wanted. I thank you for your beautiful seal, and shall send an impression of it on the outside of this letter.

Do come next Saturday, if fair weather, because the heavens may frown upon the enterprise hereafter.

Truly your friend,
Nath. Hawthorne.

1. Hillard, Henry Russell Cleveland (1809–43), a scholar from Salem, and Charles Callahan Perkins (1823–86), later a Boston art critic, had stopped at the Manse on horseback on July 11, on their way to Trenton Falls, near Utica, New York. See SH to her mother, July 15, MS, Berg; Hillard, "Memoir," in A Selection from the Writings of Henry R. Cleveland, with a Memoir (Boston: privately printed, 1844), pp. xxvii–xxviii.

2. Hillard and his wife, Susan, visited the Manse from Saturday, August 13, until Monday the 15th. See *AN*, pp. 334–37, *MOM*, pp. 17–18.

3. The cook in the Hillards' home when NH lived there. The holders were assigned to "Mr Hawthorne's wife," SH wrote to her mother on July 15 (MS, Berg).

Concord, Aug. 15th, 1842.

Dear L.

Mrs. Hillard has requested me to beg of you to come to their house, on your way to Concord; and I think it an excellent arrangement, as she will send to the stage-house, to have your name put down, and so you will escape all trouble and annoyance. Moreover, if the stage should be full on the day when you come, you can spend the night at her house. Do not, on any account, fail to take advantage of her invitation; there is no sort of reason why you should not accept it. She wished me to ask you to stay all night; and you can if you choose. The stage for Concord leaves Earle's Coffee House, Hanover-street, every day at four °clock. There is likewise one which goes early in the morning, and another at 10 °clock; but the afternoon one is the best for you, unless you spend the night at Mrs. Hillard's.

When you come, put those boot-tacks into your trunk— and also that little silver spoon. Hillard will probably have some small articles for you to take, as I am going to give him some commissions. I suppose you remember the number of their house—54 Pinckney street. By all means, go to them. Come as soon as possible after receiving this; but whenever you do come, stop at their house. We shall expect you daily.[1]

Yours in a hurry
N. H.

1. Louisa arrived on August 20 and remained until September 6.

Concord, August 20th. 1842.

My dear Sir,

Your letter, requesting contributions to the Boston Miscellany, has been received. I have likewise received a letter from Miss E. Peabody, of the same date, stating that Messrs. Bradbury & Soden have, or had, a desire that I should be more intimately connected with the Magazine, than as a mere contributor.[2] I should be glad to converse with them, or with an accredited agent, upon this subject. Without giving up some of my present engagements, I should scarcely find it possible to contribute to the Miscellany—indeed, I have almost promised the editor of the Democratic Review to send him all articles which I may have leisure to write. But as Mr. O'Sullivan is an intimate personal friend, he would probably release me from this obligation, in case of anything like an editorial connection with the Miscellany.

If you, my dear Sir, would favor me with a visit at Concord, we might perhaps hit upon some arrangement mutually agreeable; and at all events, it would give me much pleasure to see you.

Very truly Yours,
Nath. Hawthorne.

Robert Carter, Esqr.
Boston.

1. Carter (1819–79), a writer and editor, had come to Boston from Albany, N. Y. He assisted Nathan Hale, Jr., in editing the *Boston Miscellany* and in 1843 was to edit *The Pioneer* with J. R. Lowell. See *DAB*; see also 612.

2. Elizabeth's letter is unrecovered. Wymond Bradbury and Samuel S. Soden, the publishers, had become dissatisfied with Hale as editor of the *Boston Miscellany*, and on July 28 Soden had asked Elizabeth to recommend a replacement. "E. asked him why he did not engage Mr. Hawthorne & told him that she had thought so much of it that if the Hales had not been particular friends she should have spoken to him about it before. . . . Mr Soden said he had relations in Concord, & should certainly go up & see Mr. Hawthorne. . . . He asked if Mr. Hawthorne would be likely to take the editorship for 1000 dollars a year" (Mary Peabody to SH, July 28; MS, Berg). On August 11 SH wrote to her mother that she had received Mary's "proposals" (MS, Berg). As late as September 1, NH recorded, "Ellery Channing called to see us, wishing to talk to me about the Boston Miscellany, of which he had heard that I was to be Editor, and to which he desired to contribute" (*AN*, p. 357). At the end of the year, Hale was succeeded by Henry T. Tuckerman, who edited the January and February issues before publication ended; see the "Publisher's Notice," *Boston Miscellany*, II (December, 1842), 281.

Concord, August 25th, 1842.

Dear Margaret,

Sophia has told me of her conversation with you,[1] about our receiving Mr. Ellery Channing and your sister[2] as inmates of our household. I found that my wife's ideas were not altogether unfavorable to the plan[3]—which, together with your own implied opinion in its favor, has led me to consider it with a good deal of attention; and my conclusion is, that the comfort of both parties would be put in great jeopardy. In saying this, I would not be understood to mean anything against the social qualities of Mr. and Mrs. Channing—my objection being wholly independent of such considerations. Had it been proposed to Adam and Eve to receive two angels into their Paradise, as *boarders,* I doubt whether they would have been altogether pleased to consent. Certain I am, that, whatever might be the tact, and the sympathies of the heavenly guests, the boundless freedom of Paradise would at once have become finite and limited by their presence. The host and hostess would no longer have lived their own natural life, but would have had a constant reference to the two angels; and thus the whole four would have been involved in an unnatural relation—which the whole system of boarding out essentially and inevitably is.

One of my strongest objections is the weight of domestic care which would be thrown upon Sophia's shoulders by the proposed arrangement. She is so little acquainted with it, that she cannot estimate how much she would have to bear. I do not fear any burthen that may accrue from our own exclusive relation, because skill and strength will come with the natural necessity; but I should not feel myself justified in adding one scruple to the weight. I wish to remove everything that may impede her full growth and development—which, in her case, it seems to me, is not to be brought about by care and toil, but by perfect repose and happiness. Perhaps she ought not to have any earthly care whatever—certainly none which is not wholly pervaded with love, as a cloud is with warm light. Besides, she has many visions of great deeds to be wrought on canvass and in marble, during the coming autumn and winter; and none of these can be accomplished, unless she can retain quite as much freedom from household drudgery as she enjoys at present. In short, it is my faith and religion not wilfully to mix her up with any earthly annoyance.

You will not consider it impertinent, if I express an opinion about the most advisable course for your young relatives, should they retain their purpose of boarding out. I think that they ought not to seek for delicacy of character, and nice tact, and sensitive feelings, in their hosts. In such a relation as they propose, these characteristics should never exist on more than one side; nor should there be any idea of personal friendship, where the real condition of the bond is, to supply food and lodging for a pecuniary compensation. They will be able to keep their own delicacy and sensitiveness much more inviolate, if they make themselves inmates of the rudest farmer's household in Concord, where there will be no nice sensibilities to manage, and where their own feelings will be no more susceptible of damage from the farmer's family than from the cattle in his barn-yard. There will be a freedom in this sort of life, which is not otherwise attainable, except under a roof of their own. They can then say explicitly what they want, and can battle for it, if necessary; and such a contest would leave no wound on either side. Now, where four sensitive people were living together, united by any tie save that of entire affection and confidence, it would take but a trifle to render their whole common life diseased and intolerable.

I have thought, indeed, of receiving a personal friend, and a man of delicacy, into my household, and have taken a step towards that object. But in doing so, I was influenced far less by what Mr. Bradford[4] is, than by what he is not; or rather, his negative qualities seem to take away his personality, and leave his excellent characteristics to be fully and fearlessly enjoyed. I doubt whether he be not precisely the rarest man in the world. And, after all, I have had some misgiving as to the wisdom of my proposal to him.

This epistle has grown to greater length than I expected, and yet it is but a very imperfect expression of my ideas upon the subject. Sophia wished me to write; and, as it was myself that made the objections, it seemed no more than just that I should assume the office of stating them to you. There is nobody to whom I would more willingly speak my mind, because I can be certain of being thoroughly understood. I would say more,—but here is the bottom of the page.

Sincerely your friend,
Nath. Hawthorne.

1. Probably on August 20, when Fuller had come to the Manse in the afternoon and interrupted the Hawthornes' embrace in the parlor; see SH to her mother, August 22, 1842 (MS, Berg).

2. William Ellery Channing (1818–1901), son of Dr. Walter Channing and namesake of his uncle, the famous minister, and his fiancée, Ellen Kilshaw Fuller (1820–56), Margaret's sister. They were to be married on September 23, and in the following April, they moved into the "Red House," near Emerson's. See Frederick T. McGill, *Channing of Concord: A Life of William Ellery Channing II* (New Brunswick, N.J.: Rutgers University Press, 1967), pp. 69–73; *AN*, pp. 312, 357–58, 369.

3. In her journal for August 27, Fuller wrote: "I enclose here a letter received

from Hawthorne in answer to a question put at Ellery's earnest request, and with it one from Sophia received several days since. It is a striking contrast of tone between the man and woman so sincerely bound together by one sentiment" (Joel Myerson, ed., "Margaret Fuller's 1842 Journal: At Concord with the Emersons," *Harvard Library Bulletin*, XXI [July, 1973], 328). SH's letter has not been recovered, but writing to Fuller on May 11, she had invited her to "spend part of the time with us" when she visited Emerson (MS, Harvard).

4. George Bradford had left Brook Farm in the spring of 1842 to grow vegetables at Plymouth. Like NH, he was to settle in Concord at Emerson's invitation; he hoped to establish a school there. See *AN*, pp. 346–47; Emerson, *Letters*, III, 52, 87, and *JMN*, VIII, 172; James W. Mathews, "An Early Brook Farm Letter," *NEQ*, LIII (1980), 226; Mathews, "George Partridge Bradford," *Studies in the American Renaissance 1981*, pp. 135, 147.

Concord, Septr 1st. 1842.

Dear Sir,

It gives me pleasure to think that the story of "Samuel
Johnson"[1] may be useful to the Sunday School Society; and
you have my free consent to print as many copies as you
choose. I know of no impediment, except that, in the con-
tract with Messrs. Tappan & Dennett, it was provided that
no new edition of the Biographical Stories should be printed,
without their consent, until the present edition be disposed
of. I doubt not, however, that they will readily agree to such
a publication as you propose; especially as several papers have
published the story in question without credit. If you will be
kind enough to call on them, and mention my wish, I trust
that they will not withhold their consent.

I thank you for your kind remembrance of Mrs. Hawthorne. We should both be very glad to receive Mrs.
Waterston[2] and yourself under our own roof.

Very truly Yours,
Nath. Hawthorne.

Rev. R. C. Waterston,
Boston.

1. *Biographical Stories for Children*, published in April, included "Samuel Johnson." A pamphlet, *The Sunday School Society's Gift*, with a prefatory letter pre-

sumably by Waterston, offered a slightly condensed reprinting of the sketch; see *TS*, "Textual Introduction," p. 332, and "Samuel Johnson," pp. 239–48.

2. In March, 1840, Waterston had married Anna Cabot Lowell (1812–99), daughter of President Josiah Quincy of Harvard.

Concord, October 3ᵈ, 1842.

Gentlemen,

You will much oblige me by furnishing me with an account
of the sales of the edition of Twice-told Tales, at your earliest
convenience.[1]

Respectfully Yours,
Nath. Hawthorne.

Messrs. James Munroe, & Co.
Boston.

1. For the response and further details, see 279, 288, 291, and *TTT*, "Historical Commentary," pp. 524–27.

Concord, October 12th, 1842

My dear Sister,

I have just received your letter, containing the sad intelligence of Uncle Robert's death.[1] If there were a little more time, I would certainly be present at the funeral, although I should be compelled to return hither tomorrow night; but I could not arrive in Boston this evening, till between nine and ten °clock, and could scarcely be with you before the appointed hour. I cannot, at present, leave Concord for any long space; because my domestic affairs, orchard, potatoes &c have to be attended to this week; and, I have also a guest (Mr. Farley) who has been invited to stay several days—not to mention a literary matter, which must be completed within a specified time.[2] I had intended to come, with Sophia, in a week from next Saturday;—or rather, I should have come on Saturday, and Sophia would have spent Sunday in Boston, and followed me on Monday. I still purpose to come at the time above mentioned;—whether Sophia will come likewise, must depend upon your own wishes and convenience. Perhaps she had better not. We will discuss the matter when I see you.

Say everything that ought to be said on my behalf, to Mrs. Manning. Something must be done for the children.[3] This also we must talk about, when we meet. Believe me (not the less because I seldom say it) your very loving brother,

Nath. Hawthorne.

1. Robert Manning died on October 10.

2. See 255.

3. Manning was survived by Rebecca Burnham Manning and their four children: Maria, Robert, Richard, and Rebecca. NH did not assist them at this time, so far as is known.

[Concord, October 17, 1842]

I ought, some time ago, to have tendered my resignation as an associate of the Brook Farm Institute, but I have been unwilling to feel myself entirely disconnected with you.[1] As I can see but little prospect, however, of returning to you, it becomes proper for me now to take the final step.[2] But no longer a brother of your band, I shall always take the warmest interest in your progress, and shall heartily rejoice at your success—of which I can see no reasonable doubt.

1. Charles Anderson Dana (1819–97), from Buffalo, N.Y., had been forced to leave Harvard by eyestrain from overstudy in 1841, his junior year. He joined Ripley at Brook Farm, where at the meeting of September 29, 1841 (see 213.1), he was appointed recording secretary of the Brook Farm Institute, and later, a director of the Association. Eventually he was editor of the New York *Sun;* see *DAB*.

2. In December, NH and William Allen "conveyed their interest as trustees to Ichabod Morton and John S. Brown" (Swift, p. 22). NH apparently now wished to withdraw his stock, worth $1,000, but Ripley and Dana were able to pay him only $475.95. On November 7 they signed a promissory note, to pay on demand plus interest, the remaining $524.05. See 213.1 and Curtis, *A Season in Utopia*, p. 115.

Concord, October 21st. 1842.

My dear Sir,

In compliance with your request for an article, I have corrected and added some finishing touches to a sketch of character from a private Journal of mine.[2] Whether it have any interest must depend entirely on the sort of view taken by the writer, and the mode of execution. If it suit your purpose, I shall be very glad.

There is a gentleman in this town by the name of Thoreau, a graduate of Cambridge, and a fine scholar, especially in old English literature[3]—but withal a wild, irregular, Indian-like sort of fellow, who can find no occupation in life that suits him. He writes; and sometimes—often, for aught I know— very well indeed. He is somewhat tinctured with Transcendentalism; but I think him capable of becoming a very valuable contributor to your Magazine. In the Dial for July, there is an article on the Natural History of this part of the country,[4] which will give you an idea of him as a genuine and exquisite observer of nature—a character almost as rare as that of a true poet. A series of such articles would be a new feature in Magazine-literature, and perhaps a popular one; and, not improbably, he might give them a more popular tone than the one in the Dial. Would it not be worth while to try Mr. Thoreau's pen? He writes poetry also—for instance, "To the Maiden in the East"—"The Summer Rain"—and other pieces, in the Dial for October,[5] which seem to be very careless and imperfect, but as true as bird-notes. The man has stuff in him to make a reputation of; and I wish that you might find it consistent with your interest to aid him in attaining that object. In common with the rest of the public, I shall look for character and individuality in the Magazine which you are to edit; and it seems to me that this Mr. Thoreau might do something towards marking it out from the ordinary catalogue of such publications.

With my best wishes for your success, I am

Very truly Yours,
Nath. Hawthorne.

Epes Sargent, Esqr.
New-York.

1. Sargent (1813–80), journalist, poet, and dramatist, had previously worked on Boston newspapers and written for the theater there before moving to New York in 1839, where he was associated with George P. Morris and the *Mirror* and with Park Benjamin and the *World*. He was now preparing his own monthly, *Sargent's New Monthly Magazine*, which appeared from January to June, 1843. See *DAB*.

2. "The Old Apple-Dealer," published in *Sargent's*, I (January, 1843), 21–24, was expanded from a notebook entry dated January 23, 1842 (see *AN*, pp. 222–26), the day that NH was invited to the dinner for Charles Dickens (see 226). NH collected the sketch in *MOM*, 1846. "The Antique Ring" (never collected by NH) appeared in the February *Sargent's*, pp. 80–86.

3. Henry D. Thoreau (1817–62). See Anne Whaling, *Thoreau's Reading in English Poetry, 1340–1660* (Ann Arbor, Mich.: University Microfilms, 1968). He was now a frequent visitor to the Manse; see *AN*, pp. 353–58.

4. "Natural History of Massachusetts," *Dial*, III (July, 1842), 19–40, collected in *Excursions* (1863).

5. These and six other poems by Thoreau were in the issue.

Concord, Novr 25th, 1842.

Dear L.

I received the paper, with the emphatic word 'write' upon the envelope—whereby you have subjected yourself to a heavy fine, which I trust will be inflicted forthwith. Why should we write, more than you? Sophia would have written before now; but her household duties keep her busy, and latterly she has been much employed in preparing for Thanksgiving. She made a plum pudding and some pumpkin pies by the mere force of instinct—having never been taught; and they would have done credit to an old pastry-cook. We have a very good girl;[1] but she is young, and unskilled in these weightier matters of the law.

I shall not get the Salem Post-Office. If Rantoul gains his election to Congress, he will get it for Woodbury—otherwise Foote will not be removed.[2] Nevertheless, I am promised something satisfactory in the course of six months or so. Mean-time, I am very well contented to remain here. We have bought two air-tight stoves and a cooking-stove, and are now perfectly comfortable. I am sure you would like an air-tight stove in your chamber. If you get one, see that it be large; for the smaller ones are not so economical, though they cost less.

We wished for you at dinner yesterday—there being nobody but our two selves; and I suppose you dined with even a smaller party, unless you went to Mrs. Dike's. Our turkey weighed but five pounds, but was very good; and I carved it in first-rate style. Sophia read the directions from Miss Leslie's house-book,[3] sentence by sentence; so that everything was done in order. A green goose was offered us the other day; but I doubted my ability to get it apart, and therefore would not take it.

When we returned from Salem we found Pigwiggen[4] almost starved, and very melancholy. She had quite lost her playfulness; and, with my usual tenderness of heart, I was inclined to end all her ills by drowning her. However, we determined first to try the efficacy of feeding her well and making her comfortable; and it has succeeded wonderfully well. She is now quite fat, and of admirable behavior. The other morning, she jumped with all four of her feet upon a hot stove. A huge caterwauling ensued, as you may suppose; but she seems to have suffered no material damage.

We have a Lyceum here, and I have been invited to lecture. Of course, I did not hesitate a moment to accept. Wonderful to say, I attended the first lecture, which was by Mr. Emerson.[5]

Among my first epistolary performances will be a letter to the Cardinal.[6] Do you ever see him? I don't think he deserves a letter; for he treated me very ill during my visit to Salem— not inviting me to come and see him, and being otherwise intolerably rude. He is a real blackguard—which I have no hesitation in saying to you, as I have often said it to himself. You may inform his reverence, that such continues to be my opinion of him. It is not impossible that I may have occasion to come to Boston in the course of a month or so. If so, I shall come to Salem; and we shall then have an opportunity to settle our differences. I have not smoked a cigar since I saw him last—nor have any desire to smoke one.

There has been skating here in Concord; but I am not yet provided with a pair of skates.[7] I intend to have great amusement in this way, during the winter; and it is perfectly safe, as the meadows are overflowed for miles, and the water there is very shallow. There has been pleasant walking in the woods till yesterday, when we had a storm of snow and sleet, which I suppose has rendered the paths impassable.

I wish I could get a barrel of our apples to you, but the

expence would be more than their value. I half live upon apples, and never was so healthy in my life. Sophia's health is excellent likewise—and so are Pigwiggen's and the girl's.[8] I hope Mother and you and Ebe enjoy the same blessing. Why don't you write, at least once in seven centuries, and tell us how you are and what is going on?

We are going out to dine with Mr. Emerson to-day;[9] and it is time for me to put on my clean shirt and get ready. Sophia intended to have written half of this letter, and I meant that she should have written the whole; but she has had no time to write a line. Thank heaven it is accomplished. I do abominate letter-writing.

Your affectionate brother,
N. H.

1. Sarah, a Boston servant girl who had reached the Manse before the newlyweds, and welcomed them. She stayed with them into December. See AN, p. 331; SH to her mother, July 10, and to Mary Peabody, December 18 (MSS, Berg).

2. Caleb Foote had been appointed postmaster May 12, 1841, succeeding Charles W. Woodbury (see 139, and Tileston, *Caleb and Mary Wilder Foote*, p. 341). Robert Rantoul, Jr., was not elected to Congress until 1851. NH was still expecting on March 31, 1843, "prospects of official station" (AN, pp. 367, 645–46). See 265, 283.

3. Eliza Leslie, *The House-Book; or, a Manual of Domestic Economy for Town and Country* (Philadelphia: Carey and Hart, 1840), which went through five printings that year.

4. Their cat, which they had named for a fairy knight in Michael Drayton's mock-romantic poem, "Nimphidia" (1627). Pigwiggen is a rival of King Oberon for the love of Queen Mab, and confronts the jealous Oberon in single combat.

5. Emerson lectured on November 18; the subject is not known. There is no record of an invitation to NH, and his statement here is probably playful. See "The Concord Lyceum—Its Surviving Records," *The Massachusetts Lyceum During the American Renaissance*, ed. Kenneth Walter Cameron (Hartford: Transcendental Books, 1969), p. 156.

6. Horace Conolly's nickname; see 86.1.

7. See 260.

8. I.e., Sarah's.

9. Emerson wrote to his brother William on this day: "According to a custom of six years' antiquity, we keep festival this good Friday after Thanksgiving and expect Mr & Mrs S. Ripley & Gore, Elizabeth Hoar Mr & Mrs Hawthorn and Mrs. Brown to dine with us" (*Letters*, III, 100).

Concord, Novr 26th. 1842

Dear Longfellow,

I have been looking to receive somewhat in the shape of a letter of congratulation from you, on the great event of my marriage; but it does not seem to be forthcoming. Perhaps it is the etiquette that I should congratulate on your return from Outre Mer.[1] Be it done accordingly.

I exceedingly desire to see you; and the object of this present writing is, to intreat you to come to Concord and deliver a lecture before the Lyceum. Mr. Emerson, who is one of the Curators, has mentioned it to me several times. I inquired what remuneration could be offered you; and he spoke of the magnificent sum of ten dollars—which he says is the highest amount paid by country Lyceums. Do come—if not for filthy lucre, yet to gratify the good people here, and to see my wife and me. Choose your own time, only I should like to have it as soon as possible.[2]

I am very well, and very happy; so is my wife.

Truly your friend,
Nath. Hawthorne.

---

1. From late April to early November, Longfellow had been abroad. He visited France, Belgium, Germany, and England, staying principally at Marienberg on the Rhine south of Coblenz, for the water cure. NH mentioned this recreation in "The Hall of Fantasy," probably written in October or early November, and published in the February 1843 *Pioneer;* see *MOM,* p. 635.

2. Apparently Longfellow did not lecture at the Concord Lyceum in 1842–43.

Concord, Dec[r] 17th. 1842

My dear Sir,

I send you an article for your Magazine.[1] It does not seem to admit of illustration, unless by architectural designs; so that Mrs. Hawthorne has made no attempt in that way.

Epes Sargent offers me $5 per page for contributions. If you consider this a fair price, it will satisfy me; if not, you may have the article for whatever your arrangements will allow you to pay.[2]

Yours truly,
Nath. Hawthorne.

J. R. Lowell, Esqr.

---

1. *The Pioneer*, edited by Lowell and Robert Carter, began publication in January, 1843; NH's "The Hall of Fantasy" was the leading article of the February issue. Lowell wrote a favorable review of "Hawthorne's Historical Tales for Youth" in the January issue, pp. 42–43. See Sculley Bradley, introduction to *The Pioneer* (New York: Scholars' Facsimiles and Reprints, 1947), pp. xvii–xviii.

2. Probably Lowell did not pay anything; see 261, 264. He had written recently to John Sullivan Dwight, soliciting editorial help: "At first I shall not be able to pay as much as I wish. But I will give at the least $10 for every article of three pages or more and $2 a page for less"; see George Willis Cooke, *John Sullivan Dwight* (Boston: Small, Maynard, 1898), p. 70. See also Bradley, introduction, p. xiii. For a general study, see J. Albert Robbins, "Fees Paid to Authors by Certain American Periodicals, 1840–1850," *Studies in Bibliography*, II (1949), 95–104.

Concord, Dec[r] 24th. 1842.

Dear Longfellow,

I should have responded to your letter[1] sometime since; but I am very busy with the pen, and hate to ink my fingers more than is necessary. As to coming to dine with you, it is a pleasure which I cannot promise myself at present, on account of the inconvenience of leaving home, unless I take my whole establishment with me; and I believe you do not extend your invitation to my wife and maid-servant. Sometime when I am in Boston, I will come out with Hillard.[2]

Now, for your coming to see me, I do pray that so desirable an event may take place—no matter how soon. You must give us one or two days notice, so that no other engagement may interfere; not that we are much troubled with engagements; but it might happen. I have some scruples of conscience about asking you to come in mid-winter; for it would be preposterous, I suppose, to expect anybody to be comfortable or contented here, except ourselves. You will have to warm yourself by the glow of our felicity—aided by as large a wood-fire as we can pile into the chimney. If you like skating, there is enough of it, over the river, within a stone's throw of our door. I get up at sunrise to skate!!!!!!!!!!!!

I never was more surprised than at your writing poems about Slavery.[3] I have not seen them, but have faith in their excellence, though I cannot conjecture what species of ex-

cellence it will be. You have never poetized a practical subject, hitherto.

Your friend,
Nath Hawthorne.

The pamphlet has come to-day.

1. Unrecovered.

2. NH next dined with Longfellow on March 21, 1843, after returning to
Boston from a visit to Salem. See *AN*, p. 368; Longfellow, *Letters*, II, 519, 521.

3. *Poems on Slavery*, a seven-page pamphlet written during his passage from
Bristol to New York, October 23–November 6, and published by John Owen in
Boston on December 24.

Concord January 4th 1843

My dear Louisa,

"A thousand happy new years" to you all, as the Italian said in the warmth of his good will. Do not consider it a wish of doubtful good, because all those years not spent upon this planet, may be blessed upon another—for there is no end to the Future. We bade farewell to the dear old Year with grateful spirits, for it had brought us infinite benefits & felicity, & it died away in a most serene & golden sunset, like a Christian going to rest. The young Year also was born beneath a golden heaven, as if to signify its bountiful disposition, & bringing an immortal hope with it.

When Nathaniel wrote for his skates, I also on that same day indited to you a very long letter,[1] which at the last moment was put into the fire instead of into the Post Office. I thought it was no matter, since Nathaniel wrote, because the shortest letter from him must be far more precious to you than a volume from me. But I tell you, that you may not think I forgot my promise. I hoped that when the skates came, you would send his socks, because he is in great need. I was obliged at last to buy him a pair in the village, as it was of about as much use to attempt darning up the holes of some of his old ones, as it would be to darn over the crater of Mount Etna. They will not be so pleasant to his feet as if you had knitted them; but they are very stout & good. (Oh my abominable steel pen!)

He has enjoyed the skates exceedingly. I went with him once upon the river behind Peter's house,[2] & slid while he curvilineated about. Soon after he went with Mr Emerson &

Mr Thoreau on two separate expeditions, & then the meadow at the foot of our orchard froze over, & I used to go with him upon it in the afternoon at sunset. Now the snow has covered all the ice, & he does not like it at all. Do you know how majestically he skates? He looks very kingly, wrapt in his cloak, gliding to & fro. Mr Emerson called him "a perfect Ajax."[3] I think he will be very careful, because he has a wife now, & knows she could not well support any accident to befal him.

He is in the glory of health, & so am I, & we withstand the cold weather bravely. It is an oldfashioned winter in Concord. I do not hear how it is on the sea side in cities. But deep snow & steady freezing prevail here. Nathaniel has several times gone to skate before sunrise. Is not that heroic? Every morning now he writes till two o'clock alone in his study. He has written as usual as no one else can write. I think he must send you the next number of the Pioneer, in which will be a rare production of his.[4] James Lowell, one of its Editors, has sent us the first, but that has nothing of Nathaniel's. At two we dine, & by three he goes to the Athenæum & Post office, & when he comes back it is near sunset. Then he goes to the river perhaps, & I with him, if it is possible walking. We take tea early, to have a long evening. Then he reads aloud to me one or two hours or more. We have read Milton nearly in this way & Bacon's Advancement of Learning—& other less portentous & world-renowned books. You know his voice in reading is most musical thunder & I like to have great works set to such music. We take the liberty to think Milton very absurd when he goes to Heaven or endeavours to speak of GOD & His angels—but superem- inent in Paradise with Adam & Eve. We think he is pretty remarkable also in Hell. It is a high intellectual exercise to read any thing with Nathaniel, because he is so acute & profound. He winnows the chaff from the wheat at once.

Our Maid Mary[5] is quite perfect in her department, the

pink of good-nature, & very bright & also happy. So we have Paradise in the kitchen as well as in the parlor. She cooks admirably & makes nice bread. Pigwiggen waxes round & is well & lazy—& desires her love to her venerable relative Beelzebub & to young Mite. I trust your dear Mother is well—yourself & Elizabeth also. Give my love. Nathaniel shall write a little postscript to make my letter more welcome.

Yours affectionately
S. A. Hawthorne.

My pen is atrocious. I *can* write better.

[*In NH's hand:*]

Everything said in my praise and glory in the fore-going letter is no more than the simple truth.
I sent you a newspaper yesterday.

N.H.

1. On November 25; see 256.

2. Probably Peter Hutchinson (d. 1881), a black pig-butcher who lived near the Great Meadows approximately one mile east of the Old Manse near the Concord River. Or possibly Peter Robbins, another black contemporary. See Josephine Latham Swayne, *The Story of Concord*, 2nd ed. (Boston: Meador, 1939), pp. 359, 361; Emerson, "Peter's Field," *Poems* (Centenary Edition; Boston: Houghton Mifflin, 1911), IX, 363, 511–12. "Peter's Path" extended from near the Manse to Peter Hutchinson's house, which was later moved to Bedford Street in Concord.

3. Compare SH's often-quoted account of NH skating with Emerson and Thoreau, in a letter of December 30, in *Memories*, pp. 52–53.

4. "The Hall of Fantasy"; see 258.1.

5. Mary Bryan or O'Brien, a recent immigrant from Ireland. See *AN*, p. 646.

Concord, Feby 1st. 1843.

Dear Sir,

I send you another article for the Pioneer.[1]

I beg you to assure Mr. Lowell, that I did not intend to make a demand for immediate payment of my last contribution. I merely mentioned a price per page, because he had spoken to me upon the subject; and we get rid of an embarrassment by having such matters definitely fixed.[2]

It would be a great satisfaction to me to look over the proofs of this article, which might be sent me by mail; but if you are pressed for time, it is not essential. I abhor errors of the press—and but seldom escape them.

Yours truly,
Nath Hawthorne.

The second No. of the Magazine has not come to hand.[3]

1. "The Birthmark," which appeared in the *Pioneer*, I (March 1843), 113–19.

2. SH wrote to her mother on February 24: "If any money is sent to West St. for Mr Hawthorne please to send it forthwith . . . because we cannot very well come till we have it, on account of paying friend Edmund [Hosmer] for his wood first. . . . Mr Carter said he should send some on the 20th"; she wrote again on the 28th: "James Lowell owes us seventy dollars I believe. I am sorry for him but we want it. He offered Mr Hawthorne *any* price for his articles, but Mr Hawthorne would not ask any more than Epes Sargent gives though James' pages are a third larger" (MSS, Berg).

3. Carter noted at the foot of the leaf, "(I sent it yesterday)." The February number contained "The Hall of Fantasy."

Concord. Feby 1st. 1843.

Dear Margaret.

I ought to have answered your letter a great while ago;[1] but I have an immense deal of scribbling to do—being a monthly contributor to three or four periodicals;[2] so that I find it necessary to keep writing without any period at all. Now as to our friend Charles Newcomb,[3] I heartily wish that I could have the privilege of his society, next summer; and were it less than an absolute impossibility, I would undertake to be his host—though with some misgivings, chiefly as to my own proper performance of the relative duties of our position. But it is *not* possible, for a reason at present undeveloped, but which, I trust, time will bring to light.[4] We should have been compelled to eject even the impersonal Mr. Bradford, had he become our inmate.[5] So here is a second negative. How strange, when I should be so glad to do everything that you had the slightest wish for me to do, and when you are so incapable of wishing any thing that ought not to be! Whether or no you bear a negative more easily than other people, I certainly find it easier to give you one; because you do not peep at matters through a narrow chink, but can take my view as perfectly as your own. I hope Charles Newcomb will not give up the idea of coming to Concord.[6] There are many roofs besides mine; and Mr. Emerson, and Mr. Thoreau, and I, and everybody that is blessed with the knowledge of him, would gladly exert ourselves to find some proper whereabout for his reception. I should delight to anticipate long days with him on the river and in the woods.

We have been very happy this winter; we go on continually learning to be happy, and should consider ourselves perfectly so now, only that we find ourselves making advances all the time. I do suppose that nobody ever lived, in one sense, quite so selfish a life as we do. Not a footstep, except our own, comes up the avenue for weeks and weeks; and we let the world alone as much as the world does us. During the greater part of the day, we are separately engaged at our respective avocations; but we meet in my study in the evening, which we spend without any set rule, and in a considerable diversity of method—but on looking back, I do not find anything to tell of or describe. The essence would flit away out of the description, and leave a very common-place residuum; whereas the real thing has a delicate pungency. We have read through Milton's Paradise Lost, and other famous books; and it somewhat startles me to think how we, in some cases, annul the verdict of applauding centuries, and compel poets and prosers to stand another trial, and receive condemnatory sentence at our bar. It is a pity that there is no period after which an author may be safe. Forever and ever, he is to be tried again and again, and by everybody that chooses to be his Judge; so that, even if he be honorably acquitted at every trial, his ghost must be in everlasting torment.

I have skated like a very schoolboy, this winter. Indeed, since my marriage, the circle of my life seems to have come round, and brought back many of my school-day enjoyments; and I find a deeper pleasure in them now than when I first went over them. I pause upon them, and taste them with a sort of epicurism, and am boy and man together. As for Sophia, I keep her as tranquil as a summer-sunset. As regards both of us, the time that we spend together seems to spread over all the time that we are apart; and consequently we have the idea of being in each other's society a good deal more than we are. I wonder, sometimes, how she is able to dispense with all society but mine. In my own case, there is no wonder—indeed, in neither of our cases; and it is only when I get apart from myself, and take another person's view of the matter, that I think so.

I have missed Ellery Channing very much in my skating expeditions. Has he quite deserted us for good and all?[7] How few people in this world know how to be idle!—it is a much higher faculty than any sort of usefulness or ability. Such rare persons, if the world knew what was due to them or good for itself, would have food and raiment as free as air, for the sake of their inestimable example. I do not mean to deny Ellery's ability for any sort of vulgar usefulness; but he certainly *can* lie in the sun.[8]

I wish you might begin at the end of this scrawl instead of at the usual extremity; because then you would profit by the advice which I here give—not to attempt to decypher it. Sophia wants to read it, but I have too much regard for her to consent. She sends her love. Of course, you will be in Concord when the pleasant weather comes, for a month, or a week, or a day; and you must spend a proportionable part of the time at our house.

Your friend,
Nath Hawthorne.

1. January 16, 1843 (MS, Berg): Fuller portrays herself as an "interpreter" for Charles Newcomb, who wishes "to come to Concord next summer, work with you on your farm, if you have employment for him, be received as a boarder beneath your roof, if such arrangement would be pleasant for you & Sophia." Fuller had written to Newcomb on October 2, 1841, after a visit to Brook Farm, that NH spoke of him "not only with . . . warm regard . . . but with more discrimination than I have heard any person" (Fuller, *Letters,* ed. Robert N. Hudspeth [Ithaca, N.Y.: Cornell University Press, 1983], II, 238).

2. *Sargent's,* the *Pioneer,* and the *Democratic Review.* See also 272.

3. Charles King Newcomb (1820–94), from Providence, R.I., a close friend of Emerson and Fuller, had known NH at Brook Farm. See his *Journals,* ed. Judith

Kennedy Johnson (Providence: Brown University Press, 1946), pp. 138, 150. NH described Newcomb ("the young author of Dolon" in the *Dial* for July 1842) in "The Hall of Fantasy" as "involved in a deep mist of metaphysical fantasies," and alluded to him in the same sketch as "techy, wayward, shy, proud, unreasonable" (see *MOM*, pp. 636, 175). See George Willis Cooke, *Historical and Biographical Introduction to the Dial* (Cleveland: Rowfant Club, 1902), p. 146; *AN*, pp. 371, 648; Emerson, *JMN*, VIII, 377–78.

4. SH's first pregnancy. The first extant mention is in a letter of Mary Peabody to Sophia in mid-January (MS, Berg).

5. Fuller had written on January 16 that she told Newcomb that when NH "wrote declining to receive Ellery, you said you should not wish to have any man but Mr Bradford, but knowing your regard for Charles, we have thought it possible you might think again." See 250.

6. Newcomb never lived in Concord. Emerson had tried to persuade him to move there, beginning at the time of NH's decision to live in the Old Manse. See Emerson, *Letters*, III, 51, 81, 201.

7. Ellery and Ellen Channing spent the winter in Cambridge, probably with Fuller. They had been unable to find a place to live in Concord. In the spring, they returned to rent, through Thoreau's assistance, a house near Emerson's; see *AN*, p. 369; McGill, *Channing of Concord*, pp. 71–72.

8. Compare Matthew 6:24–31.

Salem, March 12th [11] (Saturday) 1843.

Own wifie, how dost thou do? I have been in some anxiety about thy little head, and indeed about the whole of thy little person.[1] Art thou qualmish, thou naughty dove? Art thou ill at ease in any mode whatsoever? I trust that thy dearest soul will not be quite worn out of thee, with the activity and bustle of thy present whereabout, so different from the intense quiet of our home. That poor home! How desolate it is now! Last night being awake, and hearing no gentle rise and fall of dove-breath at my side, my thoughts travelled back to the lonely old house; and it seemed as if I was wandering up stairs and down-stairs all by myself. My fancy was almost afraid to be there, alone. I could see every object in a sort of dim, gray light—our bed-chamber—the study, all in confussion—the parlor, with the fragments of that abortive breakfast on the table, and the precious silver-forks, and the old bronze image keeping its solitary stand upon the mantelpiece. Then, methought, the wretched Pigwiggen came and jumped upon the window-sill, and clung there with her forepaws, mewing dismally for admittance, which I could not grant her, being there myself only in the spirit. And then came the ghost of the old Doctor[2] stalking through the gallery, and down the staircase, and peeping into the parlor; and though I was wide awake, and conscious of being so many miles from the spot, still it was quite awful to think of the ghost having sole possession of our home; for I could not quite seperate myself from it, after all. Somehow, the Doctor and I seemed to be there tete-a-tete; and I wanted thee to protect me. Why wast not thou there in thought, at the same moment; and then we should have been conscious of one-another, and have had no fear, and no desolate feeling. I believe I did not have any fantasies about the ghostly kitchen-maid; but I trust Mary left the flat-irons within her reach; so that she may do all her ironing while we are away, and never disturb us more at midnight. I suppose she comes thither to iron her shroud, and perhaps, likewise, to smooth the doctor's band. Probably, during her lifetime, she allowed the poor old gentleman to go to some ordination or other grand clerical celebration with rumpled linen; and ever since, and throughout all earthly futurity (at least, as long as the house shall stand) she is doomed to exercise a nightly toil, with spiritual flat-iron.[3] Poor sinner—and doubtless Satan heats the irons for her. What nonsense is all this!—but really, it does make me shiver to think of that poor home of ours. Glad am I that thou art not there without thy husband.

I found our mother tolerably well, and Louisa, I think, in especial good condition for her, and Elizabeth comfortable, only not quite thawed. They speak of thee and me with an evident sense that we are very happy indeed, and I can see that they are convinced of my having found the very little wife that God meant for me. I obey thy injunctions, as well as I can, in my deportment towards them; and though mild and amiable manners are foreign to my nature, still I get along pretty well for a new beginner. In short, they seem content with thy husband, and I am very certain of their respect and affection for his wife.

Take care of thy little self, I tell thee! I praise heaven for this snow and 'slosh', because it will prevent thee from scampering all about the city, as otherwise thou wouldst infallibly have done. Lie abed late—sleep during the day—go to bed seasonably—refuse to see thy best friend, if either flesh or spirit be sensible of the slightest repugnance—drive all trouble out of thy mind—and above all things, think continually what an admirable husband thou hast! So shalt thou have quiet sleep and happy awaking; and when I fold thee to my bosom again, thou wilt be such a round, rosy, smiling little dove, that I shall feel as if I had grasped all cheerfulness and sunshine within the span of thy waist. [*excision*]

Thine received.

1. In early February, SH had suffered a miscarriage caused by a fall, according to her letter to her mother of February 22–24 (MS, Berg). NH's visit to Salem and SH's to Boston, planned for the first of March, were postponed to the eighth or tenth, she wrote to Louisa, because he had not received payments from editors (March 5, 1843; MS, Berg).

2. Dr. Ezra Ripley (1751–1841), pastor of the Congregational church in Concord, and occupant of the Manse from 1781 until his death. See AN, pp. 256, 619; Emerson, *Complete Works*, X, 379–95.

3. Compare "The Old Manse," *MOM*, pp. 17–18; *FIN*, p. 419.

Salem, March 16th, 1843.

Dearest wife, Thy letters have all been received; and I know not that I could have kept myself alive without them; for never was my heart so hungry and tired as it is now. I need thee continually, at bed and board, and wherever I am, and nothing else makes any approach towards satisfying me. Thou hast the easier part—being drawn out of thyself by society; but with me there is an ever present yearning, which nothing outward seems to have any influence upon. Four whole days must still intervene before we meet—it is too long—too long—we have not so much time to spare out of eternity.

As for this Mr. Billings,[1] I wish he would not be so troublesome. I put a note for him into the Boston Post-Office, directed according to his own request. His scheme is well enough, and might possibly become popular; but it has no peculiar advantages with reference to myself; nor do the subjects of his proposed books particularly suit my fancy, as themes to write upon. Somebody else will answer his purpose just as well; and I would rather write books of my own imagining than be hired to develope the ideas of an engraver; especially as the pecuniary prospect is not better, nor so good, as it might be elsewhere. I intend to adhere to my former plan, of writing one or two mythological story books,[2] to be published under O'Sullivan's auspices in New-York—which is the only place where books can be published, with a chance of profit.[3] As a matter of courtesy, I may perhaps call on Mr. Billings, if I have time; but I do not intend to be connected with this affair.

It is queer news that thou tellest me about the Pioneer. I expected it to fail in due season, but not quite so soon.[4] Not improbably we shall have to wait months for our money, if we ever get it at all. Nobody pays us. It was very unkind—at least, inconsiderate—of Mr. O'Sullivan not to send some money, my request being so urgent. Perhaps he has written to Concord. Should there be an opportunity, within a day or two, I wish thou wouldst send for any letters that may be in the Post Office there; but not unless some person is going thither, with intent to return before Wednesday next. If thou receive any, keep them till we meet in Boston.

I dreamed the other night that our house was broken open, and all our silver stolen. No matter though it be;—we have steel forks and German silver spoons in plenty, and I only wish that we were to eat our dinner with them to-day. But we shall have gained nothing on the score of snow, and slosh, and mud, by our absence; for the bad walking will be at its very *ne plus ultra,* next week. Wouldst thou not like to stay just one little fortnight longer in Boston, where the sidewalks afford dry passage to thy little feet? It will be mid-May, at least, ere thou wilt find even tolerable walking in Concord, and by that time, perhaps, our new baby will be an impediment to thy locomotion. So if thou wishest to walk while thou canst, we will put off our return a week longer. Naughty husband that I am! I know by my own heart that thou pinest for our home, and for the bosom where thou belongest. A week longer! It is a horrible thought.

We cannot very well afford to buy a surplus stock of paper, just now. By and by I should like some, and I suppose there will always be opportunities to get it cheap at auction. I do wonder—and always shall wonder, until the matter be reformed—why Providence keeps us so short of cash. Our earnings are miserably scanty at best; yet, if we could but get even that pittance, I should continue to be thankful, though certainly for small favors. The world deserves to come to a speedy end, if it were for nothing else save to break down this abominable system of credit—of keeping possession of other people's property—which renders it impossible for a man to be just and honest, even if so inclined. It is almost a pity that the comet is retrograding from the earth; it might do away with all our perversities at one smash. And thou, my little dove, and thy husband for thy sake, might be pretty certain of a removal to some sphere where we should have all our present happiness, and none of these earthly inconveniences.[5]

Ah, but, for the present, I like this earth better than Paradise itself. I love thee, thou dearest [*excision*]. It is only when away from thee, that the chill winds of this world make me shiver. Thou always keepest me warm, and always wilt; and without thee, I should shiver in Heaven. Dearest, I think I prefer to write thy name 'Mrs. Sophia A. Hawthorne', rather than 'Mrs. Nathaniel Hawthorne';—the latter gives me an image of myself in petticoats, knitting a stocking. Nevertheless, thou shalt be [*excision*] feel so sensibly that thou art my chastest, holiest, as well as intimatest little wife—a *woman* and an angel. But thou dost not love to blush in the midst of people.

Ownest, expect me next Tuesday in the forenoon; and do not look for another letter. I pray Heaven that I may find thee well, and not tired quite to death. Even shouldst thou be so, however, I will restore thee on Wednesday [*excision verso*]

1. (Charles Howland) Hammatt Billings (1818–74) had studied wood engraving with Abel Bowen, of the Bewick Company. He was listed in the *Boston Directory*, 1842, as an architect and designer. See Richard Stoddard, "Hammatt Billings, Artist and Architect," *Old-Time New England*, LXII (1972), 56–65, 76–79. He later illustrated NH's children's books for Ticknor; see 456, 487.

2. *WB* and *TT*; see *TS*, "Historical Introduction," p. 300.

3. O'Sullivan had visited NH at the Manse for three days in mid-January; see SH to Louisa, January 29, 1843 (MS, Berg). On April 7, NH wrote approvingly in his notebook of Thoreau's proposed residence in Staten Island, for the purpose of writing for New York publishers; see *AN*, p. 369; Harding, *The Days of Henry Thoreau*, pp. 145–47.

4. Robert Carter's editorial note in the March issue had promised a "fourth number," but it did not appear; see Bradley, introduction to *The Pioneer*, pp. xxiv–xxvi.

5. The great comet of 1843, first reported in New England on February 28, reached its greatest brightness about March 9. NH may be recalling an account in the Boston *Post*, March 10, 2:2, reprinted from the New York *Herald:* "Millerites in this city and Brooklyn were thrown into terrible convulsions, and several of the female disciples almost expired in hysterics." See 265.

Concord, March 25th. 1843.

Dear Bridge,

I see by the newspapers that you have had the good fortune to undergo a tremendous storm;[1]—*good* fortune I call it, for I should be very glad to go through the same scene myself, if I were sure of getting safe to dry land at last. I did not know of your having sailed; else I might have been under great apprehensions on your account; but as it happens, I have only to offer my congratulations. I hope you were in a condition to look at matters with a philosophic eye—not sea-sick, nor *too much* frightened. An idler, methinks, must be more uncomfortable in a storm than the sea-officers; taking no part in the struggle against the winds and waves, he feels himself more entirely at their mercy. Perhaps a description of the tempest may form a good introduction to your series of articles in the Democratic.[2]

I returned from my visit to Salem on Wednesday last. My wife went with me as far as Boston. I did not come to see you, because I was very short of cash—having been disappointed in money that I had expected from three or four sources. My difficulties of this sort sometimes make me sigh for the regular monthly payments at the Custom House. The system of slack payments in this country is most abominable, and ought of itself to bring upon us the destruction foretold by Father Miller.[3] It is impossible for any individual to be just and honest, and true to his engagements, when it is a settled principle of the community to be always behindhand. I find no difference in anybody, in this respect; all do wrong alike. O'Sullivan is just as certain to disappoint me in money matters, as any pitiful little scoundrel among the booksellers. On my part, I am compelled to disappoint those who put faith in my engagements; and so it goes round. The devil take such a system.

I suppose it will be sometime before you get to sea again, and perhaps you might find leisure to pay us another visit; but I cannot find in my conscience to ask you to do so, in this dreariest season of the year. It is more than three months since we have had a glimpse of the earth; and two months more must intervene, before we can hope to see the reviving verdure. I don't see how a bachelor can survive such a winter. My wife has entirely recovered her health, and seems even stronger than before—a result which is said sometimes to follow such an accident as she met with.[4] We are very happy, and have nothing to wish for, except a better-filled purse; and not improbably gold would bring trouble with it— at least, my wife says so, and therefore exhorts me to be content with little.

I have heard nothing about the office, since I saw you. They tell me in Salem that Rantoul will not probably gain his election, but that, after a few more trials, a coalition will be formed between the moderate whigs and the candidate of a fraction of the Democratic party. In that case, Woodbury will not get the Post Office, and possibly it may yet be the reward of my patriotism and public services.[5] But of this there is little prospect.

The wine came safe, and my wife sends her best acknowledgments for it. As in duty bound, however, she has made it over to me; and I shall feel myself at liberty to uncork a bottle, on any occasion of suitable magnitude. Longfellow is coming to see me soon;[6] and as he has a cultivated taste in wines, some of this article shall be submitted to his judgment. If possible, there shall be a bottle in reserve, whenever you favor us with another visit.

Do not forget your letters from Liberia. What would you think of having them published in a volume;—but it will be time enough for this after their appearance in the Magazine. I should like well to launch you fairly on the sea of literature. I have a horrible cold, and am scarcely clear-headed enough to write.

God bless you
Nath Hawthorne.

1. In early 1843 Bridge had been appointed purser of the U.S.S. *Saratoga*, under orders to the coast of west Africa. Printing this letter in *Recollections*, p. 88, Bridge added a note: "The storm here spoken of refers to a violent gale and blinding snow-storm off the coast of New Hampshire . . . in which the *Saratoga* (on her way from Portsmouth to New York, previous to the African cruise) was in imminent peril, and only escaped total shipwreck by our cutting away the masts and anchoring on a rocky lee-shore." See also Edward M. Barrows, *The Great Commodore: The Exploits of Matthew Calbraith Perry* (Indianapolis: Bobbs-Merrill, 1935), p. 161. Bridge had visited the Hawthornes in February, but because of SH's miscarriage had stayed in Concord only one night; see SH to Louisa Hawthorne, March 5, 1843 (MS, Berg).

2. In *Recollections*, pp. 87–88, Bridge noted that NH "suggested the plan of my taking such notes as would give me material for a few articles in the *Democratic Review*. This plan was afterwards, by his advice, changed to that of publishing the notes in a book." See Patrick Brancaccio, "'The Black Man's Paradise': Hawthorne's Edition of the *Journal of an African Cruiser*," *NEQ*, LIII (1980), 23–41. See 267, 299, 309.

3. William Miller (1782–1849), leader of the Adventist movement, had concluded in 1816 from study of the Bible that Christ would return to earth between March, 1843, and March, 1844. NH had discussed Miller in "The Hall of Fantasy" and "The New Adam and Eve" (*MOM*, pp. 181–85, 247). See *DAB*; Gary Scharnhorst, "Images of the Millerites in American Literature," *American Quarterly*, XXXII (1980), 19–36.

4. Her miscarriage. See 263.1, 265.1.

5. See 283.2. In his notebook on March 31, NH surveyed his "prospects of official station and emolument," concluding that "we are well content to wait; because an office would inevitably remove us from our present happy home" (*AN*, p. 367).

6. See 259.2.

[Concord, ca. May, 1843]

I am greatly troubled about that contribution for Mr. Poe.[1] Hitherto, I have never been accustomed to write during summer weather; and now I find that my thoughts fly out of the open window, and will not be enticed back again. I am compelled, indeed, to write a monthly article for the Democratic,[2] but it is with great pain and dolor, and only by the utmost force of self-compulsion. If I am to send anything to Mr. Poe, I should wish it to be worth his reception; but I am conscious of no power to produce anything good, at present. When you write to him, do make my apologies, and tell him that I have no more brains than a cabbage—which is absolutely true. He shall hear from me after the first frost—possibly sooner.

I shall not forget your promised visit.

Truly your friend,
Nath Hawthorne.

---

1. Edgar Allan Poe had written to Lowell on March 27, "I would be indebted to you if you would put me in the way of procuring a brief article (also for my opening number) from Mr Hawthorne—whom I believe you know personally" (*Letters,* ed. John Ward Ostrom [Cambridge: Harvard University Press, 1948], I, 232). Poe was planning to issue on July 1 the first number of the *Stylus,* a monthly magazine to be published in Philadelphia. He had written to Lowell on February 4 of his hopes of engaging NH as a "permanent contributor" (*Letters,* I, 222). Lowell responded on April 17, "Hawthorne writes me that he shall be able to send an article in the course of a week or two," and on May 8, "I have been delaying to write to you from day to day in the expectation that I should have received an article from Hawthorne to send with my letter" (George E.

Woodberry, *The Life of Edgar Allan Poe* [Boston: Houghton, Mifflin, 1909], II, 23, 25). The *Stylus* never appeared; see Poe, *Letters*, I, 234.

2. The following tales and sketches appeared in the *Democratic Review* in 1843: "The New Adam and Eve" in February; "Egotism; or, The Bosom-Serpent" in March; "The Procession of Life" in April; "The Celestial Rail-road" in May; "Buds and Bird-Voices" in June; "The Two Widows" (a reprinting of "The Wives of the Dead") in July; "Roger Malvin's Burial" (a reprinting) in August; and "Fire-Worship" in December.

Concord, May 3^d 1843.

Dear Bridge,

I am almost afraid that you will have departed for Africa before this letter reaches New York; but I have been so much taken up with writing for a living, and likewise with physical labor out of doors, that I have hitherto had no time to answer your's. It was perhaps as well that you did not visit Concord again;[1] for, by comparison of dates, I am led to believe that my wife and yourself were in Boston at the same time. She had gone thither to take leave of her sister Mary (the "gal," of your stage-coach story) who is now married, and has sailed in the May steamer for Europe.[2] Thus there is only one old-maid in the family.

I formed quite a different opinion from that which you express about your description of the storm. It seemed to me very graphic and effective; and my wife coincides in this judgment. Her criticism on such a point is better worth having than mine; for she knows all about storms, having encountered a tremendous one on a voyage to Cuba.[3] You must learn to think better of your powers. They will increase by exercise. I would advise you not to stick too accurately to the bare fact, either in your descriptions or narrations; else your hand will be cramped, and the result will be a want of freedom, that will deprive you of a higher truth than that which you strive to attain. Allow your fancy pretty free license, and omit no heightening touches merely because they did not chance to happen before your eyes. If they did not happen, they at least ought—which is all that concerns you. This is the secret of all entertaining travellers. If you meet with any distinguished characters, give personal sketches of them. Begin to write always before the impression of novelty was worn off from your mind; else you will begin to think that the peculiarities, which at first attracted you, are not worth recording; yet these slight peculiarities are the very things that make the most vivid impression upon the reader. Think nothing too trifling to write down, so it be in the smallest degree characteristic. You will be surprised to find, on reperusing your journal, what an importance and graphic power these little particulars assume. After you have had due time for observation, you may then give grave reflections on national character, customs, morals, religion, the influence of peculiar modes of government &c; and I will take care to put these in their proper places, and make them come in with due effect. I by no means despair of putting you in the way to acquire a very pretty amount of literary reputation, should you ever think it worth your while to assume the authorship of these proposed sketches. All the merit will be your own; for I shall merely arrange them, correct the style, and perform other little offices as to which only a practised scribbler is *au fait*.

In relation to your complaints that life has lost its charm—that your enthusiasm is dead—and that there is nothing worth living for—my wife bids me advise you to fall in love. It is a woman's prescription; but a man—videlicet, myself—gives his sanction as to its efficacy. You would find all the fresh coloring restored to the faded pictures of life; it would renew your youth—you would be a boy again, with the deeper feeling and purposes of a man. Try it—try it—first, however, taking care that the object is every way unexceptionable, for this will be your last chance in life;—if you fail, you will never make another attempt. Speaking of love, Longfellow was in love with Miss Appleton when he wrote Hyperion: but, if his own assurance to myself may be credited, he has since then never ceased to be so.[4] Except yourself, Long-fellow is my only college-acquaintance about whom I now really care much. Pierce, somehow or other, has faded out of my affections.

I suppose you will see O'Sullivan in New York. I know nothing about the prospects of office, if any remain.[5] It is rather singular that I should need an office; for nobody's scribblings seem to be more acceptable to the public than mine; and yet I shall find it a tough match to gain a respect-able support by my pen. Perhaps matters may mend; at all events, I am not very eager to ensconce myself in an office, though a good one would certainly be desirable. By the bye; I received a request, the other day, from a Philadelphia Mag-azine, to send them a daguerreotype of my phiz, for the purpose of being engraved.[6] O'Sullivan, likewise, besought my wife for a sketch of my head; so you see that the world is likely to be made acquainted with my personal beauties.[7] It will be very convenient for a retired and bashful man to be able to send these pictorial representatives abroad, instead of his real person. I know not but O'Sullivan's proposal was meant to be a secret from me; so say nothing about it to him.

Your idea of the Lake-Deities is fitter for poetry than for my humble prose. It would be excellent machinery for an Epic.

It would gladden us much to have you here for a week, now that the country is growing beautiful, and the fishing-season is coming on. But this is not to be hoped for till your return. Take care of your health, and do not forget the sketches. It is not the profit to myself that I think about; but I hope that they may contribute to give your life somewhat of an adequate purpose—which, at present, it lacks.

God bless you—

N. H.

You have not given me your address, while on the cruise.[8]

1. See 265.1.

2. Mary Peabody married Horace Mann on May 1, and they embarked on that day in the *Britannia* from Boston. Bridge apparently explained to an informant on February 27, 1868, that "the gal of the stage coach story . . . was Mrs Mann, and the first time I saw her, she was a young and extremely pretty girl of 18 or 19. I was going at the time by stage to College from my home in Augusta. I sat on the back seat and immediately in front sat this young lady and by her side a gentleman, and next to him beyond on the same seat another man, a Colonel Buttman, a man of some consequence, a village magistrate in fact. In the stage coaches of that day, it was customary for some one person to take the lead in conversation very much as it is the case at a dinner table. Colonel Buttman had been filling this part and had been discoursing for an hour on a great variety of subjects. Finally, he said: 'On one occasion Dean Swift was riding along in a stage coach just as we are doing now and he suddenly discovered a man and a woman under a hedge actually engaged Sir, yes! by God sir! actually engaged in the act of copulation!'—Just at this point the man next him kicked him on the shin, and the Colonel turning around saw the color mounting to the cheek of the young damsel. He looked entirely disconcerted and roared out in stentorian tones 'By God! Sir, I forgot the gal' " (MS in unknown hand, Berg).

3. Tharp, *The Peabody Sisters of Salem*, p. 72.

4. Longfellow had met Frances (Fanny) Appleton (1817–61) of Boston in Switzerland in 1836, shortly after the death of his first wife. Under the name Mary Ashburton she was the heroine of his romance *Hyperion* (1839). They were married July 13, 1843, having made their engagement on May 10; see Thompson, *Young Longfellow*, pp. 421–22.

5. See 283.2.

6. In his letter to Lowell of March 27 Poe had mentioned his intention to give in the *Stylus* "a series of portraits of the American literati, with critical sketches . . . we shall have medallions, about 3 inches in diameter. Could you put me in possession of any likeness of yourself?—or could you do me the same favor in regard to Mr Hawthorne?" (*Letters*, I, 232). On April 17 SH wrote to Louisa Hawthorne that NH had agreed both to write for the *Stylus*, and to have his portrait appear in it (MS, Berg). On the same date Lowell wrote to Poe that Hawthorne's "wife will make a drawing of his head or he will have a Daguerreotype taken, so that you can have a likeness of him" (Woodberry, *Life of* . . . *Poe*, II, 24).

7. No portrait of NH appeared in the *Democratic Review*.

8. This postscript was added in available space at margin after the dateline.

268. FRAGMENT, TO LOUISA HAWTHORNE, SALEM[1]

Concord, May 28, 1843.

I congratulate you upon the demise of Beelzebub. I give my assent and corroboration to the whole contents of this letter, especially to the invitations,[2] which *must* be accepted.

Nath. Hawthorne.

1. A postscript by NH to an unrecovered letter by SH sold from the estate of Rebecca B. Manning by the American Art Association, Anderson Galleries, New York, November 19–20, 1931. The catalogue describes SH's "long and newsy letter, describing in great detail the advent of spring at Concord. Hawthorne's rest from writing and his labors in the garden, news of Longfellow's engagement to Fanny Appleton (a reward *'for his long & hitherto ineffectual devotion—We expected him here this spring but perhaps his head or heart are too much occupied'*), etc." See *Hawthorne at Auction*, ed. C. E. Frazer Clark, Jr. (Detroit: Gale, 1972), p. 238.

2. Presumably to Louisa, Elizabeth, and Mrs. Hawthorne, to visit the Manse.

June 17th 1843. Concord

My dear Louisa,

I think you are very naughty indeed not to answer my letter, or rather, not to write to Nathaniel, & say whether or not you can accept our invitation. There are several other friends coming to see us, & so it is quite important to know about the exact time of each visit, that they may not interfere, because we have but one guest-chamber for them. Therefore, dear Louisa, please to write immediately & let us into the secret of your purposes. Meanwhile I assure you that you must not disappoint us. If the first week of July be not convenient for you, choose another time out of all July & August & September, & we will not let any body come to usurp your place at that given time. Tell us also whether that dear, precious mother admits the idea of coming to see her son with you. You know we have an ancient chair of great comfort for her to sit upon, & she shall, if she likes, remain in her chamber & look down on this green & bowery avenue, & hear the birds all day long, & whenever she is willing, we will pay her homage there, & carry to her fruits & flowers. Nobody shall disturb her. No visitors shall come, & she shall not even see *me* except when she desires it. Tell her we have a pleasant gallery, airy & large, where she shall walk when she pleases, & which shall be her reception-room, when she desires to behold Nathaniel. Tell her she can sit at her chamber-window & watch Nathaniel in his garden.

Also, commend me to the voluntary nun, the lady Elizabeth, & tell her I wish her to let us know what time she will come. Tell her that nobody walks in Concord but us & Mr Emerson, so that she can have all the hills, vales, woods & plains to herself, & will meet no one, & she shall sail in the boat & do every thing she pleases. Tell her she must not hesitate, for we may not be here another summer perhaps, & then she will never see the old Abbey,[1] or know how delightful Nathaniel's first—I should say—second home is.

To all these questions & petitions we beg an answer as soon as possible, that we may arrange our summer, & know who will come & when. I am in such a hurry I can say no more but that we are perfectly well. With our love to your mother & E.

truly yours,
S. A. H.

[*In NH's hand:*]

P.S. (Private) If want of cash be the hindrance, I will endeavor to send some in the course of the summer; though everybody is so dilatory in payment that I am put to considerable inconvenience.

N. H.

1. I.e., the Manse, which in her letter to Louisa of August 5 SH was to call "the old monastery" (MS, Berg).

Concord, July 2^d. 1843.

My dear Sir,

There is a mistake as to my having refused to write for Graham's Magazine; the truth is, I have heretofore had no opportunity to refuse, even had I been so inclined—your own letter being the first intimation that my contributions might be acceptable.[1]

I am never a very diligent penman in the summer time; and, moreover, I had projected a little work for children as this summer's literary labor and amusement, which is still to be begun.[2] I have likewise one engagement to fulfil for a Magazine, before I can undertake any other of the kind.[3] These matters being first disposed of, I shall be very willing to send you an article, and will agree to the terms you propose, rather than take upon myself to settle the marketable value of my productions.[4]

I am advised that the publishers of Magazines consider it desirable to attach writers exclusively to their own establishments, and will pay at a higher rate for such monopoly.[5] If this be the case, I should make no difficulty in forswearing all other periodicals for a specified time—and so much the more readily, on account of the safety of your Magazine in a financial point of view. Should you desire an arrangement of this kind, be pleased, at your leisure, to state the terms of it. I hope to free myself from other engagements by October, at furthest, and shall then be happy to become one of your contributors.

With much respect,
truly Yours,
Nath. Hawthorne.

Rev. R. W. Griswold,
Philadelphia.

1. Rufus Wilmot Griswold (1815–57), journalist and anthologist, had replaced Poe as literary editor of *Graham's Lady's and Gentleman's Magazine* in May 1842. See *DAB* and Joy Bayless, *Rufus Wilmot Griswold: Poe's Literary Executor* (Nashville: Vanderbilt University Press, 1943). Griswold had probably seen Lowell's correspondence with Poe concerning NH's possible contribution to *The Stylus:* see 266.1, 267.6.

2. Presumably the mythological narratives that were to become *WB* and *TT*. See 264.

3. See 272.

4. George Rex Graham (1813–94) was already famous as the editor who paid well-known contributors with "unprecedented liberality," having raised the circulation of *Graham's* to 40,000 by March 1842 (*DAB*). SH wrote to her mother on January 9, 1844, that Griswold had written to NH "when he took the editorship, & requested him to write, telling him that he intended to make the magazine of a higher character than it had possessed, & therefore ventured to ask his contribution—offering five dollars per page, & the liberty of drawing for the money the moment the article was published, & the number of pages thus ascertained" (MS, Berg). NH's "Earth's Holocaust" appeared in *Graham's*, XXV (May, 1844), 193–200.

5. Longfellow had written to Griswold November 27, 1842, that "if Mr. Graham will give me $50 for every article [i.e., poem] I send him, I will agree to write for no other Magazine but his" (*Letters*, II, 479). See also Bayless, *Griswold*, chapter 3. By July, 1844, *Graham's* was claiming that Longfellow, Bryant, Cooper, and "a host more of the *best* American writers" wrote for it "*exclusively*" (XXVI, 48).

[Concord] July 9th 1843.

My dear Louisa,

I recieved your very welcome letter on the 22^d June, & was truly sorry you could not come while it was warm & fresh. But as it has since proved, the first week of July was very cold, & so I am now glad. Nathaniel is quite reconciled, because he is ambitious that you should eat of his vegetables, which are not ripe yet. I am grieved that our dear mother will not be persuaded to come at all. I am sure she *would not* be ill here. But I can entirely sympathise with her shrinking from such a journey, with her delicate nerves & disuse of travelling. When the rail-road is finished[1] I shall teaze her again, & wish she would endeavour meanwhile to accustom her thoughts to the idea of coming.

We shall be very glad to have you come the first of August, & if the almanac guesses aright, the weather will be warm then.

July 14th. Dear Louisa—I have been so lazy lately that I did not finish my letter. We shall not consider ourselves badly off to have you only, I assure you, though we want the mother so much. As to Elizabeth, she cannot find any excuse for refusing our petition, & after your visit is accomplished, I shall fully expect to see her. What! would she go to Boston to see Mr Allston's pictures & not come to her own & only brother's house to see him!! Believe it not, ye Penates! Our Water-lily[2] is now beautifully painted & caulked by a sailor-friend of Nathaniel,[3] who, out of devout love to him & his own generous nautical heart,—has been most useful to us. In this newly garnished boat, Elizabeth shall explore the seas

& no one shall disturb her. The water-lilies are now abundant, & she can go on voyages & bring back rich freights, for which I will pay her with the gold of thanks. Tell her I do not have a day-visitor once a month, & she cannot concieve how retired she will be here. Cardinal flowers will bloom in August, & the Orchis grows in Concord.

My mother made us a visit the last few days of June, & before she came, Miss Anna Shaw & Mrs Frank Shaw[4] spent a day & night with us. We have had no other guests since Father in May. Tomorrow I expect Mr & Mrs Hillard, & Mr H. will leave his wife to make a short visit. I feel so indebted to Mrs H. for her admirable care of Nathaniel while with her, that I am anxious to be most hospitable to her.

We shall not put off your coming, dear Louisa, for *any body*. I know Nathaniel cares more about it than any other visit, & I should be exceedingly disappointed to miss it. I think he feels more affection for you all constantly instead of less as time wears on. His loving me does not cast you out of his heart, but rather makes more room there, & he appreciates your worth & values your regard more & more. I could not love him so much, if this were not so, for it would seem to me a great want in him not highly to respect & truly to affection such a mother & sisters. But in this, as in all other things, I find him exactly right. He satisfies my highest sense of good & nobleness, & I reverence him as profoundly as I love him. He is thinner than in winter, but perfectly well. I shall leave a space for him to tell you of his garden.

> With most affectionate regards to
> our mother & sister E yours
> very truly ever,
> .   Sophia.

[*In NH's hand:*]
(Private) I have received no money yet, and the Devil knows

when I shall. Come if you can, and I will let you have some
as soon as possible.

N. H.

1. See 283.3.

2. The boat NH had bought from Thoreau the previous September 1 for $7. It was then called the *Musketaquid*. See *AN*, p. 356.

3. Horatio Bridge.

4. Anna Blake Shaw (1817–78), who later married William Batchelder Greene (see *FIN*, pp. 676, 888), and Sarah Blake Sturgis Shaw (1815–1902), who had married Francis George Shaw (1809–82) in 1835. SH had been a close friend of Sarah, and of her cousins the daughters of Captain William Sturgis. See 97.3.

Concord, July 20th, 1843

Dear Sir,

Being pressed with other engagements, I cannot write anything more for the Boy's and Girl's Magazine at present.[2] I
therefore return the Design.

Respectfully Yours,
Nath. Hawthorne.

Samuel Colman, Esqr.
Boston.

1. Samuel Colman, a Portland bookseller and publisher, had brought out Longfellow's early grammars and readers in the 1820s. He moved to New York in the
thirties, and published Longfellow's *Hyperion* in 1839, shortly before his becoming bankrupt ruined any prospect of his publishing the two-volume *TTT*; see
Longfellow, *Letters*, II, 148. He surfaced in Boston in 1843 as manager of the
bookstore of T. Harrington Carter & Co. (*Stimpson's Boston Directory*).

2. NH's "Little Daffydowndilly" was published in the *Boys' and Girls' Magazine*, II (August, 1843), 264–69, and was collected in *SI*. The monthly, published
by T. H. Carter & Co. from January to December 1843, was edited by Colman's
wife, Pamela Atkins Chandler Colman.

Salem, August 26th. 1843

Dearest Phoebe[1] Hawthorne,

Already an age has elapsed since I parted from thee, mine own life; although, according to human measurement, it is but about twenty-seven hours. How I love thee, wife of my bosom! There is no telling; so judge it by what is in thine own deepest and widest little heart.

Sweetest, what became of that letter? Whose fault was it, that it was left behind? I was almost afraid to present myself before thy mother without it. Nevertheless, the Count[2] and I made it our first business to call at 13 West-street, where we found Madame Peabody[3] (I call her so to please my Dove) in the book room alone. She seemed quite as well as usual, and regretted, I believe, that she had not gone to Concord— and so did thy husband; but thou needest not say so to the good old gentleman who sits looking at the outside of this letter, while thou art reading the inside.[4] I gave her all the information I could about thy condition—being somewhat restrained, however, by the presence of O'Sullivan, who, methinks, might have had the tact to step out. However, there was nothing essential that could not be communicated in his presence.

Taking leave of thy mother, I went with the Count to M[r] Bancroft's door, and then parted from him, with some partial expectation of meeting him again at dinner. Then I looked in at the Athenaeum reading-room, and next went to George Hillard's office. Who should I find here but Longfellow, and with him Mr. Green, the Roman Consul,[6] whom, as thou

• 699 •

knowest, it was Bridge's plan to eject from office for thy husband's benefit. He has returned to this country on a visit. Never didst thou see such an insignificant looking personage (or person rather;) and it surprised me so much the more, as I had formed a high idea of his intellectual incarnation from a bust by Crawford,[7] at Longfellow's rooms. Longfellow himself seems to have bloomed forth and assumed solidity and substance since his marriage;[8]—never did I behold a man of happier aspect; although I know one of happier fortunes incomparably. But Longfellow appears perfectly satisfied, and to be no more conscious of any earthly or spiritual trouble than a sunflower is—of which lovely blossom he, I know not why, reminded me. Hillard looked better than I have ever before seen him, and was in high spirits on account of the success of his oration. It seems to have had truly triumphant success—superior to that of any Phi Beta Kappa oration ever delivered.[9] It gladdened me much to see this melancholy shadow of a man for once bathed and even pervaded with a sunshine; and I must doubt whether any literary success of my own ever gave me so much pleasure. Outward triumphs are necessary to him; to thy husband they are anything but essential.

From Hillard's I went to see Colonel Hall, and had a talk about politics and official matters; and the good Colonel invited me to dinner; and I concluded to accept, inasmuch as, by dining with the Count, I should have been forced to encounter Brownson—from whom the Lord deliver us.[10] These are the main incidents of the day; but I did not leave Boston till half past five, by which time I was quite wearied with the clatter and confusion of the city, so unlike our quiet brooding life at home. Oh, dear little Dove, thou shouldst have been with me; and then all the quiet would have been with me likewise.

Great was the surprise and joy of Louze when she found me at the door. I found them all pretty well; but our poor mother seems to have grown older and thinner since I saw her at last. They all inquired for thee with loving kindness. Louze intended to come and see us in about a week; and I shall not thwart her purpose, if it still continue. She thinks she may be ready in a week from to-day. And, dearest little wife, I fear that thy husband will have to defer his return to thy blessed arms till the same day. Longfellow wants me to dine with him on Friday; and my mother will not be content to give me up before Thursday; and indeed it is not altogether unreasonable that she should have me thus long; because she will not see me again, certainly, until after our child is born. How it made my heart thrill to write that sentence!

But, sweetest Phoebe, thou knowest not how I yearn for thee. Never hadst thou such love as now. Oh, dearest wife, take utmost care of thyself; for if any harm should come to thee during my absence, I should always impute blame to myself. Do watch over my Dove, now that I am away. And should my presence be needful before Saturday, I will fly to thee at a moment's warning. If all continue well, I shall proceed to Boston on Thursday, visit Longfellow on Friday, and come home (oh, happiest thought!) on Saturday-night, with Louze, if she finds it possible to come. If anything should detain her, it will be our mother's health. God bless thee. Amen.

Afternoon.—What a scrawl is the foregoing! I wrote fast because I loved fervently. I shall write once more before my return. Take care of thy dearest little self and do not get weary.

Thy best of Husbands.

---

1. NH's first extant use of this pet name, later used for the heroine of *HSG*. Phoebe ("bright") was used by Shakespeare and others as a name for the moon

and its goddess, Artemis, twin sister and counterpart of Phoebus, the sun, the god Apollo—SH's name for NH. SH wrote to Louisa on September 6 that NH returned from Salem "very lustrous and animated. His visit home and sea bathing revived him very much" (MS, Berg).

2. O'Sullivan, who was to arrive at the Manse on August 17 (SH to Louisa, August 5; MS, Berg). The title is a humorous reference to his devotion to the memory of his Irish ancestors, especially Donall O'Sullivan (1560–1618), a fierce opponent of Queen Elizabeth, and awarded by Philip III of Spain the title of Earl of Bearehaven (DNB). In "Rappaccini's Daughter," first published in the *Democratic Review*, XV (December, 1844), 545, NH alludes to that magazine as "*La Revue Anti-Aristocratique*," and to its editor as "the Comte de Bearhaven" (*MOM*, p. 93).

3. SH's mother.

4. SH's father, visiting in Concord until September 2.

5. SH was now pregnant with Una, as she had written to Louisa on August 5: "A little immortal stranger is in my bosom. . . . I think it is more than two months that we have been made happy by this promise of new life" (MS, Berg).

6. George Washington Greene (see 93.5).

7. Thomas Crawford (?1813–57), expatriate American sculptor, a close friend of Greene; he was to marry Greene's cousin. The bust, made in 1840, was much admired by Longfellow and Hillard. See Longfellow, *Letters*, II, 231, 284, 307, Plate IV; Robert C. Gale, *Thomas Crawford: American Sculptor* (Pittsburgh: University of Pittsburgh Press, 1964), pp. 18–19, Plate II.

8. See 267.4.

9. George Hillard's address to the Harvard chapter of Phi Beta Kappa on August 24, "The Relation of the Poet to His Age."

10. SH had written to her mother, December 29, 1842, that she dreaded Orestes Brownson's coming to visit the Old Manse, because he would "scare the gentle echoes of Paradise with his bellowing" (MS, Berg); see also "A Sophia Hawthorne Journal, 1843–1844," ed. John J. McDonald, *NHJ 1974*, pp. 7–10. For the literary relationship of Brownson to O'Sullivan at this time, see Arthur M. Schlesinger, Jr., *Orestes A. Brownson: A Pilgrim's Progress* (Boston: Little, Brown, 1939), pp. 155–60; Harris, pp. 145–52.

Boston, Sept 2^{d} 1843

Dear L.

You cannot call at Mrs. Hillard's on your way to Concord;[1] because she has gone to Illinois—being unexpectedly called thither by the illness of her sister-in-law. The Concord stage starts at four °clock in the afternoon. The cars leave Salem, I think, at 3/4 past two. It would not be safe to depend upon reaching the stage-house in season; so that I fear you must come to Boston in the forenoon. Is there not a stage from Salem? Perhaps it might suit you better than the cars.

Yours affectionately,
N. H.

1. SH wrote to Louisa on September 6 and 15, encouraging her to come, and offering the Peabodys' hospitality to replace Hillard's; on September 18 Louisa wrote apologizing for not having come. She finally arrived in early October, as SH indicated in a letter of October 26 (MSS, Berg). See John J. McDonald, "A Guide to Primary Source Materials for the Study of Hawthorne's Old Manse Period," *Studies in the American Renaissance*, 1977, pp. 261–312, nos. 219, 222, 223, 228.

EDITORIAL APPENDIXES

TEXTUAL COMMENTARY
THE LETTERS, 1813–1853

THE CENTENARY EDITION of Hawthorne's letters relies for the most part on the original manuscripts. It also includes transcripts from manuscripts now unknown, either handwritten by Sophia Hawthorne or by other hands, or published in newspapers, periodicals, or books. Also included are letters largely written by other persons, principally by Sophia, to which Hawthorne made contributions; the complete texts of such letters are given to put his additions into context. There are a few catalogue references to letters in private hands and not available to scholars; it is to be hoped that these letters will become accessible in future years. For the present, this edition offers the first overview of Hawthorne's correspondence, with a minimum of editorial intervention and in as clear text as is practical.

For clarity, the chronological number of every letter and the recipient's name and location are given in a headline. When Hawthorne wrote two or more letters on the same day, they are given in alphabetical order according to the recipient's last name. Also given in this headline, when necessary, is the warning that the text printed is only a fragment of the original letter. The datelines are in the majority of cases Hawthorne's own, establishing the place of origin and the date of inscription. When Hawthorne omitted one of these elements, it is provided in square brackets, and if he wrote the wrong date (based on information in the letter), the correct date follows in brackets.

The body of the letter then follows. Hawthorne's arrangement of paragraphs and his indentation (or lack of it) at the start of them have been reproduced as in the copy-texts. Similarly, the division of lines in the dateline, salutation, complimentary close, and occasional interior address have been reproduced. No attempt, however, has been made to reproduce the placement of these elements on the page; their positions have been made uniform: dateline and close flush right; salutation and interior address flush left. Also, in the case of transcripts where the MS is unavailable, housestyling of such elements (e.g., printing the signature in large and small capitals) has been ignored and uncharacteristic forms have been emended (e.g., a colon in the salutation, or the signature "Nath'l"). It has not been judged necessary to attempt to reproduce, or to comment on, the graphic embellishments that Hawthorne added to the dateline or to his signature in a few of the letters of his student days. Also, most annotations on the letters by persons other than Hawthorne (mainly by autograph collectors, indicating prices paid or identifying references in the letter) have not been reproduced or noted. When the recipient made a note on the letter of historical value, the comment is given in a historical note or textual note.

Letters written largely by another hand are treated in the same way, except that a bracketed note "[*In NH's hand:*]" directs the reader to Hawthorne's contribution and, in cases where confusion might result, a second bracketed note indicates a continuation in the other person's hand.

When catalogue references quote a portion of a Hawthorne letter not now available to scholars, the quotation, shorn of its surrounding quotation marks, is presented as the letter text, identified as a fragment in the headline. When no direct quotation is given, or when information is paraphrased in the catalogue (e.g., date and origin), the account given of the letter is printed inside square brackets to indicate that the text is the substance, but not the exact words, of the original letter.

The Introduction has discussed Sophia Hawthorne's difficulties with the editing of Hawthorne's notebooks and letters, after a proposal by James T. Fields that a biography of her husband be made from the author's own words. She studied some two hundred love letters that she had saved and whose virtues newly touched her; she transcribed extracts from a number of them and published them in *Passages from the American Notebooks*. As she read them in a new perspective, she found some letters more explicit than others, and, in fear that Philistine eyes might share the intimacies, she overmarked words and passages even of those withheld from publication: first in an easy spiraling penstroke, and later with added complexity of strokes, false ascenders and descenders, and capitalization of interior words to pretend they held initial place in covered sentences. Although her overmarking was thorough, rhythmic patterns allow the tracing of Hawthorne's text underneath, and the length of his separation of words was indicated by clear lines above or below her interference. The recovery of most of the overmarked passages has removed the necessity of noting them in the text—the removed words now reappear in context. Where passages covered by her overmarking still have not been deciphered, however, the text necessarily reads "[*obliteration*]." Wounds left by her physical destruction of manuscript, likewise, are unavoidably signaled in the text by "[*excision*]," where Sophia scissored away a passage that she did not want read, and by "[*excision verso*]," where the passage on the other side, probably innocuous, was also destroyed. The use of the terms has no relation to whether the portion lost was on the recto or verso of the manuscript leaf, only to which excision was deliberate. In all cases, the extent of overmarking and excision is described in the textual notes.

The effects of excision are summarized in printing the

final leaf of Letter 115. Hawthorne's letters were written on single leaves or folded sheets of paper, the first recto and verso and second recto holding the letter, the second verso holding the postal address. The letters were then folded into rectangles averaging four by six inches, a pocket to be sealed with wax. In writing to Sophia, he often added last-minute notes on sections of the cover that would be folded out of sight. Letter 115 may be presumed to have been in this state, for Sophia scissored away the margins of the cover, and the verso of her cut shows the recto of the leaf with its continuity lost, although the subject matter obviously needed no censoring. The right margin shows, even in printed reproduction, Hawthorne's habit of leaving an arc uninscribed where on the verso hot wax would be dropped and pressed down with a seal. For the full description of the fragmentary Letter 115, see the textual note. Obliterations and excisions made by other hands and by Hawthorne himself are handled in the same way.

Although most of the manuscript letters have otherwise survived in good condition, in some cases the sheets were torn when the wax seal was broken, tattered around the edges or at folds in the page, or trimmed by autograph collectors interested only in the valuable signature at the close. Also, Hawthorne or a later owner of the manuscript sometimes allowed a blot of ink to drop carelessly onto a page, obliterating a word or part of one. In nearly all instances, the missing letters or words can be reconstructed from their context, in which case they are restored to the printed text, with the nature and extent of the reconstruction detailed only in the textual note. If, however, continuity of the text has been lost, and no reconstruction is possible, a bracketed note— "[MS torn]," "[hole in MS]," or "[blot in MS]"—signals the loss in the text, and the note describes its extent. In the case of excised signatures, where they have been located in collections, they are returned to their proper place; otherwise, no attempt has been made to conjecture what form of close or signature Hawthorne used.

In a few cases, only a portion of a letter has survived, either in manuscript or transcript form. In such cases, where it is impossible to determine how much text has been lost at the beginning or end, or at an ellipsis in the transcript, the surviving portions are printed as they stand, after the warning in the headline, "Fragment, to. . . . " Similarly, letters that lack salutations or closes, because Hawthorne or another correspondent was interrupted or in great haste, are printed as they stand without editorial interference, and the textual or historical notes inform the reader whether the incompleteness of the text was due to loss of manuscript, editing by Sophia for print, or simple inadvertence. For reference, however, a bracketed dateline including conjectural origin and approximate date has been supplied in the few cases where Hawthorne omitted it.

Hawthorne's letters were most often carefully written, without need for alteration, and it was only after occasional haste that he had to make changes when he read over what he had written. His spellings are often unfamiliar, but of his time: "cotemporaries," "guager," "ministring," "sirname," "canvass" for cloth. Occasionally he varied spelling: "thereabouts-thereabout," "draught-draft," "parlour-parlor." No attempt is made by the Centenary text to modernize or correct Hawthorne's characteristic spellings or to regularize forms that he apparently did not differentiate. Similarly, the misspellings present in his childhood letters and in portions of letters written by other hands (e.g., his early "pleasent" and "beleive," his mother's "trimmins," and Sophia's "recieve" and "headach") appear exactly as they stand in the copy-texts.

Emendations are limited to matters of plain and unambiguous inadvertence. Occasionally Hawthorne repeated words (dittography) or left out a word obviously required by the sense (omission), especially at a line or page break; these have been emended. Spellings that are clearly slips of the pen ("eigth" for "eighth," "cetainly" for "certainly") or that are uncharacteristic of Hawthorne's usual practice ("dissapointment," "concieve") are corrected, with the original reading always given in the textual note.

When a possible compound is hyphenated at the end of a line in the copy-text, the form has been adopted that agrees with parallels within the same letter or that is most characteristic of letters closest in date to the one in question. A list of such cases is given in an appendix, along with one of words end-line in the Centenary text but hyphenated within the line in the copy-texts.

Hawthorne's heavy and often inconsistent punctuation has not been regularized, and emendation is limited to supplying an occasional period at the end of a sentence or the second in a series of quotes or parentheses when these were inadvertently omitted. Hawthorne's placement of punctuation marks, however, is often ambiguous in the manuscript, and some judgment has had to be exercised in transcribing them. His apostrophes are often far to the right of the word to which they belong: "dont'," "Sophias' "; these have been assumed to belong in their proper place. In some cases, several marks of punctuation fall simultaneously on the line; in Letter 542, for instance, commas (or semicolons), dashes, and quotation marks appear together in a vertical configuration. Rather than try for a facsimile reproduction of such punctuation, the editors have consistently placed quotation marks *outside* commas and periods, *inside* colons, semicolons, exclamation marks, and question marks, and always *before* dashes. In a few cases, where the placing of quotation marks seems clearly in error (e.g., outside a close parenthesis) they have been moved and the emendation noted in the textual notes; in all other cases, where the manuscript is ambiguous, Hawthorne has been assumed to follow standard printed conventions of his day.

No attempt has been made, however, to standardize usages that Hawthorne clearly mixed freely. Thus, his use of single, double, or no quotation marks at all around the titles of literary works is given as in the manuscripts, even when he alternated within a single letter. Also, no effort is made to standardize his free use of "Mr.-Mr-M^r-M^r." within letters. Length of dashes has been regularized to an em dash for punctuation, a hyphen for short expurgation ("h-ll-fired"), and a two-em dash for long expurgation ("Nathl H——"). Hawthorne's underscoring for emphasis has been interpreted as italics in the printed text, except in a few cases where he underscored dates for reference, not emphasis; here a rule has been printed under the date. Finally, where it is unclear whether a given dot is circular or oblong, it has been read as a period or a comma as the sense of the surrounding text requires; no effort has been spent attaching micrometers to such blots to produce a facsimile text.

In the same way, spelling and punctuation in portions of letters written by other hands have been emended only when the error is plainly the result of inadvertence. Otherwise, the copy-text appears without regularization, except that Sophia's erratic use of a small dash both within sentences and at their ends has been standardized to an em-dash internally and to a period at conclusions. As before, when the Centenary text departs from the clear reading of the copy-text, the original reading is given in the textual note.

L. N. S.

B. E.

TEXTUAL NOTES

Each textual note is keyed to the chronological number in the headline of the letter text. The repository of the MS copy-text, or the source of copy-text in transcript or printed form, is then named.

In certain cases, the condition of the manuscript is described, most notably when the headline describes the letter text as a "fragment." Hawthorne (NH) customarily wrote to Sophia (SH) on sheets that were folded in half to form two leaves, or three pages and a cover for the address. When NH used the cover for a postscript, this fact is noted. Also, if SH or another hand separated the two leaves and destroyed one, this is recorded: "First leaf of a sheet; second leaf unknown" (or vice versa). When the letter text printed in this volume is the result of detective work combining material from two or more fragments and even from early printed transcripts, the exact nature of this reconstruction is explained.

When a cover or envelope has survived, the address and evidence of posting (if any) are given. Minor variations in address form (such as the spelling-out or abbreviation of state names) are not recorded. When a postmark is legible, the town and date are transcribed (again, minor variants in abbreviations are not given); when it is visible but illegible, it is simply noted as "faint postmark." Letters addressed but lacking any postmark may have been delivered by hand or by express coach, included inside another cover, or simply not postmarked by the mail service.

All substantive alteration of a MS by NH is then identified. It was his habit to wipe off wet ink when he had a second thought or caught an error, and to write upon the same spot. When the original words or letters are legible, they are reported in this form: "NH wrote 'at' over wiped-out 'on the'." When he did not wipe off ink but simply wrote over a word or altered its letters, the fact is reported as: "NH altered 'me' to 'for'." NH's deletions were often by pen-stroke horizontally across words and infrequently by diagonal slashes; these instances are reported as: "NH cancelled 'to'." To insert an interlineation, he customarily used a caret to mark the placing; the word or words interlined and their location are given here.

Substantive alterations of portions of letters not written by NH are not recorded in these notes unless the alterations are in NH's hand.

In the note then follow any Centenary emendations of spelling, words supplied (usually articles or prepositions), and punctuation supplied (principally, periods). Some MSS are damaged, and reconstructed letters and words are shown bracketed, in this form: "Letters are supplied at break in MS: '[wa]s'." Readings conjectured from context or from surviving ascenders and descenders at the edge if an excision are also recorded as such here.

All interference with NH's text by other hands, principally SH's overmarking, excisions, and alterations, then are identified in the note. In the case of overmarkings that have been deciphered, the text has been silently restored to the letter, but the note details their extent. In the case of excisions or unrecovered overmarkings, the approximate amount of lost MS is estimated here. All of SH's changes in her husband's wording are given, and when her alteration corrects NH's inadvertent error, the note records the reading as "accepted as an emendation."

In the same way, any accidental loss of MS through tear-ing, trimming, or blotting, is detailed here, with the estimated loss of text.

If not already given in a historical note, any inscription on the letter by its recipient deemed of historical relevance is transcribed at this point (for instance, SH's marking of certain love letters as "especial").

In the case of certain letters available only in two or more independent transcripts, a list of substantive variants is given, with an indication of which have been accepted and which rejected by the Centenary text.

Finally, previous publications of letters from MS, consulted in the preparation of this volume, are noted, with indications of the most important previous errors in dating and transcription.

1. MS, Hawthorne Collection, #6249-a, Virginia. In sentence 4, 'now' before '4 weeks' is emended from 'know', inadvertently repeated from line above; in same sentence, NH's dittography 'but but' before 'it will be' has been emended. Facsimile publ., *WA*, 502–3; part publ., Lathrop, p. 68; *Works*, XII, 453; *EIHC*, LXXIV (January, 1938), 7–8.

2. MS, Berg. Address: Mr. Robert Manning, Raymond, Maine; postmark, Bowdoinham, July 31, missint [*sic*] and forwarded. At break in MS, letters are supplied: '[as ple]asent'. Part publ., Lathrop, p. 75; publ., *EIHC*, LXXIV (January, 1938), 16–17.

3. MS, Berg. Address: Mr. Robert Manning, Salem, Mass.; faint postmark. In Mrs. Hathorne's close, 'to' is supplied before 'say'. Facsimile, Rains Galleries catalogue, March, 1936, p. 101. Part Publ., Lathrop, pp. 89–90; Pickard, pp. 15–16.

4. MS, Middlebury. Address: as for 3. Part publ., Lathrop, p. 79; *Works*, XII, 456–57.

5. MS, Essex. Address: as for 2; postmark, Salem, July 27. In sentence 5, NH wrote 'would' over wiped-out 'brin' before 'bring' and interlined without caret at edge of page 'ed' above 'content'. Quoted, *EIHC*, XLI (January, 1905), 100; part publ., Pickard, pp. 16–17; *WA*, 508; *NEQ*, XI (March, 1938), 67–68.

6. MS, Morgan. Address: Miss Maria L. Hathorne, Raymond, Maine. In sentence 2 following the last verse, NH wrote 'of' over wiped-out 'in' before 'your honour'. In sentence 2 after the first verses, 'poetry' is emended from 'poety', and in sentence 2 after the last verse, 'and' is emended from 'ang' before 'good sense'. In ¶1, sentence 7, the close quotes after 'stream' are supplied. In the close, 'servant' is emended from 'sevant'. Publ., *NHHW*, I, 105–6.

7. MS, Essex. Address: Mrs. Elizabeth C. Hathorne, Raymond, Maine; postmark, Salem, March 7. In sentence 7, NH altered '8' from '7'. Part publ., Lathrop, pp. 81–82; *Works*, XII, 461; *NEQ*, XI (March, 1938), 69–70.

8. MS, Essex. Address: as for 6; postmark, Salem, March 21. In sentence 2, NH interlined 'know' before 'Mother' and in sentence 14 interlined 'no' before 'account'. Letters are supplied in sentence 9 at tear in MS, 'w[as]', and in sentence 10, 'm[ad]'. On verso an unknown hand (possibly Mary Manning's) has added this note: "Dear Brother   I want to know if when the Letter of Administration was taken out, wether you posted notices up in public places besides advertizing in the papers   send by next post."

9. MS, Essex. Address: as for 6; postmark, Salem, March 28. NH wrote three lines following ¶1 sentence 4 but obliterated them with scrawls, and repeated the process with two lines added after ¶4 sentence 1. In ¶4 sentence 4, NH inter-

lined 'one' at the end of the sentence. In ¶1 sentences 5–6, letters are supplied at break in MS: '[were comi]ng' and '[and]'. Excerpts publ., *WA*, 509–10; publ., *NEQ*, XI (March, 1938), 72.

10. MS, Essex. In postscript sentence 2, NH interlined 'I' before 'staid' and 'room' before 'till'. In the final sentence, letters are supplied at blot in MS: 'p[ag]es'.

11. MS, Morgan. In sentence 4, NH interlined 'down'. At torn foot of letter, the name is supplied: 'H[athorne.]'.

12. MS, Essex. Address: as for 7; postmark, Salem, July 25. In sentence 1, a word following 'last' was inked over by NH, as was 1/2 line after 'Saturday' at end of ¶1. Excerpt publ., *WA*, 510; publ., *NEQ*, XI (March, 1938), 77.

13. MS, Hawthorne Collection, #6249-a, Virginia. Address: as for 2; postmark, Salem, Aug. 15. Publ. *NEQ*, XI (March, 1938), 79.

14. MS, Hawthorne Collection, #6249-a, Virginia. Address: as for 2; postmark, Salem, Sept. 12. Publ., *NEQ*, XI (March, 1938), 80.

15. MS, Essex. Address: as for 7; postmark, Salem, Sept. 26. In sentence 9, 'all' before 'of his Brothers' is overmarked by unknown hand. Quoted, *EIHC*, XLI (January, 1905), 101; publ., *NEQ*, XI (March, 1938), 80.

16. MS, Essex. Address: as for 7; postmark, Salem, Oct. 31. NH's portion to his sister was written on recto and verso of the lower half of the sheet, so that she could 'cut off this part' if she liked (she did not). In ¶2 sentence 2 of this part, 'Do write me' is emended from 'Do me write me'; in sentence

3, close quotes are supplied after 'monstrous'; in final sentence, 'know' is emended from 'now'. Publ., *NEQ*, XI (March, 1938), 81.

17. MS, Huntington HM 2608. Fragment, heavily trimmed on all sides. In last sentence, one or two short words are torn away.

18. MS, Essex. Address: as for 7; postmark, Salem, Mar. 6. In sentence 12, 'am', and in sentence 13, 'that' and 'Ebe's' are supplied at tear in MS. In sentence 3 of Mary Manning's letter, her dittography 'of/of' before 'the manner' is emended. Publ., *EIHC*, LXXV (April, 1939), 119.

19. MS, Morgan. Address: as for 7; postmark, Salem, March 13. At end of ¶1, NH inked over 'contrary' but repeated it, following. In ¶2 sentence 2, he added two lines after 'studying', but wiped them out and put a period after 'studying'. In sentence 2 after verse, letters are supplied at break in MS: 'o[nl]y'.

20. MS, Berg. Address: as for 2; postmark, Salem, May 8. Publ., *NEQ*, XI (March, 1938), 85.

21. MS, Essex. Address: as for 7; postmark, May 15. NH obliterated 3/4 line after sentence 5 and 1/2 line after sentence 6—perhaps false starts.

22. MS, Essex. In sentence 3, NH altered 'dissapointed' to 'disappointed' before 'at not receiving'. Publ., *NEQ*, XI (March, 1938), 85–86.

23. MS, Essex. Address: as for 7; postmark, Salem, June 12.

24. MS, Essex. In final sentence, NH stroked closing parenthesis upon 'I', and added 'I'. Part publ., George E. Wood-

berry, *Nathaniel Hawthorne* (Boston and New York: Houghton, Mifflin, 1902), pp. 16–17; publ., Pickard, pp. 17–18; *WA*, 514; *NEQ*, XI (March, 1938), 86–87.

25. Text, *NHHW*, I, 104. 'Hathorne' is emended from 'Hawthorne', uncharacteristic of this period.

26. MS, Essex. Address: as for 7; postmark, Salem, Aug. 28. In sentence 10, NH altered 'me' to 'for' before 'me'. In sentence 3, NH interlined 'here' (the caret in error placed before 'over'), in sentence 12, 'me' before 'the cloaths', and in sentence 14, 'the' before 'vortex'. Part publ., *WA*, 514; publ., *NEQ*, XI (March, 1938), 87–88.

27. MS, Essex. Address: William Manning Esq., Salem Massachusetts; postmark, Brunswick, Oct. 9. Part publ., *WA*, 514.

28. MS, Essex. Address: as for 7; faint postmark. Quoted, *WA*, 514; publ., *NEQ*, XIII (June, 1940), 251.

28A. MS, Essex. Address: Miss Elizabeth M. Hathorne, Salem, Massachusetts; Note: favoured by Mr. McKeen. In ¶6 sentence 2, NH altered 'beleive' to 'believe' before 'it'. Publ., *NEQ*, LVI (Sept., 1983), 425–28, reading 'real hot Calvinist sermon' for 'red hot Calvinist sermon'.

29. MS, Essex. Address: as for 7; postmark, Brunswick, Oct. 31. Part publ., *WA*, 515; publ., *NEQ*, XIII (June, 1940), 254–55.

30. MS, Essex. Address: as for 7; postmark, Brunswick, Nov. 14. In ¶1, NH added 'have' before 'had' in left margin. NH inked over 2 1/3 lines before 'The Vacation'. Publ., *NEQ*, XIII (June, 1940), 256–57.

31. MS, Essex. Publ., *NEQ*, XIII (June, 1940), 257–58.

32. MS, Berg. Address: as for 3; postmark, Raymond, Jan. 16.

33. MS, Berg; MS fragment, Bowdoin. Address: as for 3; postmark, Brunswick, Feb. 20. In ¶2, NH wrote 'if' over wiped-out 'it', and in ¶3, sentence 1, 'occasion' over wiped-out 'occassion'. Publ., *NEQ*, XIII (June, 1940), 258. NH's excised signature was separately preserved at Bowdoin.

34. MS, Huntington HM 11027. Address: as for 6; postmark, Brunswick, April 15. In ¶1 sentence 3, NH interlined 'will' before 'excuse', in ¶4 sentence 3, he added 'have' before 'time' in left margin, and in ¶6 sentence 5, 'expect' before 'both'. In ¶ 5, 4 1/2 lines were lost at tear in MS.

35. MS, Essex. Address: as for 7; postmark, Brunswick, April 30. In ¶2 sentence 2, NH cancelled 'a few days' and interlined 'some time' above. Publ., *NEQ*, XIII (June, 1940), 259–60.

36. MS, Essex. Address: Mrs. Elizabeth C. Hathorne, Salem, Mass.; faint postmark. Part publ., Lathrop, pp. 117–18; Woodberry, pp. 19–20.

37. MS, Mrs. Erastus Plummer, Raymond, Maine. Address: Mark Leach, Jr. Esq., Raymond, Maine; postmark, Brunswick, June 6. Publ., Moncure D. Conway, *Life of Nathaniel Hawthorne* (London: Walter Scott, 1895), p. 25.

38. MS, Essex. Address: Miss Elizabeth Hathorne, Salem, Mass.; postmark, Brunswick, August 5. Quoted, Pickard, p. 21; *WA*, 517; part publ., Lathrop, pp. 118–19; Woodberry, pp. 20–21; publ., *NEQ*, XIII (June, 1940), 261–63.

39. MS, Huntington HM 11028. Address: Miss Maria L.

Hathorne, Salem, Mass.; postmark, Brunswick, May 6. In ¶1 sentence 2, NH interlined 'right' above cancelled 'write'. The phrase 'some of the students' follows cancelled 'the students'. In ¶4 sentence 3, dittography 'the the' before 'best' is emended. Publ., *NHHW*, I, 110–11.

40. MS, Essex. In ¶1 sentence 4, NH wrote 'Mrs.' over wiped-out 'Sarah'. In postscript, NH interlined 'before' before 'commencement'. In ¶1 sentence 4, 'were' is emended from 'where'. Part publ., Lathrop, p. 112; publ., *NEQ*, XIII (June, 1940), 268–69.

41. MS, Berg. Address: as for 39; postmark, Brunswick, Aug. 12. In ¶8 sentence 4, NH wrote 'none' over wiped-out 'of' before 'of these'. In ¶3 sentence 2, NH interlined 'all' before 'inclined', and in ¶2 of postscript, 'a letter' before 'by Monday'. In ¶7 sentence 8, 'persuade' is emended from 'persuader' before 'her'. In ¶8 sentence 2, 'to' before 'see me' is supplied where MS is damaged.

42. MS, Bowdoin. Address: as for 28A; postmark Brunswick, Me., Oct. 2. In ¶5 sentence 2, NH interlined 'been' before 'a new', in ¶7 sentence 2, 'hear' before 'from', and in postscript sentence 2, 'me' before 'in'. Facsimile, Anderson Galleries of New York, Catalogue 3911, April 29, 1931; publ., *NEQ*, XIII (June, 1940), 272.

43. MS, Huntington HM 11030. Portion of larger half, trimming showing at head and foot. Publ., *NHHW*, I, 112–13, as "1823."

44. MS, Huntington HM 11029. Address: Miss Mary Manning, Salem, Mass.; postmark, Brunswick, Nov. 28. In ¶1 sentence 2, 'disappointed' is emended from 'dissapointed'. The close 'Your affectionate nephew' and signature were lost by being torn away; they are supplied from text, *NHHW*, I,

116–17. Publ., *Second Book of Dofobs* (Chicago: Society of the Dofobs, 1909), pp. 33–34, as "1821."

45. MS, Morgan. Publ., *NHHW*, I, 117–19.

45A. MS, Essex. Address: as for 28A, with 'Mr. Dike'.

46. MS, Essex. Part publ., Lathrop, pp. 119–20, 120–21; publ., *NEQ*, XIII (June, 1940), 276–77.

47. MS, Essex. Address: Samuel Manning, Esq., New-Haven, Connecticut; postmark, Salem, Aug. 12. Publ., *EIHC*, XCIV (July, 1958), 182–83.

48. Text, without heading or signature, Lathrop, pp. 143–44, as "about 1830." Quoted, *Yesterdays*, p. 46, as "1831," and *Works*, XII, 468, as "1830."

49. MS, Hawthorne Collection, #6249-a, Virginia. Address: Mr. Samuel G. Goodrich, Boston, Mass. Publ., Barrett, pp. 5–6; Wilson, pp. 122–23.

50. MS, Mrs. Richard K. Agnew, Winnetka, Illinois. Address: Mr. John S. Dike, Steubenville, Ohio.; postmark, Salem, Feb. 20. In sentence 7, NH altered lower-case 'c' to capital in 'Court'. In sentence 36, 'y' in 'Betsey' is supplied where NH inadvertently wrote off the edge of the page. In sentences 43-44, letters are supplied at a break in MS: 'them[.]', '[I be]lieve', and 'ti[me]'. Publ., *NEQ*, VI (September, 1933), 450–53.

51. Transcript, Horatio Bridge, MS, Bowdoin, from copy furnished Bridge, February 24, 1884, by J. C. Derby. Publ., Derby, *Fifty Years among Authors, Books, and Publishers* (New York: G. W. Carleton, 1884), p. 113. Reference, Conway, p. 42, as "Nov. 9, 1830."

52. MS, Gordon Hall, Wilmette, Illinois. Address: John S. Dike, Esqr., Merchant, Steubenville, Ohio; postmark, Salem, Sep. 2. In ¶1 sentence 3, NH wrote 'I' over wiped-out 'Yo' and in sentence 9, 'dispositions of' over wiped-out '(?) of the hus'. In ¶2 sentence 4, he wrote 'he' over wiped-out 'w' and in sentence 17, 's' of 'spirituous' over wiped-out capital 'S'. In ¶3 sentence 2, NH wiped out 'h' before 're-ceived'. In ¶5 sentence 3, NH wrote 'somethings', then wiped out the final 's'. The postscript, written to the left of the signature, is put after it, following NH's usual practice. Publ., *NEQ*, VI (September, 1933), 454–57.

53. MS, Essex. Address: Miss Maria L. Hawthorne, Salem, Mass., (Care of R. Manning, Esqr.); postmark, Shaker Village, August 18. In ¶1 sentence 2, NH wrote 'at' over wiped-out 'on the'. In ¶1 sentence 7, he interlined 'day' before 'we', in 13, 'a' before 'back', and in 22, 'older' before 'than'. In ¶1 sentence 1, 'writing' is emended from 'wri-/ing', and for sentence 6 a period is supplied. In ¶2 sentence 6, letters and words lost at tear in MS are supplied: 'gro[ans]', 'lon[g]', '[more]', '[up]', 'ex[hibit]', 'a[m]'; in sentence 7, '[our]', 'til[l we]', 'surpr[ised]', '[on]', and period after 'farthest'; in ¶3 sentence 1, 'thou[gh]'. Quoted, *AM*, XXVII (February, 1871), 248, and *Yesterdays*, pp. 46–47; part publ., Lathrop, pp. 144–45; publ., *EIHC*, LXXV (April 1939), 125–28.

54. MS, Gordon Hall, Wilmette, Illinois. Address: Mr. John S. Dike, Steubenville, Ohio; postmark, Salem, Sept. 11. In ¶1 sentence 1, NH interlined 'me' before 'as', and in ¶4 sentence 1, 'father' before 'and mother'. In ¶1 sentence 2, NH blotted 'a' in 'account', then added it again before the blot. In sentence 8, he wrote 'to drink' over wiped-out 'a lit', 'broke' over 'met', and 'l' of 'limbs' over 'y'. In sentence 13, he altered 'possible' to 'possibly' and in sentence 14 wrote 'publishers' over wiped-out 'Obs'. In sentence 21, he first

wrote 'Crowinshield', then added an 'n' above the line after 'w'. In sentence 22, he wrote 'I' over wiped-out 'H' and in sentence 29 'news' over wiped-out 'knews'. In ¶3 sentence 5, he first wrote 'joing', then wiped out the 'g' and finished 'joining'; in the same sentence he wrote 'inspecting' over wiped-out 'obser'. In ¶2 sentence 7, letters are supplied at break in MS: 'oc[cu]pies'. In ¶2 sentence 9, 'recommend' is emended from 'reccommend'. Publ., *NEQ*, VI (September, 1933), 465–68.

55. MS, Morgan. Address: Miss M. L. Hawthorne, Newburyport. For ¶1 sentence 2, a period is supplied. Publ., *NHHW*, I, 126–27.

56. MS, Historical Society of Penna. Address: Messrs. Carey & Lea, Philadelphia; postmark, Salem, Jan. 30. Publ., Conway, p. 44.

57. MS, Boston Public Library. Address: Col. Franklin Pierce, Hillsboro', New-Hampshire; postmark, Salem, June 28. In ¶1 sentence 3, NH wrote 'cannot' over wiped-out 'don't' before 'see why', in sentence 4, 'then' over 'min' before 'minister', and in ¶2 sentence 1, 'Col.' over 'your'. In ¶4 sentence 2, NH wiped-out 'you' before 'you would'. Part publ., James T. Fields, *Underbrush* (Boston, J. R. Osgood, 1877), p. 35; publ., *Youth's Companion*, August 19, 1886, p. 318.

58. MS, Essex. In ¶1 sentence 3, NH interlined 'a' before 'plaguey' and 'rode' before 'with four'; in sentence 4, he interlined 'all which' before 'I galloped'; in sentence 5, he interlined 'how' before 'the thermometer'.

59. MS, Essex. Address: Miss Maria L. Hawthorne, Care of R. Manning, Esq., Salem. Publ., *Colophon*, n.s. 3 (September, 1939), unpaged.

60. MS, Essex. Quoted, Lathrop, p. 173, and *EIHC*, XLI (January, 1905), 104; publ., *Colophon*, n.s. 3 (September, 1939), unpaged.

61. MS, Morgan. In the postscript, 'perhaps' is emended from 'perhas'.

62. MS, Essex. Address: Miss Elizabeth M. Hathorne, Care of R. Manning, Esq., Salem, Mr. Dike. Publ., *Colophon*, n.s. 3 (September, 1939), unpaged; *EIHC*, XCIV (July, 1958), 187.

63. MS, Essex. Address: as for 53; In ¶1 sentence 2, NH interlined 'of' before 'Uncle Robert'. In ¶1 sentence 9, 'to' is supplied after 'obliged'. Quoted, *EIHC*, XLI (April, 1905), 105; publ., *Colophon*, n.s. 3 (September, 1939), unpaged.

64. MS, Essex. Noted in *EIHC*, XLI (April, 1905), 104, as "Feb. 4th"; part publ., Lathrop, p. 171; publ., *Colophon*, n.s. 3 (September, 1939), unpaged.

65. MS, Essex. In sentence 5, NH interlined 'have' of 'I have'; dittography 'I/I' is emended at same place. Publ., *Colophon*, n.s. 3 (September, 1939), unpaged.

66. MS, Essex. Quoted and paraphrased, *EIHC*, XLI (January, 1905), 105.

67. MS, Essex. NH erased a false start, 'The Magazine is'. Quoted, *EIHC*, XLI (January, 1905), 106; publ., *Colophon*, n.s. 3 (September, 1939), unpaged.

68. MS, Hawthorne Collection, #6249-a, Virginia, Publ., Wilson, p. 126.

69. MS, Essex. For sentence 7, a period is supplied. Quoted,

EIHC, XLI (January, 1905), 105–6; publ., reading "en feu with the" for 'no further with', *Colophon*, n.s. 3 (September, 1939), unpaged.

70. MS, Essex. In ¶1 sentence 1, '[mo]re' is supplied at a blot in MS; for sentence 2, a period is supplied. The note was written on verso of a scrap torn from the beginning of a letter from S. G. Goodrich to NH, ca. February 17, 1836. It reads: "Dr Sir, [¶] I have been hoping several days to see your face—but as I have been necessarily busy, & you do not make me a call, I have not had that pleasure. I enclose a check for the $46 due on Token account. [MS torn]" See also 63.1. Published, *Colophon*, n.s. 3 (September, 1939), unpaged.

71. MS, Essex. In sentence 7, 'to write' is emended from 'to to write' and 'it' is supplied before 'is'. Quoted, Lathrop, pp. 170–71, and *EIHC*, XLI (January, 1905), 106—with "Paul" for 'Park'; publ., *Colophon*, n.s. 3 (September, 1939), unpaged, with "transmitted to Aunties" for 'transmuted to Amber'.

72. MS, Essex. In sentence 6, NH interlined 'a' before 'poor'. For sentence 7, a period is supplied. Quoted, *EIHC*, XLI (January, 1905), 106; part publ., Lathrop, pp. 172–73.

73. MS, St. Lawrence.

74. MS, Harvard, bMS Am 1340.2 (2616). Part publ., Lathrop, p. 175; George L. Austin, *Henry Wadsworth Longfellow* (Kansas City: Van der Vaart, 1883), p. 210.

75. MS, Harvard, bMS Am 1340.2 (2616). Address: Professor H. W. Longfellow, Cambridge, Mass.; postmark, Salem, June 4. In final ¶, NH cancelled 'and make' and wrote 'in making' above. In ¶1 second sentence from end, a period is supplied at edge of page. At breaks in MS, letters are supplied: ¶2 sentence 6, 'ha[d] made'; ¶3 last sentence, 'h[ad] a

desir[e to] run'. Part publ., Lathrop, pp. 175–77; Austin, pp. 210–11; *Works,* XII, 476.

76. MS, Harvard, bMS Am 1340.2 (2616). Address: as for 75; postmark, Salem, June 20. In ¶1 sentence 4, NH interlined 'and correctness' before 'of any'. Part publ., Lathrop, pp. 177–78; Austin, p. 213; *Works,* XII, 478; publ., Longfellow, *Life,* I, 255.

77. MS, Essex.

78. MS, MHS. Publ., *NHJ* 1974, p. 38; facsimile, pp. 32, 34.

79. MS, Harvard, *45 M. 437.

80. MS, Essex, Clark Collection. Address: Joseph P. Boyd, Esqr., Cincinnati, Ohio; postmark, Salem, January 19. Facsimile, *NHJ* 1972, p. 142, and text, p. 141.

81. MS, Bowdoin. Address: Horatio Bridge, Esqr, Augusta, Maine. At breaks in MS, letters are supplied: sentence 1, '[from] you'; sentence 4, 'impossib[le]'. The excision is of 3 1/2 lines.

82. MS, Essex. Address: Postmaster, Thomaston, Maine. In ¶1 sentence 3, NH interlined 'you' before 'merely'. In sentence 4, he wiped out 'mar' before 'marriage'. Publ., Conway, pp. 61–66; *Writings,* XVII, 421–22.

83. MS, Harvard, bMS Am 1340.2 (2616). Address: as for 75. In ¶1 sentence 2, NH superceded a comma with a dash after 'of it'. Publ., Longfellow, *Life,* I, 280.

84. MS, Hawthorne Collection, #6249-a, Virginia. Address: Mrs. Lydia T. Fessenden, 53 Hancock Street, Boston,

Mass.; postmark, Salem, Apr. 12. In first part, ¶3 sentence 2, NH interlined 'it' before 'if they'; in second part, ¶2 sentence 2, he interlined 'am' before 'engaged', and ¶3, wrote 'wisdom' over wiped-out 'guidance'. The postscript, written in the right margin, opposite the last sentence, is placed after the signature, following NH's usual practice. The two parts are written on the first and second rectos of a sheet, with address on second verso. Publ., Wilson, pp. 127–28, 131; Barrett, 6.

85. MS, Hawthorne Collection, #6249-a, Virginia. Address: J. L. O'Sullivan, Esqr, Washington City. NH left a gap of 3 1/2 lines after ¶1; ¶2 has a different subject.

86. MS, St. Lawrence. Address: David Roberts, Esq., Salem, Mass.

87. MS, Harvard, bMS Am 1340.2 (2616). In ¶1 sentence 2, NH interlined 'had' before 'such' and in final sentence, 'to' before 'set'. Closing quotes of book title in ¶1 are supplied. Publ., Longfellow, *Life,* I, 298.

88. MS, Cornell. Address: J. L. O'Sullivan, Esqr, New York City; faint postmark. In dateline NH altered '6th' to '5th'. In ¶4 sentence 1, NH cancelled repeated 'do her', and in sentence 2 interlined 'not' before 'been'. A period is supplied for ¶2.

89. MS, Berg. In ¶1 sentence 2, NH wrote beginning of 'Stationers' over wiped-out 'Co'.

90. MS, Berg. Written on lower half of last leaf of MS "The Lily's Quest" (William E. Stockhausen collection) but now separated from it and trimmed. Address (split between the two MSS): Mrs. C[. H.] Gilman, Care [of] S. Gilman, D.D., [C]harleston, South Carolina.

91. MS, Hawthorne Collection, #6249-a, Virginia. Address: George Bancroft, Esq., Custom House, Boston; postmark, Salem, Jan. 12. In ¶1 sentence 2, NH interlined 'that' before 'the', and in sentence 3 'to decide', wrote 'to' over wiped-out 'for'. Facsimile, front cover, *The Month at Goodspeed's*, 28 (October-November, 1956).

92. Text, George Haven Putnam, *George Palmer Putnam* (New York: G. P. Putnam's Sons, 1912), p. 196, under dateline "Jan., 1839."

93. MS, Harvard, bMS Am 1340.2 (2616). Address: as for 75; faint postmark. In ¶1 sentence 7, NH altered 'd' to 'D' in 'Duties'. Part publ., Lathrop, p. 182; *Works*, XII, 485; Longfellow, *Life*, I, 311.

94. MS, Huntington HM 10863. Address: Miss Sophia A. Peabody, Salem, Mass. In ¶1 sentence 2, NH interlined 'our' before 'reminiscences'; in ¶2 sentence 5, he interlined 'in' above 'it' without a caret. In ¶1 of March 7 entry, letters are supplied at break in MS: 'disappointmen[t with]out', 'I [know] that', 'thing[, you] will', 'sins of [omission] or', and 'heart, [you] will', as published in *LL*, I, 3–7, perhaps from still intact MS.

95. MS, Huntington HM 10864. Address: as for 94. In the April 3 entry, ¶1 sentence 1, NH interlined 'it' before 'till' and in sentence 3, wrote 'Do' of 'Doubtless' over wiped-out 'But'; in sentence 7, a dash after 'glances' supersedes a comma. In sentence 11, NH wrote 'character' over wiped-out 'healthy'. In last sentence, he superceded a comma with a parenthesis before 'dipping'. In April 4 entry, sentence 2, he interlined 'me' after 'awaiting'. In the April 3 entry, 'Hooper's' is emended from 'Hoopers''. At the end of April 4 entry, SH trimmed away close and signature, one or two lines. The April 5 entry is on second verso cover. Excerpt

from ¶1 publ., *PAN*, I, 219–20, *Works*, IX, 224; publ., *LL*, I, 8–12.

96. MS, Huntington HM 10865. Address as for 94. NH wrote dateline 'Wednesday' over wiped-out 'Tuesday' and ¶3 sentence 3, 'noon is' over 'noonday is'; in ¶4 sentence 8, he cancelled 'to' before 'contrive' and in ¶5 sentence 3 interlined 'never' before 'seen'. Periods have been supplied for the signature and for 'P.M.', squeezed in at the bottom of the leaf. The April 19 entry is on second verso cover. In April 19 entry, SH overmarked sentence 7 'as when . . . arms.' and put a period after preceding 'tremulously'. Part publ., *NHHW*, I, 202–4; publ., *LL*,I, 13–18.

97. MS, Huntington HM 10866. Address: Miss Sophia A. Peabody, Care of Dr. N. Peabody, Salem, Mass.; postmark, Boston, May 5. In ¶1 sentence 1, NH superceded a comma with a dash before 'which'. In ¶1 sentence 3, NH wrote 'my heart' over wiped-out 'I longed for', and following 'to' over wiped-out 'for'; in May 3 entry, ¶2 sentence 2, he interlined 'not' after 'could'. The postscript, written in the left margin beside the signature, is placed after it, following NH's practice. SH overmarked ¶1 sentence 7 'And . . . friends!' and ¶4 sentence 10 'my surest . . . good man, and'. In May 3 entry, ¶2 sentence 2, 'have been' is emended from 'have', and a period is supplied for sentence 4; in sentence 11, letters are supplied at break in MS: 'hearts [hav]e' and 'na[t]urally'. Publ., *LL*, I, 19–23.

98. MS, Harvard, bMS Am 1603.3 (7). Address: Mr. B. H. [*sic*] G. Fuller, Bowdoin College, Brunswick, Maine; postmark, Boston, May 16.

99. MS, Hawthorne Collection, #6249-a, Virginia. Address: B. B. Thacher [*sic*] Esqr., Boston. NH wrote 'acceptance' over wiped-out 'assistan'. ¶2 publ., Wilson, p. 129.

100. MS, Harvard, bMS Am 1340.2 (2616). In ¶3 sentence 2, NH wrote initial 'y' of 'you may' over wiped-out 'I'. Part publ., *Final Memorials of Henry Wadsworth Longfellow*, ed. Samuel Longfellow (Boston: Ticknor, 1887), pp. 10–11.

101. MS, Robert A. Taylor. In ¶2 sentence 3, 'know' is supplied. Publ., *A Descriptive Guide to the Exhibition Commemorating the Death of Nathaniel Hawthorne* (New York: Grolier Club, 1964), pp. 15–17.

102. MS, Huntington HM 10867. Address: [Miss] Sophia A. Peabody, No. 4, Avon Place, Boston. In ¶1 sentence 3, NH wrote 'to-' of 'to-night' over wiped-out 'this'. In ¶1 sentence 6, 'you")—heaves' is emended from 'you)"—heaves', and in ¶3 sentence 5, 'by' is supplied before 'my nap'. Before ¶4 sentence 5 appears a single parenthesis, apparently to indicate the interruption; since the parenthesis was never closed, it is omitted here. In ¶1 sentence 6, SH overmarked 'or your bosom', and in ¶2 sentence 8, 'and while . . . hearts.'. Her excision in ¶3 on second recto removed 3 lines' depth, about forty words, and on the verso address, 'Miss'; remaining at right margin are words and fragments on three lines: 'be, not', 'um, but', and 'me, when'. Publ., *LL*, I, 24.

103. MS, Huntington. HM 10868. Address: as for 97; postmark, Boston, July 6. In ¶3 NH interlined 'ten' above 'disconted' to form 'discontented'. In ¶6, sentence 2, NH wrote 'You' over wiped-out possible 'Who'. In ¶1 sentence 8 and ¶2 sentence 1, NH wrote 'DOve', perhaps recalling ¶1 sentence 4 'GOD', then correcting himself midway; Centenary reads 'Dove' in both places. In last paragraph sentence 4, 'according' is emended from 'acording'. In ¶3 sentence 9, SH overmarked ', its own pillow,'. In ¶5, letters are supplied at hole in MS: '[mea]nt' and '[enjoy]'. Close and signature were excised. Quoted, *AM*, XXI (January, 1868), 106; *PAN*, I, 208–9; *Works*, IX, 213; publ., *LL*, I, 29–33.

104. MS, Huntington HM 11041. Trimmed leaf; no signature. The date is put by reference to 105; Louisa is conjectured to be the recipient by her position as manager of household routine.

105. MS, Huntington HM 2603. Small leaf, written on recto and verso. See note for 104, on recipient.

106. MS, Huntington HM 10869. Address: as for 97; postmark, Boston, July 16. In ¶1 sentence 2, NH interlined 'it' before 'in', 'it' before 'till', and 'feel' before 'as if', and he altered 'read' from 'reading' before 'them without'. In ¶2 sentence 1, he interlined 'is' before 'sick', and in sentence 4, 'be' before 'ill'. In ¶2 sentence 4, a dash after 'miracle' supersedes the original comma. In ¶2, SH awkwardly excised 3/4 line and 1/2 line, overmarking 'should' and 'her bosom . . . before'; ascenders and descenders allow recovery of 'kiss that' and 'inquire better into'. The excision affected two lines on the verso, leaving 'And this' and 'there you' isolated at left margin. Publ., *LL*, 34–35.

107. MS, Huntington HM 10870. Address: as for 97. Quoted, *Huntington Library Quarterly (HLQ)*, VII (August, 1944), 391; publ., *LL*, I, 36–37.

108. MS, Huntington HM 10871. One leaf, second leaf unknown. In ¶1 sentence 1, NH added 'my' before 'soul' in the right margin and altered 'he' to 'He'. In ¶1 sentence 11, NH interlined 'be' before 'separated', and in ¶2 sentence 7 'were' before 'made'. In July 25 entry, sentence 5, NH altered 'among' to 'in the'. In ¶1 sentences 11 and 12, letters are supplied at a break in MS: 'an[d then]', 'symbol [of]', 'than [any]', 'we [are]', 'w[e] may', 'nor [on]', 'He wi[ll]', and 'along[)]'; in July 25 entry on verso: 'neith[er la]bor', '[be be]tter', 'sur[rounded]', '[the bu]siness', 'ma[chin]e', 'an-

oth[er]', '[wh]eels', and '[bu]t', as published in *LL*, perhaps from still intact MS. In ¶1 sentence 14 'as' is supplied before 'our faith'. SH overmarked ¶1 sentence 5, 'from my bosom' and put a comma before the deletion; she overmarked sentence 9 'while . . . arms', sentence 10 'And . . . us?' sentence 14 'when I hold you in my arms', and sentences 16 and 17, 'Oh, my heart. . . . will feel it.'. Publ., *LL*, I, 38–40.

109. MS, Huntington HM 10872. One leaf; second leaf unknown. In ¶2 sentence 5, NH cancelled 'mentally' and wrote 'mutually' above it; in sentence 8, he interlined 'from' before 'yourself.' In ¶2 sentence 1, query is corrected from MS position before the quotes. Quoted, *HLQ*, VII (August, 1944), 391; publ., *LL*, I, 41–43.

110. MS, Huntington HM 10873. Address: as for 97; postmark, Boston, Aug. 10. In ¶1 sentence 3, NH cancelled 'up' before 'upward' and in sentence 8, cancelled duplicated 'for'. In ¶2 sentence 8, NH superceded a comma with a dash before 'illumine'. Letters are supplied at breaks in MS: ¶1 sentence 6, 'within [m]e'; ¶2 sentence 10, 'it, [my] Dove'; ¶5 sentence 2, 'had be[gun] to'. SH overmarked ¶1 sentences 10–11, 'In my present. . . . together?'; ¶2 sentence 11, 'Where . . . heart.'; ¶6 sentences 3–4, 'at least. . . . husband!', and put a period after 'East-Wind'. At the end of ¶3, two or three words have been excised between 'heart could' and 'if he', and 'never do so' is added above the excision in a second hand; the words are retained as possible transcript of NH, although they may also be a bowdlerization. Final words of ¶5, 'die before their birth!' and ¶6 were written on second verso cover. Quoted, *HLQ*, VII (August, 1944), 391; publ., *LL*, I, 44–48.

111. MS, Huntington HM 10874. Address: as for 97; postmark, Boston, Aug. 24. Closing 'Good bye. . . . Husband.'

written on second verso cover. In the August 23 entry, ¶1 sentence 4, NH first closed the parenthesis after 'milk', then blotted it out and superceded it with a semicolon. In ¶4 sentence 6, 'Never' of 'Nevertheless' and 'in' before 'your letter' are supplied after excision. SH overmarked ¶1 sentence 4, 'In times . . . slumber.' and in ¶6 sentence 6, 'and when . . . arms.', putting a period after 'incomings' before the comma she had overmarked. SH excised 7 1/3 lines at the start of ¶2, the excision affecting a like space on verso, in ¶4. ¶2 of August 23 entry was written on second verso cover. Publ., *LL,* I, 49–53.

112. MS. Huntington HM 10875. Address: as for 97; postmark, Boston, Aug. 28. In ¶6 last sentence, NH interlined 'I' after 'should'. In ¶4 sentence 5, 'imperial' is emended from 'imperi- / ial', and in ¶6 sentence 2, 'is' is supplied before 'strange'. SH overmarked ¶3 sentences 5–8, "He is . . . nevertheless." Quoted, *HLQ,* VII (August, 1944), 392; part of August 27 entry publ., *AM,* XXI (January, 1868), 106; *PAN,* I, 209; *Works,* IX, 213–14; publ. *LL,* I, 54–58, as "25th."

113. MS fragment, Morgan; text, *Memories,* pp. 33–34. After ¶1 *Memories* (terminated by leaders marking excision of unknown length), MS fragment recto 'of learned. . . . on me is' is inserted. *Memories* omitted 'Beloved', but followed MS fragment verso 'I am afraid. . . . say.' in ¶3. The signature 'Nathaniel Hawthorne' is rejected as uncharacteristic of this series of letters.

114. Two MS fragments, Morgan. *Memories,* pp. 32–33, after dateline 'Six o'clock, P.M.' holds ¶1; the long MS fragment holds this, with the second long passage on verso. Another fragment holds the dateline here used, and on verso, 'Beloved, . . . very late.'

115. Four MS fragments, Morgan, of a leaf and a heavily trimmed second leaf; one sentence, text, *PAN*, I, 220. Address: as for 97; postmark, Boston, Sept. 11. NH, on second recto, interlined 'you' before 'a few moments'. SH wrote '1839' after first fragment dateline, and overmarked MS first leaf verso 'Oh, kiss me. . . . too well that' (and succeeding lines, presumably, which she later excised). Her cutting of the second leaf probably was to remove NH notes on the edges of the verso cover. Rose Hawthorne in *Memories,* p. 33, published the dateline but not its verso 'Or, rather . . . self-direct,' The second fragment recto holds 'in comparison. . . . coal-vessel.' MS originally continued 'I would . . . momentous duty.' which was published in *PAN* but afterward trimmed from MS. For *Memories,* Rose joined 'coal-vessel' by leaders to 'Well—'. If she positioned the second fragment below the first, she may have seen that 'I would . . . momentous duty.' would fill the gap, but concluded that it was improper to use. She followed also SH's omission of NH's first phrase, 'in comparision with a fricaseed chicken,' and 'Sweetest Dove', below, and SH's following paraphrase. Rose did not print the versos of the fragments. The MS appearance of the mutilated second leaf recto is approximated in the present text to show SH's scissors' effect on an innocuous passage. The MS second leaf verso holds the address. Part publ., *PAN* I, 220; *Works,* IX, 224; *Memories,* p. 33.

116. MS, Huntington HM 10876. In ¶2 sentence 4, NH's dittography 'was was' before 'communing' is emended. SH overmarked in ¶1 sentence 10, 'not one kiss' and ¶3 sentences 8–12, 'Dove, come. . . . But I should', the excision preventing complete recovery. SH excised 3 1/4 lines at end of ¶1, the excision affecting verso, ¶3, first by 1/4 line after 'whenever I', then by 3 lines after 'But I should'. A second excision, involving 2/3 of the second leaf, then follows; the

excision verso trimmed away address and all but 'Bos' of the postmark. Publ., *LL*, I, 59–63.

117. MS, Huntington HM 10878. Address: as for 97; postmark, Boston, Oct. 5. In ¶2 sentence 3, 'the' is supplied before 'Athenaeum'. In ¶1, SH overmarked sentence 2, 'How could . . . lips?' and sentences 3–4, 'in a conjugal . . . . lips!' (putting a period after preceding 'spirits') and sentence 6, 'and your . . . assurance.'; and in ¶2 sentences 8–10 she overmarked 'I want . . . .evening!' and sentence 14, 'darlingest'. The final two paragraphs and the close were written on the second verso cover. Quoted, *HLQ*, VII (August, 1944), 395; publ., *LL*, I, 67–71.

118. MS, Huntington HM 10877. In ¶3 sentence 15, before 'Gardner Greene's estate', NH wrote 'hill which', wiped out 'which', and wrote 'on which'. In ¶2 sentence 6, he interlined 'of' before 'out united'. In ¶1 sentence 4, SH altered NH's 'chamber' to 'parlor', then crossed it out and wrote 'room' over it. At the MS second leaf recto excision after line 4, ascenders of letters show continued writing, but further length of the excision cannot be stated. At the end of ¶3, SH excised all but 3 1/4 lines of second leaf, trimming away address on verso. Publ., *LL*, I, 63–66.

119. MS, Huntington HM 10879. Address: as for 97; postmark, Boston, Oct. 25. In ¶1 next-to-last sentence, NH wrote 'merry' over wiped-out 'f'. In ¶2 sentence 1, NH interlined 'on' before 'by'. Lines following the ¶3 excision were written on the verso cover at a quarter-turn: letters are supplied at cut verso: 'w[ill]', '[his]', 'f[old]', '[my]', and '[Oh,]'. In ¶1, SH overmarked sentences 6–9 'Oh, beloved. . . . enchantments,', sentence 11, 'Shall she . . . couch?', and sentence 12 'that naughty . . . pillow.' (putting a period after the preceding

'no'), and sentences 21–22, she overmarked 'and his head. . . . to-night!' (putting a period after preceding 'bosom—'). In ¶2 sentences 9–10, she overmarked 'and I have. . . . too?'. In the final sentences of the letter, she overmarked 'Sweetest wife. . . . husband.'. Publ., *LL,* I, 72–75.

120. MS, Huntington HM 10881. Address: Miss Sophia A. Peabody, Salem. Part publ., *NHHW,* I, 207; *LL,* I, 77; both texts dated "15th."

121. MS, Huntington HM 10880. Address: as for 97; postmark, Boston, Nov. 14. SH overmarked ¶1 sentence 6, 'When . . . me.'. Publ., *LL,* I, 76.

122. MS, Huntington HM 10882. Address: as for 97; postmark, Boston, Nov. 18. In ¶1 sentence 6, NH interlined 'have' before 'it', in ¶2 sentence 12, 'am' before 'almost', in ¶5 sentence 7, 'shall' before 'write', in ¶6 sentence 1, 'needs' before 'strongest', and in sentence 2 'you' before 'that'. In ¶4 sentence 1, 'me' before 'with eggs' is supplied, and in ¶5 sentence 4, letters are supplied at tear in MS: '[stor]ies'. SH overmarked ¶2 sentence 7 'and with . . . close at hand.'. Part of ¶5 publ., *PAN,* I, 221; *Works,* IX, 225 (with parts of November 21 entry of 124); publ., *LL,* I, 78–82.

123. MS, Huntington HM 10883. Address: as for 97; postmark, Boston, Nov. 19. SH overmarked ¶2 sentence 3, 'held you in my arms,' and interlined above 'were with you,'. Publ., *LL,* I, 83–84.

124. MS, Huntington HM 10884. Address: as for 97; postmark, Boston, Nov. 21. In ¶2 sentence 2, NH altered 'them' to 'it.', and in sentence 3, interlined 'after' before 'all'. In ¶5 final sentence, SH interlined 'me' of 'trust me to live' after

'to', erased it, and put it before 'it'; the emendation is accepted. In ¶1 sentence 4, she overmarked 'r' of 'your' and all of following 'bosom'. In ¶4 sentence 2, she overmarked 'have' and 'in my arms' and altered preceding 'to' to 'for'. In ¶5, she overmarked sentences 1 and 2, and sentence 3 'too—' after 'now,'. November 21 entry ¶3 quoted, *PAN*, I, 221; *Works*, IX, 225; publ., *LL*, I, 85–88.

125. MS, Huntington HM 10885. Address: as for 97; postmark, Boston, Nov. 26. In ¶2 sentence 2, NH interlined 'it' before 'till', and in sentence 5, he cancelled 'in' before 'you' and interlined 'an' before 'armour'; in ¶4 sentence 4, he wrote 'a married a man' and then cancelled second 'a'. In ¶5 sentence 4, 'opened' is emended from 'openened.' SH overmarked ¶3 final sentence 'Yet . . . mine.'. Publ., *LL*, I, 89–93.

126. MS, Huntington HM 10886. Address: as for 97; postmark, Boston, Nov. 30. In ¶1 sentence 1, NH interlined 'ache' before 'this', and in the last sentence, 'and' before 'profitable' (in which he altered 'f' from 'p'). In ¶2 sentence 4, he cancelled dittography of 'both' before 'through the labyrinth'. In sentence 7, 'interpret' is emended from 'interprets'. Sentence 1 publ., *NHHW*, I, 207–8; publ., *LL*, I, 94–97.

127. MS, Huntington HM 10887. Address: as for 97; postmark, Boston, Dec. 1. SH overmarked in final sentence 'on your husband's bosom.', putting a period after 'hushed'. Publ., *LL*, I, 88–89.

128. MS, Huntington HM 10888. Address: as for 97; postmark, Boston, Dec. 3. In ¶1 sentence 10, 'disappointed' is emended from 'dissappointed'. ¶3 of December 2 entry quoted, *PAN*, I, 221, and *Works*, IX, 225, with sentences from 129 and and a garble from 149; publ., *LL*, I, 100–104.

129. MS, Huntington HM 10889. Address: as for 97; postmark mostly excised. SH's excision before ¶5 removed 4 1/2 lines. In ¶5 sentence 1, 'if' is supplied before 'other'. Part publ., *PAN*, I, 221; *Works*, IX, 225; *NHHW*, I, 208; publ., *LL*, I, 105–8.

130. MS, Huntington HM10890. One leaf; second leaf unknown. In December 12 entry, ¶1 final sentence, NH interlined 'eternal' before 'existence'. In December 11 entry, sentence 9, he wrote 'wh' at right margin, wiped it out, and wrote 'whereas' on following line. In ¶1 sentence 4, 'analogous' is altered: NH wrote 'anall', wiped out the second 'l', and added 'agous'. In ¶1, SH overmarked sentences 9–10, 'I want you. . . . whereas' and altered following 'this' to 'This'. She cut from the second leaf a strip 'not our home', which she pasted to first verso foot. Publ., *LL*, I, 109–11.

131. MS, Huntington HM 10891. Address: as for 97; postmark, Boston, Dec. 21. In December 20 entry, ¶1 sentence 9, NH interlined 'me' before 'in the midst' and in ¶3 sentence 3, 'be' before 'the source'. In the last ¶, 'Dove's' is emended from 'Doves'. In December 18 entry, sentence 4, SH overmarked the text after 'husband' through 'bosom'; at the end of sentence 6, she overmarked 'and a lonely pillow.', putting a period after 'fireside'. In sentence 8, after 'GOD-given days' she overmarked 'and nights'; in the last sentence, she overmarked 'and sleep . . . slumber.', putting a period after 'dearest'. Publ., *LL*, I, 112–16.

132. MS, Huntington HM 10892. One leaf; second leaf not now known. In ¶1 sentence 1, NH interlined 'la' above 'disconsotely' to form 'disconsolately'. In ¶1 last sentence, he wrote 'hol' of 'holiest' over wiped-out 'day'. In ¶1 sentence 2, SH overmarked 'and will mingle . . . kiss.', putting a pe-

riod after 'bosom'; in ¶1 sentence 6, 'bosom.', putting a period after 'her'; in ¶2 sentence 4, 'in my arms', altering preceding 'be in' to 'see me'; in ¶2 sentence 5, 'or at least three whole nights—'; and in ¶3 sentence 2, 'and nights', after 'long days', where SH put a comma, and 'and nights', again after 'those days'. Publ., *LL*, I, 117–18.

133. MS, Harvard, bMS Am 1340.2 (2616). Publ., Longfellow, *Life*, I, 337.

134. MS, Huntington HM 10893. Address: as for 97; postmark, Boston, Jan. 2. In ¶2 sentence 5, NH's dittography 'of of' before 'our life' is emended, and at the end of ¶4, a period is supplied. In ¶6, sentences 1–2, SH overmarked 'in my arms. . . . bosom.', putting a period after 'want you'. Part publ., *NHHW*, I, 120; publ., *LL*, I, 120–23.

135. MS, Huntington HM 10894. Address: as for 97; postmark, Boston, Jan. 3. In ¶6 sentence 3, SH overmarked 'for my pillow is very lonesome.', putting a period after 'beloved'; and ¶6 sentence 6, 'Kiss me . . . Hawthorne.'. Part publ., *NHHW*, I, 211; publ., *LL*, I, 124–27.

136. MS, Huntington HM 10896. Second leaf of a sheet? Address; as for 97; postmark, Boston, Jan. 21. SH excised about 3 lines at close.

137. MS, Huntington HM 10895. Address: as for 97; postmark, Boston, Jan. 25. In ¶2 sentence 6, NH interlined 'caused' before 'my'. SH in ¶4 sentence 1 overmarked 'but it . . . bosom.' and put a period after 'immediately'. Her excision in last ¶ removed 1/5 depth of leaf, but an indeterminate amount of MS. Part publ., *NHHW*, I, 211–13; publ., *LL*, I, 128–31.

138. MS, Huntington HM 10897. Address: as for 97; post-

mark, Boston, Feb. 7. Periods are supplied at ends of ¶4 and ¶5. In ¶5 at tear in MS, letters are supplied: 'attemp[ting]'. SH excised one line, close, and signature. ¶3 quoted, *AM*, XXI (January, 1868), 106–7; *PAN*, I, 209–10; *Works*, IX, 214; ¶2 quoted, *NHHW*, I, 213, as "February 14"; publ., *LL*, I, 132–36.

139. MS, Berg. Address: William B. Pike, Esq., Salem, Mass. In ¶1 sentence 2, NH wrote 'do' over wiped-out 'think'.

140. MS, Bowdoin. Address: as for 139. Periods are supplied at ends of ¶1 and ¶3.

141. MS, Huntington HM 10898. Address: as for 97. In ¶1 of February 13 entry, letters are supplied at break in MS: '[u]s', 'wri[tten]'. In ¶1 of February 12 entry, SH overmarked 'just tired . . . sweet one!' and put a period after 'write' to replace the dash. ¶2 and ¶3 publ., paraphrased, *AM*, XXI (January, 1868), 107; *PAN*, I, 210–11; *Works*, IX, 214–15; publ., *LL*, I, 137–41.

142. MS, Huntington HM 10899. Address: as for 97; postmark, Boston, March 12. In ¶2 of March 12 entry, NH wrote 'Dove', wiped it out, and wrote 'After Breakfast'. In ¶3 sentence 3, 'as' before 'I please.' is supplied. SH excised about 13 lines at start of ¶3, the excision verso affecting the middle of ¶1. In ¶1 sentence 2, 'decease of the other.' is conjectured from ascenders at edge of excision; in ¶3 sentence 1 after excision, letters are supplied: 'prosp[ect of] one'. SH also excised 3 lines at start of ¶5. Final sentence written on second leaf verso, cover. Publ., *LL*, I, 142–45.

143. MS, Dartmouth. Address: J. L. O'Sullivan, Esq., Washington-City, D.C.; postmark, Boston, March 17. In ¶1 sentence 5, NH interlined 'that' before ', during'.

144. MS, Huntington HM 10900. Address: as for 97; post-mark, Boston, March 16. In ¶2 sentence 1, SH overmarked 'in thy . . . heart' and interlined 'as heavy'—resulting in 'thou sittest as heavy as thy husband's heart.'. ¶3 excerpt publ., *AM*, XXI (January, 1868), 107; *PAN*, I, 211; *Works*, IX, 215–16; publ., *LL*, I, 146-50.

145. MS fragments, Huntington HM 10901, 11008. Second leaf of a sheet; first leaf unknown. Address: as for 97; post-mark, Boston, March 18. SH excised 1 1/2 lines at end of ¶1; the verso cover address was cut along the right margin but is largely readable.

146. MS, Bowdoin. Address: William B. Pike, Esqr., 35 Lafayette St., Salem. In ¶3 sentence 1, NH wrote 'Coffee' following 'Essex' and then cancelled it.

147. MS, Huntington HM 10902. Address: as for 97; post-mark, Boston, March 28. In ¶6 sentence 1, NH interlined 'husband' after 'foolish'. In ¶6 sentence 7, letters are sup-plied at break in MS: 'not th[ink h]ow', 'a yea[r a]go'. At end of ¶5 of March 27 entry, SH excised 2 1/2 lines (presumably close and signature), the excision also trimming March 28 entry verso. At end of ¶5, 'head' is conjectured from remain-ing ascenders. In ¶5 sentence 1, an apostrophe is supplied to 'husband's'. In the March 28 entry, on second verso, cover, SH overmarked 'How' but left the isolated 'th[y] head were pil-' on the line below. Part publ., *AM*, XXI (January, 1868), 108; *PAN*, I, 212–13; *Works*, IX, 216–17; publ., *LL*, I, 152–56.

148. MS, Huntington HM 10903. Address: as for 97; post-mark, Boston, April 1. In ¶1 sentence 4, NH wrote 'I dearest', then cancelled 'I' and mended 'd' to 'D'. In ¶2 sen-tence 7, he wrote 'itself', cancelled it, and interlined 'our-

selves'. In ¶5 sentence 1, he interlined 'me' after 'love'. SH
in ¶3 overmarked sentence 3 'Belovedest . . . tonight' and
upon 'tonight' superimposed 'Just' to begin a new sentence;
in ¶4 sentence 2 she superimposed 'complain' upon 'scold'.
The April 1 entries are on second verso, cover.

149. MS, Huntington HM 10904. In ¶3 sentence 4, 'wax' in
'sealing-wax', inadvertently omitted at page break, is supplied. In ¶2 sentence 8, SH overmarked 'every night', and at
end of ¶3, she excised 3/4 page, trimming address on verso;
the extent of inscription excised on recto is unknown.

150. MS, Huntington HM 10905. Address: as for 97; postmark, Boston, Apr. 8. NH in ¶3 interlined 'me' after 'make',
and in ¶4, 'not' before 'sustained'. In ¶1 sentence 2, 'days' is
emended from 'day', and in ¶2 sentence 4, 'is' before 'that
separates' is supplied. In ¶1 SH excised 1 1/2 lines after
sentence 3, then overmarked in following sentence fragment
'for, foolish heart . . . past', putting a period after 'out for
thee'. The excision affected ¶3 on verso by loss of 1/2 line,
then 1 line; at excision letters are supplied: '[hus]band's' and
'[inter]rupted'. In ¶4 sentence 3, SH erased 'vessels' and
wrote 'sets' over it before 'of coal-shovellers'. At beginning of
¶6, she also excised 2 lines after 'Dearest,'. In ¶5 sentence 1
letters are supplied at tear in MS: 'g[ossip]'. A part of April
7 entry publ., *AM,* XXI (January, 1868), 108; *PAN,* I, 213;
Works, IX, 217; publ., *LL,* I, 167–71.

151. MS, Huntington HM 10906. Address: as for 97; postmark, Boston, April 17. NH interlined in ¶1 sentence 3 'is'
before 'not a natural' and in ¶2 sentence 4, 'fit' before 'to
eat'. SH interlined in ¶1 sentence 11 'not' before 'the moments' and, in ¶3 sentence 6, altered 'hardly hardly' to 'hadst
hardly'; both emendations are accepted. In ¶1 sentence 7,
SH excised 3 or 4 words; the excision affected ¶2 sentence 5

on verso, where letters are supplied: '[re]turn'. SH also overmarked in April 17 entry (on second verso, cover) 'and want . . . kisses.'. At hole in MS at ¶3 sentence 6, letters are supplied: '[to] restore'. Publ., *LL*, I, 174–77.

152. MS, Huntington HM 10907. On second recto is an extensive trail of ink, perhaps spilled by SH; obscured readings are conjectured by help of the context: ¶3 sentence 9, 'th[ou m]ade [thy]self', sentence 10, 'Wh[en h]e', 'wear[y a]nd', 'for [thee];', 'when [he]', 'require[th]', 'the [m]ore.'; ¶4 sentence 1, 'M[y]', 'th[ou]', sentence 2, 'w[ere]', 'meth[inks,]', '[a] letter', 'ea[ch]', 'n[ot c]oming', 'Sund[ay]', 'up[on t]hee', 'state a[nd]', 'in wh[ich]', 'Sund[ay]', 'wi[th]', sentence 3, 'fan[cies]', '[o]wnest', sentence 4, '[mom]ent', sentence 5, 'Th[en]', '[he]art-quakes', 'b[e a]voided', 'o[ne] half', '[by] itself', 'gua[rd o]f', sentence 7, '[Dou]btless', 'bu[t t]hy', '[natu]re', 'w[ould]'. In ¶2 sentence 9, 'a' is supplied before 'burthen'. In ¶1 sentence 3, SH overmarked 'and sweetest kisses', putting a period after 'words'; in sentence 5 she overmarked 1/2 line after 'cured by' (not deciphered). In ¶2 final sentence, she overmarked 'he will . . . bosom; and'. After ¶4 she excised 1/3 leaf; extent of inscription is unknown. Part publ, *AM*, XXI (January, 1868), 108; publ., *LL*, I, 178–82.

153. Text, Thomas F. Madigan, *Word Shadows of the Great* (New York: Frederick A. Stokes, 1930), pp. 193–94; date, from Anderson Galleries Catalogue 1722, March 14, 1923.

154. MS, Huntington HM 10908. Address: as for 97; postmark, Boston, April 24. In ¶3 sentence 1, 'to' before 'bed' is supplied. In ¶1 sentence 7, SH interlined 'one' before 'another'; the emendation is accepted. SH excised approximately 11 1/2 lines at the beginning of ¶3 and one word before the close. Part publ., *NHHW*, I, 215–16; publ., *LL*,I, 183–86.

155. Transcript, SH, volume 2, commonplace book; MS, Berg. Facsimile, *NHJ*, 1976, p. 10, and text, pp. 11–13. In ¶2 'the x's mark a deletion in this journal transcript by SH.

156. MS fragment, Hawthorne Collection, #6249-a, Virginia, and MS Fragment, Huntington HM 11017; originally a folded sheet. Address: as for 97. The Virginia first recto runs from dateline to '*excision verso*'. The Huntington fragment recto holds ¶2 through sentence 8 'a message, while'; there the Virginia first verso begins 'I was in the midst' and runs to '*excision*'. The Huntington verso holds the May 1 entry ending at sentence 8 'and interwoven' at foot. The Virginia second recto continues 'throughout all' and holds eighteen MS lines to 'all the time:'; there, the leaf was cut across, and parted from the first leaf at the fold of the sheet. The excision on the first leaf affected 2 1/2 lines at the end of ¶1 and at the end of ¶2 verso, and that on the second leaf removed 1/3 page at the end. The first verso excision also cut across the leaf to the fold, and the upper part of the (Virginia) second leaf remained connected with the Huntington fragment by 3/4 inch depth at the fold; and when the fold was split by intention or mischance, the fragments were separated. In ¶1 sentence 4, 'to have' is conjectured from ascenders above the excision verso. In ¶2 sentence 1, letters are supplied at a tear: 'e[las]tic'. First half of ¶2 publ., *AM*, XXI (January, 1868), 108–9; *PAN*, I, 214; *Works*, IX, 218–19.

157. Transcript by Horace Conolly, MS, Bowdoin. Publ., Gilbert L. Streeter, "Some Historic Streets and Colonial Houses of Salem," *EIHC*, XXXVI (July, 1900), 210–11; Manning Hawthorne, "Hawthorne and 'The Man of God,'" *Colophon*, 2 (Winter, 1937), 269.

158. MS, Huntington HM 10911. In ¶1, NH interlined 'was' before 'restless' and in ¶2 wrote 'at noon' over wiped-out 'to

me at'. SH excised a depth of 18 lines below ¶4, from the removed passage trimmed 'I am sure thou needest it', and pasted the strip at the top edge of following MS passage remaining on second leaf recto. In ¶1 sentence 2, she cancelled 'found' and interlined 'saw'. Remnant of MS second leaf holds only 'Miss' of the address, on verso. Publ., *LL*, I, 187–90.

159. MS, Huntington HM 10912. Address: Miss Sophia A. Peabody, South St. In ¶2 sentence 10, NH wrote 'words' over 'language'. In ¶1, 'Hooper's' is emended from 'Hoopers', and in ¶2 sentence 8, SH added 'no' before 'more time'; the emendation is accepted. Postscript on second verso, cover. Part publ., *AM*, XXI (January, 1868), 109; *PAN*, I, 215; *Works*, XI, 129; publ. *LL*, I, 191–94.

160. MS, Huntington HM 10913. Address: as for 97; postmark, Boston, May 30. SH excised two lines at end of ¶1 and four lines of ¶2 following; the excision also removed five lines on the recto, after ¶1 sentence 3. On the recto words and fragments survive in both margins: 'A . . . ', 'a . . . over', 'H . . . °clock,', 'ye . . . in to', and 'fem . . . all'. On the verso fragments survive in the left margin: 'sho', 'in', 'M', 'to my', 'put t', and 'soul,'. From the indent before 'M' and context following, the heading 'M[ay 30]' is conjectured. SH also excised 2 ½ lines and signature at the end. Part publ., *AM*, XXI (January, 1868), 109; *PAN*, I, 215–17; *Works*, IX, 219–21; publ., *LL*,I, 195–99.

161. MS, National Archives. Quoted, *NEQ*, V, 2 (April, 1932), 248n; publ., *EIHC*, XCII (1956), 62–63; *American Transcendental Quarterly*, XX (1973), suppl., 145.

162. MS, Huntington HM 10914. In ¶3 sentence 3, NH interlined 'it' before 'on the shelf', and in ¶5 sentence 1,

'time' after 'breakfast'. In ¶2 SH overmarked sentence 9, 'I give . . . long.' and in ¶4 sentence 1, 'and desire . . . east.', putting a period after preceding 'day'. In ¶4 sentence 3, she altered NH's 'cuff' to buffet'; in sentence 2 she overmarked 'smiling'. At the end of ¶4, SH excised 4/5 of leaf, the excision also destroying verso address and any inscription there. Following her excision was left 'mend'—perhaps part of a longer word. She most probably wrote the words 'the more closely—' at foot of first leaf verso before the excision; the phrase is similar to NH's hand but 'closely' is placed under 'more' in a manner uncharacteristic for him. The words are kept as transcript of NH. Publ., *LL*, I, 200–203.

163. MS, Huntington HM 10915. First leaf of a sheet; second leaf unknown. Of the final phrase 'submission to thy better judgment', only end-line 'sub-' is in NH's hand; the remainder is in tiny script, taken to be SH's transcription of NH's continuation on a following leaf now unknown. In ¶1 sentence 10 NH changed 'gallery' to 'Gallery.' ¶1 and part of ¶2 publ., *AM*, XXI (January, 1868), 109–10; *PAN*, I, 217; *Works*, IX, 221–22; publ., *LL*, I, 204–7.

164. MS, Huntington HM 10916. Address: Miss Sophia A. Peabody, Care of Rev. R. W. Emerson, Concord, Massachusetts; postmarks, Boston, June 23, Concord, June 24. On cover, NH's 'Concord' struck out, 'Salem' and 'forwarded' added in other hands. In ¶1 sentence 10, NH interlined 'not' before 'know', and ¶2 sentence 3, 'will' before 'lead'. In ¶2 sentence 2, he wrote 'road' over wiped-out 'tract of', and in ¶4 sentence 6, crossed out 'it' before 'to it'. In ¶1 sentences 14-15, SH overmarked 'even when . . . dearest; but', and placed periods after preceding 'safe' and after cancelled 'but', altering following 'if' to 'If'. In ¶ 1 sentence 17, she overmarked 'to thy husband's bosom', putting a comma after pre-

ceding 'home'. Part publ., *NHHW*, I, 219–21; publ., *LL*, I, 208–12.

165. MS, Huntington HM 10964. Address: as for 97. In final paragraph, 'beseech thee not' is emended from 'beseech / not'. Publ., *LL*, II, 99–100, as "1842."

166. MS, Bowdoin. The MS is written in pencil on a leaf torn from a sheet. In sentence 2 NH interlined 'me' before 'to acceed'. Publ., *NEQ*, V, 2 (April, 1942), 248.

167. MS, Huntington HM 10917. Address: as for 97; postmark, Boston, July 11. In ¶1 sentence 3, NH interlined 'is' before 'somewhat' and in sentence 4, 'hours' before 'with'. In ¶1 sentence 1, 'moment's' is emended from 'moments', and in sentence 6, the first 'blockheads' from 'blocheads'. Part publ., *NHHW*, I, 221–22; publ., *LL*, I, 213–14.

168. MS, Huntington HM 10918. Address: Miss Sophia A. Peabody, No. 13, West-street, Boston. In ¶1 sentence 11, NH interlined 'so' after 'said'. A period is supplied after ¶3 sentence 2 'petition'. In ¶1 sentences 1–2, SH overmarked 'and ever . . . arms!' and at the end of the paragraph, 'husband did put thy'. SH excised 1/4 leaf at the end, the excision affecting ¶1 on verso, first 1/2 line, then 5 lines. Publ., *LL*, I, 215–16.

169. Transcript, SH. Publ., *AM*, XXI (January, 1868), 110; *PAN*, I, 218; *Works*, IX, 222.

170. MS, Huntington HM 10919. In ¶1 sentence 2, NH interlined 'to be' before 'borne' and in ¶4 sentence 2, 'had' before 'nothing'. In ¶4 last sentence, 'tonight' is emended from 'to night', which is considered inadvertent. In ¶3 sentences 1–3, SH overmarked comma and 'and then . . . place.'.

At the end she excised 3/4 leaf, the excision also destroying verso address and any inscription there. Quoted, *HLQ*, VII (August, 1944), 392; publ., *LL*, I, 217–19.

171. MS, Essex, Clark Collection. In ¶1, NH interlined 'upon the cash principle'. Publ., *NHJ* 1971, p. 6; facsimile, p. 2.

172. MS, Huntington HM 10920. Address: Miss Sophia A. Peabody, Care of Dr. N. Peabody, Boston. In ¶2 sentence 1, NH interlined 'for' after 'look'. In ¶1, SH overmarked sentence 2 'and longing . . . night.'. In ¶2, she overmarked sentence 2 'Oh . . . now!'. Publ., *LL*, I, 220–22.

173. MS, Huntington HM 10921. Address: as for 172; postmark, Salem, Oct. 5. In ¶1 sentence 4, NH interlined 'me' before 'and sometimes', in sentence 9, 'have' before 'become callous', and in ¶2 sentence 8, 'not' before 'a somewhat', 'have' before 'returned', and 'have' before 'been created'. In ¶1 sentence 4, NH wrote 'why it' over wiped-out 'whether it'. At the end of ¶1, a period is supplied. In ¶2 sentence 1, SH overmarked 'intimate' before 'communion'. At the end she excised the close and signature, possibly as much as 8 lines. Part publ., *AM*, XXI (January, 1868), 110–11; *PAN*, I, 218–19; *Works*, IX, 221–22; *Harper's*, XL (October, 1871), 690–91; Lathrop, p. 163; *NHHW*, I, 222–23, as "October 1840." Publ., *LL*, I, 223–26.

174. MS, Harvard, bMS Am 1340.2 (2616). Address: as for 75.

175. MS, Bowdoin. In ¶2 sentence 4, 'you' before 'shall receive' is supplied, and 'receive' is emended from 'recieve'.

176. MS, Bowdoin. Publ., *NEQ*, V (April, 1932), 249.

177. MS, Essex. Address: David Roberts, Esq., Salem, Mass. In ¶1 sentence 3, NH wrote 'for' over wiped-out 'them'. The bottom of the leaf, containing possible 'Y[ours truly]' and signature, has been torn off.

178. MS, Harvard, bMS Am 1340.2 (2616). Address: as for 75; postmark, Boston, Nov. 20. Part publ., Longfellow, *Life*, I, 362.

179. MS, Huntington HM 10922. Address: as for 172 ('Miss Sophia' and 'Care of' lost by excision). SH overmarked ¶1 last sentence, 'But . . . absence.'. At the end SH excised 1/2 leaf, extent of inscription unknown; the excision trimmed address and postmark on verso. Publ., *LL,* I, 227–30.

180. MS, Huntington HM 10951. First leaf of a sheet; second leaf unknown. Publ., *LL,* II, 72 (as "1842").

181. MS, MHS. In ¶1 sentence 2, NH wrote 'my removal' over wiped-out 'your remova'; in ¶2 sentence 3, he wrote 'as' over wiped-out 'I' and 'his' over wiped-out 'op'.

182. MS, Huntington HM 10910. Second leaf of a sheet; first leaf unknown. Postmark, Salem, Jan. 11. In ¶2, NH wrote 'here till', wiped out 'till', and wrote 'a' in the space; 'to' of 'today' is over wiped-out 'this'. SH excised the close and signature, about 2 lines.

183. MS, Huntington HM 10923. The first leaf is torn at bottom right recto and bottom left verso; however, it must have been torn before inscription, since the text shows no interruption. Address: as for 172 (presumed 'Sophia A. Pea' and 'Care of Dr. N' lost by excision). In ¶2 sentence 4, NH interlined 'be' before 'left'. SH overmarked ¶1 sentence 7, 'Why . . . within it', and ¶3 sentence 3, 'for want . . .

arms.' where she put a period after preceding 'comfortless'. She overmarked "s bosom' of ¶6 sentence 7 'husband's bosom'. After ¶5 sentence 4, SH excised 6 lines, the excision affecting address and postmark on verso. Her excision left 'of all' isolated at right margin above the line holding 'received'. Part publ., *PAN*, I, 22; *Works*, IX, 226; *NHHW*, I, 226; publ., *LL*, I, 231–34.

184. MS, MHS. In ¶1 sentence 2, NH wrote 'thing' over wiped-out 'whatever'.

185. MS, Huntington HM 10924. Address: as for 172; postmark, Salem, January 22. In ¶4 sentence 2, 'conceive' is emended from 'concieve' (SH's usual spelling but uncharacteristic of NH). In sentence 5, 'as' is supplied before 'he'. SH overmarked ¶1 sentences 2–10: 'and, now . . . better.'. At the end she excised 1/3 leaf, extent of inscription unknown. Marked 'especial' by SH. Publ., *LL*, I, 235–38.

186. MS, Harvard, fMS Am 1301.1 (11).

187. MS, University of Texas, Austin.

188. MS, Huntington HM 10927. Address: as for 172 ('Boston' after cancelled 'Salem'); faint Salem postmark. In ¶1 sentence 2 the 'ers' of 'Sinners' is written over wiped-out 'ing'. In ¶2 sentence 1, NH interlined the second 'a' of 'managest'. In entry of March 19, ¶3 sentence 1, he interlined 'not' before 'fit' and, in sentence 3, 'that' before 'thou'. SH overmarked ¶2 sentence 2 'and yet . . . lips!' and put a period before 'and'; in sentence 3, final paragraph, she overmarked 'with . . . thee.' and put a period before 'with'. Publ., *LL*, I, 243–46.

189. MS, Huntington HM 10928. Address: as for 168. In ¶3 sentence 4, NH interlined 'thou' above cancelled 'though'.

190. MS, Huntington HM 10930. Address: as for 168. In ¶2 sentence 1, NH interlined 'first' before 'lesson'. In entry of April 14, sentence 3, he wiped out the 's' of original 'Ripleys', and in ¶7 sentence 1, wrote 'has made' over wiped-out 'be- / ha'. A period is supplied for ¶4 sentence 1. SH overmarked ¶3 sentence 6, 'Thou . . . caresses.'. Part publ., PAN, II, 1–2; Works, IX, 226–28; publ., LL, II, 3–7.

191. MS, Huntington HM 10929. Address: as for 172. In ¶2 sentence 8, SH added 'which' of 'with which these'; the emendation is accepted. In ¶5 sentence 3, 'be' and 'been' are supplied at tear in MS. SH overmarked ¶1 sentence 3 'as thou hast . . . upon it' and put a period after preceding 'swell'; she overmarked sentence 5 'Thou dost . . . remedy.'; in ¶5 sentence 3, she overmarked 'and . . . nights;'. At the end, SH excised the signature and close, about 3 lines. Publ., PAN, II, 3–5; Works, IX, 228–30; LL, II, 8–11.

192. Text, PAN, II, 5. In PAN, the date alone appears, followed by four ellipsis points and first line. Publ., Works, IX, 230–31.

193. MS, Huntington HM 10931. Address: as for 172. In ¶1 sentence 3, 'throughout' is emended from 'throughought'. In ¶1, SH overmarked in sentence 3 after 'see thee' a comma and 'and hold thee in my arms,'—and in sentence 6, 'I am afraid . . . very much.'. Publ., PAN, II, 5–6; Works, IX, 231–32; LL, II, 12–16.

194. Text, PAN, II, 7-8. Publ., Works, IX, 232–33.

195. MS, Huntington HM 11035. Address: Miss Maria L. Hawthorne, Salem, Massachusetts; postmark, West Rox-

bury, May 3. In ¶1 sentence 5, NH interlined 'done' before 'various'. Part publ., *NHHW*, I, 227–28; Conway, p. 88.

196. MS, Huntington HM 10932. Address: as for 172. In ¶1 sentence 6, NH interlined 'not' above 'devour', and in ¶2 sentence 9, 'it' above 'here'. In ¶1 sentence 6 'ore' is conjectured from '–e,' where ink has soaked through the very thin paper. In ¶3 sentence 8, SH overmarked 'and desire' and just above ¶5 excision 'Oh, how I'. SH's excision at the end, of 19 lines' length, left at left margin traces of at least 13 lines of inscription.

197. Text, *PAN*, II, 9. Publ., *Works*, IX, 234.

198. MS, Huntington HM 10933. Address: as for 168. In dateline NH altered 'P' to 'A'. In ¶2 sentence 3, NH after 'comfort' cancelled 'thee' and wrote 'me' above. Part publ., *PAN*, II, 9–10; *Works*, IX, 235; publ., *LL*, II, 20–21.

199. MS, Library of Congress.

200. MS, Huntington HM 10934. Address: Miss Sophia A. Peabody. In ¶3 sentence 1, dittography 'to come to/come' is emended, and in sentence 4, 'the/the'. In ¶2 sentence 4, NH interlined 'it' before 'of such' and 'it' before 'to the wear'. In ¶3, SH overmarked 'and the . . . mine ownest' and then interlined 'with my ownest' to keep a complete sentence. At end of ¶4, she overmarked 'I kiss thee a million of times.'. Publ., *LL*, II, 22–23.

201. MS, Hawthorne Collection, #6249-a, Virginia. In ¶2 sentence 5, NH wrote 'out' over wiped-out 'of a'. Publ., Barrett, 7; facsimile, Parke-Bernet catalogue, January 23, 1945.

202. Transcript by Manning Hawthorne. In ¶5 sentence 2, 'occurred' is emended from 'occured.' At the end, the close and signature had evidently been excised before the transcript was made. Publ., "Hawthorne and Utopian Socialism," *NEQ*, XII, 4 (December, 1939), 727–29.

202A. MS, Essex. Address: as for 195; postmark, West Roxbury, Aug. 4.

203. MS, Huntington HM 10935. Address: Miss Sophia A. Peabody, Care of Mr. Daniel Newhall, Lynn, Mass.; postmark, Boston, Aug. 12. In ¶1 sentence 5, SH overmarked 'and yearning . . . breast' and placed a period after preceding 'moment'. She overmarked the last line of the letter, 'Wilt . . . kisses?'. Part publ., *NHHW*, I, 236–37; *PAN*, II, 10; *Works*, IX, 235; publ., *LL*, II, 24–26.

204. MS, Huntington HM 10936. Address: Miss Sophia A. Peabody, Boston, Mass. At ¶2 first word, letters are supplied at tear in MS: 'De[arest]', and on verso, ¶4 sentences 3 and 4, 'an[d]' and 'h[ow]'. A period is supplied for the last sentence. Sentences 1 and 2 of ¶2 publ., *PAN*, II, 10–11, and *Works*, IX, 236, as "18th"; publ., *LL*, II, 27–29, as "18th."

205. MS, Huntington HM 10937. Address: as for 168. In ¶4 sentence 2, NH interlined 'in' before 'store'. In ¶4 sentence 1, 'despondency' is written over wiped-out 'despondencies,' and in sentence 2 'He' is twice written over 'he.' SH overmarked the first two sentences of ¶2. Part publ., *PAN*, II, 11–12; *Works*, IX, 236–37; publ., *LL*, II, 30–33.

206. MS, Huntington HM 10938. Address: as for 172; faint Salem postmark. In ¶1 sentence 3, NH interlined 'a' before 'most'. In ¶3 sentence 4, SH overmarked all after 'me'. At the end SH excised the close and signature, perhaps 3 lines.

¶4 part publ., *PAN*, II, 12–13; *Works*, IX, 237–38; publ., *LL,*, II, 34–37.

207. MS, Huntington HM 10939. Address: as for 172; postmark, Salem, Sept. 9. In sentence 3, NH wrote 'ex' of 'exactly' over wiped-out 'the'. In sentence 2, NH 'dissapointment' is emended. SH overmarked the last sentence after 'continually', where she put a period. Publ., *LL*, II, 38–39.

208. MS, Huntington HM 10941. Address: as for 172; faint Salem postmark. Part publ., *PAN*, II, 13–14; *Works*, IX, 238–39; *LL*, II, 44–47.

209. MS, Huntington HM 10940. Address: as for 172; postmark, Salem, Sept. 17. In ¶8 sentence 1, NH wrote 'His' over 'his'. A period is supplied at end of ¶6. Part publ., *PAN*, II, 15–16; *Works*, IX, 239–40; *LL*, II, 40–43, as "10th."

210. MS, Huntington HM 10942. Address: as for 204. In ¶2 sentence 1, NH interlined 'shall' before 'succeed', and in sentence 7 wrote 'seriously' over wiped-out 'about'. In ¶6 sentence 2, NH's dittography 'were/were' is emended. In ¶1, SH overmarked last sentence, 'I never . . . thine arms.'. In ¶3 sentence 1, she overmarked 'kiss' and put a period after preceding 'parting'; she also overmarked last phrase, 'thou desirablest wife.'. Part publ., *PAN*, II, 16–17; *Works*, IX, 240–42; publ., *LL*, II, 48–51.

211. MS, Huntington HM 10943. Address: as for 204. In ¶1 sentence 1, SH overmarked ', when I . . . bosom.', putting a period after 'resource'. Excerpts publ., *PAN*, II, 17; *Works*, IX, 242; publ., *LL*, II, 55–57.

212. MS, Huntington HM 10944. Address: as for 204. In ¶4 sentence 1, SH overmarked 'arms.' and apparently one or two

other unrecovered words, and altered preceding 'thy' to 'thee'. Paragraphs 2 and 3 publ., *PAN*, II, 18–19; *Works*, IX, 242-43; publ., *LL*, II, 55–57.

213. MS, Huntington HM 10945. Address: as for 172. In ¶2 sentence 1, NH wrote 'to' over wiped-out 'of'. In ¶5 sentence 1, SH overmarked 'my only desirablest'. Excerpts, paragraphs 2 and 3, publ., *PAN*, II, 19; *Works*, IX, 243–44 (both as "27th"); publ., *LL*, II, 58–59.

214. MS, Huntington HM 10925. Address: as for 168. Date conjectured by reference, *Recollections*, pp. 94–95, to NH's telling Bridge of the carrying of a calf to market. In ¶1 sentence 1, NH interlined 'have' before 'seen'. Publ., *PAN*, II, 27; *Works*, IX, 247–48.

215. MS, Huntington HM 10946. Address: as for 172. Publ., *LL,*, II, 69–61.

216. MS, Huntington HM 10947. Address: as for 172. In ¶1 sentence 4, NH wrote 'a' over wiped-out 'an' before 'power' and in sentence 8 'surrendering' over wiped-out 'gi[ving]'. In ¶4, SH overmarked sentence 7, 'Thy sister . . . trumpet.'. Part publ., as "27", in *PAN*, II, 19–20; *Works*, IX, 244–45; publ., *LL*, II, 62–66.

217. MS, Huntington HM 10949. Publ., *LL*, II, 67–68.

218. MS, Huntington HM 10959. Address: as for 172. Publ., *LL*, II, 88–89, as "1842."

219. MS, Boston Public Library. Address: Jno. R. Willis, Esqr., Boston, Mass.

220. MS, Huntington HM 10950. Address: as for 172; postmark, Salem, Nov. 27. Publ., *LL*, II, 69–71.

221. MS, Berg. Address: Nathan Hale, Jr. Esqr., Boston, Mass. Publ., 1964 *Buffalo Catalogue of an Exhibition.*

222. MS, Duyckinck Collection, MSS Division, NYPL. Address: Messrs. Cornelius Mathews, and Evert A. Duyckinck, 167, Broadway, New York city; postmark, Boston, Dec. 23. In ¶2 sentence 3, NH interlined 'to receive it'. In ¶3 sentence 5, NH wrote 'eu' of 'Molineux' over wiped-out 'ex' and, after '1833', 'The' over wiped-out 'the'. A period is supplied for ¶3 sentence 6.

223. MS, Pearson, Yale. Address: Messrs. James Munroe, & Co., Present.

224. MS, Essex, Clark Collection. Publ., *NHJ* 1971, p. 9, with facsimile, p. 8.

225. MS, Huntington HM 10953. Address: as for 168. In ¶2 sentence 5, SH overmarked 'Looks . . . these' and above 'these' interlined 'Looks' before 'are a better language'. In ¶3 sentence 5, 'possibly' is emended from 'possible'. Publ., *LL,* II, 73–76.

226. MS, Adam Gimbel.

227. MS, Library of Congress. In ¶1 sentence 2, NH interlined 'mean' before 'to', and in ¶2 sentence 2, 'to both parties' after 'justice', and 'not' after 'feel'.

228. MS, Huntington HM 10955. Address: as for 172; postmark, Salem, Feb. 28. In ¶1 sentence 1, NH cancelled 'if' before 'even'; in ¶4 sentence 2, he interlined 'it' before 'is'. In ¶5 sentences 4 and 5, letters are supplied at break in MS: 'wi[ll]', '[, I w]onder' (second time) and 'ear[th w]e'. In ¶4 sentence 1, 'stretches' is emended from 'streches'. In ¶6 sentence 3, 'independently' is emended from 'indepently', and in

¶7 sentence 1, 'curiosities' from 'cuiosities'. In ¶1 sentence 4 final phrase, SH overmarked 'pressed close to my breast.' and added 'with me'. In ¶2 sentence 5, she overmarked 'on which . . . thy head.'. Publ., *LL*, II, 77–81.

229. MS, Bowdoin. Address: Charles Lanman, Esqr., Norwich, Connecticut; postmark, Boston, March 3. In the first sentence, NH altered 'summer hours' to 'Summer Hours'.

230. MS, Huntington HM 10957. Bottom half of a leaf, torn before inscription. Address: as for 172; postmark, New York, March 4. In sentence 4, 'too' before 'late' is emended from 'to'. Publ., *LL*, II, 82.

231. MS, Huntington HM 10956. Address: as for 172; postmark, Salem, March 10. Publ., *LL*, II, 83–84.

232. MS, Huntington HM 10926. Address: Miss Sophia A. Peabody, West-street, Boston. In ¶1 sentence 5, NH altered 'the' to 'my' before 'within'. In ¶3 sentence 3, NH interlined 'thee' before 'this'. Publ., *LL*, I, 241–42, as "1841."

233. MS, S. V. C. Morris, Lenox, Massachusetts. Address: Nathan Hale, Jr. Esqr. Facsimile, *Outlook, LVIII* (April 2, 1898), 843.

234. MS, Huntington HM 10958. Address: as for 172. In ¶4 sentence 2, SH overmarked 'in moments . . . tenderness.'. SH excised 4 lines at the start of ¶2, the excision affecting ¶3 verso, first 1/2 line, then 2 lines, then another 1/2 line. Publ., *LL*, II, 85–87, as "5th."

235. MS, MHS. Address: Miss E. S. Quincy, care of Josiah Quincy, Jr. Esqr.

236. MS, Huntington HM 10960. Address: as for 168. Publ., *LL*, II, 90.

237. MS, Thomas L. Hinckley, Boston. Publ., *NEQ*, XII, 4 (December, 1939), 729–30.

238. MS, Huntington HM 10961. Address: as for 168. Letters and words are supplied at tear in MS: ¶1 sentence 1 'angel [, sav]e', sentence 2 'If [they]'; ¶3 '[saw]', 'yester[day.]', '[makes fi]ne'. In ¶2 last sentence, SH overmarked approximately four words, and interlined above 'come'. In ¶2 last sentence, 'o'clock' is normalized to 'º clock'. Publ., *NHHW*, I, 238–39; *LL*, II, 91–92.

239. MS, Huntington HM 10962. Address: as for 172; postmark, Salem, June 9. In ¶1 sentence 1, SH overmarked 'kissless'. Part publ., *NHHW*, I, 239–40; publ., *LL*, II, 93–95.

240. MS, Huntington HM 10963. Address: as for 172. In ¶1 sentence 7, NH altered 'that' to 'I tell' and interlined 'I' before 'could'. Part publ., *NHHW*, I, 242. Publ., *LL*, II, 96–98.

241. MS, Huntington HM 10965. In ¶2 sentence 1, letters are supplied at tear in MS: '[Owne]st', '[thee]', 'I do n[ot]'. Publ., *LL*, II, 101–2.

242. MS, Huntington HM 10966. Address: as for 232. In ¶1 sentence 3, NH wrote 'thou' above cancelled 'though', and interlined 'find' before 'me'. Part publ., *NHHW*, I, 241–42; publ., *LL*, II, 103–4.

243. Transcript, Julian Hawthorne, MS journal, April 22, 1880, Bancroft.

244. MS, Harvard, bMS Am 1569.7 (229). Publ., *Yesterdays*, p. 118; *Works*, XII, 490.

245. MS, MHS.

246. MS, Essex. Address: as for 195; postmark, Concord, July 11. First three sentences quoted, *EIHC*, XLI (1905), 106–7; publ., Manning Hawthorne, "Maria Louisa Hawthorne," *EIHC*, LXXV (April, 1939), 130–31.

247. MS, St. Lawrence.

248. MS, Essex. Address: as for 195; postmark, Concord, Aug. [?]. In ¶2 sentence 2, NH wrote 'to' over wiped-out 'tak' before 'take'. At end of ¶1, 'Hillard's' is emended from 'Hillards''. Publ., *EIHC*, LXXV (April, 1939), 131–32.

249. MS, Berg. Address: Robert Carter, Esqr, Care of Messrs. Bradbury & Soden, Publishers, Boston, Mass.; postmark, Concord, Aug. 20. In ¶1 sentence 2, NH wrote 'or had' over wiped-out 'had'. In ¶1 sentence 5, NH first wrote 'is intimate', then awkwardly altered the first two letters of 'intimate' to 'an'; Centenary emends to 'is an intimate'. Quoted, Gordan, 207.

250. MS, Huntington HM 11036. Address: Miss Margaret Fuller, Concord. In ¶1 sentence 2, 'wife's' is emended from 'wifes'. In ¶4 sentence 1, letters are supplied at break in MS: 'friend, a[nd]'. Publ., *NHHW*, I, 252–55.

251. MS, MHS. At end of ¶1, 'withhold' is emended from 'withold'.

252. MS, Boston Public Library. Address: Messrs. James Munroe & Comp^y, Publishers, Boston, Mass.; postmark,

Boston, Oct. 4. Facsimile, *Hawthorne among His Contemporaries*, ed. Kenneth Walter Cameron (Hartford: Transcendental Books, 1968), p. 493.

253. MS, Essex. Address: as for 195; postmark, Concord, Oct. 12.

254. Text, James H. Wilson, *Life of Charles A. Dana* (New York: Harper & Brothers, 1907), pp. 45–46.

255. MS, St. Lawrence. In ¶2 sentence 5, NH interlined 'a' before 'new feature' and 'more' before 'popular'; in sentence 8 he interlined 'to' before 'make'. In sentence 7 double quotes before 'The Summer Rain' are supplied. Publ., *Harper's Weekly*, XXIII (November 1, 1879), 863; *AL*, XXIV, (March, 1962), 102.

256. MS, Essex. Address: as for 195; postmark, Concord, Nov. 25. At the end of ¶7, 'impassable' is emended from 'impassible'. Second, fourth paragraphs quoted (as "Nov. 28"), *EIHC*, 41 (1905), 107.

257. MS, Harvard, bMS Am 1340.2 (2616). Address: as for 75; postmark, Concord, Nov. 26. Published, Longfellow, *Life*, I, 422.

258. MS, St. Lawrence. Address: James R. Lowell, Esq., Boston.

259. MS, Harvard, bMS Am 1340.2 (2616). Address: Professor H. W. Longfellow, Cambridge, Mass.; postmark, Concord, Dec. 24. In ¶2 sentence 5, NH wrote possible 'it is just', wiped out 'just', awkwardly overwrote 'it', and added 'over'. The postscript is on the inside of the verso cover. Publ., Longfellow, *Life*, I, 430–31.

260. MS, Berg. Address: Miss M. L. Hawthorne, Salem, Mass.; postmark, Concord, January 4.

261. MS, Fruitlands, Harvard, Mass. Address: Robert Carter, Esqr., 4 Court-street, Boston. Facsimile, *Goodspeed's Flying Quill,* 1948, p. 1.

262. MS, Harvard, MS Am 1086 XVI 33. Address: Miss S. M. Fuller, Cambridge, Mass^{tts}; postmark, Concord, Feb. 1. In ¶1 sentence 2, NH interlined 'an' before 'absolute', in ¶2 sentence 1, 'to' before 'be happy', in ¶2 sentence 8, 'be' before 'honorably', and in ¶3 sentence 1, 'when' before 'I first'. In ¶5 sentence 1, he wrote 'because' above cancelled 'but'. In ¶1 sentence 7, dittography 'to / to' is emended. Part publ., Randall Stewart, ed., *American Notebooks* (New Haven, Conn.: Yale University Press, 1932), pp. 318–19, 402 n.

263. MS, Huntington HM 10967. Address: Mrs. Sophia A. Hawthorne, Care of Dr. N. Peabody, Boston, Mass. In ¶1 sentence 8, NH interlined 'I' before 'was', and in sentence 14, 'one-' before 'another'. In ¶1 sentence 12, 'seperate' is accepted NH spelling. In ¶1, SH overmarked sentence 3, and in sentence 8, 'and hearing . . . side,'. Part publ., *NHHW,* I, 293–94; publ., *LL,* II, 105–8.

264. MS, Huntington HM 10968. Address: as for 263. In ¶3 sentence 2, NH interlined 'to' before 'wait', in ¶4 sentence 8, 'my' before 'own heart'. In ¶1 sentence 2, SH overmarked ', at bed and board, and'; in ¶3, sentences 3 through 5. In ¶4 sentence 5, she overmarked 'and by . . . locomotion.', altering a comma to a period after 'Concord'. In ¶6 SH excised a word after 'thou dearest', then 2 full lines. In sentence 4 she overmarked 'Nevertheless, thou shalt be' and excised 1 line at the foot of the leaf, this excision affecting 1 line at the end of the last paragraph on verso. After the excision, she

over marked 'as well as intimatest little'. Publ., *LL*, II, 109–
12, as "15th."

265. MS, Bowdoin. Address: Horatio Bridge, Esq., U.S.N.,
Portsmouth, N.H. In ¶3 sentence 5, NH cancelled 'purpose'
and wrote 'purse' above. SH or Bridge excised ¶2 'O'Sullivan', supplied by reference to 264 ¶3, where SH overmarked
the name. Quoted, *Works*, XII, 493; publ., with dashes for
names of O'Sullivan, Rantoul, and Woodbury, *Harper's*,
LXXXIV (February, 1892), 364–65, as "March 23," and *Recollections*, pp. 88–91, as "March 24."

266. MS, Berg. Bottom 2/3 of a leaf; remainder unknown.

267. MS, Bowdoin. Address: Horatio Bridge, Esqr., U.S.
Ship Saratoga, New-York city; postmark, Concord, May 3.
In ¶1 sentence 4, NH altered 'of' to 'in'. In ¶3 sentence 3,
NH interlined 'find' after 'would', and in ¶6, 'us' after 'gladden'. In ¶4 sentence 7, another hand, Bridge's or SH's, interlined 'to' before 'send', and, in ¶6 sentence 1, 'us' before
'much'; both readings are accepted as emendations. After
Bridge prepared copy for *Harper's*, LXXXIV (February,
1892), 365, a strip 1 1/2 inches across each leaf, 3 lines deep,
was torn away at the fold of the sheet. On first recto, the
tear is above inscription. On first verso, ¶2 sentence 11, 'yo[u
will]', '[attracted]', and 'pecu[liarities are]' are accepted from
Harper's. Bridge published only the first four sentences of ¶3;
beginning at 'Speaking of love' a pencil cancellation is struck
across MS through 'Hyperion' and through the last two sentences: 'Except. . . . affections.'. The intervening clause
'but . . . to be so.' is overmarked by scribbling unlike SH's
overmarking, and is ascribed to Bridge. Again the tear in MS
must be taken into account: in ¶3 sentence 5, '[since then]'
and sentence 6 '[is my on]ly' and '[care m]uch' are conjec-

tured by context. Publ., *Harper's*, LXXXIV (February, 1892), p. 365; *Recollections*, p. 88.

268. Text, American Art Association, Anderson Galleries, New York, November 19–20, 1931. See *Hawthorne at Auction*, ed. C. E. Frazer Clark, Jr. (Detroit: Bruccoli-Clark, Gale Press, 1972), p. 238.

269. MS, Berg. Address: Miss M. L. Hawthorne, Herbert St., Salem, Mass.; postmark, Concord, June 17. In ¶1 sentence 5, SH's dittography 'we/we' is emended.

270. MS, Berg. Address: Rev. Rufus W. Griswold, Philadelphia Pennsylvania; postmark, Concord, July 3. Part publ., American Art Association, Anderson Galleries, New York, December 9–10, 1936; see *Hawthorne at Auction*, p. 277. Publ., *Passages from the Correspondence . . . of Rufus W. Griswold* (Cambridge, Mass.: W. M. Griswold, 1898), p. 144.

271. MS, Berg. Address: as for 195; postmark, Concord, July 14.

272. MS, Essex, Clark Collection.

273. MS, Huntington HM 10980. Address: Mrs. Nathaniel Hawthorne, Concord, Massachusetts; postmark, Salem, August 27. In ¶2 sentence 5, NH interlined 'not' before 'say'. In ¶4 sentence 3, 'have' after 'would' is supplied before 'been'. In ¶2 sentences 6–7, SH overmarked 'who, methinks . . . presence.', altering a comma to a period after 'O'Sullivan'. In ¶5 sentences 6–7, she overmarked 'certainly . . . sentence,', altering a comma to a period after 'again'. Publ., *LL*, II, 58–59, as "August 25th, 1845."

274. MS, Essex. Address: as for 195; postmark, Boston, Sept. 2.

WORD-DIVISION

1. End-of-the-Line Hyphenation in the Centenary Edition

Possible compounds hyphenated at the end of a line in the Centenary text are listed here if they are hyphenated within the line in the copy-text. Exclusion from this list means that a possible compound appears as one unhyphenated word in the copy-text. Also excluded are hyphenated compounds in which both elements are capitalized.

220.9	three-pence	399.4	oft-repeated
253.16	"sandal-shoon"	402.15	bed-room
295.35	good-natured	416.10	chimney-tops
296.6	black-faced	430.9	slang-whangers
296.7	forge-men	438.25	to-day
296.24	chimney-sweepers	439.12	coal-shovellers
318.18	dream-personages	442.31	co-operation
318.20	dream-land	450.23	salt-befrosted
335.21	one-sidedness	464.9	thirty-five
344.11	fire-side	469.14	non-arrival
345.5	coal-vessel	477.21	coal-people
348.8	salt-ship	491.18	to-night
351.5	sunset-clouds	512.25	day-light
385.1	to-night	513.9	head-ache

539.7	snow-storm	664.19	wood-fire
554.18	sea-shore	674.19	mantel-piece
557.7	sea-coast	674.19	fore-paws
566.32	horn-sounder	678.19	side-walks
568.20	penny-post	688.26	fishing-season
620.11	new-created	695.26	sailor-friend

2. End-of-the-Line Hyphenation in the Copy-Texts

The following possible compounds are hyphenated at the ends of lines in the copy-texts. The form adopted in the Centenary Edition, as listed below, represents Hawthorne's predominate usage as ascertained by other appearances or by parallels within the copy-texts.

159.20	brimstone	341.4	bedtime
212.6	handkerchief	341.20	halfway
213.35	doorsteps	343.25	sunrise
218.17	sometimes	344.8	footstool
220.14	smelling-bottle	357.4	coal-fire
220.18	town-crier	363.21	mantel-piece
232.15	wood-scratching	373.1	cotton-bagging
251.15	farewell	373.23	tomorrow
267.7	baby-house	379.3	beforehand
274.16	anybody	379.7	foregoing
298.23	fire-light	391.12	bedtime
317.19	Sometime	402.16	mantel-piece
321.13	day-light	403.9	business-people
324.6	sometimes	405.17	mud-puddles
325.3	sunset	406.19	letter-writer
331.8	ill-being	416.22	half-past
336.2	east-winds	420.7	postmaster

420.16	heartstrings	475.5	straightway
421.23	snow-flakes	510.18	broad-shouldered
425.10	due-bill	512.24	eyesight
438.28	coal-shovellers	513.14	head-ache
438.33	coal-heavers	529.1	husbandman
440.3	to-day	544.2	milking-time
441.21	to-day	555.6	forenoon
444.15	love-sick	573.10	straightway
446.18	heart-quakes	596.19	sleepy-head
450.11	stump-speeches	656.11	Indian-like
458.3	candle-light	658.19	cooking-stove
473.26	good-bye	675.4	flat-irons

3. Special Cases

The following possible compounds are hyphenated at the ends of lines in both copy-text and Centenary Edition. Words appear here in the adopted Centenary form which is obscured by line-end hyphenation.

216.5	grandmother's
262.4	dull-[excision]
298.14	east-winds
401.15	straightway
542.2	afternoon

INDEX

INDEX